REAL ESTATE FINANCE

REAL ESTATE FINANCE

SECOND EDITION

C. F. Sirmans

Professor of Finance
College of Business Administration
Louisiana State University

McGRAW-HILL BOOK COMPANY

New York   St. Louis   San Francisco   Auckland   Bogotá   Caracas   Colorado Springs
Hamburg   Lisbon   London   Madrid   Mexico   Milan   Montreal   New Delhi
Oklahoma City   Panama   Paris   San Juan   São Paulo   Singapore   Sydney   Tokyo   Toronto

This book was set in Times Roman by the College Composition Unit
in cooperation with Waldman Graphics, Inc.
The editors were Kathleen L. Loy and Cynthia L. Phelps;
the production supervisor was Louise Karam.
The cover was designed by Rafael Hernandez.
New drawings were done by Caliber Design Planning, Inc.
R. R. Donnelley & Sons Company was printer and binder.

REAL ESTATE FINANCE

2 3 4 5 6 7 8 9 0 DOC DOC 8 9 3 2 1 0 9

ISBN   0-07-057698-X

Library of Congress Cataloging-in-Publication Data

Sirmans, C. F.
    Real estate finance.
    Includes index
    1. Mortgage loans. 2. Real estate investment.
3. Dwellings--Purchasing. 4. Housing--Finance.
I. Title.
HG2040.S57 1989   332.7'22'0973   88-8333
ISBN 0-07-057698-X

CONTENTS

PREFACE

Like the first edition, this book is an introduction to the real estate financing decision. It is written for the beginner in real estate finance, whether a practicing professional (such as a broker, investor, developer, lender, or appraiser) or a student in the formal classroom. Practicing professionals will find the material useful for understanding the myriad financing methods and techniques developed in recent years. Students who have had an introductory real estate course (or professionals with the equivalent) will be adequately prepared. The only mathematical techniques used are the fundamental concepts of compound interest and present value. Readers without a background in these areas should study Chapter 2 in detail until they master it.

In recent years there have been numerous changes in markets for real estate investments. The entrance of new lenders and investors, the securitization of mortgages, governments' changing role and influence, and other factors have brought radical changes, particularly to the area of real estate finance. Although no book can discuss all these influences and changes, we outline recent financing developments.

All financial decision makers face two main decisions: how much to invest and what to invest in, and how to finance those investments. This book primarily addresses in detail the latter decision: how to finance real estate investments. Our view is that the best way to examine this key financial decision is by first studying how the financing-lending decision is made. Certain major concepts must be remembered. In any financing-lending decision there are two major participants: a borrower and a lender. For a successful transaction to occur, the criteria and objectives of both parties must be met.

There are various ways the material on real estate financing could have been discussed. Since there are two primary decision makers, the borrower and the lender, the financing decision could have been analyzed from one party's perspective, at the expense of the other's. But obviously both perspectives must be understood to reach final agreement. Alternatively, the financing of various types of real estate could have been analyzed, such as single-family houses and income properties like apartments, shopping centers, and office buildings.

If the material had been organized in this fashion, the fundamental principles would have had to be restated over and over and over. Therefore, readers familiar with real estate finance books will find that this book significantly departs from standard organization. For example, there are no separate chapters on the various financial institutions. The lender's perspective is analyzed throughout the discussion because, in my opinion, the recent deregulation of institutions has done away with (and will continue to do so) the historical distinctions between lenders.

Part One introduces the fundamental concepts of making the financing decision from both the borrower's and the lender's perspectives. Part Two discusses various alternative financing methods and techniques. Thus, the discussion about varying-rate mortgages, for example, is concerned with the additional problems (such as tax), legal or financial, the techniques create for both the borrower and the lender. The applications of the techniques to various types of real estate, such as housing or income properties, are also illustrated. The important emphasis is thus the financing methods and techniques rather than the type of real estate. Most of the financing techniques are applicable to all types of real estate investments.

Part Three discusses real estate finance decision making. The real estate financing process involves a variety of decision situations such as the optimal combination of debt and equity, the refinancing decision, pricing mortgage loans, and managing a mortgage portfolio.

OVERVIEW

The major objectives in this book are:

1 To provide the basic background and information for undertaking the borrowing-lending decision

2 To discuss in detail the major types of financing techniques and methods that are being used in the real estate marketplace

To accomplish these goals, the book is divided into three parts. Part One, "The Financing Decision," introduces readers to the major principles for understanding the decision-making process in mortgage underwriting and borrowing. In Chapter 1, the borrower-lender perspectives are blended into the financing process outlined to provide a survey of the entire mortgage market. This market represents the composite response of borrowers and lenders in determining interest rates and allocating mortgage funds. Recent developments in the major segments of the mortgage market are also discussed.

Chapter 2 discusses in detail how mortgages "work." The mechanics of the traditional fixed-rate mortgage are stressed, and coverage includes computation of mortgage payments, amortization schedules, and effective borrowing costs (yields). Chapter 3 is an in-depth look at the legal environment surrounding the financing decision.

Two major areas of concern to the lender in analyzing the risk of a loan are the borrower's willingness and ability to repay the loan and the value of the collateral securing the debt. Chapter 4 discusses borrower analysis in the financing decision. Chapters 5 and 6 discuss techniques for analyzing the value of the property. The borrower-equity investor is obviously interested in the tax effects of the financing decision. Chapter 5 details the traditional before-tax valuation methods; Chapter 6 covers the after-tax valuation decision-making techniques.

Part Two expands the basics of Part One by emphasizing and examining in detail the various alternative financing methods and techniques that have been developed by (and widely used in) the market in response to the numerous decision-making situations and problems borrowers and lenders face. Fortunately, for discussion, the methods can be classified into major categories. (As you study these techniques, remember that they are not exclusive.) Each method is analyzed according to the following questions: What are the unique property-analysis problems for the borrower? How does the method work, and when would it be used? What risk aspects are created for the borrower-lender? Each chapter has detailed examples of the various methods from both the borrower's and the lender's viewpoints. The application of the various methods to numerous types of real estate, such as single-family houses, apartments, office buildings, vacant land, and shipping centers, is also illustrated.

Chapter 7 analyzes mortgages with varying interest rates. Chapter 8 discusses the various types of government-sponsored financing methods and programs for both single-family homes and income properties. Chapter 9 covers various types of "wraparound" financing methods. Chapter 10 illustrates the popular seller financing method: installment sales. Chapters 11 and 12 analyze construction and land development financing, respectively.

Chapter 13 discusses income and equity participation mortgages. Chapter 14 analyzes the use of joint ventures in financing real estate projects. Chapter 15 illustrates the increasingly popular syndicate method to raise equity capital. Chapter 16 details leasing and sale-leaseback alternative financing methods. Chapter 17 surveys other financing methods that have been developed, such as buy down mortgages.

Chapter 18 discusses the borrower's perspective, and Chapter 19 analyzes some of the decisions that lenders must make in the real estate financing process.

ACKNOWLEDGMENTS

Anyone who has written anything knows the debts owed to those who assisted in the development of such an undertaking as a book. I am no exception. Numerous research assistants helped develop, check, recheck, and recheck again the analysis in the various chapters; particularly helpful in the first edition were Bobby Newsome, Keith Griggs, Jill Rose, John Feerick, Keith Ellenberg, Bert King,

Julie Smith and Murvyn Callo. A special note of thanks goes to Gary Sneide. For the second edition appreciation is extended to Jill Szymonski, Kris Guidry, Debbie Moran, Wendy Moran, and Shirin Jahanian. For the sometimes thankless task of typing yet another revision, appreciation is expressed to Gilda Ivory, Candace Allen, Eileen Zachary, and Elizabeth Vera. Researchers in the field of real estate finance form the basis for all the concepts and methods, and ideally the end-of-chapter references help pay the debt I owe them. I would also like to thank the following reviewers of this second edition for their valuable comments and suggestions: Ray Ackley, Ithaca College; Jaime Alvayay, University of North Texas; Donald F. Cunningham, Baylor University; Forrest E. Huffmann, Temple University; Bobby Newsome, Indiana State University; David Sher, Cornell University; and Charles Wade, Texas Technical University. Finally, an unpayable debt is due to Elaine and the kids. "Where are you going dad?" "Back to the office." "What are you doing there?" "Working on *the* book." "O.K., have fun." The true price is obviously the fun that could have been had, had there not been a chapter to revise.

C. F. Sirmans

THE FINANCING DECISION

Part One represents the basic principles to follow for making real estate financing decisions. We analyze the fundamentals of the financing decision from the perspective of both the lender and the borrower. To correctly understand the *financing decision,* we must examine how the real estate investor makes the *investment decision*—whether or not to buy a particular real estate project. From the lender's perspective, the loan is an investment. The loan represents the lender's claims (legal, cash flow, etc.) against the real estate and/or the borrower. In some types of loans, the income-producing ability and value of the collateral (the real estate) may be of prime importance. With other types of mortgages, such as for owner-occupied single-family houses, the borrower's ability and willingness to repay the loan are major concerns.

Chapter 1 introduces the financing process through an overview of the mortgage market. How does the market determine the interest rates? What are the sources of mortgage debt? What recent developments have occurred in the mortgage markets? Chapter 2 analyzes the mechanics of mortgages and discusses in detail the traditional fixed-rate mortgage. Once the reader understands these fundamentals, the alternative financing methods and techniques in Part Two are relatively easy to analyze.

Chapter 3 explores the legal environment of financing. The subject of property rights in real estate is complex and plays a major role in the decision-making process of both the lender and the borrower.

Chapter 4 analyzes the borrower, whose financial position strongly affects the financing decision. Chapters 5 and 6 consider the property that serves as collateral for mortgage loans. Chapter 5 covers property valuation on a before-tax basis. Chapter 6 discusses the effects of taxes on financing and investment decisions and the use of discounted cash flow models for property analysis.

Thus, Part One provides the fundamental legal mechanics, borrower- and property-analysis skills, and tax understanding necessary for making the real estate financing decision. Only by considering these fundamental concepts can the decision maker, whether borrower or lender, make correct decisions.

THE FINANCING ENVIRONMENT

SUMMARY
QUESTIONS
PROBLEMS
REFERENCES

Real estate is widely used as security for credit. Most real estate transactions involve large sums of capital. This capital typically comes from two sources: a lender that advances borrowed funds in exchange for future payments, and an equity investor (borrower) that provides the remainder of the capital. Real estate finance is an understanding of how to make decisions concerning the use of capital in a real estate investment of any type, from a single-family house to such income-producing property as an office building or shopping center.

This chapter introduces the environment in which these financing decisions are made by providing an overview for each aspect of financing discussed in detail in later chapters. First, basic definitions and concepts related to financing are discussed. The industry that deals with borrowing and lending, the mortgage market, is then covered. The third section covers the financing process—how the borrower and lender arrive at a decision to enter into a mortgage contract. The last section previews several major recent developments in real estate financing.

BASIC FINANCING CONCEPTS AND DEFINITIONS

Generally, financing can be defined as the *process* of borrowing (raising) or lending (providing) funds or capital. Financing is also the *system* that includes the granting of credit and the making of investments. Financing thus involves *making various decisions,* such as how much and what type of capital to use in a real estate investment.

A real estate investment deals with the commodity of capital. There are two types of capital: debt and venture (equity). The most prevalent practice is to combine a large portion of debt capital (mortgage money) with a smaller portion of venture capital (equity money). The investor undertakes an investment by using some personal equity and borrowing funds to complete the total capital required. The logic of the financial world indicates that both debt and equity capital are employed when and where they offer reasonable prospects for profitable returns. The rate of return must be expected to be more attractive than probable yields from other available capital uses.

The financing process includes a transaction between two participants: a borrower and a lender; both participants have objectives, constraints, and goals for entering into the transaction. This transaction involves a legal instrument commonly called the mortgage.

The term *mortgage* refers to both the *instrument* that pledges real estate as security for an obligation and the *process* of pledging real estate as security. The mortgage process is a transfer (or pledge) of real estate (property rights) by a debtor-borrower-mortgagor to a creditor-lender-mortgagee for the performance of an obligation. The obligation is normally the payment of a debt, evidenced by the mortgagor's promissory note. In some states and in some financing situations, the mortgage instrument is called by a different name, such as a trust deed or a purchase money mortgage, but functionally the instruments all serve the same purpose—to pledge real estate as security. Note that the lender is interested in the pledge of both the *property rights* and the *physical* real estate (land and improvements). These factors create a complex legal and economic environment for financial decision making.

Making Financing Decisions

Financing decisions are made by comparing costs and benefits. For example, suppose you are a mortgage lender and I promise to pay you $515.47 each month for 20 years (240 months) if you will give (loan) me $50,000 today. How would you analyze this situation? How would you make the decision? For all practical purposes, this situation is an example of the type of decision facing the lender in the mortgage market. It is typically called the *lending decision*.

On the other hand, we can take the borrower's viewpoint. How would the borrower decide whether to borrow $50,000 with the payment of $515.47 each month for 240 months? What factors would enter into the *borrowing decision?*

An important concept to understand is that both participants (borrower and lender) make decisions by comparing the costs and benefits associated with the decision. Returning to our simple example, note that the cost, from the lender's viewpoint, is $50,000. The benefits to the lender are the payments of $515.47 each month. But these benefits (cash inflows) take place over time. Thus the question arises of how to convert these future benefits into their present worth. The problem is even more complicated since the lender may not be certain that the borrower will honor the promise to pay each month. In addition, the borrower may pledge real estate. In this case you have to consider both the promise and the value of the real estate as security for the debt. In sum, risk is associated with the financing decision.

Risk Analysis

Real estate financing decisions are made in a risky environment. In general, *risk* refers to the possibility that what is expected to occur may not occur. In other words, the actual outcome may be different from what was expected. The lender and the borrower must consider several *types of risk* in making financing decisions.

Inflation (Purchasing Power) Risk   One type of risk associated with long-term investments is that *inflation,* a rise in all prices, may occur. As a result, the lender would be paid back in "cheaper" dollars. For example, suppose I borrow $50,000 for 1 year at an interest rate of 12 percent. The amount of interest that I pay is $6,000 ($50,000 times 0.12). Suppose that inflation during the year is 12 percent. What is the lender's "real" rate of return? It is zero. The lender earned $6,000, but in terms of purchasing power the lender is no better off. Thus the loan is essentially at a zero interest rate. Obviously no lender (investor) would enter into any investment situation with such an expected outcome. Investors must deal both with *expected* inflation and *unexpected* inflation.

Default Risk   In any financing decision there exists the possibility that the lender (investor) will not be able to obtain repayment of the loan. This possibility is referred to as *default risk*—the borrower simply is unable (or refuses) to repay the debt. If the borrower has pledged real estate as security, the lender then has the right to sell property to obtain payment of the debt. However, this creates more problems and involves more decisions. For example, suppose the sale of the property does not bring enough money to repay the debt.

Obviously, before entering into an investment, the lender will analyze both the borrower's ability and willingness to repay and the property's suitability as security. The *value* of the real estate relative to the amount of debt is an extremely important aspect of default risk analysis.

Business Risk   Business risk concerns unexpected changes in the overall investment environment. For example, the real estate market's attitude to a particular property, or to real estate in general, may change, in turn influencing the income-producing ability of a property or the situation of the borrower. The result is declining property values. Numerous other factors can alter the business environment in which the financing decision is made. For example, the government could change the legal or regulatory constraints on the lender, the borrower, or the real estate serving as security.

Liquidity Risk   Real estate financing decisions historically have dealt with long-term contracts. An investor in such a contract faces potential *liquidity* risk should it be necessary to dispose of the investment. Real estate, in general, is viewed as having relatively high liquidity risk since it cannot be converted to cash on short notice. A mortgage, as an investment, can also have liquidity problems. However, in the last several decades the mortgage market has developed a fairly efficient system of buying and selling existing mortgages, so that they are more "liquid." This system, which is referred to as the *secondary mortgage market,* is discussed in more detail later.

Financial Risk   For the borrower in the financing transaction, the use of debt creates what is known as *financial risk*. Since the debt position has priority over the equity position, and the variation in the expected return to equity is increased by using debt, the risk is greater. At the same time, it may be possible to increase the expected equity yield. This process is known as *financial leverage*.

The lender also faces financial risk in making a mortgage loan. For example, the lender "borrows" from savers to make a mortgage investment. These savers may suddenly decide that they want to withdraw the funds, but the funds are tied up in a long-term investment (a mortgage). The lender may thus be forced to sell the investment at a loss to repay the savers. From the lender's perspective, the mismatch in the time horizon of the borrowed and loaned (invested) funds is a serious problem.

The Risk Return Trade-Off

Thus, financing decisions are made in an environment that involves balancing the expected risks with the expected rewards (returns). Given a level of return, investors choose the investment(s) with the lowest expected risk; conversely, given a level of risk, investors choose the investment(s) with the highest expected return. For example, you have the following choices: mortgage A with an expected return of 12 percent and mortgage B with an expected return of 12 percent. Which would you choose? At first you may say that you are indifferent. However, we left out the vital second dimension: risk. Suppose A is riskier than B. Now you can make a choice—B. Why? Because given a choice when the return is equal, you will prefer the choice with the lowest risk.

Suppose we rewrite the example. You now know that A and B have the *same* risk level. If they had the same expected return, you would be indifferent. However, suppose A's expected return is 13 percent and B's is 12 percent. Which would you choose? Since both A and B have the same expected risk level, you will prefer the one with the highest expected return: A.

In practice, however, investors are not faced with a choice as easy as this. Often, sales pitches tout "high-return, low-risk investment." If investments of this type were indeed available, everyone would want them. Investors would then bid the price of these investments up to the point where they were no longer "high-return, low-risk." Thus, there is a definite positive relationship between expected risk and expected return. We use the term *expected* because before the investment is made, there is no absolute certainty about the return on investment. The greater the certainty of the return, the lower the risk and the lower the rate of return that can be expected. This is why an investment such as a government bond has a relatively low expected return and a speculative common stock investment, which has a higher level of risk, has a much higher expected return.

Thus, the following general principle applies to all investments. *Risk and expected return share a direct, inseparable relationship.* Figure 1-1 illustrates the risk-return trade-off. As the level of risk increases, the required rate of return also increases. Point A is called the risk-free rate. As the level of risk increases to, say, r_1, the required rate of return increases to, say, R_1. The increase in the rate from point A to r_1 is called the *risk premium*. This premium reflects all types of risk discussed previously. (Why is a positive rate required at even a zero level of risk? Don't say it's because you can take your money and put it in the bank and earn interest. *Hint:* What would you do with your money if you didn't loan it to someone?)

Another question concerns what level of risk *should* be assumed or what level

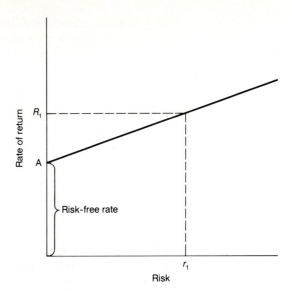

FIGURE 1-1   The risk-return trade-off.

of premium is necessary to account for risk in any investment decision. Unfortunately, there is no easy answer. When deciding the appropriate risk level to assume, each investor must consider current financial position, financial objectives, and personal factors. From the mortgage lender's perspective, the risk level assumed depends on the lender's willingness and ability (based on regulatory constraints) to risk depositor's funds. From the borrower's perspective, the appropriate risk level is based on the borrower's current financial position and objectives.

To summarize, financing decisions are made by comparing the *expected* rate of return on an investment with the *required* rate of return. To illustrate, let's return to our example of a $50,000 loan with payments of $515.47 per month, or $6,185.64 per year. A simple measure of the rate of return on this investment is to divide $6,185.64 by $50,000; the result is 12.37 percent. Would you (the lender) make the loan? To make your decision, you must have a measure of the required rate of return. Suppose your required rate, given the expected risk you must take, was 15 percent. In this case you would not make the loan since you require 15 percent but the loan (investment) is expected to yield only 12.37 percent. Since the element of risk is present in all investment decisions, the borrower and the lender apply the same basic principle in analyzing the investment situation.

THE REAL ESTATE FINANCE INDUSTRY

In the real estate marketplace, lenders (suppliers) compete to make loans and borrowers (demanders) compete to obtain loans. The arena for the transactions between lenders and borrowers is the *finance industry*. The *mortgage market* via such participants as mortgage bankers, mortgage brokers, and various financial institutions, works to bring together these two types of decision makers. In essence, the industry deals with the market for mortgage funds.

Financial Markets

The mortgage market is only one of the many *financial markets* in the United States today. In a broad sense, financial markets include all the institutions and procedures for bringing together buyers and sellers of all types of financial instruments. To understand the operation of the mortgage market, it is important to first understand the operation and purpose of *any* financial market.

Financial markets allocate surplus funds (savings) at the least cost to ultimate users, for either consumption or investment in real assets. Obviously, if those economic units that saved, i.e., individuals, households, partnerships, corporations, were the same as those units that invested, there would be no need for financial markets, including the mortgage market. However, in our modern economy, certain economic units (savings-deficient units), generally nonfinancial corporations, invest an amount(s) greater than their excess savings in real assets. Other economic units (savings-plus units), usually households and individuals, have total savings in excess of total investment. Hence, without financial markets, there would be no balance between investment and savings. The greater the divergence between savings and investment patterns of different economic units, the greater the requirement for efficient financial markets to channel savings to ultimate users.

Financial Intermediaries   Various financial intermediaries satisfy the demand for an efficient method of bringing savers and investors together. Financial intermediaries essentially operate as brokers, for example, mortgage brokers, who specialize in simply bringing savers and borrowers together. The broker is usually able to perform this function more efficiently and cheaper than the individual savings and investment units. The enhanced efficiency these financial agents provide helps facilitate the operation of primary markets for financial securities (including mortgages and mortgage markets).

Financial agents are able to divide a primary security into smaller amounts more compatible with the preferences of savings-surplus units. Thus the attractiveness of primary securities and the flow of savings to users of funds can be improved. The agent may also underwrite the issuing of primary securities by buying them from the borrower and reselling them to savers. The agent thus undertakes the risk of selling the primary securities, and this service makes it easier for savings-deficient units to finance their excess investment in real assets over savings.

Another method of enhancing the efficiency of the interchange between savings-surplus and savings-deficient units is by developing *secondary markets,* where existing securities may be bought or sold. Secondary markets further the liquidity and efficiency of primary markets. With a viable secondary market, savings-surplus units have the flexibility to sell their purchased primary securities, which encourages savers to make their excess funds available to savings-deficient units rather than holding them as money balances.

Financial Institutions and Their Roles   Financial institutions provide many services. Institutions such as commercial banks, savings banks, savings and loan associations, and pension funds act as *financial intermediaries*. But unlike the agents just discussed, these institutions purchase primary securities and in turn issue their own securities, called *indirect securities*. As examples, a mortgage is the primary security a savings and loan association buys; the corresponding indirect security is a savings account or certificate of deposit the association issues. A life insurance company buys stocks, bonds, or mortgages and issues life insurance policies. Figure 1-2 illustrates the relationship among savers, borrowers, financial institutions, and the different kinds of securities.

Thus financial institutions operate to make the transferring of funds more attractive to both savings-surplus and savings-deficient units. Indirect securities are more attractive to savers than direct or primary securities, and borrowers are able to sell primary securities to financial intermediaries much more readily and on more attractive terms than if the securities were sold directly to savers.

Because financial institutions specialize in purchasing primary securities and selling indirect securities, they are able to obtain *economies of scale* the individual borrower or saver cannot. Economies of scale result when the per unit cost of providing a product or service (in this case, primary and indirect security transactions) decreases as the quantity produced (number of transactions) increases.

Financial institutions are able to transform indirect securities of varying *sizes* into primary securities of a specific size. Since indirect securities are generally smaller than primary securities, this process often involves pooling the resources of many individual indirect securities. Because different economic units save in different amounts, financial institutions generally offer indirect securities in many sizes, contributing greatly to the financial institution's attractiveness to the saver. The borrower gains the advantage of dealing with only one or a few financial institutions as opposed to a large number of savers.

By purchasing a variety of different primary securities, a financial institution is able to *diversify,* or spread, the risk associated with any single primary security. Individual savers are generally unable to adequately diversify on their own. For example, a savings and loan association can minimize the effect of any one mortgage's going into default by pooling many different mortgages. Financial institutions are able to pass on the benefits of reduced risk to the indirect security holders. Consequently, indirect securities give the saver a higher degree of liquidity than a single primary security does.

Maturity is the length of time it takes a loan or financial security to become

FIGURE 1-2   Flow of funds and securities: an economy with financial institutions.

due. Financial institutions are able to transform indirect securities of different and variable maturities into primary securities of a *specific maturity*. If a loan were direct from saver to borrower, the two parties would have to inconveniently negotiate a mutually acceptable maturity on the loan. Financial institutions must try to solve this problem. Consequently, the maturities on the primary and indirect securities may be more attractive to the borrower and the saver.

As a result of their specialization in purchasing primary securities and selling indirect securities, financial institutions have developed a level of *expertise* that eliminates the borrower's and the saver's inconvenience of being involved in direct transactions. For example, most individuals are not familiar with the procedures and intricacies of making a mortgage loan, and they rarely have the inclination or the time to learn. Most savers are happy to purchase indirect securities by placing deposits into a savings account, money market fund, certificate of deposit, etc., letting the financial institution loan funds to purchase primary securities. In addition to their ability to handle borrowers, most financial institutions also know how to deal with savers—expertise most borrowers lack.

For these reasons financial institutions make a profit by investing in primary securities that yield more than the return the institutions must pay on indirect securities sold and the cost of operations. To make the profits, the institutions must be able to transfer funds from savers to borrowers more efficiently and at a lower cost than would be possible if ultimate savers directly bought primary securities.

Figure 1-3 illustrates the distribution of total residential mortgage debt outstanding among the various types of financial institutions. Note the decline in the role of thrift institutions. Also note the importance of increased holdings of mort-

FIGURE 1-3 Residential mortgage assets by type of holder. (*Source:* Federal Reserve Bulletin, *December 1987.*)

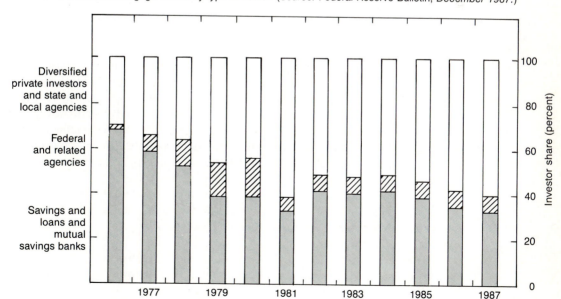

gages by diversified private investors, investors that have bought loans in the secondary mortgage market. These securities are issued by the various intermediaries, such as the Federal National Mortgage Association (FNMA), with mortgages as the collateral. Finally, note the increased role of state and local agencies through the issuance of tax-exempt bonds to subsidize home borrowers.

Mortgage Market

The *mortgage market* is the mechanism by which the capital available for mortgage loans can be allocated among the competing users either for investment in real estate or consumption (use). Funds go to the potential users that bid the most for the scarce resource (capital). The interaction between the supply of and the demand for loanable funds determines the price of funds in the mortgage market; this price is the *interest rate*.

The mortgage market has developed a variety of financing methods for bringing together the borrower (demand) and the lender (supply). The financing process is governed by a host of laws and regulations designed to protect both borrowers and lenders. Also, in recent years there has been an increase in the various types of government programs that influence the operation of the mortgage market.

The mortgage market is divided into two segments: *primary* and *secondary*. Each has different participants and roles within the mortgage market.

The Primary Market   The primary mortgage market is composed of lenders that originate (make) the loans and the ultimate borrowers of these loans. The lenders are savings and loan associations, commercial banks, life insurance companies, finance companies, credit unions, mutual savings banks, and government agencies. The borrowers are individuals who buy homes, and private and corporate investors that buy real estate for investment or use in their businesses.

Because of its high visibility, the primary market is responsible for the popular image of the mortgage market. Yet lenders and borrowers alike often do not realize the full impact of the mortgage market on the economy: Mortgage debt alone is the single largest type of debt in the United States. Table 1-1 shows the mortgage debt outstanding up to the second quarter of 1987, the most recent figures available at this writing. Total mortgage debt is listed in **bold** print in the top line and broken down by type of property financed (lines 2 to 5) and by lending institutions (lines 6 to 63). To put the total debt in perspective, note that total mortgage debt outstanding at the end of the second quarter of 1987 was 2.74 trillion.

The major borrowers in the primary market are households, and, as Table 1-1 shows, the major type of lender is the savings and loan association, accounting for $823 billion in outstanding mortgages at the end of the second quarter of 1987, or over 30 percent of total mortgage debt outstanding.

The Secondary Market   The secondary mortgage market deals with buying and selling mortgages that have been originated in the primary mortgage market.

TABLE 1-1 MORTGAGE DEBT OUTSTANDING[a]
(Millions of dollars, end of period)

Type of holder, and type of property	1984	1985	1986	1986			1987	
				Q2	Q3	Q4	Q1	Q2
1 **All holders**	**2,035,238**	**2,269,173**	**2,565,867**	**2,386,022**	**2,471,574**	**2,565,867**	**2,658,942**	**2,744,930**
2 1- to 4-family	1,318,545	1,467,409	1,666,357	1,544,392	1,607,799	1,666,357	1,709,863	1,770,953
3 Multifamily	185,604	214,045	246,879	229,405	237,661	246,879	259,309	266,913
4 Commercial	419,444	482,029	555,825	511,038	526,535	555,825	596,507	615,264
5 Farm	111,645	105,690	96,806	101,187	99,579	96,806	93,263	91,800
6 Major financial institutions	1,269,702	1,390,394	1,506,422	1,435,437	1,464,213	1,506,422	1,557,014	1,600,779
7 Commercial banks[b]	379,498	429,196	502,534	456,163	474,658	502,534	517,271	542,575
8 1- to 4-family	196,163	213,434	235,814	221,640	228,593	235,814	241,512	251,701
9 Multifamily	20,264	23,373	31,173	26,799	28,623	31,173	31,745	33,585
10 Commercial	152,894	181,032	222,799	195,484	204,996	222,799	230,771	243,399
11 Farm	10,177	11,357	12,748	12,240	12,446	12,748	13,243	13,890
12 Savings institutions[c]	709,718	760,499	777,312	768,435	772,175	777,312	809,967	823,217
13 1- to 4-family	528,791	554,301	558,412	556,039	557,938	558,412	557,065	567,262
14 Multifamily	75,567	89,739	97,059	92,563	94,227	97,059	103,698	105,649
15 Commercial	104,896	115,771	121,236	119,195	119,406	121,236	148,688	149,804
16 Farm	464	688	605	638	604	605	516	502
17 Life insurance companies	156,699	171,797	192,975	180,041	185,269	192,975	194,689	198,089
18 1- to 4-family	14,120	12,381	12,763	12,608	12,927	12,763	12,832	12,832
19 Multifamily	18,938	19,894	20,847	20,181	20,709	20,847	20,820	20,820
20 Commercial	111,175	127,670	148,367	135,924	140,213	148,367	150,592	154,192
21 Farm	12,466	11,852	10,998	11,328	11,420	10,998	10,445	10,245
22 Finance companies[d]	23,787	28,902	33,601	30,798	32,111	33,601	35,087	36,898
23 Federal and related agencies	158,993	166,928	203,800	161,398	159,505	203,800	199,509	196,498
24 Government National Mortgage Association	2,301	1,473	889	876	887	889	687	665
25 1- to 4-family	585	539	47	49	48	47	46	45
26 Multifamily	1,716	934	842	827	839	842	641	620
27 Farmers Home Administration[e]	1,276	733	48,421	570	457	48,421	48,203	48,085
28 1- to 4-family	213	183	21,625	146	132	21,625	21,390	21,157
29 Multifamily	119	113	7,608	66	57	7,608	7,710	7,808
30 Commercial	497	159	8,446	111	115	8,446	8,463	8,553
31 Farm	447	278	10,742	247	153	10,742	10,640	10,567
32 Federal Housing and Veterans Administration	4,816	4,920	5,047	5,094	4,966	5,047	5,177	5,254
33 1- to 4-family	2,048	2,254	2,386	2,449	2,331	2,386	2,447	2,504
34 Multifamily	2,768	2,666	2,661	2,645	2,635	2,661	2,730	2,750
35 Federal National Mortgage Association	87,940	98,282	97,895	97,295	97,717	97,895	95,140	94,064
36 1- to 4-family	87,175	91,966	90,718	90,460	90,508	90,718	88,106	87,013
37 Multifamily	5,765	6,316	7,177	6,835	7,209	7,177	7,034	7,051
38 Federal Land Banks	52,261	47,498	39,984	43,369	42,119	39,984	37,362	35,833
39 1- to 4-family	3,074	2,798	2,353	2,552	2,478	2,353	2,198	2,108
40 Farm	49,187	44,700	37,631	40,817	39,641	37,631	35,164	33,725
41 Federal Home Loan Mortgage Corporation	10,399	14,022	11,564	14,194	13,359	11,564	12,940	12,597
42 1- to 4-family	9,654	11,881	10,010	11,890	11,127	10,010	11,774	11,172
43 Multifamily	745	2,141	1,554	2,304	2,232	1,554	1,166	1,425

TABLE 1 MORTGAGE DEBT OUTSTANDING[a] *(Continued)*

(Millions of dollars, end of period)

Type of holder, and type of property	1984	1985	1986	1986 Q2	1986 Q3	1986 Q4	1987 Q1	1987 Q2
44 Mortgage pools or trusts[f]	332,057	415,042	529,763	475,615	222,721	529,763	571,705	612,408
45 Government National Mortgage Association	179,981	212,145	260,869	229,204	241,230	260,869	277,386	290,512
46 1- to 4-family	175,589	207,198	255,132	223,838	235,664	255,132	271,065	283,892
47 Multifamily	4,392	4,947	5,737	5,366	5,566	5,737	6,321	6,620
48 Federal Home Loan Mortgage Corporation	70,822	100,387	171,372	125,903	146,871	171,372	186,295	200,284
49 1- to 4-family	70,253	99,515	166,667	123,676	143,734	166,667	180,602	194,238
50 Multifamily	569	872	4,705	2,227	3,137	4,705	5,693	6,046
51 Federal National Mortgage Association	36,215	54,987	97,174	72,377	86,359	97,174	107,673	121,270
52 1- to 4-family	35,965	54,036	95,791	71,153	85,171	95,791	106,068	119,540
53 Multifamily	250	951	1,383	1,224	1,188	1,383	1,605	1,730
54 Farmers Home Administration[e]	45,039	47,523	348	48,131	48,216	348	351	342
55 1- to 4-family	21,813	22,186	142	21,987	21,782	142	154	149
56 Multifamily	5,841	6,675	n.a.	7,170	7,353	n.a.	n.a.	n.a.
57 Commercial	7,559	8,190	132	8,347	8,409	132	127	126
58 Farm	9,826	10,472	74	10,627	10,717	74	70	67
59 Individuals and others[g]	274,486	296,809	325,882	313,572	325,135	325,882	330,714	335,245
60 1- to 4-family	154,315	165,835	180,896	175,107	183,255	180,896	179,517	180,442
61 Multifamily	48,670	55,424	66,133	61,198	63,886	66,133	70,146	72,809
62 Commercial	42,423	49,207	54,845	51,977	53,396	54,845	57,866	59,190
63 Farm	29,078	26,343	24,008	25,290	24,598	24,008	23,185	22,804

[a] Based on data from various institutional and governmental sources, with some quarters estimated in part by the Federal Reserve. Multifamily debt refers to loans on structures of five or more units.

[b] Includes loans held by nondeposit trust companies but not bank trust departments.

[c] Includes savings banks and savings and loan associations. Beginning 1987:1, data reported by FSLIC-insured institutions include loans in process and other contra assets.

[d] Assumed to be entirely 1- to 4-family loans.

[e] FmHA-guaranteed securities sold to the Federal Financing Bank were reallocated from FmHA mortgage pools to FmHA mortgage holdings in 1986:4, because of accounting changes by the Farmers Home Administration.

[f] Outstanding principal balances of mortgage pools backing securities insured or guaranteed by the agency indicated.

[g] Other holders include mortgage companies, real estate investment trusts, state and local credit agencies, state and local retirement funds, noninsured pension funds, credit unions, and other U.S. agencies.

Source: Federal Reserve Bulletin, December 1987, p. 439.

The secondary mortgage market is made up of those lenders that originate mortgages and other lenders that purchase the loans from the originators—virtually all major public and private financial institutions are included. A major purpose of the secondary market is to allow a mortgage lender to make a loan, sell it, and with the funds received from the sale, make another loan in the local market. This way, areas of the country with insufficient savings (deposit) inflows to meet the mortgage loan demand may meet this need by drawing on other areas where savings inflows exceed mortgage demand. In effect, funds are shifted from capital-rich areas to those that are capital-poor. The secondary market is also a readilyavailable place for investors to invest funds in mortgages without having to wait for a borrower to apply for funds, as happens in the primary market.

Federal credit agencies—the FNMA, Federal Home Loan Mortgage Corporation (FHLMC), Government National Mortgage Association (GNMA), Federal Land Banks,and Farmers Home Administration (FmHA)—help create a national market for existing mortgages to facilitate the leveling of the peaks and valleys in available financing and shift funds from capital-rich to capital-poor areas. These agencies have grown phenomenally over the past decade because of restrictions on savings institutions, limiting the maximum rates that could be paid to depositors. These restrictions narrowed the ability of savings institutions in capital-poor areas to attract additional funds from outside sources to meet local mortgage loan demand. In addition, the government (primarily GNMA) issued pass-through securities; the securities are backed by a pool of mortgages, and a government agency guarantees the principal and interest payments to the investors, even if the borrower is delinquent in payments. Exhibit 1-1 summarizes the federal agencies' functions.

This broadening of the market for mortgage loans has led to considerable nationwide standardization of mortgage loan instruments, allowing easier comparison of market risk and return for mortgages vis-à-vis other investment vehicles. As a result, the secondary mortgage market has a computerized information system similar to that used by the stock market, whereby market prices and yields for various mortgages available in the secondary market can be quickly obtained.

Interest and Determination The mortgage interest rate takes into account both the lender's and the borrower's numerous expectations and assumptions. Figure 1-4 conceptually illustrates the mortgage market. The interest rate i is on the vertical axis, and the flow of funds Q in the mortgage market is on the horizontal axis.

The *SS* curve represents the supply of funds for mortgage lending. The greater the interest rate, the greater the supply of funds. This curve is drawn holding constant the risk that the lender perceives. If, for example, the risk declines, the lender will be willing to loan more funds at a given interest rate. Thus there will be a shift (outward) in the supply curve.

The *DD* curve illustrates the demand for funds. The quantity of funds demanded decreases as the interest rate increases. If, for example, home ownership for an area increases, a greater amount of funds will be demanded. Thus there will be a shift upward in the demand curve.

The equilibrium price of loanable funds (the interest rate) is subject to the laws of supply and demand. In Figure 1-4, i_e is the equilibrium interest rate and Q_e is the equilibrium quantity. Changes in factors influencing the supply and/or demand will obviously influence the equilibrium interest rate and quantity.

Interest Rates and Risk When making a mortgage loan, the lender faces the types of risk discussed earlier; in other words, the *realized yield* on the loan may

EXHIBIT 1-1   SELECTED HOUSING CREDIT AGENCIES

The *Federal National Mortgage Association* (FNMA or Fannie Mae) provides funds to mortgage originators through its purchases of mortgages on the secondary market. It became a privately owned corporation in 1968. Previously, it was wholly owned by the Federal Government (1938-54) and under mixed ownership (1954-68). FNMA is subject to supervision by the Secretary of Housing and Urban Development and, regarding its issues of securities, by the Secretary of the Treasury.

FNMA acquires home mortgages through three types of programs. First, biweekly auctions are held at which FNMA offers commitments to purchase home mortgages. Mortgage originators who want to obtain a commitment from FNMA submit bids that specify the volume of mortgages for which commitments are sought and the yield to FNMA. Delivery of the mortgages during the 4-month commitment period is at the option of the mortgage originator.

Second, FNMA sells 9- and 12-month convertible, standby commitments at posted prices, i.e., outside the auction system. After holding a standby commitment for 4 months, the holder may convert it to a 4-month commitment, with the yield to FNMA being the weighted average yield at the most recent auction. Under a standby commitment, delivery of the mortgages is at the option of the mortgage originator.

Third, FNMA initiated a number of new mandatory delivery programs in 1981. For each of these, FNMA specifies a yield at which it will purchase mortgages; generally, delivery must be made within 1 to 4 months.

FNMA finances its operations by the sale of debentures and notes in capital markets and by charging commitment fees. Although its notes and debentures are classified as "Federal Agency Securities," they are not obligations of the Federal Government and are not federally guaranteed.

The *Government National Mortgage Association* (GNMA or Ginnie Mae) assists in providing mortgage credit and in stabilizing the financing of selected types of mortgages. It was established within the Department of Housing and Urban Development in 1968 to take over some of the activities that previously had been performed by FNMA. Many of those activities—notably the servicing and disposal of mortgages it purchased or that were transferred to it, and the purchase and resale of mortgages at yields that subsidized housing—have since been reduced to very low levels.

Currently, GNMA's primary involvement in the mortgage market is through its mortgage-backed securities program. Since 1970, GNMA has guaranteed the timely payment of principal and interest on passthrough certificates backed by pools of federally underwritten mortgages. (In a pool backing GNMA passthroughs, the individual mortgages are insured by the Federal Housing Administration or guaranteed by the Veterans Administration. Thus, GNMA's guarantees of the passthrough certificates mainly cover the timing of the cash flow.)

The *Federal Home Loan Mortgage Corporation* (FHLMC, The Mortgage Corporation, or Freddie Mac) provides assistance to the secondary market for home mortgages by supplying liquidity through its purchases of mortgages. Its primary concern is the secondary market for conventional home mortgages, i.e., those not insured by the Federal Housing Administration or guaranteed by the Veterans Administration. The FHLMC was chartered by Congress in 1970 as a private corporation. It is owned by the 12 Federal home loan banks (which, in turn, are owned by their member institutions).

FHLMC periodically auctions commitments to purchase mortgages. Auctions for 8-month commitments, with delivery at the option of the mortgage originator, are held monthly. Auctions for the "immediate purchase" of mortgages—under which mortgages must be delivered to FHLMC within 60 days—are held weekly. Like FNMA, FHLMC decides after each auction which bids to accept.

Mortgages acquired by the FHLMC are placed in pools and used to back the issuance of two kinds of certificates: participation certificates and guaranteed mortgage certificates. FHLMC guarantees the timely payment of interest and principal to owners of participation certificates, and the semi-annual payment of interest and annual repayment of principal to owners of guaranteed mortgage certificates. Sales of the two kinds of certificates provide FHLMC with most of the funds it needs to operate its mortgage purchase programs.

The *Federal Home Loan Bank System* has supervisory and regulatory authority for system members and provides credit to members to stabilize their mortgage lending. The System was established by an act of Congress in 1932. It is supervised by the Federal Home Loan Bank Board, an agency in the executive branch of the Federal Government. The System consists, in addition to the Board, of 12 Federal home loan banks, which are owned by their member institutions.

The Board has supervisory and regulatory authority for all federally chartered savings and loan associations. These associations are required by law to be members of the System. In addition, about 2,000 State-chartered savings and loan associations have joined voluntarily in order to qualify for insurance by the Federal Savings and Loan Insurance Corporation, as have over 80 mutual savings banks and few life insurance companies.

The 12 banks make loans ("advances") to their member institutions, serving as a central source of credit. These advances meet heavy withdrawals of deposits, smooth seasonal imbalance between deposits and loan disbursements, and allow expansion of mortgage lending. The primary source of financing for the banks' advances is the sale of consolidated obligations in the money and capital markets. (Like FNMA's debt, these obligations are classified as "Federal Agency Securities," but they are not obligations of the Federal Government and are not federally guaranteed.) Deposits received from member banks also help finance advances.

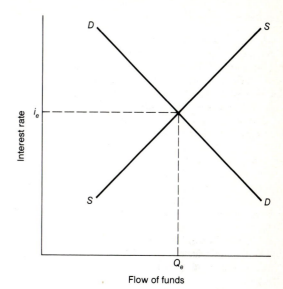

FIGURE 1-4   Mortgage market supply and demand.

be different from the *expected yield*. To adjust for the risk, the lender adds a "risk" premium to the base (risk-free) rate. The risk premium is influenced by many factors, such as default possibilities, liquidity, and inflation expectations. Changes in any of these factors will change the equilibrium interest rate through shifts in the supply curve.

Figure 1-5 shows the relationship between inflation and interest rates from 1970 to 1987. During the early 1970s the average mortgage interest rate was about 8 percent. There was a sharp rise in 1974, with a downward cycle in 1976. Another up-down cycle occurred over the 1979–1981 period. Mortgage rates generally declined during the mid-1980s.

Mortgage Submarkets

The mortgage market is divided into various submarkets: short-term versus permanent (long-term) financing, insured (by government or private mortgage insurance company) versus conventional (uninsured) loans, and various types of properties. The market creates these divisions in response to many factors, primarily differing risk-return characteristics.

Income Property Mortgage Market   An important segment of the mortgage market is the long-term financing of income properties. Because various types of income properties involve different risk factors, the financing costs change according to the property type. And since the factors influencing the risk for a loan change by geographical area in the United States, the financing also varies.

Table 1-2 summarizes the financing cost for various subgroups within the in-

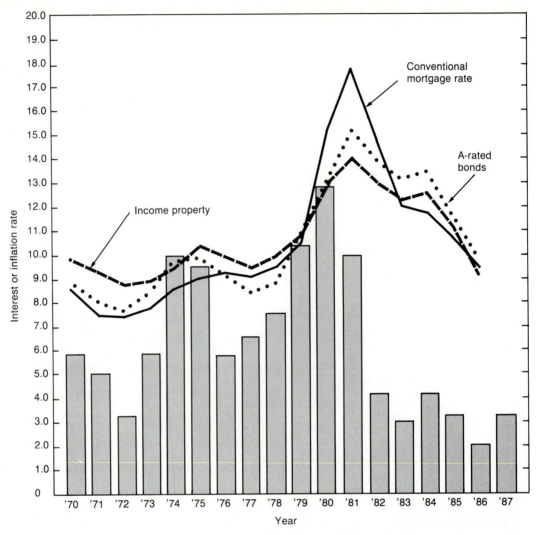

FIGURE 1-5 Relationship between inflation and interest rates from 1970 to 1987. (*Sources: Federal Home Loan Bank Board and the American Council of Life Insurance.*)

come property mortgage market. The averages for the period 1979 to 1987 are based on life insurance companies' financing terms for such types of income property loans as apartments, commercial and retail establishments, office buildings, individual properties, and hotels and motels.

Residential Mortgage Markets The residential mortgage market is subdivided into "conventional," or noninsured, mortgage loans and loans insured by a government agency. The Federal Housing Administration (FHA) is the primary gov-

TABLE 1-2 TERMS OF MORTGAGE LOAN COMMITMENTS MADE ON INCOME PROPERTIES

Period	No. of loans	Amount committed ($000)	Loan amount ($000)	Interest rate (% by no.)	Interest rate (% by $)	Loan/value (%)	Capitaliza-tion rate (%)	Debt coverage ratio	Percent constant	Maturity (years/months)
					Averages					
1979:										
1st quarter	647	2,565,725	3,966	10.03	10.02	74.5	10.2	1.24	11.1	20/7
2nd quarter	786	3,399,869	4,326	10.23	10.26	74.5	10.4	1.25	11.1	21/5
3rd quarter	742	2,974,591	4,009	10.45	10.42	73.9	10.6	1.28	11.2	22/1
4th quarter	462	1,821,356	3,942	10.91	10.95	73.0	10.7	1.27	11.7	21/4
Year	2,637	10,761,541	4,081	10.36	10.36	74.1	10.5	1.26	11.3	21/5
1980:										
1st quarter	194	1,021,201	5,265	10.32	12.10	73.6	11.8	1.26	12.8	20/8
2nd quarter	83	634,865	7,649	13.20	12.95	73.6	12.6	1.27	13.6	17/7
3rd quarter	214	1,531,289	7,156	12.58	12.40	74.3	12.1	1.27	13.0	18/3
4th quarter	165	992,934	6,018	13.04	12.90	71.6	12.2	1.28	13.4	16/8
Year	656	4,180,289	6,372	12.69	12.53	73.3	12.1	1.27	13.1	18/6
1981:										
1st quarter	155	692,842	4,470	13.90	13.48	72.3	12.8	1.32	14.2	14/3
2nd quarter	144	1,206,421	8,378	14.28	13.48	69.0	13.0	1.29	14.5	17/8
3rd quarter	107	916,068	8,561	14.47	14.34	71.4	13.1	1.28	14.7	17/3
4th quarter	87	446,974	5,138	14.98	14.77	67.4	13.4	1.34	15.2	13/8
Year	493	3,262,305	6,617	14.32	13.90	70.3	13.0	1.30	14.6	15/10
1982:										
1st quarter	135	1,098,020	8,133	15.23	14.63	66.2	12.9	1.39	15.5	14/3
2nd quarter	137	847,589	6,187	15.23	14.74	66.4	12.8	1.36	15.3	12/2
3rd quarter	139	750,754	5,401	14.75	14.49	64.9	12.0	1.28	15.1	10/0
4th quarter	260	2,132,089	8,200	13.26	13.30	67.6	11.6	1.30	13.7	9/6
Year	671	4,828,452	7,196	14.36	14.04	66.5	12.2	1.33	14.7	11/1
1983:										
1st quarter	285	2,009,854	7,052	12.89	12.85	69.8	11.4	1.30	13.2	8/9
2nd quarter	334	2,723,891	8,155	12.25	12.28	70.7	11.0	1.26	12.6	10/0
3rd quarter	328	2,894,789	8,826	12.29	12.29	69.2	10.8	1.28	12.6	9/10
4th quarter	234	2,337,340	9,989	12.67	12.57	70.5	11.1	1.23	13.1	9/10
Year	1,118	9,965,874	88,439	12.49	12.46	70.0	11.1	1.27	12.8	9/7
1984:										
1st quarter	357	3,482,348	9,754	12.59	12.55	70.3	10.8	1.26	12.8	10/0
2nd quarter	285	3,345,201	1,738	12.97	12.95	68.1	10.5	1.27	13.2	9/10
3rd quarter	142	2,131,375	15,010	13.40	12.85	72.5	11.2	1.16	13.6	9/9
4th quarter	354	4,009,911	11,327	12.91	12.90	70.5	10.8	1.22	13.2	9/1
Year	1,138	12,968,835	11,396	12.88	12.81	70.1	10.8	1.24	13.1	9/8
1985:										
1st quarter	528	4,405,871	8,344	12.38	12.28	70.0	10.5	1.25	12.7	8/7
2nd quarter	473	4,973,043	10,514	12.17	11.98	70.8	10.2	1.23	12.4	8/1
3rd quarter	603	5,234,854	8,681	11.42	11.40	71.5	9.9	1.24	11.7	8/3
4th quarter	555	6,020,011	10,847	11.25	11.20	71.5	9.8	1.25	11.5	8/1
Year	2,159	20,633,779	9,557	11.77	11.67	71.0	10.1	1.24	12.1	8/3
1986:										
1st quarter	549	5,986,204	10,904	10.39	10.25	71.6	9.5	1.28	10.9	8/10
2nd quarter	720	7,769,458	10,791	9.62	9.47	71.2	9.3	1.28	10.4	9/3
3rd quarter	423	4,713,001	11,142	9.40	9.30	71.4	9.1	1.32	10.1	9/0
4th quarter	443	5,595,257	12,630	9.36	9.03	70.2	9.1	1.40	10.0	8/9
Year	2,135	24,063,920	11.27	9.72	9.53	71.1	9.3	1.32	10.3	9/0
1987:										
1st quarter	394	3,998,061	10,147	9.16	8.97	72.0	9.1	1.31	9.8	8/9

Note: Data represent new commitments for future disbursement. Similar data for a smaller sample of companies are available beginning in 1951. Except for the dollar-weighted interest rate, averages are based on number of loans for which the data were available. In the latest quarter, an interest rate was not available for one commitment amounting to $7.3 million. Rates vary in part with the changing composition of loans as to property type, location, purpose of loans, amortization, call, and prepayment provisions and are particularly affected by such loan provision.
Source: Investment Bulletin, American Council of Life Insurance, Washington, D.C., July 1987.

19

ernment agency involved in insuring mortgage loans. The FHA does not actually loan money. For an annual insurance premium of one-half of 1 percent of the outstanding loan balance, paid by the borrower, the agency will insure loans made by approved lenders according to specific regulations. Under the program, buyers are able to obtain 40-year loans at up to 97 percent of the value of a newly constructed home. Historically, the interest rate allowed on an FHA-insured loan was fixed by the Secretary of Housing and Urban Development. The FHA rate is typically one- to three-quarters of a percentage point lower than the rate on conventional noninsured loans. Congressional action has moved toward allowing the interest rate on FHA loans to be determined by the market.

Another type of residential mortgage is a Veterans Administration (VA) guaranteed mortgage, often called a VA or GI mortgage. Under a VA mortgage, the VA guarantees a percentage of a veteran's mortgage loan from a qualified lender, up to some specified maximum amount. The amount of the maximum loan guarantee, the rate of interest, and the mortgage maturity can be changed by an act of Congress.

Conventional mortgages are loans made without FHA insurance or VA guarantees, generally at lower loan-to-value ratios and with higher interest rates than government-guaranteed or -insured loans. Table 1-3 shows the average interest rate, fees and charges, terms to maturity, and loan-to-value ratio on conventional mortgage loans from 1984 through September, 1987. Table 1-4 gives the interest rates for various loan-to-value ratios. As discussed earlier, the higher the loan as

TABLE 1-3 TERMS ON ALL CONVENTIONAL HOME MORTGAGE LOANS

Period	Contract interest rate (%)	Initial fees and charges (%)	Effective rate (%)	Term to maturity (years)	Loan amount ($000)	Purchase price ($000)	Loan-to-value ratio (%)
1984	11.87	2.67		27.8	73.7	96.8	78.7
1985	11.12	2.53		26.9	77.4	104.1	77.1
1986	9.82	2.48		26.6	86.2	118.1	75.2
1987							
Jan	9.14	2.23		27.7	97.3	132.6	75.5
Feb	8.87	2.21		27.6	99.1	135.6	75.3
March	8.77	2.20		27.1	95.0	130.2	74.3
April	8.84	2.23		27.1	100.9	136.9	75.2
May	8.99	2.26		28.0	99.0	132.9	76.1
June	9.05	2.40		28.0	97.5	131.8	75.9
July	9.01	2.42		27.9	99.4	134.6	75.4
Aug	9.01	2.19		27.8	102.6	141.2	75.0
Sept	9.03	2.08		27.3	100.8	140.2	74.6

Source: Federal Reserve Bulletin, December 1987, p. A38.

TABLE 1-4   INTEREST RATES FOR DIFFERENT LOAN-TO-VALUE RATIOS

Period	Contract interest rate (%) Loan-to-price ratio					Effective interest rate (%) Loan-to-price ratio				
	50	75	80	90	95	50	75	80	90	95
1979	10.94	11.00	11.05	11.23	11.28	11.20	11.27	11.32	11.54	11.63
1980	13.60	13.63	13.66	13.80	13.86	13.97	14.00	14.02	14.21	14.30
1981	16.21	16.24	16.25	16.40	16.49	16.68	16.71	16.72	16.92	17.05
1982	16.07	16.09	16.08	16.22	16.24	16.57	16.59	16.59	16.77	16.82
1982:										
Jan.	16.80	16.83	16.84	17.00	17.13	17.31	17.34	17.35	17.56	17.72
Feb.	16.96	16.99	17.01	17.20	17.31	17.47	17.50	17.52	17.75	17.90
Mar.	16.98	17.00	17.02	17.16	17.24	17.49	17.51	17.54	17.72	17.83
Apr.	16.85	16.87	16.89	17.03	17.05	17.37	17.39	17.41	17.59	17.64
May	16.75	16.77	16.77	16.90	16.91	17.26	17.28	17.29	17.46	17.50
June	16.63	16.64	16.65	16.80	16.80	17.14	17.16	17.16	17.35	17.39
July	16.70	16.71	16.72	16.88	16.91	17.21	17.23	17.23	17.44	17.50
Aug.	16.48	16.50	16.50	16.63	16.67	16.99	17.01	17.02	17.20	17.25
Sept.	15.66	15.68	15.67	15.76	15.69	16.17	16.18	16.18	16.31	16.26
Oct.	15.10	15.12	15.09	15.20	15.21	15.60	15.62	15.59	15.74	15.78
Nov.	14.14	14.15	14.11	14.25	14.16	14.62	14.63	14.59	14.77	14.70
Dec.	13.75	13.76	13.74	13.87	13.83	14.20	14.22	14.21	14.38	14.35

Source: Federal Home Loan Bank Board Journal, March 1983.

a proportion value of the real estate, the higher the risk to the lender. Note in Table 1-4 how the mortgage rate increases with higher loan-to-value ratios.

With this background on the overall real estate finance industry, we can now discuss the process by which financing decisions are made.

THE FINANCING PROCESS

Figure 1-6 illustrates the *process* of making real estate lending-borrowing decisions. Following is an overview of the steps the lender takes to arrive at a decision to make a loan to the borrower.

The Borrowing Decision

The financing process is initiated by the borrower (equity investor). The borrower analyzes the expected return of a proposed real estate purchase (or a currently owned property) and the risks involved and then makes a decision whether to possibly borrow funds to finance (or refinance) the property. Through informal inquiry prior to formal application, the prospective borrower obtains an estimation of the various types of financing available and their respective terms and costs. These factors are also used in the analysis of

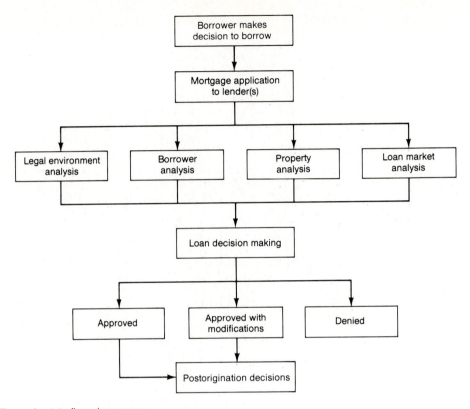

FIGURE 1-6 The real estate financing process.

the investment decision. Many times, the investor enters into a sales contract with a seller contingent on the buyer (borrower) obtaining financing. The decision to *invest* in a project is a separate but interrelated decision from the *financing* decision. The financing decision is of main concern in this book. The borrower makes the financing decision by comparing the costs and the benefits; numerous factors, such as taxes, influence this decision, as we see in Chapter 7.

The Mortgage Loan Application

Once the prospective borrower has decided to apply, the borrower makes a formal mortgage application to a lender in the mortgage market. Sometimes applications are submitted to more than one lender simultaneously, to broaden the borrower's financing options; this practice is of course costly.

The nature of both the borrower and the property partly determines the choice of lender(s). As discussed earlier, lending preferences vary among institutions. For example, historically, the most likely source of funds for the purchase of a single-family residence has been a savings and loan association or a commercial bank. The lenders' affinities for different types of loans are based on their risk-return preferences and, to some extent, regulatory constraints, although recent deregulation has loosened many constraints.

In the loan-application stage, various types of information have to be collected through documents like an application form, requests for credit reports, requests for verification of assets and employment, borrower's financial statement, and sales contract on property. Using these documents, the lender analyzes various aspects of the environment in which the lending decision is to be made.

The Environment for Financing Decisions

The economic environment influences both the lender's and the borrower's decision-making process. The various risk categories discussed earlier have to be formally analyzed.

Legal Environment Analysis In this stage, the lender applies general legal principles to the application at hand. The property title must be examined for accuracy and the existence of any legal claims against the property. The laws relating to the types of loans and terms that may be offered must be known. Government restrictions on the property in the form of police power and taxation must be considered. In addition, the rights of tenants currently leasing the property must be considered, insofar as their rights may affect the lender's position. Finally, the mortgage document and promissory note must be drafted in a manner that makes it legally binding on the parties. This process is done to ensure that the lender's interest is not impaired. Chapter 3 analyzes the financing legal environment in detail.

Borrower Analysis The lender requires assurance that there is a reasonable likelihood of the borrower's repaying the loan. *Default risk* plays a major role in the lender's decision making. There are several central issues. First, does the borrower have the financial *ability* to repay the loan? To make this determination, the lender examines the borrower's current and expected future financial status, the amount of proposed equity investment, and the proposed debt service or payments. Second, the lender wants to know if the buyer *intends* to pay back the loan. Intent is generally measured by past fiscal responsibility, as evidenced by the borrower's credit rating. With this information and the use of various ratios, the lender can analyze the risk associated with the borrower regarding the probability that default on the loan will occur. Chapter 4 covers borrower analysis.

Property Analysis Since real estate is serving as collateral for a mortgage loan, the lender must examine various aspects of the property to ensure that the property is of sufficient value to cover the loan amount. A professional appraiser is hired to estimate the property's market value. In addition, the future value of the property must be estimated to determine whether the property will continue to provide sufficient collateral until the loan is repaid. If the proposed loan is to be paid back partially or totally from income generated by the property, current and future estimates of the property's income-producing ability must be considered. Chapters 5 and 6 describe the techniques for property analysis from the borrower's and the lender's perspectives.

Market Analysis Before making the decision to loan, the lender also considers the implications external economic factors may have on the mortgage loan (investment) in particular and the lender's total investment portfolio in general. The liquidity and marketability of loans in the secondary market must be considered, as well as the availability of funds to lend, current conditions in financial markets, and inflation expectations. Since a mortgage is an investment for the lender, other investment options must be considered along with their respective risk-return relationships and the lender's portfolio objectives. The lender is concerned with the *business* and *inflation risks* surrounding the investment decision.

Finance Decision Making

Using the information obtained from the analysis of the factors expected to influence the loan's profitability, the lender must then make the decision: approve (make the loan) or deny (do not make the loan). Occasionally, the lender will agree to make the loan provided that certain items in the original application are modified.

How does the lender make the investment decision? What types of decisions must the lender analyze? The lender must answer many questions. For example, what should the "price" (interest rate) of the loan be? Will the loan be marketable should the lender decide to sell the mortgage? What types of restrictions, such as due-on-sale clauses, should be placed in the loan document? Can there be a prepayment penalty? What type (and how much) of origination fees should be charged? What is the expected yield on the loan? All these (and other) questions must be answered before a decision can be arrived at.

If the lender decides to make the loan, a written approval, called a *firm commitment,* is issued to the borrower. The borrower then has a specified amount of time to accept or reject the commitment. If the commitment is accepted, the borrower then has a specified length of time to borrow the committed funds.

If the lender agrees to make the loan subject to certain modifications, such as a lower loan-to-value ratio, private mortgage insurance, modified payment schedule or interest rate, or additional collateral, typically a *conditional commitment* will be issued. If the borrower agrees to the modifications, the conditional commitment becomes firm and the borrower has a stated amount of time in which to borrow the committed funds.

A loan denial means that the legal, borrower, property, or market analysis, or some combination thereof, made the proposed loan appear unsatisfactory as an investment for the lender. At this point the borrower must ascertain the reasons for the denial and, if able, correct the problem. Possibly another lender will perceive the situation differently and consent to make the loan.

Postorigination Decisions

If borrower and lender reach an agreement, the necessary forms are drawn and signed and the funds are transferred—a mortgage loan has been made. *After* the loan has been originated (accepted), both the borrower and the lender must make more decisions. For example, the loan must be "serviced." Loan servicing involves keeping records of payments, sending out overdue notices, and making certain that the various mortgage covenants, such as payment of taxes and insurance, are being kept. The lender might have to decide whether to dispose of the loan by selling it in the secondary mortgage market. When would be the optimal time to sell? Should the lender retain the servicing of the loan after sale? How can the risk associated with the mortgage portfolio be minimized? What about mortgages that are delinquent or in default? How is the foreclosure to be handled? How can the lender work with the borrower to cure the delinquency? A key decision for the borrower is whether to keep the loan or refinance with a new loan. For example, if interest rates decline, the borrower might find it advantageous to pay off the loan by refinancing. Chapter 7 discusses these types of decisions.

RECENT DEVELOPMENTS IN REAL ESTATE FINANCING

Over the past decade there have been several major changes in real estate financing. The industry is currently undergoing a traumatic transition, particularly in the area of housing finance. The end result will likely be a dramatically altered way of doing business, for both the borrower and the lender. Government policies toward home ownership, lender attitudes toward mortgage investments, and the methods used to finance housing will all undergo changes. This section briefly explains several of the changes so that the reader can better understand the changing environment in which financing decisions are made. These issues are explored in specific detail in later chapters.

Changing Attitudes toward Inflation

Lenders and other suppliers of capital have changed their attitudes toward inflation. Generally, prior to 1980, most lenders ignored inflation or believed that whenever it went up, it would soon return to "reasonable" levels. However, after years of basically negative real interest rates, the financial community has drastically revised its expectations concerning inflation. If the future inflation rate could be forecasted reliably, lenders would write in advance loan contracts that contained interest rates that would offset future price increases. The difficulty, of course, is that the actual inflation rate may be different from the expected one.

Alternative Mortgage Instruments

Although the fixed-rate mortgage historically has been the mainstay of real estate financing, recent volatile economic conditions have rendered it less desirable because it no longer meets the requirements of the market participants. Thus, borrowers and lenders alike have been forced to search for alternative financing techniques that better fit their demands in light of changing economic conditions. This change, coupled with the demand for loans that serve special purposes in real estate financing, led to the development of the various financing techniques we examine in Part Two.

Inflation has altered the nature of real estate mortgages. First, it has necessitated the changing of regulations that prohibited lenders from shifting the unexpected changes in interest rates, called *interest rate risk,* to the borrower. The mortgage market currently uses numerous financing methods designed to protect against unexpected inflation, including the *adjustable-rate* mortgage, which allows the interest rate to change based on an inflation-sensitive index.

Second, the market has developed loans that have to be renegotiated at frequent intervals to allow the interest rate to "catch up" to changing conditions. These loans are *renegotiable-rate* (rollover) mortgages. Some loans allow the lender to directly participate in the income that the real estate is expected to generate. In certain instances, other methods let the lender acquire an equity position: *income-equity participation mortgages, convertible mortgages, and joint ventures.*

Deregulation of Lenders

Another major change in real estate financing is the decline in viewing housing as a favored position in the credit market. For decades, housing financing was favored over other capital markets because of government regulations, such as federal ceilings (called Regulation Q), rates that thrift institutions and banks could pay savings depositors, and portfolio restrictions that required thrift institutions to invest most of their assets in home mortgages. However, as a result of these restrictions, money market funds developed. The funds pay relatively higher rates, so savers have thus moved massive amounts of capital from low-interest-rate accounts to money market funds.

Changes in Tax Laws

Housing has enjoyed a favored position because of the tax advantages of "investing" in home ownership. Mortgage interest and property taxes can be deducted from taxable income. However, the major tax advantage of home investment is that homeowners are not taxed on the value of the flow of services derived from living in the house.

The 1986 Tax Reform Act produced significant changes in the area of real estate investment. The benefits of tax shelters have been eradicated by passive loss limitations, investment interest limitations, and a change in the depreciable life of real estate. Chapter 6 discusses the tax impact on property analysis.

Changes in Government Policies

The government has been involved in the operation of the mortgage market for housing. Prior to 1980, many states had usury ceilings that limited the interest rate on mortgage loans. As with all attempts to implement price controls, usury ceilings tended to make the condition of the mortgage market worse as the market rate began to approach the ceiling rate and the market began to allocate funds based on factors other than the interest rate. In addition, numerous government programs aimed at financing housing have been developed under various fiscal policy programs. Chapter 9 discusses these government-sponsored financing methods.

Another major change in real estate financing is the dramatic shifts in the nation's basic monetary fiscal policies. Because of rising inflation, the Federal Reserve, which controls the money supply, has altered its monetary policies by attempting to control growth in the money supply. Such policies slowed the inflation fire in 1982 and 1983 but also increased the financial market's uncertainty about future interest rates.

Changes in the direction of fiscal policies have also altered the mortgage market. The most dramatic was the concept of "supply-side" economics, based on the belief that increased incentives for production and investment are the key to future economic growth.

Developments in the Secondary Market

The secondary mortgage market has also undergone changes in recent years. The federal credit agencies have developed numerous pass-through securities that have given home mortgage borrowers broader access to the capital market. These securities are essentially issued against mortgage loans. The loan thus becomes the collateral for the pass-through security.

Changes in Commitment Policies

Mortgage lenders typically have made commitments to provide long-term credit well before the funds have been scheduled for disbursement. These commitments were at a fixed interest rate, and borrowers had the option of accepting the commitment. In recent years, many lenders have been reluctant to make such commitments because of the possibility of unexpected changes in the interest rate. The market has made adjustments by imposing larger nonrefundable commitment fees to discourage cancellations when market rates fall. Lenders have also shortened the period of time over which a stated interest rate will be guaranteed.

Changes in Real Estate Markets

The real estate financing process and decision making have also been influenced greatly by changes in the real estate markets. Shifts in the types of housing demanded by a changing demographic structure of the population, migration pattern shifts, and varying regional growth rates have all affected the demand for mortgage funds.

Shifts in the types of income-producing properties being developed and equity investors' changing attitudes toward the use of debt in the capital structure of investments have also influenced real estate financing. New investors, such as pension funds, real estate syndications, and foreign investors, have caused new problems and a complex environment for decision making.

SUMMARY

This chapter reviewed the environment in which financing decisions are made. Both the lender and the borrower face many questions and problems that must be answered and solved before the decision to borrow and/or lend can be made. Both participants make the decisions based on the expected costs and benefits in a risky environment.

The finance industry is concerned with the transaction between borrowers and lenders. The mortgage market, which includes both primary and secondary markets, allocates mortgage funds according to the "price" (interest rate). This rate reflects the demand and supply of funds given the risks of borrowing and lending.

The financing process considers the factors involved in making the borrowing-lending decisions: analyses of the legal environment, borrower, property, and market factors. And even after the decision to borrow and/or lend has been made, both participants still face a series of postorigination decisions.

The real estate finance environment has changed dramatically in recent years. Influences, such as inflation, deregulation and other government policy changes, changes in the secondary market, and fundamental changes in real estate markets, have all created a complex environment in which financing decisions are made.

QUESTIONS

1 Define the following terms:
   a mortgage
   b primary mortgage market
   c inflation risk
   d default risk
   e business risk
   f liquidity risk
   g financial risk
   h interest rate
   i secondary mortgage market
   j mortgagee
   k mortgagor
   l equity
   m risk premium
   n maturity

2 Describe how the interest rate on a mortgage is determined.
3 Who are the major lenders on single-family house mortgages? Income property mortgages?
4 Discuss the role of financial institutions in the mortgage market.
5 Outline the real estate financing process.
6 Discuss several recent developments in real estate finance. What types of problems do both borrowers and lenders face? What would you propose as solutions to these problems?
7 Analyze the following statement:
   Housing is a necessity. Therefore the government should ensure that the interest rate on mortgages is low enough so that every household can afford a house.
8 Why would the lender want to analyze the property value in a mortgage loan?
9 What would happen to the contract interest rate and the effective interest rate on a mortgage loan with and without the following types of clauses?
   a prepayment penalty
   b due-on-sale
   c deficiency judgment
   d points
10 Explain the distinction between the primary and secondary mortgage markets.

PROBLEMS

1 Suppose you faced the following choices:

Situation A:. You can invest your money in a mortgage with an expected yield of 12 percent or in another mortgage with a yield of 13 percent. Both have the same level of risk. Which would you prefer?

Situation B:. You can invest your money in a mortgage with an expected yield of 12 percent or in another mortgage with the same expected yield (12 percent). The first choice is riskier than the second. Which would you prefer?

Situation C:. You can invest your money in a mortgage with an expected yield of 12 percent or in a U.S. Treasury bond with an expected yield of 10 percent. The mortgage is riskier. Which would you prefer?

2 From a copy of the most recent *Federal Reserve Bulletin,* analyze the amount of mortgage debt for the different types of lenders.

3 What are the relationships between inflation and mortgage interest rates? Suppose mortgage interest rates were 10 percent with 7 percent expected inflation. Suddenly inflation expectations changed to 10 percent. What is likely to be the new level of mortgage interest rate?

4 Using the data in Table 1-4, plot and explain the relationship between the interest rate and the loan-to-value ratio.

5 From a copy of the most recent *Federal Home Loan Bank Board Journal,* analyze the trend in mortgage interest rates over the past 12 months.

6 Using the data in Table 1-3, discuss the relationship between the contract and the effective interest rates.

7 Suppose you are a real estate investor and decide to buy an apartment building for $500,000. You have two alternatives: pay 100 percent cash or borrow 75 percent and invest 25 percent of your own money. Which option would you select? Why?

8 Suppose you are a mortgage lender and a borrower wants to borrow $300,000 and make a payment of $3,303 each month for 20 years. Another borrower wants the same amount but is willing to pay $3,500 each month for 20 years. Which loan would you make? Why?

9 Using a diagram such as Figure 1-4, show what would happen in the mortgage market if the following events occurred:
  a All mortgage loans suddenly became riskier or less risky.
  b The mortgage suddenly became a more attractive investment.
  c The demand for housing suddenly increased.

10 Discuss the role of the secondary mortgage market. Obtain copies of the most recent *Federal Home Loan Bank Board Journal* and *The Wall Street Journal* and examine the yields in the secondary market.

REFERENCES

Beaton, William R.: *Real Estate Finance,* 2nd ed., Prentice-Hall, Englewood Cliffs, N.J., 1982.

Brueggeman, William B., and Leon D. Stone: *Real Estate Finance,* 7th ed., Irwin, Homewood, Ill., 1981.

Dasso, Jerome, and Gerald Kuhn: *Real Estate Finance,* Prentice-Hall Englewood Cliffs, N.J., 1983.

Dennis, Marshall: *Fundamentals of Mortgage Lending,* Prentice-Hall, Englewood Cliffs, N.J., 1978.

Downs, Anthony: "The Triple Revolution in Real Estate Financing," *Real Estate Review,* vol. 15, Spring 1983, pp. 97–103.

Epley, Donald R., and James A. Mellar: *Basic Real Estate Finance and Investments,* Wiley, New York, 1980.

Larkins, Daniel J.: "Recent Developments in Mortgage Markets," *Survey of Current Business,* vol. 62, February 1982, pp. 19–36.

The Mortgage and Real Estate Executives Report, Warren, Gorham & Lamont, Boston, monthly.

Plander, John: "A Survey of the Commercial Real Estate Market in the United States," *The Economist,* February 7, 1981, pp. 1–17.

Reidy, Mark J.: "The Real Estate Market in Transition," Graduate School of Business, Indiana University, Bloomington, December 1982.

Seiders, David F.: "Changing Patterns of Housing Finance," *Federal Reserve Bulletin,* vol. 67, no. 6, June 1981, pp. 461–472.

Wiedemer, John P.: *Real Estate Finance,* 3d ed., Prentice-Hall, Englewood Cliffs, N.J., 1980.

COMPOUND INTEREST AND MORTGAGE MECHANICS

KNOW TERMS

The decision to purchase or finance real estate is made for the purpose of increasing the investor's or the lender's wealth. Any investment, whether an equity interest or a mortgage interest, involves laying out some sum of money today in expectation of a return of and return(s) on that money in the future. The measurement of these returns is the basis for *compound interest*. This chapter presents the compound interest concepts that are used throughout the rest of the book. Only by thoroughly understanding compound interest can you grasp the nature of the return on an investment.

Every compound interest problem is concerned with four variables:

1 The amount of the initial investment or loan
2 The amount of the future returns(s) or payment(s) expected from the investment
3 The time element—that is, the specified times when **1** and **2** occur
4 An interest rate

If we know, or make assumptions about, any three of these variables, the fourth can be determined by the use of compound interest relationships.

LUMP SUM AMOUNTS

One type of compound interest problem is to find the future or present value of a *lump sum*. A lump sum is only one amount. If you borrow a lump sum today (the present), you want to know what lump sum you will have to pay back in the future. Conversely, if you know the lump sum you will have in the future, you want to know what present amount (present value) you can borrow.

Future Value of a Lump Sum

Suppose you have the following problem. You want to borrow $10,000 today and repay it in one lump sum (with 10 percent interest) 1 year from now. How much would you owe at the end of the year?

To solve this problem, first determine which of the four compound interest variables you do know and which you do not:

1 Amount of original investment (loan): *$10,000*
2 Amount of future return (payment): *unknown*
3 Time $10,000 received (invested, loaned) today, where *time = 0*; future return received 1 year from now, where *time = 1*
4 Interest rate: *10 percent*

Since the lender expects a return *of* the principal amount, $10,000, plus a return (interest) *on* it of 10 percent, the amount that must be paid at the end of the year is $10,000 + (10% of $10,000), or $11,000.

This can be expressed in equation form as

$$FV = PV(1 + i)^1$$

where FV = future value of lump sum
 PV = present value of lump sum
  i = interest rate

Substituting the numbers from our example, we have

$$FV = \$10,000(1 + 0.10)^1$$
$$= \$11,000$$

This works fine for our 1-year example. However, what if the period were 3 years? Would the interest then be $3,000? No, because the interest is accruing (or being added on) yearly, so that for any given year, the interest rate is applied to the sum of principal plus interest, if any, accrued in prior years and still owing. Essentially then, the borrower is paying interest on interest. Stated another way, the interest is *compounded,* and in our example, the compounding period is 1 year (that is, interest is computed and added on annually).

If the $10,000 were borrowed for 3 years at 10 percent, the future value could be computed as follows:

Year	Present amount ($) (beginning of year)	×	(1 + i)	=	Future amount ($) (end of year)
1	10,000		1.1		11,000
2	11,000		1.1		12,100
3	12,100		1.1		13,310

Note that the beginning amount for each year is the principal plus interest, if any, accrued in prior years. Also note that because of the effect of compounding the interest, total interest of $3,310 rather than $3,000 will be owed.

Alternately, the future value (FV) can be expressed in a general equation, as follows:

$$FV_{i,n} = PV(1 + i)^n \qquad (2\text{-}1)$$

where n = number of compounding periods
  i = interest rate per period

In our example, the number of compounding periods is 3 (years), and the interest rate is 10 percent per year. Thus, for our example,

$$FV_{10\%,3} = \$10,000(1 + 0.1)^3$$
$$= \$13,310$$

We apply Equation 2-1 whenever we have a known present amount and known interest rate and are trying to find the future amount of the lump-sum payment required at the end of a given period to yield the given interest rate.

Because the $(1 + i)^n$ calculation can be tedious, tables that give the future value of $1 can be used. These tables thus perform the $(1 + i)^n$ calculation for the user. The $(1 + i)^n$ is called the future value factor (FVF). The present value is merely multiplied by the appropriate factor in the table. Table 2-1 lists future values of the lump sum of $1 for various periods.

Using Table 2-1 to solve our example, we first choose the appropriate interest column (10%) and find the FVF for the appropriate number of periods (3). We then multiply the factor, 1.33100, by the PV to derive the FV. Thus,

$$FVF_{i,n} = (1 + i)^n$$

TABLE 2-1 FUTURE VALUE OF $1 AT END OF N PERIODS
$FVF_{i,n} = (1 + i)^n$

Period (n)	Rate (%) per period				
	8	10	12	15	20
1	1.08000	1.10000	1.12000	1.15000	1.20500
2	1.16640	1.21000	1.25440	1.32250	1.45203
3	1.25971	1.33100	1.40493	1.52088	1.74969
4	1.36049	1.46410	1.57352	1.74901	2.10838
5	1.46933	1.61051	1.76234	2.01136	2.54059
6	1.58687	1.77156	1.97382	2.31306	3.06142
7	1.71382	1.94872	2.21068	2.66002	3.68901
8	1.85093	2.14359	2.47596	3.05902	4.44525
9	1.99900	2.35795	2.77308	3.51788	5.35653
10	2.15892	2.59374	3.10585	4.04556	6.45462
11	2.33164	2.85312	3.47855	4.65239	7.77781
12	2.51817	3.13843	3.89598	5.35025	9.37227
13	2.71962	3.45227	4.36349	6.15279	11.29358
14	2.93710	3.79750	4.88711	7.07571	13.60876
15	3.17217	4.17725	5.47357	8.13706	16.39856
16	3.42594	4.59497	6.13039	9.35762	19.76026
17	3.70002	5.05447	6.86604	10.76126	23.81112
18	3.99602	5.55992	7.68997	12.37545	28.69240
19	4.31570	6.11591	8.61276	14.23177	34.57434
20	4.66096	6.74750	9.64629	16.36654	41.66208
21	5.03383	7.40025	10.80385	18.82152	50.20281
22	5.43654	8.14027	12.10031	21.64475	60.49438
23	5.87146	8.95430	13.55235	24.89146	72.89573
24	6.34118	9.84973	15.17863	28.62518	87.83935
25	6.84848	10.83471	17.00006	32.91895	105.84642
30	10.06266	17.44940	29.95992	66.21177	268.91276
35	14.78534	28.10244	52.79962	133.17552	683.19809
40	21.72452	45.25926	93.05097	267.86355	1735.72883

and

$$FV_{i,n} = PV(FVF_{i,n})$$

Substituting from our example,

$$FVF_{10\%,3} = (1 + 0.1)^3$$
$$= 1.33100$$

and

$$FV_{10\%,3} = \$10,000(1.33100)$$
$$= \$13,310$$

which is identical to the value obtained using Equation 2-1.

Present Value of a Lump Sum

Suppose you are in the following situation: You will receive an inheritance of $13,310 3 years from today. Since you want the money today, you would like to borrow as much as you can now and use the inheritance to pay off the loan in one lump sum. You know that the current interest rate is 10 percent. How much can you borrow today so that the lump-sum payment in 3 years is exactly $13,310?

We know that the future value is $13,310, the interest rate 10 percent, and the period of time 3 years. What we do not know is the *present value*. This is essentially the same as our future value problem, except we must solve for the present rather than the future value. Using Equation 2-1, $FV = PV(1 + i)^n$,

$$PV_{i,n} = \frac{FV}{(1 + i)^n} \qquad (2\text{-}2)$$
$$= FV \frac{1}{(1 + i)^n}$$

Using our facts and solving the equation for the PV, we have

$$PV_{10\%,3} = \$13,310 \frac{1}{(1.1)^3}$$
$$= \$10,000$$

The reciprocal of the FVF is the present value factor (PVF):

$$PVF_{i,n} = \frac{1}{(1 + i)^n}$$

or

$$PVF_{i,n} = \frac{1}{FVF_{i,n}}$$

For our example, we can solve for the PVF three ways:

$$PVF_{10\%,3} = \frac{1}{FVF_{10\%,3}} = \frac{1}{1.331} = 0.7513$$

or

$$PVF_{10\%,3} = \frac{1}{(1.1)^3} = \frac{1}{1.331} = 0.7513$$

or we can use Table 2-2, which lists the present values of $1. Looking at Table 2-2

TABLE 2-2 PRESENT VALUE OF $1 DUE AT END OF N

$$PVF_{i,n} = \frac{1}{(1 + i)^n}$$

Period (n)	Rate (%) per period				
	8	10	12	15	20
1	0.92593	0.90909	0.89286	0.86957	0.83333
2	0.85734	0.82645	0.79719	0.75614	0.69444
3	0.79383	0.75131	0.71178	0.65752	0.57870
4	0.73503	0.68301	0.63552	0.57175	0.48225
5	0.68058	0.62092	0.56743	0.49718	0.40188
6	0.63017	0.56447	0.50663	0.43233	0.33490
7	0.58349	0.51316	0.45235	0.37594	0.27908
8	0.54027	0.46651	0.40388	0.32690	0.23257
9	0.50025	0.42410	0.36061	0.28426	0.19381
10	0.46319	0.38554	0.32197	0.24718	0.16151
11	0.42888	0.35049	0.28748	0.21494	0.13459
12	0.39711	0.31863	0.25668	0.18691	0.11216
13	0.36770	0.28966	0.22917	0.16253	0.09346
14	0.34046	0.26333	0.20462	0.14133	0.07789
15	0.31524	0.23939	0.18270	0.12289	0.06491
16	0.29189	0.21763	0.16312	0.10686	0.05409
17	0.27027	0.19784	0.14564	0.09293	0.04507
18	0.25025	0.17986	0.13004	0.08081	0.03756
19	0.23171	0.16351	0.11611	0.07027	0.03130
20	0.21455	0.14864	0.10367	0.06110	0.02608
21	0.19866	0.13513	0.09256	0.05313	0.02174
22	0.18394	0.12885	0.08264	0.04620	0.01811
23	0.17032	0.11168	0.07379	0.04017	0.01509
24	0.15770	0.10153	0.06588	0.03493	0.01258
25	0.14602	0.09230	0.05882	0.03038	0.01048
30	0.09938	0.05731	0.03338	0.01510	0.00421
35	0.06763	0.03558	0.01894	0.00751	0.00169
40	0.04603	0.02209	0.01075	0.00373	0.00068

under the appropriate rate (10%) for the stated time period (3 years), we see the same result obtained by the other two methods: 0.7513. To solve our example, we can rewrite Equation 2-2 as

$$PV = FV(PVF_{10\%,3})$$
$$= \$13,310(0.7513)$$
$$= \$10,000$$

Of course, we would have expected the PV to be $10,000. Thus, we could borrow $10,000 today at 10 percent interest, and the inheritance of $13,310 at the end of the third year would be just enough to pay off the loan.

ANNUITIES

Up to now, we have discussed only those loans that are borrowed (or paid off) in one lump sum. But what if there is a series of equal payments made at equal time intervals? This series is called an *annuity*. The annuity can be paid at the beginning of each time period (*annuity due*) or at the end (*regular annuity*).

Future Value of an Annuity Due

Suppose you want to borrow $10,000 *per year* at the beginning of each year for 3 years. How much would you owe at the end of the 3 years? The interest rate is 10 percent.

This problem can be solved two ways. First, we can assume that we have three separate loans, each for $10,000. The initial loan will be outstanding for 3 years, the second loan for 2 years, and the third loan for 1 year.

Recalling our future value of a lump-sum equation,

$$FV = PV(FVF_{i,n})$$

Using this equation to solve for the future value of each loan, we have

Loan 1:
$$FV = \$10,000(FVF_{10\%,3})$$
$$= \$10,000(1.331)$$
$$= \$13,310$$

Loan 2:
$$FV = \$10,000(FV_{10\%,2})$$
$$= \$10,000(1.210)$$
$$= \$12,100$$

Loan 3:
$$FV = \$10,000(FVF_{10\%,1})$$
$$= \$10,000(1.10)$$
$$= \$11,000$$

The total amount owed at the end of year 3 would be the sum of the future values of all three loans: $36,410.

Recall that equal payments made at the beginning of each period constitute an *annuity due* (AD). We can express an annuity due in a general equation as follows:

$$FVAD_{i,n} = ANN(1 + i)^n + ANN(1 + i)^{n-1} + ANN(1 + i)^{n-2} \cdots$$
$$+ ANN(1 + i)^1$$

where $FVAD_{i,n}$ = future value of annuity due at rate i for n periods
i = rate per period
n = number of periods
ANN = amount of annuity

In our example, we would substitute as follows:

$$FVAD_{10\%,3} = \$10,000(1 + 0.1)^3 + \$10,000(1 + 0.1)^2 + \$10,000(1 + 0.1)^1$$
$$= \$36,410$$

Obviously, this method could involve very long and tedious calculations if the number of periods were substantial, say 24, 100, or even 300. Fortunately, the equation can be simplified as follows:

$$FVAD_{i,n} = ANN \frac{(1 + i)^{n+1} - (1 + i)}{i} \tag{2-3}$$

In our example,

$$FVAD_{10\%,3} = \$10,000 \frac{(1.1)^4 - 1.1}{0.1}$$
$$= \$10,000(3.641)$$
$$= \$36,410$$

Future Value of a Regular Annuity

The future value of a regular annuity is similar to the future value of an annuity due. In fact, the only difference is that the regular annuity occurs at the end rather than the beginning of the period. To illustrate, suppose you want to save for the down payment on a piece of real estate. If you can deposit $10,000 at the end of each year into a savings account, how much will you accumulate for a down payment at the end of 3 years if the savings account pays 10 percent interest compounded annually? To answer this problem, we use the following equation:

$$FVA_{i,n} = ANN(1 + i)^{n-1} + ANN(1 + i)^{n-2} + \cdots + ANN(1 + i)^0$$

where FVA is the future value of a regular annuity. Simplified, the equation can be written as

$$FVA_{i,n} = ANN\frac{(1 + i)^n - 1}{i}$$

(2-4)

or

$$FVA_{i,n} = ANN(FVAF_{i,n})$$

where FVAF is the future value of a regular annuity factor. We have a table for the FVAF to simplify our calculations (see Table 2-3).

TABLE 2-3   FUTURE VALUE OF ANNUITY FACTORS

$$FVAF_{i,n} = \frac{(1 + i)^n - 1}{i}$$

Period (n)	Rate (%) per period				
	8	10	12	15	20
1	1.00000	1.00000	1.00000	1.00000	1.00000
2	2.08000	2.10000	2.12000	2.15000	2.20000
3	3.24640	3.31000	3.37440	3.47250	3.64000
4	4.50611	4.64100	4.77933	4.99338	5.36800
5	5.86660	6.10510	6.35285	6.74238	7.44160
6	7.33593	7.71561	8.11519	8.75374	9.92992
7	8.92280	9.48717	10.08901	11.06680	12.91590
8	10.63663	11.43589	12.29969	13.72682	16.49908
9	12.48756	13.57948	14.77566	16.78584	20.79890
10	14.48656	15.93742	17.54874	20.30372	25.95868
11	16.64549	18.53117	20.65458	24.34928	32.15042
12	18.97713	21.38428	24.13313	29.00167	39.58050
13	21.49530	24.52271	28.02911	34.35192	48.49660
14	24.21492	27.97498	32.39260	40.50471	59.19592
15	27.15211	31.77248	37.27971	47.58041	72.03510
16	30.32428	35.94973	42.75328	55.71747	87.44213
17	33.75023	40.54470	48.88367	65.07509	105.93056
18	37.45024	45.59917	55.74971	75.83636	128.11667
19	41.44626	51.15909	63.43968	88.21181	154.74000
20	45.76196	57.27500	72.05244	102.44358	186.68800
21	50.42292	64.00250	81.69874	118.81012	225.02560
22	55.45676	71.40275	92.50258	137.63164	271.03072
23	60.89330	79.54302	104.60289	159.27638	326.23686
24	66.76476	88.49733	118.15524	184.16784	392.48424
25	73.10594	98.34706	133.33387	212.79302	471.98108
30	113.28321	164.49402	241.33268	434.74515	1181.88157
35	172.31680	271.02437	431.66350	881.17016	2948.34115
40	259.05652	442.59256	767.09142	1779.09031	7343.85784

Substituting into Equation 2-4, we have

$$FVA_{10\%,3} = \$10,000(3.310)$$
$$= \$33,100$$

Thus, we would be able to accumulate $33,100 for a down payment by the end of the third year.

At this point, note that regular annuities are more common in practice than annuities due, so to simplify terminology, *all annuities from this point on will be assumed to be regular, unless specifically stated that the annuity is an annuity due.*

The Sinking Fund Factor

The *sinking fund factor* is similar to the future value of an annuity. To illustrate, suppose in the previous example you knew the amount of the down payment you wished to accumulate by the end of the 3-year period—that is, $33,100 by the end of 3 years—and you wanted to know how much you must set aside in an account paying 10 percent interest per year.

We can rewrite Equation 2-4 to solve for the unknown, which is the annuity:

$$ANN_{i,n} = FVA \frac{(1 + i)^n - 1}{i} \tag{2-5}$$

or, alternatively,

$$ANN_{10\%,3} = FVA \frac{1}{FVAF_{10\%,3}}$$

Substituting the facts from our example,

$$ANN_{10\%,3} = \$33,100 \frac{1}{FVAF_{10\%,3}}$$
$$= \frac{\$33,100}{3.310}$$
$$= \$10,000$$

Thus, we must set aside $10,000 each year to accumulate $33,100 by the end of the third year at an interest rate of 10 percent. The reciprocal of the FVAF is called the *sinking fund factor* (SFF). There are tables for the SFF. Using SFF Table 2-4, in the 10% column for 3 years we have a factor of 0.30211:

$$ANN_{10\%,3} = \$33,100(0.30211)$$
$$= \$10,000$$

exactly the result obtained by using Equation 2-5.

TABLE 2-4 SINKING FUND FACTORS

$$SFF_{i,n} = \frac{i}{(1 + i)^n - 1}$$

Period	Rate (%) per period				
(n)	8	10	12	15	20
1	1.00000	1.00000	1.00000	1.00000	1.00000
2	0.48077	0.47619	0.47170	0.46512	0.45455
3	0.30803	0.30211	0.29635	0.28798	0.27473
4	0.22192	0.21547	0.20923	0.20027	0.18629
5	0.17046	0.16380	0.15741	0.14832	0.13438
6	0.13632	0.12961	0.12323	0.11424	0.10071
7	0.11207	0.10541	0.09912	0.09036	0.07742
8	0.09401	0.08744	0.08130	0.07285	0.06061
9	0.08008	0.07364	0.06768	0.05957	0.04808
10	0.06903	0.06275	0.05698	0.04925	0.03852
11	0.06008	0.05396	0.04842	0.04107	0.03110
12	0.05270	0.04676	0.04144	0.03448	0.02526
13	0.04652	0.04078	0.03568	0.02911	0.02062
14	0.04130	0.03578	0.03087	0.02469	0.01689
15	0.03683	0.03147	0.02682	0.02102	0.01388
16	0.03298	0.02782	0.02339	0.01795	0.01144
17	0.02963	0.02466	0.02046	0.01537	0.00944
18	0.02670	0.02193	0.01794	0.01319	0.00781
19	0.02413	0.01955	0.01576	0.01134	0.00646
20	0.02185	0.01746	0.01388	0.00976	0.00536
21	0.01983	0.01562	0.01224	0.00842	0.00444
22	0.01803	0.01401	0.01081	0.00727	0.00369
23	0.01642	0.01257	0.00956	0.00628	0.00307
24	0.01498	0.01130	0.00846	0.00543	0.00255
25	0.01368	0.01017	0.00750	0.00470	0.00212
30	0.00883	0.00680	0.00414	0.00230	0.00085
35	0.00580	0.00369	0.00232	0.00113	0.00034
40	0.00386	0.00226	0.00130	0.00056	0.00014

Present Value of Annuities

Suppose we want to know the present value of an annuity rather than the future value. For example, suppose a borrower will be able to repay a proposed loan with payments of $10,000 per year for 3 years. How much would you be willing to loan this borrower, given that your required rate of return is 10 percent?

To answer this problem, the equation is

$$PVA_{i,n} = ANN \underbrace{\frac{1 - [1/(1 + i)^n]}{i}} \qquad (2\text{-}6)$$

Present value of an
annuity factor (PVAF)

where PVA = present value of annuity

        i = rate per period

       n = number of periods for which annuity is paid

  ANN = annuity

Substituting the facts from the problem into Equation 2-6,

$$PVA_{10\%,3} = \$10,000 \frac{1 - [1/(1 + 0.1)^3]}{0.1}$$

$$= \$10,000(2.4869)$$

$$= \$24,869$$

In other words, you could loan $24,869 today, and if you received payments of $10,000 per year for 3 years, you would be earning your 10 percent required rate of return. (Conversely, the borrower would be paying a 10 percent rate of interest, which is the cost of borrowing.)

As in our previous problems, there is an easier method for computing the present value of an annuity. In Equation 2-6, note the expression called the present value of an annuity factor (PVAF). Thus, Equation 2-6 can be rewritten as

$$PVA_{i,n} = ANN(PVAF_{i,n})$$

Table 2-5 gives PVAFs for selected rates of interest and time periods. Looking at the 10% column for 3 years, we find a factor of 2.4869, which is the same factor we found previously when we solved the PVAF in Equation 2-6.

At this point, it is useful to look at the relationship between the PVF and PVAF. Compare Tables 2-2 and 2-5. The PVAF at any given rate and number of periods is the same as the *sum* of the PVFs for all prior periods up to and including the given period. For example, the PVFs in the 10% column are 0.90909, 0.82645, and 0.75131 for periods 1, 2 and 3, respectively. Adding these factors, we get 2.4869, which is the same as the PVAF for three periods at 10 percent. Logically, this makes sense, for an annuity of $1 is simply a series of lump-sum payments, so adding the present values of three lump-sum $1 payments received in three consecutive periods is the same as an annuity of $1 received for three periods.

MONTHLY AND OTHER COMPOUNDING PERIODS

In all the examples so far in this chapter, we have assumed the compounding period to be 1 year. If the compounding period changes to, say, monthly, will our results change?

For the most part, our analysis remains the same. Recall than n denotes the compounding period and i the rate per period. Since n and i are commonly expressed in years and the rate per year, respectively, even if the compounding pe-

TABLE 2-5   PRESENT VALUE OF ANNUITY OF $1 PER PERIOD

$$PVAF_{i,n} = \frac{1 - [1/(1 + i)^n]}{i}$$

Period	Rate (%) per period				
(*n*)	8	10	12	15	20
1	0.92593	0.90909	0.89286	0.86957	0.83333
2	1.78326	1.73554	1.69005	1.62571	1.52778
3	2.55710	2.48685	2.40183	2.28323	2.10648
4	3.31213	3.16987	3.03735	2.85498	2.58873
5	3.99271	3.79079	3.60478	3.35215	2.99061
6	4.62288	4.35526	4.11141	3.78448	3.32551
7	5.20637	4.86842	4.56376	4.16042	3.60459
8	5.74664	5.33493	4.96764	4.48732	3.83716
9	6.24689	5.75902	5.32825	4.77158	4.03097
10	6.71008	6.14457	5.65022	5.01877	4.19247
11	7.13896	6.49506	5.93770	5.23371	4.32706
12	7.53608	6.81369	6.19437	5.42062	4.43922
13	7.90378	7.10336	6.42355	5.58315	4.53268
14	8.24424	7.36669	6.62817	5.72448	4.61057
15	8.55948	7.60608	6.81086	5.84737	4.67547
16	8.85137	7.82371	6.97399	5.95423	4.72956
17	9.12164	8.02155	7.11963	6.04716	4.77463
18	9.37189	8.20141	7.24967	6.12797	4.81219
19	9.60360	8.36492	7.36578	6.19823	4.84350
20	9.81815	8.51356	7.46944	6.25933	4.86958
21	10.01680	8.64869	7.56200	6.31246	4.89132
22	10.20074	8.77154	7.64465	6.35866	4.90943
23	10.37106	8.88322	7.71843	6.39884	4.92453
24	10.52876	8.98474	7.78432	6.43377	4.93710
25	10.67478	9.07704	7.84314	6.46415	4.94759
30	11.25778	9.42691	8.05518	6.56598	4.97894
35	11.65457	9.64416	8.17550	6.61661	4.99154
40	11.92461	9.77905	8.24378	6.64178	4.99660

riod is not annual, we must convert the *n* and *i* to numbers that truly reflect the number of compounding periods and the rate for that period. For example, a 3-year loan with monthly payments has 12 payments for each year, so we must multiply 3 years times 12 to get the correct number of periods: 36.

Similarly, we must change the interest rate *i* to a number that correctly represents the rate per period, in this case, per month. This applies to all compound interest equations we have studied. The equations can be modified as shown in Table 2-6, where *n* is the number of years, *i* the interest rate per year, and *m* the number of compounding periods in 1 year.

Note that the Appendix has monthly and annual compound interest tables. *When using the tables, be certain to consult the one appropriate for the compounding period you are considering.*

TABLE 2-6 COMPOUND INTEREST AND PRESENT VALUE FACTORS WITH COMPOUNDING AT TIME LENGTH *M*

Factor	Symbol	Equation
Future value of lump-sum factor	FVF	$\left(1 + \dfrac{i}{m}\right)^{mn}$
Future value of an annuity factor	FVAF	$\dfrac{\left(1 + \dfrac{i}{m}\right)^{mn} - 1}{i/m}$
Sinking fund factor	SFF	$\dfrac{i/m}{\left(1 + \dfrac{i}{m}\right)^{mn} - 1}$
Present value of lump-sum factor	PVF	$\dfrac{1}{\left(1 + \dfrac{i}{m}\right)^{mn}}$
Present value of an annuity factor	PVAF	$\dfrac{1 - \left[1 \Big/ \left(1 + \dfrac{i}{m}\right)^{mn}\right]}{i/m}$
Mortgage constant	MC	$\dfrac{i/m}{1 - \left[1 \Big/ \left(1 + \dfrac{i}{m}\right)^{mn}\right]}$

SERIES OF UNEQUAL PAYMENTS

Occasionally in mortgage lending and real estate investing, unequal payments are made (or received), sometimes at unequal time intervals. To deal with this situation, *each payment should be treated as a lump sum*. To illustrate, suppose a mortgage loan calls for the annual payments shown in Table 2-7. The lender's required rate of return is 12 percent per year. How much is the lender willing to loan this borrower?

The present value of this unequal series of future amounts must be determined. This is done by discounting each amount as a lump sum and finding the total (Table 2-7). Multiplying the annual payment by the present value factor at 12 percent for each year yields the present value of each payment. For example, the payment in year 5 is $4,000. Multiplying this payment by the present value factor of 0.56743 gives the present value of $2,270. Adding all the present values results in a total present value of $16,194. This is the amount the lender would be willing to loan, given the required return of 12 percent and the unequal payments.

To determine the *future value* of this unequal series, multiply the future value factor for each year by the payment and then add all the future values.

TABLE 2-7 PRESENT VALUE OF UNEQUAL SERIES

Year	Payment($)	Present value factor at 12%	Present value($)
1	2,500	0.89286	2,232
2	3,000	0.79719	2,392
3	2,750	0.71178	1,957
4	3,500	0.63552	2,224
5	4,000	0.56743	2,270
6	2,000	0.50663	1,013
7	2,250	0.45235	1,018
8	2.750	0.40388	1,111
9	3,250	0.36061	1,172
10	2,500	0.32197	805
			16,194

THE MECHANICS OF MORTGAGES

With this background on compound interest, we can now consider certain major mechanical aspects of mortgages that the lender and the borrower must be familiar with: how to calculate the payment, how to allocate each payment between the interest and principal repayment, how to calculate the outstanding balance at any point in the life of the loan, and how to calculate the yield (borrowing cost).

The Mortgage Constant

The *mortgage constant* is similar to the present value of an annuity and is used to find the amount of annuity (payment) necessary to amortize (pay off) a given amount at a specific interest rate over a given period of time.

Suppose a borrower wants to take out a $100,000 mortgage loan. The lender wants to earn a 12 percent interest rate (annual) and be repaid in equal monthly payments over 20 years (240 months). What is the monthly payment?

Using Equation 2-6,

$$PVA_{i,n} = ANN \, \frac{1 - [1/(1 + i)^n]}{i}$$

Substituting our facts

$$\$100,000 = ANN \, \frac{1 - [1/(1.01)^{240}]}{0.01}$$

Note that the present value is $100,000, the interest rate is 1 percent per month (12 percent divided by 12), and the maturity is 240 months (20 times 12).

Thus, we know everything except the "annuity." In mortgage problems, this is called the payment. Solving for the payment yields

$$\text{Payment} = \$100,000 \; \frac{0.01}{1 - [1/(1.01)^{240}]}$$

$$= \$1,101.09$$

Thus, the payment to amortize this loan is $1,101.09 per month for 240 months. In general form, the equation for finding the payment on a fixed-rate mortgage is

$$\text{Payment} = \text{amount borrowed} \; \underbrace{\frac{i}{1 - [1/(1 + i)^n]}}_{\text{Mortgage constant}} \qquad (2\text{-}7)$$

Always remember that the interest rate i and the length of time n must be measured in the same unit, that is, days, weeks, months, quarters, semiannually, or annually.

Note the *mortgage constant* in Equation 2-7. Tables of mortgage constants at various interest rates and maturities can be developed. Table 2-8 assumes *monthly* compounding.

The Amortization Schedule   *Know*

In the mortgage constant example we determined the amount of the payment necessary to amortize (or pay off) a $100,000 loan with monthly payments over 240 months. Each payment included interest on the balance outstanding for the period preceding each payment; the balance of the payment is applied to the reduction of the principal amount owing. A table showing the amount outstanding and the allocation between interest and principal is called an *amortization schedule*. Table 2-9 illustrates how this concept works.

Consider the loan facts: $100,000 amount, $1,101.09 per month payment, 12 percent interest rate (annual). For the first month, the amount outstanding is $100,000. The interest rate is 1 percent per month; thus the interest owed is $1,000 (0.01 × $100,000). The total payment is $1,101.09. The principal payment is $101.09 in the first month. This leaves an amount owed of $99,898.91 ($100,000 − $101.09). The interest owed for the second month is $998.99 (0.01 × $99,898.91). Since the total payment in month 2 is $1,101.09, the principal payment is $102.10. This process in continued for each of the 240 months. Notice in Table 2-9 that the amount outstanding declines each month, the payment is remaining constant, the interest amount is declining, and the principal payment is increasing. In the early life of the mortgage, almost all of the payment is interest, with little principal repayment.

TABLE 2-8   MORTGAGE CONSTANTS WITH MONTHLY COMPOUNDING

$$MC = \frac{i/12}{1 - [1/(1 + i/12)^{n \times 12}]}$$

	Rate(%)					
Years	8	10	12	15	20	Months
1	0.08698843	0.08791589	0.08884879	0.09025831	0.09263451	12
2	0.04522729	0.04614493	0.04707347	0.04848665	0.05089580	24
3	0.03133637	0.03226719	0.03321431	0.03466533	0.03716358	36
4	0.02441292	0.02536258	0.02633384	0.02783075	0.03043036	48
5	0.02027639	0.02124704	0.02224445	0.02378993	0.02649388	60
6	0.01753324	0.01852584	0.01955020	0.02114501	0.02395283	72
7	0.01558621	0.01660118	0.01765273	0.01929675	0.02220620	84
8	0.01413668	0.01517416	0.01625284	0.01794541	0.02095320	96
9	0.01301871	0.01407869	0.01518423	0.01692434	0.02002650	108
10	0.01213276	0.01321507	0.01434710	0.01613350	0.01932557	120
11	0.01141545	0.01251988	0.01367788	0.01550915	0.01878634	132
12	0.01082453	0.01195078	0.01313420	0.01500877	0.01836609	144
13	0.01033074	0.01147848	0.01268666	0.01460287	0.01803522	156
14	0.00991318	0.01108203	0.01231430	0.01427040	0.01777265	168
15	0.00955652	0.01074605	0.01200168	0.01399587	0.01756297	180
16	0.00924925	0.01045902	0.01173725	0.01376770	0.01739466	192
17	0.00898257	0.01021210	0.01151216	0.01357700	0.01725903	204
18	0.00874963	0.00999844	0.01131950	0.01341691	0.01714936	216
19	0.00854501	0.00981259	0.01115386	0.01328198	0.01706046	228
20	0.00836440	0.00965022	0.01101086	0.01316790	0.01698825	240
21	0.00820428	0.00950780	0.01088700	0.01307117	0.01692948	252
22	0.00806178	0.00938246	0.01077938	0.01298997	0.01688159	264
23	0.00793453	0.00927182	0.01068565	0.01291899	0.01684251	276
24	0.00782054	0.00917389	0.01060392	0.01285929	0.01681060	288
25	0.00771816	0.00908701	0.01053224	0.01280831	0.01678452	300
26	0.00762598	0.00900977	0.01046952	0.01276740	0.01676320	312
27	0.00754280	0.00894098	0.01041449	0.01272738	0.01674574	324
28	0.00746759	0.00887960	0.01036613	0.01269540	0.01673146	336
29	0.00739946	0.00882477	0.01032359	0.01266797	0.01671977	348
30	0.00733765	0.00877572	0.01028613	0.01264444	0.01671019	360
31	0.00728148	0.00873178	0.01025311	0.01262424	0.01670234	372
32	0.00723038	0.00869238	0.01022398	0.01260688	0.01669591	384
33	0.00718382	0.00865703	0.01019827	0.01259197	0.01669064	396
34	0.00714137	0.00862527	0.01017557	0.01257916	0.01668632	408
35	0.00710261	0.00859672	0.01015550	0.01256813	0.01668278	420
36	0.00706719	0.00857105	0.01013776	0.01255865	0.01667988	432
37	0.00703480	0.00854793	0.01012206	0.01255050	0.01667750	444
38	0.00700516	0.00852712	0.01010817	0.01254348	0.01667555	456
39	0.00697800	0.00850836	0.01009588	0.01253744	0.01667395	468
40	0.00695312	0.00849146	0.01008500	0.01253224	0.01667264	480

TABLE 2-9 MONTHLY AMORTIZATION SCHEDULE: $100,000 AT 12% ANNUAL INTEREST RATE, 240 MONTHLY PAYMENTS

Month	Amount outstanding	Payment	Interest	Principal
0	$100,000			
1	99,898.91	$1,101.09	$1,000.00	$101.09
2	99,796.81	1,101.09	998.99	102.10
3	99,693.69	1,101.09	997.97	103.12
4	99,589.54	1,101.09	996.94	104.15
5	99,484.35	1,101.09	995.90	105.19
6	99,378.10	1,101.09	994.84	106.25

The Amount Outstanding

Another common real estate finance problem is to find the balance remaining on a loan at a point in time. An amortization schedule supplies this information, but a simpler method uses the *proportion outstanding*. The proportion outstanding is the percentage of the original loan amount that remains outstanding at a point in the life of the loan.

The amount outstanding at the end of any period is the present value of the remaining payments. Recall from Equation 2-6 that the total amount loaned is the present value of all the payments. Thus, the same equation applies for calculating the balance at any time, except that the number of periods of the total loan maturity $n \times m$ must be reduced by the total number of payments made $t \times m$. Thus, Equation 2-6 may be modified as follows:

$$\text{Amount outstanding at end year } t = \text{payment } (\text{PVAF}_{i, nm - tm}) \qquad (2\text{-}8)$$

From our previous example, to find the amount outstanding at the end of month 1:

$$\begin{aligned}
\text{Amount outstanding at end month 1 } (t = \tfrac{1}{12}) &= \$1,101.09(\text{PVAF}_{1\%, 239}) \\
&= \$1,101.09(90.727609) \\
&= \$99,898.91
\end{aligned}$$

which is the balance shown at the end of month 1 in the amortization schedule in Table 2-9.

The *proportion outstanding* is the percentage of the original loan that remains outstanding:

$$\text{Proportion outstanding} = \frac{\text{amount outstanding end period } t \times m}{\text{original amount of loan}}$$

The original amount of the loan is the present value of all the payments. Thus,

$$\text{Proportion outstanding} = \frac{\text{ANN}(\text{PVAF}_{nm-tm})}{\text{ANN}(\text{PVAF}_{nm})}$$

Canceling the ANNs out of the right side of the equation,

$$\text{Proportion outstanding} = \frac{\text{PVAF}_{i,nm-tm}}{\text{PVAF}_{i,nm}} \tag{2-9}$$

Table 2-10 gives the proportion outstanding at various interest rates, mortgage maturities, and holding periods assuming monthly compounding.

The proportion outstanding is useful in setting up amortization schedules. Table 2-11 illustrates this concept. Suppose we have the same $100,000 at 12 percent with monthly payments for 240 months. We want to know the *annual* amount of interest and principal for years 1 through 5. We could go through the process discussed previously for each of the 60 months. However, using the proportion outstanding, the task is much easier.

The proportions outstanding in Table 2-11 are taken from Table 2-10 under the 12 percent interest rate, 20-year-maturity column. This shows the proportion at the end of year 1 as 0.98718. Since the original amount borrowed was $100,000, the amount outstanding at the end of year 1 is $98,718. The total annual payment in year 1 is $13,213 ($1,101.09 × 12). If we owed $100,000 at the beginning and $98,718 at the end of year 1, we must have paid off the difference, or $1,282. Since the total payment is $13,213, the interest amount would be $11,931 ($13,213 − $1,282). Notice that the interest payment is less than 12 percent of $100,000 ($12,000) since we have monthly compounding.

At the end of the second year, the proportion outstanding (of the original amount) is 0.97273. Therefore, the amount outstanding is $97,273 (0.97273 × $100,000). The principal payment in year 2 is the difference between the amount owed at the beginning of the second year (end of year 1), $98,718, and the amount owed at the end of year 2, $97,273, or $1,445. Since the total payment is $13,213, the interest amount would be $11,768 in year 2. This process is continued for each year.

Effective Yield (Effective Borrowing Cost)

The *effective yield* on a mortgage loan is the interest rate the lender earns. (The effective borrowing cost is the interest rate the borrower pays.) Normally, the effective yield (effective borrowing cost) is the same as the *contract rate* of interest on which the loan payments are computed. However, certain modifications to loans alter the "true" rate of interest the lender earns (or the borrower pays).

TABLE 2-10 PROPORTION OUTSTANDING ON MORTGAGES: VARIOUS INTEREST RATES, MATURITIES, AND HOLDING PERIODS ASSUMING MONTHLY COMPOUNDING

Mortgage maturity	Holding period (years)	Interest rate (%)															
		8	8.25	8.5	8.75	9	9.25	9.5	9.75	10	10.25	10.5	10.75	11	11.25	11.50	11.75
20 years (240 months)	1	.97886	.97949	.98010	.98069	.98127	.98184	.98239	.98293	.98345	.98396	.98446	.98495	.98542	.98558	.98632	.98676
	2	.95597	.95722	.95844	.95963	.96079	.96192	.96303	.96412	.96517	.96620	.96721	.96819	.96915	.97008	.97099	.97187
	3	.93118	.93304	.93486	.93664	.93838	.94009	.94176	.94339	.94498	.94653	.94806	.94954	.95099	.95241	.95379	.95514
	4	.90433	.90679	.90920	.91156	.91388	.91614	.91837	.92054	.92267	.92475	.92679	.92879	.93074	.93265	.93451	.93633
	5	.87526	.87829	.88127	.88420	.88707	.88989	.89265	.89537	.89802	.90063	.90319	.90569	.90814	.91054	.91289	.91519
	6	.84377	.84735	.85088	.85434	.85775	.86110	.86439	.86762	.87080	.87392	.87698	.87998	.88293	.88582	.88865	.89143
	7	.80966	.81376	.81779	.82177	.82568	.82953	.83332	.83705	.84072	.84433	.84788	.85137	.85480	.85816	.86147	.86472
	8	.77273	.77729	.78178	.78622	.79060	.79492	.79917	.80336	.80750	.81157	.81558	.81952	.82341	.82723	.83099	.83470
	9	.73273	.73769	.74259	.74744	.75223	.75696	.76163	.76624	.77079	.77528	.77971	.78408	.78839	.79264	.79682	.80095
	10	.68941	.69470	.69994	.70513	.71026	.71534	.72036	.72533	.73024	.73510	.73990	.74464	.74932	.75394	.75851	.76302
25 years (300 months)	1	.98691	.98742	.98791	.98838	.98884	.98929	.98972	.99013	.99053	.99092	.99129	.99165	.99199	.99232	.99264	.99295
	2	.97293	.97376	.97475	.97571	.97664	.97754	.97841	.97925	.98007	.98085	.98161	.98235	.98305	.98374	.98440	.98503
	3	.95738	.95892	.96043	.96188	.96329	.96466	.96599	.96727	.96851	.96971	.97087	.97200	.97308	.97413	.97515	.97613
	4	.94075	.94282	.94484	.94679	.94869	.95054	.95233	.95406	.95574	.95737	.95895	.96048	.96196	.96339	.96478	.96612
	5	.92274	.92534	.92787	.93033	.93272	.93505	.93731	.93951	.94164	.94371	.94571	.94766	.94955	.95138	.95315	.95487
	6	.90324	.90636	.90940	.91237	.91526	.91807	.92081	.92347	.92606	.92857	.93102	.93339	.93570	.93794	.94011	.94222
	7	.88211	.88575	.88930	.89277	.89615	.89945	.90266	.90579	.90884	.91181	.91470	.91752	.92025	.92291	.92550	.92801
	8	.85294	.86338	.86743	.87139	.87525	.87903	.88272	.88632	.88983	.89325	.89659	.89984	.90301	.90610	.90911	.91203
	9	.83446	.83909	.84362	.84805	.85239	.85664	.86079	.86485	.86882	.87270	.87648	.88017	.88378	.88730	.89073	.89407
	10	.80763	.81272	.81771	.82260	.82739	.83209	.83669	.84120	.84561	.84993	.85415	.85828	.86232	.86627	.87012	.87389
30 years (360 months)	1	.99165	.99205	.99244	.99281	.99317	.99351	.99383	.99414	.99444	.99472	.99499	.99525	.99550	.99573	.99596	.99617
	2	.98260	.98342	.98421	.98497	.98570	.98639	.98706	.98769	.98830	.98888	.98944	.98997	.99048	.99096	.99142	.99186
	3	.97280	.97405	.97526	.97641	.97752	.97858	.97960	.98058	.98152	.98241	.98327	.98409	.98487	.98562	.98634	.98702
	4	.96219	.96388	.96551	.96708	.96858	.97003	.97141	.97274	.97402	.97525	.97642	.97754	.97862	.97965	.98064	.98158
	5	.95070	.95284	.95490	.95689	.95880	.96064	.96241	.96411	.96574	.96731	.96822	.97026	.97165	.97297	.97425	.97547
	6	.93825	.94085	.94336	.94577	.94810	.95035	.95251	.95459	.95660	.95852	.96038	.96215	.96386	.96551	.96708	.96859
	7	.92477	.92783	.93079	.93365	.93640	.93907	.94163	.94411	.94649	.94879	.95100	.95313	.95518	.95715	.95904	.96086
	8	.91018	.91370	.91711	.92041	.92361	.92669	.92967	.93255	.93533	.93801	.94060	.94309	.94549	.94781	.95003	.95218
	9	.89437	.89836	.90223	.90598	.90961	.91313	.91653	.91982	.92300	.92608	.92905	.93192	.93468	.93736	.93993	.94242
	10	.87725	.88170	.88603	.89022	.89430	.89825	.90208	.90579	.90938	.91286	.91622	.91948	.92263	.92567	.92860	.93144

Mortgage maturity	Holding period (years)	Interest rate (%)																
		12	12.25	12.5	12.75	13	13.25	13.5	13.75	14	14.25	14.5	14.75	15	15.25	15.5	15.75	16
20 years (240 months)	1	.98718	.98759	.98799	.98838	.98876	.98912	.98948	.98983	.99016	.99049	.99081	.99111	.99141	.99170	.99198	.99225	.99252
	2	.97273	.97357	.97439	.97519	.97596	.97672	.97745	.97816	.97885	.97953	.98018	.98082	.98144	.98204	.98263	.98319	.98374
	3	.95646	.95774	.95899	.96021	.96140	.96256	.96369	.96479	.96586	.96690	.96792	.96891	.96987	.97080	.97171	.97260	.97646
	4	.93811	.93985	.94155	.94321	.94483	.94641	.94795	.94946	.95092	.95235	.95375	.95511	.95643	.95773	.95898	.96021	.96140
	5	.91744	.91965	.92180	.92391	.92597	.92798	.92995	.93188	.93376	.93559	.93738	.93913	.94084	.94251	.94414	.94572	.94727
	6	.89415	.89682	.89944	.90200	.90451	.90696	.90937	.91172	.91402	.91628	.91848	.92064	.92274	.92480	.92681	.92878	.93070
	7	.86791	.87104	.87411	.87713	.88008	.88298	.88583	.88861	.89135	.89402	.89665	.89922	.90173	.90420	.90661	.90897	.91128
	8	.83834	.84191	.84543	.84889	.85229	.85562	.85890	.86212	.86528	.86838	.87143	.87442	.87735	.88022	.88304	.88580	.88851
	9	.80501	.80901	.81296	.81684	.82065	.82441	.82811	.83175	.83533	.83884	.84230	.84570	.84904	.85232	.85555	.85871	.86182
	10	.76746	.77185	.77618	.78045	.78466	.78881	.79289	.79692	.80089	.80481	.80866	.81245	.81618	.81986	.82348	.82703	.83054
25 years (300 months)	1	.99325	.99354	.99381	.99408	.99433	.99457	.99481	.99503	.99525	.99546	.99566	.99585	.99604	.99621	.99638	.99654	.99670
	2	.98564	.98623	.98680	.98735	.98788	.98838	.98887	.98934	.98979	.99023	.99065	.99105	.99143	.99180	.99216	.99250	.99283
	3	.97707	.97799	.97887	.97971	.98053	.98132	.98208	.98282	.98352	.98420	.98486	.98548	.98609	.98667	.98723	.98777	.98829
	4	.96741	.96867	.96988	.97105	.97218	.97327	.97432	.97533	.97631	.97726	.97817	.97904	.97989	.98070	.98149	.98224	.98297
	5	.95653	.95814	.95970	.96121	.96267	.96407	.96544	.96675	.96803	.96926	.97044	.97159	.97269	.97376	.97479	.97578	.97674
	6	.94427	.94625	.94817	.95004	.95184	.95359	.95528	.95692	.95850	.96004	.96152	.96295	.96434	.96568	.96697	.96822	.96943
	7	.93045	.93282	.93512	.93736	.93952	.94163	.94367	.94564	.94756	.94941	.95121	.95295	.95464	.95627	.95785	.95938	.96086
	8	.91488	.91765	.92034	.92296	.92551	.92798	.93038	.93271	.93498	.93717	.93931	.94138	.94338	.94533	.94721	.94904	.95081
	9	.89733	.90051	.90361	.90662	.90955	.91241	.91519	.91789	.92052	.92307	.92556	.92797	.93032	.93259	.93480	.93695	.93904
	10	.87756	.88115	.88465	.88807	.89140	.89465	.89781	.90090	.90390	.90683	.90968	.91245	.91515	.91778	.92033	.92282	.92523
30 years (360 months)	1	.99637	.99656	.99675	.99692	.99709	.99724	.99739	.99753	.99767	.99780	.99792	.99803	.99814	.99825	.99834	.99844	.99852
	2	.99228	.99268	.99306	.99343	.99377	.99410	.99441	.99471	.99499	.99526	.99551	.99576	.99599	.99620	.99641	.99661	.99679
	3	.98767	.98830	.98889	.98946	.99000	.99051	.99100	.99147	.99191	.99234	.99274	.99312	.99348	.99383	.99416	.99447	.99477
	4	.98248	.98334	.98417	.98495	.98570	.98642	.98710	.98775	.98837	.98897	.98953	.99007	.99058	.99107	.99153	.99197	.99239
	5	.97663	.97775	.97882	.97984	.98082	.98175	.98264	.98349	.98431	.98508	.98583	.98653	.98721	.98785	.98846	.98904	.98960
	6	.97004	.97143	.97276	.97403	.97526	.97642	.97754	.97861	.97963	.98061	.98155	.98244	.98329	.98411	.98488	.98563	.98633
	7	.96261	.96429	.96590	.96744	.96893	.97035	.97171	.97301	.97426	.97546	.97660	.97770	.97875	.97975	.98071	.98163	.98250
	8	.95424	.95622	.95813	.95996	.96172	.96341	.96504	.96659	.96809	.96952	.97090	.97221	.97347	.97468	.97584	.97695	.97801
	9	.94481	.94711	.94933	.95147	.95353	.95550	.95741	.95923	.96099	.96268	.96430	.96586	.96735	.96879	.97016	.97148	.97275
	10	.93418	.93682	.93937	.94183	.94420	.94648	.94868	.95080	.95284	.95480	.95669	.95850	.96025	.96193	.96354	.96509	.96658

TABLE 2-11   ANNUAL AMORTIZATION SCHEDULE: $100,000 MORTGAGE, 12% INTEREST RATE, 240 MONTHS

Year	Proportion outstanding*	Amount outstanding	Annual debt service†	Interest	Principal
0	1.0	$100,000			
1	0.98718	98,718	$13,213	$11,931	$1,282
2	0.97273	97,273	13,213	11,768	1,445
3	0.95646	95,646	13,213	11,586	1,627
4	0.93811	93,811	13,213	11,378	1,835
5	0.91744	91,744	13,213	11,146	2,067

*See Table 2-10.
†Annual debt service is $1,101.09 (monthly) times 12.

These modifications are *loan discounts, loan origination fee, prepayment penalties,* and other payments.

Lenders sometimes negotiate with the borrower to actually disburse less cash proceeds than the amount that the loan documents. For example, the borrower agrees to monthly payments of $1,101.09 for 20 years at 12 percent interest based on a $100,000 loan, but the borrower also agrees that the lender will disburse $98,000 instead of $100,000. The $2,000 difference is called a *loan discount* and is usually expressed as a percentage of the face amount of the mortgage; each percentage is called a *discount point.* In this example, the number of discount points is 2 ($2,000/$100,000 = 0.02). Note that the borrower is required to pay back $100,000 at the terms specified but is actually receiving only $98,000 in loan proceeds. The major distinction between discount points charged on government loans and those charged on conventional loans is that the *seller* of the real estate *rather than the borrower-buyer is required to pay the points* on government loans. (More about this in Chapter 8.)

Lenders charge loan discounts for the fundamental reason that the discount raises the lender's effective yield on the mortgage above the interest rate specified (the contract rate) in the mortgage documents. Why not simply charge a higher interest rate to raise the yield, rather than confusing the issue with loans that are not for the amount that the loan document specifies? One reason for this practice is the psychological impact of interest rates on borrowers. For competitive reasons, it sounds better to quote a 12 percent rate of interest with 3 points rather than 12½ percent (but who's fooling who?).

A second reason is that usury ceilings often limit the interest rate that can be charged but not the number of discount points. If a lender requires a mortgage interest rate higher than the law allows, the lender will not make the loan unless discount points can be charged to increase the mortgage's yield to the lender's required rate.

A loan discount that compensates the lender for costs spent setting up the loan is called a *loan origination fee.* The loan origination fee covers costs of processing the loan application, such as credit reports, preparation of documents related to the loan, payment books and amortization schedules, periodic inspection of new construction, and any other costs the lender incurs in setting up the loan. These costs are normally charged to the borrower as an origination fee because they might not be recoverable under the loan's interest payments if the borrower pays off the loan soon after closing.

The origination fees are charged to the borrower at closing. The net effect is the same as if the origination fee were discount points. For example, suppose a 2 percent loan origination fee is charged to the borrower on a $100,000 loan. The borrower would pay the $2,000 fee to the lender, and the lender would give the borrower the loan proceeds of $100,000. The net effect of course is that the lender really disburses $98,000. The basic difference between the two discounts is the purpose for which the charge is levied against the borrower.

For example, what is the effective borrowing cost on a $100,000 loan with a $2,000 discount, with monthly payments of $1,101.09 for 20 years and a 12 percent contract rate? Recall that the present value of a loan is the discounted value of the remaining payments. So,

$$\text{Loan amount} = (\text{PVAF}_{i,m}) \text{ payment}$$

Substituting the facts from our problem,

$$\$98,000 = (\text{PVAF}_{i\%,240 \text{ months}}) \$1,101.09$$

we know that

$$\$100,000 = (\text{PVAF}_{i\%,240 \text{ months}}) \$1,101.09$$

What rate, i percent, will make the given payment stream equal to $98,000 rather than $100,000?

Solving the equation for the unknown PVAF, we have

$$\frac{\$98,000}{\$1,101.09} = \text{PVAF}_{i\%,240 \text{ months}}$$

$$89.002715 = \text{PVAF}_{i\%,240 \text{ months}}$$

To approximate the effective rate more closely, we can use a process called *linear interpolation*, which is determining the ratio of the difference between one table factor and our desired factor to the differences between the two table factors. This ratio is then applied to the differences in the rates.

In our example, we interpolate as follows:

$$\text{PVAF}_{12\%,240 \text{ months}} = 90.819416$$
$$\text{PVAF}_{13\%,240 \text{ months}} = 85.355132$$

$$\text{Difference in factors} = 5.464284$$
$$\text{Difference in rate} = 1.000000\%$$
$$\text{PVAF}_{12\%, 240 \text{ months}} = 90.819416$$
$$\text{Desired PVAF} = 89.002715$$
$$\text{Difference} = 1.816701$$

$$\frac{1.816701}{5.464284} = 33\% = \text{ratio of differences}$$

Thus, we know that the desired PVAF is 33 percent of the difference between the 12 and 13 percent factors. Therefore, the effective rate of interest is about 33 percent of the difference between the 12 and 13 percent rates. So, 33 percent × 1 percent = 0.33 percent, and 12 percent + 0.33 percent = 12.33 percent. Our effective rate is therefore approximately 12.33 percent, assuming the loan is not paid off before maturity. The reason we say approximately is that linear interpolation will not yield the exact answer because compound interest relationships are not linear. However, it does give a very close approximation.

Effect of Early Repayment In the example, would paying off the loan before maturity affect the yield? If there is no loan discount, prepayment at any time does not change the effective rate of interest. However, if there is a loan discount, *shortening the loan term by prepayment raises the effective yield.* So, using our example where we figured the effective yield as 12.33 percent, if the loan is amortized to maturity, we will see the results of prepayment on the effective yield if the loan is to be paid off at the end of, say, the fifth year.

To begin, we must visualize the payment stream as being different from the 20-year annuity it was. We know the following:

$$\text{Present value of loan} = \$98,000$$
$$\text{Monthly payment} = \$1,101.09$$
$$\text{Term} = 5 \text{ years (60 months)}$$
$$\text{Contract amount of loan} = \$100,000$$

We also know that there will be one final payment at the end of the fifth year, which is the balance outstanding at that time (see Table 2-11) of $91,745.[1] Our $100,000 loan then has 5 years of monthly payments of $1,101.09 plus a final lump-sum payment at the end of the fifth year, all of which must be discounted back to the present at some rate that will equal a present value of $98,000. In equation form,

$$\$98,000 = (\text{PVAF}_{i\%, 60 \text{ months}}) \, \$1,101.09 + (\text{PVF}_{i\%, 60 \text{ months}}) \, \$91,745$$

[1] Difference is due to rounding off of figures in Table 2-11.

We must use trial and error to find the rate whose PVAF and PVF will, when multiplied by the payments and lump sum, respectively, make the right side of our equation equal to $98,000. Let's try, say, 12 percent.

Substituting the 12 percent, 5-year PVF and PVAF into the equation, we have

$$\$98,000 = (44.955038)\$1,101.09 + (0.550450)\$91,745$$
$$\$98,000 < \$100,000.58$$

Trying 13 percent and substituting into our equation,

$$\$98,000 = (43.950107)\$1,101.09 + (0.523874)\$91,745$$
$$= \$48,393.02 + \$48,062.64$$
$$\$98,000 > \$96,455.66$$

We know that the effective rate is somewhere between 12 and 13 percent. To determine the rate more closely, we again use interpolation:

$$PV_{12\%} = \$100,000.58$$
$$PV_{13\%} = \underline{\$\ 96,455.66}$$
$$\text{Difference} = \$\ \ \ 3,544.92$$
$$\text{Difference in rate} = 1\%$$
$$PV_{12\%} = \$100,000.58$$
$$\text{Desired PV} = \underline{\$\ 98,000.00}$$
$$\text{Difference} = \$\ \ \ 2,000.58$$
$$\frac{\$2,000.58}{\$3,544.92} = 56\%$$
$$56\% \times 1\% = 0.56\%$$
$$12\% + 0.56\% = 12.56\%$$

Note that when a loan discount is charged, paying off the loan before maturity results in an increase in the effective yield (borrowing cost) above that for the fully amortized loan.

Effect of Prepayment Penalties   Lenders sometimes impose a penalty fee on the borrower if the loan is paid off before maturity. This *prepayment penalty* is usually expressed as a percentage of the balance outstanding at the time of prepayment. From the lender's perspective, the sudden inflow of funds from a mortgage prepayment might not be readily invested in another mortgage, and in a period of declining interest rates, the lender might not be able to reinvest the funds at a rate equivalent to that of the old mortgage. In recent years, however, with interest rates rising rapidly, lenders have been only too happy to have borrowers pay off old, low-interest loans and, in some cases, have offered borrowers a bonus (rather than penalizing) as an inducement to prepay.

Most mortgage loans today include a clause stipulating provisions and penalties for prepayment. However, if a mortgage is silent on the issue, prepayment is *not* allowed, and a borrower who wants to prepay will have to attempt to negotiate the prepayment privilege with the lender. Most single-family home loans do not have penalties, whereas most income property loans do.

To understand the effect of a prepayment penalty on yield and borrowing costs, let us return to our previous example. Suppose that instead of a 2 percent loan discount there is a 2 percent prepayment penalty, and we want to pay off the loan at the end of 5 years. Reviewing what we know,

$$\text{Loan amount (PV)} = \$100,000$$

$$\text{Payment (annuity)} = \$1,101.09 \text{ per month}$$

$$\text{Period of time} = 5 \text{ years (60 months)}$$

$$\text{Balance owing (end year 5)} = \$91,745$$

$$\text{Prepayment penalty} = 2\% \text{ of } \$91,745$$

$$= \$1,835$$

$$\text{Total lump sum payment at end year 5} = \$91,745 + \$1,835$$

$$= \$93,580$$

We are trying to find the effective rate of interest, so our equation can be constructed as follows:

$$\$100,000 = (\text{PVAF}_{i\%,60 \text{ months}}) \, \$1,101.09 + (\text{PVF}_{i\%,60 \text{ months}}) \, \$93,580$$

To find the rate, we must use trial and error, as before. Trying 12 percent factors, we have

$$\$100,000 = (44.955038)\$1,101.09 + (0.550450)\$93,580$$

$$= \$49,499.54 + \$51,511.11$$

$$\$100,000 \neq \$101,010.65$$

Substituting 13 percent factors, we have

$$\$100,000 = (43.950107)\$1,101.09 + (0.523874)\$93,580$$

$$= \$48,393.02 + \$49,024.13$$

$$\$100,000 \neq \$97,417.15$$

Therefore, we know the rate lies between 12 and 13 percent. Using interpolation,

$$PV_{12\%} = \$101,010.65$$

$$PV_{13\%} = \underline{\$\ 97,417.15}$$

$$\text{Difference} = \$\ \ 3,593.50$$

$$\text{Difference in rate} = 1\%$$

$$PV_{12\%} = \$101,010.65$$

$$\text{Desired PV} = \underline{\$100,000.00}$$

$$\text{Difference} = \$\ \ \ 1,010.65$$

$$\frac{\$1,010.65}{\$3,593.50} = 28\%$$

$$28\% \times 1\% = 0.28\%$$

$$12\% + 0.28\% = 12.28\%$$

Thus, a 2 percent prepayment penalty increases the yield on this loan from 12 to 12.28 percent.

Combined Yield Effects: Discounts and Prepayment Penalties   Some mortgages contain a discount, origination fees, and a prepayment penalty. Suppose the $100,000 loan in prior examples had a 2 percent origination fee and a 2 percent prepayment penalty and was prepaid at the end of year 5. What would the effective yield (borrowing cost) be on this loan? Looking at what we know,

$$\text{Amount loaned}$$
$$(\text{less 2\% origination fee}) = \$98,000$$

$$\text{Annuity (payment)} = \$1,101.09 \text{ per month}$$

$$\text{Term of loan} = 5 \text{ years (60 months)}$$

$$\text{Balance at end year 5}$$
$$(\text{including prepayment penalty}) = \$93,579.54$$

We are trying to find the rate that will make the discounted value of the payment stream equal to $98,000, the amount loaned. Our equation would appear as follows:

$$\$98,000 = (PVAF_{i\%,60\ months})\$1,101.09 + (PVF_{i\%,60\ months})\$93,580$$

By trial and error, substitute, say, 12 percent factors:

$$\$98,000 = (44.955038)\$1,101.09 + (0.550450)\$93,580$$

$$= \$49,499.54 + \$51,511.11$$

$$\$98,000 \neq \$101,010.65$$

Trying 13 percent factors, we have

$$\$98,000 = (43.950107)\$1,101.09 + (0.523874)\$93,580$$
$$= \$48,393.02 + \$49,024.13$$
$$\$98,000 \neq \$97,417.15$$

As before, we can see that the effective rate will lie between 12 and 13 percent. Interpolating, we have

$$PV_{12\%} = \$101,010.65$$
$$PV_{13\%} = \underline{\$\ 97,417.15}$$
$$\text{Difference} = \$\ \ \ 3,593.50$$
$$\text{Difference in rate} = 1\%$$
$$PV_{12\%} = \$101,010.65$$
$$\text{Desired PV} = \underline{\$\ 98,000.00}$$
$$\text{Difference} = \$\ \ \ 3,010.65$$
$$\frac{\$3,010.65}{\$3,593.50} = 84\%$$
$$84\% \times 1\% = 0.84\%$$
$$12\% + 0.84\% = 12.84\%$$

Thus, the combined effect of the origination fee and prepayment penalty is to raise the yield on a contract 12 percent loan to 12.84 percent if the loan is paid off at the end of year 5. The effect on yield becomes greater the earlier the loan is repaid.

FINANCIAL CALCULATORS

Financial calculators are now commonly used in the analysis of investment and lending decisions. Programmed with compound interest formulas, these minicomputers can perform compound interest calculations with such speed and accuracy that the use of tables and formulas has become somewhat obsolete. We say "somewhat" because not all financial calculators can do all compound interest problems, so a thorough knowledge of the application of tables and formulas is still necessary in some situations. In addition, a complete understanding of the concepts of compound interest can be gained only through a familiarity with the formulas and tables. With such a background, you can then enjoy the capabilities of financial calculators.

SUMMARY

This chapter presented the fundamentals of compound interest and mortgage mechanics that the borrower and lender need. These concepts must be completely mastered so you will have an excellent foundation for learning the topics presented in later chapters. We suggest that you work all the various problems in this chapter as a superb way of understanding these concepts.

QUESTIONS

1 Define the following terms:

   a compound interest

   b present value of a lump sum

   c future value of a lump sum

   d future value of an annuity

   e present value of an annuity

   f sinking fund factor

   g mortgage constant

   h amortization schedules

   i proposition outstanding on a mortgage

   j effective yield

   k prepayment penalty

   l discount points

   m borrowing costs

2 What is the relationship between the future and present values of a lump-sum factor?

3 Discuss the difference between a regular annuity and an annuity due.

4 What is the relationship between the sinking fund factor and the future value of an annuity factor?

5 What are the unknowns in any compound interest problem?

6 Describe when you would use the

   a mortgage constant

   b sinking fund factor

   c present value of an annuity factor

   d present value factor

7 Using Tables 2-2 and 2-4, explain the relationship between the present value of a lump-sum factor and the present value of an annuity factor.

8 Discuss how you would calculate the mortgage amortization schedule.

9 What happens to the effective interest rate on a mortgage loan if

   a the lender charges points

   b the lender charges a prepayment penalty

   c for a given amount of points the loan is paid off early (prior to maturity)

10 Discuss the following statement:

The government should set the interest rate at 10 percent since that is the rate which borrowers can afford.

PROBLEMS

1 Mr. and Mrs. Graves have just married. They had planned to work and save enough money to make a down payment on a house in 5 years. They have instead inherited $15,523 from a rich uncle. If they invest this amount for 5 years at 10 percent per year, how much can they put down on a home? Rework the problem assuming monthly compounding.

2 Robos and Carroll, Inc., has decided to purchase in 4 years a building to use in their business. They expect the purchase price to be $100,000. What amount must Robos and Carroll deposit in an account that pays 8 percent annual interest to accumulate $100,000 at the end of 4 years? Rework the problem assuming monthly compounding.

3 Debbie has just graduated from college and has accepted a good job. She wants to buy her childhood home from her parents (in 10 years her parents will no longer require such a large house). If she deposits $6,000 per year beginning tomorrow for 10 years at 9 percent interest per year, how much money will she accumulate to apply toward the purchase price of the house? Rework the problem assuming monthly compounding.

4 The Chance Company has decided to lease a small warehouse to the Harrison Corporation. The lease terms include an annual rent of $6,000 due on December 31 each year for 10 years. The Chance Company elects to add the rent proceeds to an existing employee pension fund that earns 9 percent per year. How much of the funds' total amount after 10 years is attributable to the lease agreement with Harrison Corporation? Rework the problem assuming monthly compounding.

5 John D. Investor owns an apartment building. Each apartment has certain items, such as refrigerators, garbage disposals, and carpets, that are expected to require replacement in 10 years. The total cost of replacement at the end of 10 years is expected to be $50,000. How much must John deposit in an account earning 8 percent per year (compounded yearly) to have the required $50,000? Rework the problem assuming monthly compounding.

6 An investor has purchased an apartment complex. He anticipates cash flows from rents at $180,000 per year for the next 5 years. What is the present value of these cash flows if the investor's required rate of return is 12 percent? Rework the problem assuming monthly compounding.

7 Ms. Hall has entered the housing market in search of a suitable home. She has saved $15,000 for a down payment and has found a house that sells for $100,000. Ms. Hall can obtain a mortgage for the difference for 30 years at 12 percent per year. The mortgage payment is due monthly, and Ms. Hall cannot afford a payment greater than $900. Can she purchase this house?

8 Suppose Ms. Hall (from problem 7) learns she is being transferred. She must now sell her house and pay off the mortgage debt outstanding after 6 months. Determine the amount outstanding by using (1) an amortization schedule and (2) the present value of remaining payments.

9 Suppose that instead of transferring after 6 months, Ms. Hall is transferred after 4 years. Use the proportion outstanding method to determine the mortgage amount to be paid off.

10 The Dowless Company has decided to buy and develop a tract of land. Dowless secures a $200,000, 20-year, 12 percent mortgage on the property from D & D Mortgage Company. D & D charges 1 discount point on this loan as well as a 2 percent prepayment penalty on early debt retirement. After 4 years, Dowless changes plans and decides to sell the property and develop another site. Determine the effective yield (borrowing cost) on this loan.

REFERENCES

Assell, Robert, Helen Assell, and David C. Flaspohler: *Mathematics of Finance,* Houghton Mifflin, Boston, 1982.

Butcher, Margorie V., and Cecil J. Nesbitt: *Mathematics of Compound Interest.* Edwards Brothers, Ann Arbor, Mich., 1971.

Estes, Jack C.: *Interest Amortization Tables,* McGraw-Hill, New York, 1976.

Goebel, Paul R., and Norman G. Miller: *Mortgage Mathematics and Financial Tables,* Prentice-Hall, Englewood Cliffs, N.J., 1981.

THE FINANCING LEGAL ENVIRONMENT

Chapter 2 introduced the mechanics of mortgages. That information is essential for understanding mortgage loan yields, costs of borrowing, and return on invested capital. For the direct participants—whether lenders or equity investors (borrowers)—in the financing process to acquire the *right* to the returns on an investment, certain legal principles and procedures must be followed. However, once acquired, the right to receive these returns is not absolute; it is conditioned on the rights of other participants in the financing arena and the responsibilities of all the participants to each other. Here we introduce the direct and indirect participants in the financing process and explain the legal relationship among them, including their basic rights and responsibilities as founded in general U.S. property law. We also introduce the documents and contracts that tie the participants together with the real estate.

THE PARTICIPANTS

There are four basic participants in the real estate finance process: the equity investor (the borrower); the mortgage lender; the tenant, or whoever physically occupies or uses the real estate; and the government. Figure 3-1 is a relational chart of all participants involved in the process.

The Equity Investor

The *equity investor* owns or holds title to real estate, and risks venture capital today with the expectation of future returns from the property. The equity investor is the decision maker that decides what to buy, when to buy it, how much to pay, and, most importantly for this book, whether to finance it and, if so, how and when. The equity investor thus is the entity that starts the financing process rolling.

Forms of Real Estate Ownership   There are four basic forms of equity ownership of real estate. The forms differ regarding liability, tax consequences, and the number of individuals owning the property together. Chapter 6 fully discusses these four forms of ownership; following is a brief explanation.

Individual and *partnership* forms of ownership are the most common, primarily because they have relative tax advantages over corporate ownership. (This topic is explained further in subsequent chapters.) However, individual owners and partners in a general partnership are exposed to unlimited personal liability. *Corporate* ownership shields the owners' (stockholders') assets from liability for business debts and actions but has the disadvantage of double taxation. (The corporate profits are taxed, and dividends paid to stockholders out of what is left are also taxed as income to the individual stockholders.) A modified form of partnership, called the *limited partnership*, combines many of the advantages of corporate ownership without the double-taxation disadvantage. To qualify for this special tax treatment, however, the limited partnership is under several restrictions, most notably that the limited partners may have no voice in management.

The *real estate investment trust* (REIT) is similar to the mutual fund for stock

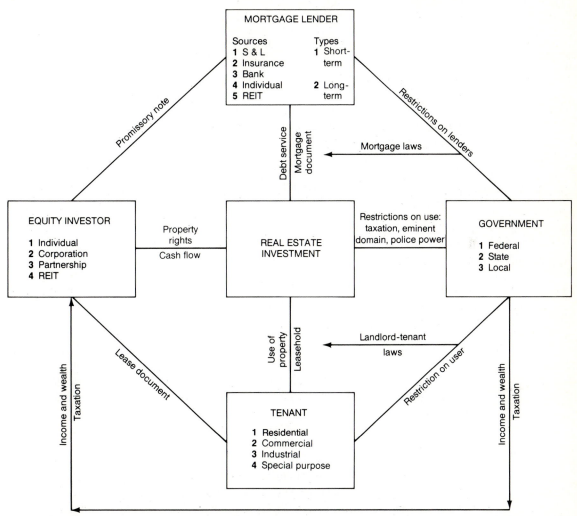

FIGURE 3-1 Participants in the real estate financing process. (*Source: Austin J. Jaffe and C. F. Sirmans,* Real Estate Investment Decision Making, *Prentice-Hall, Inc., Englewood Cliffs, N.J., 1982. Reprinted by permission.*)

ownership. Investors buy shares in the REIT, whose management then invests in various real estate interests.

Regardless of the form of ownership, generally the equity investor expects to receive the "bundle of rights" that accrues to equity ownership, including the right to use the property, the right to sell or leave it to heirs, and the right to its rents and profits. These rights can be given up individually, however. For instance, the right to use the property is often given up to others in exchange for rent. And, as a borrower (or mortgagor), the equity investor gives up the right to unencumbered ownership as long as the mortgage remains in effect.

The Mortgage Lender

The *mortgage lender* is the entity that invests money in the real estate in the form of a mortgage loan. Unlike the equity investor, however, the rights of the lender (also called the *mortgagee*) in the real estate are usually limited to the right to receive payment of the debt from the borrower. To ensure repayment of the debt, the lender requires from the borrower assurance that the loan will be repaid and a pledging of the property as security in the event it is not. To protect their interests, lenders carefully establish their rights through properly drawn legal documents. The lender may be an individual, a commercial lending institution (such as a bank, an insurance company, or a savings and loan), or an REIT.

The Tenant

The *tenant* is the user of the property. Although the tenant is not a direct participant in the financing process, the extent of the duration, quality, and value of the tenant's right to possession and use are often significant determinants of the investment and financing decisions. Thus, the tenant's legal rights and responsibilities vis-à-vis the property and equity investor are important considerations.

The tenant's use of the property usually is restricted to that for which the property is suited or for which it was designed. Tenants fall into four broad subclassifications based on the allowed use: residential, commercial, industrial, or special-purpose.

The Government

Like the tenant, the *government* is an indirect participant in the financing process. At the federal, state, and local levels, the government places restrictions on the other participants and their interrelationships. It restricts the lender with laws relating to mortgages and lending practices. It restricts the tenant by land-use controls (i.e., zoning) and laws relating to tenant rights and responsibilities. Finally, it restricts the equity investor the same way it affects the lender and the tenant and also taxes the income the investment generates. Thus, the government provides the legal framework within which the other participants operate. Within this framework, let us more clearly define the legal ties among the participants and the real estate investment.

THE LEGAL RELATIONSHIPS

Today's laws relating to real estate ownership and mortgage interests evolved from the early Greek and Roman civilizations. However, the most significant influences on the substance and terminology of our current system of laws are rooted in English common law. Over the years, our laws have been constantly modified and shaped by social, economic, and political events and forces. In the 1960s and 1970s, the consumer movement caused a major upheaval in the traditional caveat approach to the law. The Truth-in-Lending Law, Real Estate Settlement and Procedures Act, and various implied warranties were aimed at protecting the consumers of housing.

More recently, the inflationary trend of the late 1970s and early 1980s has caused a tremendous upheaval in real estate finance law. The effects of inflation have forced changes in the types of allowable financing methods, the maximum interest rates that can be charged, and the lender's rights to foreclosure. The recent deregulation of the banking industry and the revision of the Federal Income Tax Code are likely to cause further changes in the financing of real estate.

One aspect of the legal environment that complicates its study is that real estate finance is affected by both federal and individual state laws. Here we provide the overall basics of real property and mortgage law with modifications, as practicable, for the laws of the individual states. This chapter is thus an overview of real property and mortgage law. It is *not* an exhaustive treatment of the legal environment; thus, you should obtain competent counsel whenever legal issues arise.

The Contractual Obligation

As mentioned, the participants in the financing process have interrelationships. These interrelationships are based on the concept of *quid pro quo,* literally "this for that." In other words, one party agrees to perform an act, and the other party agrees to perform another act. Each party agrees to do something that the other desires. For instance, A agrees to sell her house to B, and B agrees to pay a specified amount for it. Or one party agrees to perform an act if and only if the other party performs. For instance, A agrees to pay B a commission if B obtains a ready, willing, and able buyer for A's house. If B does not find such a buyer, then A is not obligated to pay. Because the relationships among the participants take the form of legal contracts, a general background in contract law is necessary because a contract without the legal "teeth" to compel the parties to perform is valueless.

Contract Validity   For a contract to compel the performance of the parties, it must be *valid*. A valid contract is binding and enforceable on the parties. (The elements necessary to make any contract valid are listed below.) At the other extreme, a *void* contract is not binding or enforceable on either party, such as a contract that has been drawn but not signed (agreed to) by both parties. A *voidable* contract may or may not be binding, at the option of the parties. Finally, an *unenforceable* contract is binding but not enforceable; that is, one party cannot bring a court action to compel the other part to act.

Essentials of a Valid Contract

1 Parties who are competent to contract
2 An offer and acceptance
3 Consideration
4 A legal purpose
5 Compliance with the statute of frauds

The parties to a contract must be *competent,* or able to understand the nature of the agreement. Generally, most persons are assumed competent, except minors and persons adjudged insane or under the influence of drugs or alcohol at the time of the contract. In addition, when one party acts on behalf of another, as an individual signing a contract on behalf of a corporation, church, charitable organization, or another individual, for the contract to be valid on the other, the signer must have the legal authority to bind the other. A contract made with an incompetent party is considered voidable, at the option of the incompetent party or that party's legal agent.

The second essential element to a valid contract is the *offer and acceptance.* This means that there must be a "meeting of the minds": One party makes a proposal (offer) to another. If and when the other party properly accepts the offer, there is assumed to be a meeting of the minds and the contract becomes binding. If there is no acceptance, or if the offer is withdrawn prior to acceptance, there is no contract.

The third essential element is *consideration,* which is the benefit received or sacrifice made by the parties by the terms of the contract. It is the quid pro quo concept mentioned earlier. Consideration can take the form of money, goods, or promises. The amount of consideration is not an issue in determining whether consideration exists in the contract, as long as some consideration is agreed on. The key element determining whether consideration exists is whether each party to the contract must do something that would not have to be done in absence of the contract. For example, if A agrees to give B $1,000 but B has to do nothing, then there is no consideration on B's part and there is no legal obligation on A to pay the money.

The fourth essential element is *legal purpose.* If the contract requires one or both parties to perform an illegal act, the contract is void. For instance, if A agrees to provide B space for the express purpose of warehousing stolen property, there is no contract: B cannot compel A to perform an illegal act.

Finally, in many cases a contract is not considered valid unless it is in writing. This requirement dates back to the *statute of frauds* in English common law. All states have adopted some form of the statute of frauds. There are minor differences, but generally real estate sales and financing transactions and leases covering more than 1 year must be in writing to be valid. Oral contracts for these transactions are considered *unenforceable* under the statute of frauds.

Now that basic contractual requirements have been discussed, let us examine the specifics of the legal relationships among the four participants and the real estate.

Investor-Borrower Rights in the Real Estate

The investor or equity owner of real estate obtains a "bundle of rights" in the real estate when it is purchased. These rights include the right to possess, control, enjoy, use, exclude others from, dispose of, and will to heirs. These rights pertain to the land surface itself, and generally all attachments, including those things built on, growing on, or permanently affixed to the land. The rights also pertain to the earth below the surface area, in the shape of a pyramid with its point at the earth's center, and the airspace above the surface as far as necessary to permit peaceable enjoyment of the land. The equity owner may acquire all or only a portion of these rights and may subsequently sell or otherwise transfer all or a portion of them to others.

Estates in Land The quality of ownership in real estate is based on the interest, or *estate,* held. There are various types of estates, which are classified by the duration or quality (number of included rights) of the interest. These types fall into two broad categories. *Freehold estates* are basically ownership interests, and *nonfreehold estates* are nonownership rights to use the real estate. Table 3-1 shows the types of estates in each category. *The fee simple (absolute)* freehold estate is the fullest form of private ownership and also the most common. Although most or all of the bundle of rights are included, a fee simple estate is still subject to public or government restrictions (i.e., zoning laws) and private encumbrances (i.e., easements, mortgages).

There are two types of *conditional fee* estates: the *fee simple determinable* and *fee subject to a condition subsequent.* These estates are contingent on some act, event, or condition specified by the grantor (seller) of the land that is under the control of the grantee (buyer). For instance, if A grants land to B so long as B does not marry, B essentially owns the property as long as he complies. But if B marries, in the case of fee simple determinable he loses this ownership right automatically and the property reverts to the grantor. With a fee subject to a condition subsequent, B's ownership is not automatically terminated, but the grantor retains the right to reclaim the property if desired.

The *life estate* permits the grantee full rights in the property so long as a cer-

TABLE 3-1   FREEHOLD AND NONFREEHOLD ESTATES

Freehold (Ownership)	Nonfreehold (Tenants)
1. Fee simple (absolute)	1. Estate from year-to-year
2. Conditional fee estates	2. Estate for years
a. Fee simple determinable	3. Estate at will
b. Fee subject to a condition subsequent	4. Estate at sufferance
3. Life estates	
4. Remainder	
5. Reversion	

tain person lives. This person, called the *specified life,* is often the grantee, but it may be any other person. At the termination of the specified life, the property passes to another, called a *remainderman,* as specified by the grantor.

A *reversion* is an interest the grantor retains, whereby the ownership of a property reverts to the grantor or the grantor's heirs at the termination of a life estate or a conditional fee estate.

Generally, the fee simple absolute freehold estate is the only type that is mortgageable. The other types theoretically may have value, but lenders are usually unwilling to extend funds for loans secured by property where the interest is limited or subject to some condition over which there is no control.

Nonfreehold estates pertain to renting the rights to use and possess real estate. They are discussed later in the "Tenant-Owner-Property Relationship" section.

Number of Owners Ownership in a parcel of real estate may rest with one or more owners at the same time. Ownership by two or more persons may take one of several forms: joint tenancy, tenancy in common, tenancy by the entireties, community property, or condominium ownership.

In *joint tenancy* ownership, each owner has an equal, undivided interest in the property and the "right of survivorship," which means that if one of the joint tenants dies, his or her share passes to the surviving joint tenant(s). This arrangement is common for husband-wife ownership, especially in states without community property law. Joint tenants must ordinarily acquire and dispose of their interests at the same time.

In *tenancy in common* ownership, each owner has an undivided interest in the property, although the interests do not have to be equal. The tenants in common may sell or otherwise dispose of their interests separately, unless forbidden by contract. And if one owner dies, the deceased's interest goes to her or his heirs, not to the other tenants in common. Business partners generally hold property as tenants in common.

Tenancy by the entireties pertain to only husband-wife ownership and includes the rights of survivorship. This arrangements is used in few states because the practical differences between it and joint tenancy are slight.

Several states, namely, Arizona, California, Idaho, Louisiana, Nevada, New Mexico, Texas, and Washington, have *community property* law. This concept recognizes two kinds of property that spouses can own: separate property, generally the property each spouse owned at the time of marriage; and community property, generally the property acquired during the marriage. Separate property is wholly owned by the spouse who acquired it and is not subject to claims from the other spouse. Community property is considered an acquisition made through the joint efforts of the marriage partners and thus owned by both husband and wife, even if the deed states otherwise.

Laws relating to *dower, curtesy,* and *inchoate* interests provide for an automatic interest to the surviving spouse in property the deceased spouse owned. *Dower* is the wife's rights in the husband's property; *curtesy* is the husband's right in the wife's property. Traditional dower and curtesy laws provide for a one-third minimum interest. Dower and curtesy have been replaced in some states with a statutory *inchoate* interest. ''Inchoate'' means ''dormant until death''; that is, a spouse's rights are dormant until the other spouse dies. Although dower and curtesy are inchoate interests, the laws replacing them modify the minimum percentage of interest the surviving spouse obtains. These provisions prevent one spouse from leaving the other spouse destitute in the event of death by keeping property in one name, either through oversight or by design. These rights do not apply to property owned jointly and equally by husband and wife (as in joint tenancy) and are extinguished on dissolution of the marriage or joint sale of the property.

Note that the laws of various states differ greatly regarding husband-wife rights in jointly and separately owned real estate. However, in most states, husband and wife *both* must sign documents when conveying any of their real estate to a new purchaser. This effectively extinguishes all inchoate and community rights in the real estate and is often advised, even if not required by state law, to prevent any future uncertainties of title.

The *condominium* concept is another form of multiple ownership. Under condominium (condo) ownership, the equity owner generally has a fee simple title to one unit in a multiunit building, sharing ownership of and responsibility for common areas and features with the rest of the owners in the building.

A *cooperative* (co-op) apartment building is owned by a corporation, whose stockholders are the residents of the building. Each stockholder obtains a proprietary lease from the corporation to occupy an apartment unit and pays rent to the corporation.

Although both condo and co-op ownership have increased in recent years, the condo form generally has more financial and legal advantages for individual owners. Because each condo unit is separately owned, it can be financed individually by a first mortgage. In contrast, there is a single mortgage on the entire co-op property. Thus, individual co-op owners cannot obtain new financing on their individual units because they do not own them. As a result, condos tend to be much more easily disposed of (sold). Co-ops typically have the advantage of better control over choice of residents, however, because of the closely held nature of the corporation.

Identifying the Property Owned   As stated, the ownership of real estate extends to the bundle of rights in the land itself, including generally whatever is erected on, affixed to, and growing on it. We just examined the owners' rights; we now define the property in which these rights are vested.

In any contract or document where real estate is part of the consideration, a clear, unambiguous description of the property is essential. Street or mailing addresses are not sufficient. An unambiguous *legal description* clearly defines the boundaries of the property so that they can be determined with acceptable accuracy by anyone who follows the stated legal description and has the proper surveying expertise and equipment. An accurate legal description in all contracts and conveyance documents is necessary to ensure a meeting of the minds.

Legal descriptions take various forms, depending on the location of the property in question. The *government rectangular survey method* is used in 30 states, primarily the western states. Florida is the only eastern state that uses the rectangular survey system. This system was the original means by which land was divided and sold by the government after 1785.

The government survey system begins at the intersection of a north-south line (the *principal meridian*) and an east-west line (the *base line*). The several principal meridian–base line combinations throughout the United States were located where convenient at the time. From the principal meridian, the land is divided into 6-mile-wide vertical strips called *ranges,* and from the base line, 6-mile-wide horizontal strips called *tiers.* The 6-mile square of land outlined by the intersection of a tier and range is called a *township.* Tiers are numbered consecutively north and south of the base line; ranges are numbered consecutively east and west of the principal meridian. This numbering system allows a particular township to be precisely located.

Townships are then divided up into 36 *sections,* each 1 mile square. The sections are then quartered (or halved), and the quarters are identified by their compass location. The quartered sections may be quartered (or halved) again and again and identified by the compass quadrant using the center of the quarter section as a reference point.

The second type of survey system, called *metes and bounds,* is similar in operation to following a treasure map. From a known, unambiguous point, such as a surveyor's monument, the distance and compass direction to the nearest corner of the property are determined. Then the property boundaries are determined from this *point of beginning* by noting the distance and compass direction to the next corner, and the next corner, and so on, until the property has been circumscribed, back to the point of beginning. This method works well for describing irregular or smaller parcels within other land description methods, and it is employed in those states not using the rectangular survey system.

Quite often, large areas of cities, towns, and counties are subdivided into many small parcels. It would be very cumbersome to describe these small lots by either the rectangular survey or the metes and bounds methods, so the large area (the *subdivision*) is laid out with numbered blocks and lots, and if approved by the local government, recorded. This recorded subdivision is now a matter of public record, and the parcels within it may be legally described using their respective lot and block numbers.

Restrictions on Rights   In addition to the limitations on the owner of real estate by the estate received, the number of owners, and the property boundaries, other private interests may place *voluntary* or *involuntary* restrictions on the owner.

A common form of voluntary restriction on use is an *easement,* which is the right to use or cross the land of another for a specific purpose. A utility company's right to use one's land for running utility lines over (or under) the ground is a common example. The landowner may use the property included in the easement only if the purpose does not impede the easement owner's rights. Thus, the landowner may be prevented from erecting a building over (or under) a utility line because doing so would impede the utility company's ability to repair the line.

Another voluntary restriction is a *deed restriction,* which "goes with the land" from owner to owner. It has been placed on the land by a prior owner and generally binds subsequent owners. Deed restrictions are most commonly used for properties located in areas with few government restrictions on land use. To preserve property values within a subdivision, for example, the subdivider will often include in the deed limitations that regulate the type or intensity of use for the parcels within the subdivision. In a residential subdivision, four common deed restrictions are

1 Residential construction only.
2 Building footage must be a specified minimum.
3 No farm animals may be kept.
4 No mobile homes or prefabricated structures are allowed.

Other contractual voluntary limitations are *leases,* where a tenant is given the right of use and/or possession, and *mortgages,* where the lender is given the right to force a sale of the property to pay the debt if the owner-borrower defaults. These restrictions are discussed later.

Involuntary restrictions on the landowner by private interests include liens and encroachments. Nonpayment of income or property taxes, court judgments, creditors' claims, and contractors and material suppliers who have provided labor or materials to the property may cause a *lien* to be placed on the property. The lien is a formal claim for payment, under which the sale of the real estate may be demanded to effect payment.

An *encroachment* is the unauthorized use of an owner's property. This may take the form of a building erected partially or totally on the lot of another or the use of another's property as a route of passage from one place to another. Because they are unauthorized, the landowner can prevent encroachments by initiating appropriate action. However, obvious encroachments that continue uninterrupted for a long time may become *prescriptive easements,* whereby the landowner may lose the right to stop the encroachment and the party using the land may be allowed to continue.

The Borrower-Lender-Property Relationship

When granting a loan, the mortgage lender wants assurance of repayment. This assurance is twofold: The lender may require a promise from the borrower to repay the loan, so the borrower signs a document called the promissory note. The lender also requires that the owner pledge the real estate as security (or collateral) for the loan via a mortgage (or trust deed). If the owner-borrower then defaults on the loan payments, the lender acquires some of the rights in the "bundle" and may force a sale of the real estate to pay off the debt.

The rights of borrower and lender under the mortgage vary from state to state, depending on the theory of law to which each state adheres. In *lien theory* states—which form the majority—the lender has a lien against the real estate while the borrower holds title to it. At the other extreme are *title theory* states, where the lender holds title to the real estate until the loan is paid, at which time title is transferred to the borrower. The title theory is a throwback to English common law and today is not applied in its purest form in the United States. Some states, however, follow a position between the title and lien theories, called the *intermediate theory,* whereby mortgagees (lenders) have legal title but only for the purpose of protecting their security interests. As a practical matter, borrowers in all states have the right of possession and most other rights to the real estate until a default occurs.

Types of Security Instruments Depending on the state, the lender's security interest may take three basic forms. The standard *mortgage* or *mortgage deed,* which is used in most states, is a document that conveys the property from the borrower to the lender. If the debt noted in the mortgage is paid, the document becomes null and void.

Deeds of trust or *trust deeds* involve a third party, called a *trustee,* that receives title to the real estate from the borrower and holds it in trust for the lender's benefit until the loan is paid. The trustee's title is dormant as long as the borrower does not default on the loan. If default occurs, the trustee has the right to sell the real estate to pay off the debt to the lender. For the lender, the deed of trust has an advantage over the mortgage deed in that foreclosure by trustee's sale is often speedier than foreclosure under a regular mortgage.

Some states use the *deed to secure debt* method to avert long foreclosure proceedings. This instrument substitutes for the warranty deed and mortgage combined. It transfers title to the lender but notes that the deed secures payment of the debt and allows the lender to sell the property in case of default. When the debt is fully paid, the deed to secure debt is either canceled or title to the property conveyed back to the borrower. In practice, the only substantive differences among the mortgage deed, trust deed, and security deed are the foreclosure provisions and the removal of the debt from the record (or transfer of title back to the borrower) when the loan is fully paid.

The *promissory note* accompanies the mortgage, deed of trust, or deed to secure the debt and specifically outlines the amounts the borrower owes. Exhibit 3-1 is a typical FNMA-FHLMC standard form. The note sets forth the principal amount, the interest rate, and the time, manner, place, and amount of the payments. In addition, late charges are specified, and penalties for repaying the loan, if any, are noted. Generally, unless specifically allowed in the note, mortgages must be paid in the time and manner agreed on and are not freely prepayable.

NOTE

US $...................

.........................., Florida
City

........................., 19....

    FOR VALUE RECEIVED, the undersigned ("Borrower") promise(s) to pay...........................
...., or order, the principal sum of
....Dollars, with
interest on the unpaid principal balance from the date of this Note, until paid, at the rate of...................
......................percent per annum. Principal and interest shall be payable at......................
...., or such other place as the Note holder may
designate, in consecutive monthly installments of...
.........................Dollars (US $..........................), on the....................
.............day of each month beginning.........................., 19..... Such monthly installments
shall continue until the entire indebtedness evidenced by this Note is fully paid, except that any remaining indebtedness, if not sooner paid, shall be due and payable on...

    If any monthly installment under this Note is not paid when due and remains unpaid after a date specified by a
notice to Borrower, the entire principal amount outstanding and accrued interest thereon shall at once become due
and payable at the option of the Note holder. The date specified shall not be less than thirty days from the date such
notice is mailed. The Note holder may exercise this option to accelerate during any default by Borrower regardless of
any prior forbearance. If suit is brought to collect this Note, the Note holder shall be entitled to collect all reasonable
costs and expenses of suit, including, but not limited to, reasonable attorney's fees.

    Borrower shall pay to the Note holder a late charge of.........................percent of any monthly
installment not received by the Note holder within.........................days after the installment is due.

    Borrower may prepay the principal amount outstanding in whole or in part. The Note holder may require that
any partial prepayments (i) be made on the date monthly installments are due and (ii) be in the amount of that
part of one or more monthly installments which would be applicable to principal. Any partial prepayment shall be
applied against the principal amount outstanding and shall not postpone the due date of any subsequent monthly
installments or change the amount of such installments, unless the Note holder shall otherwise agree in writing.

    Presentment, notice of dishonor, and protest are hereby waived by all makers, sureties, guarantors and endorsers
hereof. This Note shall be the joint and several obligation of all makers, sureties, guarantors and endorsers, and shall
be binding upon them and their successors and assigns.

    Any notice to Borrower provided for in this Note shall be given by mailing such notice by certified mail addressed
to Borrower at the Property Address stated below, or to such other address as Borrower may designate by notice to
the Note holder. Any notice to the Note holder shall be given by mailing such notice by certified mail, return receipt
requested, to the Note holder at the address stated in the first paragraph of this Note, or at such other address as may
have been designated by notice to Borrower.

    The indebtedness evidenced by this Note is secured by a Mortgage, dated............................
........................, and reference is made to the Mortgage for rights as to acceleration of the indebtedness
evidenced by this Note.

                                                    ....(Seal)

....(Seal)

....(Seal)
         Property Address
                                                        (Execute Original Only)

FLORIDA—1 to 4 Family—8/79—FNMA/FHLMC UNIFORM INSTRUMENT

EXHIBIT 3-1   NOTE

The Lender's Security Interest To be legal, a mortgage must have all the essentials of a valid contract. In addition, within the standard mortgage two or three clauses are necessary to effect a security interest in the real estate. The *acceleration clause* generally provides that if the borrower defaults in the mortgage terms, the lender may immediately call the entire balance owing due and payable. Where it is legal, the *power of sale clause* allows the lender or a government official (say, a sheriff), without a court action, to sell the property to pay off the debt. The *defeasance clause* defeats the mortgage instrument if and when the borrower pays the amounts owed.

Although not a requirement for validity, the mortgage has to be immediately *recorded* to preserve its priority status as a line against the property. Recording the mortgage documents serves as *constructive notice* to all other parties that the lender holds a security interest in the property. An unrecorded mortgage is valid, but subsequent liens and mortgages that have been previously recorded usually attain priority over it. The lender who intends to make a loan secured by a first-mortgage lien examines the title to the property to be sure no other party has a first lien. If no other liens are found, the lender grants the loan and immediately records the mortgage to ensure its first-place standing. Recording laws differ from state to state, so in some situations the first lien recorded may not be the first priority. Nonetheless, in *every* state, prompt recording is essential for minimizing lien-priority problems.

Prompt recording generally ensures priority over liens subsequently filed by other individuals, but it does not provide priority over equity claims, such as those by a surviving spouse of a prior owner who is entitled to a dower or curtesy interest that was never received. As a result, lenders frequently insist that the borrower provide a title insurance policy to protect them from any equity claims that may arise.

In addition, recording the mortgage does not prevent priority of government claims, such as federal tax liens or property tax liens. These claims supersede all others, regardless of the date of filing.

General Rights and Responsibilities of the Parties The rights and responsibilities of mortgagor and mortgagee vary, depending on the provisions in the mortgage and state laws. Generally, however, mortgagors have the rights to possession of the property and to the rents and profits it generates. However, mortgagors cannot "commit waste" on the property—that is, they may not diminish its value and thus damage the lender's security position. In addition, they must perform all the covenants or promises made in the document and pay back the amount owed. Finally, mortgagors have the right to redeem their interest in the property if default occurs and the lender invokes the acceleration clause.

Mortgagees have the right to receive *full payment* at the times and in the manner agreed to in the mortgage. They also have the right to *full performance* of other covenants the mortgagor made as well as the right to *foreclose* if these conditions are not met. However, the lender generally cannot dispossess the borrower from the property or interfere with the right of quiet enjoyment until fore-closure is complete.

Unless specifically restricted by the mortgage's provisions, both the borrower and the lender have the right to freely assign their respective interests to anyone of their choosing. Thus, unless expressly forbidden, mortgages are assumable and assignable.

Specific Rights and Responsibilities of the Parties   In addition to general provisions, most mortgages contain a number of clauses that further define the rights and responsibilities of borrower and lender. Exhibit 3-2 is the FNMA-FHLMC standard mortgage used in the state of Florida. (Similar forms are used in other states, modified to comply with state laws.)

Certain of these clauses deserve specific mention. Clause 2 provides that the borrower shall pay into an account each month one-twelfth of the annual property taxes, special assessments, hazard insurance premiums, mortgage insurance premiums, and ground rents. The lender may waive this requirement (or in some cases, laws may forbid it). The clause's main purpose is to protect the lender because unpaid taxes and ground rents may attain priority over the mortgage. In addition, hazard insurance canceled because of nonpayment leaves the security for the loan unprotected, and a canceled mortgage insurance policy leaves the lender unprotected if the borrower defaults. Even if not required by the lender, however, borrowers often escrow for these items for budgeting convenience. For example, suppose that insurance and property taxes are $900 per year for a parcel of real estate. The borrower would place $75 each month in an account with the lender to cover these charges.

Clauses 4 and 5 in Exhibit 3-2 relate to the same issues. Clause 4 requires the borrower to discharge liens that may attain a priority over the mortgage. Clause 5 specifies the type and form of hazard insurance the borrower is required to carry. It also specifies that the proceeds from any claim shall be applied to the restoration of the property, if economically feasible—otherwise, the proceeds are to be applied to the balance owing on the loan.

Clause 7 allows the lender to take whatever action is necessary to protect its security interest in the property when the borrower fails to perform any of the mortgage's covenants, including paying mortgage insurance and repairing the property if waste has been committed or building or housing codes are being violated. All costs the lender incurs become additional borrower indebtedness under the mortgage, and the lender may demand payment at any time.

Clause 8 allows the lender to enter the property for reasonable cause associated with its security interest.

Clause 9 specifies the allocation of proceeds between borrower and lender in the event the property is condemned. If the property is totally condemned, the proceeds are applied to the loan balance, with any excess going to the borrower. In a partial taking by condemnation, the proportion of proceeds applied to the loan balance is based on the loan-to-value ratio at the time of the taking. Clause

This instrument was prepared by:

....

....

MORTGAGE

THIS MORTGAGE is made this.........................day of.........................., 19...., between the Mortgagor,.. ....(herein "Borrower"), and the Mortgagee,................. ...., a corporation organized and existing under the laws of......................................, whose address is................. ....(herein "Lender").

WHEREAS, Borrower is indebted to Lender in the principal sum of.................................... ....Dollars, which indebtedness is evidenced by Borrower's note dated.........................(herein "Note"), providing for monthly installments of principal and interest, with the balance of the indebtedness, if not sooner paid, due and payable on........................ ....;

To SECURE to Lender (a) the repayment of the indebtedness evidenced by the Note, with interest thereon, the payment of all other sums, with interest thereon, advanced in accordance herewith to protect the security of this Mortgage, and the performance of the covenants and agreements of Borrower herein contained, and (b) the repayment of any future advances, with interest thereon, made to Borrower by Lender pursuant to paragraph 21 hereof (herein "Future Advances"), Borrower does hereby mortgage, grant and convey to Lender the following described property located in the County of......................................, State of Florida:

which has the address of..., ...,
                               [Street]   [City]

..........................(herein "Property Address");
[State and Zip Code]

TOGETHER with all the improvements now or hereafter erected on the property, and all easements, rights, appurtenances, rents, royalties, mineral, oil and gas rights and profits, water, water rights, and water stock, and all fixtures now or hereafter attached to the property, all of which, including replacements and additions thereto, shall be deemed to be and remain a part of the property covered by this Mortgage; and all of the foregoing, together with said property (or the leasehold estate if this Mortgage is on a leasehold) are herein referred to as the "Property".

Borrower covenants that Borrower is lawfully seised of the estate hereby conveyed and has the right to mortgage, grant and convey the Property, that the Property is unencumbered, and that Borrower will warrant and defend generally the title to the Property against all claims and demands, subject to any declarations, easements or restrictions listed in a schedule of exceptions to coverage in any title insurance policy insuring Lender's interest in the Property.

FLORIDA—1 to 4 Family—6/75—FNMA/FHLMC UNIFORM INSTRUMENT

EXHIBIT 3-2 MORTGAGE

UNIFORM COVENANTS. Borrower and Lender covenant and agree as follows:

1. Payment of Principal and Interest. Borrower shall promptly pay when due the principal of and interest on the indebtedness evidenced by the Note, prepayment and late charges as provided in the Note, and the principal of and interest on any Future Advances secured by this Mortgage.

2. Funds for Taxes and Insurance. Subject to applicable law or to a written waiver by Lender, Borrower shall pay to Lender on the day monthly installments of principal and interest are payable under the Note, until the Note is paid in full, a sum (herein "Funds") equal to one-twelfth of the yearly taxes and assessments which may attain priority over this Mortgage, and ground rents on the Property, if any, plus one-twelfth of yearly premium installments for hazard insurance, plus one-twelfth of yearly premium installments for mortgage insurance, if any, all as reasonably estimated initially and from time to time by Lender on the basis of assessments and bills and reasonable estimates thereof.

The Funds shall be held in an institution the deposits or accounts of which are insured or guaranteed by a Federal or state agency (including Lender if Lender is such an institution). Lender shall apply the Funds to pay said taxes, assessments, insurance premiums and ground rents. Lender may not charge for so holding and applying the Funds, analyzing said account, or verifying and compiling said assessments and bills, unless Lender pays Borrower interest on the Funds and applicable law permits Lender to make such a charge. Borrower and Lender may agree in writing at the time of execution of this Mortgage that interest on the Funds shall be paid to Borrower, and unless such agreement is made or applicable law requires such interest to be paid, Lender shall not be required to pay Borrower any interest or earnings on the Funds. Lender shall give to Borrower, without charge, an annual accounting of the Funds showing credits and debits to the Funds and the purpose for which each debit to the Funds was made. The Funds are pledged as additional security for the sums secured by this Mortgage.

If the amount of the Funds held by Lender, together with the future monthly installments of Funds payable prior to the due dates of taxes, assessments, insurance premiums and ground rents, shall exceed the amount required to pay said taxes, assessments, insurance premiums and ground rents as they fall due, such excess shall be, at Borrower's option, either promptly repaid to Borrower or credited to Borrower on monthly installments of Funds. If the amount of the Funds held by Lender shall not be sufficient to pay taxes, assessments, insurance premiums and ground rents as they fall due, Borrower shall pay to Lender any amount necessary to make up the deficiency within 30 days from the date notice is mailed by Lender to Borrower requesting payment thereof.

Upon payment in full of all sums secured by this Mortgage, Lender shall promptly refund to Borrower any Funds held by Lender. If under paragraph 18 hereof the Property is sold or the Property is otherwise acquired by Lender, Lender shall apply, no later than immediately prior to the sale of the Property or its acquisition by Lender, any Funds held by Lender at the time of application as a credit against the sums secured by this Mortgage.

3. Application of Payments. Unless applicable law provides otherwise, all payments received by Lender under the Note and paragraphs 1 and 2 hereof shall be applied by Lender first in payment of amounts payable to Lender by Borrower under paragraph 2 hereof, then to interest payable on the Note, then to the principal of the Note, and then to interest and principal on any Future Advances.

4. Charges; Liens. Borrower shall pay all taxes, assessments and other charges, fines and impositions attributable to the Property which may attain a priority over this Mortgage, and leasehold payments or ground rents, if any, in the manner provided under paragraph 2 hereof or, if not paid in such manner, by Borrower making payment, when due, directly to the payee thereof. Borrower shall promptly furnish to Lender all notices of amounts due under this paragraph, and in the event Borrower shall make payment directly, Borrower shall promptly furnish to Lender receipts evidencing such payments. Borrower shall promptly discharge any lien which has priority over this Mortgage; provided, that Borrower shall not be required to discharge any such lien so long as Borrower shall agree in writing to the payment of the obligation secured by such lien in a manner acceptable to Lender, or shall in good faith contest such lien by, or defend enforcement of such lien in, legal proceedings which operate to prevent the enforcement of the lien or forfeiture of the Property or any part thereof.

5. Hazard Insurance. Borrower shall keep the improvements now existing or hereafter erected on the Property insured against loss by fire, hazards included within the term "extended coverage", and such other hazards as Lender may require and in such amounts and for such periods as Lender may require; provided, that Lender shall not require that the amount of such coverage exceed that amount of coverage required to pay the sums secured by this Mortgage.

The insurance carrier providing the insurance shall be chosen by Borrower subject to approval by Lender; provided, that such approval shall not be unreasonably withheld. All premiums on insurance policies shall be paid in the manner provided under paragraph 2 hereof or, if not paid in such manner, by Borrower making payment, when due, directly to the insurance carrier.

All insurance policies and renewals thereof shall be in form acceptable to Lender and shall include a standard mortgage clause in favor of and in form acceptable to Lender. Lender shall have the right to hold the policies and renewals thereof, and Borrower shall promptly furnish to Lender all renewal notices and all receipts of paid premiums. In the event of loss, Borrower shall give prompt notice to the insurance carrier and Lender. Lender may make proof of loss if not made promptly by Borrower.

Unless Lender and Borrower otherwise agree in writing, insurance proceeds shall be applied to restoration or repair of the Property damaged, provided such restoration or repair is economically feasible and the security of this Mortgage is not thereby impaired. If such restoration or repair is not economically feasible or if the security of this Mortgage would be impaired, the insurance proceeds shall be applied to the sums secured by this Mortgage, with the excess, if any, paid to Borrower. If the Property is abandoned by Borrower, or if Borrower fails to respond to Lender within 30 days from the date notice is mailed by Lender to Borrower that the insurance carrier offers to settle a claim for insurance benefits, Lender is authorized to collect and apply the insurance proceeds at Lender's option either to restoration or repair of the Property or to the sums secured by this Mortgage.

Unless Lender and Borrower otherwise agree in writing, any such application of proceeds to principal shall not extend or postpone the due date of the monthly installments referred to in paragraphs 1 and 2 hereof or change the amount of such installments. If under paragraph 18 hereof the Property is acquired by Lender, all right, title and interest of Borrower in and to any insurance policies and in and to the proceeds thereof resulting from damage to the Property prior to the sale or acquisition shall pass to Lender to the extent of the sums secured by this Mortgage immediately prior to such sale or acquisition.

6. Preservation and Maintenance of Property; Leaseholds; Condominiums; Planned Unit Developments. Borrower shall keep the Property in good repair and shall not commit waste or permit impairment or deterioration of the Property and shall comply with the provisions of any lease if this Mortgage is on a leasehold. If this Mortgage is on a unit in a condominium or a planned unit development, Borrower shall perform all of Borrower's obligations under the declaration or covenants creating or governing the condominium or planned unit development, the by-laws and regulations of the condominium or planned unit development, and constituent documents. If a condominium or planned unit development rider is executed by Borrower and recorded together with this Mortgage, the covenants and agreements of such rider shall be incorporated into and shall amend and supplement the covenants and agreements of this Mortgage as if the rider were a part hereof.

7. Protection of Lender's Security. If Borrower fails to perform the covenants and agreements contained in this Mortgage, or if any action or proceeding is commenced which materially affects Lender's interest in the Property, including, but not limited to, eminent domain, insolvency, code enforcement, or arrangements or proceedings involving a bankrupt or decedent, then Lender at Lender's option, upon notice to Borrower, may make such appearances, disburse such sums and take such action as is necessary to protect Lender's interest, including, but not limited to, disbursement of reasonable attorney's fees and entry upon the Property to make repairs. If Lender required mortgage insurance as a condition of making the loan secured by this Mortgage, Borrower shall pay the premiums required to maintain such insurance in effect until such time as the requirement for such insurance terminates in accordance with Borrower's and

Lender's written agreement or applicable law. Borrower shall pay the amount of all mortgage insurance premiums in the manner provided under paragraph 2 hereof.

Any amounts disbursed by Lender pursuant to this paragraph 7, with interest thereon, shall become additional indebtedness of Borrower secured by this Mortgage. Unless Borrower and Lender agree to other terms of payment, such amounts shall be payable upon notice from Lender to Borrower requesting payment thereof, and shall bear interest from the date of disbursement at the rate payable from time to time on outstanding principal under the Note unless payment of interest at such rate would be contrary to applicable law, in which event such amounts shall bear interest at the highest rate permissible under applicable law. Nothing contained in this paragraph 7 shall require Lender to incur any expense or take any action hereunder.

8. Inspection. Lender may make or cause to be made reasonable entries upon and inspections of the Property, provided that Lender shall give Borrower notice prior to any such inspection specifying reasonable cause therefor related to Lender's interest in the Property.

9. Condemnation. The proceeds of any award or claim for damages, direct or consequential, in connection with any condemnation or other taking of the Property, or part thereof, or for conveyance in lieu of condemnation, are hereby assigned and shall be paid to Lender.

In the event of a total taking of the Property, the proceeds shall be applied to the sums secured by this Mortgage, with the excess, if any, paid to Borrower. In the event of a partial taking of the Property, unless Borrower and Lender otherwise agree in writing, there shall be applied to the sums secured by this Mortgage such proportion of the proceeds as is equal to that proportion which the amount of the sums secured by this Mortgage immediately prior to the date of taking bears to the fair market value of the Property immediately prior to the date of taking, with the balance of the proceeds paid to Borrower.

If the Property is abandoned by Borrower, or if, after notice by Lender to Borrower that the condemnor offers to make an award or settle a claim for damages, Borrower fails to respond to Lender within 30 days after the date such notice is mailed, Lender is authorized to collect and apply the proceeds, at Lender's option, either to restoration or repair of the Property or to the sums secured by this Mortgage.

Unless Lender and Borrower otherwise agree in writing, any such application of proceeds to principal shall not extend or postpone the due date of the monthly installments referred to in paragraphs 1 and 2 hereof or change the amount of such installments.

10. Borrower Not Released. Extension of the time for payment or modification of amortization of the sums secured by this Mortgage granted by Lender to any successor in interest of Borrower shall not operate to release, in any manner, the liability of the original Borrower and Borrower's successors in interest. Lender shall not be required to commence proceedings against such successor or refuse to extend time for payment or otherwise modify amortization of the sums secured by this Mortgage by reason of any demand made by the original Borrower and Borrower's successors in interest.

11. Forbearance by Lender Not a Waiver. Any forbearance by Lender in exercising any right or remedy hereunder, or otherwise afforded by applicable law, shall not be a waiver of or preclude the exercise of any such right or remedy. The procurement of insurance or the payment of taxes or other liens or charges by Lender shall not be a waiver of Lender's right to accelerate the maturity of the indebtedness secured by this Mortgage.

12. Remedies Cumulative. All remedies provided in this Mortgage are distinct and cumulative to any other right or remedy under this Mortgage or afforded by law or equity, and may be exercised concurrently, independently or successively.

13. Successors and Assigns Bound; Joint and Several Liability; Captions. The covenants and agreements herein contained shall bind, and the rights hereunder shall inure to, the respective successors and assigns of Lender and Borrower, subject to the provisions of paragraph 17 hereof. All covenants and agreements of Borrower shall be joint and several. The captions and headings of the paragraphs of this Mortgage are for convenience only and are not to be used to interpret or define the provisions hereof.

14. Notice. Except for any notice required under applicable law to be given in another manner, (a) any notice to Borrower provided for in this Mortgage shall be given by mailing such notice by certified mail addressed to Borrower at the Property Address or at such other address as Borrower may designate by notice to Lender as provided herein, and (b) any notice to Lender shall be given by certified mail, return receipt requested, to Lender's address stated herein or to such other address as Lender may designate by notice to Borrower as provided herein. Any notice provided for in this Mortgage shall be deemed to have been given to Borrower or Lender when given in the manner designated herein.

15. Uniform Mortgage; Governing Law; Severability. This form of mortgage combines uniform covenants for national use and non-uniform covenants with limited variations by jurisdiction to constitute a uniform security instrument covering real property. This Mortgage shall be governed by the law of the jurisdiction in which the Property is located. In the event that any provision or clause of this Mortgage or the Note conflicts with applicable law, such conflict shall not affect other provisions of this Mortgage or the Note which can be given effect without the conflicting provision, and to this end the provisions of the Mortgage and the Note are declared to be severable.

16. Borrower's Copy. Borrower shall be furnished a conformed copy of the Note and of this Mortgage at the time of execution or after recordation hereof.

17. Transfer of the Property; Assumption. If all or any part of the Property or an interest therein is sold or transferred by Borrower without Lender's prior written consent, excluding (a) the creation of a lien or encumbrance subordinate to this Mortgage, (b) the creation of a purchase money security interest for household appliances, (c) a transfer by devise, descent or by operation of law upon the death of a joint tenant or (d) the grant of any leasehold interest of three years or less not containing an option to purchase, Lender may, at Lender's option, declare all the sums secured by this Mortgage to be immediately due and payable. Lender shall have waived such option to accelerate if, prior to the sale or transfer, Lender and the person to whom the Property is to be sold or transferred reach agreement in writing that the credit of such person is satisfactory to Lender and that the interest payable on the sums secured by this Mortgage shall be at such rate as Lender shall request. If Lender has waived the option to accelerate provided in this paragraph 17, and if Borrower's successor in interest has executed a written assumption agreement accepted in writing by Lender, Lender shall release Borrower from all obligations under this Mortgage and the Note.

If Lender exercises such option to accelerate, Lender shall mail Borrower notice of acceleration in accordance with paragraph 14 hereof. Such notice shall provide a period of not less than 30 days from the date the notice is mailed within which Borrower may pay the sums declared due. If Borrower fails to pay such sums prior to the expiration of such period, Lender may, without further notice or demand on Borrower, invoke any remedies permitted by paragraph 18 hereof.

NON-UNIFORM COVENANTS. Borrower and Lender further covenant and agree as follows:

18. Acceleration; Remedies. Except as provided in paragraph 17 hereof, upon Borrower's breach of any covenant or agreement of Borrower in this Mortgage, including the covenants to pay when due any sums secured by this Mortgage, Lender prior to acceleration shall mail notice to Borrower as provided in paragraph 14 hereof specifying: (1) the breach; (2) the action required to cure such breach; (3) a date, not less than 30 days from the date the notice is mailed to Borrower, by which such breach must be cured; and (4) that failure to cure such breach on or before the date specified in the notice may result in acceleration of the sums secured by this Mortgage, foreclosure by judicial proceeding and sale of the Property. The notice shall further inform Borrower of the right to reinstate after acceleration and the right to assert in the foreclosure proceeding the non-existence of a default or any other defense of Borrower to acceleration and foreclosure. If the breach is not cured on or before the date specified in the notice, Lender at Lender's option may declare all of the sums secured by this Mortgage to be immediately due and payable without further demand and may foreclose this Mortgage by judicial proceeding. Lender shall be entitled to collect in such proceeding all expenses of foreclosure, including, but not limited to, reasonable attorney's fees, and costs of documentary evidence, abstracts and title reports.

19. Borrower's Right to Reinstate. Notwithstanding Lender's acceleration of the sums secured by this Mortgage, Borrower shall have the right to have any proceedings begun by Lender to enforce this Mortgage discontinued at any time

EXHIBIT 3-2 *(Continued)*

prior to entry of a judgment enforcing this Mortgage if: (a) Borrower pays Lender all sums which would be then due under this Mortgage, the Note and notes securing Future Advances, if any, had no acceleration occurred; (b) Borrower cures all breaches of any other covenants or agreements of Borrower contained in this Mortgage; (c) Borrower pays all reasonable expenses incurred by Lender in enforcing the covenants and agreements of Borrower contained in this Mortgage and in enforcing Lender's remedies as provided in paragraph 18 hereof, including, but not limited to, reasonable attorney's fees; and (d) Borrower takes such action as Lender may reasonably require to assure that the lien of this Mortgage, Lender's interest in the Property and Borrower's obligation to pay the sums secured by this Mortgage shall continue unimpaired. Upon such payment and cure by Borrower, this Mortgage and the obligations secured hereby shall remain in full force and effect as if no acceleration had occurred.

20. Assignment of Rents; Appointment of Receiver. As additional security hereunder, Borrower hereby assigns to Lender the rents of the Property, provided that Borrower shall, prior to acceleration under paragraph 18 hereof or abandonment of the Property, have the right to collect and retain such rents as they become due and payable.

Upon acceleration under paragraph 18 hereof or abandonment of the Property, Lender shall be entitled to have a receiver appointed by a court to enter upon, take possession of and manage the Property and to collect the rents of the Property, including those past due. All rents collected by the receiver shall be applied first to payment of the costs of management of the Property and collection of rents, including, but not limited to, receiver's fees, premiums on receiver's bonds and reasonable attorney's fees, and then to the sums secured by this Mortgage. The receiver shall be liable to account only for those rents actually received.

21. Future Advances. Upon request by Borrower, Lender, at Lender's option within twenty years from the date of this Mortgage, may make Future Advances to Borrower. Such Future Advances, with interest thereon, shall be secured by this Mortgage when evidenced by promissory notes stating that said notes are secured hereby. At no time shall the principal amount of the indebtedness secured by this Mortgage, not including sums advanced in accordance herewith to protect the security of this Mortgage, exceed the original amount of the Note plus US$. . . . .

22. Release. Upon payment of all sums secured by this Mortgage, Lender shall release this Mortgage without charge to Borrower. Borrower shall pay all costs of recordation, if any.

23. Attorney's Fees. As used in this Mortgage and in the Note, "attorney's fees" shall include attorney's fees, if any, which may be awarded by an appellate court.

IN WITNESS WHEREOF, Borrower has executed this Mortgage.

Signed, sealed and delivered
in the presence of:

. . . . (Seal)
—Borrower

. . . . (Seal)
—Borrower

STATE OF FLORIDA, ...County ss:

I hereby certify that on this day, before me, an officer duly authorized in the state aforesaid and in the county aforesaid to take acknowledgements, personally appeared. . . . .
. . . ., to me known to be the person(s) described in and who executed the foregoing instrument and acknowledged before me that. . . . . .executed the same for the purpose therein expressed.

WITNESS my hand and official seal in the county and state aforesaid this. . . . . .day of . . . ., 19. . . . . . .

My Commission expires:

[Seal]

. . . .
Notary Public

———————— (Space Below This Line Reserved For Lender and Recorder) ————————

9 also allows the lender to collect the condemnation proceeds if the borrower abandons the property or fails to respond and apply these proceeds to repair of the property or to the loan balance.

Clause 17 is typically called a "due-on-sale" clause and has been the cause of much litigation in recent years. Basically, it provides that the lender may accelerate the sums owed under the mortgage if the property is sold, unless the lender agrees to the assumption of the loan. Thus, the borrower's implicit right to assign personal interest to another is ostensibly revoked by this clause.

Clauses 18 and 19 relate to specific acceleration clauses and redemption provisions of Florida law. In other states, depending on foreclosure and redemption provisions, the clauses are different. Note that clause 20 partially revokes the earlier-mentioned general provision of the borrower's right to the rents for the property. This clause entitles the rents to the lender if the loan is accelerated as under clause 18.

In addition to these clauses, the borrower and the lender are free to agree on any other clauses that do not violate applicable law.

Default, Redemption, and Foreclosure   When a borrower defaults, typically the lender works with the borrower to resolve the problem and cure the default. If the problem (and default) cannot be solved, the lender's final alternative is *foreclosure* of the mortgage, whereby the borrower's title to the property is taken away and the property is sold to pay off the debt. Prior to foreclosure, borrowers in all states have what is called *equity of redemption:* The borrower may retain title to the property if, at any time after the acceleration clause is involved and prior to the foreclosure sale, the borrower pays the balance due on the mortgage, along with accrued interest and any expenses the lender incurred in starting foreclosure proceedings. In addition, some states provide for a *statutory right of redemption* for a stated period *after* the foreclosure sale, whereby the borrower may redeem interest by paying the balance due, accrued interest, and lender's foreclosure costs.

In most states, the lender's right to foreclose takes two basic forms: *foreclosure by judicial sale* and *foreclosure by power of sale*. Foreclosure by judicial sale is accomplished through a lawsuit, whereby the lender sues to foreclose. A hearing is held; the lender must prove a default has occurred. If this is proved, the court issues a judgment in favor of the lender, and arrangements are made to hold the foreclosure sale. This process is lengthy, time-consuming, and costly compared with foreclosure by power of sale.

Foreclosure by power of sale is favored over foreclosure by judicial sale where it is permitted, which includes most states. No judicial hearing or judgment is necessary. The arrangements for the sale generally are made according to state statute. These arrangements include giving specific notice of the sale to parties in possession of the premises and general notice to the public at large, usually through newspaper advertisements. State laws typically specify the minimum amount of time that these notices must be given prior to the sale.

At the foreclosure sale—whether by judicial decree or power of sale—the property is put up for public auction, with the sale being conducted by the sheriff, the mortgagee, or, in the case of a deed of trust, the trustee. The mortgagee typically bids for the property in the amount outstanding on the loan together with accrued interest and foreclosure costs. Unless there is a higher bidder, the mortgagee may be the ultimate purchaser at the foreclosure sale.

After the sale, all the mortgagor's rights are extinguished unless of course applicable state law provides for the statutory right of redemption. If so, the purchaser at the sale does not obtain title to the property until the redemption period expires and the mortgagor fails to redeem. This could mean a wait of from 6 months to 2 years.

Table 3-2 outlines the types of security instruments used, typical foreclosure remedies, typical foreclosure times, and statutory redemption periods, if any, in all states except Hawaii.

Once foreclosure is completed and the property is sold, one of two situations may occur. The price obtained at the foreclosure sale may be *more than* necessary to pay off the borrower's debt to the lender, including legal fees and costs of foreclosure. If so, the surplus is distributed first to other parties, if any, that have liens on the property, and the balance to the mortgagor. Or, the foreclosure sale proceeds may be less than the amount necessary to retire the full amount of the debt. In this case, the lender may have the right to sue for a *deficiency judgment* against the borrower for the balance due. If the deficiency judgment is valid, the court may seize and sell other assets of the borrower to fully retire the debt. To ensure that the deficiency judgment is valid, a burden of proof is on the lender to show that the foreclosure sale price reasonably reflects the property's fair market value at that time. The stringency of this requirement varies from state to state, and some states have abolished deficiency judgments altogether.

There are two other methods of foreclosure: *strict foreclosure* and *foreclosure by writ of entry*. Their use is often restricted, so they are little used and are of local interest only.

The Tenant-Owner-Property Relationship

As noted, the tenant that leases the real estate gains the right of possession and use of the property from the original bundle of rights. For this right, the tenant pays a consideration called *rent*. The extent of the tenant's interest is defined by the estate the tenant holds.

Nonfreehold Estates   As noted in Table 3-1, possessory rental interests in real estate are referred to as *nonfreehold estates*. The four basic estates are

1 Estate from period to period (month to month, year to year)
2 Estate for years
3 Estate at will
4 Estate at sufferance

Under *estate from period to period,* no specific term of the rental is agreed to and the rent is paid periodically, usually monthly, quarterly, or annually. The estate continues until one party or the other gives notice of intent to terminate the tenancy. A tenant who rents an apartment and pays monthly rent but has no fixed minimum or maximum rental period has an estate from month to month. Rules for termination of this type of estate are usually set forth in state law. Generally, a minimum of one rental period's advance notice to the other party is required, unless the parties agree to a longer notice period.

An *estate for years* is a tenancy with a definite term. At the end of the tenancy, the tenant may lose possessory rights unless renewal provisions are set forth in the original agreement.

An *estate at will* is a tenancy with an indefinite term and continues as long as both parties agree. It may be terminated at the will of either party. Generally, no notice of termination is required, although some states require a minimum notice when the rental property is residential.

An *estate at sufferance* is a wrongful tenancy, whereby the tenant holds over in the rental premises after the legal right to do so has expired. It is typically not enforceable by the tenant.

The Lease   The lease is a *contract* between landlord and tenant. It is also a *conveyance* in that it conveys to the tenant the rights to possession and use. It requires all the elements of a valid contract: competent parties, an offer and acceptance, consideration, a legal purpose, and compliance with the statute of frauds. In most states, oral agreements (leases) between landlord and tenant are legal, except those for longer than 1 year. As a practical matter, however, an oral lease leads to misunderstandings between the parties, and the true content and intent of the oral agreement become more difficult to reconstruct as time goes on. For this reason, written leases, even for month-to-month tenancies, are recommended.

Under the lease, whether oral or written, the tenant and the landlord each have general rights and responsibilities. The tenant has purchased the exclusive right to possess and use the premises and is entitled to that right without interference from the landlord; entry by the landlord constitutes a trespass, unless expressly provided for in the lease. The tenant may use the property for any legal purpose, unless the lease expressly restricts the use. For this reason, clauses such as "The premises may be used for residential use only" or "for use as a jewelry store only" are usually inserted into the lease.

In absence of any agreement to the contrary, the rent for the lease's premises is not due until the end of the rental period. Few landlords, however, will wait until the end of the rental period, so there is usually a clause in the lease requiring the rent to be paid at the beginning of each rental period.

Rental increases during the lease's term are not allowed unless expressly provided for in the lease. Generally, states provide that the landlord must give the tenant reasonable notice of rental increases. When the rent is to be raised at the time of lease renewal, the notice of increase must usually be for a period at least

TABLE 3-2 FORECLOSURE-REDEMPTION SUMMARY

State	Security instrument used	Typical foreclosure remedies	Length of time to complete foreclosure	Period of redemption
Alabama	Mortgage	Power of sale	4 to 6 weeks plus redemption period	1 year
Alaska	Mortgage	Power of sale	4 to 6 weeks	None
Arizona	Mortgage and deed of trust	Judicial sale for mortgages, trustee sale for deed of trust	3 months	None with deed of trust; 6 months with mortgage (30 days if property abandoned)
Arkansas	Mortgage	Judicial sale	3 to 4 months	Usually waived
California	Deed of trust	Trustee sale	4 months	None
Colorado	Deed of trust	Trustee sale	4 to 6 months	75 days
Connecticut	Mortgage	Judicial sale	8 to 9 months	None
Delaware	Mortgage	Judicial sale	3 to 7 months	None
District of Columbia	Deed of trust	Trustee sale	4 weeks	None
Florida	Mortgage	Judicial sale	3 to 4 months	10 days confirmation after sale 60 days appeal prior to sale
Georgia	Deed of trust	Power of sale	1 month	None
Idaho	Deed of trust	Power of sale	4 months	None
Illinois	Mortgage	Judicial sale	6 months plus redemption period	6 months after sale or longer as court prescribes; 2 months after sale possible if house abandoned
Indiana	Mortgage	Judicial sale	Mortgage originated prior to 1958—14 months; 1958–7/1/75—8 months; after 7/1/75—5 months	12 months 6 months 3 months
Iowa	Mortgage	Judicial sale	4 to 6 weeks plus redemption period	6 months if deficiency is waived; otherwise 12 months

TABLE 3-2 FORECLOSURE-REDEMPTION SUMMARY (*Continued*)

State	Security instrument used	Typical foreclosure remedies	Length of time to complete foreclosure	Period of redemption
Kansas	Mortgage	Judicial sale	3 months plus redemption period	6 months
Kentucky	Mortgage	Judicial sale	4 months	None
Louisiana	Mortgage	Judicial sale	3 to 4 months	None
Maine	Mortgage	Judicial sale	3 weeks	12 months after first advertisement; 90 days before sale
Maryland	Mortgage	Power of sale	60 to 90 days	30 days ratification
Massachusetts	Mortgage	Power of sale	3 to 4 months	None
Michigan	Mortgage	Judicial sale	1 month	12 months; over 3 acres 6 months; 90 day strict foreclosure; 30 days if abandoned
Minnesota	Mortgage	Power of sale	2 months	6 months
Mississippi	Deed of trust	Trustee sale	1 month	None
Missouri	Deed of trust	Trustee sale	1 month	None
Montana	Deed of trust and mortgage	Judicial sale	3 months plus redemption period	Trust deed—4 months Mortgage—12 months
Nebraska	Deed of trust and mortgage	Trustee sale; Judicial sale	3 to 4 months	None
Nevada	Deed of trust	Judicial sale	4 months	None
New Hampshire	Mortgage	Power of sale	4 to 6 weeks	None
New Jersey	Mortgage	Judicial sale	8 months	None
New Mexico	Mortgage	Judicial sale	4 to 6 months plus redemption period	1 month standard, but court may extend to 9 months
New York	Mortgage	Power of sale	5 months	None
North Carolina	Mortgage	Trustee sale	1 to 2 months	10 days confirmation

State	Instrument	Sale Method	Foreclosure Period	Redemption Period
North Dakota	Mortgage	Judicial sale	4 to 6 weeks	6 months if 10 acres or less
Ohio	Mortgage	Judicial sale	8 to 12 months	None
Oklahoma	Mortgage	Judicial sale	6 to 8 months including redemption period	6 months, expiring *prior* to sale
Oregon	Deed of trust and mortgage	Judicial sale for mortgage; trustee sale for deed of trust	4 months	Trust deed—none; Mortgage—1 year
Pennsylvania	Mortgage	Judicial sale	3 to 4 months	None
Puerto Rico/Virgin Islands	Mortgage	Judicial sale	12 months for noncontested cases	30 days-PR; 6 months-VI
Rhode Island	Mortgage	Power of sale	4 weeks	None
South Carolina	Mortgage	Judicial sale	3 to 4 months	30 days
South Dakota	Mortgage	Power of sale	6 months	6 months
Tennessee	Deed of trust	Trustee sale	1 month	None
Texas	Deed of trust	Judicial sale or trustee sale	3 weeks	None
Utah	Deed of trust or mortgage	Trustee sale	3 months plus 3 weeks	Mortgage—3 months; deed of trust—none
Vermont	Deed of trust and mortgage	Judicial sale for mortgage; trustee sale for deed of trust	3 months for deed of trust, 12 months for mortgage	3 months after notice of default or 12 months before sale
Virginia	Deed of trust	Trustee sale	4 weeks	None
Washington	Deed of trust and mortgage	Judicial sale for mortgage; trustee sale for deed of trust	6 months	Trust deed—None; Mortgage—1 year
West Virginia	Deed of trust	Trustee sale	8 to 10 weeks	None
Wisconsin	Mortgage	Judicial sale	14 months; 8 months without deficiency	12 months; 6 months before sale with deficiency
Wyoming	Mortgage	Power of sale	8 to 11 months	3 months

Source: Mortgage Guaranty Insurance Corporation, Milwaukee, November 1983. Reprinted with permission.

as long as the notice required from the tenant to vacate if the tenant should decide not to renew. A landlord has no obligation to justify to the tenant the reason for the increased rental amount, unless this is expressly provided in the lease or local rent control laws require it.

The provisions of the lease usually determine the responsibility for repair and maintenance of the premises. If the lease is silent on this issue, the landlord is usually required to maintain the structural integrity of the premises, and the tenant is required to make minor repairs to prevent deterioration. This is not always true, however. The thorny issue of responsibility and liability for repairs and maintenance has been addressed at length by many court cases and state statutes, especially for residential-use properties. Most states adhere to the notion that the residential tenant obtains an *implied warranty of habitability* with the property; that is, it is implied that the property is habitable and usable for the tenant's contemplated purpose. Thus, the landlord is obligated to maintain the premises in a habitable condition and is often liable for damages for failure to do so. A breach by the landlord of this obligation is called *constructive eviction*.

Whether the landlord is obligated to make repairs by either the lease terms or the implied warranty of habitability, the tenant may generally use four basic remedies if the landlord breaches the duties: (1) abandon the premises and terminate the lease obligation if the property is nonhabitable; (2) make the necessary repairs and deduct the cost from the rent; (3) continue to occupy the premises "as-is," deducting from the rent the fair value of the loss of use occasioned by the landlord's failure to repair; (4) continue to occupy the premises, paying full rent, and sue the landlord for the decrease in rental value caused by the landlord's failure to repair. Options 2 and 3 are risky, however, because the tenant's assessment of the situation may be incorrect. In some areas, a safer option is for the tenant to place a portion or all of the rent into an escrow account, to be turned over to the landlord or tenant depending on the court's judgment of the situation.

The tenant is obligated to surrender the property at the end of the tenancy in as good a condition as received, normal wear and tear excepted. Landlords generally require a deposit in advance as security against nonpayment of rent or damages to the premises. In addition, a clause is often inserted into the lease requiring tenants to pay on demand the cost of any damages they caused. This payment is in the form of increased rent for that rent-payment period; thus, nonpayment for tenant-caused damages is considered the same as a default in the payment of rent. Historically, some landlords have retained tenant's security deposits unreasonably, so most states have passed laws that make the landlord accountable for retained security deposits.

If the leased premises are damaged or destroyed or otherwise rendered unsuitable for use as intended after the lease has been agreed to but *before* the tenant takes possession, it is universally held that the tenant has the option of terminating the lease with no obligation to the landlord. However, if the building is damaged or destroyed after the tenant takes possession, in certain states the tenant may be liable for payment of rent for the balance of the lease if the land *and* building are rented. If only the building (and not the land) is rented, the untenantability of the building relieves the tenant of liability under the lease. Many states have abolished this rule by statute, providing that the destruction of the building relieves the tenant of liability. Generally, most lease forms provide for this event with a clause that terminates the lease automatically if the premises are destroyed.

The lease interests, as in any other legal contract, are freely assignable unless specifically prohibited in the contract. Lease assignment by the tenant may take two forms. In an *assignment,* the tenant assigns rights to possession and use for the remainder of the lease term to another tenant, who assumes the rental-payment obligation along with the obligation to comply with other covenants within the lease. Another form of assignment is a *sublease,* whereby the tenant conveys the right of possession and use to a new tenant via a new lease. The original tenant, then, acts as an intermediate landlord, collecting rent from the new tenant under the new lease and paying rent to the landlord under the old lease. Thus, a tenant paying below-market rent on the premises may prefer to sublet the premises to the new tenant at the fair market rent, paying the lower rent to the landlord and pocketing the difference, rather than simply assigning the original lease interest directly to the new tenant. Whether the original tenant transfers under an assignment or sublease, however, the tenant is not absolved of responsibility under the lease if the new tenant defaults, unless the landlord specifically exempts the tenant in writing. Most landlords insert a clause in their leases forbidding or restricting the tenant's right to assign and sublet.

If the tenant breaches the lease agreement, the landlord has the remedy of *actual eviction* if the tenant refuses to leave the premises voluntarily. Actual eviction is the legal, physical removal of the lessee from the premises. Eviction must be accomplished through court action and varies considerably from state to state. The time it takes to evict a tenant may vary from as little as 2 weeks to several months.

Types of Leases   Leases are generally classified by the rental amount and the inclusions. Under a *gross lease,* the landlord pays all taxes, property insurance, maintenance and repairs, and other operating expenses (including in some cases utilities) connected with the property. Under a *net lease,* the tenant pays utilities and some or all of the other expenses in addition to the rent. Net leases are more common in commercial and industrial rentals; residential rentals are most often gross leases. A *percentage lease* typically requires a commercial tenant to pay a minimum base rental plus a percentage of the sales volume and may be combined with a gross or net lease. A *step lease* provides that the rent payments be increased or decreased by fixed amounts at fixed time intervals. An *index lease* provides that the rent payments increase or decrease at periodic intervals, with the amount of increase or decrease based on the percentage change in some business index (such as the Consumer Price Index) over the period. *Escalation clauses* for taxes, insurance, utilities, and other operating expenses provide that the landlord may raise the rent during the lease term to account for increases in expenses. Step leases, index leases, and escalation clauses are typically found in leases that run for more than 1 year, but occasionally they are included in shorter-term leases.

A *ground lease* refers to the ground (land) only. It is the tenant's responsibility and expense to effect improvements, which generally become part of the real estate and revert to the landlord when the lease term expires. As a result, most ground leases are long-term, say 25 to 50 years, or long enough for the tenant to recoup any investment in the building.

Government Restrictions

The final participant in the real estate financing process is the government. Here is an overall view of the constraints it places on the other participants.

Limitations on the Owner-Borrower   The equity owner's rights in the real estate are restricted by the government's three basic powers: taxation, eminent domain, and police power.

The right of *taxation* is vested in all levels of government. They may assess taxes against the real estate, which are used to pay local government operations and to support the school system. Property taxes are generally assessed on an *ad valorem* basis, whereby the amount of the tax bears some relationship to the property's value. Property taxes become a lien on the real estate until they are paid and are enforceable through a forced sale of the property to satisfy the lien.

In addition, federal, state, and in some areas, local governments have the right to tax both the income the real estate generates and the owner's income from other sources. When a property owner fails to pay income taxes, the government may place a lien against the property; the lien is enforceable much like a property tax lien. Federal tax liens have absolute priority over all other liens, with property tax liens next in line, regardless of the order of recording or the effective date of the lien. Other liens generally follow behind, according to the individual state's recording statutes. Chapter 6 discusses income taxation in detail.

Eminent domain is the right of government agencies (and some private agencies that are "affected with the public interest," such as utilities) to acquire a portion or all of the owner's rights in the property, provided that (1) the acquisition is deemed in the "public interest," i.e., for a public purpose or use, and (2) the owner is paid "just compensation." Examples are the acquisition of private property for highways, public buildings, and parks; the acquisition of air rights for airport runway approaches; and the acquisition of an easement for utility lines. If an owner refuses to voluntarily give up the rights in the property, a *condemnation proceeding* is held in court to determine whether the taking is "in the public interest" and if so, the amount of just compensation that should be paid. If it is determined that the taking is in the public interest, the property is condemned (i.e., the bundle of rights is transferred to the government or private agency) and just compensation is determined and paid to the dispossessed owner.

The government's *police power* is its right to regulate private property, as long as the regulation is in the interest of public health, safety, morals, or general welfare. Police power is generally delegated to local and state governments. Examples of police power include *zoning ordinances,* which regulate the uses for property; *building codes,* which specify minimum standards for building construction; *housing codes*, which regulate the safety and habitability of residential rental property; and *other land-use controls* that regulate wetlands and navigable waters, land development and subdivision, and historical landmark preservation.

Table 3-3 is a comprehensive list of various government land-use and other controls.

The government has the additional right to prohibit *racial discrimination* in selling or renting housing. State laws often extend the prohibition to discrimination based on religion, national origin, sex, marital status, or status with regard to public assistance or disability.

Limitations on the Lender   The government restricts the lender with regard to the granting of mortgage loans. *Discrimination* in lending is forbidden on the same basis as discrimination in renting or selling (this topic is discussed further in Chapter 4). Governments, state and federal, determine the types of loans and loan terms that may be offered, along with other mortgage regulations, such as foreclosure procedures and security instruments.

Limitations on the Tenant   Since the tenant has essentially purchased the right to use the property, the tenant's right is modified by all regulations affecting owner use, such as zoning laws and housing codes, and other regulations involving tenant responsibilities.

TRANSFERRING REAL ESTATE OWNERSHIP

Certain legal concepts are involved when title to real estate is transferred. These concepts are different from those involved in the ownership period itself. Here we present the legal environment associated with the title and the contracts used to transfer title from one owner to another.

Land Title Considerations

Title to land is defined as *proof of ownership* of the land. For an owner to sell or transfer the interest held, it must be satisfactorily proven to the received (purchaser) of the property that the seller in fact does hold the interest claimed and has the right to convey it to another. Because of the indestructible nature of land, the chain of ownership goes back to the earth's beginning, but from a practical standpoint, land titles in the United States are traced back to the time the land was acquired by the government (through purchase, conquest, or annexation). A purchaser of real estate requires assurance that prior interests in the property no longer exist; if these interests do exist, they may have priority over the purchaser's ownership rights.

TABLE 3-3   GOVERNMENT CONTROLS ON REAL ESTATE

1 Policy and Assessment Tools
a Planning
b Carrying capacity
c Fair-share housing allocation
d Cost-revenue analysis/fiscal impact analysis
e Environmental assessment
2 Regulatory Mechanisms
a Use controls
  (1) Zoning
  (2) Special permits/special exceptions/conditional use permits
  (3) Variances
  (4) Floating zones
  (5) Conditional zoning
  (6) Contract zoning
  (7) Cyclical rezoning
  (8) Comprehensive plan consistency requirements
  (9) Zoning referendum
  (10) "Prohibitory" zoning
  (11) Agricultural zoning/large lot zoning/open space zoning
  (12) Phased zoning/holding zones/short-term service area
  (13) Performance zoning/performance standards
  (14) Planned Unit Development (PUD)
b Bulk controls
  (1) Subdivision regulations
  (2) Minimum lot size
  (3) Minimum lot size per dwelling unit
  (4) Minimum lot size per room
  (5) Setback, frontage, and yard regulations
  (6) Minimum floor area
  (7) Height restriction

  (8) Floor-area ratio (FAR)
  (9) Land-use intensity rating
  (10) Flexible zoning/cluster zoning/density zoning
c Allocation controls
  (1) Adequate public facilities ordinance
  (2) Permit allocation system
  (3) Facility allocation system
  (4) Development moratorium/interim development controls
d Special controls
  (1) Special-protection districts/critical areas/environmentally sensitive areas
  (2) Developments of regional impact
  (3) Extraterritorial zoning and subdivision powers
e Compensatory controls
  (1) Transferable development rights (TDR)
  (2) Compensable regulation
  (3) Zoning by special assessment Financed eminent domain (ZSAFED)
f Miscellaneous controls
  (1) Official mapping
  (2) Timed conditional annexation
  (3) Long-term service area/Long-term limit line/urban-rural service areas
  (4) Total population limitation/growth cap
g Private market incentives
  (1) Restrictive covenants
  (2) Nonzoning
  (3) Bonus and incentive zoning

  (4) Land acquisition assistance
  (5) Special development districts/municipal utility districts
3 Capital Expenditures
a Facilities construction
  (1) Facility location
  (2) Capital improvements programming
b Land acquisition
  (1) Fee simple acquisition
  (2) Advance land acquisition/project land banking
  (3) General land banking
  (4) Less than fee simple acquisition
4 Revenue Mechanisms
a Property taxes
  (1) Conventional property taxation
  (2) Use-value taxation
  (3) Deferred taxation
  (4) Restricted-use taxation
  (5) Differential taxation
  (6) Land value taxation
  (7) Tax base sharing
b Special taxes and fees
  (1) Land gains tax/special capital and real estate windfall taxes (SCREWTS)/incremental value taxes
  (2) Special assessment
  (3) Variable service fees/marginal cost pricing
c Exactions
  (1) Mandatory dedication
  (2) Fees in lieu of mandatory dedication
  (3) Development impact fee
  (4) Mandatory low-cost housing

Source: "Land Management: A Technical Report on Controls and Incentives for Use by State and Local Government," Washington, D.C., Public Technology, Inc., 1977.

As a result, the seller's title to the real estate must be examined to assure the buyer that the seller has *merchantable or marketable title*. A merchantable or marketable title is proof of ownership, sufficient to meet currently acceptable standards and thus acceptable to buyers in the marketplace.

Examination of the title involves hiring an attorney to pursue the courthouse records in the county in which the property is located. All records affecting the property in question are examined, to ascertain (1) that all prior ownership interests have properly signed away their interests to subsequent owners and (2) the existence of any other claims or interests that may affect the purchaser's rights in the property liens, mortgages, easements, and so on. The lender also needs assurance that no prior interests exist; the purchaser must have marketable title to give the lender mortgage lien rights. Because the examination of courthouse records is a lengthy process, most states have two processes that simplify the operation: the *abstract of title* and the *Torrens land registration system*.

The Abstract of Title   The abstract of title is a summary of all the recorded documents affecting the title to a parcel of land. The abstract is compiled by a registered abstractor, who certifies that as of a certain date all recorded documents affecting title are included and that no liens or other encumbrances appear on the records, except as noted in the abstract. The abstract is typically updated by the abstractor just prior to the title examination so that all entries are included. The attorney then examines the abstract and renders an opinion as to the marketability of the seller's title.

The Torrens Land Registration System   Although the abstract considerably reduces the time and expense necessary for examining land title, the lawyer's title opinion may not be sufficient because of prior *unrecorded* claims or an error the attorney may have made when examining a lengthy and complex chain of title dating back 100 or more years. To help protect against these risks, the Torrens land registration system was developed. Under this system, which is available as an option in certain states, the property owner makes a formal request to the county recorder that his or her title to the property be registered, or "torrensed." Arrangements are made for a court hearing, at which any other persons claiming an ownership interest must appear and state their claim. Prior to the hearing, public notice of the hearing must be published for a statutory time period, and any parties known to have an interest must be served with specific notice. If the owner is the only party appearing at the hearing, the court issues a judgment in favor of the owner, and all prior ownership claims, if any, are extinguished. The owner is issued a *certificate of title* subject to any recorded encumbrances (such as mortgages). When the owner sells the property, this certificate and the deed conveying the property to the purchaser must be turned over to the county recorder. The purchaser is then issued a new certificate of title in her or his name. Due to the extinguishing of prior ownership rights, a lawyer's title examination is very inexpensive and quick and is not even considered necessary in many instances where the property has been torrensed.

However, Torrens registration does have its drawbacks. The registration process itself is costly, and it does not fully protect the registered owner against errors, omissions, fraudulent acts, or prior owners. Thus, the system has not been widely used.

Title Insurance   To protect the owners of real estate against title defects, *title insurance* is available in all states and is becoming increasingly popular as a means of eliminating title risk. As a condition of making a loan, many lenders require that borrowers provide a title insurance policy to protect the lender.

The title insurance company initially examines the title, and if the title is found marketable, the company issues a policy that protects the owner, or lender, or both against claims made because of events that occurred *prior* to the date of the policy. It does not cover claims caused by events that occur *after* the policy is in force. The company will not insure a title that is knowingly defective; all known defects must be resolved before a title policy may be obtained. The policy premium is typically paid at the time of issue, and the policy continues in force as long as the insured or the insured's heirs retain an interest in the property. If the insured is a mortgage lender, the policy terminates when the mortgage is removed through payoff or foreclosure.

In the event of a valid adverse claim, the company will pay damages to the insured and defend the insured's rights in court at no expense to the insured. Note that a lender's title insurance policy provides no protection for the owner's interest. Thus, even though a lender may require the borrower to provide a title policy, that policy does not protect the owner-borrower from covered losses. In any event, a title insurance policy is the best title protection available.

Title to Attachments to the Land   When title to the land is acquired, title to all things that are part of the real estate is implicitly acquired. As noted, real estate includes the land and generally all attachments, including those things built on, growing on, or otherwise permanently affixed to the land. Thus, the purchaser of land also is entitled to the buildings, plants, trees, crops, and other "permanent" attachments. Although it may be obvious to the owner of real estate what is hers, when she sells the property it is not always obvious to the seller and the buyer what is intended to be included in the sale. The buyer and the seller may explicitly agree to include with or exclude from the sale of the real estate any items they wish, but problems arise when items are not explicitly accounted for and the buyer and the seller make differing assumptions about the inclusion of these items in the sale. Certainly this is one area of real estate law that causes a large share of litigation. For this reason, an understanding of *the law of fixtures* is necessary.

We already defined real estate. All other property that is not real estate is called *personal property*. In general, personal property is movable and not attached to land or buildings. Personal property may become part of the real estate by being attached to it permanently. For instance, a dishwasher in an appliance store is considered personal property, but when it is purchased by a homeowner and permanently installed in the home's kitchen, it becomes a part of the real estate and is known as a fixture. The homeowner may remove this fixture at the time of sale if the removal is by mutual agreement between the buyer and the seller. If the seller removes it without such express agreement and the buyer expects the dishwasher to be there when he obtains title because it is a fixture and therefore part of the real estate, the law of fixtures will likely provide the buyer with a cause for action against the seller. This case is rather clear-cut, but many others are not. A fixture is tested by the following questions:

1 *What is the intent of the parties?* This is the most important question. If the parties express mutual intent, this intent determines the status of the item as real estate or personal property. Unfortunately, the parties do not always express their intent, and so the other tests are used to determine the intent.

2 *How is the item attached to the property?* If the item is attached in such a way that its removal would cause damage or leave the property incomplete, the intent is assumed to be that the item was originally installed as a fixture. Our dishwasher is such a case.

3 *What is the character of the item?* This test covers those items which if removed might not cause substantial damage but were added to increase the property value and for which the buyer paid an implicit price. Landscaping items, custom-made storm windows, and expensive chandeliers all fall into this category and are generally adjudged fixtures.

4 *What is the relationship of the parties?* This question relates primarily to the treatment of fixtures used in a trade or business. The courts generally hold that trade fixtures, even though installed in a more or less permanent fashion, are not considered a part of the real estate.

Note that the fixture tests apply not only to the transfer of ownership of real estate but in a rental situation to the transfer of possessory rights from tenant back to the landlord.

The Transfer of Ownership Process

The process by which ownership is transferred typically takes the form shown in Figure 3-2. At the time the owner decides to sell (dispose of) the real estate, a

FIGURE 3-2   The ownership transfer process.

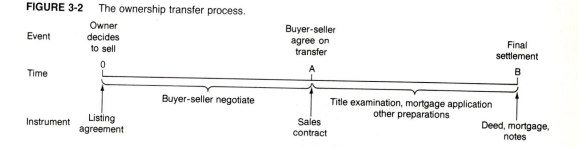

decision must be made whether to list the property with an agent and if so, which one. The formal agreement between agent and owner is called a *listing agreement*.

The Listing Agreement   This agreement spells out the legal relationship between the real estate broker and the property owner. It may take one of three forms: an open listing, exclusive agency listing, or exclusive-right-to-sell listing.

An *open listing* states that the owner owes the broker a commission if the broker procures a buyer who is ready, willing, and able to purchase the property at the asking price and terms, or at other mutually agreeable terms. In addition, the owner is free to make the same arrangement with any other brokers or may sell the property personally; in any case, the owner owes the broker a commission only if that broker actually was the procuring cause of the sale. If a sale occurs and the broker(s) with whom the open listing was signed was (were) not the procuring cause of the sale, the open listing automatically terminates and the broker(s) is (are) not entitled to a commission. In addition to automatic termination upon sale, the open listing typically has an expiration date if the property is not sold.

The *exclusive agency listing* is similar to the open listing, but it gives the listing broker the right to be the owner's exclusive agent. The seller owes the exclusive agent a commission if the property is sold (i.e., if a ready, willing, and able buyer is provided) by any other agent. This type of listing, however, gives the owner the right to sell the property personally without paying the broker a commission. The exclusive agency listing automatically terminates if the owner personally sells the property. It also typically has an expiration date in the event neither agent nor owner sells the property during the term of the listing.

As a rule, brokers are reluctant to take open or exclusive agency listings because of the difficulty of ascertaining who was the "procuring cause" of the sale. For example, a broker's promotional efforts may have been the cause of sale, but the buyer chose to deal directly with the owner. Unless the broker knows (and can prove) that personal efforts indeed were the procuring cause of the sale, the broker is not entitled to a commission under an open or exclusive agency listing. For this reason, a broker who agrees to take an open or exclusive agency listing typically spends little time, effort, and money in promotion.

The *exclusive-right-to-sell listing* is similar to the exclusive agency listing except that the owner owes the broker a commission no matter who procured a ready, willing, and able buyer—the owner, the listing broker, or another broker. The agreement terminates at sale or at a fixed expiration date, whichever occurs first. This type of listing is the most legally restrictive on the owner, but it gives the broker a greater assurance of being paid as a result of sales efforts.

Generally, listing agreements are drafted such that the owner owes a commission if the broker "procures a ready, willing, and able buyer" who will purchase the property at the "asking price and terms." The implication here is that if the broker presents an offer to purchase from such a buyer at the asking price and terms but the seller refuses to accept the offer, the seller nonetheless owes the broker a commission, even though a sale is not made.

The *multiple listing* concept deserves special mention. Under multiple listing, the owner lists the property with one broker on an exclusive right-to-sell basis. The owner gives consent to the broker to list the property with an organized multiple listing service composed of the listing broker and other member brokers, who may all offer the property for sale. If a purchase offer is obtained, the seller broker (if different from the listing broker) pursues negotiations through the listing broker, who continues to represent the owner throughout the negotiations and sales process. The owner owes a commission only to the listing broker, who shares the commission with the selling broker according to a predetermined split arrangement. Exhibit 3-3 is a typical exclusive-right-to-sell listing with multiple listing provisions.

The Sales Agreement   Once the property is offered for sale and a prospective purchaser is found, the purchaser makes an offer in writing to the seller, either directly or through the broker if the property is listed. The offer spells out the price and terms of the proposed agreement, together with any contingencies on which the offer depends. If the seller agrees to the offer, the seller signs it, the acceptance is communicated back to the offerer (buyer), and a binding agreement is made.

The variety of sales contracts is unlimited; Exhibit 3-4 is a typical one. It includes space for the legal description and address of the property and the explicit inclusion of fixtures, which often is a common cause of disputes. The offering price and the amount of earnest money that accompanies the offer are inserted. The time and manner of payment of the balance are inserted next, along with any financing proposals and a clause that voids the contract if the buyer cannot obtain the necessary funds from a lender.

The projected closing date is then inserted. Note that the contract provides that the seller shall furnish marketable title and that the purchaser has the right to have the title examined prior to closing. In the space at the bottom, any special stipulations of the sale may be inserted.

The agreement is first signed by the purchaser at the time the offer is made and by the agent, if any. If the offer is accepted, the seller signs and the agreement becomes binding when the purchaser is notified of the acceptance.

Because the sales contract spells out the entire agreement between the parties, it is generally regarded as the most important contract in the sale or purchase of real estate, and so it must be carefully worded and understood by the parties involved. If in doubt, competent legal counsel should be obtained.

The Closing   Once all the terms of the agreement have been complied with and all contingencies to the sale have been satisfied, the *closing* of the sale takes place. This is the time of settlement. The buyer pays the remainder of all sums owed to the seller, the seller conveys title to the buyer, and expenses of the sale are paid by buyer and seller according to the terms of the agreement.

The *deed* is the document that effects the transfer of ownership from seller to buyer. It is essentially a "bill of sale for real estate." Generally, most transactions require that the seller provide a *warranty* deed, in which the seller makes

EXHIBIT 3-3   LISTING AGREEMENT

To: _____   _____
        Broker   Date

For One Dollar ($1.00) and other good and valuable considerations, I hereby grant to you, commencing the date hereof, and terminating on the _____ day of _____ , 19 _____ at 12:00 o'clock midnight, the exclusive right and privilege to sell or exchange the following described property for the sum of $_____ or at such lesser price or terms to which I may consent.

Land Lot _____ Dist. _____ Section _____ County _____
Lot _____ Block _____ Subdv. _____ Unit _____
Street Address _____
City _____ State _____ Zip Code _____
As recorded in Plat Book _____ , Page _____ , _____ County Records.

The gross sales price shall be payable as follows: _____ or with my consent for a lesser sum or upon other terms. Earnest money deposit shall be held in escrow until delivery of possession with the escrowee allowed to retain expenses incurred for me and to pay escrow into court in the event of a dispute.

If, during the listing period, anyone, including myself, produces a purchaser ready, willing and able to purchase said property, or if, within three months after the expiration of said listing period a sale is made without incurring a commission to another broker, to any person to whom the property has been shown by anyone, including myself, during said listing period, I agree to pay you a commission of _____ percent of such gross sale price which becomes due on signing of a contract and shall be paid no later than the stated time of closing or upon my default. I further agree to cooperate to a reasonable degree with you toward the making of such sale and refer to you all inquiries made to me. The term "sale" as used herein shall be construed to include any exchange to which I consent in writing. In the event of an exchange, you are authorized to represent and to receive compensation from both parties, provided that I am advised of your dual interest prior to my acceptance of the exchange proposal. The "gross sale price" in an exchange shall be the list price of the property at the time for the purpose of computing the commission. "Listing period" means the original listing term and renewal thereof.

You are hereby authorized to advertise the property during this agreement and extension thereof, to place your FOR SALE sign on said property, to remove all other FOR SALE signs, if any, and to photograph said property and use such photographs in promoting the sale. I agree to refer all inquiries concerning the sale of the property to you during the term of this agreement. I further agree to consider your recommendations to enable you to show this property to its best advantage, to allow you to show it at all reasonable hours and otherwise cooperate with you.

I warrant that I have furnished you a complete and accurate legal description of the property and I further warrant that I have title to the property described herein and/or have full authority to enter into this agreement.

I hereby acknowledge receipt of a copy of this agreement.

Agreed to and accepted by:

_____   _____
Broker   Owner

_____   _____
By   Owner

CONTRACT FOR SALE OF REALTY   STANDARD SALES CONTRACT

The undersigned Purchaser agrees to buy, and the undersigned Seller agrees to sell the following described property through_____a licensed Broker:

The improvements thereon consist of   which is known as
No.   Street according to the present system

of numbering in

Included as a part of such property are all lighting fixtures and TV antenna attached thereto; all heating, water heating and plumbing equipment therein, and all plants, trees and shrubbery now on the premises, and

The purchase price of said property shall be:

                    Dollars, $ to be paid as follows:

Purchaser has paid to the undersigned Broker, receipt whereof is hereby acknowledged by such Broker, $, as earnest money, which earnest money is to be applied as part payment of the purchase price of said property at the time the sale is consummated.

The balance of the purchase price shall be paid

This transaction shall be closed as soon as practical after the parties have complied with the title matters as hereinafter provided but not later than   after the last party hereto signs.

Seller agrees to furnish good, valid and marketable title in fee simple to said property and agrees to convey said property at his expense by warranty deed, with state transfer tax paid, if applicable, to Purchaser at the time the sale is consummated, subject to: 1. All restrictions of record; 2. Zoning ordinances affecting the same; 3. Encumbrances as specified in this contract; 4. Existing leases, and purchaser assumes Seller's responsibilities under said lease.

Purchaser shall have reasonable time after acceptance of this contract in which to examine the title and in which to furnish Seller with a written statement of objections, if any, affecting the validity of said title. Seller shall have reasonable time after receipt of such objections to satisfy all valid objections and if Seller fails to satisfy such valid objections within a reasonable time, then at the option of Purchaser, upon written notice to Seller, this contract may be cancelled and shall be null and void.

Purchaser agrees that he will pay for the preparation of any note and security deed provided for herein, for the recording of the warranty deed and any security deed and for any Georgia intangible tax on such security deed.

Seller warrants that when the sale is consummated the improvements on the property will be in the same condition as they are on the date this contract is signed by the Seller, natural wear and tear excepted. However, should the premises be destroyed or substantially damaged before the sale is consummated, then, at the election of the Purchaser: (a) This contract may be cancelled; or (b) Purchaser may consummate the purchase and receive the benefit of such insurance as accrues to the Seller on account of such loss or damage. This election is to be exercised within ten (10) days after the amount of the Seller's damage is determined.

In negotiating this contract Broker has rendered a valuable service and is made a party to this contract to enable Broker to enforce his commission rights hereunder against the parties hereto on the following basis: Seller agrees to pay Broker a commission as hereinafter provided when the sale is consummated; Seller agrees that if he defaults and fails to consummate the sale except for his exercise of some elective or optional right of cancellation hereunder or for his inability to cure any title defects, he shall pay Broker the full commission and Broker shall return the earnest money to Purchaser; Purchaser agrees that if he defaults and fails to consummate the sale, except for the exercise of some elective or optional right of cancellation hereunder or Seller's inability to cure title defects, he shall pay Broker the full commission and Purchaser and Seller agree that Broker may apply the earnest money deposited by Purchaser toward payment of the commission, and turn the balance, if any, over to Seller to be applied to Seller's damages, and Purchaser agrees that thereupon Broker is released from any and all liability for return of the earnest money to Purchaser. All parties hereto agree that if Seller or Purchaser has any elective or optional rights of cancellation hereunder and such rights are exercised and the sale is not consummated, or Seller is unable to cure title defects and the sale is not consummated, then the earnest money shall be returned to Purchaser and no party shall have any right to commissions or damages.

The commission to be paid in this transaction shall be

This contract constitutes the sole and entire agreement between the parties hereto and no modification of this contract shall be binding unless attached hereto and signed by all parties to this agreement. No representation, promise, or inducement not included in this contract shall be binding upon any party hereto.

The following SPECIAL STIPULATIONS shall, if conflicting with printed matter, control:

This instrument shall be regarded as an offer by the Purchaser or Seller, who first signs, to the other and is open for acceptance by the other until noon on the   day of   19   , by which time written acceptance of such offer must have been actually received by Broker, who shall promptly notify the other party, either by giving written notice of such acceptance, or by delivering an executed copy of this contract.

Executed by Seller   , 19   Executed by Purchaser   , 19

_____   _____
            (Seller)   (Purchaser)

                                                          _____
                                                                    (Purchaser)

EXHIBIT 3-4   STANDARD SALES CONTRACT   **97**

EXHIBIT 3-5 GENERAL WARRANTY DEED

(1)

THIS DEED, made the 30th day of September 19XX, between H. O. Mowner and Jane Mowner, his wife, of Anywhere, State, hereinafter referred to as "Grantors," and Will C. Carter and Tammy Carter, his wife, Anywhere, State, hereinafter referred to as "Grantees."

(2)

WITNESSETH, that Grantors, in consideration of the sum of ten dollars ($10.00), receipt whereof is hereby acknowledged, do grant, sell, and convey unto Grantees, their heirs and assigns, all that tract or parcel of land with improvements thereon located in State County, State, described as follows:

Part of the S.E. ¼ of Section 14, T. 57 N., R. 35 W., of the 5th P.M., State County, State of Anywhere, beginning at a point being 202 feet east of the S.E. ¼ so said Section 14, running thence north 72 degrees east 200 feet to an iron pin; running thence east 103 degrees 100 feet to an iron pin; running thence south 70 degrees west 300 feet to an iron pin; running thence west 103 degrees 100 feet to the point of beginning. This property is that described as Lot 8, Block J, of the Harris West Estate, as recorded in Plat Book 5 page 49, in the Office of the Clerk of the Circuit Court of State County, State.

(3)

TO HAVE AND TO HOLD the premises hereby granted to Grantees, their heirs and assigns in fee simple forever.

(4)

The Grantors warrant that the premises are free from all encumbrances except for the following:

(a) The underground utility easement running along the eastern boundary within five feet thereof.

(b) All other restrictions of record.

(5)

The Grantors, having a fee simple interest and the right to convey such interest, warrant that Grantees, their heirs and assigns shall enjoy quietly and peaceably possession of the premises.

(6)

It is further warranted that Grantors shall procure and execute any further assurances of the title to the premises and that Grantors will forever defend the title to the premises against all claims.

IN WITNESS WHEREOF, Grantors have set their signatures and seals, the day and year first written above.

_____ (seal)
H. O. Mowner

_____ (seal)
Jane Mowner
Signed, sealed, and delivered in the presence of:

_____

_____

Notary Public, State County, State

certain promises or covenants to the buyer: (1) The seller has good title and also has the right to convey the property; (2) the buyer has "quiet enjoyment" of the property—that is, no other persons have ownership claims; (3) there are no encumbrances against the property other than those specified in the deed; and (4) the seller will warrant title and defend it, as necessary, to provide the buyer with marketable title. Exhibit 3-5 is a typical warranty deed.

Other types of deeds are sometimes used to transfer an interest in real estate, depending on the situation. A *quitclaim deed* provides for transfer of whatever interest the owner has to the buyer. (The owner may have little or no interest.) It contains no warranties of any kind, however. It is typically used to remove title defects, such as the extinguishing of dower interests or the voluntary termination of a life estate by the life tenant. The *bargain and sale deed* falls between the warranty and quitclaim deeds, in that it assumes the seller has good title but provides no further warranties. *Probate deeds, executors deeds,* and *administrator deeds* convey property on behalf of a deceased owner's estate. Typically, these deeds provide few if any warranties, but they are generally accepted as being equivalent to a warranty deed when property is being purchased from an estate.

At the same time as the seller gives the deed to the buyer and the buyer pays the seller the balance due, the expenses both parties incurred in the transaction must be paid. Typically, the mortgage lender (if one is involved), real estate broker, or seller's attorney supervises the closing, collecting monies and disbursing payments to the individuals involved, with the buyer and the seller given a statement of settlement costs. These settlement costs include attorney's fees for title examination and document preparation, appraisal and credit report fees, recording taxes and fees, sales commissions, loan discounts, and other financing costs. Chapter 4 covers the topic of settlement costs in more detail.

SUMMARY

This chapter overviewed real estate property law in general and, more specifically, the law as it relates to the borrower-lender-property relationship. It also provided insight into the effects of tenants' rights and government intervention on the borrower and the lender. Finally, it examined the specific nature of the title transfer process, with emphasis on the documents used to effect the transfer. You should now have the basics necessary for understanding the more specific relationships between the participants illustrated in subsequent chapters.

QUESTIONS

1 Define the following terms:
   a mortgagee
   b mortgagor
   c fee simple estate
   d lease
   e easement
   f trust deed
   g deed

2 Discuss the interrelationships among the four major participants in the real estate finance process.

3 What are some of the major contracts used in real estate financing? What are the essentials of a valid contract?

4 What are the various types of estates in land?

5 What are the methods for legally describing a parcel of real estate?

6 What are the major distinctions between a trust deed and a mortgage? What type of security instrument is used in your state?

7 What is the role of the promissory note in the financing process? Analyze Exhibit 3-1 carefully.

8 What would produce default on a mortgage? Analyze Exhibit 3-2 in detail. If possible, obtain a standard mortgage contract from your state and analyze the various types of clauses.

9 Discuss the various methods of foreclosure on a mortgage.

10 What types of government restrictions influence the real estate market?

11 What methods are used to examine the title to a parcel of real estate? Why is the lender interested in the borrower's title?

12 What are the typical steps involved in selling a parcel of real estate?

PROBLEMS

1 You give Mr. A a mortgage covering your land on January 1. On January 15, you sell your land to Ms. B. who does not record the deed. You default on the mortgage debt, and Mr. A institutes foreclosure proceedings. Mr. A buys the land at the foreclosure sale. Who has title to the property?

2 Maria loans Tommy $150,000 to start a business. In return for this Tommy gives a deed covering his house to Ryan. Tommy pays $100,000 of the loan back and then refuses to pay any more. What may Maria do to get her remaining $50,000?

3 Victoria takes out a loan from Jay in return for a mortgage. Victoria pays four monthly installments, then misses two straight payments. Who has title in an immediate theory state?

4 Juan borrows $50,000 from Kimi in return for a mortgage on Juan's house and land. Juan pays six monthly installments of $150 each and then defaults on the mortgage. At Kimi's request, the local court orders the property sold. This foreclosure sale brings a price of $42,000. The cost of conducting the foreclosure sale was $500. How much will Kimi receive from the proceeds of this sale, and how much, if any, may she seek from Juan in a deficiency judgment?

5 What is the advantage of an acceleration clause?

6 Michelle borrows money from Lillie in return for a mortgage in a title theory state. The mortgaged property is an apartment building whose tenants pay a total of $1,000 rent to Michelle. If Michelle defaults on the mortgage and Lillie takes over management of the apartment building, does Michelle still have the right to receive the tenants' rent payments?

7 Discuss the difference between a fee simple and an easement.

8 Oneil sells to Roy and Fay as joint tenants. Roy pays 85 percent of the purchase, while Fay pays 15 percent. If Roy dies before Fay, how much of the property does Fay own?

9 From a taxation perspective, which form of multiple real estate ownership is the least advantageous to the investor and why?

10 Why is the concept of constructive notice necessary?

REFERENCES

Caswell, Christopher: "The New Mortgages: A Functional Legal Analysis," *Florida State University Law Review*, vol. 10, no. 1, Winter 1982, pp. 95–128.

Freedman, Ronald M., and Benjamin N. Henszey: *Real Estate Law*, Warren Gorham & Lamont, Boston, 1979.

Kratovil, Robert, and Raymond J. Werner: *Modern Mortgage Law and Practice*, 2d ed., Prentice-Hall, Englewood Cliffs, N.J., 1981.

Nelson, Grant S., and Dale A. Whitman: *Real Estate Finance and Development*, West Publishing, St. Paul, Minn., 1976.

Osborne, George E., Grant S. Nelson, and Dale A. Whitmen: *Real Estate Finance Law*, West Publishing, St. Paul, Minn., 1979.

BORROWER ANALYSIS

Chapters 2 and 3 examined the legal environment and the mechanics of mortgages as fundamental aspects of the financing decision. Two other major compo-

nents of the financing process are the analyses of the borrower and of the property serving as collateral for the mortgage. This chapter discusses borrower analysis; Chapters 5 and 6 consider property analysis. Specifically, here we explain the process of borrower analysis for long-term conventional financing. The analysis of the borrower is of major concern to the lender, to minimize the risk associated with the loan. This type of risk is called *default risk*. Generally, the lender is concerned with the borrower's ability and willingness to meet the debt's obligations. Even if the borrower is not personally liable for the debt, the borrower analysis is an important component of the financing decision.

First we discuss the various documents lenders use to analyze the borrower for lending decisions. Then we discuss loan underwriting policies and procedures for borrower analysis. Finally, we discuss government involvement in the borrower-lender relationship.

LOAN DOCUMENTATION

Typically, after the sales contract between a buyer and a seller has been executed, the buyer (borrower) contacts the lender and begins processing the several documents the lender will use to make the decision to loan (invest) the money requested. These documents include a (1) loan-application form, (2) verification of deposit, (3) verification of employment, (4) good faith estimate provided by the lender detailing the charges and fees that the applicant will pay, and (5) credit report. This discussion centers around a loan request to purchase a single-family residence. The process is illustrated by a detailed example.

For the most part, the process of analyzing the borrower also applies to other types of real estate. However, if the applicant is a partnership or a corporation, additional documents may be required. These documents are discussed at the end of this section.

Loan-Application Form: Single Family

The first form processed is the loan application. Standardized forms and underwriting policies will be used if the lender anticipates participating in the secondary mortgage market. On the loan application, the borrower supplies such data as desired loan terms; description of the subject property; personal and employment information, including gross monthly income, monthly housing expenses, and terms of purchase; other income and previous employment; legal history; assets and liabilities, including existing loans; and previous credit references.

The loan application is the most important source an underwriter (who rates the acceptability of the loan) uses to judge a prospective property buyer's ability and willingness to fulfill the mortgage loan agreement. The underwriter will be able to ascertain from this document whether the prospects of making the loan are good, marginal, or unpromising.

Exhibit 4-1 is a standardized loan-application form completed by Will Carter and Tammy Carter for property located at 209 Boweevil Street, Crete, Any State. We will follow the preparation of this loan application section by section.

Background Information   Both Carters have been working for their current employers since graduating from college 3 years ago. They have been renting an apartment in a complex with swimming pools, saunas, and tennis courts. They own a 1974 Datsun and a 1982 Dodge. When they were first employed, they purchased as much furniture as their apartment could hold and have just recently paid off all their accounts.

Several months ago, Will's father died and left Will $20,000. Will and Tammy have decided to use this money as a down payment on their first home.

After several weeks of looking, the Carters have decided to buy a house priced at $85,000 and located in Cotton Hills Estates. They tender a contract to purchase through Homes Realty, paying $1,000 as an earnest money deposit, with the contingency that they will be able to obtain an 80 percent loan from Pike County Savings and Loan at 12 percent interest for 30 years. The seller accepts and signs the contract. Will and Tammy now take their copy of the sales contract to Pike Savings and Loan to apply for the financing.

Subject Property   The subject property section of the application in Exhibit 4-1 asks for such information as the loan amount and terms of repayment, property address and legal description, title information, source of down payment, and closing charges. The Carters are applying for a $68,000 conventional mortgage with monthly payments of $699.46.

Borrower and Coborrower   This information about the borrower and coborrower concerns ages, education, phone numbers, and so on. Since Will and Tammy will be taking title as joint tenants and both their names will be considered in the analysis, it does not matter who is listed as borrower and who as coborrower.

Gross Monthly Income, Monthly Housing Expenses, and Purchase Details   The housing and income sections in Exhibit 4-1 include a breakdown of projected gross monthly housing expenses compared with current housing expenses and details of the property purchase.

A stable monthly income is the borrower's gross monthly income from primary employment base earnings, plus any recognized secondary income. A borrower's secondary income (commission, bonuses, overtime, or part-time employment) is considered stable monthly income if it is typical for the occupation, it is substantiated by the borrower's previous 2 years' earnings, and its continuation is probable based on foreseeable circumstances. The Carters have a combined monthly income of $3,117.

Information under the monthly housing expenses section reveals that the Carters will more than double these expenses. They will have to pay $2,730 in closing costs and $555 in prepaid escrows. The $1,000 earnest money deposit will

RESIDENTIAL LOAN APPLICATION

MORTGAGE APPLIED FOR	[X] Conventional [ ] FHA [ ] VA [ ]	Amount $ 68,000	Interest Rate 12 %	No. of Months 360	Monthly Payment Principal & Interest $ 699.46	Escrow/Impounds (to be collected monthly) [X] Taxes [X] Hazard Ins. [ ] Mtg. Ins. [ ]

Prepayment Option

No prepayment penalty

SUBJECT PROPERTY

Property Street Address 209 Boweevil Street	City Crete	County Pike	State Any State	Zip	No. Units

Legal Description (Attach description if necessary) Lot 10, Block B, Cotton Hills Estates	Year Built 19xx

Purpose of Loan: [X] Purchase [ ] Construction-Permanent [ ] Construction [ ] Refinance [ ] Other (Explain)

Complete this line if Construction-Permanent or Construction Loan [→]	Lot Value Data Year Acquired N/A $	Original Cost $	Present Value (a) $	Cost of Imps. (b) $	Total (a + b) $	ENTER TOTAL AS PURCHASE PRICE IN DETAILS OF PURCHASE.

Complete this line if a Refinance Loan N/A	Purpose of Refinance	Describe Improvements [ ] made [ ] to be made
Year Acquired	Original Cost $	Amt. Existing Liens $		Cost: $

Title Will Be Held In What Name(s) Will C. and Tammy Carter	Manner In Which Title Will Be Held Joint Tenancy

Source of Down Payment and Settlement Charges

Savings Account and Inheritance

This application is designed to be completed by the borrower(s) with the lender's assistance. The Co-Borrower Section and all other Co-Borrower questions must be completed and the appropriate box(es) checked if [ ] another person will be jointly obligated with the Borrower on the loan, or [ ] the Borrower is relying on income from alimony, child support or separate maintenance or on the income or assets of another person as a basis for repayment of the loan, or [ ] the Borrower is married and resides, or the property is located, in a community property state.

BORROWER				CO-BORROWER			

Name Tammy Carter	Age 26	School Yrs 16	Name Will C. Carter	Age 26	School Yrs 16

Present Address No. Years ___ [ ] Own [ ] Rent	Present Address No. Years ___ [ ] Own [ ] Rent
Street 5665 College Avenue	Street 5665 College Avenue
City/State/Zip Crete, Any State 00000	City/State/Zip Crete, Any State 00000
Former address if less than 2 years at present address	Former address if less than 2 years at present address
Street N/A	Street N/A
City/State/Zip	City/State/Zip
Years at former address [ ] Own [ ] Rent	Years at former address [ ] Own [ ] Rent

Marital Status	[X] Married [ ] Separated [ ] Unmarried (incl. single, divorced, widowed)	DEPENDENTS OTHER THAN LISTED BY CO-BORROWER NO. AGES	Marital Status	[X] Married [ ] Separated [ ] Unmarried (incl. single, divorced, widowed)	DEPENDENTS OTHER THAN LISTED BY BORROWER NO. AGES

Name and Address of Employer Dependable Electric Co. 135 Industry Drive Crete, Any State 00000	Years employed in this line of work or profession? 3 years Years on this job 3 [ ] Self Employed*	Name and Address of Employer American Monitor Corp. 127 Work Street Crete, Any State 00000	Years employed in this line of work or profession? 3 years Years on this job 3 [ ] Self Employed*

Position/Title Hard Worker	Type of Business Electric Motors	Position/Title Hard Worker	Type of Business Monitor Products

Social Security Number*** 004-06-8967	Home Phone 555-1865	Business Phone 555-1279	Social Security Number*** 005-06-8968	Home Phone 556-1865	Business Phone 556-2000

GROSS MONTHLY INCOME / MONTHLY HOUSING EXPENSE** / DETAILS OF PURCHASE

Item	Borrower	Co-Borrower	Total	(Housing)	Present	Proposed	Details of Purchase	
Base Empl. Income	$1500	$1417	$2933	Rent	$ 350.		a. Purchase Price	$ 85,000
Overtime	—	—		First Mortgage (P&I)		$ 699.46	b. Total Closing Costs (Est.)	2,730
Bonuses	100	100	200	Other Financing (P&I)		—	c. Prepaid Escrows (Est.)	555
Commissions				Hazard Insurance		25.00	d. Total (a + b + c)	$ 88,285
Dividends/Interest				Real Estate Taxes		85.00	e. Amount This Mortgage	(68,000)
Net Rental Income				Mortgage Insurance		—	f. Other Financing	(—)
Other† (Before completing, see notice under Describe Other Income below.)				Homeowner Assn. Dues		—	g. Other Equity	(—)
				Other:			h. Amount of Cash Deposit	(1,000)
				Total Monthly Pmt.	$	$ 809.46	i. Closing Costs Paid by Seller	(—)
				Utilities	100.	150.00	j. Cash Reqd. For Closing (Est.)	$ 19,285
Total	$1600	$1517	$3117	Total	$ 450	$ 956.46		

DESCRIBE OTHER INCOME

NOTICE: † Alimony, child support, or separate maintenance income need not be revealed if the Borrower or Co-Borrower does not choose to have it considered as a basis for repaying this loan.

B—Borrower C—Co-Borrower

		Monthly Amount
B	None	$
C	None	

IF EMPLOYED IN CURRENT POSITION FOR LESS THAN TWO YEARS COMPLETE THE FOLLOWING

B/C	Previous Employer/School	City/State	Type of Business	Position/Title	Dates From/To	Monthly Income
						$

THESE QUESTIONS APPLY TO BOTH BORROWER AND CO-BORROWER

If a "yes" answer is given to a question in this column, explain on an attached sheet.	Borrower Yes or No	Co-Borrower Yes or No	If applicable, explain Other Financing or Other Equity (provide addendum if more space is needed).
Have you any outstanding judgments? In the last 7 years, have you been declared bankrupt?	No	No	
Have you had property foreclosed upon or given title or deed in lieu thereof?	No	No	
Are you a co-maker or endorser on a note?	No	No	
Are you a party in a law suit?	No	No	
Are you obligated to pay alimony, child support, or separate maintenance?	No	No	
Is any part of the down payment borrowed?	No	No	

*FHLMC/FNMA require business credit report, signed Federal Income Tax returns for last two years, and, if available, audited Profit and Loss Statements plus balance sheet for same period.

**All Present Monthly Housing Expenses of Borrower and Co-Borrower should be listed on a combined basis.

***Neither FHLMC nor FNMA requires this information.

FHLMC 65 Rev. 8/78

FNMA 1003 Rev. 8/78

EXHIBIT 4-1   RESIDENTIAL LOAN APPLICATION

This Statement and any applicable supporting schedules may be completed jointly by both married and unmarried co-borrowers if their assets and liabilities are sufficiently joined so that the Statement can be meaningfully and fairly presented on a combined basis; otherwise separate Statements and Schedules are required (FHLMC 65A/FNMA 1003A). If the co-borrower section was completed about a spouse, this statement and supporting schedules must be completed about that spouse also.

☐ Completed Jointly ☐ Not Completed Jointly

ASSETS		LIABILITIES AND PLEDGED ASSETS			
		Indicate by (*) those liabilities or pledged assets which will be satisfied upon sale of real estate owned or upon refinancing of subject property.			
Description	Cash or Market Value	Creditors' Name, Address and Account Number	Acct. Name if Not Borrower's	Mo. Pmt. and Mos. left to pay	Unpaid Balance
Cash Deposit Toward Purchase Held By	$	Installment Debts (include "revolving" charge accts)		$ Pmt./Mos.	$
Homes Realty	1,000	Mastercharge		/	85.00
Checking and Savings Accounts (Show Names of Institutions/Acct. Nos.) Pike County Savings & Loan 21-5579	19,450			/	
				/	
Stocks and Bonds (No./Description) None	None			/	
				/	
Life Insurance Net Cash Value Face Amount ($)	None	Other Debts Including Stock Pledges		/	
SUBTOTAL LIQUID ASSETS	$20,450				
Real Estate Owned (Enter Market Value from Schedule of Real Estate Owned)	None	Real Estate Loans			
Vested Interest in Retirement Fund	None				
Net Worth of Business Owned (ATTACH FINANCIAL STATEMENT)	None				
Automobiles (Make and Year) 1982 Dodge Charger 1974 Datsun 610	6,500 1,800	Automobile Loans Ajax Credit Association 111-11111		145/24	6,000
Furniture and Personal Property	3,800	Alimony, Child Support and Separate Maintenance Payments Owed To			
Other Assets (Itemize)					
		TOTAL MONTHLY PAYMENTS		$	
TOTAL ASSETS	A $ 32,550	NET WORTH (A minus B) $ 26,465		TOTAL LIABILITIES	B $ 6,085

SCHEDULE OF REAL ESTATE OWNED (If Additional Properties Owned Attach Separate Schedule)

Address of Property (Indicate S if Sold, PS if Pending Sale or R if Rental being held for income)	◇	Type of Property	Present Market Value	Amount of Mortgages & Liens	Gross Rental Income	Mortgage Payments	Taxes, Ins. Maintenance and Misc.	Net Rental Income
None			$	$	$	$	$	$
TOTALS →			$	$	$	$	$	$

LIST PREVIOUS CREDIT REFERENCES

◇ B–Borrower C–Co-Borrower	Creditor's Name and Address	Account Number	Purpose	Highest Balance	Date Paid
B&C	First Citizens Bank, Crete, Any State	311-60142	Auto	$ 2,600	7-10-xx
B&C	Warsaw Furniture, Crete, Any State	011-3164	Furniture	4,500	8-24-xx
B&C	Buy Cheap Furniture, Crete, Any State	299-1492	Furniture	1,800	7-15-xx

List any additional names under which credit has previously been received   None

AGREEMENT   The undersigned applies for the loan indicated in this application to be secured by a first mortgage or deed of trust on the property described herein, and represents that the property will not be used for any illegal or restricted purpose, and that all statements made in this application are true and are made for the purpose of obtaining the loan. Verification may be obtained from any source named in this application. The original or a copy of this application will be retained by the lender, even if the loan is not granted.   The undersigned ☐ intend or ☐ do not intend to occupy the property as their primary residence.

I/we fully understand that it is a federal crime punishable by fine or imprisonment, or both, to knowingly make any false statements concerning any of the above facts as applicable under the provisions of Title 18, United States Code, Section 1014.

_____ Date 9-15-xx   _____ Date 9-15-xx
Borrower's Signature   Co-Borrower's Signature

INFORMATION FOR GOVERNMENT MONITORING PURPOSES

Instructions: Lenders must insert in this space, or on an attached addendum, a provision for furnishing the monitoring information required or requested under present Federal and/or present state law or regulation. For most lenders, the inserts provided in FHLMC Form 65-B/FNMA Form 1003-B can be used.

FOR LENDER'S USE ONLY

(FNMA REQUIREMENT ONLY) This application was taken by ☐ face to face interview ☐ by mail ☐ by telephone

_____   _____
(Interviewer)   Name of Employer of Interviewer

FHLMC 65 Rev. 8/78   REVERSE   FNMA 1003 Rev. 8/78 be credited at closing, leaving an additional $19,285 the Carters need to pay to close the loan.

Other Income and Previous Employment The Carters have no additional income to report. Since the Carters have each been with only one employer, the section on previous employment is not applicable here.

Legal History This section determines if there are outstanding judgments, pending litigation, and/or any other legal obligations the borrower is required to honor. The Carters are able to answer no to these questions, so no further information is necessary.

Statement of Assets and Liabilities The reverse side of the application in Exhibit 4-1 is the borrower's or borrowers' financial statement. Assets are all items of value the prospective borrower owns; they may be owned free and clear or encumbered with debt. Assets include savings and checking accounts, stocks, bonds, and net cash values of insurance policies. Assets are classified as liquid (easily convertible to cash without substantial loss) and nonliquid. Nonliquid assets include ownership of real estate, automobiles, furniture, and personal property.

The lender is concerned with the borrower's assets because in the case of default, the lender may, through appropriate legal action, claim assets of the borrower that stand behind the loan. In a situation where the borrower is personally liable, as described above, it is a recourse loan. A nonrecourse loan is a loan in which the borrower's assets are not available to the lender if the borrower defaults on his or her loan. The Carters will have a recourse loan.

All long-term (and certain semi-long-term outstanding debts are shown on the statement as liabilities. These include such items as charge accounts and money owed to banks, finance companies, and businesses.

A borrower's ability to repay a loan is determined partly by income. Income growth and continuity depend on the borrower's occupation, future opportunities, employment history, age, educational background, training for the position, credit history, and consumption patterns. The borrower's total gross annual income is determined as follows:

$$\text{Gross annual income} = \text{base employment income} + \text{overtime} + \text{bonuses} \\ + \text{commissions} + \text{dividends and interest earned} \\ + \text{net rental income} + \text{other income}$$

The borrower's debt-management history and net worth are also important in predicting probability of repayment according to the terms of the loan. Income and debt on improved real estate require special consideration. The net rental income from real estate owned is itemized and recognized as stable income *only* after the underwriter relates the property type to the net income. For example, the gross income from a single-family property may only offset any mortgage payments and operating expenses, with the owner's profit being created by debt reduction, appreciation, refinance, or sale. Rising vacancy rates, real estate taxes, and operating expenses can materially offset obligations the borrower is required to honor. Since the Carters have answered no to all the questions, no additional information is required in this section. If the Carters had answered yes to any of the questions, they would have had to explain the reasons for the answer on a separate sheet.

The Carters' liquid assets total little more than the $20,000 inheritance. The rest of their assets are their automobiles and furniture. Their liabilities are a small amount on their charge cards and the amount owed on their car to Ajax Credit Association. The Carters own no other real estate, and their creditors are listed as references.

Verification of Deposit and Verification of Employment

At the time the applicant submits the loan application, the loan officer may have the applicant sign requests for *verification of deposit and verification of employment*. These forms authorize the disclosure of requested information.

The borrowers provide certain information about their accounts at various depository institutions, as Exhibit 4-2 shows. The depository then verifies the amounts and balances for previous months. Each account of the borrower should be identified and verified. Obviously, if the accounts are at different depository institutions, separate forms will be used for each account.

To confirm the borrower's statements concerning employer, salary, or other income from employment, the lender usually requires a verification of employment from the borrower's employer. This form also shows the past 12 months of wages paid and the employee's position. Exhibit 4-3 is a request for verification of employment addressed to Tammy Carter's supervisor at her place of employment. A similar form was sent to Will Carter's employer. The verification adds to the salary and stability-of-income information on the loan application.

The short-term stability of the borrower's income is critical in determining the borrower's ability to make the mortgage payments and maintain the property. It is difficult to predict income beyond 3 to 5 years, and typically it is during this time that the borrower will experience the most difficulty in meeting loan obligations. Therefore, the underwriter looks at these short-term salary predictions to ascertain whether or not the borrower has income sufficient and stable enough to support the debt service.

The underwriter also considers earnings from a second job. Many individuals' primary income is from jobs they work at only part of the year; they supplement this income with a second job. The secondary income source must be relatively stable if the primary income is insufficient to carry the loan.

If the borrower is self-employed, the documents necessary for verifying income are acceptable profit and loss statements (income statements) and balance sheets for the previous years or completed federal income tax returns for the same period. These documents should show that the income is the same as that

Federal National Mortgage Association

REQUEST FOR VERIFICATION OF DEPOSIT

🏛 FNMA

INSTRUCTIONS: LENDER - Complete Items 1 thru 8. Have applicant(s) complete Item 9. Forward directly to depository named in Item 1.
DEPOSITORY - Please complete Items 10 thru 15 and return DIRECTLY to lender named in Item 2.

PART I - REQUEST

1. TO (Name and address of depository)	2. FROM (Name and address of lender)
Pike County Savings & Loan 129 Deposit Boulevard Crete, Any State 00000	Larry Lender 1234 Dollar Avenue Crete, Any State 00000

3. SIGNATURE OF LENDER	4. TITLE Loan Officer	5. DATE	6. LENDER'S NUMBER (Optional) 1717

7. INFORMATION TO BE VERIFIED

TYPE OF ACCOUNT	ACCOUNT IN NAME OF	ACCOUNT NUMBER	BALANCE
Now		21732983	$ 19,450
			$
			$
			$

TO DEPOSITORY: I have applied for a mortgage loan and stated in my financial statement that the balance on deposit with you is as shown above. You are authorized to verify this information and to supply the lender identified above with the information requested in Items 10 thru 12. Your response is solely a matter of courtesy for which no responsibility is attached to your institution or any of your officers.

8. NAME AND ADDRESS OF APPLICANT(s)	9. SIGNATURE OF APPLICANT(s)
Will C. Carter 5665 College Avenue Crete, Any State 00000	

TO BE COMPLETED BY DEPOSITORY

PART II - VERIFICATION OF DEPOSITORY

10. DEPOSIT ACCOUNTS OF APPLICANT(s)

TYPE OF ACCOUNT	ACCOUNT NUMBER	CURRENT BALANCE	AVERAGE BALANCE FOR PREVIOUS TWO MONTHS	DATE OPENED
		$	$	
		$	$	
		$	$	
		$	$	

11. LOANS OUTSTANDING TO APPLICANT(s)

LOAN NUMBER	DATE OF LOAN	ORIGINAL AMOUNT	CURRENT BALANCE	INSTALLMENTS (Monthly/Quarterly)	SECURED BY	NUMBER OF LATE PAYMENTS
		$	$	$ per		
		$	$	$ per		
		$	$	$ per		

12. ADDITIONAL INFORMATION WHICH MAY BE OF ASSISTANCE IN DETERMINATION OF CREDIT WORTHINESS:
(Please include information on loans paid-in-full as in Item 11 above)

13. SIGNATURE OF DEPOSITORY	14. TITLE	15. DATE

The confidentiality of the information you have furnished will be preserved except where disclosure of this information is required by applicable law. The form is to be transmitted directly to the lender and is not to be transmitted through the applicant or any other party.

FNMA Form 1006
Rev. June 78

PREVIOUS EDITION WILL BE USED UNTIL STOCK IS EXHAUSTED

EXHIBIT 4-2 VERIFICATION OF DEPOSIT FORM

FNMA

Federal National Mortgage Association

REQUEST FOR VERIFICATION OF EMPLOYMENT

INSTRUCTIONS: LENDER- Complete items 1 thru 7. Have applicant complete item 8. Forward directly to employer named in item 1.
EMPLOYER-Please complete either Part II or Part III as applicable. Sign and return directly to lender named in item 2.

PART I - REQUEST

1. TO *(Name and address of employer)*	2. FROM*(Name and address of lender)*
Dependable Electric Co. 135 Industry Drive Crete, Any State 00000	Peak Federal Savings & Loan 1234 Dollar Avenue Crete, Any State 00000

3. SIGNATURE OF LENDER	4. TITLE Loan Officer	5. DATE 10-19-xx	6. LENDER'S NUMBER *(optional)* 1717

I have applied for a mortgage loan and stated that I am now or was formerly employed by you. My signature below authorizes verification of this information.

7. NAME AND ADDRESS OF APPLICANT *(Include employee or badge number)* Tammy Carter 5665 College Avenue Crete, Any State 00000	8. SIGNATURE OF APPLICANT

PART II - VERIFICATION OF PRESENT EMPLOYMENT

EMPLOYMENT DATA

PAY DATA

| 9. APPLICANT'S DATE OF EMPLOYMENT
July 5, 19xx | 12A. CURRENT BASE PAY (Enter Amount and Check Period) ☐ ANNUAL ☐ HOURLY ☒ MONTHLY ☐ OTHER ☐ WEEKLY (Specify)
$ _____ | 12C. FOR MILITARY PERSONNEL ONLY
PAY GRADE |

10. PRESENT POSITION	

| 11. PROBABILITY OF CONTINUED EMPLOYMENT
Good |

	12B. EARNINGS				
13. IF OVERTIME OR BONUS IS APPLICABLE, IS ITS CONTINUANCE LIKELY?	TYPE	YEAR TO DATE	PAST YEAR	TYPE	MONTHLY AMOUNT
	BASE PAY	$ 18,000	$ 17,500	BASE PAY	$
				RATIONS	$
	OVERTIME	$	$	FLIGHT OR HAZARD	$
	COMMISSIONS	$	$	CLOTHING	$
OVERTIME ☐ YES ☐ NO				QUARTERS	$
BONUS ☒ YES ☐ NO	BONUS	$ 1,000	$ 900	PRO PAY	$
				OVER SEAS OR COMBAT	$

14. REMARKS *(if paid hourly, please indicate average hours worked each week during current and past year)*

PART III - VERIFICATION OF PREVIOUS EMPLOYMENT

15. DATES OF EMPLOYMENT	16. SALARY/WAGE AT TERMINATION PER (Year) (Month) (Week) BASE _____ OVERTIME _____ COMMISSIONS _____ BONUS _____

17. REASON FOR LEAVING	18. POSITION HELD

19. SIGNATURE OF EMPLOYER	20. TITLE	21. DATE

The confidentiality of the information you have furnished will be preserved except where disclosure of this information is required by applicable law. The form is to be transmitted directly to the lender and is not to be transmitted through the applicant or any other party.

PREVIOUS EDITION WILL BE USED UNTIL STOCK IS EXHAUSTED

FNMA Form 1005
Rev. June 78

EXHIBIT 4-3   VERIFICATION OF EMPLOYMENT FORM

stated on the application and that the business can be expected to continue to earn this net income. If the borrower is retired or about to retire, the underwriting should be based on retirement income and the financial reserves accumulated for living expenses and debt service.

Good Faith Estimate of Closing Costs

When taking the application, the lender requires a good faith estimate of the settlement charges; a copy is then given to the applicant. This estimate details the costs the borrower will be charged when the loan is consummated or closed. Exhibit 4-4 is the good faith estimate for the Carters' application (more about this later).

Credit Report

The credit report must adhere to the Fair Credit Reporting Act of 1971, which imposes controls on both the consumer reporting agencies and the businesses using their reports. The purpose of the act is to ensure accuracy and relevancy and confidential treatment of credit data and a disclosure of the credit agency's findings to the investigated party (under certain circumstances). The loan processor should remember that reports based only on facts and not on the applicant's character, personal characteristics, or manner of living are acceptable. Once the credit report is received, it must be handled with the utmost confidentiality.

Credit reports are both historical and current. However, according to the Fair Credit Reporting Act, certain past data may not be used when the principal amount of the loan is below $50,000, including:

1 Tax liens that were paid more than 7 years prior to the report

2 Bankruptcies that, from the date of adjudication of the most recent bankruptcy, antedate the report by more than 14 years

3 Accounts placed for collection or charged to profit and loss more than 7 years prior to the report

4 Suits and judgments that, from date of entry, precede the report by more than 7 years (or the governing statute of limitations)

5 Records of arrest, indictment, or conviction for a crime that, from date of disposition, release, or parole, antedate the report by more than 7 years

6 Any other adverse data that preceded the report by more than 7 years

A credit report gives the lender information about the applicant's debt-repayment history at those firms identified on the loan application. The report also includes data from other creditors and any information from public records that reveals any pending suits against the applicant.

The report may include date of the applicant's employment, position, job security, annual salary, and net worth. It may also list the opening dates of the applicant's various retail accounts, available credit, date of last transaction, terms of sales, past repayment record, and amount past due.

GOOD FAITH ESTIMATE
OF SETTLEMENT CHARGES

Listed below is the Good Faith Estimate of Settlement Charges made pursuant to the requirements of the Real Estate Settlement Procedures Act (RESPA). These figures are only estimates and the actual charges due at settlement, may be different. This is not a commitment.

		Estimated Charge	or	Range	of	Charges
801	Loan Origination Fee *(POINTS)*					
	(Includes Item No.)	$ 680.00			to	
802	Loan Discount = *POINTS*					
803	Appraisal Fee	$1,360.00			to	
804	Credit Report	$ 100.00			to	
805	Lender's Inspection Fee	$ 15.00			to	
806	Mortgage Insurance Application Fee	$ --			to	
807	Assumption Fee	$ --			to	
901	Interest	$ --			to	
902	Mortgage Insurance Premium	$ --			to	
1101	Settlement or Closing Fee	$ --			to	
1102	Abstract or Title Search	$ --			to	
1105	Document Preparation	$ 25.00			to	
1106	Notary Fees	$ --			to	
1107	Attorney Fees	$ 175.00			to	
	(Includes Item No.)				to	
1108	Title Insurance	$ 250.00			to	
	(Includes Item No.)					
1201	Recording Fees	$ 35.00			to	
1301	Survey	$ 90.00		/	to	
1302	Pest Inspection	$			to	
	Total	$ 2,730.00			to	
					to	

In lieu of individual settlement charges, the lender at its option may elect to absorb all settlement charges and charge a fixed amount. If so, instead of amounts, all of the services and items checked above are included in the following fixed amount, in accordance with Section 3500.7(f) and 3500.8(d)(2), of the Real Estate Settlement Procedures Act. $ _____

This form does not cover all items you will be required to pay in cash at settlement, for example, deposits in escrow for real estate taxes and insurance. You may wish to inquire as to the amounts of such other items, as you may be required to pay other additional amounts at settlement.

THIS SECTION TO BE COMPLETED BY LENDER ONLY IF A PARTICULAR PROVIDER OF SERVICE IS REQUIRED

Listed below are providers of service which we require you use. The charges or range indicated in the Good Faith Estimate above are based upon the corresponding charge of the below designated providers.

Designated Charge Item No.	Phone No.	Item No.	Phone No.
Service Provided			
Providers Name			
Address			
We (☐ do), (☐ do not), have a business relationship with the above named provider.		We (☐ do), (☐ do not), have a business relationship with the above named provider.	

Delivery of the above Good Faith Estimate and the booklet entitled "Settlement Costs and You" is hereby acknowledged.

Applicant's Signature,
or Mailed By:

Address of Subject Property   Date

EXHIBIT 4-4   GOOD FAITH ESTIMATE

One method of evaluating credit risk is based on the five C's of credit quality:

1 *Character.* The probability that the borrower will attempt to honor obligations

2 *Capacity.* The subjective judgment of a borrower's ability to pay

3 *Capital.* As measured by the borrower's financial position and a financial ratio analysis

4 *Collateral.* The assets that a borrower offers as security

5 *Conditions.* The impact of general economic trends or certain developments in regions that may affect the borrower's ability to repay the loan

After the credit report on the Carters has been examined, all appears acceptable.

Loan Application: Income Property

Exhibit 4-5 is a loan application for a multifamily dwelling. There are major differences between this application and the residential application in Exhibit 4-1. First, the *purpose of loan* section is expanded. It requires a description of significant improvements noted in the refinance section. This information may imply an increase in the value of the property since the original loan was made. Also, in the case of new construction, detailed information is requested. Note that copies of all pertinent documents relating to the construction of the property have to be attached.

The *subject property* section requests estimated gross rental income, vacancy allowances, other income, and operating expenses. These data yield net effective income before debt service and depreciation. The borrower must disclose if the property is subject to rent control; if so, the rent control ordinance must be attached. The lender also wants to know if the apartments are rented furnished or unfurnished and which utilities are included in the rent. In addition, the borrower must indicate the name of the current residential manager, the proposed manager, and a list of properties the proposed manager oversees. Finally, signed, certified, current statements of income and expense and balance sheets must be attached, along with copies of such financial statements for the 2 preceding calendar years. If the property is new, pro forma statements are required. The lender also requires current rent schedules.

The borrower can be an individual, a partnership, a corporation, or some other entity. In the *borrower information* section, the name of the borrower is filled in and the name in which title will be vested is indicated. If the borrower is a partnership, the type of partnership must be checked and a copy of the partnership agreement must be attached. In addition, the principal business of the partnership and its address and phone number are included. If the borrower is a corporation, the address, phone number, and date and state of incorporation are requested.

In the *personal information* section, the name, phone number, age, address, title, and percentage of ownership of the individual borrowers, general partners, or corporate officers are filled in. Also, an employment summary of each principal must be included. If the loan is to be personally guaranteed, the names of the guarantors must be listed.

The multifamily residential loan application requires more information since the property generates income and the borrower frequently is more than one person (such as a partnership or corporation). Credit reports, financial statements, and employment and deposit verifications must also be submitted by all the parties. Exhibit 4-6 is a financial statement that would accompany the income loan application.

Loan Application: Other Types of Property

The loan-application process for other types of real estate, such as condominiums, follows the same procedure as that for the single-family house. The borrower has to provide the lender with all necessary information on similar types of forms. The lender then uses this information to analyze the acceptability of the loan application. We now turn to this analysis.

UNDERWRITING PROCEDURES FOR BORROWER ANALYSIS

Once the lender has received all the necessary documents and verified the information, the lender is in a position to determine the borrower's ability and willingness to honor the debt obligations under the terms of the mortgage application.

A borrower who has demonstrated strong job stability and/or is in a line of work in continuing demand and where advancement is possible should receive favorable consideration, given that an ability to manage financial affairs has been shown. Education and/or training that might strengthen job opportunities and earning ability should be received favorably. Table 4-1 illustrates other sources of income considered in borrower analysis.

A borrower who has changed jobs often for advancement within the same line of work should receive positive consideration if there is evidence the borrower is successful in the work but perhaps has outgrown the opportunities a previous employer provided. A certain number of job changes are considered normal in various lines of work. Frequent job changes without advancement or from one line of work to another can lead to unstable income. However, if in the past, stable income was maintained, job hopping without advancement should not receive negative consideration. Sometimes job hopping occurs because of race or sex discrimination. Unstable employment history may also be neutralized by the borrower's savings and consistent ability to meet financial obligations when due. In our single-family example, each Carter worked for one employer only, so Tammy and Will's income level is noted as stable.

Ratio Analysis

A mortgage lender is concerned with minimizing risk while enhancing the yield on each loan and on the lender's entire mortgage portfolio. To achieve these

MULTIFAMILY LOAN APPLICATION

LOAN APPLIED FOR ▶	Amount	Interest Rate	Monthly Payment Principal & Interest	Amortization Basis	Term	Escrow/Impounds (to be collected monthly)
	$	%	$	Mos.	Mos.	☐ Taxes ☐ Hazard Ins. ☐ _____

Prepayment Option

PURPOSE OF LOAN

☐ **PURCHASE SUBJECT PROPERTY** — Settlement Date _____ per sales agreement (attach copy)

Sales Price	Cash Down Paymt.	Source of Equity Funds (cash down and/or other - explain)
$	$	

Secondary Financing	Interest Rate	Monthly Payment Principal & Interest	Term	To Be Payable To:
$	%	$	Mos.	

☐ **REFINANCE SUBJECT PROPERTY**

Describe Significant Improvements Made.

FUNDS TO BE USED TO PAY:▼	Date Acquired	Purchase Price
		$

Cost $ _____

First Lien Balance	Maturity Date	Payable To:	(name & address)	Account No.
$				

Second Lien Balance
$

Remaining Funds to be used to

☐ **CONSTRUCT NEW MULTIFAMILY BUILDING(S)**   Estimated time to complete construction _____ mos.

Date Property Acquired	Cost	Existing Lien(s)	Payable to:	(Name & Address)
	$	$		

USE OF FUNDS: ▼		SOURCE OF FUNDS: ▼		
Pay Existing Lien(s)	$	Loan Applied For	$	Attach copies of plans; specifications; site plan; construction contract (if applicable); detailed breakdown of estimate of land development, direct & indirect construction costs; and, if applicable, details of performance and payment bonds or completion bond.
Land Dev. Costs	$	Funds invested by Owner	$	
Direct Constr. Costs	$	Other:	$	
Indirect Constr. Costs	$		$	
TOTAL:	$	TOTAL:	$	

General Contractor (name & address)	Explain source of funds to be invested by owner and/or other.

SUBJECT PROPERTY

Street Address	City	County	State	ZIP Code

Legal Description (attach separate sheet, if necessary)	Site/Lot Size	No. Bldgs.	No. Stories	No. Units	No. Pkg. Spaces	Yr. Built

Title is in ☐ Fee Simple   Brief Description of Improvements, incl. type structural frame, exterior walls, heat & A/C system, recreation facilities.
☐ Leasehold (attach copy of ground lease)

☐ Annualized estimates based on present levels of income & expenses—OR ☐ Pro-forma estimates for:

Gross Rental Income from apartments . . . . $_____
Other gross rental income from _____ $_____
Less vacancy (_____ %) . . . . (_____)
Other income (explain) _____ $_____
Less operating expenses . . . . (_____)
Net effective income before debt service and depreciation . . . . $_____

No. Apts. Vacant	Is project subject to rent control?	Name of current resident manager	Telephone No. ( )
	☐No ☐ Yes If yes, attach copy of Rent Control Law	Management will be by: (individual or firm's name & address)	

Apts. are rented	☐ Furnished	No. _____	Individual or firm manages following multifamily buildings:
	☐ Unfurnished	No. _____	(Address) (No. Units)

Utilities Incl. in rent ☐ Water   ☐ Gas   ☐ Elec.
☐ Heat   ☐ A/C ☐ _____

Attach signed, certified **current income and expense statement** and balance sheet for subject property as well as statements for the previous two calendar or fiscal years (pro-forma statements are required for new properties). Attach signed, certified **current rent schedule** showing occupant's name (if vacant, so indicate); apartment no. and type; monthly rent and lease expiration date; whether rented furnished or unfurnished; and type of utilities furnished by owner.
Expense statements should itemize expenditures for repairs and/or replacements.

BORROWER(S) TYPE

BORROWER(S) WILL BE ☐ Individual(s)   ☐ Partnership   ☐ Corporation   ☐ _____

Name of Borrower(s) (name of individual[s], partnership, corp.)	Title Will Be Vested In: (name of individual[s], partnership, corp.)

PARTNERSHIP TYPE ☐ General   ☐ Limited   ☐ Joint Venture   **(Attach partnership agreement)**

Principal Business of Partnership	Partnership Address	Telephone No. ( )

	Corporation Address	Telephone No. ( )	Date of Incorp.	State of Incorp.
CORPORATION				

FHLMC FORM 75 9/80

EXHIBIT 4-5   MULTIFAMILY LOAN APPLICATION

114

List below names of: individual borrowers; general partners, if partnership; or officers, if corporation. Under "Title", indicate "Indiv.". Gen'l Ptnr", "Pres." "V. Pres." "Treas.", etc. "Stockholder", as appropriate.

PERSONAL INFORMATION

	Name	Phone	Age	Home Address	Title	Ownership
A						%
B						%
C						%
D						%

ENTER INFORMATION BELOW ON LINES WITH LETTER CORRESPONDING TO THE PERSON NAMED ABOVE

EMPLOYMENT SUMMARY

	Primary Employer (name & address)	Type Business	Position	Years in this Business	Social Security No.
A					
B					
C					
D					

NAME OF GUARANTORS OF LOAN (If none, so state) ➤

FINANCIAL STATEMENTS. Satisfactory financial statements are required to be submitted with this application. Use of FHLMC Form 75A as a form of **personal financial statement** is optional.

ATTACHMENTS

CHECK ITEMS ATTACHED TO THIS APPLICATION

☐ Sales agreement (if purchase)
☐ Ground lease (if leasehold)
☐ Partnership agreement (if partnership)
☐ Recorded plat or survey
☐ Area map with arrow to site
☐ Copy of rent control laws or ordinances (if applicable)

☐ Construction contract or breakdown of est. costs; plans, specs., & site plan (if construction)
☐ Property income & exp. statements for previous 2 years (or pro-forma, if new or proposed)
☐ Description of repairs; replacements (if indicated in expense statement)

☐ Current income & expense statement and balance sheet regarding subject property.
☐ Current rent schedule, per instructions on front (unless construction)
☐ Financial statements
☐ Statement of management plan
☐ Statement of borrower's experience in owning, managing or building multifamily buildings
☐ Other _____

FOR LENDER'S USE

INFORMATION FOR GOVERNMENT MONITORING PURPOSES (complete if borrower[s] are individual[s])

Instructions: Lenders must insert in this space, or on an attached addendum, a provision for furnishing the monitoring information required or requested under present Federal and/or present state law or regulation. For most lenders, the inserts provided in FHLMC Form 65-B/FNMA Form 1003-B may be used.

AGREEMENT: The undersigned applies for the loan indicated in this application to be secured by a first mortgage or deed of trust on the property described herein, and represents that the property will not be used for any illegal or restricted purpose, and that all statements made in this application and the attachments, are true and are made for the purpose of obtaining the loan. Verification may be obtained from any source named in this application and/or in attachments.

I/we fully understand that it is a federal crime punishable by fine or imprisonment, or both, to knowingly make any false statements concerning any of the above facts as applicable under the provisions of Title 18, United States Code, Section 1014.

_____ Date _____   _____ Date _____

_____ Date _____   _____ Date _____

FHLMC Form 75 9/80   REVERSE

PERSONAL FINANCIAL STATEMENT — Supplement to FHLMC FORM 75

(USE OF THIS FORM IS OPTIONAL. OTHER FORMS OF PERSONAL FINANCIAL STATEMENTS CONTAINING SUBSTANTIALLY SIMILAR INFORMATION ARE ALSO ACCEPTABLE)

The following information is provided to become a part of the application by _____
(name of borrower(s) as shown on FHLMC Form 75)

for a mortgage loan in the amount of $ _____ with interest at _____% for a term of _____ months, to be secured by property known

as: _____
(property street address, city, state)

PERSONAL FINANCIAL STATEMENT
as of _____ (Date)

NOTE: THE FOLLOWING SENTENCE APPLIES IF THIS STATEMENT IS BEING COMPLETED ABOUT INDIVIDUALS AS BORROWER/CO-BORROWER:

The Co-Borrower section and all other Co-Borrower questions must be completed and the appropriate box(es) checked if ☐ another person will be jointly ob-ligated with the Borrower on the loan, or ☐ the Borrower is relying on income from alimony, child support or separate maintenance or on the income or assets of another person as a basis for repayment of the loan, or ☐ the Borrower is married and resides, or the property is located, in a community property state.

1 | Name of ☐ Individual as Borrower, or ☐ Partner, Officer or Stockholder of Borrowing Entity, or ☐ Guarantor

2 | Name of Individual ☐ As Co-Borrower ☐ Not as Co-Borrower

Home Address

Home Address

Employer (name and address)

Employer (name and address)

Years with this Employer | Current Position

Years with this Employer | Current Position

GROSS ANNUAL INCOME	ENTER INFORMATION APPLICABLE TO PERSON NAMED IN BLOCK 1 IN COLUMN 1, INFORMATION APPLICABLE TO PERSON NAMED IN BLOCK 2 IN COLUMN 2.	COLUMN 1	COLUMN 2
	Base Employment Income	$	$
	Overtime		
	Bonuses		
	Commissions		
	Dividends/Interest		
	Net Rental Income		
	Other* (describe)		
	*Alimony, child support or separate maintenance income need not be revealed if individuals do not choose to have it considered as a basis for repaying this loan. TOTAL:	$	$

Social Security Number | / / | / /

OTHER INFORMATION		Yes	No	Yes	No
	If a "Yes" answer is given to any of the following questions, explain on an attached sheet.				
	Have you any outstanding judgments? In the last 7 years, have you been declared bankrupt?	☐	☐	☐	☐
	Have you had property foreclosed upon or given title or deed in lieu thereof?	☐	☐	☐	☐
	Are you a co-maker or endorser on a note?	☐	☐	☐	☐
	Are you a party in a law suit?	☐	☐	☐	☐
	Are you obligated to pay alimony, child support, or separate maintenance?	☐	☐	☐	☐
	Is any part of the down payment borrowed?	☐	☐	☐	☐
	Marital Status: (M) Married; (S) Separated; (U) Unmarried, including single, divorced, widowed (circle appropriate letter symbol)	M S U		M S U	

Identify the person to whom the following information relates by entering the number corresponding to the person named in blocks 1 and 2 above.

IF EMPLOYED IN CURRENT POSITION FOR LESS THAN TWO YEARS COMPLETE THE FOLLOWING

#	Previous Employer/School	City/State	Type of Business	Position/Title	Dates From/To	Annual Income
						$

LIST PREVIOUS CREDIT REFERENCES

#	Creditor's Name and Address	Account Number	Purpose	Highest Balance	Date Paid
				$	

List any additional names under which credit has previously been received _____

FHLMC Form 75A (9/80)

EXHIBIT 4-6 PERSONAL FINANCIAL STATEMENT

This statement and any applicable supporting schedules may be completed jointly by both married and unmarried co-borrowers if their assets and liabilities are sufficiently joined so that the statement can be meaningfully and fairly presented on a combined basis; otherwise separate statements and schedules are required on FHLMC Form 75A. If the Co-Borrower section was completed about a spouse, this statement and supporting schedules must be completed about that spouse also.

☐ Completed Jointly ☐ Not Completed Jointly

ASSETS			LIABILITIES AND PLEDGED ASSETS			
Indicate by (*) those liabilities or pledged assets which will be satisfied upon sale of real estate owned or upon refinancing of subject property.						
Description	Cash or Market Value		Creditors' Names, Addresses and Account Nos.	Acct. Name if Not Borrower's	Mo. Pmt. and Mos. left to pay	Unpaid Balance
Cash Deposit Toward Purchase Held By	$		Installment Debts (include "revolving" charge accts.)		$ Pmt./Mos. /	$
Checking and Savings Accounts (show names of institutions/acct. nos.)					/	
					/	
_____ Acct. # _____					/	
_____ Acct. # _____					/	
_____ Acct. # _____			Other Debts including stock pledges		/	
_____ Acct. # _____					/	
			Real Estate Loans			
Stocks and Bonds (no./description)						
Life Insurance Net Cash Value						
Face Amount ($)						
SUBTOTAL LIQUID ASSETS	$					
Real Estate Owned (enter Market Value from Schedule of Real Estate Owned)						
Vested Interest in Retirement Fund						
Net Worth of Business Owned (ATTACH FINANCIAL STATEMENT)						
Automobiles (make and year)			Automobile Loans			
Furniture and Personal Property			Alimony, Child Support and Separate Maintenance Payments Owed To			
Other					/	
			TOTAL MONTHLY PAYMENTS		$	
TOTAL ASSETS	A $		NET WORTH (A minus B) $		TOTAL LIABILITIES	B $

STATEMENT OF ASSETS AND LIABILITIES

SCHEDULE OF REAL ESTATE OWNED (if additional properties owned, attach separate schedule)

Address of Property (indicate S if sold, PS if pending sale or R if rental being held for income)		Type of Property	Present Market Value	Amount of Mortgages & Liens	Gross Rental Income	Mortgage Payments	Taxes, Ins. Maintenance and Misc.	Net Rental Income
			$	$	$	$	$	$
TOTALS ⟶								

I/we fully understand that it is a federal crime punishable by fine or imprisonment, or both, to knowingly make any false statements concerning any of the above facts as applicable under the provisions of Title 18, United States Code, Section 1014.

_____ Date _____   _____ Date _____
Signature   Signature

Home Phone: _____ Bus. Phone _____ Home Phone _____ Bus. Phone _____

NOTE: Self-employed persons must submit, as attachments to this statement, signed copies of their individual Federal Income Tax Returns for the last two years.

FHLMC Form 75A (9/80)   REVERSE

TABLE 4-1 OTHER INCOME SOURCES

Type of income	Explanation
Overtime income	If the type of employment requires continual overtime as a normal routine, overtime pay is counted.
Part-time income	Counted if there is a history of regularity and continuity.
Commission and fees	Duration and quality are the guidelines. A past record as evidenced by tax statements is sufficient.
Bonuses	Generally considered optional and not counted unless there is a long, consistent history of such payments.
Spouse's income	Included only if it is long-term and high quality. Pregnancy or sex factors should not affect the decision.
Disability benefits	Countable if stable (VA, Social Security), but educational payments are temporary and so are not countable.
Armed services reserve income	Usually excluded because of duration limitations.
Child support and alimony	Counted if the history of payments indicates commitment.
Investment income	Duration and quality of the investment are the major factors, i.e., net income from rental properties, stocks, bonds, CDs, savings accounts, and Treasury debt.

goals, flexible but standard and defensible analytical techniques (i.e., ratio analysis and underwriting standards) must be used. Using these techniques helps the lender detect both high-quality and very bad loans as well as questionable ones. We now discuss some of the more common ratios and industry standards used to evaluate the borrower and assets; Table 4-2 summarizes the forms.

Loan-to-Value Ratio One risk-minimization guideline is the *loan-to-value ratio*. This ratio protects the lender by assuring the lender that the borrower has sufficient equity invested in the property to properly maintain the property and to make mortgage payments on time. The ratio also protects the lender by ensuring an ample margin between the property value and the loan amount, in case of foreclosure on the property. Maximum loan-to-value ratios vary according to the type of property and state and federal requirements. Higher ratios can be granted with private mortgage insurance (to be discussed later) or government loan insurance (FHA, VA). In general, the average loan-to-value ratios range from 65 to 80 percent. The loan-to-value ratio of an income property loan usually ranges from 65 to 75 percent, and that of a residential loan from 75 to 95 percent. The loan-to-value ratio of FHA and VA loans ranges from 97 to 100 percent.

Monthly Housing Expenses The underwriter also considers the impact of the *monthly housing expenses ratio* on the borrower's ability to pay the debt service and maintain the property. The energy efficiency of the property must be considered, because items that reduce the energy costs permit a greater portion of the

TABLE 4-2 UNDERWRITING RATIOS AND TYPICAL INDUSTRY STANDARDS

Ratio	Typical standard
$\dfrac{\text{Total mortgage expense}}{\text{Stabilized gross income}}$	0.25 to 0.35
$\dfrac{\text{Total housing expense}}{\text{Stabilized gross income}}$	0.30 to 0.35
$\dfrac{\text{Total fixed expenses}}{\text{Stabilized gross income}}$	0.45 to 0.55
$\dfrac{\text{Total monthly income} - \text{fixed monthly debt}}{\text{Total monthly mortgage payments}}$	3.5 to 5.0
Affordable mortgage amount	Gross household income $\times$ 2.0
Affordable house price	Investor income $\times$ 2.25 to 2.75

borrower's income to be applied to other housing expenses. An underwriting rule of thumb is that the monthly housing expense should not exceed a 25 to 35 percent range of the borrower's stable monthly income. Another rule to use is that total monthly debt payments (housing, installment debt, alimony) should not exceed 30 to 35 percent of the borrower's stable monthly income. Higher ratios may be justified by the following seven factors:

1 Borrower's demonstrated ability to allocate a greater proportion of income to basic needs, such as housing expenses

2 Energy efficiency of the property

3 Borrower's demonstrated ability to sustain a good credit history, accumulate savings, and maintain a low-debt position

4 Potential for increased earnings indicated by education or job training relative to time employed

5 Large down payment on the purchase of the property

6 Amount, nature, and terms of child support payments

7 Borrower's net worth more than sufficient to evidence a high propensity to repay the mortgage

In our example, the Carters have a good monthly income, and the expenses for the new house are expected to be $959.46 per month. This means that 31 percent of the Carters' gross income will go for covering housing expenses. These expenses plus their car payment constitute about 35 percent of their income. Note that the Carters have recently paid off several loans on one of their cars and their furniture. The price of the house is about 2.25 times their gross annual income.

Private Mortgage Insurance

Another aspect of the borrower analysis is private mortgage insurance (PMI). PMI is issued through the lender by a private company to cover the first 20 to 25 percent of the mortgage balance. Any loan-to-value ratio greater than 80 percent for a conventional loan typically requires PMI. Usually, the lender considers the first few years of payments the most risky because the owner's equity in the property is relatively low.[1]

What Is PMI? In high-ratio loans, home buyers are in low-equity positions. Mortgage insurance provides loss coverage so that if a borrower defaults, the top 20 to 25 percent of a mortgage loan can be subject to loss claims by the lender. Insurance coverage substitutes for the reduced equity in high-ratio loans, to make them acceptable to a lender's risk-management policies. It helps make the conventional high-ratio mortgage an acceptable investment, relying less on property location and other nonquantifiable underwriting criteria. It also enables lenders to settle for low (often as little as 5 percent) down payments from buyers with adequate, steady incomes to meet monthly payments but with little accumulated savings.

There are presently 13 mortgage insurance companies (MICs) actively engaged in insuring lenders against loss resulting from default on one-to-four-family home mortgages. All have met the qualifications of the Federal National Mortgage Association (FNMA or Fannie Mae) and the Federal Home Loan Mortgage Corporation (FHLMC or Freddie Mac), both of which purchase conventional loans in excess of 80 percent loan-to-value ratio on the strength of MIC insurance. FNMA and FHLMC require a qualified MIC to maintain a minimum policyholder's surplus of $5 million and limit outstanding insurance risk to 25 times its policyholder's surplus. Some state regulators require that MICs be "monoline," that is, not write insurance on loans for real property other than the one-to-four-family dwellings an MIC can insure. Thirteen MICs are members of Mortgage Insurance Companies of America (MICA), representing 100 percent of the market.

The 13 MICA members conduct their insurance operations through 230 main and regional underwriting offices. There are 36 states served by 7 or more members, and no state is served by fewer than 3. Mortgage originators who seek the services of MICs apply for master policies with one or more MICs. Insurance of a master policy is not perfunctory since prudence, reinforced by FHLMC and FNMA requirements, requires the MIC's evaluation of the lender's (1) net worth and quality of assets, (2) servicing ability, (3) methodology for handling delinquent loans, and (4) appraisal and underwriting staffs' professional capability. Moreover, once a master policy is issued, each application for insurance of a mortgage is subject to the MIC's underwriting procedures.

Insurance commitments generally are issued within 24 hours of the MIC's receiving the following documents from the lender: application for insurance, credit report, appraisal, affidavit of purchase price, sales contract, and verification of income.

MICs are chartered by the states and regulated by state insurance depart-

---

[1] This section is adapted from *Factbook and Directory,* Mortgage Insurance Companies of America, Washington, D.C.

ments. State laws and regulations limit an MIC's exposure to no more than the top 25 percent of the mortgage. Most policies cover the top 20 percent, with 25 percent coverage generally limited to 95 percent loan-to-value mortgages. Actuarial experience supports the conclusion of industry pioneers that 20 to 25 percent represented the risk portion of a mortgage with a low down payment and hence the valid insurable portion.

The industry is highly competitive, and MICs offer their lender customers a variety of premium plans. In all cases, initial-year premiums vary, depending on the loan-to-value ratio and the level of coverage (12 to 30 percent). For example, a premium could be 1 percent of the mortgage for the first year on a 95 percent loan with 25 percent coverage, three-quarters of 1 percent on a 90 percent loan with 25 percent coverage, or one-half of 1 percent on a 90 percent loan with 20 percent coverage. In most cases, the premium plans are offered by most MICs, and the premiums vary from 1½ percent for a 5-year policy to 2¼ percent for 15 years with 20 percent coverage on a loan over 90 percent.

The lender determines the duration of mortgage insurance; at any time the lender may opt to not renew the policy. The average term of an MIC policy is approximately 8 years.

PMI Example   The essence of mortgage insurance is to protect the lender from loss resulting from default by the borrower. MIC's master policies require the lender to report delinquencies to the MIC and to institute foreclosure or other appropriate proceedings after continuing delinquencies. A lender generally must have evidence of salable title to the property at the time a claim is submitted. Upon receipt of the claim, the MIC will proceed according to one of the following options:

1 Pay the entire claim to the lender and take title to the property
2 Pay 20 to 25 percent (depending on the policy) of the total claim

In most cases, the loss claims include such lender costs as accumulated interest, real estate taxes, fire and hazard insurance premiums, attorney's or trustee's fees, court costs, property maintenance fees, and unpaid balance due on the mortgage.

The following table is an example of a claim settlement:

Principal balance due	$40,946
Accumulated interest (excludes penalty interest and late charges)	3,200
Subtotal	44,146
Attorney's fees (maximum 3% of subtotal)	1,324
Property taxes paid	584
Hazard insurance	242
Preservation of property (includes such items as securing the property and winterizing)	160
Disbursement and foreclosure proceeding	386
Subtotal	$46,842
Less escrow balance and rent received	280
Total Claim	$46,562

The total claim is $46,562. Under an MIC's first option, this amount would be paid to the insured lender in return for merchantable title to the property. Under the second option, the lender would keep title to the property and receive cash payment equal to that percentage of the total claims which is the percentage coverage originally selected in the lender policy. For example, if it were 25 percent coverage, the cash payment to the insured would be $11,640.50.

Advantages of PMI PMI differs in many respects from insurance on government loans (see Chapter 10). For example, PMI covers only that part of the loan repaid in the early years of the loan, whereas FHA insurance covers the total loan. PMI offers the borrower several advantages:

1 With PMI, the borrower can buy a house that might not pass VA or FHA inspection.
2 The borrower can obtain a loan with a small down payment because the lender's risk of capital loss is minimized within the first few years of the loan.
3 The PMI insurance premium is much lower than that of the FHA because it does not cover the entire mortgage.
4 A request for insurance commitment under PMI can usually be processed quicker than an FHA application.
5 PMI can be canceled when the risk is sufficiently reduced (when the loan-to-value ratio drops below 80 percent).
6 Private mortgage insurance insures at market rates.

PMI also offers the lender certain advantages:

1 It protects the lender against loss from interest, taxes, hazard insurance, attorney's fees, foreclosure costs, property maintenance, and falling property value.
2 The PMI also enables the lender to offer an investment package to sell to a secondary mortgage market investor (see Chapter 1).

Borrower Analysis in Mortgage Pricing

The lender wants to earn a return consisting of four elements:

1 Real return (i.e., compensation for deferred consumption)
2 Inflation premium (i.e., compensation for the declining value of the dollar)
3 Inflation risk premium (i.e., compensation for the possibility that the inflation premium was underestimated and that the loan will be paid back in even cheaper dollars than expected)
4 Default risk premium (i.e., compensation for the possibility that the loan may not be repaid as agreed to)

Changes in the level of interest rates result mainly from changes in the three premiums. The inflation premium will move up and down in accordance with inflation trends in the economy. The inflation risk premium varies with the perceived accuracy of the inflation forecast. The default risk premium, on the other hand, is a function of the safety and liquidity of the particular loan. The better the collateral (the higher the quality of the real property assets) and the wealthier the borrower, the lower will be the default risk premium demanded by the lender.

Borrower analysis helps determine the risk of default. The Carters, with stable incomes, little outstanding debt, and a good credit history, will probably receive a lower default risk premium than someone who does not have these attributes. After determining the riskiness of a loan, the lender can adjust the interest rate charged or the amount of the loan it is willing to extend. For example, if a proposed loan is riskier than normal, the lender can charge a higher interest rate or the lender may reduce the amount it is willing to lend.

GOVERNMENT INVOLVEMENT IN BORROWER-LENDER RELATIONSHIP

In recent years, the government has been involved in trying to protect borrowers affected by lending practices on single-family homes that either discriminate against borrowers or fail to provide enough information so that borrowers can compare loan terms among competing institutions. Consequently, Congress enacted three significant pieces of legislation to protect borrowers purchasing or refinancing single-family homes: the Consumer Protection Act (Truth-in-Lending Law), which was effective July 1, 1969; the Real Estate Settlement Procedures Act (RESPA), which was effective June 20, 1975; and the Equal Credit Opportunity Act (ECOA), which was effective October 28, 1975. We now discuss the pertinent details of these acts and follow our example of the single-family home loan through the preparation of the relevant documents that will satisfy the requirements of this legislation. For the most part, the government has not become involved in the borrower-lender relationship on income property loans.

Consumer Protection Act (Truth-in-Lending Law)

The Consumer Protection Act of 1969 requires that the lender (any person who as part of his or her business regularly provides consumer credit) inform the borrower in advance of all terms and conditions of the loan so that the borrower can readily compare various available credit terms. The Federal Reserve Board is responsible for implementing the law; the board prepared the so-called *Regulation Z.* The law does not apply to business loans extended to corporations, partnerships, trusts, cooperatives, associations, or units of the government because they usually involve large sums of money and are assumed sophisticated enough to perform their own research.

A disclosure statement must be provided. The statement includes the annual percentage rate (APR), the number, amount, and due dates of payments; terms of the repayment clause; components of the finance charge; and the sum of all monthly payments. The APR is the sum of the interest charged on the loan and the total of all prepaid expenses. It represents the relationship between total finance charge and the total amount financed. Exhibit 4-7 is the truth-in-lending disclosure statement for the Carters. The total finance charge consists of all costs the borrower paid and that the lender required. These costs include interests, points, service charges, and premiums for mortgage insurance. Not included in the calculation are costs for credit reports, hazard insurance premiums, taxes, legal fees, title insurance, and the like. The APR is calculated by dividing the total finance charges by the net amount financed, to determine the finance charge per $100 financed. Then, the Federal Reserve System APR tables are used to match the financed cost per $100 with the applicable APR (rounded to the nearest ¼ percent).

Not all loans are subject to the Truth-in-Lending Law. Several exceptions are (1) when the loan proceeds of the mortgage are used for investment purposes, (2) for owner-occupied multifamily dwellings, and (3) in connection with a first mortgage to purchase or build a dwelling.

Another aspect of the law is the *right of recision*. If a borrower pledges her home as collateral for a loan (except of course if she is buying or building the home), she can cancel the loan within 3 business days after the pledge or after receipt of the disclosure statement. The creditor is obligated to inform the borrower of this right of recision by giving the borrower two copies of the notice in the form outlined by Regulation Z. The notice states that the arrangement may be canceled during the 3-day period and that the borrower cannot be held liable for any of the lender's expenses during that period. Waiver of the right of recision is allowed, but the borrower must sign and date a personal statement. In the case of joint ownership, the right may be exercised by either joint owner, but it is still binding on the other parties in the transaction. If the Truth-in-Lending Law is not complied with, there are civil and criminal remedies.

Real Estate Settlement and Procedures Act (RESPA) DETAIL INFO ON CLOSING COST

This law provides the borrower with sufficient detailed information about closing costs to allow the borrower an opportunity to effectively compare the terms of the loans being offered. In addition, the law requires that the borrower and the seller be given detailed data on closing costs over a 12-day waiting period prior to settlement. The amount a lender can escrow for real estate taxes and insurance is limited. The seller (or agent) must furnish the buyer with the property's previous sale price. Finally, the act prohibits kickbacks to anyone providing settlement services. In its final form, RESPA contains the following specific basic requirements:

1 At the time of the loan application, the lender must give the borrower a booklet prepared by HUD.

2 At the time of the loan application, the lender must give the prospective borrower a good faith estimate of the charges the borrower must pay at closing.

3 The borrower must be allowed an opportunity to inspect the settlement

FEDERAL TRUTH-IN-LENDING DISCLOSURE STATEMENT
For use with Secured Loans

Date: <u>October 6</u>, 19 <u>XX</u> Loan No.: _____

Borrowers: <u>Will C. & Tammy Carter</u> _____

_____

Address: <u>209 Boweevil Street</u> _____

<u>Lot 10, Block B, Cotton Hill Estates</u>

<u>Crete Peak, Any State</u>

ANNUAL PERCENTAGE RATE	FINANCE CHARGE	Amount Financed	Total of Payments
The cost of your credit as a yearly rate.	The dollar amount the credit will cost you	The amount of credit provided to you or on your behalf.	The amount you will have paid after you have made all payments as scheduled.
12.4 maturity 12.7 7 years			
%	$	$68,000	$251,805.60

You have the right to receive at this time an itemization of the Amount Financed.
☐ I want an itemization. ☐ I do not want an itemization.

Your payment schedule will be:

Number of Payments	Amount of Payments	When Payments are Due
360	$ 699.46	1st of each month, beginning Dec. 1, 19xx
	$	
	$	

☐ This obligation has a demand Feature.

Insurance: Credit life insurance and credit disability insurance are not required to obtain credit, and will not be provided unless you sign and agree to pay the additional cost. No such insurance will be in force until you have completed an application, the insurance company has issued the policy, the effective date of that policy has arrived and the required premium has been paid.

Type	Premium	Term	Signature
Credit Life	$		I want to apply for credit life insurance. _____ Signature
Credit Disability	$		I want to apply for credit disability insurance. _____ Signature
Credit Life and Credit Disability	$		I want to apply for credit life and disability insurance. _____ Signature

You may obtain property insurance from anyone you want that is acceptable to this institution. If you get the insurance from _____ _____ you will pay $_____ for a term of _____

Security: You are giving a security interest in:
☐ the goods or property being purchased
☐ _____
Filing fees $_____ Non-filing insurance $_____

Late Charge: If payment is_____late, you will be charged $_____/_____% of the payment.

Prepayment: If you pay off early, you
☐ may ☒ will not have to pay a penalty.
☐ may ☒ will not be entitled to a refund of part of the finance charge.

☐ **Required Deposit:** The annual percentage rate does not take into account your required deposit.

See your contract documents for any additional information about nonpayment, default, any required repayment in full before the scheduled date, and prepayment refunds and penalties.
<u>e means an estimate</u>

I/We hereby acknowledge receipt of this disclosure.

_____ / _____
                                                                DATE

_____ / _____
                                                                DATE

EXHIBIT 4-7 TRUTH-IN-LENDING DISCLOSURE

statements on the day before the closing. The statements must be as complete as possible.

4 The HUD settlement statement must be used at closing.

5 Payment or receiving a kickback for unearned fees is prohibited.

6 The seller cannot condition the sale on the buyer's buying title insurance from a particular title company.

7 Escrows for taxes, insurance, and other charges the lender requires cannot exceed the amount necessary to make payments, plus a 2-month deposit.

8 If the loan is being made to a fiduciary, the party receiving the beneficial interest must be disclosed to any FDIC- and FSLIC-insured lenders.

9 Lenders are prohibited from charging fees for preparation of statements in accordance with RESPA or the Truth-in-Lending Law.

Certain transactions are excluded from the RESPA: loans for property of 25 or more acres; any loans where the proceeds are not used to purchase or transfer legal title to the property; loans for the purchase or transfer of a vacant lot, unless the proceeds are used to construct a one- to four-family home or to buy a mobile home; assumptions and so on of preexisting loans, unless a construction loan is used as is or converted to a permanent loan to finance the purchase by a first user; construction loans to developers; the proceeds of a permanent loan used to finance construction of a one- to four-family home, where the borrower already owns the lot; and loans for purchasing property that is intended for immediate resale.

Settlement Statement: Single-Family Example   Exhibit 4-8 is the standard settlement statement for our single-family house. The Carters bought the house from H.O. Mowner for $85,000. The Carters' total settlement charges amounted to $2,985, which included the loan origination fees, loan discount, the appraisal fee, credit report, escrow deposits for property taxes, and other title and recording charges. The total amount due from the borrowers (Carters) is thus $87,985. They have already deposited $1,000 earnest money, and they have taken out a loan of $68,000. In addition, they have an adjustment of $935 for property taxes the seller did not pay. The amount of cash (equity) necessary for the buyers to close the transaction is $18,050.

From the seller's perspective, the seller owes a total of $5,105 in closing costs (primary brokerage commission). In addition, the seller is paying off existing first and second mortgages. The total cash to the seller is thus $29,785, as shown in Exhibit 4-8.

Equal Credit Opportunity Act (ECOA)

The 1975 Equal Credit Opportunity Act requires that all financial institutions and other firms engaged in the extension of credit make credit equally available to all creditworthy applicants, without regard to race, color, religion, national origin, age, sex, and marital status. The lender and the borrower are also concerned with

A.	U.S. DEPARTMENT OF HOUSING AND URBAN DEVELOPMENT SETTLEMENT STATEMENT.	B. TYPE OF LOAN

Peak Federal Savings and Loan Association
202 College Avenue
Crete, Any State 30601

Conventional Single Family

6. FILE NUMBER:	7. LOAN NUMBER:
021-315	57-311
8. MORT. INS. CASE NO.: N/A	

C. NOTE: This form is furnished to give you a statement of actual settlement costs. Amounts paid to and by the settlement agent are shown. Items marked "(p.o.c.)" were paid outside the closing; they are shown here for informational purposes and are not included in the totals.

D. NAME OF BORROWER:	E. NAME OF SELLER:	F. NAME OF LENDER:
Will and Tammy Carter	H. O. Mowner	Peak Federal Savings and Loans

G. PROPERTY LOCATION:	H. SETTLEMENT AGENT:	I. SETTLEMENT DATE:
209 Boweevil Street 108 Cotton Hills Estates Crete, Any State	PLACE OF SETTLEMENT:	29 Oct. 19xx

J. SUMMARY OF BORROWER'S TRANSACTION:		K. SUMMARY OF SELLER'S TRANSACTION:	
100. GROSS AMOUNT DUE FROM BORROWER		400. GROSS AMOUNT DUE TO SELLER	
101. Contract sales price	85,000	401. Contract sales price	85,000
102. Personal property	--	402. Personal property	
103. Settlement charges to borrower (line 1400)	2,985	403.	
104.		404.	
105.		405.	
Adjustments for items paid by seller in advance		Adjustments for items paid by seller in advance	
106. City/town taxes to		406. City/town taxes to	
107. County taxes to		407. County taxes to	
108. Assessments to		408. Assessments to	
109.		409.	
110.		410.	
111.		411.	
112.		412.	
120. GROSS AMOUNT DUE FROM BORROWER	87,985	420. GROSS AMOUNT DUE TO SELLER	85,000
200. AMOUNTS PAID BY OR IN BEHALF OF BORROWER		500. REDUCTIONS IN AMOUNT DUE TO SELLER	
201. Deposit or earnest money	1,000	501. Excess deposit (see Instructions)	
202. Principal amount of new loan(s)	68,000	502. Settlement charges to seller (line 1400)	5,105
203. Existing loan(s) taken subject to		503. Existing loan(s) taken subject to	
204.		504. Payoff of first mortgage loan	36,675
205.		505. Payoff of second mortgage loan	12,500
206.		506.	
207.		507.	
208.		508.	
209.		509.	
Adjustments for items unpaid by seller		Adjustments for items unpaid by seller	
210. City/town taxes to		510. City/town taxes to	
211. County taxes 1-1-xx to 12-1-xx	935	511. County taxes 1-1-xx to 12-1-xx	935
212. Assessments to		512. Assessments to	
213.		513.	
214.		514.	
215.		515.	
216.		516.	
217.		517.	
218.		518.	
219.		519.	
220. TOTAL PAID BY/FOR BORROWER	69,935	520. TOTAL REDUCTION AMOUNT DUE SELLER	55,215
300. CASH AT SETTLEMENT FROM OR TO BORROWER		600. CASH AT SETTLEMENT TO OR FROM SELLER	
301. Gross amount due from borrower (line 120)	87,985	601. Gross amount due to seller (line 420)	85,000
302. Less amounts paid by/for borrower (line 220)	69,935	602. Less reduction amount due seller (line 520)	55,215
303. CASH BORROWER	18,050	603. CASH SELLER	29,785

HUD-1A

REV. 10/77

EXHIBIT 4-8   SETTLEMENT STATEMENT

legal protection of their investment via clear title. To ascertain and protect title, the Torrens system (used in certain states; see Chapter 3), title abstract, legal opinion, or title insurance may be used. The lender must also avoid the practice of redlining: the discriminatory limiting or restricting of funds based on race, income, or housing factors.

SUMMARY

This chapter discussed the analysis of the borrower in the financing process. The lender is concerned with the borrower's willingness and ability to repay the mortgage debt. To make the lending decision, data are obtained from various documents, such as the loan application, credit reports, and financial statements. Using the data provided, the lender then applies various types of underwriting rules and techniques to assess the likelihood of borrower default, to minimize the risk associated with the loan. In recent years, the government has introduced numerous regulations and laws concerning the borrower-lender relationship. Lenders must be careful to conform to these restrictions.

The examples in this chapter are primarily single-family properties. For the most part, borrower analysis on income properties is the same; the following two chapters consider property analysis.

QUESTIONS

1 Define the following terms:
   a default risk
   b private mortgage insurance
   c credit report
   d loan-to-value ratio
   e closing statement
   f Real Estate Settlement and Procedures Act
2 Discuss the types of information usually required when applying for a single-family house loan. Analyze Exhibit 4-1 in detail.
3 What is the purpose of a
   a request for verification of deposit?
   b request for verification of employment?
   c good faith estimate of settlement costs?
4 What types of information does a credit report provide?
5 What additional information (over a single-family house) is required when applying for an income property loan? Analyze Exhibit 4-5 in detail.
6 What decision-making techniques do lenders use to judge the acceptability of a mortgage application? What criteria are illegal?
7 Discuss the role of private mortgage insurance in mortgage loans. Describe how it works.
8 The following federal legislation affects the borrower-lender relationship:
   a Real Estate Settlement and Procedures Act
   b Truth-in-Lending Law
   c Equal Credit Opportunity Act
   What problem(s) is each act or law designed to correct? What problem(s) does the legislation create?
9 What is the closing statement? Describe how a closing statement works (see Exhibit 4-8).

PROBLEMS

1 Imagine that you are in the market for a home. Gather information concerning a home that is currently for sale in your area. Fill out the necessary paperwork.

2 The Wangs have a good monthly income of $2,400. The expenses for a new home are expected to be $675.49 per month. These expenses constitute what percentage of their income? If the home they have purchased is valued at $250,000, have they overstepped their limits for an affordable home by typical industry standards?

3 What would be the total claim for the PMI example if the attorney's fees amount to 1 percent of the subtotal and the MIC agrees to pay 23 percent of the total claim?

4 Rework the settlement statement for the single-family-home example if the home is purchased for $100,000 instead of $85,000.

5 How does private mortgage insurance affect conventional loans?

REFERENCES

Boykin, James H.: *Financing Real Estate,* Lexington Books, Lexington, Mass., 1979.

Farrell, Michael D.: "Notes and Comments: Valuation of Income-Producing Properties for Loan Underwriting Purposes," *Appraisal Journal,* October 1980, pp. 576–579.

Hall, Kenneth F.: *Mortgage Loan Disclosure Handbook,* Clark Boardman Co., New York, 1987.

Keenan, Patrick D.: "Private Mortgage Insurance and the Real Estate Appraiser," *Real Estate Appraiser and Analyst,* July–August 1979, pp. 13–17.

Siegelaub, Harold: "The Mortgage Application," *The Journal of Property Management,* March/April 1976, pp. 57–62.

Underwriting Guidelines: Home Mortgages, Federal Loan Mortgage Corporation, Washington, D.C., 1979.

Vidger, Leonard P.: *Borrowing and Lending on Residential Property,* Lexington Books, Lexington, Mass., 1981.

PROPERTY ANALYSIS:
PART 1

Here and in Chapter 6 we focus on the analysis of the value of the real property securing the mortgage debt. The tools used in this analysis are fundamentally the same for borrower and lender and for all types of real estate—both residential and income-producing—although the emphasis changes, depending on the nature of the property and the equity investor or lender positions.

    To gain a perspective on mortgage collateral analysis, we first look at the objectives of the two participants: the equity investor (borrower) and the mortgage lender. Their objectives are similar in that both risk investment capital with the expectation of a return on and a return of their investments. But the level of risk that each assumes is different, so each participant looks at investments from a somewhat different perspective.

The mortgage lender is concerned primarily with the safety of the principal of the loan and the expectation that the payments will be made, either from income generated by the property or the borrower's income. If the lender is assured of these factors, the equity investor's concerns, such as profit potential from rents, aesthetic characteristics, intangible benefits of the property, and future property appreciation, will also be of importance since they may affect the riskiness of the lender's position.

OWNER-OCCUPIED VERSUS INCOME PROPERTY ANALYSIS

As noted, the analysis of mortgage collateral depends on the nature of the property, whether it is an owner-occupied residence or a nonowner-occupied income-generating property. In *both* owner-occupied residential and income property financing, a major concern of both lender and borrower is that the value of the real estate is sufficiently high to cover the outstanding debt in the event of foreclosure. The underwriting differs, however, according to the source of funds for repayment. Lenders (and equity investors, for that matter) generally expect an investment property to generate sufficient income to cover its expenses and debt and to provide a return to the equity investor. Although the borrower's credit history and financial position are of concern to the lender, the property's value and income are important to both borrower and lender. Since owner-occupied residences do not generate income and were not designed for that purpose, the lender looks to the borrower's ability and willingness to repay the loan. The value of the property, however, is just as important to the lender.

THE VALUATION PROCESS

The process for estimating value is generally called the appraisal process. The valuation of mortgage loan collateral is of primary importance to the lender because the property's current value is a determinant of the maximum amount of money that can be prudently lent on the property to maintain the desired level of security in case of default. Similarly, the valuation of the property is important to the borrower-investor because it determines the maximum price one should pay for the property based on the collective thinking of buyers in the marketplace. This process of valuation is equally important for owner-occupied residential and income property financing.

The appraiser searches for the *market value,* which is traditionally defined as the highest price in terms of money that a property will bring in a competitive and open market under all conditions requisite to a fair sale, assuming the buyer and seller are each acting prudently and knowledgeably and the price is not affected by undue stimulus. Alternatively, market value at a certain time is the most probable selling price which could be realized at that time.

An appraisal, in strict terms, is the appraiser's opinion of value. This opinion is based on generally accepted methods and techniques that have been applied to factual material from the market and the appraised property itself. To arrive at a value for a particular property, an appraiser is guided by the (1) highest and best use, (2) principle of anticipation, (3) principle of substitution, (4) principle of change, (5) principle of contribution, and (6) principle of diminishing returns.

The *highest and best use* of a property is the use that will bring the owner the highest economic benefit over the long run. Determining highest and best use is central to estimating market value because the use of a property for other than the current (or proposed) use may yield higher benefits to both the investor and the lender regarding greater investment returns and/or less risk than originally anticipated.

The *principle of anticipation* states that a property's market value is based on the investor's expectation about the future benefits the property will provide and the present value of those benefits.

The *principle of substitution* states that a prudent buyer will pay no more for a property than the cost of a substitute property that will provide equivalent usefulness.

The *principle of change* states that the real estate market is dynamic rather than static; socioeconomic forces are constantly changing, causing constant changes in value. Thus, market value today may not be the same as market value yesterday or tomorrow.

The *principle of contribution* states that the value of a given feature of a property is worth only as much as the amount of money it contributes to the value of the property as a whole. For example, improvements to property may add more, less, or as much value to the property as they cost, depending on what the market is willing to pay for the added features.

The *principle of diminishing returns* states that with each additional unit of improvement, the marginal utility of each unit declines until the point at which any additional units cost more than the additional value they add to the property.

The estimate of value is the final step in solving the appraisal problem. Figure 5-1 outlines the appraisal process. The appraiser must (1) define the appraisal problem; (2) plan the appraisal; (3) collect relevant data on the area, subject property, construction costs, sales data, and income data; (4) compute the three approaches to value; and (5) reconcile the three approaches to arrive at one final estimate of value. We concentrate our discussion on the three appraisal methods.

COST APPROACH
INCOME APPROACH

Market Comparison Approach

The market comparison approach, also called the market data or direct sales comparison approach, is based on the principle of substitution. In other words, a property's value is no more than what the market will pay for an equally desirable substitute. Very simply, the appraiser notes the sales prices of recently sold, similar properties (comparables) and bases the value of the subject property on these

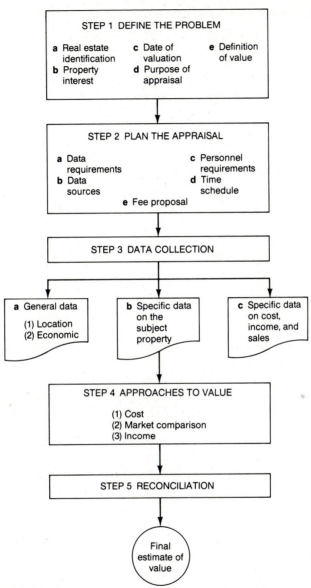

FIGURE 5-1 The appraisal process. *(Source: William M. Shenkel,* Modern Real Estate Appraisal, *McGraw-Hill Book Company, New York, p. 116. Reprinted with permission.)*

prices. However, since no two parcels of real estate are identical, the appraiser often must make adjustments to the comparable's sales price to account for differences between the comparable property and the subject property. For example, if the comparable has a feature that is better than that in or nonexistent in the subject, its sales price will be adjusted downward to reflect the price it would have sold for if it were more like the subject. Conversely, if the comparable has a feature that is inferior to that of the subject, its sales price will be adjusted upward.

The amount of the adjustment is determined by the principle of contribution—that is, the amount which the presence of (or absence of) the feature contributes to value. The comparable's adjusted sales price (price after all differences between the comparable and subject have been noted and adjusted for) is the indicated value of the subject property.

The appraiser attempts to select the comparables most similar to the subject in size, quality, location, financing, bargaining strength of the parties, and other significant details. The fewer differences that must be adjusted for, the better an indicator of value the comparable is likely to be.

The reliability of this approach as an accurate indicator of value depends on the availability of data on several recent sales of similar properties. One or two comparable sales are generally not good indications of value since the sales price of each sale was arrived at through negotiations between one buyer and one seller. Their actions under their unique set of circumstances may not reflect or predict accurately the actions of the market in general. The more comparable, the better the value estimate.

The following process is used in applying the market comparison approach:

1 Research the market to find recently sold, similar properties and determine accurate data from these properties.

2 Qualify the comparables by rejecting those that may not be good value indicators for the subject.

3 Compare the comparables and the subject regarding such factors as physical characteristics, location, time of sale, conditions of sale, and financing.

4 Where the subject and the comparable differ, adjust the comparable's selling price according to the market reaction to those differences.

5 From the analysis, determine a final value estimate for the subject property.

Market Comparison Approach Example To illustrate the comparison approach to value, suppose an investor is considering buying an apartment building. Table 5-1 is the information collected on six comparable properties and shows the unadjusted prices per apartment and per room. Notice that the sales price indicates a range from $16,000 to $18,929 per apartment, and the sales price per room ranges between $4,000 and $4,732. Also given is the gross income multiplier (more on this later), which ranges between 5.26 and 6.0.

Table 5-2 is the adjustment grid for the comparables. To make property adjustments, think of the property being appraised as 100 percent; comparable properties thus observed to be inferior to the subject property (i.e., 90 percent of the subject property, for example) require a positive (upward) adjustment to get to the 100 percent level. Properties perceived superior to the subject property (i.e., 110 percent of the subject property) require a negative (downward) adjustment. The idea is that if the comparable has a particular attribute which is better

TABLE 5-1 COMPARABLE APARTMENT SALES

Compa-rable	Date of sale (months ago)	Sale price	Number of apart-ments	Number of vacant apart-ments	Price per apart-ment	Number of rooms	Price per room	Effective gross income	Gross income multi-plier	Average rent per unit per month	Operat-ing expenses	Net operat-ing income
1	2	$275,000	16	1	$17,188	64	4,297	$50,000	5.50	$278	$21,300	$28,700
2	6	288,000	18	2	16,000	67	4,299	49,500	5.82	258	18,800	30,700
3	8	450,000	24	1	18,750	100	4,500	76,500	5.88	277	32,800	45,700
4	1	265,000	14	0	18,929	56	4,732	50,400	5.26	300	23,200	27,200
5	5	525,000	30	2	17,500	120	4,375	87,500	6.00	260	34,100	53,400
6	6	340,000	20	2	17,000	85	4,000	58,200	5.84	270	21,650	36,550

TABLE 5-2   ADJUSTMENT GRID: APARTMENT BUILDING EXAMPLE

	Comparable Sale					
Factor	1	2	3	4	5	6
Sale price	$275,000	$288,000	$450,000	$265,000	$525,000	$340,000
Number of rooms	64	67	100	56	120	85
Price per room	$ 4,297	4,299	4,500	4,732	4,375	4,000
Time adjustment	0	+5% (+$215)	+5% (+$225)	0	+5% (+$219)	+5% (+$200)
Condition of building	+5% (+$215)	0	+5% (+$225)	−15% (−$710)	0	0
Location	0	0	−10% (−$450)	+10% (+$473)	−5% (−$219)	+5% (+$200)
Net adjustment	+$215 $4,512	+$215 $4,514	0 $4,500	−$237 $4,495	0 $4,375	$400 $4,400
Indicated value of subject property (105 rooms)	$473,760	$473,970	$472,500	$471,975	$459,375	$462,000

than that same attribute in the subject, we assume that the comparable's superiority would be reflected in its sales price; it sold for the indicated price because of the attribute, so logically the subject should sell for less, all else being equal. So the basic question we are attempting to answer is, What would the comparable have sold for, given that it has the same attributes as the subject? This adjusted price, then, is the price the appraiser estimates the subject would bring, or the indicated value of the subject.

In this example, we adjusted only for time, location, and condition of the building. The adjustments are based on the price per room. Notice that sale 1 is not adjusted for time or location but is adjusted upward by 5 percent for building condition. Obviously, the appraiser feels that the building condition on comparable 1 is 5 percent inferior to that of the subject. Sales 2, 3, 5, and 6 are adjusted upward by 5 percent for time. Sales 3 and 5 are adjusted downward for location, indicating that they have a superior location relative to the subject. Remember that positive adjustments are made if the comparable is inferior to the subject; negative adjustments are made if the comparable is superior. The net result is a sales price per room that ranges from $4,375 for comparable 5 to $4,514 for comparable 2.

The subject property contains 105 rooms. Multiplying the number of rooms by the estimated value per room gives a total value, as shown in the last line of Table 5-2, between $459,375 and $473,970. The final value estimate depends on the appraiser's judgment about the reliability of each comparable.

Limitations of Comparison Approach   As stated earlier, the strength of this approach is the availability of data on similar properties that have sold recently; therein also lies this approach's greatest weakness.

Some types of property rarely are sold, such as churches, schools, and special types of industrial property; all are difficult to appraise accurately by the market comparison approach because of a lack of close comparables. In addition, the subjective nature of the appraiser's adjustments leaves a potential for bias in the value estimation, based on that appraiser's perceptions, knowledge, and experience.

The market approach is based on historical information and on expectations for the future. Therefore, rapid, extreme changes in market conditions since the comparables were sold could render the conditions useless as indicators of value. Finally, one-of-a-kind properties, for which no close substitutes are available, are hard to appraise by this method.

Generally, the market comparison approach is the best indicator of value for single-family residences. It can provide accurate value estimates for other types of property depending on the relative strength of the data used in the appraisal.

Cost Approach

The cost approach also relies on the principle of substitution in that no one will pay more for a property than the cost of building a property of equal utility or usefulness.

The cost approach is best used in situations where there is a lack of data for the market comparison and income approaches. To implement the cost approach accurately and effectively, the appraiser must be able to determine *precisely* construction costs and depreciation amounts, as illustrated later in this discussion. For these reasons, the cost approach is the one most used to appraise churches, special-use industrial and commercial properties, public buildings, and other types of property where market turnover is low and the building itself is not designed for generating income.

The cost approach is also very useful for deciding whether to build a new structure. The values derived by the market and cost approaches are compared. If the value from the market comparison approach exceeds the value from the cost approach, the finished property will be worth more than it costs to build and therefore should be built. Conversely, if the value from the market approach is less than the value from the cost approach, the complete project will not be worth its cost and therefore should be rejected. (When making this kind of comparison, note that both value conclusions are assumed to be well-supported.)

The cost approach is fundamentally a five-step process:

1 Estimate the cost (new) to reproduce or replace the structure and other improvements to the land, not including the land value.
2 Estimate the loss in property value (depreciation) that has been caused by

    a physical deterioration
    b functional deficiencies
    c economic obsolescence
3 Deduct total depreciation from the estimated cost new, arriving at a depreciated value for the building and other improvements.
4 Estimate the value of the land as if it were vacant, typically using the market comparison approach.
5 Add the land value to the depreciated value of the improvements to arrive at a total value estimate for the property.

Each step is now discussed in detail.

    Estimating Cost of Improvements   To estimate the cost of improvements, two strategies can be employed; reproduction cost or replacement cost. *Reproduction cost* is the cost of producing an exact replica of the property being appraised, using the same building materials and construction techniques. *Replacement cost* is the cost of producing a building of similar utility or usefulness as the subject property, applying currently used materials and building techniques.

    Reproduction cost is difficult to apply with older buildings, particularly those that are functionally obsolete or have such ornate features as carved woodwork and leaded glass windows. A functionally obsolete building would not be built today, and ornate features, although desirable, are not commonly installed because of their prohibitively high cost, which often exceeds the value they add to the property.

    Replacement cost also involves implementation difficulties due to the necessity of determining the type of structure that will provide the same utility as the subject without being identical. Since a new building would be built in a functionally efficient design, the deduction for functional obsolescence is inappropriate when using replacement cost. In the majority of situations, however, reproduction cost is the method to use, according to currently accepted appraisal standards.

    There are three methods for estimating reproduction cost: *quantity survey, unit-in-place,* and *aggregate cost per unit*. The *quantity survey* technique is perhaps the most difficult and expensive to apply because skill in cost estimating is required and time and expense are involved. Thus the method is generally used only by contractors and experienced cost estimators. The cost is estimated by determining the amounts and costs of all materials and labor required to complete the structure. Such detail in estimating reproduction cost is rarely necessary for typical appraisals.

    The *unit-in-place* method is easier to apply than the quantity survey. The appraiser estimates the cost (installed) of each major component of the structure. Accurate unit-in-place cost data are available on such components as foundation, wiring, plumbing, heating and cooling systems, floor, partition walls, and roofs. The unit-in-place method is often used when an accurate and detailed cost estimate is required.

The *aggregate cost per unit* method is based on per square foot or per cubic foot costs. Since many properties are constructed with similar materials, techniques, and design features, the aggregate costs per square or cubic foot are also similar, thus providing an easy yet usually sufficiently accurate means of estimating cost in most situations. Unit-cost estimating manuals such as the Boeckh *Building Valuation Manual* and the *Marshall Valuation Service* give appraisers accurate, up-to-date building costs for a great variety of structures in all areas of the country. Because the method is easily applied, it is also easily explained and understood by appraisers and their clients.

Estimating Loss in Value (Depreciation)   The first step in the cost approach is to estimate the cost (new) of replacement. Since the structure most likely is not new, depreciation must be deducted for wear and tear and functional and economic obsolescence that have occurred so that the reproduction cost of the improvements accurately reflects their value in their current situation and state of repair.

One way to estimate loss in value is the *straight-line method,* where overall loss in value is based on the property's age and remaining economic life. There are various ways to apply this method, but in general it is difficult to apply because of the subjective judgments the appraiser must make regarding the effective (not actual) age of the property, depending on the property's level of upkeep and modernization and its remaining economic life. Because of these very subjective judgments and the simplistic nature of the straight-line method, it often does not reflect the actual market situation or the myriad of different factors that can affect depreciation of a particular property.

More commonly used is the *breakdown method.* The factors causing a property loss in value are broken down into three basic forms of depreciation: physical, functional, and economic. *Physical deterioration* is caused by wear and tear on the property as a result of day-to-day usage, aging, and damage from the elements or other causes. *Functional obsolescence* is a loss in the property's value, usefulness, or desirability caused by poor or obsolete design, structure, or materials. *Economic obsolescence* is a loss in value caused by adverse factors external to the property itself and over which the property owner has no direct control. Table 5-3 lists the forms of depreciation.

There can be *curable* or *incurable* forms of physical deterioration and functional obsolescence. Although technically any physical or functional defect can be cured if enough money is expended, the distinction between curable and incurable forms is whether it is economically feasible to cure the defect. A basic question to be asked is, Is it cheaper to expend the funds to cure the defect or to suffer the loss in value to the property if we do not cure it? If it is less costly to fix the defect, the cost to cure it will be the amount to deduct. If it is less expensive to live with the defect, then the resulting dollar loss in value (as seen by the market) is the amount to deduct.

In contrast, *economic obsolescence* is generally considered *incurable.* Since the obsolescence is caused by external adverse influences, one assumes that

TABLE 5-3   FORMS OF DEPRECIATION: COST APPROACH

Physical deterioration	Functional obsolescence	Economic obsolescence
Peeling paint	Old-style plumbing fixtures	Encroachment of
Worn carpeting or other floor	Outdated decorating	incompatible land uses
coverings	Outmoded or inadequate	Noise, dust, obnoxious
Leaky roof or deteriorated	heating-cooling, wiring, or	odors
roofing	plumbing systems	Poor access to property
Structural wear and tear	Awkward floor plan	
Wear and tear on heating/	Obsolete architecture	
cooling, electrical, or	Rooms of inadequate size	
plumbing systems	Inadequate storage or closet	
	space	

owners cannot change surrounding properties they do not own and have no control over.

Depreciated Value of Improvements   The third step in the cost approach is to deduct the total amount of depreciation from the reproduction cost of the improvements new.

Land Value Estimation   The fourth step in the cost approach is to estimate the value of the land. To estimate land value, the market comparison approach is typically used. Although simple in concept, it becomes difficult to apply in areas that are completely "built up" because there is no vacant land; hence there are no vacant land sales with which to compare the subject land. In this case, the appraiser must attempt to find vacant land comparables, often in newer, developing areas with similar market appeal to use as an indicator of value. The appraiser must then adjust if necessary for the subject land's difference in appeal.

Value Estimation by Cost Approach   The final step in the cost approach is to add the land value to the depreciated value of the improvements, to arrive at a total value estimate.

Cost Approach Example   To illustrate the application of the cost approach, consider the earlier apartment building example. The reproduction cost is estimated with the unit comparison (per square foot) method. The unit method is also used to calculate the depreciation. The property is an apartment building with 105 rooms in 24 units, with a total of 27,000 square feet. Table 5-4 summarizes the cost approach for the apartment building.

The subject property has a 4-acre lot size. Recent sales figures on three comparable lot sizes were obtained and indicated a value of $18,750 per acre. Thus, the estimated land value is $75,000.

The depreciated value of the site improvements, such as utilities (on-site

TABLE 5-4 COST APPROACH: APARTMENT BUILDING EXAMPLE

Property component	Reproduction cost	Percent of depreciation	Depreciated value	Market value
Land value: 4 acres at $18,750 per acre, or 24 apartment units at $3,125 per unit				$75,000
Site improvements:				
Utilities	6,500	5	$6,175	
Paving	12,000	20	9,600	
Walkways	2,000	15	1,700	
Landscaping	3,000	0	3,000	
Outside lighting	1,000	15	850	
	24,500			$21,325
Buildings:				
Apartments (27,000 sq ft at $21)	$567,000	30	$396,900	$396,900
Indicated value from cost approach				493,225
Total estimated value (rounded)				$493,000

sewer, water main and storm sewers, paving, walkways, landscaping, outside lighting), was estimated separately (Table 5-4) as $21,325.

The depreciated value of the apartments is estimated as $396,000. Adding the site value to the value of the site improvements and the apartments gives a total estimated value of (rounded) $493,000 using the cost approach.

Limitations of Cost Approach Ideally, the cost approach should be an accurate, reliable indicator of value if accurate cost figures are used, land value is well-supported, and depreciation charges are made properly. In practice, however, cost estimates can be difficult to measure accurately, land value may be difficult to estimate, and depreciation estimates are highly subjective. For these reasons, reliance on the cost approach should be limited to cases where the property is relatively new and does not suffer significantly from functional or economic obsolescence. In these cases, construction costs for a newer structure generally should be easier to estimate; comparables for determination of land value are often easier to find, and depreciation deductions will be minimized so that their accuracy is not as great a factor.

Income Approach

The income approach is based on the principle of anticipation; that is, the value of a property is the present worth of benefits (income) the property is expected to provide in the future to its owner.

Operationally, the basic income approach equation is

$$V = \frac{I}{R} \qquad (5\text{-}1)$$

where V = value
I = expected net operating income
R = overall capitalization rate

Value can be determined if we know the expected income for the subject property and the appropriate capitalization rate. We first discuss how the income is forecast and then cover how to determine the appropriate capitalization rate.

Since the cash receipts from an income-producing property usually must cover the repayment of debt and a return on the owner's equity, it is necessary to forecast, as accurately as possible given available information, the future net returns of the property for the expected period that the capital (mortgage or equity funds) is expected to be invested ("tied up") in the property.

These future net returns take the forms of annual cash flows from operations and net proceeds from the disposition (sale) of the investment at some future date. In this chapter we consider only the before-tax returns; Chapter 6 covers taxes and their effect on investment returns.

Income from Operations Before-tax cash flow (BTCF) is the annual amount of money the investment yields after all the expenses of operation and the payments on the debt have been paid. Table 5-5 illustrates the determination of BTCF; here we discuss how the amount of each component is determined and each component's impact on BTCF.

Potential gross income (PGI) is the amount of rent that would be generated if the property were rented at full occupancy for each year. PGI is calculated by multiplying the expected rent per unit times the number of units. Ideally, the "expected rent" estimate should be based on fair market comparisons with prices on similar rented properties in the area. However, care should be taken if the property is locked into long-term leases, as is common with commercial and industrial

TABLE 5-5 DETERMINATION OF BEFORE-TAX CASH
FLOW FROM OPERATION

Potential gross income (PGI)
− vacancy and bad debt allowance (VBD)
+ miscellaneous income (MI)
effective gross income (EGI)
− operating expenses (OE)
net operating income (NOI)
− debt service (DS)
before-tax cash flow (BTCF) from operation

space, because the expected rent projections are made according to the lease provisions. Thus, a property leased at below-market rates for a very long remaining period of time is evaluated on the below-market rent, resulting in a market value and loan value substantially less than comparable properties because of the below-market income the property will generate.

Over the long run, it is doubtful whether any investment will be occupied to capacity with tenants who always pay their rent. For this reason, a prudent investor or lender should always make an allowance for loss of income through *vacancies and bad debts* (VBD). The amount of this allowance is usually expressed as a percentage of PGI. Determination of the percentage allowance of VBD is extracted, like the rents, from data on other similar properties in the marketplace.

Often an investment provides income other than rent from the use of space. Coin-operated vending machines, laundry facilities, parking spaces, and optional services to tenants fall into this category of *miscellaneous income* (MI).

Effective gross income (EGI) is the total amount of money the property can reasonably be expected to generate annually. It is calculated by deducting allowances for VBDs from PGI and adding MI. The importance of accurately measuring EGI is the income the investment is expected to take in; it is the entire right-hand (revenue) side of the property's income statement, and out of it must be paid all expenses of operation, debt repayment, and cash flow, if any, to the investor. Relatively small percentage errors made in estimating EGI can greatly affect BTFC and return-on investment computations.

Operating expenses (OE) are those cost items that are expended to generate rent from the property. Examples of common operating expenses are real estate taxes, property insurance, utilities, management fees, advertising, supplies, workers' salaries, and repairs and maintenance.

Certain additional types of expenses, although possibly deductible from the federal income tax, are not necessary for generating rent from the property. Expenses in this category are building depreciation and personal business expenditures.

Capital expenditures constitute a cash flow to the owner. Generally, a capital expenditure is a significant improvement in the property and it has a useful life of more than 1 year. In many ways it is similar to a repair or maintenance item, except that it is generally a relatively large expenditure with a relatively long life. Examples of capital expenditures are room additions, building expansions, and construction of a new swimming pool. These items are *not* deductible as operating expenses, although their cost can be recovered other ways, as explained in Chapter 6. Occasionally the distinction between an item as a maintenance expense or capital improvement is not at all clear-cut.

One common failure of investors and lenders alike is to accept operating expenses submitted to them as realistic projections for the future without so much as a perfunctory investigation or analysis. Statements owners or their agents submit are generally historical, actual-cost data. The lender and the equity investor must make their own projections from the best available market data regarding the amounts of taxes, insurance, utilities, and other expenses that will likely be incurred in the future. As with the EGI computation, relatively small percentage errors in operating expense forecasts will have a much larger percentage effect on BTCF and return-on-investment computations.

Net operating income (NOI) is the amount of money left after all operation expenses have been paid. It is obtained by subtracting operating expenses from effective gross income and is one of the components used in investment analysis. It can also be viewed as the amount of money available for debt service and cash flow to the owner.

Debt service (DS) is the annual amount of money needed to "service the debt" on the investment. It is the total of all principal and interest payments for the year based on the proposed mortgage loan for the investment. In a level monthly payment loan, it is the amount of the monthly payments multiplied by 12.

Before-tax cash flow is the amount of income to the investor after all expenses and debt payments for the year have been paid out of the rent collected; it is the owner's "profit" for the year, before tax consequences are considered. It is calculated by deducting debt service from net operating income. The following example is a complete computation of BTCF.

Operating Income Computation: Apartment Building Example You have the following information about a 24-unit apartment investment:

Rents. Market rents are $280 per month for each apartment, and at these rents, vacancy and credit losses are 5 percent of PGI.

Miscellaneous income. $1,000 per year from coin-operated laundry facilities.

Operating expenses. These are estimated for the coming year as

Insurance	$ 2,250
Management fees	3,880
Real estates taxes	10,125
Utilities	6,500
Repairs and maintenance	6,345
Total	$29,100

Debt service. The proposed loan is for $350,000. It will be amortized over 25 years at 12 percent interest, with monthly payments of $3,686.20, or $44,235 per year.

Table 5-6 shows our computation of projected BTCF for year 1 of operation.

Income from Sale Another benefit of real estate ownership is the proceeds received when the property is sold at some future date. These sale proceeds are called the equity reversion. Here we discuss the before-tax equity reversion (BTER); in Chapter 6 we add the tax impact on the sale, to arrive at the after-tax equity reversion (ATER).

The equity reversion is composed of the investor's original capital investment

TABLE 5-6   INCOME FROM OPERATION: APARTMENT
BUILDING EXAMPLE

Potential gross income (PGI)*	$80,640
− vacancy and bad debt (VBD)†	−4,032
+ miscellaneous income	+1,000
effective gross income	$77,608
− operating expenses (OE)	−29,100
net operating income (NOI)	$48,508
− debt service (DS)	−44,235
BTCF	$ 4,273

*Rent of $280 per month for each apartment; total of 24 apartments.
†5% of potential gross income.

(down payment), principal reduction on the mortgage over the period of time the property was owned (holding period), and appreciation (depreciation) in value over the holding period. From the lender's perspective, the potential equity reversion is very important because the lender wants to ascertain that the loan-to-value (LTV) ratio over the life of the mortgage is not expected to increase; that is, the property value will not decline or at least will not decline at a faster rate than the principal balance on the loan, so the security of the loan will not be impaired.

The borrower is interested in the equity reversion because it has been a significant portion of the return on many real estate investments. Thus, an accurate projection of the equity reversion is vital to an accurate projection of the return on the investment. Table 5-7 illustrates the computation of income from sale.

The first step in computing BTER is to make an assumption of the expected holding period and to estimate the price the property will be expected to sell for at that time. The length of the holding period may vary, depending on the investor's objectives with regard to the property, tax status, and many other variables. Generally, however, most investors hold property for 5 to 10 years, as evidenced by the average length of time mortgages remain outstanding. It is customary then for projections to be made over this length of time.

Expected selling price (ESP) at the end of the assumed holding period is based on the best-guess expectation of the future value changes over the holding period.

TABLE 5-7   MEASUREMENT OF CASH FLOW
FROM SALE

Expected selling price (ESP)
− selling expenses (SE)
net sale proceeds (NSP)
− unpaid mortgage (UM)
Before-tax equity reversion (BTER)

These value changes are generally expressed as an annual percentage change in value over the holding period. The assumptions one makes about ESP are most important, and since the equity reversion is often the largest portion of the cash benefits received from the investment, it is the major factor in determining the investor's return on investment. Thus, crude, ill-informed judgments about the ESP can have a disastrous effect.

Next, *selling expenses (SE)* must be deducted from ESP. Selling expenses are such items as brokerage commissions, attorney fees, and transfer costs that one normally incurs in disposing of a property. Selling expenses are estimated based on actual costs for the area and are sometimes expressed as a percentage of the ESP, typically 5 to 8 percent.

Net sales proceeds (NSP) is the amount of cash the seller realizes on the sale before the loan balance is paid off and before any income taxes due on the sale are paid.

The *unpaid mortgage balance (UM)* is the balance on the loan remaining unpaid at the assumed date of sale. The computation of the amount outstanding on a mortgage was discussed in Chapter 2.

Before-tax equity reversion is the amount of money the investor has in hand after paying all costs of sale and the loan balance but before paying income taxes due as a result of the sale.

Income from Sale: Apartment Building Example To illustrate the BTER computation, let us return to the example used in the operation analysis. We must make assumptions about the length of the holding period, the change in value over the holding period, and the selling expenses.

Holding period. We assume the property is held for a 5-year period.

Change in value. Based on our analysis of the market, we assume the property increases in value to $600,000.

Selling expenses. The costs of selling this type and size of property generally amount to about 8 percent of the expected sales price.

Table 5-8 is our computation of income from sale. We now focus on determining the second component of the income approach: the capitalization rate.

Determining the Capitalization Rate To illustrate how to determine the capitalization ("cap") rate, let us estimate the NOI for the apartment building as

TABLE 5-8 CASH FLOW FROM SALE: APARTMENT BUILDING EXAMPLE

Expected sale price (ESP)	$600,000
− selling expenses (SE)	− 48,000
net sale price (NSP)	$552,000
− unpaid mortgage (UM)	− 334,786
BTER	$217,214

$48,500 per year. There are several methods for determining the capitalization rate, including *market extraction, band of investment,* and *Ellwood.*

The *market extraction method* "extracts" the rate from market comparison. By taking our basic equation and solving for R, we have

$$V = \frac{I}{V}$$

Thus, by knowing the sales price (value) and net operating incomes of similar properties in the market that have recently sold, we can determine the overall cap rate for each similar property, which translates into a rate that the market expects for this type of investment. Table 5-9 illustrates this process. We see that the market rate is between 9.71 and 10.75 percent. By applying this to the $48,500 (rounded) NOI (see Table 5-6) for our subject property, we arrive at the following estimated range in values:

$$V = \frac{\text{NOI}}{R}$$

$$= \frac{\$48,500}{0.0971} \qquad V = \frac{\$48,500}{0.1075}$$

$$= \$499,485 \qquad\quad = \$451,163$$

It is important to stress that the properties used in the market extraction procedure must be similar to the subject property in location, age, quality, condition, market appeal, and other significant factors. Since the market expects different returns based on these risk factors, attempting to use a rate derived from dissimilar properties is entirely inappropriate.

Another frequently used method of deriving the cap rate is the *band of investment* technique. The proportion of funds each participant (borrower and lender) supplies to the proposed purchase of the investment is multiplied by the rate of return each participant expects on the personal portion; these figures are added to derive the overall rate.

TABLE 5-9 MARKET-EXTRACTED OVERALL CAP RATE: APARTMENT BUILDING EXAMPLE

Comparable*	Sale price	NOI	Overall rate
1	$275,000	$28,700	0.1044
2	288,000	30,700	0.1066
3	450,000	43,700	0.0971
4	265,000	27,200	0.1026
5	525,000	53,400	0.1017
6	340,000	36,550	0.1075

*See Table 5-1.

The participants are of course the equity investor and the lender. The lender's required rate is expressed in terms of the mortgage constant for the appropriate interest rate and loan maturity. The equity investor's return is expressed in terms of the *equity dividend rate* (EDR), which is simply the BTCF divided by the equity investment. The band of investment method can be expressed in equation form as follows:

$$R = \frac{L}{V} \, MC + \frac{E}{V} \, EDR \qquad (5\text{-}2)$$

where $\frac{L}{V}$ = loan-to-value ratio, or proportion to total value of mortgage

MC = annual mortgage constant

$\frac{E}{V}$ = equity-to-value ratio, or proportion of equity to total value of mortgage

To illustrate this method, suppose that the appraiser surveys the market and finds that for this type of investment, lenders are willing to loan 75 percent of value for 25 years with monthly payments. The investors in the market generally demand a 5 percent EDR on this type of property. The rate would be derived as follows:

Investment	% of value	×	Rate (MC, EDR)	Weighted rate
Mortgage	0.75		0.1264	0.0948
Equity	0.25		0.05	0.0125
			$R =$	0.1073
				or 10.73%

The appraiser is concerned with typical requirements of investors and lenders in the current market, not with conditions that existed when the present mortgage on the property was taken out.

Using the rate derived by this method, we can determine the value of our subject property as follows:

$$V = \frac{NOI}{R}$$

$$= \frac{\$48,500}{0.1073}$$

$$= \$452,004$$

A third commonly used technique of deriving the capitalization rate is the *Ellwood method*. This method is also based on the present value of the future returns on the investment, but it has a more inclusive approach in that *equity buildup* as a result of mortgage amortization and appreciation (or loss of equity through decreases in value) is considered. Also, an additional assumption is required to implement this technique: the expected length of the holding period for the investment. Thus, given the market's required rate of return on equity (before tax), the terms of the loan, and changes in property value over a given holding period, we can determine the overall rate and thus the property's value.

The mathematical derivation of the Ellwood method is beyond the scope of this book, but the equation for determining the overall capitalization rate is

$$R = y - \frac{L}{V}(C) \frac{+ \text{dep}}{- \text{app}} (\text{SFF}_{y\%,n})$$

where R = overall rate

y = equity yield rate (required before-tax internal rate of return on equity)

$\dfrac{L}{V}$ = loan-to-value ratio

C = mortgage coefficient = $y + P(\text{SFF}_{y\%,n}) - \text{MC}$

P = proportion of loan paid off over holding period

MC = annual mortgage constant

dep = proportionate decrease in property value expected over holding period

app = proportionate increase in property value expected over holding period

$\text{SFF}_{y\%,n}$ = sinking fund factor at rate y for holding period

n = length of holding period, years

To illustrate, recall the facts from our previous example, which had a NOI of $48,500: 75 percent financing is available at 12 percent, with monthly payments for 25 years. In addition, investors expect that the property will increase in value by 15 percent over the 5-year expected holding period. If the market requires an 18 percent return before tax, what is the appropriate cap rate?

Using the Ellwood equation and definitions,

$$R = 0.18 - \{0.75[0.18 + 0.04347(0.1398) - 0.1264]\} - 0.25(0.1398)$$
$$= 0.10029$$

The estimated value of the property, then, with a $48,500 NOI is:

$$V = \frac{\$48,500}{0.10029}$$
$$= \$483,600$$

Uses and Limitations of Income Approach   The income approach provides a reliable value estimate for those properties that generate an income stream. Since single-family residences generally do not provide income, and for the relatively few that do data are usually not available, this approach has little or no application to single-family housing; so it is generally not used to estimate value for single-family residences.

Another limitation of the income approach is the formulation of the appropriate rate to be used in a given situation. Even though the rates developed by these methods were close, the value estimate varied substantially. Thus, the value estimate is very sensitive to the rate, so the accuracy of rate analysis is an all-important factor.

Finally, the projection of the future income stream is subject to question. Many appraisers, investors, brokers, and developers have different opinions about future appreciation and changes in income from operations. Despite these drawbacks, however, the income approach is widely used and relied upon for estimating the value of income-producing real estate.

Reconciliation of the Three Approaches

At this point, the appraiser has three estimates of value: one from each of the three approaches. Ideally, in perfect market conditions with perfect knowledge, all three approaches are identical. After all, they all rely on market data for their analyses, so theoretically, they are all market comparison approaches.

In practice, however, the appraiser finds that the indicated values outline a range of dissimilar values. The appraiser must now view the entire appraisal process and ask several questions. Which approach has the strongest, most reliable data supporting it? Based on the strengths and weaknesses of each approach, which one lends itself best to the property under appraisal? Finally, and most importantly, since the purpose of an appraisal is to estimate the market value, i.e., the price buyers and sellers would likely settle on, which approach best defines the thought process of typical buyers and sellers of this type of property in the market?

Once these questions have been answered, usually one approach stands out as the "best," and the estimated value of the subject property is determined by that approach. Generally, current appraisal thought dictates the selection of one approach rather than an average of some sort. Does this mean that only one approach need be computed since only one will be used anyway? No, it is useful to do all three approaches because the approaches check and balance each other. Also, it is not possible to select the best approach until the data have been collected and analyzed.

In our apartment building example, we found values for the three approaches that must be reconciled:

Comparison approach	$459,000–$474,000
Cost approach	$493,000
Income approach	
Market extraction	$470,000
Band of investment	$452,000
Ellwood method	$483,600

In reconciling these approaches, most likely the cost approach will be least favored because of the relatively high percentage of depreciation taken. Between the market and income approaches, then, the appraiser must look at the closeness of the comparable sales, the perceived accuracy of the income data, and the cap rate determination; the market tendency to rely on one or the other of these approaches must be examined as well. Since this is a fictitious example, it is not possible to narrow our choice further because the absolute validity of the data is assumed and the investor would likely use income and market data for an apartment project of this size.

Appraisal Example: Single-Family Residence

To further illustrate the appraisal process, we will appraise a single-family home.

Will Carter and Tammy Carter recently put an earnest money down payment on their first home and entered into an agreement with the sellers, Mr. and Mrs. H. O. Mowner, to purchase. The Carters have applied to Peak County Federal Savings and Loan for a conventional mortgage loan to complete the purchase. Peak County Federal, like any lender-participant in the investment decision, wants to be certain that making this loan will be a good "investment" for them, so they want to check out the Carters' creditworthiness and determine that there is enough value in the home they are buying to secure the 30-year loan, which will be 80 percent of the value of the home.

Peak County Federal begins the loan process by ordering a credit report on the Carters and sends a memo to the staff appraiser requesting that a market value appraisal be performed on the house.

The appraiser first gathers some factual data on the subject property:

Address: 209 Boweevil, Crete, Peak County, Any State 30000
Legal description: Lot 10, Block B, Cotton Hills
Sale price: $85,000
Sale date: October 2, 1988
Real estate taxes: $1,020
Occupant: Mr. and Mrs. H. O. Mowner
Lot size: 75 feet × 130 feet
Zoning: Single-family residential
Age: 18 years

Once these data are entered onto the appraisal form (see Exhibit 5-1, a standard "form" appraisal report), the appraiser makes an appointment with the Mowners to personally inspect the home.

Neighborhood Analysis   After driving to the subject property, the appraiser first gathers information about the immediate neighborhood in which the property is located: The location is within the city, fully built-up, and developed. The property is well-located with respect to transportation access, schools, shopping centers, and employment.

RESIDENTIAL APPRAISAL REPORT

File No. _____

Census Tract _____   Map Reference _____

To be completed by Lender

Borrower	Will C. and Tammy Carter
Property Address	209 Boll Weevil

City __Crete__   County __Peak__   State __Anystate__   Zip Code __30000__

Legal Description __Lot 10, Block B, Cotton Hills__

Sale Price $ __85,000__   Date of Sale __10/2/xx__   Loan Term __30__ yrs   Property Rights Appraised [X] Fee [ ] Leasehold [ ] DeMinimis PUD

Actual Real Estate Taxes $ __1,020__   (yr) Loan charges to be paid by seller $ _____   Other sales concessions _____

Lender/Client __Peak County Federal Savings and Loan__   Address __Crete, Anystate 30000__

Occupant __H. O. Mowner__   Appraiser __Ima Student__   Instructions to Appraiser _____

NEIGHBORHOOD

Location	[X] Urban	[ ] Suburban	[ ] Rural	
Built Up	[X] Over 75%	[ ] 25% to 75%	[ ] Under 25%	
Growth Rate	[X] Fully Dev. [ ] Rapid	[ ] Steady	[ ] Slow	
Property Values	[X] Increasing	[ ] Stable	[ ] Declining	
Demand/Supply	[ ] Shortage	[X] In Balance	[ ] Over Supply	
Marketing Time	[X] Under 3 Mos.	[ ] 4–6 Mos.	[ ] Over 6 Mos.	

Present Land Use __90__% 1 Family __10__% 2-4 Family __0__% Apts. __0__% Condo __0__% Commercial __0__% Industrial __0__% Vacant __0__%

Change in Present Land Use [X] Not Likely [ ] Likely (*) [ ] Taking Place (*)

(*) From _____ To _____

Predominant Occupancy [X] Owner [ ] Tenant __0__% Vacant

Single Family Price Range $ __75,000__ to $ __90,000__   Predominant Value $ __80,000__

Single Family Age __12__ yrs to __22__ yrs   Predominant Age __15__ yrs

	Good	Avg.	Fair	Poor
Employment Stability	X			
Convenience to Employment	X			
Convenience to Shopping	X			
Convenience to Schools	X			
Adequacy of Public Transportation	X			
Recreational Facilities	X			
Adequacy of Utilities		X		
Property Compatibility	X			
Protection from Detrimental Conditions	X			
Police and Fire Protection	X			
General Appearance of Properties	X			
Appeal to Market	X			

Note: FHLMC/FNMA do not consider race or the racial composition of the neighborhood to be reliable appraisal factors.

Comments including those factors, favorable or unfavorable, affecting marketability (e.g. public parks, schools, view, noise) __One of the more desirable residential neighborhoods in the city. Sewer line serving neighborhood is troublesome and due for replacement. Homes in neighborhood are neat appearing and well-maintained, showing pride of ownership.__

SITE

Dimensions __75 x 130'__ = __9750__ Sq. Ft. or Acres   [ ] Corner Lot

Zoning classification __Single Family__   Present improvements [X] do [ ] do not conform to zoning regulations

Highest and best use: [X] Present use [ ] Other (specify) _____

	Public	Other (Describe)
Elec.	[X]	
Gas	[X]	
Water	[X]	
San.Sewer	[X]	

[X] Underground Elect. & Tel.

OFF SITE IMPROVEMENTS

Street Access: [X] Public [ ] Private
Surface __Paved__
Maintenance: [ ] Public [ ] Private
[X] Storm Sewer [X] Curb/Gutter
[X] Sidewalk [X] Street Lights

Topo __flat, slightly sloping toward street__
Size __average for neighborhood__
Shape __rectangular - average for neighborhood__
View __good - park across street__
Drainage __good__

Is the property located in a HUD Identified Special Flood Hazard Area? [X] No [ ] Yes

Comments (favorable or unfavorable including any apparent adverse easements, encroachments or other adverse conditions) __city park is located across the street.__

IMPROVEMENTS

[X] Existing [ ] Proposed [ ] Under Constr.   No. Units __1__   Type (det, duplex, semi/det, etc.) __detached__   Design (rambler, split level, etc.) __rambler__

Yrs. Age: Actual __18__ Effective __10 to 12__   No. Stories __1__

Exterior Walls __wood siding__

Roof Material __asphalt shingles__   Gutters & Downspouts [ ] None __yes__

Window (Type): __double hung__   [ ] Storm Sash [ ] Screens [X] Combination

Insulation: [ ] None [ ] Floor [X] Ceiling [ ] Roof [ ] Walls

[ ] Manufactured Housing

Foundation Walls __poured concrete perimeter__

[ ] Slab on Grade [X] Crawl Space

BSMT
__0__% Basement [ ] Outside Entrance [ ] Concrete Floor [ ] Floor Drain [ ] Sump Pump __%__ Finished   Evidence of: [ ] Dampness [ ] Termites

Finished Ceiling _____ Finished Walls _____ Finished Floor _____ [ ] Settlement

Comments __Improvements are in average condition__

ROOM LIST

Room List	Foyer	Living	Dining	Kitchen	Den	Family Rm.	Rec. Rm.	Bedrooms	No. Baths	Laundry	Other
Basement											
1st Level		1	1	1				3	1.5		
2nd Level											

Finished area above grade contains a total of __7__ rooms __3__ bedrooms __1.5__ baths. Gross Living Area __1792__ sq. ft. Bsmt Area __0__ sq. ft.

Kitchen Equipment: [ ] Refrigerator [ ] Range/Oven [X] Disposal [X] Dishwasher [X] Fan/Hood [ ] Compactor [ ] Washer [ ] Dryer [ ]

HEAT: Type __forced air__ fuel __not gas__ Cond. __good__   AIR COND: [X] Central [ ] Other _____   [X] Adequate [ ] Inadequate

INTERIOR FINISH & EQUIPMENT

Floors	[ ] Hardwood	[X] Carpet Over _____ [ ]
Walls	[ ] Drywall	[ ] Plaster
Trim/Finish	[X] Good	[ ] Average [ ] Fair [ ] Poor
Bath Floor	[X] Ceramic	[ ]
Bath Wainscot	[ ] Ceramic	[ ]

Special Features (including energy efficient items) __ceramic kitchen floor; oak trim; insulated ductwork__

ATTIC: [X] Yes [ ] No [ ] Stairway [ ] Drop-stair [ ] Scuttle [ ] Floored [ ] Heated

Finished (Describe) _____

CAR STORAGE: [ ] Garage [ ] Built-in [ ] Attached [ ] Detached [X] Car Port

No. Cars __2__   [X] Adequate [ ] Inadequate   Condition _____

PROPERTY RATING

	Good	Avg.	Fair	Poor
Quality of Construction (Materials & Finish)	X			
Condition of Improvements	X			
Room sizes and layout	X			
Closets and Storage	X			
Insulation—adequacy			X	
Plumbing—adequacy and condition		X		
Electrical—adequacy and condition		X		
Kitchen Cabinets—adequacy and condition	X			
Compatibility to Neighborhood	X			
Overall Livability	X			
Appeal and Marketability	X			

Yrs. Est. Remaining Economic Life __35__ to __45__. Explain if less than Loan Term.

FIREPLACES, PATIOS, POOL, FENCES, etc. (describe) __masonry fireplace in living room.__

COMMENTS (including functional or physical inadequacies, repairs needed, modernization, etc.) __new carpeting and bath and kitchen remodeling done within last 5 years.__

FHLMC Form 70 Rev. 7/79   ATTACH DESCRIPTIVE PHOTOGRAPHS OF SUBJECT PROPERTY AND STREET SCENE   FNMA Form 1004 Rev. 7/79

EXHIBIT 5-1   RESIDENTIAL APPRAISAL REPORT

VALUATION SECTION

Purpose of Appraisal is to estimate Market Value as defined in Certification & Statement of Limiting Conditions (FHLMC Form 439/FNMA Form 1004B). If submitted for FNMA, the appraiser must attach (1) sketch or map showing location of subject, street names, distance from nearest intersection, and any detrimental conditions and (2) exterior building sketch of improvements showing dimensions.

COST APPROACH

Measurements	No. Stories	Sq. Ft.
32 x 56	x 1	= 1792
x	x	=
x	x	=
x	x	=
x	x	=

Total Gross Living Area (List in Market Data Analysis below) 1792

Comment on functional and economic obsolescence: Functional obsolescence due to lack of wall insulation and an inefficient fireplace. Cost to cure these deficiencies, $2,000.

No economic obsolescence evident.

ESTIMATED REPRODUCTION COST – NEW – OF IMPROVEMENTS:

Dwelling 1792 Sq. Ft. @ $ 44	=	$ 78,848
Sq. Ft. @ $	=	
Extras fireplace	=	3,000
Built-in appliances	=	900
Special Energy Efficient Items	=	
Porches, Patios, etc.	=	
Garage/Car Port 500 Sq. Ft. @ $ 4	=	2,000
Site Improvements (driveway, landscaping, etc.)	=	3,000
Total Estimated Cost New	=	$ 87,748
Less Depreciation: Physical $ 10,000 Functional $ 2,000 Economic $ -0-	=	$ (12,000)
Depreciated value of improvements	=	$ 75,748
ESTIMATED LAND VALUE (If leasehold, show only leasehold value)	=	$ 10,000
INDICATED VALUE BY COST APPROACH		$ 85,748

MARKET DATA ANALYSIS

The undersigned has recited three recent sales of properties most similar and proximate to subject and has considered these in the market analysis. The description includes a dollar adjustment, reflecting market reaction to those items of significant variation between the subject and comparable properties. If a significant item in the comparable property is superior to, or more favorable than, the subject property, a minus (-) adjustment is made, thus reducing the indicated value of subject; if a significant item in the comparable is inferior to, or less favorable than, the subject property, a plus (+) adjustment is made, thus increasing the indicated value of the subject.

ITEM	Subject Property	COMPARABLE NO. 1	Adjustment	COMPARABLE NO. 2	Adjustment	COMPARABLE NO. 3	Adjustment
Address	209 Boll Weevil	215 Robert St.		172 Mary Lane		182 Broken Bucket Dr.	
Proximity to Subj.		1/2 block		2 blocks		3 blocks	
Sales Price	$ 85,000	$ 89,500		$ 82,000		$ 86,900	
Price/Living area	$ 47.43	$ 45.25		$ 45.45		$ 46.82	
Data Source	Lender	Appraiser's file		Appraiser's file		Appraiser's file	
Date of Sale and Time Adjustment	Oct. 19xx	Sept. 19xx	0	May 19xx	+1000	April 19xx	+1600
Location	Quiet Street	Similar		Busy Street	+2000	Similar	
Site/View	Average	Similar		Similar		Larger lot	-4500
Design and Appeal	Good	Similar		Similar		Similar	
Quality of Const.	Good	Similar		Similar		Similar	
Age	18 yrs.	20 yrs.		19 yrs.		17 yrs.	
Condition	Good	Similar		Similar		Good-Fair	+2000
Living Area Room Count and Total	Total 7 B-rms 3 Baths 1.5	Total 7 B-rms 3 Baths 2		Total 7 B-rms 3 Baths 1.5		Total 6 B-rms 3 Baths 2	
Gross Living Area	1792 Sq.Ft.	2000 Sq.Ft.	-4000	1804 Sq.Ft.	-0-	1856 Sq.Ft.	-800
Basement & Bsmt. Finished Rooms	None	Similar		Similar		Similar	
Functional Utility	very good	Similar		Similar		Similar	
Air Conditioning	Central	Similar		Similar		Similar	
Garage/Car Port	2-car	Similar		Similar		1-car	+600
Porches, Patio, Pools, etc.	None	Similar		Similar		Similar	
Special Energy Efficient Items	Insulated	Similar		Similar		Similar	
Other (e.g. fireplaces, kitchen equip., remodeling)	Dishwasher, Disposal, Fan and Hood	Additional Kitchen Appliances	-800	Similar		Similar	
Sales or Financing Concessions							
Net Adj. (Total)		☐Plus ☒Minus $ 4,800		☒Plus ☐Minus $ 3,000		☐Plus ☒Minus $ 1100	
Indicated Value of Subject		$ 84,700		$ 85,000		$ 85,800	

Comments on Market Data All three comparables were quite similar to subject, with comparable 2 being most similar in size and design, and comparable 1 most similar in location.

INDICATED VALUE BY MARKET DATA APPROACH $ 85,000

INDICATED VALUE BY INCOME APPROACH (If applicable) Economic Market Rent $ 530 /Mo. x Gross Rent Multiplier 163 = $ 86,390

This appraisal is made ☒ "as is" ☐ subject to the repairs, alterations, or conditions listed below ☐ completion per plans and specifications.

Comments and Conditions of Appraisal: Market data was easily obtained due to the high market activity. Depreciation was difficult to estimate due to the extensive remodeling and redecorating of the home. Rental data for this type of home was also readily available.

Final Reconciliation: In this appraisers opinion, the market data approach is probably the best indicator of value, although all three approaches had closely correlated value estimates.

Construction Warranty ☐ Yes ☒ No Name of Warranty Program _____ Warranty Coverage Expires _____

This appraisal is based upon the above requirements, the certification, contingent and limiting conditions, and Market Value definition that are stated in

☐ FHLMC Form 439 (Rev. 10/78)/FNMA Form 1004B (Rev. 10/78) filed with client 10-2-xx 19 ___ ☐ attached.

I ESTIMATE THE MARKET VALUE, AS DEFINED, OF SUBJECT PROPERTY AS OF October 10, 19 xx to be $ 85,000.

Appraiser(s) _____ Review Appraiser (If applicable) _____

☐ Did ☐ Did Not Physically Inspect Property

FHLMC Form 70 Rev. 7/79   REVERSE   FNMA Form 1004 Rev. 7/79

The city has a diversified economic base and has fared better than most cities in economic downturns. Several recreation areas are within 2 miles of the subject property, and the police and fire protection for this neighborhood are deemed adequate. Being an urban area, the neighborhood is well-served by all city (public) utilities, although the sanitary sewer main serving this neighborhood has had numerous breaks in the past few years and is expected to be replaced in about 2 years, with a subsequent assessment to the affected property owners. Nevertheless, the neighborhood has been characterized as one of the more desirable residential neighborhoods in the city. As a result, a steady demand for properties in this area has kept property values increasing, and most houses placed on the market are sold within 60 days. Most of the properties in the area are owner-occupied, single-family residences, with an occasional duplex. Homes tend to fall in the $75,000 to $90,000 range and were built between 1960 and 1970, with the majority being built around 1967 to 1968. The homes in the area are neat and well-maintained, showing pride of ownership.

The homes were built by a single contractor, and although they are generally similar in design, style, and appearance, there is enough variation to eliminate the "tract development" look. The appraiser completes the neighborhood section of the appraisal form (see Exhibit 5-1).

Site Analysis   Once on the site, the appraiser examines the lot and its improvements. Located near the middle of the block, the lot is flat and slightly sloping toward the street, and its size and rectangular shape appear about average for the neighborhood. The public street out front is paved, with curbs and gutters, sidewalks, street lights, and storm sewer. The site is served by all the city utilities, with all wiring underground. A city park is located across the street. The site portion of the appraisal form is now completed.

Improvement Analysis   The appraiser next observes the exterior of the house itself: It is a one-story rambler-style home with wood siding, gutters and downspouts, asphalt shingle roof, and mostly double-hung sash windows with combination storm windows. Although the home is one of the oldest in the neighborhood, its exterior appears in good condition, except for the roof shingles, which appear to be original and will need replacing within a year or two. The home is built on a poured concrete perimeter foundation, with crawl space and no basement. Both the attic floor and the forced-air heating ducts in the crawl space are insulated. The appraiser then measures the exterior of the home and finds it to be 32 feet by 56 feet. The improvements section of the appraisal form is filled in.

The appraiser then enters the house, meets Mr. and Mrs. Mowner, and makes the inspection. He finds the house has 3 bedrooms, 2½ baths, kitchen, a separate dining room, and family and living rooms. Not including the baths, there are 7 rooms total. The kitchen has a built-in dishwasher, garbage disposal, and exhaust fan with hood. The baths and kitchen floors are ceramic tile; all other floors are covered in good-quality nearly new carpet. The furnace is natural gas, forced air, with central air-conditioning; it appears to be in good condition. The bath and kitchen have been remodeled within the past 5 years. There is oak trim throughout the house. There is a masonry fireplace in the living room, and an attached carport for two cars. Overall, the quality of construction is quite good. The floor plan is well-designed and very livable, with a good traffic pattern, plenty of closet space, and a nicely designed, efficient kitchen. The plumbing and wiring meet the minimum standards required of new homes built today, although the lack of insulation in the walls and the inefficient fireplace are throwbacks to the days when fuel was cheap and plentiful. The home's appearance blends well with the neighborhood and should have good sales appeal. The appraiser estimates that although the home is 18 years old, its effective age is between 10 to 12 years and it should have a remaining economic life of about 40 years. The appraiser now completes the remainder of the first page of the appraisal form.

When finished with the inspection, the appraiser returns to the office to complete the second page of the report.

Cost Approach To determine the value by the cost approach, the appraiser consults the *Marshall Valuation Service Handbook* and finds the reproduction cost of this type and quality of structure to be about $42 per square foot. In addition, the fireplace cost is $3,000 and the built-in appliances cost about $900 installed. The carpet cost is $2,000, and the site improvements amount to $3,000.

When viewing the house and location, the appraiser noted no detrimental neighborhood conditions that could cause a loss in value. However, there has been some physical deterioration due to the aging of components, which must be accounted for. The appraiser estimates the physical depreciation at $10,000. The appraiser also feels that the house's energy inefficiencies need to be cured, at an estimated cost of $2,000. In examining comparable lot sales, the appraiser finds the subject lot should be worth about $15,000. Using this information, the appraiser estimates a value by the cost approach and completes this portion of the appraisal form.

Market Comparison Approach In doing the market comparison approach, the appraiser finds three recent sales in the file that are similar to and within three blocks of the subject. They are all rambler-style homes with perimeter foundations and crawl spaces and are similar to the subject in most respects. More detailed information follows:

Comparable 1. 215 Robert Street. Sold for $89,500 last month. 2,000 square feet, 7 rooms, 3 bedrooms, 2 baths, built-in oven and range and trash compactor in addition to dishwasher, disposal, and range hood and fan. Similar to subject in other respects. The appraiser feels the square footage difference requires a $4,000 adjustment and the additional kitchen appliances are worth $800 to the value differential.

Comparable 2. 172 Mary Lane. Sold for $82,000 last May. 1,804 square feet, 7 rooms, 3 bedrooms, 1½ baths. Very similar to subject, except it is located at the edge of the neighborhood on a busy street. The appraiser feels that the comparable would have sold for $1,000 more today than it did 4 months ago. The location is such that the home would have sold for $2,000 more if it were on a quieter, less-traveled street. The appraiser also feels the difference in square footage between comparable 2 and the subject will be viewed as insignificant in the marketplace.

Comparable 3. 182 Broken Bucket Drive. Sold for $86,900 last April. 1,856 square feet, 6 rooms, 3 bedrooms, 2 baths, one-car carport. Lot is about 1½ times the size of subject lot. Exterior of house is run down, needs painting and general upkeep. The appraiser makes the following adjustments in comparable 3: time of sale, $1,600; lot size, $4,500; condition, $2,000; additional square footage and bath, $800; one-car carport, $600.

The appraiser takes this information, notes significant differences between each comparable, and makes appropriate adjustments for them on the appraisal form. The guiding principle the appraiser uses in making these adjustments is the principle of contribution. That is, the amount is based on the value that each feature or item of difference contributes to the value, as evidenced in the market. (This value is not necessarily the same as the cost of the item.)

Income Approach   To complete the income approach, the appraiser first looks in the file for similar homes that have been sold and that also have been rented. Three are found, from which a gross rent multiplier is extracted:

Comparable	Sale price	Monthly rent	Multiplier
1	$88,000	$550	160
2	83,200	500	166
3	83,000	510	163

Second, the appraiser must estimate the market rent for the subject property. It is estimated that the subject will rent for $530 per month. The appraiser computes the indicated value by this approach.

Reconciliation   In reconciling the three approaches, the appraiser must weigh the comparative validity of each method, based on the accuracy of the available data. In this instance, the market data approach is probably the best indicator of value because of the close similarity of the comparables to the subject. The cost approach is likely the second best indicator of value because of the subjective nature of depreciation. The income approach, although used in single-family appraisals to the extent illustrated here, is generally the least valid of the three, most often because of the poor availability and reliability of data for single-family house rentals.

Market Value Estimate   Although in this instance, the three approaches are not equally valid, their values correlate well with one another, as evidenced by the range of values. After weighing all the evidence, the appraiser determines a final market value estimate for the property and submits the completed appraisal to the loan committee.

The final value estimate our appraiser arrives at is $85,000. Since there is adequate security for the lender because the credit reports were favorable, Peak Federal now notifies the Carters that it will be happy to make the loan.

RULES OF THUMB AND RATIO ANALYSIS

Investors and mortgage lenders also employ simple rules of thumb and ratio analysis to help them in their decision to invest capital. The following discussion includes the most commonly used ratios. Because many of them are based on income generation, they are primarily useful for analyzing income-producing properties.

Rules of Thumb

One common rule of thumb is the *overall capitalization rate,* which was analyzed under valuation methods as

$$R = \frac{\text{NOI}}{V}$$

Its reciprocal, the *net income multiplier* (NIM), is defined as

$$\text{NIM} = \frac{V}{\text{NOI}}$$

For example, suppose an income property is offered on the market for $100,000. Projected NOI is $10,000. As a lender, you are concerned that the market price is fair because your position on the maximum amount to loan and the security of your institution's position will be based to a great extent on the property's market value. As an investor-borrower, you are always concerned that you are paying no more than a fair market price for the property. *Given that reliable capitalization rates for this type of property are available in the market,* you can compare the rate derived from the asking price with that of the market, as the following calculations illustrate:

$$
\begin{aligned}
R &= \frac{\text{NOI}}{V} \\
&= \frac{\$10,000}{\$100,000} \\
&= 10\%
\end{aligned}
$$

Suppose that after comparing other properties of this type you decide that the market R is 10.4 percent. Is this property overpriced? Substituting 10.4 percent for the rate into the equation and solving for value,

$$V = \frac{\$10,000}{0.104}$$

$$= \$96,154$$

Hence, it is overpriced.

Conversely, NIM could be used as a tool to determine the time necessary to cover the investment cost, if all the NOI were allocated to recovery.

$$\text{NIM} = \frac{V}{\text{NOI}}$$

$$= \frac{\$100,000}{\$10,000}$$

$$= 10$$

If, from our overall rate example, the market value was $96,200, the market payback period would be

$$\text{NIM} = \frac{\$96,200}{\$10,000}$$

$$= 9.62 \text{ years}$$

Gross Income Multiplier   Similar to the NIM is the *gross income multiplier (GIM)*, which has been very widely used. If an income approach is used at all for a single-family residence, most often it is the GIM, which is defined as

$$\text{GIM} = \frac{V}{\text{gross income, potential or effective}}$$

$$V = \text{GIM (gross income)}$$

In practice, the GIM is usually expressed this way for income-producing properties, using annual growth income in the calculation. For single-family residences, however, the gross *monthly* rent is generally used, and the multiplier is expressed as the *gross rent multiplier (GRM)* as follows:

$$\text{GRM} = \frac{V}{\text{monthly rent}} \quad \text{and} \quad V = \text{GRM (monthly rent)}$$

Multipliers are derived from sales in the market and then used with the rent to determine value.

For instance, suppose an apartment building has an effective gross income of $77,600 and buildings of this type are selling for 5.25 times their gross (i.e., the GIM is 5.25). What is the value of the property?

$$V = \text{GIM (gross income)}$$
$$= 5.25(\$77,600)$$
$$= \$407,400$$

Or suppose a single-family residence is expected to be able to rent for $400 per month and that the market GRM for homes of this type is 130. What is the property's value?

$$V = \text{GRM (monthly rent)}$$
$$= 130(\$400)$$
$$= \$52,000$$

Equity Dividend Rate   The *equity dividend rate*, or "cash-on-cash" rate, is another commonly used rule of thumb, especially by equity investors. It measures the ratio of the amount of cash received before taxes from the investment (BTCF) to the amount of equity cash invested, hence the name cash-on-cash. Operationally, it is computed as

$$EDR = \frac{BTCF}{\text{equity investment}}$$

For example, if the expected BTCF for a proposed investment were $6,000 and the down payment (equity investment) were $50,000, the EDR would be

$$EDR = \frac{BTCF}{\text{equity investment}}$$
$$= \frac{\$6,000}{\$50,000}$$
$$= 12\%$$

The EDR for this investment can then be compared with similar investments' EDRs to determine whether the investment is worthwhile. Obviously, this method requires not only an accurate estimate of NOI but reasonable assumptions about currently available financing terms.

Ratio Analysis

We now turn our attention to commonly used ratios for property analysis.

Loan-to-Value Ratio   The most commonly used ratio by lenders and borrowers alike for residential and income property is the *loan-to-value (L/V) ratio,* which expresses the proportion the loan is of the total property value. In equation form,

$$\frac{L}{V} = \frac{\text{mortgage outstanding}}{\text{property value}}$$

Usually lenders have certain guidelines setting the maximum acceptable L/V ratios for various types of property. These guidelines are set in some instances by government regulations or by internal policy. If, for instance, a lender will loan a maximum of 80 percent of value (i.e., the L/V ratio is 0.80), the largest loan that can be obtained on a $50,000 residence is $40,000.

The L/V ratio is a measure of risk for the lender. The higher the L/V ratio, the more likely the occurrence of default. Studies have shown that the risk of default is relatively low for L/V ratios less than 80 percent. Beyond this, the default risk rises as the L/V ratio increases from 80 percent to 100 percent. Since the property is security for the debt, the lender is concerned that the L/V ratio does not increase over the amortization period.

For the borrower, the L/V ratio is a determination of the amount of down payment required. This can be expressed, alternately, as the *equity-to-value (E/V) ratio*.

Since $E/V + L/V = 1.0$,

$$\frac{E}{V} = 1.0 - \frac{L}{V}$$

Hence, E/V and L/V are simply complements of each other. For example, if $L/V = 0.8$, determine E/V:

$$\frac{E}{V} + \frac{L}{V} = 1.0$$

$$\frac{E}{V} = 1.0 - 0.8$$

$$= 0.20$$

Therefore, a 20 percent down payment is required with an 80 percent L/V ratio.

Debt Coverage Ratio   The *debt coverage ratio (DCR)* is a popular tool lenders use to determine the ability of an income property to cover its proposed debt service. It is defined as

$$DCR = \frac{NOI}{\text{debt service}}$$

A DCR of 1 means that there is exactly enough net operating income from the investment (after operating expenses are paid) to cover the debt-service payments. Ideally, a property should have a DCR of something greater than 1, to have a cushion if there is a decline in expected NOI. Since debt-service payments are typically known and NOI is not, the lender usually insists on a DCR greater than 1, unless the borrower's financial position and credit history are so favorable as to warrant making the loan on a DCR of 1 or less. Historically, many lenders have taken the position that a DCR of 1.1 to 1.2 is the minimum acceptable figure for most income property loans.

Default Ratio Similarly, the *default ratio (DR)* is a measure of financial feasibility of the investment from the viewpoint of the lender. In equation form,

$$DR = \frac{OE + DS}{EGI}$$

The default ratio measures the amount of cash outflow (OE + DS) as a proportion of cash inflow (EGI) from the investment. The higher the percentage, the higher the risk of default.

From the borrower's perspective, the DR can be used as a measure of the property's proximity to its break-even point: The closer the ratio approaches 1, the closer the property is to break-even. If it exceeds 1, the property is below its break-even point. Alternately, the DR can be called the *break-even cash flow ratio* when used in this manner.

Operating Expense Ratio

The *operating expense ratio (OER)* is the proportion of operating expenses to effective gross income:

$$OER = \frac{OE}{EGI}$$

The larger the OER, the greater the proportion of income required to cover operating expenses.

This ratio is useful to both the lender and the borrower. Since OER data for many properties are usually compiled by lenders, appraisers, and brokers, the lender can use the OER as a perfunctory check on the figures the borrower presents in the loan application. If OER is lower than normal for the type of property under consideration, further investigation may be warranted.

For borrowers, the OER can be used the same way, to check the figures sellers or their agents present. In addition, a relatively high OER may point up to existing owners the necessity of cost-saving measures or to a purchaser the opportunity to turn a previously unprofitable investment into a profitable one.

Limitations of Ratios and Rules of Thumb

Ratios and rules of thumb are useful in that they provide analyses of important relationships about the investment and are relatively easy to calculate. Indeed, they could be used alone in making the investment decision except that they do not, separately or combined, present the total picture for making the optimum decision. Inherent in these simple analyses is the fact that they omit several important considerations. The equity reversion is a large portion of the return on many investments, yet it is not considered in these analyses. Similarly, income tax effects are omitted, and with GIM, even the operating expenses are not considered.

Despite their limitations, however, ratios and rules of thumb do give the lender useful insights and the borrower first approximations of investment worth.

SUMMARY

This chapter examined the methods and techniques used to estimate the value of the real estate used as collateral for the mortgage debt. Both lenders and borrowers are interested in the property value. We illustrated the techniques for both owner-occupied residences and income-producing properties.

This chapter also analyzed the various ratios and rules of thumb for analyzing real estate investments. These simplified criteria give both lenders and borrowers information about the feasibility of a real estate investment.

Chapter 6 continues our analysis of real estate by discussing the more complex discounted cash flow models, and it also examines the tax impacts of real estate financing and investment decisions.

QUESTIONS

1 What is the role of property analysis in real estate finance?
2 Outline the appraisal process.
3 What are the three major appraisal methods? What is the premise underlying each method? Outline the steps for each approach.
4 Define the following terms:

a market value	g overall capitalization rate
b highest and best use	h gross income multiplier
c market comparison approval	i equity dividend rate
d cost approach	j debt coverage ratio
e functional obsolescence	k operating expense ratio
f net operating income	

5 What are the limitations of the market comparison approach? Cost approach? Income approach?
6 What are some examples of economic obsolescence? Functional obsolescence? How would you estimate the loss in property value from each factor?
7 A property has a net operating income of $50,000. The indicated overall capitalization rate is 10.5 percent. What is the value? Discuss the relationship among value, cap rate, and net income.
8 Analyze how the net operating income from a real estate investment is determined.
9 Describe how to calculate the cash flow from sale.
10 What are the questions for the various methods of determining the overall capitalization in the income approach?
11 Name several ratios used in property analysis. Give the equation for each ratio. What are the limitations?

PROBLEMS

1 Recompute the result of the market data approach for the apartment example in the chapter, using the price per apartment instead of the price per room as the unit of com-

parison (the subject property has 24 apartment units). Will this change your range of indicated values? Discuss.

2 A real estate investor is considering the purchase of a small office building and has requested that you appraise it. The following data on recent sales of small office buildings similar to and competitive with the subject have been obtained:

Comparable number	Sale price	Effective gross income	Average vacant space per year (square feet)	Operating expenses	Offices (rooms)	Net rentable square feet
1	$360,000	$65,070	520	$20,770	36	8,650
2	345,000	62,400	500	20,000	35	8,300
3	382,000	69,400	550	22,600	38	9,225
4	373,500	67,560	535	22,000	38	8,980

The subject property contains 38 rooms (offices) and 8,900 square feet of net rentable area. The site has a total area of 16,000 square feet. Neighboring office building sites are bringing average sales prices of $5 per square foot.

From our cost manual, we find that the reproduction cost of a building of this type, quality, and size is $40.10 per square foot of net rentable area, thus yielding a cost new for the building of $356,890. However, the building is 15 years old and has suffered, in your judgment, 15 percent physical depreciation; in addition, it is not energy efficient, resulting in an additional 5 percent for curable functional obsolescence. For site improvements, your cost manual gives a total of $15,500, and you estimate they are about 40 percent depreciated.

It is assumed that a 75 percent loan at 12 percent interest with monthly payments for 20 years is available. Investors demand a 9.5 percent EDR on this type of investment. Stabilized NOI is estimated to be $46,000.

The property is to be held for 5 years, with it appreciating 13 percent over that period. The before-tax required rate of return on equity is 20 percent.

Comparable 1 is a very recent sale, so no adjustment is made for time. However, comparable 1 is estimated to be 4 percent superior in condition in an essentially similar location. Comparable 2 is an older sale, so you should adjust for the change in the market since the sale date. If the current annual rate of appreciation is 10 percent, then the time adjustment for comparable 2 should be +5 percent. In addition, it is essentially similar in condition to the subject, except that it has an all-new heating system and roof. (The subject's heating system and roof are 15 years old.) You therefore estimate a −4 percent adjustment for these items. The location is superior to that of the subject, resulting in a −2 percent adjustment, in your opinion. Comparable 3, which is located next door to the subject, was built at the same time as the subject by the same builder and is nearly identical in many respects. However, it is an older sale, requiring a +7.5 percent adjustment to account for the difference. Comparable 4, also very similar physically, is in a poorer location: estimated adjustment, −5 percent. Also, 6 months have passed since it was sold, requiring a +5 percent time adjustment.

Apply the cost, income, and market comparison approaches to estimate the value of the office building.

3 Recompute the result of the market data approach for the office building example using a price-per-room basis rather than price per square foot. How will this change affect the range of indicated values?

4 You are given the following unit-in-place costs for erecting a duplex residence:

Foundation, complete	$25,000
Structural framing, complete	63,000
Partition walls, per unit	8,000
Floor covering, per unit	5,500
Heating/cooling system, per unit	10,000
Kitchen cabinets, per unit	2,600
Electrical system, per unit	10,000
Bath fixtures, per unit	7,200
Plumbing system, complete	12,000

In addition, the lot on which the structure will be built has a market value of $30,000. Utility lines will cost $6,000; landscaping, $10,000; paving of driveways and sidewalks, $6,000. Estimate the reproduction cost new of this duplex.

5 Assuming the duplex will have a market value of $235,000 when completed, should it have been built? Why or why not?

6 In the apartment example, suppose the capitalization rate were 9 percent. What would happen to value? At 11 percent?

7 Using the market extraction technique, determine the overall capitalization rate for the following sales:

Sale	Sales price	NOI
1	$285,000	$29,200
2	300,000	30,000
3	450,000	38,700
4	325,000	32,000

For the data given, would you say these four were all similar comparable sales? Why or why not?

8 In the office building example, suppose stabilized NOI is raised to $47,500. What happens to value? At an NOI of $44,500?

REFERENCES

American Institute of Real Estate Appraisers: *The Appraisal of Real Estate*, 8th ed., Chicago, 1983.

American Institute of Real Estate Appraisers: *Appraising in a Changing Economy*, Chicago, 1982.

Case, Frederick E., and Sanders A. Kahn: *Real Estate Appraisal and Investment*, 2d ed., Ronald Press, New York, 1977.

Dyer, Robert O., Woodring M. Fryers, and Wayne L. King (eds.): *Income Property Appraising*, National Association of Independent Fee Appraisers, St. Louis, 1981.

Friedman, Jack P., and Nicholas Ordway: *Income Property Appraisal and Analysis*, Reston, Reston, Va., 1981.

Jennings, Curtis A., Wayne L. King, and William H. Steele (eds.): *Principles of Residential Real Estate Appraising,* National Association of Independent Fee Appraisers, St. Louis, 1982.

Murman, F. H.: "Band of Investment Premise and High Ratio Mortgages," *Appraisal Institute Magazine,* April 1977, pp. 31–32.

Pollack, Bruce: "Ratios and Formulae: Talking the Lenders' and Appraisers' Language," *Real Estate Appraiser,* January–February 1978, pp. 39–41.

PROPERTY ANALYSIS: PART 2

This chapter continues our discussion of analyzing the property serving as collateral for a mortgage loan. Chapter 5 examined the traditional appraisal methods and the various rules of thumb and ratios lenders and borrowers use. Here we extend our analysis to consider the *tax aspects* of real estate investments and the more complex investment criteria called *discounted cash flow models*.

Because the tax effects on the real estate investment have such significant impact, both the investor-borrower and the lender should consider these factors. Traditional analysis suggests that tax impacts are of primary interest to the borrower-investor rather than to the lender because the tax benefits (or consequences) of the investment accrue to the equity investor; however, it is important that the lender also analyze tax consequences inasmuch as they may alter the borrower's financial position.

Readers may find this material complex. Unfortunately, the myriad of tax laws and their applications are difficult, so to gain a clear, accurate picture for our analysis, we must study the laws as they occur in the real world. We attempted to sort out the "wheat from the chaff" so that tax impacts for the investments will be handled accurately by partly eliminating little-used rules or those that do not apply directly to real estate investments. Material of this nature must be read and reread until it is thoroughly understood. All the numerical examples and problems should be worked through carefully. Finally, it is important at this point to stress one fundamental rule regarding taxes on real estate investments: *The taxes on the BTCF and BTER amounts are not computed as they were in Chapter 5;* the incomes from operations and disposition (sale) of the investment that are subject to taxation are computed in an entirely different manner. Keeping this fact in mind will reduce confusion later.

ANALYZING TAX IMPACTS: OVERVIEW

There is a five-step procedure for analyzing the tax impacts on the investment:

1 Determine the investment's tax classification.
2 Determine the investor's tax status (i.e., form of business organization).
3 Estimate the investor's marginal tax rate.

4 Forecast the taxable income resulting from operations and from the disposition (sale) of the investment

5 Using the investor's marginal tax rate and the taxable income figures, compute the estimated taxes.

We now look at each step in detail.

DETERMINING THE TAX CLASSIFICATION

For tax purposes, real estate is classified into four categories, depending on the owner's purpose for holding it: (1) property held to produce income or investment, (2) property held for sale to customers, (3) property held for use in trade or business (commonly called section 1231 property), and (4) property held as a personal residence. Each category is subject to different tax rules. Since most real estate investments fall into the personal residence and trade or business categories, most of our discussion is about these two classifications.

Income from real estate has been further classified by the Tax Reform Act of 1986 (TRA 1986). A taxpayer's income has been subdivided into these categories: active, passive, and portfolio income. Table 6-1 depicts the three categories and gives some examples.

Property Held for Investment

Most real estate investments do *not* fall into this category. Those that do typically are unimproved land and property subject to a net lease. The real estate investments in this category are subject to a limitation not imposed on other types of real estate investments. For the noncorporate taxpayer, the interest on indebtedness incurred to purchase or carry the property may not be fully deductible. The interest-deduction limit is the net investment income.

Property Held for Sale to Customers

This classification primarily refers to the owner as a *dealer*. A *dealer* is an entity that sells real estate for a profit relatively frequently; the property is thus not held

TABLE 6-1   CLASSIFICATION OF TAXPAYER'S INCOME

1. Active income:
   Wages, salaries
2. Portfolio income:
   Interest, dividends
3. Passive income:
   a. Trade of business in which the investor does not materially participate
   b. Rental activities
   c. Limited partnership activities

for very long. For tax purposes, the dealer's profits on the sale are treated as *ordinary income,* just as a storekeeper's profits on the sale of inventory are treated. An investor is entitled to take the depreciation deduction, whereas the dealer is not. Although most real estate investors are classified as "investors" for tax purposes, the IRS is wary of investors who buy and sell several properties in a year and thus often classifies them as dealers.

Property Held for Use in Trade or Business (Section 1231)

This is the category into which most real estate investments fall. *Real estate owned and operated for the purpose of deriving rental income* are the key words that distinguish property in this category from property held for investment and held for sale to customers. Section 1231 property receives the most favorable tax treatment: All operating expenses, mortgage interest, and a depreciation allowance are fully deductible from rental income.

Property Held as Personal Residence

Property held as a personal residence applies to owner-occupied residences only. The major differences between this category and the others are:

1 Capital gain on the sale can be deferred.
2 Losses on the sale are not deductible, nor are most operating expenses.
3 Property taxes and interest are deductible as itemized deductions on the owner's tax returns.
4 The depreciation deduction is not allowed.

Active, Portfolio, or Passive Income

The basic implication of this categorization is that losses derived from passive activities cannot be used to offset income from either active or portfolio income; however, these losses may be carried forward (termed "suspended losses") to offset future passive income. Passive activities are defined as activities in which the investor does not materially participate; specifically included in this are rental and limited partnership activities.

Active participation in real estate rental activities does not change the status to active. However, an exception is granted to individuals who actively participate in a rental real estate activity with at least 10 percent interest. The exception results in a $25,000 loss deduction (total deductions and equivalent credits) against active and portfolio income. A limitation is imposed on this exemption for taxpayers with income greater than $100,000. For every dollar greater than $100,000, the exemption is reduced 50 percent, therefore resulting in a total phaseout for incomes exceeding $150,000. Thus, this exception allows taxpayers of medium incomes to offset some of their current rental losses.

DETERMINING THE INVESTOR'S TAX STATUS

Determining the investor's tax status basically involves identifying the form of business organization to be used: either corporate or noncorporate. Most real estate investments are held in a noncorporate form of ownership because of the tax advantages over corporate ownership. With sole proprietorship and general and limited partnerships, the tax losses or profits the property provides "flow through" directly to the investor(s) in that they are included on the investor's personal income tax return. With corporate ownership, however, the tax losses or profits are considered income or loss to the corporation and are accounted for on the corporation tax return. Any dividends paid to the shareholders (owners) are treated as ordinary taxable income to the investors on their individual tax returns.

Real estate investment trusts (REITs) are a special case in that they are subject to a modified flow-through provision—i.e., tax losses cannot exceed the cash distributions made to the investor. Since most investors favor noncorporate ownership, we consider only this form of ownership in the remainder of this book.

ESTIMATING THE INVESTOR'S TAX RATE

To estimate the investor's tax impacts from an investment, we must know the applicable tax rate. The federal income tax is progressive: The proportion of income that is taxed increases as taxable income increases. The percentage of income taxed depends on both the amount of taxable income and the investor's filing status: single taxpayer, married taxpayer filing joint return, married taxpayer filing separate return, or unmarried taxpayer qualifying as head of household. Table 6-2 illustrates 1988 tax rates and taxes due under each filing status for various levels of income. For example, see the column "Married filing joint return." Married taxpayers filing a joint return whose taxable income is, say, $57,000, would pay a tax of $4,463 plus 28 percent of $27,250, or $12,093. Any additional income would be taxed at 28 percent. Also, any losses that reduced taxable income would save these taxpayers 28 percent of the loss in taxes, provided the loss brought down taxable income to a level within the 28 percent bracket.

TABLE 6-2   TAX RATES FOR 1988 AND THEREAFTER

Tax rate (%)	Married filing joint return	Married filing separate return	Head of household	Single
15	0–$29,750	0–$14,875	0–$23,900	0–$17,850
28	above $29,750	above $14,875	above $23,900	above $17,850
Income levels subject to 5 percent additional tax*				
	$71,900–$149,250	$35,950–$113,300	$61,650–$123,790	$43,150–$89,560

*The benefit of the 15 percent bracket is phased out for taxpayers with taxable income exceeding specified levels. The tax liability of such taxpayers is increased by applying a 5 percent additional tax to taxable income within the levels of taxable income shown below. If the benefit of the 15 percent bracket is entirely phased out, the effect is to impose a straight 28 percent tax rate on the individual.

When considering the tax impacts of a proposed investment on the investor, we assume that all income the investor has from other sources—that is, wages, dividends, interest—is given and that the taxable income or loss from the proposed investment will add to, or detract from, this given amount. *The additional tax owed (or saved) as a result of owning the investment is the tax impact of the investment.*

To illustrate, suppose a proposed real estate investment is expected to generate $1,000 in taxable income for our investors (married, filing jointly), who expect to have $57,000 in taxable income from other sources. Without the real estate investment, their tax will be $12,093. With the real estate investment, their tax will be $4,463 + 28 percent of $28,250, or $12,373, a $280 difference. Thus, the investors will pay an additional $280 of tax on the additional $1,000 of taxable income. This represents a *marginal tax* rate of 28 percent.

Suppose, however, that the investment is expected to generate a $1,000 taxable *loss*. With the real estate investment, the couple's tax will now be based on a taxable income of $57,000 minus $1,000, or $56,000. The tax will be $4,463 plus 28 percent of $26,250, or $11,813. This is $280 less than the tax would be without the real estate investment. Thus the investment will *save* the taxpayers $280, or 28 percent of the taxable loss of $1,000, in taxes they otherwise will owe. The tax impact of the investment is thus a tax savings of $280.

It is possible for the investment's tax impacts to raise or lower the investor's taxable income above or below the limits of his or her bracket. When this occurs, to accurately predict the tax impact, investors should apply the appropriate tax rate for the amount of income or loss that falls within each bracket. For simplicity's sake, however, the examples in this book assume that the marginal tax rate will remain constant even if the investment's taxable income (or loss) raises (or lowers) the investors' total taxable income above (or below) their original tax bracket. For example, for our taxpayers in the 28 percent bracket, we assume that 28 percent of the additional dollars of taxable income the investment will generate will be the taxes owed as a result of the investment. Similarly, 28 percent of all taxable losses the investment generates will be the taxes saved as a result of the investment.

FORECASTING TAXABLE INCOME

As mentioned, the tax classification of the real estate investment decides the rules that can be applied to determine tax impacts. At this point, we discuss separately the classification of most real estate investments: property held for use in a trade or business (Section 1231 property). Taxes arise during two stages of investment ownership: the year-to-year operations and the disposition stages.

Taxable Income from Operations

Recall from Chapter 5 that we computed the expected before-tax cash flows (BTCFs) for an investment over the expected period of ownership. Although the

BTCF is the investor's before-tax earning, *it is not the amount that is taxed*. That is, the IRS does not consider the BTCF as the taxable income (TI) upon which the tax rate is applied. Table 6-3 illustrates the computation of taxable income. Note that the BTCF and TI computations are similar down to the NOI figure, but there the similarity ends. Since you should already have an understanding of NOI and its components, we now discuss the computation of taxable income from operations.

Replacement Reserves (RR)   Recall from Chapter 5 that RR expenses for computing BTCF were set aside for replacement of appliances, carpeting, and the like and so were not considered cash flow to the investor. In general, all other expenses of operating, maintaining, and repairing real estate investments are fully deductible in the year paid or incurred; the notable exception is the fund for RRs. Because we had previously included RR in operating expenses, thus reducing NOI, we must now add it back in because it is not a deductible expense item for the taxable-income computation.

Interest (I) Expenses   The *interest* paid on mortgage indebtedness is deductible up to investment income for tax purposes, but the principal paid is not. For cash flow purposes, recall that we deducted the entire amount of the debt service (principal and interest) because it was a cash outflow for the investor. To compute taxable income, however, the repayment of principal is considered neither income to the lender nor a deductible expense to the borrower. Interest, on the other hand, is considered income to the lender and a deductible item to the borrower.

Depreciation (D) Deduction   Depreciation is another major deduction when computing taxable income. Depreciation allows the taxpayer to recover the cost of the investment property or asset. With types of trade or business property other than real estate, such as motor vehicles, machinery, and equipment, the

TABLE 6-3   HOW TO COMPUTE TAXABLE INCOME AND TAXES FROM OPERATIONS

Effective gross income (EGI)
− operating expenses (OE)
net operating income (NOI)
+ replacement reserves (RR)
− interest (I)
− depreciation (D)
− amortized financing costs (AFC)
taxable income (TI)
× marginal tax rate
taxes from operations (TO)

property loses value as it wears out, wastes away, or becomes obsolete; thus, in these cases depreciation of the asset is a very real expense to the investor because the cost of the property most likely will not be recovered when the asset is disposed of or sold. Real estate investments, however, generally do not lose value over time; in fact, they have risen quite substantially in value during certain periods. The depreciation allowance on real estate is an item that can be expensed, or written off, where no real or actual loss in value has occurred, and therein lies the tax sheltering benefit of real estate: The investor can write off depreciation expense as a deductible item even though it is generally not a cost (cash outflow) of operating the property.

Depreciation is an allowable deduction for property classified as trade or business or investment but not personal residence. In addition, only property that has a limited useful life, such as buildings and machinery, is depreciable. Land is not depreciable since, at least for tax purposes, its useful life is considered unlimited. The depreciation of land improvements such as landscaping and paving generally depends on whether they permanently improve the land or improve it only so long as a particular building or structure remains useful.

Three factors determine the amount of depreciation that can be deducted in any year:

1 Cost (or basis) of the property, not including the nondepreciable items (land)
2 Recovery period of the property, that is, the number of years over which the property is to be depreciated
3 Method of depreciation

First, the *depreciable basis* must be calculated. The basis will be used here to compute the annual depreciation deductions and then the gain or loss on the disposition (sale) of the property. *The basis is the price the investor pays plus the cost of capital improvements and acquisition costs.*

The *depreciable amount* is generally the basis less the value (cost) of the nondepreciable land. The price the investor pays is the total cash, mortgages, and other property the investor gives up in exchange for the investment.

The *capital improvements* are expenditures that substantially *improve* the value of the property or *increase* its useful life. These costs should be distinguished from operating expenses, which are expenditures that only *maintain* the value or useful life of the property. Capital improvements include structural additions to the property and, generally, the installation of such items as air conditioning, appliances, and carpeting, which are additions to the property, not merely replacements for units already there.

Acquisition costs are such expenses as transfer fees, legal expenses, and title insurance that the investor incurs when purchasing the real estate investment. The tax code allows these costs to be added to the basis and depreciated.

In determining the depreciable amount, an allocation must be made between the cost of the depreciable items (buildings) and the cost of the nondepreciable items (land). The portion of the total cost to be allocated to each item is based on the market value of each at the time the investor acquires the property. This allocation can be made by either hiring a professional appraiser to determine the allocation or using the proportion of total value the local tax assessor placed on each item. For instance, if the local tax assessor valued land at $25,000 and the building at $75,000, total property value is $100,000. These proportions (25 percent land, 75 percent building) can be applied to the purchase price of the property to determine the depreciable portion. If the purchase price was $150,000, then the depreciable portion is 75 percent, or $112,500. To this amount add capital improvements and acquisition costs to find the depreciable amounts to be used in the annual depreciation calculation.

The second factor that determines the amount of the depreciation deduction is the *useful life* (also called *recovery period*), or the number of years over which the investment will be depreciated. This useful life is specified in the 1986 tax revision, which sets the useful life of real estate investments at 27.5 years for residential real property and 31.5 years for nonresidential real property.

The *depreciation method* allowed is the *straight-line* method. Depreciation in the year the property is placed in service is based on the midmonth convention. This assumes that an asset is placed in service on the fifteenth of the month regardless of the actual day. Table 6-4 shows the percentage deduction for residential property depreciated on a 27.5-year basis and nonresidential property depreciated on a 31.5-year basis for the years in service. To use this table, one chooses the vertical column which shows the recovery year and moves across to the month of depreciation. The percentage will be applied to the total amount to be depreciated. For example, if a residential real estate investment was placed in service in June, the first year's proportion would be 0.020 and the second year's proportion would be 0.036. A similar proportion would be used over the balance

TABLE 6-4 STRAIGHT-LINE DEPRECIATION FOR REAL PROPERTY ASSUMING MIDMONTH CONVENTION
(Unofficial Table)

Recovery year(s)*	1	2	3	4	5	6	7	8	9	10	11	12
				27.5-year residential real property*								
1	0.035	0.032	0.029	0.026	0.023	0.020	0.017	0.014	0.011	0.008	0.005	0.002
2–27	0.036	0.036	0.036	0.036	0.036	0.036	0.036	0.036	0.036	0.036	0.036	0.036
28	0.029	0.032	0.035	0.036	0.036	0.036	0.036	0.036	0.036	0.036	0.036	0.036
29	0	0	0	0.002	0.005	0.008	0.011	0.014	0.017	0.020	0.023	0.026
				31.5-year nonresidential real property								
1	0.030	0.028	0.025	0.022	0.020	0.017	0.015	0.012	0.009	0.007	0.004	0.001
2–31	0.032	0.032	0.032	0.032	0.032	0.032	0.032	0.032	0.032	0.032	0.032	0.032
32	0.010	0.012	0.015	0.018	0.020	0.023	0.025	0.028	0.031	0.032	0.032	0.032
33	0	0	0	0	0	0	0	0	0	0.001	0.004	0.007

*The applicable percentage is: (use the column for the month in the first year the property is placed in service).

TABLE 6-5 DEPRECIATION DEDUCTION FOR APARTMENT BUILDING
EXAMPLE: $113,500 BASIS

Year	Straight-line deduction
1	$ 3,973 (rounded)
2–27	4,086
28	3,292 (rounded)
29	0
Total	$113,500

of the life. If the property is sold before the end of the life, the deduction for the year of disposition is based only on the number of months the property was in service during that year.

Depreciation Deduction: An Example   We want to determine the depreciation for a 5-year holding period of an apartment building investment with the following data:

Type of investment: Apartment building
Depreciation method: Straight-line with midmonth convention
Purchase price: $140,000
Acquisition costs: $1,500
Percentage of price depreciable: 80 percent
Recovery period: 27.5 years

The depreciable basis is the building cost (80 percent of $140,000) plus the acquisition costs ($1,500), for a total of $113,500. We will assume the property is placed in service at the beginning of the year. To compute the straight-line amount with the midmonth convention, we multiply the $113,500 depreciable basis by the applicable percentage, 0.035 (found in Table 6-4), deriving the first year's depreciation amount of $3,973 (rounded). The depreciation over the life of the asset is shown in Table 6-5.

Amortized Financing Costs   Another deductible item in computing taxable income from operations is *amortized financing costs*. Financing costs are those incurred when obtaining financing, such as lender appraisal fees, loan discounts, lender's title insurance policies, and loan-origination fees. When the property is classified as trade or business (Section 1231), these costs are not deductible as expense items when incurred at the beginning of the loan; they must be amortized in equal amounts over the term (number of years) of the mortgage. If the loan is paid off before maturity, the unamortized portion of the financing costs can be deducted in the year the loan is paid off.

To illustrate this concept, let us return to the apartment building example, with the following assumptions:

Mortgage amount: $112,000
Financing costs: 2 percent of loan amount ($2,240)
Term of loan: 25 years
Holding period: 5 years

To compute the amount deductible each year, we divide the $2,240 cost by the term of the loan, 25 years. Therefore, $90 per year is deductible as amortized financing costs. Note, however, that we expect to hold the property for only 5 years, disposing of (selling) the property at the end of the fifth year and (presumably) paying off the mortgage. The entire unamortized portion of the financing costs, $1,890, is deductible in year 5, the year the loan will be paid off.

Prepayment Penalty In many income property loans, the lender charges a penalty for early repayment of the loan. For tax purposes, such a penalty is deductible as interest in the year the borrower pays it. Remember: A prepayment penalty is also a cash outflow in the year paid.

Taxes from Operation: Apartment Building Example

Now that each component of taxable income has been discussed, let us determine the taxable income for our apartment building investment. Table 6-6 is a summary of salient facts; Table 6-7 contains the forecasted taxes from operation of this building.

1 *Net operating income* is expected to be $15,764 for year 1. For years 2 to 5, it is expected to increase at 5 percent per year (compounded).
2 *The interest on the debt* is computed according to the methods outlined in Chapter 2. Table 6-8 contains the amortization schedule.
3 The *depreciation deduction* was computed in a previous section.
4 *Amortized financing costs* are $2,240 divided by 25, or $90 per year. Note that in year 5, the unamortized balance is deductible.

TABLE 6-6 APARTMENT BUILDING EXAMPLE: FACTS AND ASSUMPTIONS

Net operating income	$15,764 for year 1, expected to increase at 5% per year for years 2–5
Acquisition costs	$1,500
Asking price	$140,000
Reserves for replacement	$800 each year
Financing	L/V ratio, 80%; interest rate, 12%; term, 25 years; monthly payment, $1,179,62; financing cost, $2,240
Depreciation	80% of price depreciable; useful life, 27.5 years; method: straight-line with midmonth convention
Holding period	5 years
Investor's tax rate	28%

TABLE 6-7 EXPECTED TAXES FROM OPERATION: APARTMENT BUILDING EXAMPLE

	Year				
	1	2	3	4	5
Net operating income (NOI)	$ 15,764	$ 16,552	$ 17,380	$ 18,249	$ 19,161
− interest on debt (I)	13,399	13,303	13,195	13,074	12,936
− depreciation deduction (D)	3,973	4,086	4,086	4,086	4,086
− amortized financing costs (AFC)	90	90	90	90	1,880*
+ replacement reserves (RR)	800	800	800	800	800
ordinary taxable income (OTI)	(898)	(127)	809	1,799	(1,059)
× investor's marginal tax rate	0.28	0.28	0.28	0.28	0.28
taxes (savings) from operation (TO)	(251)	(36)	227	504	(297)

*Unamortized balance is deductible.

5 Replacement reserves of $800 per year have been deducted as operating expenses for the NOI computation. Since they are not allowable expenses for tax purposes, the RRs must be added back in the taxable-income computation.

The total is the ordinary taxable income (or tax loss) of the investment for each of the 5 years in the holding period. This amount is then multiplied by the investor's marginal tax rate (in this case, 28 percent) to find the taxes (or tax savings) from operations each year.

Note that the property is expected to generate a taxable loss in 2 of the 5 years (see Table 6-7). As a result, this investor will have an expected tax *savings* in 2 of the years as a result of owning the property. For example, in year 1, the investor will save $251 in taxes by owning the building. Or viewed from another perspective, the investor will have to pay an additional $251 in taxes if the investor does not own the building. This tax savings is in effect a cash flow from the investor's perspective because the investor's income tax liability is reduced each year as a direct result of owning the property.

TABLE 6-8 ANNUAL AMORTIZATION SCHEDULE: APARTMENT BUILDING EXAMPLE, YEARS 1–5

Year	Debt service	Principal	Interest	Ending balance
0	$0	$0	$0	$112,000
1	14,155	756	13,399	111,244
2	14,155	852	13,303	110,392
3	14,155	960	13,195	103,432
4	14,155	1,081	13,074	108,351
5	14,155	1,219	12,936	107,132

TABLE 6-9   TAXES DUE ON SALE

Taxable income	Taxes due on sale
Expected selling price (SP) − selling expenses (SE)	Total gain (TG)
amount realized (AR) − adjusted basis (AB)	× investor's marginal tax rate
total gain (TG)	taxes due on sale (TDS)

Taxable Income from Sale

We just discussed the tax computation on the year-to-year earnings from the operation of the investment. When an investment is sold or otherwise disposed of, it may also generate income to the investor. We now turn to the computation of the taxable income (total gain) and the taxes due on the sale of the investment.

Table 6-9 shows the method of computing taxable income and taxes due on sale with straight-line depreciation with the midmonth convention.

Expected Selling Price (SP)   The first step in calculating taxable income and taxes due on sale is to estimate the price the property is expected to sell for at the end of the holding period. This price includes cash received plus the market value of any other property the seller received as payment. It also includes the liabilities against the property sold, such as mortgages or back taxes, which the buyer assumes or takes "subject to."

Selling Expenses (SE)   The tax code lets the seller deduct *selling expenses*— brokerage commissions, transfer fees, attorney fees, advertising expenses incident to the sale, etc.—incurred during sale of the investment.

Amount Realized (AR)   The *amount realized* is the expected selling price minus the selling expenses. Generally, the investor is taxed on the difference between the amount realized and the adjusted basis.

Adjusted Basis (AB)   This is the original price the investor paid for the investment plus acquisition costs, less the cumulative depreciation deductions taken over the holding period, plus the cost of any capital improvements made to the property during the holding period. Since the investor generally pays tax on the difference between the amount realized and the adjusted basis, subtracting the cumulative depreciation deductions effectively reduces taxable income from operations over the holding period, but now the deductions must be accounted for. Similarly, adding capital improvements *reduces* tax liability on the sale because capital improvements add to the price paid for the investment and thus increase the investment's value; therefore, the improvements should not be considered a part of the gain on the sale.

Total Gain (TG)   The total gain is the difference between the amount realized and the adjusted basis.

Other Tax Consequences on Disposition

Other than an outright sale, the *installment sale* and *tax-deferred exchange* methods may reduce or defer the taxes due on disposition. The installment sale is the topic of Chapter 11.

Taxes Due on Sale: Apartment Building Example

Let us now return to our apartment building example. Table 6-10 has the facts and assumptions needed to compute the TDS. Our results are presented in Table 6-11.

TABLE 6-10   CALCULATING TAXES DUE ON SALE: APARTMENT BUILDING EXAMPLE

Purchase period	$140,000
Acquisition costs	$1,500
Capital improvements	0
Depreciation	$113,500 basis, 27.5 years; straight-line with midmonth convention method; total depreciation taken years 1–5, $20,317
Holding period	5 years
Expected selling price, end year 5	$178,679
Selling expenses	8% of expected selling price
Investor's marginal tax rate	28%

TABLE 6-11   COMPUTATION OF TAXES DUE ON SALE: APARTMENT BUILDING EXAMPLE

Taxable income	
Selling price (SP) (given)	$178,679
− selling expenses (SE) (8% of $178,679)	14,294
amount realized (AR)	164,385
− adjusted basis (AB) ($141,500 − $20,317)	121,183
total gain (TG)	43,202

Taxes due on sale	
Total gain (TG)	$43,202
× investor's marginal tax rate	0.28
taxes due on sale (TDS)	12,097

TABLE 6-12 EXPECTED CASH FLOW FROM OPERATION: APARTMENT BUILDING EXAMPLE

	Year				
	1	2	3	4	5
Net operating income (NOI)	$15,764	$16,552	$17,380	$18,294	$19,161
− debt service (DS)	14,155	14,155	14,155	14,155	14,155
before tax cash flow (BTCF)	1,609	2,397	3,225	4,139	5,006
− taxes (savings) from operation (TO)*	(251)	(36)	227	504	(297)
after tax cash flow (ATCF)	1,860	2,433	2,998	3,635	4,709

*See Table 6-7.

AFTER-TAX CASH FLOWS

Once the tax consequences of the investment have been determined, they may be added to (in the case of a tax savings) or deducted from (in the case of a tax due) the before-tax cash flows (BTCFs) from operations and sale to derive the after-tax cash flows (ATCFs) and after-tax equity reversion (ATER), respectively. To illustrate, we return to our apartment building example. Table 6-12 recaps the BTCF calculations we demonstrated earlier and adds the tax savings from operations to derive the ATCFs. Table 6-13 similarly recaps the before-tax equity reversion (BTER) and deducts the taxes due on sale to derive the ATERs.

The ATCFs are of greatest interest to the investor because they are the actual net cash amounts the investor expects to receive after paying all expenses, including taxes.

AFTER-TAX ANALYSIS OF INVESTMENT RETURNS

We have seen how the ATCFs and ATERs are calculated; the next step is to use these cash flows as a basis for decision making. Chapter 5 introduced the two basic decision-making tools: traditional valuation methods and rules of thumb and ratios. Since traditional valuation methods and most ratios do not explicitly use after-tax figures in their analysis, here we cover only one commonly used rule of thumb along with new techniques called discounted cash flow models.

Rule of Thumb: The After-Tax Rate (ATR)

The ATR is similar to the equity divided rate described in Chapter 5, except that the initial year's ATCF is substituted for the BTCF. Operationally,

$$ATR = \frac{ATCF}{equity\ investment}$$

For instance, the expected ATCF for our apartment building example was $1,860 for the first year (Table 6-12), and the equity investment is the $140,000 price plus the acquisition costs ($1,500) and the financing costs ($2,240) less the $112,000

TABLE 6-13 EXPECTED CASH FLOW FROM SALE: APARTMENT BUILDING
EXAMPLE

Expected selling price (SP)	$178,679
− selling expenses (SE)	14,294
net sale proceeds (NSP)	164,385
− unpaid mortgage balance (UM)	107,132
before-tax equity reversion (BTER)	57,253
− taxes due on sale (TDS)*	12,097
after-tax equity reversion (ATER)	45,156

*See Table 6-10.

mortgage, or $31,740; the ATR then would be 5.86 percent. As a basis for decision making, the ATR is subject to the same limitations as the EDR, and all comments about the EDR made in Chapter 5 apply to the ATR.

Discounted Cash Flow Models

Discounted cash flow models discount the expected future income from the property over an assumed holding period at a specific rate of return. This process is much the same as the process described in Chapter 2 in the section "Series of Unequal Payments."

There are two discounted cash flow models: *net present value* (NPV) and *internal rate of return* (IRR). Here we use these models with the ATCFs and ATERs just computed to make investment decisions for the apartment building example.

Net Present Value   The net present value of an investment is the present value of the cash inflows minus the present value of the cash outflows, discounted at the rate of return required by the investor. For example, recall from Tables 6-11 and 6-12 that our apartment building investment is expected to provide a stream of after-tax income over the expected 5-year holding period; assume also that the investor's required after-tax rate of return is 14 percent.

Table 6-14 contains the NPV computation for our apartment building example using the ATCFs, the ATER, and the initial investment equity of $31,740, which is the sum of the $28,000 down payment, the $2,240 financing costs, and the $1,500 acquisition costs. As Table 6-14 illustrates, each cash flow is discounted to the present as a lump sum (the ATCF and ATER for year 5 are assumed to be received together at the end of the year and thus are added and discounted once). The present values are then added to arrive at NPV, which is $1,869.

There are two rules to follow when using NPV for decision making.

1 If the investment is worth at least as much as it costs, it should be bought.
2 If the investment is worth less than it costs, it should be rejected.

TABLE 6-14 AFTER-TAX NPV COMPUTATION: APARTMENT BUILDING EXAMPLE USING 14% REQUIRED RATE

Year	Equity	ATCF	ATER	PVF	PV
0	($31,740)			1.0	($31,740)
1		$1,860		0.8772	1,632
2		2,433		0.7695	1,872
3		2,998		0.6750	2,024
4		3,635		0.5921	2,152
5		4,709	$45,156	0.5194	25,900
				Net present value	$ 1,840

In our example, the "cost" of the investment is the $31,740 down payment (equity investment). The "worth" is the present value of all future cash returns, discounted at the investor's required 14 percent return. This total present value for the returns is $33,609. Hence, this investment is worth $1,869 more (at 14 percent) than it costs and should be purchased (i.e., its NPV is a positive $1,869). Thus, we can rewrite our decision-making rules as:

1 If NPV ≥ 0, the investment is worth at least as much as it costs and should be purchased.

2 If NPV < 0, the investment is worth less than it costs and should be rejected.

The NPV is useful in investment decision making because it is a measure of the total increase (or decrease) in the investor's wealth as a result of making the investment. The investor can use NPV for determining whether a given investment is worth what it costs (as shown here) and for choosing among investments based on the highest NPV.

Internal Rate of Return (IRR) The IRR on an investment is the rate that makes the NPV exactly equal to zero. For instance, in the previous NPV example, if the present value of the cash inflows discounted at 14 percent had been exactly $31,740 (i.e., the same as the cash outflow), the NPV would have equaled zero and the rate of return (or IRR) would have been exactly 14 percent. However, the net present value of the cash inflows was $1,869, implying that the expected rate of return is higher than 14 percent. How do we find the rate of return? We discount the cash inflow at various rates by trial-and-error and interpolation until we find a rate at which the present value of the inflows exactly equals the present value of the outflows. This rate then is the internal rate of return.

At this point, our discussion sounds familiar because the section from Chapter 2, "Effective Yield (Effective Borrowing Cost)," applied virtually the same concept. The IRR on a mortgage loan is simply its effective yield, or borrowing cost.

With this in mind, let us determine the IRR for our example. Since NPV is positive, the 14 percent rate is too low. Let us try, say, 17 percent: Table 6-15 illustrates the process. Since the present value of the cash inflows at 17 percent is

TABLE 6-15   AFTER-TAX NPV COMPUTATION: APARTMENT BUILDING EXAMPLE USING 17% REQUIRED RATE

Year	Equity	Cash inflows	×	PVF$_{17\%}$	=	PV
0	($31,740)			1.0		($31,740)
1		$1,860		0.8547		1,590
2		2,433		0.7305		1,777
3		2,998		0.6244		1,872
4		3,635		0.5337		1,940
5		4,709 + 45,156		0.4561		22,743
				Net present value		($ 1,818)

less than the cash outflow of $31,740 (NPV = 0), we know that the 17 percent rate is too high. Therefore, the rate (the IRR) must be between 14 and 17 percent. By interpolation, we can more closely approximate the rate:

NPV$_{14\%}$	$1,840	NPV$_{20\%}$	$1,840
NPV$_{17\%}$	(1,818)	Desired NPV	0
Difference	3,658	Difference	1,840

Difference in rates 17 − 14 = 3%

$$\frac{1,840}{3,658} = 0.5030 \qquad 0.5030 \times 3\% = 1.51\%$$

$$14 + 1.51 = 15.51\%$$

For our decision-making purposes, we see that the IRR on the investment, 15.53 percent, is higher than the investor's required 14 percent rate of return; thus, the investment should be bought.

Comparison of NPV and IRR   Although it appears that NPV and IRR are interchangeable when making the investment decision, *there are significant differences in practice, and any assumption otherwise may lead to incorrect or misleading analyses.*

First, *NPV and IRR may present conflicting advice when used to rank investment alternatives.* If we assume wealth maximization is the overriding investor objective, then NPV, which is a measure of the increase in wealth as a result of making the investment, should point to the optimal decision. Wouldn't IRR do the same thing? Only if the required capital investment were the same for all alternatives. For example, suppose we have the following information:

Project	Required capital	NPV$_{10\%}$	IRR (%)
A	$10,000	$1,980	17.9
B	6,000	1,300	19.6
C	16,000	2,730	15.1
D	9,000	1,764	17.6

By using NPV, the investments would be ranked according to the size of NPV, or (from highest to lowest) C, A, D, B. However, when using IRR, the ranking is B, A, D, C. An investor with a limited amount of investment capital should select the combination of investments that provides the greatest increase in wealth. This maxim necessitates the use of NPV as the criterion.

Another problem with IRR calculations is that where cash flows change from plus to minus more than once [i.e., an initial cash outflow (−) is followed by a series of inflows (+) and another outflow (−)], *multiple IRRs may result*. The question then is, Which IRR is appropriate, since they are both mathematically correct? There is no answer.

A third problem with IRR is that *it does not discount the cash flows at the required rate of return*. Both NPV and IRR have an implicit assumption that cash flows will be reinvested at the rate of return used in the analysis. Since NPVs use investors' required rate, which is the rate at which they can invest in other investments, no problem arises. With IRRs, however, the cash inflows are assumed to be reinvested at the IRR, not at the actual rate at which investors can invest. This can lead to misleading analyses and wrong decisions.

RISK ANALYSIS

In our previous discussion and example, we made several assumptions about rates of return—"The investor requires a 14 percent rate of return," "The lender expects to earn 12 percent on the mortgage," "The investor's expected return (IRR) on the property is 15.53 percent"—that were often givens for the problem at hand. When finding the NPV and IRR in the apartment building example, we essentially solved the following equation:

$$\text{NPV} = \sum_{t=1}^{n} \frac{\text{ATCF}_t}{(1 + k)^t} + \frac{\text{ATER}_n}{(1 + k)^n} - \text{equity}$$

where n = number of years in holding period
t = each year of holding period
k = interest rate—either required rate, or if NPV set equal to zero, IRR

Thus far, we have analyzed the top halves (numerators) in the equation—the ATCFs, ATER, and equity—given a rate of return, k. Now we examine the rate at which we have been discounting the cash flows.

Risk versus Return

With all types of investments, there is a direct relationship between risk and return. That is, the higher the expected return, the riskier the investment is likely to be. Unscrupulous investment dealers' claims that tout "high returns with no risk" are misstating the investment's relative risk, return, or both. Why? Because if there were such an investment, everyone would want to own it, and the high demand would bid its price up to the point where investors would pay for this lower risk, thus driving the rate of return down to a level where risk and return were commensurate with one another. Similarly, an investment that is perceived as relatively risky and priced so high that it promises relatively small returns is likely to have few, if any, bidders. The seller will be forced to reduce the price to the point where the market perceives risk to be commensurate with return. Figure 6-1 illustrates the positive relationship between risk and return.

Investment y has return k_1 and risk level r_1. Investment z, at risk level r_2, requires a commensurately higher return, k_2. Investment x has a zero risk level (i.e., it is risk-free); even with no risks, however, a rate of return k_0 is needed because this is the rate the market requires to give up present use of the money for future use—the "time value of money" or present value concept discussed in Chapter 2.

Moving from investment x to investment y, the additional rate of return the investor expects $(k_1 - k_0)$ is called the *risk premium,* or the additional rate of return required for taking on risk level r_1. This risk premium is a composite of basically two types of risk: *inflation,* or the risk of losses in purchasing power caused by nominal price increases for goods and services; and *business and financial risk,* or the risk that expected income will not materialize, causing a loss of equity capital, default on borrowed funds, and/or a reduction in return on investment. Regardless of the kinds of risk, however, risk and return are inseparable.

FIGURE 6-1   The risk-return relationship.

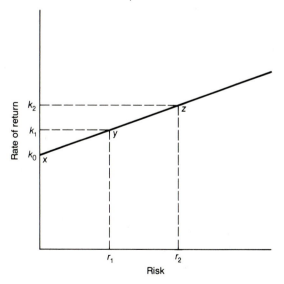

Expected, Required, and Actual Rates of Return

The *expected rate of return* is the rate investors expect the investment to provide in the future, given a set of assumptions. These assumptions are based on estimates about what will occur in the future with items like rents, expenses, and tax consequences.

The *required rate of return* is the rate investors demand for a certain type of investment given the riskiness perceived inherent in it. In the apartment building example, we compared the required rate with the investment's expected rate to determine whether we should buy the building. Since the expected rate exceeded our required rate, we made the decision to buy.

Both the expected and the required rates are based on future expectations and are used to make the investment decision. The *actual rate of return,* however, can be computed only *after* the investment has been made. It is thus a historical, after-the-fact rate that is not directly useful in making the investment decision. And it may differ from the required and expected rates since they are based on estimations of the future.

This distinction between various rates is fundamentally important in real estate investing. The investor unwilling to assume large risks will have a lower required rate and will search out those investments whose variability of income is low. In addition, this investor will be wary of investments that promise high rates of return *and* low risk, based on historical (actual) rates of return. The past is not necessarily representative of the future, and if the elements of risk are still present, then the investment's risk level is not really "low." But all else being equal, given two investments with equivalent returns, the investor will always choose the one with the lower risk. Conversely, for investments offering the same risk level, the investor will choose the one with the higher return.

Dealing with Risk in the Investment Decision

Before investigating alternative investments, the investor must determine the desired levels of risk and return. Determining risk and assigning a risk premium to an investment are highly subjective undertakings. Nevertheless, a number of methods have been used to put risk in perspective. By using these risk-analysis methods, the investor and the lender can obtain better insight into the risk associated with an investment. (Risk is discussed further in Chapter 7.)

Conservatism Traditionally, investors dealt with risk by being conservative about future expectations. Rents were adjusted downward and expenses upward, to duplicate a "worst case" situation. If the investment still looked acceptable under the worst of expectations, it was bought. Unfortunately, use of this investment strategy caused the investor to reject potentially acceptable investments because the method ignored the best-guess approximations of what would occur.

The Risk-Adjusted Discount Rate When accounting for risk in the discounted cash flow models, we can change the rate at which cash flows are discounted. To illustrate, assume that in our apartment building example we discount the cash flows at 17 instead of 14 percent because we perceive that the level of risk inherent in the apartment building is higher. This computation was performed in Table 6-15. As indicated, the negative NPV of $1,792 signals a "no-buy" decision. If our assessment of risk on this investment parallels the market's assessment, to sell the property the seller will have to lower the price to the point where the NPV at 17 percent is greater than or equal to zero. The elusive part of this assessment is the *quantification* of this investment's risk premium. Why should the required rate be 17 percent instead of, say, 14 percent? Although relative risk levels are fairly easy to determine, absolute risk (regarding a risk premium) is difficult to quantify.

Sensitivity Analysis Sensitivity analysis is a natural extension of the risk-adjusted discount rate. Essentially, we change one or more assumptions about the future to see how the NPV or IRR is affected.

For instance, in our apartment building example, we assumed the property value would increase at 5 percent per year over the holding period. How would NPV and IRR be affected if, say, the property value increased at only 2.5 percent per year? To answer this question, we simply substitute the new expected selling price and selling expenses into the TDS and ATER computations, as shown in Tables 6-16 and 6-17. Note that the figures changed from those in Tables 6-11 and 6-13 and 6-13 are the sales price, selling expenses, taxes from sale, and the resulting totals. Also note that the adjusted basis and depreciation amounts are not

TABLE 6-16 TAXES DUE ON SALE: APARTMENT BUILDING EXAMPLE

Selling price (SP) (EOY5)	$158,397
− selling expenses (SE) (8%)	12,672
amount realized (AR)	145,725
− adjusted basis (AB)	121,183
total gain (TG)	24,542
× investor's tax rate (28%)	.28
taxes due on sale (TDS)	6,872

TABLE 6-17 EXPECTED CASH FLOW FROM SALE

Expected selling price (SP)	$158,397
− selling expenses (SE)	12,672
net sale proceeds (NSP)	145,725
− unpaid mortgage balance (UM)	107,132
before-tax equity reversion (BTER)	38,593
− taxes due on sale (TDS)*	6,872
after-tax equity reversion (ATER)	31,721

*See Table 6-16.

TABLE 6-18   AFTER-TAX NPV COMPUTATION WITH REVISED ATER AMOUNTS

Year	Equity	ATCF	ATER	PVF$_{14\%}$	PV
0	($31,740)			1.0	($31,740)
1		$1,860		0.8772	1,632
2		2,433		0.7695	1,872
3		2,998		0.6750	2,024
4		3,684		0.5921	2,181
5		4,709	$31,721	0.5194	18,922
				Net present value	(5,109)

IRR = 12.66%

affected by a change in the expected selling price. Table 6-18 computes the NPVs given the new ATER amounts and shows the resulting IRRs. See how sensitive the NPV and IRR are to a relatively small change in the rate of appreciation expected. This is typical with investments that are highly leveraged, such as real estate. Similarly, sensitivity analysis can be used to modify assumptions about rental income, operating expenses, financing, and tax rates, to see their effects on NPV and IRR.

TAX IMPACTS ON PROPERTY HELD AS PERSONAL RESIDENCE

The "personal residence" real estate tax classification constitutes a large segment of the real estate market. Some of the tax rules applicable to property held as a personal residence are similar to the rules for trade or business property, but other rules are unique to this classification. Since the tax impacts occur at or during the acquisition, ownership, and disposition (sale) of the residence, our discussion of these rules concerns these three stages.

Tax Impacts at Acquisition

When a taxpayer purchases property for personal use, two tax consequences affect the income tax due for the year in which the property was purchased: *the proration of property taxes and the deductibility of financing costs.* In addition, the taxpayer's basis in the residence should also be considered at the time of acquisition. Although the basis will not have any consequence until the disposition stage, it is generally beneficial to compute it at the time of acquisition while records are still available and details of the purchase are still fresh. Computation of the basis now also helps when planning tax strategy for the future.

Proration of Property Taxes   When a residence is purchased, the IRS considers that property taxes for the year of sale are imposed on the seller up to, but not including, the date of sale. Similarly, the IRS considers the remainder of the property tax for the year to be imposed on the buyer. By this method, then, the buyer and the seller must apportion the taxes, regardless of which party actually paid them. The buyer and the seller then deduct these itemized amounts for the income tax year in which ownership was transferred. It is important to note that often a situation occurs in which either the party who assumes payment of the taxes will be able to deduct only her or his prorated share; similarly, the party who did not pay any portion of the taxes will nonetheless have a deduction for his or her share.

Other complications that arise are the variability of property tax years from state to state and the terminology used to denote the years. For example, some states' property tax years run from January 1 to December 31, whereas others run from April 1 of one year to March 31 of the following year. In some states, property taxes for a given year are payable the following year but not commonly identified as such. For these reasons, the purchaser of real estate should hire a competent accountant or other tax adviser in the locale where the property is located to determine the proper apportionment for income tax purposes.

Deductibility of Financing Costs   Interest paid on mortgage indebtedness for a personal residence is deductible as an itemized deduction on the owner's tax return to the extent of the taxpayer's basis plus the cost of capital improvements. At acquisition, however, the lender often charges the borrower a loan discount, or "points," to increase the yield to the lender. Our discussion of trade or business property noted that these charges had to be amortized over the term of the mortgage. When the property is for personal use, however, these points are fully deductible in the year of purchase as interest paid. Other closing costs related to the borrowing procedure, such as credit reports, appraisal fees, attorney's fees, and credit insurance, are nondeductible personal expenses for income tax purposes.

Basis Computation   Determining the adjusted basis in a personal residence is similar in many respects to that for trade or business property; original purchase price plus capital improvements and certain acquisition costs minus casualty loss deductions taken during the ownership stage and payments received for easements or rights-of-way given up. The original purchase price and capital improvements items for a personal residence are defined the same way they are for trade or business property. (You might want to refer to our earlier discussion of these items for clarification.)

Certain *acquisition costs* expended in the purchase of a personal residence can be added to the basis *if the buyer paid them.* These include title insurance, transfer taxes, and fees for appraisal, attorney services, advertising, escrow, survey, title opinion, recording, and abstracting. Note that there is no "cumulative depreciation" reduction of the basis, as there is with trade or business property, because for a personal residence the taxpayer is not allowed a deduction for depreciation. However, casualty losses (from fire, flood, windstorm, etc.) that have reduced the value of the property are considered itemized deductions (with limitations) in the year of occurrence and are considered reductions in the basis to the extent they have been taken as itemized deductions during the period of ownership. This topic is explained more fully in the following section.

Tax Impacts during Operation Period

The homeowner-taxpayer is bound by certain tax considerations in the year-to-year ownership of a personal residence. As noted, the homeowner is not allowed to deduct depreciation expense. However, mortgage interest and property taxes paid during the taxable year are fully deductible as itemized deductions.

Repairs and maintenance and other operating expenses are *not* deductible for a personal residence as they are for trade or business property. However, if the taxpayer uses a portion of the principal residence as a principal place of business, to be used exclusively and on a regular basis by clients, patients, or customers to meet or deal with the taxpayer, a portion of the operating and home-maintenance expenses are deductible as business expenses. Utilities, insurance, taxes, maintenance, and other operating expenses are usually apportioned on a basis of either the proportion of rooms or proportion of square feet in the residence used for business purposes. An employee who maintains an office at home may also be allowed these deductions, but only if the use is for the convenience of the employer.

In recent years, "business use of residence" deductions have been closely scrutinized by the IRS, and many deductions have been disallowed. As a result, the advice of a competent tax consultant is recommended when considering this type of deduction.

As mentioned in the "Basis Computation" section, the homeowner may deduct *casualty losses* to the personal residence in the year of occurrence. To be considered a *casualty loss,* the casualty must be an identifiable event that is sudden, unexpected, and swift, such as a fire, windstorm, or flood. The *loss* is the resulting loss in value to the property *or* the adjusted basis of the property just prior to the loss, whichever is less; it is reduced by the amount of insurance or other compensation received. A casualty loss is also subject to a $100 minimum; that is, the loss is deductible only to the extent that it exceeds $100.

Tax Impacts on Disposition

Since for tax purposes a personal residence is considered a "capital asset," the treatment of a gain on the sale is similar to that for trade or business property in that property held for more than 1 year qualifies for long-term capital gain treatment. However, although a gain on the sale of trade or business property must be *recognized* (i.e., it is taxable) in the year of sale, special provisions in the tax code permit the taxpayer to defer, or not recognize until later, the gain on the sale of a personal residence and in many cases to never owe taxes on disposition.

Computation of Realized and Recognized Gain   The *realized gain* is the actual amount of gain for tax purposes, but it may not need be *recognized* (that is, it may not be taxable) in the year of sale. The taxpayer can defer the recognition of all this realized gain if another principal residence is purchased within 24 months before or after the date of sale and if the price of the replacement residence equals or exceeds the old residence's adjusted sales price (ASP). If the ASP of the old residence is less than the purchase price of the new residence, then the amount that the new residence purchase price exceeds the ASP of the old is the portion which must be recognized in the year of sale. The gain is usually reported within the 24-month period after the sale by amending the tax return for the year of sale.

Adjusted Sale Price (ASP)   To determine the ASP, we must first determine the selling price, fixing-up expenses, and selling expenses for the old residence. The *selling price* is simply the gross contract price received for the property, including any assumed or "subject to" mortgage taken over by the buyer. The *fixing-up expenses* are expenditures for work performed on the old residence to make it more attractive for sale. To qualify as a fixing-up expense, expenditures must be incurred for work performed within 90 days of the date of the sales contract and must be paid for within 30 days of the date of sale. In addition, the expenditures must not be allowable as deductions in computing taxable income (for instance, as business-use-of-home deductions) or otherwise included in computing the amount realized from the sale of the old residence (for instance, as capital improvements would be). The *selling expenses* are expenses incurred in selling the residence, just as they are for the Section 1231 property. Brokerage commissions, legal fees, and advertising are examples of selling expenses.

Treatment of Unrecognized Gain   When a personal residence is sold, all or part of the realized gain may go unrecognized in the year of sale if a replacement residence is purchased within the statutory time period. What happens to this portion of the realized gain that is not recognized? *It reduces the taxpayer's basis in the replacement residence.* Thus, the purchase price of the replacement would immediately be reduced by the amount of gain that was not recognized on the old residence.

Treatment of Recognized Gain   What if the taxpayer chooses not to purchase another principal residence within the 24-month period following the date of sale? Ordinarily, the entire realized gain or loss must be recognized in the year of sale and is treated just as a gain or loss on trade or business property. However, for most taxpayers, it is possible to eliminate the recognition of gain altogether, as the following rule illustrates.

Exclusion: Taxpayers Age 55 or Older   If the taxpayer is 55 or older when the residence is sold and chooses to not purchase a replacement residence, up to $125,000 of realized gain ($62,500 for married taxpayers filing separately) may be excluded from income in the year of sale. Besides the age requirement, the taxpayer must have owned and occupied the residence for at least 3 of the last 5 years ending on the date of sale. Also, the taxpayer and spouse *combined* are entitled to take this election only once is a lifetime.

SUMMARY

This chapter addressed the tax consequences of real estate ownership, primarily from the standpoint of the investor purchasing property under the trade or business (Section 1231) and personal residence classifications. We included all rules that are generally applicable to the majority of real estate investments and investors. You should now have a solid background for the more specific financing applications discussed in Part Two.

QUESTIONS

1 Define the following terms:

a marginal tax rate	h adjusted basis
b taxable income from operation	i depreciable basis
c recovery period	j selling expenses
d depreciation	k discounted cash flow model
e replacement reserves	l net present value
f acquisition costs	m internal rate of return
g amortized financing costs	

2 Outline the steps for analyzing the tax impacts on a real estate investment.

3 What are the four tax categories of real estate? What are the major differences among the categories?

4 Outline and discuss briefly major forms of business organization. How are the tax rules different for each form? How would you decide the appropriate form of organization for owning a real estate investment?

5 Discuss the concept of the marginal tax rate. Why is this the appropriate rate in making investment decisions?

6 How are the taxable income and the taxes from operation calculated? Discuss briefly each component in the calculation of taxable income from operation.

7 Discuss how to calculate the depreciation deduction.

8 Explain the meaning of the negative taxable income in Table 6-7. Suppose that the before-tax cash flow from a real estate investment is negative; how can the after-tax cash flow be positive?

9 How are the taxable income and the taxes due on sale calculated? Discuss briefly each component in the calculation of taxable income from sale.

10 What does the adjusted basis of a real estate investment mean? How is it calculated?

11 a Suppose you buy a real estate investment for $100,000 and sell it 5 years later for $100,000 (net of selling expenses). During this period you have taken depreciation deductions of $27,500. What is your total gain on sale?

b Suppose you were in a 28 percent tax bracket. What is the amount of taxes due on sale?

12 Explain how to calculate the after-tax cash flow from operation.

13 What does a discounted cash flow model mean? What are the two discounted cash flow models?

14 Explain the concept of net present value. Using the cash flows in Table 6-14, calculate the net present value if the required rate of return is 15 percent, 18 percent, and 25 percent. Plot the relationship between the net present value and the required rate of return. What is the significance of a positive (negative) net present value?

15 Discuss the concept of the required rate of return. How would you calculate this rate? How is it used in investment analysis? Compare the concept of the lender's required rate of return on the mortgage and the equity investor's required rate of return on equity.

16 Explain the concept of the internal rate of return. How is it calculated? How is it used in making investment decisions?

17 Suppose you are trying to decide whether to buy an apartment building. The net present value is positive at a required rate of 15 percent. What does this imply about the internal rate of return? Does your decision to buy or not differ if you use the net present value or the internal rate of return methods?

18 When might the net present value and the internal rate of return methods yield conflicting conclusions?

19 Explain the concept of sensitivity analysis. How does the investor use sensitivity analysis in investment decision making?

20 Discuss the unique tax aspects of real estate held as a personal residence.

PROBLEMS

1 How do you compute the after-tax equity reversion (ATER)?

2 The depreciation deduction cannot be taken on real estate that falls into which of the four classifications?

3 What are the major differences in tax treatment between property held for investment, property held for use in a trade or business, and property held for sale to customers?

4 Given the following facts, prepare a straight-line depreciation schedule for years 1–5:

Purchase price: $1,000,000
Depreciable portion: 80 percent
Type of investment: Shopping center
Acquisition costs: $5,000

5 Do you think that taxable income from operations should be based on before-tax cash flow (i.e., TI = BTCF)? Why or why not? What would be the impact on the investment community if this proposal were enacted? What would happen to property values?

6 Your real estate agent has just called to inform you of an apartment building that she recently listed for sale. She gave you the following facts concerning the property:

   Seller's asking price is $3,000,000. The 160 apartment units rented for $250 per month each; expected to increase at 5 percent per year beginning in year 2. Vacancy factor has been 4 percent of potential gross income (PGI). Miscellaneous income from late charges on overdue rents has been averaging $8 per year per apartment unit and is not expected to change over the next 5 years. Operating expenses average 35 percent of EGI. With 8 percent appreciation, the agent figures the property should be worth $4,400,000 at the end of 5 years, with 10 percent going to selling expenses. A new 12 percent, 20-year, $2,400,000 mortgage is available, with monthly payments.

   Given these facts, do the following:

a Compute the BTCF for the 5-year holding period.
b Assuming the investor paid all cash, compute the BTCF.
c Compute the ATCF for the 5-year holding period.
d Compute the BTER at the end of year 5.
e Compute the ATER at the end of year 5.

7 Rest Easy Apartments, Inc., needs to compute its taxable income and wants you to assist. The effective gross income (EGI) was $56,000; operating expenses were $23,235, of which $2,000 was put into a fund for future replacement of stoves and refrigerators; debt service was $26,662, of which $25,126 was interest; depreciation was $17,000. Compute the TI.

8 Why do you suppose that depreciation is an allowable deduction when computing taxes from operation but replacement reserves are not?

9 Why do you think that the IRS makes a distinction between dealers and investors in real estate?

10 What are the impacts on taxes due on sale if financing costs increase over what was expected?

REFERENCES

Cooper, James R., and Stephen A. Pyhrr: *Real Estate Investment Strategy, Analysis, Decisions,* Wiley, New York, 1982.

Higgins, J. Warren: *A Federal Tax Guide for Real Estate Decisions,* rev. ed., rept. no. 31, Center for Real Estate and Urban Economic Studies, Storrs, Conn., January 1982.

Jaffe, Austin J., and C. F. Sirmans: *Real Estate Investment Decision Making,* Prentice-Hall, Englewood Cliffs, N.J., 1982.

Kau, James B., and C. F. Sirmans: *Tax Planning for Real Estate Investors,* 3d ed., Prentice-Hall, Englewood Cliffs, N.J., 1985.

Robinson, Gerald J.: *Federal Income Taxation of Real Estate,* 5th ed., Warren, Gorham & Lamont, Boston, 1988.

PART **TWO**

FINANCING METHODS AND TECHNIQUES

Part One introduced the principles for making the borrowing-lending (financing) decision using the traditional fixed-rate mortgage. Part Two expands those basics by examining various alternative financing methods and techniques. These techniques have been developed by the market in response to the many decision-making situations and problems borrowers and lenders face.

This discussion *assumes that you understand the material in Part One*. The analysis of each method centers around the following questions: What are the unique legal implications? What are the unique tax implications? What are the unique borrower- and property-analysis problems? How does a particular method work and when would it be used? What risks are created for the borrower and the lender? Each chapter provides detailed examples of a particular financing method(s) from both the borrower's and the lender's viewpoint. We apply the methods to the various types of real estate, such as single-family houses, apartments, office buildings, vacant land, and shopping centers.

Chapter 7 analyzes varying-rate mortgages. Chapter 8 then discusses the government-sponsored financing methods and programs for both single-family homes and income properties. Chapter 9 covers the various wraparound financing methods. Chapter 10 illustrates the popular seller financing method: the installment sale. Chapters 11 and 12 analyze construction and land-development financing, respectively. Chapter 13 discusses participation mortgages. Chapter 14 analyzes the use of joint ventures in financing real estate projects. Chapter 15 dissects the increasingly popular syndication method of raising equity capital. Chapter 16 covers leases and sale-leaseback as financing methods. Finally, Chapter 17 discusses several other alternative financing methods that have been developed in recent years.

As mentioned, the chapters are structured around the various financing methods. Also, the methods are *not* exclusive of each other; for example, installment sales are often structured around wraparound mortgages. Thus you must understand "wraps" before you can complete a thorough analysis of installment sales. Likewise, construction loans and land-development loans share many risks and mechanical similarities, and participation mortgages, joint ventures, and syndications have many similar characteristics. However, the chapters are self-contained: They can be read in any order.

If you are interested in the financing of single-family houses, read Chapters 7, 8, 9, and 17, which discuss the most widely used methods for housing finance. Remember, however, that these methods are also applicable to income properties, as we illustrate.

VARYING-RATE MORTGAGES

/|\\

Chapter 2 introduced the mortgage with a fixed interest rate and level monthly payments over a term generally extended 20 to 30 years. This type of mortgage had been the mainstay of mortgage lending, but changes in the mortgage market over the past decade led to the creation of a *varying-rate mortgage,* in which the interest rate is not fixed over the term of the loan.

This chapter first examines why varying-rate mortgages were created. Because such loans were a radical departure from the market's notions about mortgages, they conflicted with many of the existing laws and regulations that had been instituted when fixed-rate mortgages were the only type available. Since ancient times, the charging of interest by lenders has been viewed with a critical eye, as evidenced by the public contempt toward money lenders who charged *any* interest during Biblical times and the various usury and truth-in-lending laws enacted in recent years. Thus we first look at the various laws and regulations that pertain to each type of varying-rate loan.

The advent of varying-rate loans also changed the nature of risk analysis, causing lenders and borrowers alike to rethink (or scrutinize more closely) some aspects of mortgage loans. Here we identify these areas of concern. Finally, varying-rate loans differ from fixed-rate mortgages in the mechanics of calculating payments, constructing the amortization schedule, and determining yield and borrowing cost. A step-by-step example illustrates these computations for each type of varying-rate mortgage.

WHY VARYING-RATE MORTGAGES?

To understand why varying-rate mortgages were created, we must first examine the components of the interest rate that lenders charge. The rate charged (or the *nominal rate*) is composed of the risk-free rate, which is the rate of interest one would expect to earn on an investment in an economy in which there was no risk; the *risk premium,* which is the additional return lenders require as a result of the risk they take in loaning money to a borrower who might default; and the *inflation premium,* which is the additional return necessary to compensate lenders for the loss in purchasing power that they expect to incur over the life of the loan due to inflation. In equation form,

$$\text{Nominal rate} = \text{risk-free rate} + \text{risk premium} + \text{inflation premium}$$

Generally, the fixed-rate, level-payment mortgage was quite satisfactory for many years. Since inflation was relatively low, the inflation premium had little effect on the nominal rate, and since inflation remained fairly constant over time, it was easy to predict. However, this situation changed during the late 1960s as inflation rose rapidly. Since the inflation premium is a function of *expected* inflation and inflation had become much higher and more unpredictable, lenders found themselves saddled with older, low-interest loans that were made with low inflationary expectations. Although legally obligated to carry these low-interest loans for the remainder of the term, lenders simultaneously had to pay increasingly higher interest rates to savings depositors. The result was that the average yield the lenders earned on their mortgage portfolios often fell *below* the current interest rates paid to depositors.

On the other hand, borrowers benefited from this unanticipated inflation because they were repaying these fixed-rate loans with cheaper dollars; in effect, they were gaining the wealth the lenders were losing. Consequently, lenders required alternative mortgage instruments to protect themselves from the ravages of unexpected inflation. Although the mechanics of these instruments differ, their *basic* purpose is *to adjust the nominal interest rate periodically to account for changes in inflation expectations.*

TYPES OF VARYING-RATE MORTGAGES AND THEIR UNIQUE CHARACTERISTICS

There are many variations of flexible-rate loans in today's market, all classified into three categories:

1 Adjustable-rate mortgage (ARM)
2 Renegotiable-rate mortgage (RRM)
3 Price-level-adjustable mortgage (PLAM)

The mortgages in all three categories have many basic features unique to varying-rate mortgages. The features of a typical varying-rate mortgage are presented in Table 7-1.

Index The interest rate on a varying-rate mortgage varies (up or down) in accordance with the movement of some index. Several of the more common indexes to which interest rate adjustments are tied are the national average mortgage contract rate for major lenders on the purchase of previously occupied homes [Federal Home Loan Bank Board (FHLBB)]; the average cost of funds to FSLIC-insured savings and loan associations for each of the 12 districts; the monthly average auction rates for 3- to 6-month Treasury bills; and the monthly average yields on 1-, 2-, and 5-year U.S. Treasury securities.

The method used to apply the index to certain rate changes can take one of two forms: (1) the *date certain method* or (2) the *moving average method.* With the date certain method, an index value called the *base index rate* is selected at the date of loan origination and then subtracted from the index in effect at the

TABLE 7-1 FEATURES OF A TYPICAL VARYING-RATE MORTGAGE

1. Indexed to Treasury bills
2. Rate and monthly payment adjusted annually
3. Rate and payment adjustments limited by periodic caps of 2% or 6% over the life of the loan
4. Change in principal balance (negative amortization) not permitted
5. Change in loan term not permitted
6. Fully amortized
7. 30-year loan term
8. Maximum loan-to-value ratio 95%
9. Private mortgage insurance required when loan-to-value ratio is 80–95%

adjustment date to derive the new interest rate on the loan for the coming period. With the moving average method, all values of the index from the origination or prior rate-change adjustment date to the current rate-change adjustment date are added together; this total is then divided by the number of index values to derive an average index value for the adjustment period.

Adjustment Period   The adjustment period is the time between changes in the interest rate on the loan. These periodic changes correlate directly with changes in the chosen index during the stated period. Adjustment periods on varying-rate mortgages vary from 1, 3, or 6 months to 1, 3, or 5 years.

Margin   The margin is the percentage amount added to the index rate. The total amount is used to determine the interest rate on a varying-rate mortgage, i.e.,

$$\text{Index rate} + \text{margin} = \text{varying-rate mortgage interest rate}$$

This margin is used primarily to compensate the lender for the increased risk associated with the uncertainty of a varying-rate mortgage.

Caps   Caps limit the upward (or downward) adjustment of rates or payments on varying-rate mortgages. The issuance of such caps protects the borrower from volatile changes in interest rates or monthly payments. Caps can take the form of periodic or lifelong limits. A periodic interest rate cap prevents the mortgage rate and the security yield from changing more than a specified amount at any adjustment, whereas a lifelong cap prevents the rate and yield from changing more than a larger specified amount from the initial interest rate at any time during the life of the loan.

Negative Amortization   Negative amortization is an increase in the unpaid loan balance because the monthly payment is insufficient (due to payment caps) to cover the accrued interest on the loan. The excess of accrued interest due over the monthly payment is added to the outstanding balance each month until the payment can be increased to an amount that exceeds the interest due thereafter, and normal amortization occurs.

Convertibility   Many varying-rate mortgages allow convertibility into fixed-rate mortgages. The new interest rate on the converted loan is usually set at the current market rate for a fixed-rate mortgage with similar maturity outstanding.

Assumability   All varying-rate mortgages contain due-on-sale clauses. A due-on-sale clause gives the lender the right to require the outstanding mortgage balance immediately due if the mortgaged property is sold; thus, the new property owner may not be allowed to assume the mortgage. Upon sale, if current interest rates are above that on the old mortgage, the lender will require the indebtedness due. If current rates are below that on the outstanding mortgage, the lender will be better off allowing assumption of the old mortgage. Therefore, the due-on-sale clause is quite valuable to lenders; it assists lenders in avoiding being locked into below-market-rate loans.

Prepayment Prepayment clauses are common to varying-rate mortgages; they allow the borrower to prepay the loan after some specified date with little or no penalty. As interest rates fall, the borrower prepays; if rates rise, the option to prepay expires without exercise.

Teasers A lender hoping to reorganize its portfolio uses a teaser in order to entice the borrower to purchase an ARM over a fixed-rate mortgage. The lender usually quotes an initial rate indicating that it is "discounting" the normal index plus margin rate. However, the costs associated with the low initial rate are disguised and passed through to the borrower in various other ways.

Adjustable-Rate Mortgage (ARM) An adjustable-rate mortgage is one which adjusts its interest rate, level of payment, and/or term to maturity in accordance with adjustments in a certain rate index. ARMs offer interest rate immunization; they protect the lender hesitant to lend long-term at a fixed rate of interest during times of interest rate fluctuation. Usually, the interest rate on an ARM is lower than that on a fixed-rate mortgage in order to compensate the borrower for the increased risk in holding an instrument whose future rate level is contingent on market conditions. ARMs are also referred to as variable-rate mortgages (VRMs).

There are two forms of ARMs: the variable-payment and the variable-term. With both forms, the interest rate may be modified at some specific interval in an amount dictated by some specific index that is not controlled by either the borrower or the lender. When the rate is changed, either the payment amount or the term of the (maturing) loan fluctuates accordingly to account for the change in amortization.

Table 7-2 outlines the major standards of the eight types of ARMs currently accepted by the Federal National Mortgage Association (FNMA) in the secondary mortgage market. The liquidity of ARMs in this market has been a major factor in their development and use by lenders.

The lender's freedom to structure ARMs depends on direct federal and state regulations and indirect secondary market influences. Table 7-3 outlines the major characteristics of recent federal regulations governing ARMs when used for financing single-family housing. Note that the regulations differ for federal savings and loan and national banks. Finally, individual state regulations may affect the magnitude of rate adjustments, may not allow negative amortization, or may forbid the use of ARMs altogether.

Exhibit 7-1 is an example of an ARM uniform rider. This rider is used to ac-

TABLE 7-2   FNMA OPTIONS FOR ARMs

Interest rate index	Life cap (%)	Periodic adjust-ment cap (%)	Margin with rate reduction (%)	Gross maximum margin (%)	Maximum shortfall with rate reduction (%)
1-year Treasury bill	6	0	1.70	3	1.50
1-year Treasury bill	6	1	2.00	3	2.00
1-year Treasury bill	6	2	1.90	3	2.00
1-year Treasury bill	6	2	2.25	3	1.25
1-year Treasury bill	5	1	2.00	3	1.00
1-year Treasury bill	6	2	2.00	3	1.25

count for the differences between the ARM and the standard fixed-rate mortgage and is attached to the standard mortgage document widely used for home mortgages. (The standard mortgage was illustrated in Chapter 3.) The major difference is the interest rate and monthly payment changes (part A, Exhibit 7-1). The initial interest rate, the exact date of the first rate change, and the frequency of rate changes thereafter are to be indicated on the form. The initial index figure is to be indicated as well. Part C of the rider contains the provisions for notification, which differ from those stated in the standard mortgage. The remaining parts of the rider are intended to protect the lender in the event of state or federal laws that conflict with provisions within the mortgage.

Renegotiable-Rate Mortgage (RRM)   Also known as the *rollover mortgage,* the RRM has gained popularity in recent years. An RRM is simply a fixed-rate level-payment mortgage with a 20- to 30-year amortization period, but with a balloon payment due at the end of a period of time, typically 3 to 5 years. At that time, the amount of the balloon is refinanced for the remaining years in the amortization period at the then-current mortgage rate, with a balloon payment coming at the end of another 3- to 5-year period, when the process repeats itself.

For single-family house financing, this RRM is typically subject to regulations, including the following: these are restrictions on the magnitude of the interest rate change; the lender may not have the option to demand payment at the time of adjustment (i.e., the lender *must* refinance the loan at the current "renegotiated" rate if the borrower accepts the new rate); the borrower may be free to refinance the balance with another lender; the lender cannot collect points or loan fees, and prepayment penalties at the time of adjustment and any time after the first renewal period are forbidden; and interest rate increases not accounted for because of the renegotiated-rate ceiling cannot be accumulated and added in future periods.

The RRM is one of the most popular alternative financing vehicles for investment property, but the regulations just cited do not apply to investment property loans. Hence, the investment borrower should beware. In the strictest sense, an RRM should have specific provisions for the calculation of the new rate at the

TABLE 7-3   MAJOR FEDERAL REGULATIONS FOR ARM HOME LOANS

Major characteristics	Federal savings and loans and mutual savings banks	National banks
Must offer fixed-rate mortgage instrument to borrower	None	None
Limits amount of ARMs that may be held	None	None
Indexes governing mortgage-rate adjustments	Any interest rate index that is readily verifiable by the borrower and not under the control of the lender, including national or regional cost-of-funds indexes for savings and loans	One of three national rate indexes—a long-term mortgage rate, a Treasury bill rate, or a 3-year Treasury bond rate
Limits frequency of rate adjustments	None	Not more often than every 6 months
Limits size of periodic rate adjustments	None	None
Allowable methods of adjustment to rate changes	Any combination of changes in monthly payment, loan term, or principal balance	Changes in monthly payment or rate of amortization
Limits amount of negative amortization	No limit, but monthly payments must be adjusted periodically to amortize fully the loan over the remaining term	Limits are set, and monthly payments must be adjusted periodically to amortize fully the loan over the remaining term
Advance notice of rate adjustments must be given	30–45 days before scheduled adjustment	30–45 days prior to scheduled adjustment
Prepayment restrictions or changes	None	Prepayment without penalty permitted after notification of first scheduled adjustment
Disclosure requirements	Full disclosure of ARM characteristics no later than time of loan application	Full disclosure of ARM characteristics no later than time of loan application

time of renegotiation and a covenant by the lender that the refinancing of the unpaid balance at the new rate is guaranteed. Many so-called RRMs for investment property are not specific about renegotiation of rates and make no promises to refinance the unpaid balance. Thus, the unwary borrower may be caught with a sizable balloon payment, with no lender willing to refinance it. At the very least, the borrower may be placed in a disadvantageous bargaining position.

Price-Level Adjustable Mortgages (PLAM)   The PLAM has been used for several years in other countries. It is unique because the contract interest rate is set

ADJUSTABLE RATE RIDER

THIS ADJUSTABLE RATE RIDER is made this .... day of .... 19........, and is incorporated into and shall be deemed to amend and supplement the Mortgage, Deed of Trust, or Deed to Secure Debt (the "Security Instrument") of the same date given by the undersigned (the "Borrower") to secure Borrower's Adjustable Rate Note to .... (the "Lender") of the same date (the "Note") and covering the property described in the Security Instrument and located at:

....

(Property Address)

The Note Contains Provisions Allowing for Changes in the Interest Rate. Increases in the Interest Rate will Result in Higher Payments. Decreases in the Interest Rate will Result in Lower Payments.

ADDITIONAL COVENANTS. In addition to the covenants and agreements made in the Security Instrument, Borrower and Lender further covenant and agree as follows:

A. INTEREST RATE AND MONTHLY PAYMENT CHANGES

The Note provides for an Initial Rate of Interest of ....%. Section 4 of the Note provides for changes in the interest rate and the monthly payments, as follows:

"(A) Change Dates
Beginning in 19........, the rate of interest I will pay may change on the .... day of the month of ...., and on that day every ☐ **6th** ☐ **12th** ☐ **30th** ☐ **60th** *[Check only one box]* month thereafter. Each date on which the rate of interest could change is called a "Change Date."

(B) The Index
Any changes in the rate of interest will be based on changes in the Index. The "Index" is the monthly average yield on United States Treasury securities adjusted to a constant maturity of ☐ **6 months** ☐ **1 year** ☐ **3 years** ☐ **5 years** as made available by the Federal Reserve Board, or ☐ the "Contract Interest Rate, Purchase of Previously Occupied Homes, National Average for all Major Types of Lenders" as made available by the Federal Home Loan Bank Board.
[Check only one box]
If the Index is no longer available, the Note Holder will choose a new index which is based upon comparable information. The Note Holder will give me notice of this choice.
The first Index figure for this Note is ....%. It is called the "Original Index."
The most recently available Index figure as of the date .... days before each Change Date is called the "Current Index."

(C) Calculation of Changes
Before each Change Date, the Note Holder will determine any change in my rate of interest. The Note Holder will calculate the amount of the difference, if any, between the Current Index and the Original Index. If the Current Index is higher than the Original Index, the Note Holder will add the difference to the Initial Rate of Interest. If the Current Index is lower than the Original Index, the Note Holder will subtract the difference from the Initial Rate of Interest. The Note Holder will then round the result of this addition or subtraction to the nearest one-eighth of one percentage point (0.125%). This rounded amount will be the new rate of interest I am required to pay.
The Note Holder will then determine the new amount of my monthly payment that would be sufficient to repay the outstanding principal balance in full on the maturity date at my new rate of interest in substantially equal payments. The result of this calculation will be the new amount of my monthly payment.

(D) Effective Date of Changes
The new rate of interest will become effective on each Change Date. I will pay the new amount of my monthly payment each month beginning on the first monthly payment date after the Change Date until the amount of my monthly payment is again changed or I have fully repaid the loan.

(E) Notice of Changes
The Note Holder will mail or deliver to me a notice of any changes in the amount of my monthly payment before the effective date of any change. The notice will include information required by law to be given me and also the title and telephone number of a person who will answer any question I may have regarding the notice."

B. CHARGES; LIENS

Uniform Covenant 4 of the Security Instrument is amended to read as follows:

4. Charges; Liens. Borrower shall pay all taxes, assessments, and other charges, fines and impositions attributable to the Property which may attain a priority over this Security Instrument, and leasehold payments or ground rents, if any, in the manner provided under paragraph 2 hereof or, if not paid in such manner, by Borrower making payment, when due, directly to the payee thereof. Borrower shall promptly furnish to Lender all notices of amounts due under this paragraph, and in the event Borrower shall make payment directly, Borrower shall promptly furnish to Lender receipts evidencing such payments. Borrower shall promptly discharge any lien which has priority over this Security Instrument; provided, that Borrower shall not be required to discharge any such lien so long as Borrower: (a) shall agree in writing to the payment of the obligation secured by such lien in a manner acceptable to Lender; (b) shall in good faith contest such lien by, or defend against enforcement of such lien in, legal proceedings which in the opinion of Lender operate to prevent the enforcement of the lien or forfeiture of the Property or any part thereof; or (c) shall secure from the holder of such lien an agreement in a form satisfactory to Lender subordinating such lien to this Security Instrument.

ADJUSTABLE RATE RIDER—Single Family-7/81—**FNMA Uniform Instrument**

EXHIBIT 7-1   ADJUSTABLE RATE RIDER

If Lender determines that all or any part of the Property is subject to a lien which may attain a priority over this Security Instrument, Lender shall send Borrower notice identifying such lien. Borrower shall satisfy such lien or take one or more of the actions set forth above within ten days of the giving of notice.

C. NOTICE

Uniform Covenant 14 of the Security Instrument is amended to read as follows:

14. Notice. Except for any notice required under applicable law to be given in another manner, (a) any notice to Borrower provided for in this Security Instrument shall be given by delivering it or by mailing it by first class mail addressed to Borrower at the Property Address or at such other address as Borrower may designate by notice to Lender as provided herein, and (b) any notice to Lender shall be given by first class mail to Lender's address stated herein or to such other address as Lender may designate by notice to Borrower as provided herein. Any notice provided for in this Security Instrument shall be deemed to have been given to Borrower or Lender when given in the manner designated herein.

D. UNIFORM MORTGAGE; GOVERNING LAW; SEVERABILITY

Uniform Covenant 15 is amended to read as follows:

15. Uniform Mortgage; Governing Law; Severability. This form of Security Instrument combines uniform covenants for national use and non-uniform covenants with limited variations by jurisdiction to constitute a uniform security instrument covering real property. This Security Instrument shall be governed by federal law and the law of the jurisdiction in which the Property is located. In the event that any provision or clause of this Security Instrument or the Note conflicts with applicable law, such conflict shall not affect other provisions of this Security Instrument or the Note which can be given effect without the conflicting provision, and to this end the provisions of this Security Instrument and the Note are declared to be severable.

E. NO FUTURE ADVANCES

Non-Uniform Covenant 21 of the Security Instrument ("Future Advances") is deleted.

F. LOAN CHARGES

If the loan secured by the Security Instrument is subject to a law which sets maximum loan charges, and that law is finally interpreted so that the interest or other loan charges collected or to be collected in connection with the loan exceed permitted limits, then: (1) any such loan charge shall be reduced by the amount necessary to reduce the charge to the permitted limits; and (2) any sums already collected from Borrower which exceeded permitted limits will be refunded to Borrower. Lender may choose to make this refund by reducing the principal owed under the Note or by making a direct payment to Borrower. If a refund reduces principal, the reduction will be treated as a partial prepayment under the Note.

G. LEGISLATION

If, after the date hereof, enactment or expiration of applicable laws have the effect either of rendering the provisions of the Note, the Security Instrument or this Adjustable Rate Rider (other than this paragraph G) unenforceable according to their terms, or all or any part of the sums secured hereby uncollectable, as otherwise provided in the Security Instrument and this Adjustable Rate Rider, or of diminishing the value of Lender's security, then Lender, at Lender's option, may declare all sums secured by the Security Instrument to be immediately due and payable. In such event, Borrower shall not have the right to reinstate otherwise provided in Non-Uniform Covenant 19 of the Security Instrument.

IN WITNESS WHEREOF, Borrower has executed this Adjustable Rate Rider.

....(Seal)
-Borrower

....(Seal)
-Borrower

....(Seal)
-Borrower

(Sign Original Only)

at the rate that would prevail if zero inflation were expected, and the rate remains constant over the life of the mortgage. However, the outstanding principal balance and the monthly payments are adjusted periodically by a factor that accounts for the current inflation rate. This adjustment keeps the mortgage payment the same in *real* dollars, although the actual (nominal) payment changes. Because of this inflation indexing and difficulties related to tax treatment of interest, the PLAM is not used in the United States for single-family housing. But because of the PLAM's accuracy in keeping constant the real return to the lender, PLAM is likely to be a mortgage instrument of the future if unexpected inflation continues to occur.

A PLAM significantly departs from the traditional fixed-rate mortgage. Here we outline these major differences; the PLAM mechanics are covered in detail later in the chapter. Since the initial payment under a PLAM is based on a low real rate, in current dollars, the initial payments are much lower than those for a fixed-rate mortgage, ARM, or RRM. This condition permits a buyer to take out a larger mortgage (hence, buy a more expensive home) than might be affordable under a fixed-rate mortgage. However, because the outstanding balance (and payment) is adjusted by the inflation rate, the payment increase could become an unaffordable burden if the borrower's income did not rise at the same rate as inflation.

Another potential disadvantage is if the property value fails to increase at the rate of inflation. There could be situations where the loan-to-value ratio increases to the point where the loan balance exceeds the value of the property. Studies have indicated that this type of situation increases the likelihood of default.

The PLAM appears a very attractive instrument in many ways, but the U.S. tax code inhibits its use because the indexing of the loan balance represents income to the lender. Since most lenders are accrual-basis taxpayers, they are required to pay taxes as the balance is indexed. However, the lender does not receive an immediate cash flow upon balance indexing; the increased loan balance is, in effect, refinanced over the remaining term of the mortgage. The lender's cash flow from each loan's balance indexing is extended over several years; therefore the PLAM is not attractive to the lender because of this mismatch of cash flow and tax payments.

There are other problems with PLAM financing. For instance, equity accumulates slower with a PLAM than with a fixed-rate mortgage. With a PLAM, the parties to the financing do not know exactly what the total cost of the loan will be prior to the beginning of the term. Federally chartered lenders are not permitted by regulations to use PLAMs. State chartered associations are permitted to use them but are subject to applicable state laws.

IMPACTS ON LOAN ANALYSIS
AND THE LOAN-SUBMISSION PACKAGE

Theoretically, flexible-rate mortgages eliminate the unexpected inflation risk to the lender. In practice, they may not and may introduce other risks as well. For instance, with a flexible-rate loan, the regulations regarding the frequency and magnitude of the changes restrict the lender's ability to absorb inflation. Rate- and payment-adjustment ceilings (caps) and the lag in rate adjustments that can occur with frequent rate-change intervals may benefit the borrower but not the lender in a period of rapidly rising inflation. In addition, there is the risk that an index chosen as a basis for rate changes may not correlate well with the lender's future cost of funds and thus will not serve the intended purpose.

Flexible-rate mortgages are considered higher in default risk than fixed-rate mortgages. One reason is that in an inflationary period, there is a possibility that the borrower's income will not keep pace with inflation, making it more difficult or impossible for the borrower to meet the debt service. Thus the borrower's expected future income must be scrutinized closely. Also, although not always required by law, the worst-case comparison between the proposed flexible-rate loan and a fixed-rate mortgage should always be made for the benefit of the borrower *and* and the lender. When a flexible-rate loan is considered, comparison of the borrower's expected future income to the worst-case flexible-rate loan should indicate whether underwriting is advisable.

Another reason for higher default risk with flexible-rate loans is the negative-amortization provisions. With a fixed-rate, level-payment mortgage, the loan balance gradually falls over the term. Thus, even if the nominal value of the property does not change, the loan-to-value ratio becomes smaller (as illustrated in Figure 7-1). With a flexible-rate mortgage that allows negative amortization, it is possible for the loan balance to increase above the original amount. Unless the property's value increases proportionally, the loan-to-value ratio increases.

FIGURE 7-1   Amortization comparison: fixed-rate mortgage versus an ARM with negative amortization.

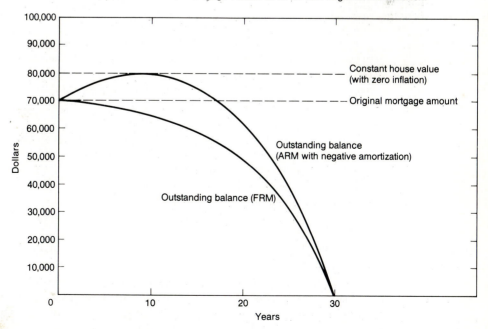

Therefore, when underwriting flexible-rate loans, lenders must consider the local market's property appreciation rate relative to the original loan-to-value ratio and the amount of negative amortization permitted. Risk studies and simulations have indicated a significant increase in the probability of default in varying-rate mortgages compared with default on fixed-rate mortgages.

The lender usually conducts some amount of financial analysis to determine the borrower's ability to repay the loan so as to substantially lessen default risk. In order to guard against the resulting risk, varying-rate mortgages are often insured by a few private companies that offer mortgage insurance; such a policy is referred to as private mortgage insurance (PMI). Private mortgage insurance companies offer insurance to approved lenders against financial loss on the default of first mortgages. The insurance costs are paid by the borrower—usually as a one-time lump sum or an annual percentage of the mortgage's declining balance (see Chapter 4 for a complete discussion of PMI).

MECHANICS OF VARYING-RATE MORTGAGES

We now turn to the computational aspects of varying-rate loans. Each type of flexible-rate mortgage is illustrated by calculating the payment, amortization schedule, and yield (effective borrowing cost). Special consideration is given to the similarities and differences in each mortgage type, with only minor changes in the numerical assumptions.

A Review of Present Value Concepts in Relation to the Varying-Rate Mortgage

Before beginning the examples, a brief review and expansion of present value concepts is necessary. In Chapter 2 we found the present value of a stream of equal payments (i.e., an annuity) by multiplying the amount of the payment by the appropriate factor, given the rate of interest and the number of payments. Thus, if the payment is $400 per month for 3 years and the rate is 10 percent, the present value is computed as

$$PV = \$400(PVAF_{10\%/12,36}) = \$400(30.99124) = \$12,396$$

With a varying-rate mortgage, however, the payment stream changes periodically over the term of the loan. Thus, we have several different series of equal-payment streams that must be discounted back to the present. For example, suppose we have a payment stream calling for monthly payments of $350 for the first 12 months (year 1), $400 for the second 12 months (year 2), and $450 for the third 12 months (year 3). We thus have three annuities occurring during consecutive time intervals. To find the present value of this stream of payments, we must *separately* discount each annuity back to the present. Assuming the rate at which we wish to discount this stream of payments is 10 percent, we may discount each annuity back to its beginning point using the PVAF to derive the present value *at*

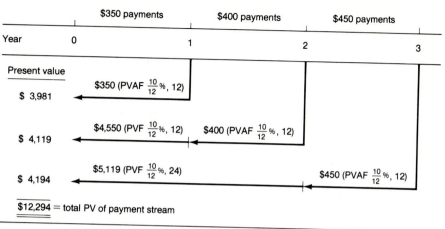

FIGURE 7-2   Time-line illustration of a 3-year uneven annuity.

that point; then we must discount these values to the present (time zero) as lump sums using the PVF. Figure 7-2 illustrates this process. Note that the $350 payments for the first year are discounted to the present by using the PVAF, and no further discounting is necessary. For year 2, however, the $400 payments are discounted to the beginning of year 2 (end of year 1), where the value at that time is $4,550. This value must then by discounted for 1 year by using the PVF for 12 months. The payments for year 3 are discounted in a similar fashion. First, the payments for year 3 are discounted to their beginning point (EOY 2) to derive a lump-sum value, which is then discounted the remaining 24 months to the present, as shown in Figure 7-2. This concept is important in understanding how to compute the yield on varying-rate mortgages in the following examples.

Adjustable-Rate Mortgage Example

Assume we have a $70,000 mortgage at 8.5 percent original interest rate, with a 30-year term and monthly payments. The interest rate can be adjusted at the end of each year, and we assume the rate increases 0.25 percent after the first year and another 0.25 percent after the second year. What are the monthly payments for the first, second, and third years of the loan?

Variable-Rate, Variable-Payment Mortgage Example

The computation for the first year's monthly payment is

$$\text{Monthly payment} = \text{original balance} \times MC_{8.5\%/12,360}$$
$$= \$70,000 \times 0.007689$$
$$= \$538.23$$

To compute payments for the second year, we must first find the balance at the end of year 1:

$$\text{Monthly payment}_{\text{year 1}} \times \text{PVAF}_{8.5\%/12,348} = \text{loan balance}_{\text{EOY 1}}$$
$$\$538.23 \qquad \times \qquad 129.07049 \quad = \$69,470$$

Now the monthly payments for the second year can be calculated by using the same basic formula as before but reducing the term by the number of months (12) that have already passed and increasing the rate 0.25 percent:

$$\text{Loan balance} \times \text{MC}_{8.75\%/12,348} = \text{monthly payment}_{\text{year 2}}$$
$$\$69,470 \qquad \times \qquad 0.007924 \quad = \$550.48$$

Note that the monthly payments for year 2 are now $550.48, up $12.25 from year 1.

For year 3, we assume the interest rate will increase another 0.25 percent, to 9.0 percent. Proceeding as before, we first find the balance outstanding at EOY 2:

$$\text{Monthly payment}_{\text{year 2}} \times \text{PVAF}_{8.75\%/12,336} = \text{loan balance}_{\text{EOY 2}}$$
$$\$550.48 \qquad \times \qquad 125.20264 \quad = \$68,922$$

Next we find the monthly payments for year 3:

$$\text{Loan balance}_{\text{EOY 2}} \times \text{MC}_{9.0\%/12,336} = \text{monthly payment}_{\text{year 3}}$$
$$\$68,922 \qquad \times \qquad 0.008163 \quad = \$562.61$$

The year 3 payments have risen $12.13 above the payments for year 2. For subsequent years, the same process is used.

The preceding results can be used to derive the amortization schedule for this loan. Table 7-4 is the annual amortization schedule. Since we have already determined the balances for the end of each of the first 3 years, we can subtract these balances to obtain the amount of principal reduction each year. Also, we

TABLE 7-4 3-YEAR ANNUAL AMORTIZATION SCHEDULE—$70,000 VARIABLE-RATE, VARIABLE-PAYMENT MORTGAGE

Year	Rate (%)	Balance	Annual debt service*	Principal	Interest
0		$70,000			
1	8.5	69,470	$6,459	$530	$5,929
2	8.75	68,922	6,606	548	6,058
3	9.0	68,350	6,751	572	6,179

*This is the monthly payment multiplied by 12. For example, the monthly payment in year 1 is $538.23. Multiplying this payment by 12 yields the annual debt service in year 1 of $6,459.

have already calculated the debt service for each year, and we know that subtracting the amount of principal from the debt service yields the amount of interest paid for each year.

To calculate the lender's yield (borrower's cost), we must make an assumption about the number of years the loan will be outstanding. Will the loan be paid off at the end of year 3? Or will the loan continue to maturity (36 years)? If we assume the loan continues past year 3, we must also make an assumption about future rate adjustments.

First, let us compute the yield assuming the loan is paid off at the end of year 3:

$$\begin{aligned}
\text{Present value of loan (\$70,000)} = {} & \$538.23(\text{PVAF}_{i\%/12,12}) \\
& + \$550.48(\text{PVAF}_{i\%/12,12})(\text{PVF}_{i\%/12,12}) \\
& + \$562.61(\text{PVAF}_{i\%/12,12})(\text{PVF}_{i\%/12,24}) \\
& + \$68,350 \times \text{PVF}_{i\%/12,36}
\end{aligned}$$

To solve for the rate in this equation, we must first set up a table like Table 7-5, where by trial and error and subsequent interpolation we can determine the yield. Since the nominal rate begins at 8.5 percent and rises no higher than 9.0 percent, we know the effective rate (yield) will be somewhere between. In the table, the present value of the payments is $70,428 when discounted at 8.5 percent and $69,023 when discounted at 9.0 percent. The desired present value, $70,000, falls between these values; thus the yield is between 8.5 and 9.0 percent. We can interpolate as follows:

TABLE 7-5   YIELD CALCULATION—ARM EXAMPLE, LOAN PAYOFF EOY 3

Year	Monthly payment	Balloon payment	$\text{PVAF}_{8.5\%}$	$\text{PVF}_{8.5\%}$	$\text{PV}_{8.5\%}$	$\text{PVAF}_{9.0\%}$	$\text{PVF}_{9.0\%}$	$\text{PV}_{9.0\%}$
1	$538.23	—	11.465	—	$ 6,171	11.435	—	$ 6,155
2	550.48	—	11.465	0.91879	5,799	11.435	0.19424	5,261
3	562.61	—	11.465	0.84417	5,445	11.435	0.83583	5,377
		$68,350	—	0.77561	53,013	—	0.76415	52,230
Total present value					$70,428			$69,023

Interpolation:

$\text{PV}_{8.5\%}$	$70,428	$\text{PV}_{8.5\%}$		$70,428
$\text{PV}_{9.0\%}$	69,023	Desired PV		70,000
Difference	$ 1,405	Difference	$	428

$$\frac{\$428}{\$1,405} \times 0.5\% = 0.15\%$$

$$8.5\% + 0.15\% = 8.65\% \text{ yield}$$

1 Find the difference between the present values at 8.5 and 9.0 percent ($70,428 − $69,023 = $1,405).

2 Calculate the difference between the present value at the lower rate and the desired present value ($70,428 − $70,000 = $428).

3 Divide the result in step 2 by the result from step 1 ($428 ÷ 1405 = 0.3046).

4 Multiply the quotient in step 3 by the difference in the two percentage rates (9.0 − 8.5 = 0.5 × 0.3046 = 0.15).

5 Add the result in step 4 to the lower rate (8.5 + 0.15) to get the approximate yield of 8.65 percent.

Next, let us compute the yield on this same loan, but assume the loan continues to maturity with no rate increases after year 3. Thus,

$$\$70,000 = \$538.23(PVAF_{i\%/12,12})$$
$$+ \ \$550.48(PVAF_{i\%/12,12})(PVF_{i\%/12,12})$$
$$+ \ \$562.61(PVAF_{i\%/12,336})(PVF_{i\%/12,24})$$

Table 7-6 illustrates this yield calculation. Note that the yield in this case is higher than in the previous example because of the 9.0 percent rate being maintained from the third through the thirtieth years of the loan.

Variable-Rate, Variable-Term Mortgage Example

In another type of ARM, the mortgage term is changed but the payment is held constant. Assume we have the same facts as in the variable-payment example,

TABLE 7-6 YIELD CALCULATION—ARM EXAMPLE, LOAN RUNS TO MATURITY, NO RATE INCREASE AFTER YEAR 3

Year	Monthly payment	PVAF$_{8.5\%}$	PVF$_{8.5\%}$	PV$_{8.5\%}$	PVAF$_{9.0\%}$	PVF$_{9.0\%}$	PV$_{9.0\%}$
1	$538.23	11.465	—	$ 6,171	11.435	—	$ 6,155
2	550.48	11.465	0.91879	5,799	11.435	0.19424	5,755
3–20	562.61	128.00	0.84417	60,792	122.504	0.83583	57,607
Total present value				$72,762			$69,517

Interpolation:

PV$_{8.5\%}$	$72,762	PV$_{8.5\%}$	$72,762
PV$_{9.0\%}$	69,517	Desired PV	70,000
Difference	$ 3,245	Difference	$ 2,762

$$\frac{\$2,762}{\$3,245} \times 0.5\% = 0.43\%$$

8.5% + 0.43% = 8.93% yield

except that instead of changing the payment when the rate increases, the term of the loan is lengthened and the monthly payment remains at the original $538.23 level. Thus, this loan parallels the previous loan for year 1. When the rate increases to 8.75 percent at the beginning of year 2, however, we increase the term to compensate. The term then is our unknown. The problem is to find the number of payments that will fully amortize the balance owing at the end of year 1, given the higher 8.75 percent interest rate. Our equation is as follows:

$$\text{Balance outstanding}_{EOY\ 1} \times MC_{8.75\%/12,\ months} = \$538.23$$

Our next step is to compute the balance outstanding at EOY 1. This has already been calculated for the previous example in Table 7-4 and is the same for this example. Inserting this balance into our equation,

$$\$69,470 \times MC_{12\%/12, months} = \$538.23$$
$$MC_{12\%/12, months} = \frac{\$538.23}{\$69,470}$$
$$= 0.00775$$

This number 0.00775 is the mortgage constant at 8.75 percent for the unknown number of payments remaining. Solving this equation, we find a maturity between years 30 and 33 that yields a constant of 0.00775. By interpolation, we find the remaining maturity of the loan to be approximately 32 years and 6 months (see Table 7-7).

At the end of year 2, however, we have another rate increase, to 9.0 percent. When this occurs, the remaining term must once again be changed. We repeat the previous process. Our equation is as follows:

TABLE 7-7   DETERMINING REMAINING LOAN TERM

$MC_{8.75\%/12,360} = 0.00786$

$MC_{8.75\%/12,396} = 0.00773$

Desired $MC_{8.75\%/12,n} = 0.00775$

Interpolation:

$MC_{8.75\%/12,360}$	0.00786	$MC_{8.75\%/12,360}$	0.00786
$MC_{8.75\%/12,396}$	0.00773	Desired MC	0.00775
Difference	0.00013		0.00011

$\dfrac{0.00011}{0.00013} = 0.85$; thus maturity is about 85% of the way from years 30–33

30 years + (0.85 × 3 years) = 32 years 6½ months

$$\text{Balance outstanding}_{EOY\ 2} \times MC_{9.0\%/12,\text{months}} = \$538.23$$

We must first calculate the outstanding balance at end of year 2 (EOY 2) as follows:

$$\begin{aligned}
\text{Loan balance}_{EOY\ 2} &= \$538.23(PVAF_{8.75\%/12,378\text{months}}) \\
&= \$538.23(128.343) \\
&= \$69,078
\end{aligned}$$

Substituting into the mortgage-constant equation,

$$\begin{aligned}
\$69,078 \times MC_{9.0\%/12,\text{months}} &= \frac{\$538.23}{\$69,078} \\
&= 0.00779
\end{aligned}$$

The remaining loan term corresponding to a 9.0 percent rate and a loan constant of 0.00779 is between 36 and 37 years. By interpolation, we can determine it as 36 years and 9 months.

The preceding results can again be used to derive the amortization schedule for this variable-term loan, as illustrated in Table 7-8. As noted, the balance at the end of year 1 is the same as in the variable-rate, variable-payment example because the loans amortize at the same rate over the first year. We computed the balance for the end of year 2 as $69,078. For year 3, the balance is computed in the same fashion as we followed previously:

$$\begin{aligned}
\text{Outstanding balance}_{EOY\ 3} &= \$538.23(PVAF_{9.0\%/12,429\text{months}}) \\
&= \$538.23(127.92815) \\
&= \$68,854
\end{aligned}$$

We can determine the amount of principal reduction for each year by subtracting the outstanding balance for that year. Subtracting the principal reduction from the total debt service yields the interest paid over the year.

To solve for the yield in this example, we must again make an assumption

TABLE 7-8 3-YEAR ANNUAL AMORTIZATION SCHEDULE—$70,000

Year	Balance	Annual debt service*	Principal	Interest
0	$70,000			
1	69,470	$6,459	$530	$5,929
2	69,078	6,459	392	6,867
3	68,855	6,459	223	6,236

*This is the monthly payment ($538.23) multiplied by 12.

about the number of years the loan will remain outstanding. Let us assume that the loan is held the entire length of maturity, with no rate increases past year 3. The total term of the loan was calculated at 36 years, 9 months.

Our equation is as follows:

$$PV = \$70,000 = \$538.23(PVAF_{i\%/12,441 \text{ months}})$$

We know that the rate i will be between 8.5 and 9.0 percent, so we can determine the present values of the $538.23 payment stream using these two rates, as shown in Table 7-9. We find that the PV at 8.5 percent is $92,606 and at 9.0 percent $69,104. Our desired PV, $70,000, lies between these two. Therefore, by interpolation, we find the effective rate to be 8.87 percent, as Table 7-9 illustrates.

You may want to compare the yield on this loan with that on the variable-rate, variable-payment example, where we assumed the same facts but varied the payment rather than the term (see Table 7-6). The yield in Table 7-6 is 8.93 percent, very close to the 8.87 percent obtained in this example. Actually, the yields are equivalent; the differences are caused by rounding. Note that this will always be the case if the loans run full-term and no points or prepayment penalties are levied.

Capped, Change in Adjustment Period Example

Assume we have the same initial facts as in the variable-payment example; i.e., we want to borrow $70,000 on an ARM for 30 years with monthly payments and initial interest rate of 8.5 percent. However, now the rate may be changed every 6 months with a corresponding change in the payment, but the new payment cannot increase more than 7.5 percent over the previous payment. Assume also that the index used is the 6-month Treasury bill rate and the loan originated on June 1.

TABLE 7-9   YIELD CALCULATION—VARIABLE-RATE, VARIABLE-TERM MORTGAGE EXAMPLE; LOAN RUNS TO MATURITY, NO RATE INCREASES AFTER YEAR 3

Payment (annuity)	$PVAF_{8.5\%}$, 36 yr, 9 mo	PV	$PVAF_{9.0\%}$, 36 yr, 9 mo	PV
$538.23	134.89709	$72,606	128.39171	$69,104

Interpolation:

$PV_{8.5\%}$	$72,606	$PV_{8.5\%}$	$72,606
$PV_{9.0\%}$	69,104	Desired PV	70,000
Difference	$ 3,502	Difference	$ 2,606

$$\frac{\$2,606}{\$3,502} \times 0.5\% = 0.37\%$$

$$8.5\% + 0.37\% = 8.87\%$$

At the end of every 5 years, the payment cap is lifted so that the payment can be increased to the amount necessary to amortize the loan over the remaining term.

Payment Computation and Amortization Schedule We calculate the payments for the first 6 months as we would for any 8.5 percent, 30-year loan:

$$\$70,000 \times MC_{8.5\%/12,360} = \text{payment}$$
$$\$70,000 \times 0.007689 = \$538.23$$

At the time of the first rate adjustment (Dec. 1, year 1), the Treasury bill rate has increased from 7.20 to 9.40 percent, an increase of 2.20 percent (see Table 7-10). This amount is added to the previous 8.5 percent mortgage interest rate to derive the new rate of 10.7 percent, which will be used to calculate the indicated payments for the second 6 months as follows:

$$\text{Outstanding balance}_{\text{month 6}} \times MC_{10.7\%/12,354} = \text{payment}$$

First we must find the outstanding balance from the previous 6 months of amortization:

$$
\begin{aligned}
\text{Outstanding balance}_{\text{EOM 6}} &= \$538.23(\text{PVAF}_{8.5\%/12,354}) \\
&= \$538.23 \times 129.572 \\
&= \$69,739
\end{aligned}
$$

Substituting into our equation,

$$\$69,739 \times MC_{10.7\%/12,354} = \text{payment}$$
$$\$69,739 \times 0.009319 = \$649.90$$

The indicated payment to amortize the balance of this loan over the remaining 354-month term is $649.90. However, the increase in the payment each 6 months is limited to 7.5 percent of the previous payment. In this case, the previous payment was $538.23. Increasing it by 7.5 percent yields a maximum capped payment of $578.60, which is the payment the borrower will actually make and the one that will be used to compute the amortization schedule.

Note that in Table 7-10 the loan amortization has been calculated. The outstanding balance column lists the beginning-of-period balance rather than the end-of-period balance, as in previous examples. The principal reduction, as a result of the first 6 months of payments, is $70,000 − $69,739, or $261. The interest for the first 6 months is the debt service $538.23 × 6, − the $261 principal reduction, or $3,238.

To calculate the payment for the third 6-month period, we first must determine the new rate. The index is now 9.06 percent, or 1.86 percent higher than the 7.20

TABLE 7-10 PAYMENT COMPUTATIONS AND AMORTIZATION SCHEDULE—ARM EXAMPLE

Date/year	Index rate (%)	Index change (%)	Indicated mortgage rate (%)	Indicated payment	% change in payment	Actual (capped) payment	Payment shortage	6-month interest	6-month principal	Beginning outstanding balance at period
June 1/1	7.20	...	8.5	$538.23	...	$538.23	$0	$3,238	261	$70,000
Dec. 1/1	9.40	2.20	10.7	649.90	7.5	578.60	71.30	3,472	(265)	69,739
June 1/2	9.06	1.86	10.4	638.39	7.5	622.00	16.39	3,638	94	70,004
Dec. 1/2	11.85	4.65	13.2	787.69	7.5	668.65	119.04	4,012	(619)	69,910
June 1/3	7.22	0.02	8.5	551.01	−17.59	551.01	0	2,992	314	70,529
Dec. 1/3	14.77	7.57	16.1	953.78	7.5	592.34	361.44	3,554	(2,170)	70,215
June 1/4	13.95	6.75	15.3	938.38	7.5	636.77	301.61	3,821	(1,772)	72,385
Dec. 1/4	12.57	5.37	13.9	881.62	7.5	684.53	197.09	4,107	(1,078)	74,157
June 1/5										75,235

percent rate effective at loan origination. The mortgage rate is now 8.5 percent + 1.86 percent, or 10.4 percent rounded to the nearest 0.1 percent. The indicated payment for the third 6-month period is computed as follows:

$$\text{Outstanding balance}_{\text{EOM 12}} \times \text{MC}_{10.4\%/12,348} = \text{payment}$$

As before, we must determine the outstanding balance at the end of month 12. However, since the capped payments during the previous period were not sufficient to cover the interest accruing each month, at the end of this 6-month period we will owe the balance as if we made the indicated payment, plus the *future value* of that portion of the indicated payment we did not make over the 6 months.

The balance (if the indicated payment were made) is derived as before:

$$\$649.90 \times \text{PVAF}_{10.7\%/12,348} = \text{balance}_{\text{EOM 12}}$$
$$\$649.90 \times 107.04267 = \$69,567$$

The portion of the indicated payment that has not been made is $649.90 − $578.60, or $71.30. To find the value of this annuity, which is building up each month at (10.7 percent)/12 interest, we compute its future value as follows:

$$\$71.30(\text{FVAF}_{10.7\%/12,6}) = \text{balance owed on payment shortage, EOM 12}$$
$$\$71.30(6.13535) = \$437$$

Adding the $437 to the $69,567, we obtain $70,004, which is the total balance outstanding at the end of month 12 (or beginning of month 13). Subtracting $70,004 from the previous period's balance of $69,739 yields a negative amortization of $265. Since the entire debt service was allotted to interest, the 6 months' interest is $578.60 × 6 = $3,472. Now that the beginning balance for the third 6-month period has been determined, we can substitute this into the payment equation:

$$\$70,004 \times \text{MC}_{10.4\%/12,348} = \text{payment for months 13–18}$$
$$\$70,004 \times 0.009119 = \$638.39$$

The indicated payment is thus $638.39. But with the 7.5 percent limitation on the payment increase, the actual capped payment may rise to only $622 (578.60 × 1.075 = 622). We therefore have a payment shortage of $16.39 per month.

To compute the outstanding balance at the end of the third 6-month period, we again must calculate the amount owing as if the indicated payment were made and then add the future value of the monthly payment shortage for the 6 months in the period:

$638.39(\text{PVAF}_{10.4\%/12,342})$ = balance if indicated payment were made, EOM 18

$638.39(109.35284)$ = \$69,810

$16.39(\text{FVAF}_{10.4\%/12,6\text{months}})$ = compounded balance of payment shortage at month 18

$16.39(6.1315)$ = \$100

$69,810 + \$100 = \$69,910 \qquad$ balance at EOM 18

This balance owing is subtracted from the previous balance owing to obtain the principal reduction over the period, \$94. The total debt service over the period is 622.00×6, or \$3,732. Subtracting the principal reduction from the debt service yields the interest amount of \$3,638 for the period.

For the future periods, the computations follow this same procedure. *It is important to remember, however, that whenever there is a payment shortage, the future value of each month's shortage must be compounded forward to the date for which the outstanding balance is being computed.*

Note the effect of negative amortization on the outstanding balance of this loan, especially during the periods of high interest rates beginning December 1, year 3, and June 1, year 4. Remember that after every 5 years in our example, the payment cap is lifted so that the payment can be increased (if necessary) to amortize the loan over the remaining term.

Cost of Borrowing (Yield)   To calculate the yield to the lender (or the cost to the borrower), we proceed just as we did for the ARM example with variable payments. We must discount each payment stream to the beginning using the PVAF and then discount this amount back to the present as a lump sum, using the PVF. Assuming we wish to calculate the yield as if the loan were to be paid off at the end of year 4, our equation appears as follows:

$$\$70,000 = \$538.23(\text{PVAF}_{i\%/12,6\text{months}}) + \$578.60(\text{PVAF}_{i\%/12,6\text{months}})(\text{PVF}_{i\%/12,6\text{months}})$$

$$+ \$622.00(\text{PVAF}_{i\%/12,6\text{months}})(\text{PVF}_{i\%/12,12\text{months}})$$

$$+ \$688.65(\text{PVAF}_{i\%/12,6\text{months}})(\text{PVF}_{i\%/12,18\text{months}})$$

$$+ \$551.01(\text{PVAF}_{i\%/12,6\text{months}})(\text{PVF}_{i\%/12,24\text{months}})$$

$$+ \$592.34(\text{PVAF}_{i\%/12,6\text{months}})(\text{PVF}_{i\%/12,30\text{months}})$$

$$+ \$636.77(\text{PVAF}_{i\%/12,6\text{months}})(\text{PVF}_{i\%/12,36\text{months}})$$

$$+ \$684.53(\text{PVAF}_{i\%/12,6\text{months}})(\text{PVF}_{i\%/12,42\text{months}})$$

$$+ \$75,235(\text{PVF}_{i\%/12,48\text{months}})$$

We must solve for the rate by trial and error. To roughly approximate the rate, we can take an average of the rates over the 4-year term, which is 12.08 percent. Thus, we can begin the trial-and-error process by using, say, 12 percent as the rate and determining the present value. This has been done in Table 7-11, where each payment is multiplied by the appropriate 12 percent PVAF and/or PVF to derive the present value. The present value of the payments is $69,637 at 12 percent. Since we desire a PV of $70,000, we have discounted the payments at too high a rate. If we try, say, 11 percent, the PV of the payment stream is $71,966. Since the desired PV of $70,000 falls between $69,637 and $71,966, we know that the actual yield is between 11 and 12 percent. We may interpolate to derive the yield of 11.84 percent, as shown in Table 7-11.

Renegotiable-Rate Mortgage Example

In this example, the same $70,000 amount is borrowed for 30 years, there are monthly payments, and the initial interest rate is 8.5 percent. The adjustment period is 3 years, at which time the outstanding balance is computed and then refinanced at the new rate for the remaining 27 years. The new rate is expected to increase at 0.5 percent per year, for a total of 1.5 percent over the 3-year adjustment period.

Payment Calculation To compute the payments of this RRM in years 1 through 3, we follow the process used previously:

$$\text{Loan amount} \times MC_{8.5\%/12,360} = \text{monthly payment}$$
$$\$70,000 \times 0.007689 = \$538.23$$

TABLE 7-11 YIELD CALCULATION—ARM EXAMPLE

Period	Payment amount	12% PVAF	12% PVF	12% PV	11% PVAF	11% PVF	11% PV
0 – 6 months	$538.23	5.795	. . .	$3,119	5.812	. . .	$3,128
6 mo – 1 yr	578.60	5.795	0.9420	3,159	5.812	0.9467	3,184
1 – 1½ yr	622.00	5.795	0.8874	3,199	5.812	0.8963	3,240
1½ – 2 yr	668.65	5.795	0.8360	3,239	5.812	0.8485	3,297
2 – 2½ yr	551.01	5.795	0.7876	2,515	5.812	0.8033	2,573
2½ – 3 yr	592.34	5.795	0.7419	2,547	5.812	0.7605	2,618
3 – 3½ yr	636.77	5.795	0.6989	2,579	5.812	0.7200	2,665
3½ – 4 yr	684.53	5.795	0.6584	2,612	5.812	0.6816	2,712
EOY 4	75,235		0.6203	46,668		0.6453	48,549
Total PVs				69,637			71,966

Interpolation:

PV$_{11\%}$	$71,966	PV$_{11\%}$	$71,966
PV$_{12\%}$	69,637	Desired PV	70,000
Difference	2,329	Difference	1,966

$$\frac{\$1,966}{\$2,329} = 0.844$$

0.844 × 1% rate difference = 0.84%

11% + 0.84% = 11.84% yield

In years 4 through 6, we use the same general operation, but we first need to find the balance outstanding on the loan at the beginning of year 4 (end of year 3), as follows:

$$Balance_{EOY\ 3} = monthly\ payment\ (PVAF_{8.5\%/12,324})$$
$$= 538.23 \times 126.83579$$
$$= \$68,267$$

Now the monthly payment for years 4 through 6 can be computed at the new 10 percent rate:

$$Balance_{EOY\ 3} \times MC_{10\%/12,324} = monthly\ payment\ for\ years\ 4–6$$
$$\$68,267 \times 0.008940 = \$610.31$$

This process is repeated every 3 years for the life of the mortgage.

Amortization Schedule   The amortization schedule for the RRM is calculated much like previous amortization schedules. Table 7-12 is the annual amortization schedule for our RRM example.

To compute the amortization for year 1, we first find the balance outstanding at the end of year 1:

$$Balance\ outstanding_{EOY\ 1} = \$538.23(PVAF_{8.5\%/12,348})$$
$$= (\$538.23)(129.0715)$$
$$= \$69,470$$

We then subtract the EOY 1 balance from the beginning balance to obtain the principal reduction of $530. Subtracting the principal reduction from the debt service for year 1 gives us the interest paid that year.

TABLE 7-12   ANNUAL AMORTIZATION SCHEDULE—YEARS 1–6 FOR RRM EXAMPLE

Year	Outstanding balance EOY	Annual debt service*	Principal	Interest
0	$70,000			
1	69,470	$6,459	$530	$5,929
2	68,894	6,459	576	5,883
3	68,267	6,459	626	5,833
4	67,746	7,324	521	6,803
5	67,171	7,324	575	6,749
6	66,627	7,324	644	6,680

*This is the monthly debt service multiplied by 12.

For year 2, we first find the balance outstanding at EOY 2:

$$\text{Balance outstanding}_{\text{EOY 2}} = \$538.23(\text{PVAF}_{8.5\%/12,336})$$
$$= \$538.23(128.0004)$$
$$= \$68,894$$

Subtracting this amount from the previous year's balance yields a principal reduction of $576, which when subtracted from the debt service gives the interest amount of $5,883. This process is followed for the remaining years of the loan. In Table 7-12 the debt service changes after year 3 because of the rate change.

Effective Cost of Borrowing To calculate the yield for this loan, we must make an assumption about the length of time the loan will remain outstanding. This term determines the timing and amounts of the cash inflows to the lender. In this case, we assume the loan is paid off at the end of year 6. The equation for the yield calculation is

$$\text{Loan amount} = \text{payment}_{\text{years 1-3}}(\text{PVAF}_{i\%/12,36})$$
$$+ \text{ payment}_{\text{years 4-6}}(\text{PVAF}_{i\%/12,36})(\text{PVF}_{i\%/12,36})$$
$$+ \text{ balance}_{\text{EOY 6}}(\text{PVF}_{i\%/12,72})$$

We may obtain the payment amounts and balance from the amortization schedule in Table 7-12, substituting into the equation:

$$\$70,000 = \$538.32(\text{PVAF}_{i\%/12,36}) + \$610.31(\text{PVAF}_{i\%/12,36})(\text{PVF}_{i\%/12,36})$$
$$+ \$66,527(\text{PVAF}_{i\%/12,72})$$

We solve this equation for the rate by trial and error, as in previous examples. We know the rate is between 8.5 and 10 percent. Let us try 9 and 10 percent as our bracketing rates. Table 7-13 outlines the process. The annuities and final payment are discounted using the appropriate PVFs at the assumed rates. We see that the PV of the payment stream is $70,439 at 9 percent, $67,315 at 10 percent. By interpolation, we estimate the rate to be 9.14 percent, as in Table 7-13.

Price Level-Adjustable Mortgage Example

We now compute the payments, amortization schedule, and effective yield for the PLAM, using a $70,000, 30-year monthly payment mortgage as before, but assuming the "real" loan rate is 3 percent, with inflation rates of 12, 10, and 9 percent for years 1, 2, 3, respectively. We also assume that adjustments are made annually in the outstanding balance, and we find the payment by applying the inflation rate to them.

TABLE 7-13   YIELD CALCULATION—RRM EXAMPLE

Year	Monthly payment	Final payment	9%			10%		
			PVAF	PVF	PV	PVAF	PVF	PV
1–3	$538.32		31.447		$16,929	30.991	. . .	$16,683
4–6	610.31		31.447	0.7641	14,665	30.991	0.7417	14,029
EOY 6		$66,527		0.5839	38,845		0.5502	36,603
Total PV					70,439			67,315

Interpolation:

$PV_{9\%}$	$70,439	$PV_{9\%}$	$70,439
$PV_{10\%}$	67,315	Desired PV	70,000
Difference	3,124	Difference	439

$$\frac{\$439}{\$3,124} = 0.14$$

$$0.14 \times 1\% \text{ difference in rate} = 0.14\%$$

$$9\% + 0.14\% = 9.14\% \text{ yield}$$

Payment Computation   For the first year of the PLAM, the payment computation is just like that of the fixed-rate mortgage. Assuming a loan amount of $70,000, a 3 percent rate, and a 360-month term, we have

$$\$70,000(MC_{3\%/12,360}) = \text{payment}$$
$$\$70,000(0.004216) = \$295.12$$

For year 2, we must first find the balance owing at EOY 1:

$$\text{Balance}_{EOY\ 1} = \$295.12(PVAF_{3\%/12,348})$$
$$= \$295.12(232.237)$$
$$= \$68,538$$

Because of the 12 percent inflation rate during year 1, we must now increase the balance outstanding for the beginning of year 2 by 12 percent:

$$\$68,538 \times 1.12 = \$76,763$$

To compute the year 2 payments, we use this inflated balance and determine the payments necessary to amortize this balance over the remaining 29 years at 3 percent interest:

$$\$76,763(MC_{3\%/12,348}) = \text{monthly payment during year 2}$$
$$\$76,763(0.004306) = \$330.54$$

To compute payments for year 3, we follow the same procedure. The balance at EOY 2 is determined as follows:

$$\$330.54(PVAF_{3\%/12,336}) = \text{balance}$$

$$\$330.54(227.1347) = \$75,077$$

Since we assume the inflation rate in year 2 is 10 percent, we increase the $75,077 to $82,585 and use this amount in our payment calculation. The third-year payments are

$$\$82,585(MC_{3\%/12,336}) = \$363.59$$

This same process is repeated each year for the life of the mortgage.

Amortization Schedule   Table 7-14 is the annual amortization schedule for the PLAM example. The figures were obtained from the payment calculations, except for the end of year 3 balance. The EOY 3 balance (uninflated) is computed as

$$\text{Balance}_{EOY\,3} = \$363.59(PVAF_{3\%/12,324})$$

$$= \$363.59(221.8768)$$

$$= \$80,672$$

The inflated balance is 9 percent higher, or $87,932. Note that we have not separated the principal and interest paid in each year since there is no consensus about whether increases in the balance should be treated as interest or principal.

Effective Cost of Borrowing   To compute the yield (cost) on the PLAM example, we must first make an assumption about the remaining term of the loan. Assume that the debt will be paid off at the end of year 3. Our yield equation is

$$\$70,000 = \$259.12(PVAF_{i\%/12}) + \$330.54(PVAF_{i\%/12,12})(PVF_{i\%/12,12})$$

$$+ \$363.59(PVAF_{i\%/12,12})(PVF_{i\%/12,24}) + \$87,932(PVF_{i\%/12,36})$$

TABLE 7-14   ANNUAL AMORTIZATION SCHEDULE—PLAM EXAMPLE

Year	End of period balance	Inflation rate (%)	End of period inflated balance	Debt service	Real rate (%)
0	$70,000				
1	68,538	12	$76,763	$3,541	3
2	75,077	10	82,585	3,966	3
3	80,672	9	87,932	4,363	3

TABLE 7-15   YIELD CALCULATION—PLAM EXAMPLE

Year	Monthly payment	Balance	12%			13%		
			PVAF	PVF	PV	PVAF	PVF	PV
1	$295.12		11.255	· · ·	$ 3,322	11.196	· · ·	$ 3,304
2	330.54		11.255	0.88745	3,302	11.196	0.87871	3,252
3	363.59		11.255	0.78757	3,223	11.196	0.77213	3,143
EOY 3		$87,932		0.69892	61,458		0.67848	59,660
Total PV					71,305			69,359

Interpolation:

PV$_{12\%}$	$71,305	PV$_{12\%}$	$71,305
PV$_{13\%}$	69,359	Desired PV	70,000
Difference	1,946	Difference	1,305

$$\frac{\$1,305}{\$1,946} = 0.67$$

$0.67 \times 1\%$ difference in rates $= 0.67\%$

$12\% + 0.67\% = 12.67\%$ yield

Table 7-15 illustrates the yield computation.

Since trial and error must be used to calculate the yield, let us try 12 and 13 percent as our bracketing rates. At 12 percent, the present value is $71,305. At the 13 percent rate, the present value is $69,359 ($69,360 rounded off). Since our $70,000 desired present value is in between, the loan yield (cost) must be between 12 and 13 percent. As can be seen from the table, the yield is 12.67 percent.

Note that although the real rate on the PLAM is only 3 percent, the yield over a 3-year term is 12.67 percent. In contrast, the payments on a fixed-rate mortgage at 12.67 percent for the same amount and term would be $756.33, considerably higher that the $295.12 to $363.59 range for the first 3 years of the PLAM loan. Clearly, the PLAM offers benefits to both borrowers and lenders, but it is hindered by legal and institutional difficulties.

SUMMARY

This chapter introduced alternative methods of financing that are becoming more widespread. These instruments alleviate the fixed-rate mortgage problems by helping lenders with their "spread" problem (cost of funds exceeding portfolio yields). Adjustable-rate mortgages attempt to solve the problem of borrowing "short" and lending "long." Such financing methods enable mortgage lenders to improve market conditions and better align assets and liabilities to protect their value during high-inflation periods. Most of the methods are structured to allow institutions to charge a market rate and to adjust it to market fluctuations. The chapter also discussed the indexes, legal aspects, negative-amortization aspects, rate-change factors, payment-adjustment rules, and risk analysis of these adjustable loans, including examples of how these financing methods work.

QUESTIONS

1 Define the following terms:
  a varying-rate mortgage
  b inflation premium
  c renegotiable-rate mortgage
  d price-level adjustable mortgage
  e teaser
  f margin
  g interest rate risk

2 The mortgage with a varying interest rate is designed to solve what problems facing the mortgage market? What problems does it create for the borrower? the lender?

3 Discuss the indexes and methods of adjusting used in ARMs.

4 Analyze the ARM. Discuss Exhibit 7-1 in detail. What unique legal problems do ARMs create?

5 What unique loan-analysis problems do ARMs create?

6 Suppose the interest rate on a fixed-rate mortgage is 12 percent. What is the expected interest rate on an ARM? Why? Suppose that the interest rate on an ARM is 11 percent. What does the 1 percent difference represent?

7 What are the conceptual differences between adjustable-rate and renegotiable-rate mortgages? How are these types similar?

8 Describe how the price-level-adjustable mortgage works. What unique risks does it create for the borrower? the lender?

9 Describe how to calculate the effective yield (cost of borrowing) on an ARM.

10 Collect some data on varying-rate mortgages in your local market. Compare and contrast the different options and choices available.

PROBLEMS

1 Suppose a variable-rate loan of $100,000 is made at an interest rate of 10 percent with monthly payments over 25 years. At the end of the first year, the interest rate has increased to 10.85 percent.
  a Determine the new monthly payment.
  b Hold the original monthly payment constant and determine the length of time over which the loan should be amortized.

2 Assume a borrower obtains a 30-year $250,000 mortgage at 13 percent with monthly payments. This loan is pegged to an index with a beginning value of 11.5. If the payments were to adjust every 2 years, and the index moved to 10.5, calculate the amortization of this loan for its first 3 years.

3 Assume the following information on a PLAM:

Mortgage amount: $100,000
Mortgage term: 20 years (monthly payments)
Current real rate: 5%
Expected inflation rates: 7 and 10% respectively, for the next 2 years

  a What is the monthly payment in the first year?
  b What is the monthly payment in the second year?

4 Assume the following information on an RRM:

Mortgage amount: $80,000

Mortgage term: 20 years (monthly payments)

Initial interest rate: 8.5%

Adjustment period: 3 years—at which time the outstanding balance is computed and then refinanced at the new rate for the remaining 17 years.

New rate: expected to increase 0.5 percent for a total of 1.5 percent over the 3-year adjustment period.

    a Compute the payments on the RRM in years 1 through 3.

    b Compute an amortization schedule for years 1 through 5.

5 A loan is made by a local bank for $25,000 at 8.5 percent interest, with a 20-year term. The initial rate is to adjust every year, and payments will adjust every 2 years. At the end of the first year the index moves from 8.00 to 9.00, and ending the second year, it moves from 9.00 to 9.50.

    a What is the new monthly payment after the payment adjustment date 2 years later?

    b Assume that the loan is held the entire length of maturity, with no rate increases past year 3. Solve for the yield in this example.

6 The dual-rate mortgage is a special form of adjustable-rate mortgage. There are two interest rates: one the rate at which interest on the loan accrues and one the rate on which the payment is based and which is lower (at least initially) that the accrual rate. Suppose a lender offers to lend $70,000 on a dual-rate ARM, with $587.44 monthly payment based on a 9 percent annual interest rate with 25-year amortization and an initial accrual rate of 11 percent. The outstanding balance balloons at the end of year 5. Payments will not change over the loan term, but the accrual interest rate is expected to increase at 0.5 percent per year at the beginning of years 2 through 5. Determine both the outstanding balance that must presumably be refinanced at the end of year 5 and the yield to the lender.

7 Suppose that you are considering an adjustable-rate loan with the following characteristics:

Mortgage amount: $50,000

Margin: 2.5 percent

Maturity: 20 years

Maximum annual adjustment: 2 percent

Index: 1-year Treasury bill yield

Lifetime cap: 5 percent

Payment adjustment period: annual

    a If the Treasury bill yield is 7.5 percent at the outset and then moves to 9.5 percent at the beginning of year 2, what is the monthly payment for year 2?

    b If the loan is paid off at the end of year 2, what is the effective yield?

REFERENCES

Asay, Michael R.: "Pricing and Analysis of Adjustable Rate Mortgages," *Mortgage Banking,* December 1984, pp. 60–64.

Erdevig, Eleanor, and George G. Kaufman: "Improving Housing Finance in an Inflationary Environment: Alternative Residential Mortgage Instruments," *Economic Perspectives,* Federal Reserve Bank of Chicago, July/August 1981.

McCulloch, J. Huston: "Price Level Adjusted Mortgage: Affordability and Inflation Protection," *Mortgage Banking,* September 1982, pp. 8–10.

Melton, Carroll R.: "Alternative Mortgage Instruments—Who Wins?," *Illinois Business Review,* vol. 35, no. 2, March 1978, pp. 9–12.

Olin, Virginia K., and Stephen T. Zabrenski: "Characteristics of Adjustable Mortgage Loans by Large Associations," *Federal Home Loan Bank Board Journal,* vol. 15, no. 8, August 1982, pp. 21–24.

"The Risks of Creative Financing," *Economic Review,* Federal Reserve Bank of Atlanta, vol. 117, no. 12, December 1982, pp. 4–13.

Zearley, Thomas: "Alternative Mortgage Instruments and Lenders' Risks," *Banker's Magazine,* November/December 1981, pp. 61–64.

GOVERNMENT-SPONSORED FINANCING METHODS

////

In recent years, governments have played a prominent role in financing various types of housing. To encourage home ownership and investment in income-producing housing, federal, state, and, in some instances, local governments provide assistance to prospective homebuyers and investors. This assistance ranges from insurance or guaranty programs to low-interest rate loans and rent subsidies. In some instances, to induce lenders to provide mortgage funds at lower-than-market terms, the government provides lenders insurance against borrower default. In other situations, a government agency grants outright loans to homebuyers. The government has also been involved in the financing of income-producing rental housing, such as apartments, particularly for low-income residents.

This chapter introduces assorted government financing methods and outlines the important aspects of several programs offered, comparing the advantages and disadvantages with those of conventional loans. We also introduce the mechanics and loan-submission packages for government-sponsored financing methods.

FEDERAL HOUSING ADMINISTRATION (FHA) LOANS

An FHA loan is a mortgage made with funds advanced by a local lender, like a conventional loan. The difference is that the FHA insures the lender against a loss on the loan caused by the borrower's defaulting. The borrower pays the cost of this insurance. (This cost is added to the monthly mortgage payment.) In addition, on certain loans the FHA subsidizes a portion of the interest rate via a monthly cash payment to the lender, to allow low-income borrowers to pay lower monthly payments.

Background on the FHA

The FHA was created in 1934 by the National Housing Act as a vehicle to use the federal government's credit to insure home loans, improve housing standards, encourage lending from private sources, and stabilize the mortgage market. The Federal National Mortgage Association (FNMA, or Fannie Mae) was formed in 1938 as a government agency to provide a secondary market for FHA-insured loans. As a result of the economic problems of the 1930s, the FHA also encouraged lenders to begin implementation of an amortization schedule with monthly payments. Previously, home mortgages were single-payment, short-term notes, which were renewed at the lender's discretion. In the 1940s, the pressures of World War II caused the FHA to expand its activities in order to encourage increased housing in defense-designated locations and to allow financing of multifamily projects. As more and more housing programs were developed, the Department of Housing and Urban Development (HUD) was formed in 1965, and the FHA was made part of it.

The FHA acts primarily as an insurance institution, entirely self-supported by insurance premiums on the loans it insures. These underwritings insure private lenders against losses resulting from borrower default. In some rare cases, the

FHA will make direct loans from its own funds; the funds are advanced by an FHA-approved lender.

Another FHA goal is to advantageously influence the stability of the mortgage market. By underwriting the lenders of mortgage capital, the government lowers the lenders' risks. In theory, this causes a greater inflow of funds into home mortgage lending.

Table 8-1 outlines several of the FHA home mortgage insurance programs. Historically, the most widely used program is 203(b), for one- to four-family dwellings, for new or existing structures.

Other popular insurance programs over the years have been the Title I, Sec. 2 loans, for owners of existing homes to finance major improvements. Section 235 enables eligible lower-income families to purchase new homes that meet FHA standards. To reduce the interest cost to the borrower to as low as 4 percent (depending on income level), HUD insures the mortgages and makes monthly payments to lenders.

Finally, the Sec. 245(a) graduated-payment mortgage (GPM) program was enacted in 1974 to enable borrowers to buy homes with lower initial monthly payments, with the payments rising in subsequent years as the borrowers' incomes presumably increase, thus allowing the borrowers to buy more expensive houses today than they could afford under a fixed-rate, level-payment mortgage. For a variety of reasons, the Sec. 245(a) program has not experienced a high degree of popularity in the market. We discuss GPMs later in this chapter.

The remainder of the programs in Table 8-1 are primarily special-purpose. Table 8-2 illustrates in more detail the important aspects of Secs. 203(b), 203(i), 235, and 245(a). FHA financing requirements are subject to change or government policy changes.

Unique Characteristics of FHA Loans

Much of the form and substance of conventional loans are determined by the laws and regulations of the individual states. In contrast, FHA loans (and VA loans), because they are federal programs, are exempt from state statutes and are administered under uniform regulations nationwide. As a result, FHA loan requirements are fairly rigid, whereas lenders typically have more leeway in structuring conventional loans. Depending on the applicable state laws, FHA regulations, and the characteristics of the local market, FHA loans may have advantages or disadvantages vis-à-vis conventional loans in such areas as assumability, prepayment, determination of interest rate, property qualification, and loan-to-value ratio. Table 8-3 shows the unique characteristics of an FHA loan compared with a conventional loan.

Loan Assumption   At this writing, FHA loans place no restrictions on loan assumption. FHA loans are assumable, according to the terms and conditions of the original mortgage. However, the original borrower remains liable on the loan.

TABLE 8-1 FHA HOME MORTGAGE INSURANCE PROGRAMS

Title	Section	Authorized	Program synopsis
I	2	1934	Property improvements
I	2	1969	Mobile homes
II	203(b)	1934	Proposed, under construction, or existing one- to four-family homes
II	203(b)	1954	Disaster-victim housing
II	203(i)	1954	Farm housing
II	203(k)	1964	Urban renewal areas
II	213	1950	Cooperative housing projects
II		1974	Graduated payment mortgages
II	221(d)(2)	1954	Housing for displaced families
II	222	1954	Single-family purchase by armed forces persons
II	223(a, b, c)	1954	Permanent housing sold by government
II	223(d)	1961	Excess of expenses over gross income
II	223(e)	1968	Declining urban area housing
II	225	1954	Additional advances on one- to four-family homes
II	233	1961	New or untried construction methods
II	234	1961	Condominiums
II	235	1968	Single-family with interest reduction plans
II	236	1968	Rental and co-op with interest-reduction plans
II	237	1968	Single-family at less than FHA credit requirements
II		1965	Rent-supplement program
II	240	1968	Purchases of fee simple title to property
II	241	1968	Supplemental loans for multifamily changes
II	242	1968	Construction or rehabilitation of hospitals
II	244	1974	Coinsurance by private lenders
VIII	809	1956	Department of Defense civilian employees
VIII	810	1959	Off-base housing for military
X		1965	Land and development for new communities
XI		1966	Group practice facilities
II	202	1974	Direct loans to elderly and handicapped
V	518(a)	1964	One- to four-family homes with structural defects
V	518(b)	1974	Assistance to owners to correct defects
V	245(a)	1974	Graduated payment mortgages
II	223(f)	1974	Co-insurance program

Source: FHA.

TABLE 8-2 MAJOR CHARACTERISTICS OF FHA 203(b), 203(i), 235, AND 245(a) PROGRAMS*

	Programs			
	203(b)	203(i)	235	245(a)
Special borrower qualifications	None	None	Low income—owner-occupants only	Owner-occupants only
Special property qualifications	One–four family structures, new or existing; must meet FHA-MPS	One-family structures, new or existing; rural location; must meet FHA-MPS	New or substantially rehabilitated one-family or condominium; must be approved prior to construction or rehabilitation	Same as 203(b) but for single-family only
Maximum amount insurable (most areas)	One-family—$67,500 Two-family—$76,000 Three-family—$92,000 Four-family—$107,000	Same as 203(b)	One-family—$40,000 plus $7,500 additional for four-bedroom units purchased by families of five or more persons.	$67,500
Maximum loan-to-value ratio	97% of first $25,000 of value plus closing costs, owner-occupants; 95% in excess of $25,000 plus closing costs, owner-occupants; 85% of value plus closing costs, non-owner-occupants	97% of value plus closing costs for owner-occupants; 85% of value plus closing costs for non-owner-occupants.	97% of value	97% of first $25,000 of value plus closing costs; 95% of value plus closing costs in excess of $25,000
Maximum term	30 years	30 years	30 years	30 years
Interest rate	Current HUD-FHA rate	Current HUD-FHA rate	Current HUD-FHA rate—borrower's payments subsidized by the amount payment exceeds 20% of adjusted income	Current HUD-FHA rate
Insurance premium	½%	½%	7/10%	½%
Payments	Level monthly payments	Level monthly payments	Borrower payments vary with income	Five possible plans available, with payments increasing 2–7½% each year for the first 5 or 10 years of the loan
Tax and insurance escrow	Required	Required	Required	Required

*Current as of 1983. Limitations, maximum amounts, and other features are subject to change. Any regional office of the FHA or approved lender can provide current information on program requirements.

TABLE 8-3   FHA FINANCING COMPARED WITH CONVENTIONAL LOANS

	FHA loan with minimum down payment for owner-occupied home	Conventional loan with 95% loan-to-value ratio for owner-occupied home
Down payment:		
For loans with acquisition cost* of $50,000 or less	3%	Minimum 5% of the lesser of price or appraised value.
For loans with acquisition cost above $50,000	3% of the first $25,000 and 5% of the balance	At least 5% must be buyer's own savings.
Closing costs	Must be financed into loan.	Must be paid in cash at closing.
Gifts	Relatives and related parties accepted.	Relatives only
Coborrowers	OK	Must live in home.
Assumability	New buyer may assume without qualification.	Not assumable.
Refinancing to lower interest	Buyer does not need to qualify.	Buyer must qualify.

*Acquisition cost is the lesser of sale price or appraised value plus FHA allowable closing costs for the area.
Source: Dennis Creps: "Financing a Home through FHA," *Real Estate Today,* May 1986, p. 13.

The buyer who plans to assume the loan may be required to submit to a qualifying procedure similar to that followed for obtaining a new loan. If the new buyer is approved, the seller (original buyer) is relieved of liability on the loan and is eligible to obtain another FHA loan.

Prepayment   FHA loans have no restrictions on or penalties for prepayment of the loan before maturity. In contrast, conventional mortgages may penalize prepayment, except in states where such practice is illegal.

Interest Rate   Historically, the interest rate on FHA loans was set on a nationwide basis by the Secretary of the Department of Housing and Urban Development. The rate has often been below, and occasionally above, the current market rate of interest on conventional loans. To account for regional rate differences and to induce lenders to make below-market-rate FHA loans, lenders are permitted to charge *discount points* to raise their yield above the contract rate. Although points are often charged on conventional loans as well, the FHA's regulations stipulate that the maximum the borrower can be charged is 1 percent—essentially, the origination fee. The *seller* pays the discount points on an FHA mortgage. The empirical evidence indicates that sellers add at least part of the expected cost of any points to the selling price of the house. In 1983, the FHA interest rate regulations were changed to allow the rate to be determined by the mortgage market.

From the lender's perspective, each discount point charged to the seller raises the effective yield on the loan by *approximately* one-eighth of 1 percent. (Recall our discussion in Chapter 2, where we indicated that the points necessary to increase the yield by a specific amount depend on the contract rate, amortization period, and expected loan term.) To illustrate, suppose a borrower wants to take out a $60,000 FHA loan to purchase a home and the current FHA interest rate is 12 percent, while the conventional market rate is 12.5 percent. The lender requires a 1 percent origination fee. What are the charges to the borrower and seller?

The borrower must pay the origination fee of 1 percent of the loan amount, or $600. The seller of the home will be required to pay the discount points, as determined by the lender. Generally, but not always, lenders will use the one-eighth of 1 percent rule to determine the appropriate points to charge. Thus, to raise the yield from 12 to 12.5 percent, an 0.5 percent difference, the lender must charge four points (0.5 percent ÷ ⅛ percent = 4 points); 4 points, or 4 percent of the $60,000 mortgage, is $2,400 that the seller must pay for the buyer to receive this mortgage.

Property Standards   When underwriting a conventional loan, the lender has the property appraised mainly to determine whether it is sufficient collateral for the loan. When determining whether to insure a loan, however, the FHA goes beyond the valuation aspect and requires that the dwelling meet FHA's minimum property standards (MPSs). FHA uses approved appraisers for this purpose. On new construction, mandatory periodic inspections are performed to ensure that the dwelling is built according to the MPSs for new construction. For existing structures, which may or may not have been built to FHA standards, MPSs for existing housing must be complied with. Typically, the FHA completely rejects dilapidated, substandard houses or requires the owners to make certain improvements or changes before they will insure a loan on such property.

Loan Amounts   Whereas conventional loans typically do not exceed 80 to 90 percent of value, FHA loans can be made up to 97 percent of value, depending on the circumstances. This condition has been a major attraction of FHA loans. The maximum insurable mortgage is limited, however. As of this writing, under the Sec. 203(b) program, the limits range from $67,500 for a single-family structure up to $107,000 for a four-family structure, although these limits can be increased for certain geographical locations. In contrast, conventional mortgages have no maximum loan amount.

Liquidity   The secondary mortgage market agencies, such as the FNMA, GNMA, and FHLMC, were created to even out fluctuations in availability of mortgage credit. By purchasing mortgages from local lenders when money is tight, the agencies put the funds back into the local economy so that the lenders can make more loans. When lenders have more money available for investment than their borrowers need, these government agencies sell mortgages to the lenders, thus providing a place for investing these excess funds. The uniformity of FHA underwriting standards and the backing of the government make the loans especially attractive and easily tradable on the secondary market. In fact, there is no limit to the amount of funds any one institution can invest in out-of-state FHA-insured loans.

Default Provisions   With conventional financing, a default by the borrower may ultimately lead to foreclosure to pay off the loan. If the proceeds from the foreclosure sale are insufficient to retire the debt, the lender may sue the borrower (in some states) for a *deficiency judgment,* which is the difference between the foreclosure sale proceeds and the amount needed to pay off the debt. If the lender wins, the borrower will have to pay this difference. The FHA, however, requires that lenders provide a greater degree of forbearance when default is beyond the borrower's control. A lender may recast or extend the mortgage of a borrower who defaulted because of unemployment caused by a serious medical ailment, for example, if there is a good chance that the borrower can and will resume regularly scheduled payments. Also, the FHA does not generally seek a deficiency judgment against a borrower.

In 1985, a new foreclosure relief program for FHA-insured mortgages was instituted. The new program disallows lenders to foreclose on a mortgagor until it has been determined whether the mortgagor meets all the federal criteria for an assignment. An assignment includes the transfer in writing of the rights or interest in a mortgage. If the mortgagor is eligible for the federal program, the mortgage is assigned to HUD. Such an assignment assists homeowners experiencing financial difficulties.

Processing Time and Complexity   Two disadvantages of FHA loans compared with conventional mortgages are the longer time required for processing and the large amount of paperwork. Often, special certifications are required, and other items that are understood or assumed in the conventional loan-submission package need formal, written documentation in FHA loans. The additional paperwork, plus the introduction of another party (FHA) to the loan underwriting process, often cause considerably longer processing times. Processing time for FHA loans can exceed 60 to 90 days, depending on the circumstances, whereas conventional loans usually are processed in 15 to 30 days.

Insurance Premiums   The lender is insured by the FHA against loss as a result of borrower default. The premium as paid by the borrower and amounts to (generally) one-half of 1 percent of the outstanding loan balance annually. The annual premium is divided by 12 and the result added to each monthly payment (this concept is illustrated later in the FHA loan examples).

Escrow Requirements   In addition to the principal and interest payments, all borrowers on FHA loans must place in escrow a sum equal to one-twelfth of the annual real estate taxes and monthly hazard insurance premium on the property. A tax and insurance escrow account may not be required with conventional loans.

Fraud   In order to reduce the incidence of fraud against the Federal Housing Administration, new restrictions were placed on FHA-insured mortgages in 1986. Among the restrictions are the following:

1 The FHA will discourage buydowns.

2 The FHA will not insure a loan for anyone on whom it has paid a claim in the past 3 years.

3 The FHA will perform a credit check on any individual who assumes an FHA-backed loan during the first 2 years of the loan.

The new limitations arose from an investigation of builders, real estate agents, and others which resulted in many indictments and convictions on charges of defrauding the insurance program through various methods, such as falsified credit and employment records.

FHA Loan Examples

To illustrate the computational aspects of FHA loans, we present examples of a standard Sec. 203(b) loan and graduated-payment Sec. 245(a) mortgage. The following facts are used in both examples.

1 Buyers are applying for a maximum loan on a home valued at $58,000.

2 Loan term is 30 years.

3 Annual real estate taxes and hazard insurance premiums on the property are $900.

4 Buyers' closing costs are estimated at $1,900, including a 1 percent origination fee.

5 The sellers will be charged 2 discount points.

6 The current FHA interest rate is 12 percent.

Level-Payment, Sec. 203(b) Loan   A Sec. 203(b) loan is quite similar to a conventional fixed-rate, level-payment mortgage in that monthly principal and interest payments are computed the same way. However, as we indicated, there are special rules for determining the maximum loan amount and required down payment on FHA loans. In addition, points must be determined, and the FHA insurance premium and tax and insurance escrow amounts must be calculated and added to the principal and interest payments.

To determine the *maximum loan amount,* the purchase price (value) must first be added to the closing costs:

Purchase price (value)	$58,000
closing costs	1,900
total cost	59,900

Of this amount, 97 percent loan-to-value ratio applies to the first $25,000, and 95 percent applies to the remaining $34,900:

$$0.97 \times 25{,}000 = \$24{,}250$$
$$0.95 \times 34{,}900 = 33{,}155$$
$$\$24{,}250 + \$33{,}155 = \$57{,}405 \text{ maximum loan} \qquad (\$57{,}400 \text{ rounded})$$

The *required down payment* is derived by subtracting the $57,400 from $59,500, which gives us $2,100. Notice that in this example the loan-to-total-cost ratio is about 96.5 percent.

Since the sellers are paying 2 points, the amount of the points must be deducted from the sellers' proceeds: 2 percent of the $57,400 mortgage amount is $1,148. The purchase price of $58,000 reduced by $1,148 yields proceeds to the sellers (not including other items the sellers owe) of $56,852. From the sellers' perspective, then, this $58,000 purchase price under these FHA terms is roughly equivalent to a $56,852 offer with no points.

To determine the *total monthly payment* on an FHA loan, we must first calculate the principal and interest payments in the usual fashion:

$$\$57{,}400 \times MC_{12\%/12{,}360} = \text{payment}$$
$$\$57{,}400 \times 0.010286 = \$590.42$$

Then, the *FHA insurance premium* must be calculated. The annual FHA insurance premium is 0.5 percent of the $57,500 outstanding balance for the first year, or $287. This is $23.92 per month added to the payment. For succeeding years, this process is repeated on each anniversary of the loan, using the outstanding balance at that time. Thus, the premium decreases slightly each year.

The amount of tax and insurance escrow is $900. This is an amount of $75 per month added to the payment. The total loan payment in this example is the sum of the principal and interest, tax and hazard insurance escrow, and FHA insurance premium:

$$\$590.42 + \$75 + \$23.92 = \$689.34$$

Graduated-Payment Loan Example   The graduated-payment loan originated in the 1970s, when interest rates began to rise rapidly. Recall from earlier chapters that the nominal interest rate is composed of the real rate plus the rate for expected inflation. When inflation is expected to be high, the nominal interest rate on loans is increased by the expected inflation rate, causing the monthly payment on a level-payment loan to increase as well. The payments on new loans increase immediately when the interest rates rise, but the borrower's income does not—thus, fewer borrowers are able to qualify for a new mortgage. This is referred to as the *tilt effect*. The graduated-payment mortgage (GPM) is an attempt to better equate mortgage payments and borrower income over time. Although the GPM originated as a government-sponsored program, the concept is not limited to FHA-insured loans; there are GPMs issued by conventional lenders.

Figure 8-1 illustrates the problem and the solution the GPM offers. BI_1 is the borrower's income level in dollars over the term of the loan, assuming the income does not change and no inflation. FRM_1 is the amount of the monthly payment on a fixed-rate, level-payment mortgage over its life, assuming no inflation. Note that without inflation, the initial relationship between borrower income and mortgage payments does not change over time. Suppose, however, that expected inflation increases the monthly payment to FRM_2, a substantial increase. It may now be higher that what the borrower can "afford." However, with inflation, the borrower's income may be expected to increase as well, as line BI_2 illustrates. Thus, the borrower cannot afford these payments now but could afford them in the future years after the BI_2 line increases sufficiently.

The solution would be a loan that provides for a payment at the same rate as the borrower's income, as line GPM_1 illustrates. In practice, however, the typical FHA/GPM loan that is used provides for five to seven stepped payment increases, one each year, for the first 5 to 7 years of the loan. Subsequently, the payments remain level for the remaining term of the loan. Line GPM_2 illustrates how the payments would increase on a typical FHA/GPM loan.

The GPM is a partial solution to the affordability problem caused by inflation, but it does not adjust the lender's yield as inflation expectations change over the loan term. In addition, it results in *negative amortization* in the early years of the loan since the balance outstanding increases because the initial payment is insufficient to cover the interest accruing each month. As long as property values in-

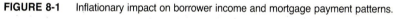

FIGURE 8-1   Inflationary impact on borrower income and mortgage payment patterns.

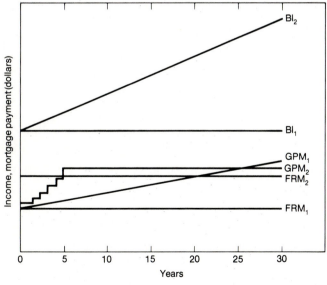

crease, there is no problem. But if they do not, the loan-to-value ratio will increase rather than decrease over the early years, thus increasing the lender's risk. The lender's risk is also affected by the possibility that the borrower's income might not keep pace with inflation.

To find the monthly payments for an FHA Sec. 245(a) GPM loan, first determine the amount of the initial payment and then increase it by the appropriate percentage each year for the number of years that the payment is to be graduated. In our example, assume that the payments will be graduated at the rate of 7.5 percent per year for 5 years. To determine the initial payment, we determine the mortgage constant for the GPM loan by using the following formula:

$$MC = \cfrac{1}{PVAF_{i\%/12,12}(FVAF_{u\%,T}) + (1 + g)^T \cfrac{PVAF_{i\%/12}(N - T)12}{FVF_{i\%/12,T(12)}}}$$

where MC = mortgage constant
 PVAF = present value of annuity factor
 FVAF = future value of annuity factor
 FVF = future value of lump sum
 u = sinking fund rate, defined as $(1 + g/FVFi\%/12,12) - 1$
 T = total number years over which payments will be graduated
 N = term of loan, years
 g = percentage rate of payment graduation
 i = mortgage interest rate

The first step is to find the value of u:

$$u = \frac{1 + g}{FVF_{i\%/12,12}} - 1$$

$$= \frac{1 + 0.075}{FVF_{12\%/12,12}} - 1$$

$$= \frac{1.075}{1.126825} - 1$$

$$= -0.0459920$$

Note that u is a *negative* value.

Next, we compute the FVAF at rate u for time T (5 years):

$$FVAF_{u,T} = \frac{(1.0 - 0.0459920)^5 - 1}{-0.0459920}$$

$$= 4.560751$$

Finally, we substitute all values into the MC formula:

$$MC = \cfrac{1}{PVAF_{12\%/12,12months}(4.560751) + \cfrac{(1 + 0.075)^5(PVAF_{12\%/12,360-60})}{FVF_{12\%/12.60}}}$$

$$= \cfrac{1}{(11.255078)(4.560751) + \cfrac{(1.435629)(94.956551)}{1.816697}}$$

$$= \cfrac{1}{51.331608 + 75.03069}$$

$$= 0.00791375$$

Now we multiply the mortgage constant by the mortgage amount of $57,400 to derive the initial payment of $454.25. To this amount, we add the $75 escrow and the $23.92 FHA insurance premium amounts, which were computed for the Sec. 203(b) loan and which are the same for the Sec. 245(a). Thus, we derive the total payment of $553.17. Contrasting this with the $689.34 payment under the Sec. 203(b) loan, it is evident that the GPM can substantially reduce payments *initially*. For subsequent years, the graduated payments are as shown in Table 8-4. Note that the payments increase at 7.5 percent per year for years 2 through 6, leveling off at $652.13 for years 6 through 30.

Table 8-5 is the *annual* amortization schedule for the GPM. Note the *negative amortization* in years 1 to 5, when the payments are not sufficient to cover the interest accruing each month. In year 1, this excess of interest owing over debt service paid is $1,519 and is included as "negative" principal in the table. In essence, it is *added* to the balance outstanding rather than subtracted, as with normal amortization. This process continues until year 6, when the payments finally increase to the point where they will cover the accrued interest and also somewhat reduce the principal.

VETERANS ADMINISTRATION (VA) LOANS

A VA loan is a mortgage made by a local lender that is insured and *guaranteed* by the federal government. Thus, the VA *guarantees* and insures a loan; the FHA

TABLE 8-4 PAYMENT SCHEDULE—GPM LOAN EXAMPLE

Year	Rate of graduation (multiply by year 1 payment)	=	New payment
1	. . .		$454.25
2	1.075^1		488.32
3	1.075^2		524.94
4	1.075^3		564.31
5	1.075^4		606.64
6–30	1.075^5		652.13

TABLE 8-5   ANNUAL AMORTIZATION SCHEDULE, YEARS 1–6—GPM EXAMPLE

Year	Annual debt service*	Principal	Interest	Balance
0	. . .	. . .	. . .	$57,400
1	$5,451	($1,519)	$5,451	58,919
2	4,860	(1,279)	5,860	60,198
3	6,299	(977)	6,299	61,175
4	6,772	(602)	6,772	61,777
5	7,280	(141)	7,280	61,918
6	7,826	418	7,408	61,500

*Monthly payment for each year multiplied by 12.

only *insures* a loan. There is no cost for this guarantee, but VA loans are made only to eligible veterans of the armed forces and a select few others.

Background on VA Loan Guaranty Program

In 1944, the VA was authorized via the Serviceman's Readjustment Act to guarantee home loans made by lenders to veterans of World War II. The term *veterans* was subsequently broadened to include

1 Persons who were members of the U.S. armed services during World War II (September 16, 1940, to July 25, 1947) for no less than 90 days or were discharged or released from active duty because of a service-related disability

2 Persons who were members of the armed forces during the Korean Conflict (June 27, 1950, to January 31, 1955) serving anywhere in the world for no less than 90 days or were discharged or released because of a service-related disability

3 Persons considered Cold War veterans who, as members of the armed services, served 180 days or longer on active duty since January 1955

4 Unremarried widows of veterans who died from a service-related disability, are MIAs, or are POWs as a result of performing in the line of duty for 90 or more days

5 American citizens who, during World War II, served as members of armed services of a government allied with the United States and who are U.S. residents

6 Vietnam-era veterans with active duty of 90 days or more

Like the FHA, the VA acts primarily to indemnify the lender in the event of borrower default. Generally, the VA does not loan money, although there are some direct VA loan programs. The Serviceman's Readjustment Act granted the VA three major powers concerning mortgage loans:

1 To *partially guarantee* loans made to veterans by any firm, person, corporation, or government body

2 To *insure* loans made to veterans by a supervised leader (subject to examination and supervision by a state or federal government agency)

3 To make *direct loans* to veterans in areas where mortgage funds are not readily available

Loans may be guaranteed for a variety of reasons. Table 8-6 describes the various programs available to the veteran-borrower. Section 1810 is by far the most popular program for home financing. In 1986, the VA guaranteed $21.8 billion in loans to finance purchases of 307,747 conventionally constructed homes and condominium units.

Unique Characteristics of VA Loans

VA loans bear similarities to FHA loans. The *interest rate* as set by the Secretary of HUD is used for VA loans, and *prepayment penalties* are forbidden on VA loans, as they are on FHA loans.

Loan Assumption   Veterans may allow their VA loans to be assumed by anyone, veteran or nonveteran, but are not relieved of liability unless the VA and the lender who granted the loan deem the new borrower a good credit risk. In addition, veterans are not eligible to obtain other VA loans until the original loans are paid off, unless the buyer (who must also be a veteran) is willing to substitute personal "entitlement" (discussed below) for that of the original veteran-borrower.

Property Requirements   The VA, like the FHA, uses its own approved appraisers to estimate the property value. However, the VA's purpose is primarily valuation, but the FHA's is valuation and minimum property standards. The vet-

TABLE 8-6   VETERANS ADMINISTRATION TITLE III PROGRAMS

Section	Program description
1810	Loan guarantees to purchase, construct, or repair owner-occupied, one- to four-family homes, condominiums, or mobile homes for up to 60% of loan's balance with a maximum guarantee of $27,500.
1811	Direct loans to those eligible veterans who are unable to secure other loans on property in certain areas that are capital-poor. These funds are provided by the U.S. Treasury Department and limited to $21,000.
1812	Guarantees of loans to buy, construct, alter, or improve farm residences at 60%, or $17,500; and other farm property, equipment or outbuildings at 50%, or $4,000.
1813	Guarantees of loans to purchase, alter, construct or improve business properties, businesses, and business equipment (limited to 50%, or $4,000 on the latter).
1814	Guarantees for loans to refinance delinquent indebtedness on existing mortgages or liens at 60%, or $17,500.
1815	Provides a VA-established insurance fund for the lender based on 15% of the lender's total portfolio of VA loans, not to exceed the set maximum guaranteeable amount for these loans. (Rarely used by VA.)

eran must intend to occupy the property as a personal home but can use the loan benefits to purchase a home; to purchase a condominium unit; to build a home; to repair or improve a home; to improve a home by installing energy conservation or solar heating measures; to refinance an existing home loan; to purchase a manufactured home, with or without a lot; or to purchase a lot for a manufactured home owned by the veteran.

Loan Terms Although the FHA insures the lender against loss, the VA guarantees that if the lender suffers a loss as a result of borrower default, the VA will pay that loss up to the dollar limits of what is called ''veterans entitlement.'' Any regional VA office or approved lender can provide current information about these requirements.

There is no limit on the amount of mortgage loan that can be granted to a veteran, except that the dollar amount of veteran's entitlement must not be less than 15 percent of the loan amount. For example, a veteran's entitlement of $27,500 translates into a maximum loan of $183,333. Of course, the veteran must qualify financially like any other borrower, but the maximum the VA will guarantee is $27,500. There is no charge for this guarantee, as there is for FHA insurance.

No down payment is required on a VA loan, as long as the reasonable value of the property as determined by the VA equals or exceeds the amount of the mortgage. Lenders are allowed to charge points on a VA loan in the same fashion as FHA loans; that is, the seller pays the points, except where there is no seller involved in the transaction (i.e., new construction, refinance, or home improvement situations).

The *maximum term* for a VA home loan is 30 years and 32 days. Also, as with FHA loans, tax and hazard insurance escrow accounts are required. The VA loan is a typical fixed-rate, level-payment amortized loan, although term loans (with no amortization) may be granted under some programs for not more than 5 years.

VA Loan Example

To illustrate the mechanics of a VA loan, assume that a qualified veteran wants to buy a home priced at $60,000. The veteran applies to the local lender for a 100 percent loan (i.e., no down payment). The veteran has $27,500 of the entitled benefits. The FHA-VA interest is 12 percent, and the veteran wants a 30-year loan term. The lender requires a 4 percent discount that the seller will pay. We must determine the principal and interest payments on this loan and the maximum guarantee to the lender.

The payment will be computed in the usual fashion.

$$\$60,000 \times MC_{12\%/12,360} = \text{payment}$$
$$\$60,000 \times 0.01012861 = \$617.71$$

The maximum guarantee is the veteran's entitlement of $27,500, or 60 percent of the loan amount, whichever is less. Since 60 percent of $60,000 is $36,000, the maximum guarantee is $27,500.

GOVERNMENT FINANCING OF INCOME PROPERTIES

We discussed the involvement of HUD-FHA and the VA in home financing, primarily for owner occupants. As part of its goal to ensure decent shelter for all Americans, HUD-FHA also provides programs to facilitate the financing of other types of housing, primarily rental property. Now we examine the financing methods for income property; Table 8-7 outlines some of the methods.

Note that the HUD-FHA programs discussed here are not the only government financing methods for income property. Recall that the FHA Sec. 203(b) and 203(i) programs may be used to finance a structure with up to four rental units for nonowner occupants. In addition, the veteran owner-occupant may finance a building with up to four units under the VA Sec. 1810 program. Also, various other government programs (such as state or local), which are discussed in the last section of this chapter, can be used on a limited basis for financing income properties. However, the HUD-FHA programs outlined in Table 8-7 cover most of the government methods of financing larger-scale income properties. HUD also provides programs to

1 Give technical assistance and loans to nonprofit sponsors of certain HUD-assisted housing
2 Give federal aid to local public housing agencies to provide shelter for low-income tenants
3 Give direct loans for the financing of housing and related facilities for the elderly or handicapped
4 Provide mortgage insurance for the construction and rehabilitation of hospitals and equipment
5 Provide joint mortgage insurance with state housing finance agencies to facilitate financing of rental housing

Unique Characteristics

There are several unique aspects to the HUD-FHA programs regarding borrower and property requirements, legal and financial aspects, and income tax considerations. These characteristics separate the HUD-FHA loan programs from each other as well as from standard conventional loans.

Note that a very detailed analysis of these loan programs is futile, primarily because each Congress amends program requirements and eliminates some programs altogether. Thus a *general* discussion of these programs is of most use. For more detailed information about currently active programs, consult the HUD-FHA area office or a HUD-FHA-approved lender.

TABLE 8-7 HUD-FHA INCOME PROPERTY FINANCING

Program	Nature of program	Eligibility	Authority	Office	Source	Status	Scope
Multifamily rental housing	HUD insures mortgages made by private lenders to finance the construction or rehabilitation of multifamily rental housing by private or public developers. Applicable to projects of five or more units at reasonable rents.	Investors, builders, developers, and others who meet HUD requirements. The project area must be approved by HUD as an area with a demand for such housing.	Section 207, National Housing Act (1934), (P.L. 79-479), as amended.	Assistant Secretary for Housing, Federal Housing Commission, Department of HUD.	. . .	Active	2,501 projects with 323,874 units. Amount insured is $412 billion (as of 1986).
Mobile home courts	To aid financing construction or rehabilitation of mobile home courts, HUD insures private mortgages on the entire site. Mortgage limit is $3,250 per mobile home space within each park. The park area must be approved and deemed needed by HUD.	Investors, builders, developers, cooperatives, and others who meet HUD requirements can apply to an FHA-approved institution conferring with the local HUD office.	Section 207, National Housing Act (1934), (P.L. 73-479).	Same	HUD field offices	Active	66,148 spaces insured for $205 million (as of 1986).
Existing multifamily rental housing	HUD insures mortgages to purchase or refinance existing multifamily projects originally financed with or without federal mortgage insurance. The projects must contain no less than eight units and be at least 3 years old.	Investors, builders, developers, and others who meet the HUD requirements.	Section 223(f), NHA (1934), (P.L. 73-479), added by Sec. 311, Housing & Community Dev. Act of 1974 (P.L. 93-383).	Same	HUD field offices	Active	481 projects were insured on 108,473 units valued over $1.67 billion.
Multifamily rental housing for low- and moderate-income families	To aid in the financing of the construction or rehabilitation of multifamily (five or more units) rental or cooperative housing for low- and moderate-income or displaced families. HUD may insure only 90% of the project cost for any type mortgagor.	Public agencies; nonprofit, limited-dividend or cooperatives, private builders or investors who sell completed projects to said organizations. Also, mortgages may be obtained by profit-motivated sponsors.	Section 221(D)(4), NHA (1934), (P.L. 73-479), added by Housing Act of 1954 (P.L. 83-560).	Same	HUD field offices	Active	Cumulative through May 1986: 10,657 projects with 1,136,200 units for a value of over $27 billion.

Program	Description	Authority	Administering agency	Status	Statistics
Lower-income rental assistance	A rent subsidy for lower-income families to aid them in affording fair housing in the private market. Proposals are submitted to HUD for rehabilitation or new construction by nonprofit and profit-motivated developers.	Tenants must earn income of 80% of the area median income or less. Project sponsors may be private owners, profit-motivated and nonprofit or cooperative organizations, public or state housing agencies.	Section 8, U.S. Housing Act of 1937, (P.L. 73-479), added by the Housing and Community Dev. Act of 1974 (P.L. 93-383).	Assistant Secretary for Housing, Federal Housing Commission, Department of HUD.	HUD field offices	Active	As of October 31, 1986: over 2 million units either available or reserved.
Mortgage insurance for housing for the elderly	To assure a supply of rental housing suited to the needs of the elderly or handicapped, HUD insures mortgages to rehabilitate or build multifamily projects of no less than eight units.	Investors, builders, public bodies, developers, and nonprofit sponsors may qualify for mortgage insurance. Renters must be at least 62 years old.	Section 231, NHA (1934), (P.L. 73-479), added by Section 201 of Housing Act of 1959 (P.L. 86-372).	Same	HUD field offices	Active	As of 1986: 499 projects with 66,394 insured for over $1.17 billion.
Nursing homes and intermediate care facilities	HUD insures mortgages to finance construction or renovation of facilities to accommodate 20 or more patients requiring skilled nursing care and related medical services—major equipment may also be included in the mortgage.	Investors, builders, developers, and private nonprofit corporations licensed in the field.	Section 232, NHA (1934), (P.L. 73-479), added by Section 115, Housing Act of 1959 (P.L. 86-372).	Same	HUD field offices	Active	As of 1986: 1,538 projects with 182,656 beds were insured at over $2.75 billion.

Borrower Eligibility   The basic distinction HUD-FHA makes regarding the borrowers eligible for particular programs is whether the borrower is a private, profit-motivated entity or a public or nonprofit organization. More specifically, the following programs are available to investors, builders, developers, and others who meet HUD requirements: multifamily and mobile home court programs under Secs. 207 and 223(f); the Sec. 221(D) (4) low-income multifamily program; and the housing for the elderly and nursing home programs under Secs. 231 and 232, respectively. For nonprofit organizations and public agencies, the low-income multifamily programs(s) [Secs. 221(D) (3) and (4)] and the housing for the elderly and nursing home programs(s) [Secs. 231 and 232] are available (see Table 8-7).

The Sec. 8 program is a special case in that it involves a rent subsidy paid to owners on behalf of tenants in approved low-income housing. It typically applies to newly constructed or substantially rehabilitated buildings, but it is also available to tenants occupying existing nonrehabilitated apartment dwellings. Section 8 gives owners of approved units subsidy payments (the difference between the tenants' ability to pay and the HUD-determined "contract rents") and escalation of rents due to inflation and hardship and a partial subsidy for vacant units. Although Sec. 8 is not a financing method per se, when Sec. 221(D) (4) financing is used, Sec. 8 rent subsidies are coupled with it. Since the typical contract between the investor-owner and HUD under Sec. 8 is for a term of 20 or more years, depending on financing terms, the expected Sec. 8 rental income will be a major determinant of a project's feasibility from the investor's perspective.

Property Requirements   HUD loan programs are generally divided between those for existing structures and those for construction of new buildings or substantial rehabilitation of existing structures. As noted in Table 8-7, programs under certain sections provide mortgage insurance for the financing of new construction and rehabilitation. Few programs are available for financing existing multifamily buildings.

Generally, more favorable terms are available for new construction and "rehab" loans. These properties are periodically inspected during construction or rehabilitation to ascertain that the construction techniques and materials used conform to approved plans and FHA's MPSs. Existing structures' conformance with FHA's MPSs are judged by viewing the finished product. As a result, a relatively greater economic life is expected and a longer loan term is typically granted on new construction and rehab loans.

There are limitations on the minimum size of projects that may be financed. For new construction or rehabilitated property to receive loans, the property must have a minimum of five living units; existing projects and those for the elderly under Sec. 231 must have at least eight units. Thus, there is a void for those investors who want government financing on existing five- to seven-unit structures that are not being rehabilitated; financing on one- to four-family units is available under Sec. 203(b), and eight units and above may be financed under Sec. 223(f).

Legal and Financial Aspects   HUD-FHA income property mortgages typically have the same assumption privileges as home loans; that is, they are assumable, according to their terms and conditions, by most potential buyers.

Loan-to-value ratios may be as high as 90 percent for profit-motivated investors and as high as 100 percent for nonprofit or public agencies. The loan term generally may not exceed 75 percent of the estimated remaining economic life, or up to 40 years, whichever is less. Since conventional loans generally do not exceed 80 percent of value and are made for shorter, 20- to 30-year, terms, the more highly leveraged HUD-FHA loans offer attractive financing alternatives to certain investors.

As is typical of FHA home loans, the income property loan program has no prepayment restrictions. Thus, the lender may not charge a prepayment penalty to increase loan yield. The yield can be increased only through front-end points, if permitted under the specific program. The borrower, however, must pay the mortgage insurance premium to the FHA and thus should include this factor when calculating the effective borrowing cost. In addition, the FHA may charge a processing rate of 2 percent of the mortgage on new construction and rehab property when construction inspections are required.

Tax Aspects   HUD-FHA loans on properties that are not low-income have no unique tax aspects. However, on approved low-income properties, the Tax Reform Act of 1986 creates three tax credits available for the following projects: construction and rehabilitation of existing housing without federal subsidies construction, rehabilitation of existing housing financed by federal subsidies, and acquisition costs for existing buildings.

In order for the low-income housing (LIH) credit—9 percent per year for 10 years for construction and rehabilitation of existing housing without federal subsidies, and 4 percent per year for 10 years for construction and rehabilitation of existing housing financed by federal subsidies, and acquisition costs for existing buildings—to be granted, the following requirements must be met:

1 Rehabilitation costs for previously owned buildings must be $2,000 per rental unit and must be incurred within 2 years of the start of the project.

2 Newly acquired buildings must have been in service for more than 10 years and not substantially improved during that time period.

3 Twenty percent of the units must be rented to tenants with income less than 50 percent of the community's median income, or 40 percent of the units must be rented to tenants with income less than 60 percent of the community's median income. Tenant incomes are adjusted for family size.

4 Gross rent must be less than 30 percent of the tenants' qualifying income.

5 Low-income housing does not include transient housing.

6 Rental units must remain low-income for 15 years.

7 For investor incomes less than $250,000, a portion of the credits may offset nonpassive income—for investor incomes less than $100,000, up to $25,000 may be used against nonpassive income; the amount of credit to be used against nonpassive income is reduced by 50 percent of the amount over $100,000.

The credit for 1 year is computed by multiplying the building's qualified basis by the applicable credit percentage. The building's qualified basis is the lesser of

$$\text{Eligible basis} \times \frac{\text{number of LIH units in building}}{\text{total number of units in building}}$$

or

$$\text{Eligible basis} \times \frac{\text{total floor space in LIH units}}{\text{total floor space in all units}}$$

where the eligible basis is the adjusted basis of the building at the time the building is put into service. The eligible basis remains constant throughout the entire compliance period. The credit begins the year the project is placed into service.

Government-Financed Low-Income Apartment Building Example

An investor is considering constructing and operating a 50-unit apartment complex, to be financed under a typical government-sponsored low-income-housing program. The property will qualify such that the low-income tenants may obtain Sec. 8 rental assistance, and the investor intends to enter into a long-term Sec. 8 contract with HUD. To make the investment decision, the investor wants to assess the feasibility of the project.

The data for the project are as follows: The total project cost is estimated at $950,000, including purchase of the site. When construction is completed, the rental units are expected to be rented for an average fair market rental of $300 per unit per month, including Sec. 8 subsidy payments when applicable to individual tenants. HUD has examined the local market and the building plans and has approved these rental amounts. Each unit in the complex contains 1,000 feet of floor space. Fifty percent of the units are designated as low-income housing. Rents are expected to increase 5 percent per year.

Vacancy and bad debt losses are estimated at 7 percent of potential gross income, according to HUD-FHA guidelines. Operating expenses are estimated at $70,000 for the first year of operations and expected to increase 5 percent per year thereafter.

The loan terms currently available under the program are

1 90 percent loan-to-value ratio
2 12 percent interest rate
3 35-year term
4 2 percent origination fee—1 percent payable on the commitment date and 1 percent payable at closing (when construction is completed)
5 FHA mortgage insurance premium of 1 percent for the first year, due at closing, plus an additional 0.50 percent per year on the unpaid balance (to simplify calculations, the 0.50 percent will be added to the interest rate on the loan)

Special construction financing is to be obtained for the 1-year construction period in the amount of the FHA permanent loan (90 percent × $950,000 = $855,000). The investor will receive construction-period advances to pay subcontractors as work is completed, inspected, and approved by the FHA. However, to simplify calculations, we assume that all monies for construction costs and expenses incurred during the construction period will be paid at the end of the period. Interest and real estate taxes over the construction period are assumed to be $60,000 and $3,000, respectively.

The investor intends to depreciate the $857,000 structure using the straight-line method over a 27.5-year life. In addition, the investor will have appraisal fees, title insurance, and other acquisition costs totaling $6,000, which will be added to the depreciable basis. Thus, the depreciation deduction is $31,382 per year.

The expected holding period is 5 years from the completion of construction, or a total of 6 years from project inception. The property is expected to be sold for $1,100,000 at the end of year 6, with selling expenses totaling 5 percent of the sales price.

The investor is assumed to be in the 28 percent tax bracket and requires an 8 percent after-tax return on this type of investment.

After-Tax Cash Flow (ATCF) Calculations Table 8-8 shows the ATCFs from the beginning of the project through the entire holding period. In year 0, the $95,000 equity investment is made, as HUD generally requires all project funds to be placed in escrow with the lender prior to the start of construction. In addition, one-half of the origination fee (1 percent) must be made at this time. The investor's before-tax cash flow (BTCF) at the beginning of the project is thus −$103,550, and since there are no tax impacts at this time, the ATCF is −$103,550 as well. This means that the investor must invest $103,550.

For year 1 (the construction period), we have the permanent loan proceeds of $855,000 coming in, which will cover the $855,000 construction costs and expenses. In addition, the investor must pay the remaining one-half of the origination fee, the 1 percent FHA insurance premium, and the $6,000 acquisition costs. The BTCF for year 1 is thus −$23,100. However, the FHA insurance premium is deductible. This translates into a taxable loss of $8,550 and a tax savings of $2,394 that, when added to the −$23,100 BTCF, yields a −$20,706 ATCF for year 1.

At this point, the property is placed in service and the operations phase of the project begins. For simplicity, we are assuming that full rent up occurs instantaneously at this time. Thus, in year 2, the potential gross income (PGI) is $180,000 (50 units × $300/month × 12 months) and increases at 5 percent per year for years 3 through 6. The 7 percent vacancy and the operating expenses are deducted, to yield $97,400 net operating expenses (NOI) for year 2. (Remember, operating expenses also are expected to increase at 5 percent per year for years 3 through 6.) Debt service (DS) is calculated on a 12.5 percent interest (including FHA insurance), 35-year, $855,00 mortgage with level monthly payments. As is customary with FHA loans, there is no prepayment penalty; thus DS in year 6

TABLE 8-8 AFTER-TAX CASH FLOWS FOR SIMPLIFIED LOW-INCOME APARTMENT BUILDING EXAMPLE

				Year			
	0	1	2	3	4	5	6
Construction period—cash inflows:							
Loan proceeds	0	$ 855,000					
Minus—cash outflows:							
Equity investment	$ 95,000						
Origination fee	8,550	8,550					
FHA insurance premium		8,500					
Acquisition costs		6,000					
Construction costs		855,000					
Total outflows	103,550	878,100					
BTCF during construction period	(103,550)	(23,100)					
Operating period cash flows:							
Potential gross income (PGI)			$180,000	$189,000	$198,450	$208,373	$218,791
− 7% vacancy			12,600	13,230	13,892	14,586	15,315
effective gross income			167,400	175,770	184,558	193,787	203,476
− operating expenses			70,000	73,500	77,175	81,034	85,085
net operating income (NOI)			97,400	102,270	107,383	112,753	118,391
− debt service (DS)			108,269	108,269	108,269	108,269	108,269
before-tax cash flow (BTCF)			(10,869)	(5,999)	(886)	4,448	10,122
Taxable income:							
Net operating income (NOI)			97,400	102,270	107,383	112,753	118,391
− interest		0	106,792	106,597	106,375	106,125	105,841
− amortized financing costs		8,550*	489	489	489	489	489
− depreciation		0	31,382	31,382	31,382	31,382	31,382
taxable income (loss)		(8,550)	(41,263)	(36,198)	(30,863)	(25,243)	(33,976)
× tax rate		0.28	0.28	0.28	0.28	0.28	0.28
taxes (savings) before credit	0	(2,394)	(11,554)	(10,135)	(8,642)	(7,068)	(9,513)
− credit	0	0	0	17,260	17,260	17,260	17,260
taxes (savings)	0	(2,394)	(11,554)	(27,395)	(25,902)	(24,328)	(26,773)
BTCF	(103,550)	(23,100)	(10,869)	(5,999)	(886)	4,484	10,122
− taxes (savings)	0	(2,394)	(11,554)	(27,395)	(25,902)	(24,328)	(26,773)
ATCF	(103,550)	(20,706)	685	21,396	25,016	28,812	36,895

*Amount consists of the first year's FHA insurance premium paid at closing.

252

(the year of sale) is the same as in other years. Note the negative BTCFs in year 2 through 4.

Taxable income must now be calculated in the usual fashion. Both interest on the mortgage and depreciation are deducted. The 2 percent origination fee on the mortgage must be amortized equally over the 35 years of the loan ($8,550 + $8,550 = $17,100 total origination fee; $17,000 ÷ 35 years = $489 per year). Note that in year 6 the entire unamortized portion of these costs can be deducted. The tax credit for each year is computed by applying the following formula: $863,000 × 50 percent × 0.04 = $17,260.

After-Tax Equity Reversion (ATER) Calculations   Next, the expected after-tax cash flow from sale must be determined, as shown in Table 8-9. First, we must find taxes due on sale. The selling expenses are deducted from the $1,100,000 expected sales price, to derive the amount realized of $1,045,000. The adjusted basis at the time of sale is computed as follows:

Cost	$950,000
+ acquisition costs	6,000
total costs	956,000
− accumulated depreciation	125,528
adjusted basis	830,472

The total gain is thus $214,528. We multiply this figure by the investor's tax rate to arrive at taxes due on sale of $60,068.

The ATER is then calculated in the usual fashion and yields $139,548.

TABLE 8-9   AFTER-TAX EQUITY REVERSION FOR SIMPLIFIED LOW-INCOME APARTMENT BUILDING EXAMPLE

Taxes Due on Sale:	
Selling price (EOY 6)	$1,100,000
− selling expenses (5%)	55,000
amount realized	1,045,000
− adjusted basis	830,472
total gain	214,528
× tax rate	0.28
taxes due on sale	60,068
Selling price	$1,100,000
− selling expenses	55,000
− unpaid mortgage	845,384
− taxes due on sale	60,068
after-tax equity reversion	139,548

NPV and IRR Computations Table 8-10 illustrates the NPV computation and the investor's required 8 percent after-tax rate of return. Note that the NPV is positive, yielding a 14.62 percent IRR. This relatively high rate of return can be expected, because of the leveraging effects of the 90 percent financing and the favorable tax treatment of depreciation and construction period interest and taxes for low-income housing. Of course, the riskiness of the investment is directly related to the expected return; thus, this investment is probably riskier than one financed under conventional mortgage terms.

OTHER GOVERNMENT-SPONSORED FINANCING PROGRAMS

Historically, the HUD-FHA and VA loans have provided the bulk of government-sponsored financing programs. However, other programs have become increasingly popular in recent years: The Farmers Home Administration (FmHA), Federal Land Bank, and State Housing Finance Agencies (SHFAs).

Farmers Home Administration (FmHA)

FmHA began as a farm loan agency in the 1930s and 1940s, but as the population in rural areas shifted away from farming, FmHA developed into a rural and small-town development institution. Although still providing farm loans for ownership and operation of family farms, the FmHA also renders financing assistance to low- and moderate-income persons for purchasing or improving single-family homes.

FmHA programs typically grant financing to rural residents and communities unable to obtain affordable credit in the private market. Thus FmHA loans can be made only to persons whose incomes fall below fairly strict limitations. FmHA programs are intended to supplement, rather than compete with, private lending sources. In addition, generally, the property to be financed must be located in a rural area of a community with a population of 10,000 or less, although some communities of up to 50,000 population may qualify for certain programs. Some

TABLE 8-10 NPV AND IRR CALCULATIONS—SIMPLIFIED LOW-INCOME APARTMENT BUILDING EXAMPLE

Year	Equity	ATCF	ATER	PVF$_{8\%}$	PV
0	($103,550)	. . .		1.0000	($103,550)
1		(20,706)		0.926	(19,174)
2		685		0.857	587
3		21,396		0.794	16,988
4		25,016		0.735	18,387
5		28,812		0.681	19,621
6		36,895	$139,548	0.630	111,159
				Net present value	$ 44,018
				IRR	14.62%

FmHA loans are direct loans, at below-market rates; others are made by private lenders under an FmHA guarantee of payment, similar to the VA-guaranteed loans. In addition, FmHA makes direct grants-in-aid under certain circumstances.

The programs the FmHA offers provide loan and/or grant assistance in five general areas: farming, single- and multifamily housing, community facilities, business and industry, and area development.

The *farm programs* give funding for the ownership and operation of family-sized farms and ranches. To qualify as a "family farm," the operation must be of the size that one family can manage and operate by itself, with minimal reliance on hired help. Direct and guaranteed loans are made for

Land acquisition
Debt refinancing
Building construction and rehabilitation
Development of water facilities
Establishment of farm-based, agricultural, or nonagricultural supplemental businesses
Purchase of operating equipment, feed, livestock, and fertilizer
Payment for hired labor, medical care, insurance, and living expenses

Maximum loan amounts currently vary between $100,000 and $300,000, depending on the program. Terms for operating loans generally range from very short (3 to 9 months) up to 7 years, depending on the purpose of the loan and the borrower's repayment ability. For ownership and improvement loans, the loan term may be as high as 40 years if adequately secured by the real estate. Loan-to-value ratios may be as high as 100 percent. Interest rates may vary, depending on the government's cost of funds, but lower rates are available to borrowers with limited resources. FmHA provides (and may require) supervision and counseling services to assist the borrower in financial and agricultural management.

FmHA's *housing programs* provide loans for home ownership of modest single-family dwellings that meet minimum government standards of quality. Loans can be obtained for up to 100 percent of appraised value, at interest rates as low as 1 percent, depending on the borrower's income. The maximum term is 33 years. Loans for home repair and weatherization are available in amounts ranging from $5,000 to $7,500, repayable over 5 to 25 years, at interest rates as low as 1 percent. The maximum loan amount, term, and interest rate depend on the nature of the loan and the borrower's repayment ability. FmHA also provides loans to groups of families wishing to help each other build their own homes and grants to provide technical assistance to such families.

Loans are also given for multifamily housing, to either purchase and rehabilitate or build new. Loan terms may not exceed 50 years, and the interest rate is typically based on the government's cost of funds. The borrower may be an individual, cooperative, corporation, or public agency. To get the loan, applicants must show that they cannot provide low- or moderate-cost rental units with other types of financing.

FmHA also provides financing programs for farm labor housing and congregate, semi-independent housing for the elderly and infirm. In addition, there is a rental assistance program similar in design and function of FHA's Sec. 8

FmHA's *community facilities programs* provide loans and grants for the planning and building of better rural community facilities such as water and waste-disposal systems. FmHA provides loans for other community facilities such as hospitals, schools, fire and police departments, and other essential community installations.

To encourage *business and industrial development* in rural areas, FmHA provides loan guarantees for existing as well as new enterprises. An existing business loan may have a loan-to-value ratio as high as 90 percent, but new business loans have higher equity requirements. FmHA does not impose a "no credit available elsewhere" provision on these borrowers, but the loans must be sound credit risks and must be expected to provide lasting benefit to the rural community. FmHA also provides grants for industrial-site development to attract private enterprises to rural areas.

Finally, FmHA provides *area-development grants* for comprehensive planning efforts in rural areas. These grants are available to government bodies, from the community to state levels.

Federal Land Bank

The Federal Land Bank was created in 1916 to make loans to farmers through the sale of its own Federal Land Bank Bonds. Like FmHA, the Federal Land Bank evolved into a financier of rural housing and makes direct loans. There are 12 regional Federal Land Banks nationwide that make loans through national farm loan associations.

Rural housing loans are made for up to 85 percent of value, with a maximum term of 35 years. Unlike FmHA, the Federal Land Bank does not restrict its program to modest housing for low- to moderate-income persons, although borrowers must meet standard income and credit guidelines applicable to all mortgage loans. The interest rate is adjusted periodically, depending on the bank's cost of funds.

Agricultural loans are somewhat more restrictive. They are limited to 65 percent of value for a maximum term of 40 years. Borrowers must meet both typical credit and income requirements and have farming as their principal occupation. Loans are available for land acquisition, debt refinancing, construction of buildings, and other agricultural purposes and must be secured by a first mortgage on the real estate to which the loan applies. Interest rates are determined in a fashion similar to that for rural housing loans.

State Housing Finance Agencies (SHFAs)

SHFAs are entities set up by state governments to encourage the purchase and development of housing by and for lower-income persons. SHFA programs differ widely, depending on the agency and the types of programs in which it chooses to become involved. However, SHFAs typically sell tax-exempt mortgage bonds that, because of their tax-exempt nature and government backing, bear interest rates below the cost of funds of commercial lending institutions. As a result of this lower cost of funds and their public, nonprofit status, SHFAs can provide mortgage funds at below conventional market interest rates. Typically, SHFAs obtain federal loan guarantees for their loans through the HUD-FHA programs discussed earlier. SHFAs also may provide loans to borrowers not classified as low- to moderate-income, and rather than granting loans directly may purchase approved mortgages from local lenders and sell them in the secondary market. Also, some agencies may subsidize the interest rates. Since the types of programs each state offers vary greatly, prospective borrowers should contact the agency for their states for a detailed list of available programs.

Mortgage Revenue Bonds

Mortgage revenue bonds are tax-exempt bonds issued by state and local governments. The revenues generated by these bonds are applied to lower interest rates for first-time homebuyers.

The benefits of mortgage revenue bonds have been disputed. When analyzed by the U.S. General Accounting Office, mortgage revenue bonds seemed to adversely affect the cost of other tax-exempt borrowing by consequently damaging the financing of traditional municipal needs such as roads, etc. It was also found that many mortgage revenue bonds substituted for loans that would have been made without the subsidy. In summary, mortgage revenue bonds seemed to have a high cost relative to their benefits and only marginal effectiveness.

The major costs with these bonds were borne by the federal government in the form of lost tax revenues. In order to limit the volume of bonds issued and to restrict their use to low- and moderate-income families, Congress enacted the Mortgage Subsidy Bond Tax Act in 1980.

SUMMARY

This chapter was a rather broad overview of the government's involvement in financing various types of real estate, including a discussion of the Federal Housing Administration (under the Department of Housing and Urban Development), the Veterans Administration, Federal Land Bank, and state housing finance agencies. The variety of programs offered was introduced, along with the basic borrower and property-qualifying procedures. Consequently, many of the details and requirements involved in applying and qualifying for and processing these various loans have been omitted. The various agencies may be consulted for currently available programs and their requirements.

QUESTIONS

1 Define the following terms:

a graduated-payment mortgage   f tilt effect
b FHA mortgage   g negative amortization
c VA mortgage   h 200 percent declining balance depreci-
d FHA insurance premium   ation
e mortgage revenue bonds

2 What is the FHA's role in the housing finance market? What are its benefits? What are its costs?

3 You have been selected to advise Congress on how the government should be involved in mortgage financing of houses. What programs and policies would you recommend?

4 Discuss the following statement:The government sets the interest rate on FHA and VA mortgages.

5 Outline some unique characteristics of FHA loans that distinguish them from conventional mortgages.

6 Visit or write your regional HUD office or an approved FHA/VA lender and obtain information about current government programs, interest rates, terms, and other aspects of the types of loans they offer.

7 On an FHA-VA loan, the points charged are to be paid by the seller, not the buyer-borrower. Explain how this influences the housing market. Suppose you were a real estate appraiser and had two properties that were *exactly* alike except one was financed with an FHA loan and the other with a conventional mortgage. Would you expect the selling price to be the same? Why or why not?

8 Who pays for the "insurance" that an FHA loan provides to the lender against default?

9 Discuss the characteristics of a graduated-payment mortgage. What problems is it designated to solve? Discuss thoroughly the tilt effect.

10 Outline briefly what is meant by a VA loan. Contact a local VA-approved lender and collect information about current VA loan requirements, terms, and so forth.

11 What types of government-sponsored income property loans are available? Discuss several of their unique characteristics relative to those of a conventional income property mortgage. What unique tax aspects do low-income-property mortgages create?

12 Explain how the depreciation percentages in Table 8-8 were obtained. When and how are they used to calculate the depreciation deduction?

13 Explain briefly the role of the Farmers Home Administration.

14 Does your state have a housing finance agency? Collect some information about the types of loans made, interest rates, and so forth.

15 Has your local government issued any bonds for use in financing housing? What was the interest rate? Who could qualify for a loan? Do you consider these bonds good or bad? Why?

PROBLEMS

1 Assume the following facts apply to an FHA loan:

1 Buyers are applying for a maximum loan on a home valued at $70,000.
2 The loan term is 30 years.
3 Annual real estate taxes and insurance premiums on the property total $1,000.
4 Buyers' closing costs are estimated at $2,000 including the 1 percent origination fee.
5 Sellers are charged 4 discount points.
6 Current FHA interest rate is 11.5 percent.

a Find the maximum loan amount.

    b Find the required down payment.

    c Calculate the total loan payment.

2 Find the monthly payments for a $60,000 FHA Sec. 245(a) GPM loan at 11 percent interest for a 30-year term. Assume that the payments will be graduated at the rate of 4 percent per year for 5 years.

3 Suppose you can get a GPM loan of $50,000 at 10 percent interest for 30 years, no points.

    a If the growth rate of payments (g) is 7.5 percent, what would the monthly payment during each of the first 5 years be?

    b Set up an amortization schedule for the first 5 years.

4 Assume the following on a VA loan:

    1 A qualified veteran wants to buy a home for $75,000.

    2 He has applied to a local lender for a 100 percent loan.

    3 The veteran has $27,500 entitled benefits.

    4 The FHA-VA interest is 11.00 percent.

    5 The veteran wants a 30-year loan term.

    6 The lender requires a 5 percent discount the seller will pay.

    a Determine principal plus interest payments.

    b What is the maximum guarantee?

5 Assume, on a VA loan, that a qualified veteran wants to purchase a house for $100,000. She has $25,000 of entitled benefits. The VA rate is 13 percent for the 30-year loan term that she has requested. The veteran applies to the local lender for a 100 percent loan (no down payment). The lender requires a 6 percent discount that the seller will pay.

    a What is the maximum guarantee of the veteran's entitlement?

    b What are the principal and interest payments?

6 Assume, on an FHA loan, a buyer is applying for a maximum loan on a home valued at $82,000. The current FHA interest rate is 10 percent and he has applied for a loan term of 30 years. The annual real estate taxes and hazard insurance premiums on the property are $1,200. Buyer's closing costs are estimated at $3,000, including the 1 percent origination fee. The seller will be charged 3 discount points.

    a What is the maximum loan amount?

    b What is the required down payment?

    c Find the total loan payment.

7 Assuming the following:

    A buyer is applying for a maximum loan on a home valued at $65,000, and she wishes to obtain a 30-year loan term.

    Annual real estate taxes and insurance premiums on the property total $1,500.

    Sellers are charged 4 discount points.

    Comparing an FHA loan with an 11.5 percent interest rate to a conventional loan with an 11.75 interest rate,

    a Calculate the down payment on both types of loan.

    b Can closing costs be financed? In which type of loan?

    c Which loan would be assumable?

    d Which loan could be refinanced at a lower rate with no requalification?

    e What would the monthly principal and interest payments be on each type of loan?

    f Considering all factors, which option would you choose? Why?

8 An investor is considering constructing and operating an apartment complex to be financed under the low-income-housing program. The total project cost is estimated at

$502,000, of which $75,000 represents the purchase price of the site. When construction of the 100-unit complex is completed, the units are to be rented at $550 per unit per month. Each unit has the same amount of total floor space. Rents are expected to increase 4 percent per year. It is expected that 75 percent of the units will be designated as low-income housing. Vacancy and bad debt losses are estimated at 7 percent of potential gross income. Operating expenses are estimated at $100,000 for the first year of operations and expected to increase 5 percent per year thereafter. The loan terms available are

1 A 90 percent LTV
2 A 10 percent interest rate
3 A 35-year term
4 A 2 percent origination fee—1 percent payable on commitment date and 1 percent payable at closing
5 An FHA mortgage insurance premium of 1 percent for the first year, due at closing, plus an additional 0.50 percent on the unpaid balance

Special construction financing is to be obtained for the 1-year construction period in the amount of the FHA permanent loan. Interest and real estate taxes are assumed to be $100,000 and $5,000, respectively. The investor will have appraisal fees, title insurance, and other acquisition costs totaling $5,000, which will be added to the depreciable basis. The expected holding period is 3 years from the completion of construction, or a total of 4 years from project inception. The selling expenses total 5 percent of the sales price. The investor is in the 28 percent bracket and requires a 15 percent after-tax return on this type of investment.
a   Compute ATCF's and ATER for the holding period.
b   Compute NPV and IRR. Should this investment be made?

REFERENCES

Catalog of Federal Domestic Assistance, Office of Management and Budget, Washington, D.C., 1987.

Clifton, Russell B.: "The Secondary Market Concerns with Real Estate Appraising," *Appraisal Journal,* January 1975, pp. 51–61.

"Costs and Benefits of Single-Family Mortgage Revenue Bonds: Preliminary Report," U.S. General Accounting Office, Washington, D.C., 1983.

Creps, Dennis: "Financing a Home through FHA," *Real Estate Today,* May 1986, pp. 13–15.

Douglas, James A., and Rosa Koppel: *Real Estate Financing Forms Manual,* Warren, Gorham & Lamont, Boston, 1987.

Jacobs, Barry G., Kenneth R. Harney, Charles L. Edson, and Bruce S. Lane: *Guide to Federal Housing Programs,* Bureau of National Affairs, Washington, D.C., 1982.

Huhnle, John H.: "The Federal National Mortgage Association Conventional Mortgage Program," *Real Estate Appraiser,* November-December 1973, pp. 19–29.

Lewis, Bertram: "Government-Assisted Housing as a Tax Shelter," *Evaluating Tax Shelter Offerings,* 1981, pp. 771–781.

York, John C., Jr.: "Section 223(f): A Viable Method of Financing Apartment Buildings," *Journal of Property Management,* vol. 46, July-August 1981, pp. 224–227.

CHAPTER 9

WRAPAROUND FINANCING METHODS

/ / /

WHAT IS A WRAP MORTGAGE?

RISK ANALYSIS OF WRAPAROUND LOANS
  Legal Implications
  Borrower-Lender Risk Implications
  Income Tax Implications

WRAPAROUND FINANCING EXAMPLES
  Simultaneous-Term Wrap
  Partially Amortized Wrap
  Extended-Term Wrap
  Extended-Term–No-Funds-Advanced Wrap
  Shorter-Term Wrap
  After-Tax Yield for Wrap Lender: An Example
  Yield and Cost-of-Borrowing Considerations
  Blended-Rate Mortgages

SUMMARY

QUESTIONS

PROBLEMS

REFERENCES

This chapter discusses a real estate financing technique called the wraparound (''wrap'') mortgage. The wrap is a major financing method and has been the catalyst for many real estate transactions. First is an overview of the types of situations in which a wrap could be used. Next, we discuss the legal, risk, and tax implications of wraps for the borrower and the lender. The last section provides several detailed examples of various types of wraps. Since the tax aspects from the wrap lender's perspective are unique, we conclude with an example of how to calculate the after-tax yield.

WHAT IS A WRAP MORTGAGE?

The concept of wraparound mortgages is not new. However, the use of wraps in real estate financing grows significantly during periods of increasing interest rates because of the benefits it offers both the borrower and the wrap lender. To illustrate how a wrap mortgage works and its benefits, let us examine two common situations in which wraparound mortgages might be used.

First, suppose a buyer wants to buy a $100,000 property. The seller's existing mortgage has a $40,000 balance, a 6 percent interest rate, and is assumable with annual payments of $3,439. However, the buyer has only $20,000 in cash for a down payment and therefore cannot simply assume the existing loan; the buyer requires another $40,000 to complete the transaction. The buyer seeks *new* financing from a lender for the $80,000 required and will no doubt pay the current market rate of interest—say, 12 percent. Obviously, it could benefit the borrower to be able to leave the 6 percent loan on the property and borrow the additional $40,000 elsewhere. This may be done by assuming the existing mortgage and taking out a second mortgage for $40,000. Since a second mortgage is considered riskier, the borrower probably would be required to pay a higher rate—say, approximately 14 percent. But all else being equal, it is certainly better to pay 6 percent on half the money and 14 percent on the other half with this option rather than 12 percent overall, as with the new $80,000 loan option.

However, there is a third alternative. Suppose the seller, or a mortgage lender, is willing to carry the existing first mortgage and continue to make payments on it if the buyer signs a new $80,000 wraparound mortgage at say, 10 percent interest with annual payments of $9,264. The buyer would then make payments on the $80,000 wrap loan to the seller or wrap lender, as the case may be. Out of each payment received, the seller (or wrap lender) would then make payments on the first mortgage and keep the difference. The seller (or wrap lender) earns the 10 percent rate on the entire $80,000 but is only extending $40,000 in funds to the borrower while paying off the prior $40,000 obligation at the lower 6 percent rate. The lender is thus earning a rate in excess of 10 percent on the $40,000 extended. Indeed, the simple cash-on-cash return is 14.6 percent [($9,264 − 3,439)/40,000], which is why the lender is willing to offer this wrap mortgage at the "below market" rate of 10 percent. (We illustrate the mechanics involved with this wrap loan later in the chapter.)

The other common situation in which a wrap mortgage is beneficial is in refinancing. Using the same facts, suppose the owner of a $100,000 property requires additional cash. The owner realizes that only $40,000 is owed on the property and that lenders are willing to finance up to 80 percent of the value: $80,000 in this case. The owner could take out a $40,000 second mortgage at, say, 14 percent and pocket the cash proceeds from the loan. Alternatively, the owner could obtain a wraparound loan for $80,000 at, say, 10 percent, with the wrap lender assuming payments on the existing $40,000 mortgage and giving the borrower $40,000 in cash.

In these examples, the lender earns a yield close to 14 percent (we illustrate this concept later) while the borrower obtains a 10 percent rate, which is lower than if a completely new loan was taken out and the old one was paid off. The "loser" in wrap financing is the existing mortgagee, who remains saddled with the below-market interest rate loan.

RISK ANALYSIS OF WRAPAROUND LOANS

Although the wraparound mortgage can be a useful financing tool, various laws, additional risks imposed on the lender and the borrower, and income tax consequences must be considered.

Legal Implications

There are several legal issues involved with wrap financing methods. These include usury laws and restrictive clauses.

Usury Laws   Before a wraparound mortgage is structured, state usury laws should be fully reviewed. In some states, the interest the lender receives on money not advanced is attributable to money actually advanced. Thus, in some states, the wrap lender needs to be concerned about not only the interest rate charged on the wrap but also the method used to compute that rate. In addition, some state laws prohibit charging interest on interest, which often occurs in wraparound mortgage financing.

Restrictive Clauses   The existing first mortgage must be reviewed to ascertain that there are no restrictions on the use of wrap mortgages. *Due on sale clauses* have been the subject of much litigation in recent years, with somewhat inconclusive results. The essence of most due-on-sale clauses is that the acceleration provisions of the mortgage are invoked if the equity interest in the property is sold or transferred in any manner. Thus the mortgage is "due on sale." Many existing mortgages restrict the use of second or wrap mortgage financing.

Nonassignment or nonassumption clauses restrict the borrower from assigning the mortgage to another party. This could present problems when structuring a wraparound mortgage because of the wrap lender's assumption of the payments on the first mortgage. *Prepayment penalties* or a *nonprepayment clause* may also exist in the mortgage. Although a prepayment penalty will not prevent the making of a wrap loan, both borrower and lender should be aware of the effect it can have on the yield (borrowing cost) and hence on the financing (or refinancing decision). A nonprepayment clause strictly forbids the borrower from prepaying the mortgage. Although quite rare in mortgages granted in recent years, the provision exists in a few older mortgages and generally stipulates that the borrower may prepay the loan if the principal and *all* interest to be earned under the original terms are paid to the lender. The nonprepayment provision will not prevent a wraparound mortgage from being structured, but the combination of a nonassignment clause and a nonprepayment clause in a mortgage essentially prevents the borrower from selling the property to anyone during the term of the loan. Courts have universally held that this combination is a ''restraint on alienation'' and illegal. As a result, structuring a wrap when the first mortgage includes *both* nonassignment and nonprepayment provisions may be permissible.

Because this area of the law is still being tested in the courts, be careful about structuring a wraparound mortgage when these restrictive clauses are in the first mortgage; *retain competent legal advisers with experience in this area.*

Mortgage Registry Tax   Mortgage registry tax is paid in the county in which the property is located; the tax is used to record the mortgage documents. Where it exists, the mortgage tax is generally based on some percentage of the mortgage amount. The method of computation varies among states, some charging the tax on the face amount of the wraparound mortgage, even though only a portion of that amount is extended. The cost the lender incurs in recording the mortgage is generally passed on to the borrower. Because it can affect yield and borrowing cost, the registry tax must be considered in the financing decision.

Borrower-Lender Risk Implications

A wraparound mortgage entails potential risks and problems for both the wrap lender and the borrower.

Lender Risks   As with any mortgage, the wrap lender faces the possibility that the borrower might default on the loan. However, the wrap lender (unlike the first mortgage lender) must be prepared to continue the payments on the first mortgage that was assumed when the wraparound was originated, to protect the status of the wrap loan. Should the wrap lender find it necessary to foreclose, the lender may face the burden of immediately retiring the balance on the first mortgage, especially if there is a due-on-sale clause.

In addition, because of the legal status of the wrap loan as an inferior lien to the existing mortgage, there can be a lag in distributing funds from insurance proceeds and condemnation awards. First, the wrap lender should ascertain that the borrower's casualty insurance policy names the wrap lender in the loss-payable clause behind the first mortgagee and that the property is insured for its full replacement cost at all times. Although insuring the property is the borrower's responsibility, the wrap mortgage should include a clause that requires the borrower to do so.

Even with these precautions, however, there is a greater likelihood that the wrap lender rather than the first mortgagee will suffer losses if a substantial casualty or condemnation occurs. In a total or near-total loss or taking of the property, the first mortgagee is usually entitled to complete payment before any other party. Depending on the amounts and factors involved, it is conceivable that the wrap lender may be left with an amount insufficient to cover the debt and with a property that is no longer adequate security.

To account for the additional risks, the wrap lender will attempt to increase the yield on the wrap by increasing the interest rate, using front-end points, or lowering the loan-to-value ratio. The effect of points on yield is greater with a wrap than with a standard first mortgage because of the wrap's leveraging effect. This effect is calculated by reducing the amount of new money initially advanced by the amount of points collected. This concept is illustrated in the later examples in this chapter.

Borrower Risks   As the equity investor, the borrower is in the riskiest position of all the participants in the wrap mortgage. The borrower's main concern is gaining free, unencumbered title after completely paying off the wrap lender. This can be accomplished by the borrower's making timely payments on the wrap loan *and* the wrap lender's making timely payments on the first mortgage. Therefore, some degree of cooperation and trust is necessary among the first mortgagee, wrap lender, and borrower. There can be situations in which the borrower who has made regular payments finds that free, unencumbered title is not available because the wrap lender is unwilling or unable to perform according to the contract.

There could also be difficulties over title to the property. Consider the situation in which the seller of the property acts as the wrap lender for the purchaser-borrower and does not have marketable title to the property. Unless the borrower demands title evidence and is assured of marketable title prior to the closing, lengthy and expensive litigation may be necessary to resolve the issue. Some sellers have been unwilling or unable to bear the costs of providing good title after receiving all the borrower's money. Some sellers may, due to circumstances beyond their control, be unable to provide good, marketable title at any cost. For this reason, a purchaser should obtain a title opinion or title insurance policy prior to the closing.

Another difficulty for the borrower is a default by the wrap lender. Suppose the borrower dutifully makes payments on the wrap loan but the wrap lender fails to pay on the first mortgage, thus creating a default. The first mortgagee subsequently invokes the acceleration clause in the mortgage and forecloses on the property, extinguishing the rights of the wrap lender and the borrower. Although the borrower has a cause of action against the wrap lender, prolonged and costly litigation is often the result, with no assurance of a monetary settlement.

A similar situation occurs when the amortization on the wrap loan proceeds at a faster rate than on the first mortgage. The wrap lender collects the relatively high payments on the wrap mortgage and then pays the relatively low payments on the longer-term first mortgage and pockets the difference. When the wrap loan is completely paid, a balance is still owed on the first loan. The borrower needs the assurance that this balance will be paid as agreed. Since the amount can be substantial, the borrower may stipulate in the loan agreement that the wrap lender pay higher monthly payments on the first mortgage so that it will amortize at or above the rate of amortization on the wrap loan. In this fashion, the borrower's payments always equal or exceed the payments on the first mortgage. Coupled with a provision allowing the borrower to pay the first mortgagee directly if the wrap mortgagee defaults, this should minimize or eliminate potential losses.

Escrow Agents   Probably the best, although costliest, method of prevention against wrap lender default is the use of a disinterested third party acting as an escrow agent. This could be another lender, a broker, an attorney, or anyone who has no financial interest in the transaction. The escrow agent receives the payment from the borrower, pays the agreed-upon amount to the first mortgagee, sends any balance to the wrap lender, and records all transactions for the borrower and the lender. The escrow agent also charges the borrower or the wrap lender or both a fee for servicing the loan.

The use of an escrow agent is relatively rare in wraparound mortgage transactions, especially where the wrap lender is an established lending institution of sound financial reputation. An agent's use is much more common when the wrap lender is an individual, especially if the individual is also the seller in the transaction.

Income Tax Implications

The tax implications are no different for the borrower on a wraparound mortgage than for the borrower on a typical mortgage. The interest paid on the wraparound mortgage is fully deductible as an interest expense on trade or business property or as an itemized deduction for property used as a personal residence. The interest on the underlying first mortgage, however, is now the obligation of the wrap lender and therefore is not deductible by the borrower.

For the wrap lender, the before-tax cash flow is the annual wraparound intake minus the annual first mortgage outflow. The interest earned on the wrap loan is treated as ordinary income, and the interest paid on the first mortgage is deductible from taxable income. So the *net* interest earned is the amount taxed at ordinary income tax rates. Note that it does not matter that more principal is being paid on the first mortgage than is being taken in on the wraparound mortgage. In addition, the IRS assumes that for tax purposes the buyer in a wraparound has taken the property subject to the existing mortgage. The major benefit for the wrap seller is that he or she may avoid tax treatment on any excess of liabilities over the property's basis in the year the wraparound loan is initiated. Thus, the seller gains both significant tax benefits and nontax benefits. We illustrate how to analyze the tax aspects in a later example. Now we discuss the mechanics of wraparound financing methods.

WRAPAROUND FINANCING EXAMPLES

There are numerous variations of wrap financing. This section illustrates some of the more common methods of structuring wrap mortgages.

Simultaneous-Term Wrap

Probably the simplest and most commonly used wrap mortgage is the *simultaneous-term,* in which the remaining term of the wrap coincides with the term remaining on the underlying first mortgage and with level payments on each loan fully amortizing their respective balances over the term. Example 9-1 illustrates this situation: The remaining term of the $40,000, 6 percent first mortgage is 20 years, and the loan fully amortizes over that time period with equal monthly payments of $286.57. The $80,000, 10 percent wrap mortgage could be structured with a 20-year term and equal monthly installments of $772.02. In this case, both loans are paid off simultaneously. The wrap lender collects $772.02 from the borrower each month and pays out $286.57 to the first mortgagee, retaining the difference: $485.45. The resulting yield is 13.6 percent to the wrap lender.

Partially Amortized Wrap

A second alternative is to leave the actual term of the wrap loan the same as that of the first mortgage, but with partial amortization. Example 9-2 illustrates this

---

EXAMPLE 9-1

SIMULTANEOUS-TERM WRAPAROUND MORTGAGE

Existing first mortgage		New wraparound mortgage	
Balance	$40,000	Balance	$80,000
Remaining term	20 years	Term	20 years
Interest rate	6 percent	Interest rate	10 percent
Monthly payment	$286.57	Monthly payment	$772.02

1 The funds the wrap lender extends is the wrap amount minus the first mortgage balance assumed ($80,000 − $40,000 = $40,000).
2 The funds the wrap lender collects is the difference between the monthly payment inflow and outflow ($772.02 − $286.57 = $485.45).
3 The equation for computation of the yield is

$$PV = \text{net payment inflow} \times PVAF_{i\%/12,240}$$

$$\$40,000 = \$485.45 \times PVAF_{i\%/12,240}$$

Solve for $i\%$ and interpolate; the yield is 13.59%.

EXAMPLE 9-2

SIMULTANEOUS-TERM WRAPAROUND MORTGAGE WITH BALLOON PAYMENTS

Existing first mortgage		New wraparound mortgage	
Balance	$40,000	Balance	$80,000
Remaining term	20 years	Amortization period	30 years
Interest rate	6%	Term	20 years
Monthly payment	$286.57	Rate	10%
		Monthly payment	$702.06
		Balloon payment	$53,125

1 Funds extended by wrap lender: $40,000
2 Net funds collected by wrap lender
  a Annuity (monthly payment) years 1–20:

$$\$702.06 - \$286.57 = \$415.49$$

  b Balloon payment, EOY 20: $53,125
3 Yield computation:

$$\$40,000 = \$415.49 \, (PVAF_{i\%/12,240}) + \$53,125 \, (PVF_{i\%/12,240})$$

Solve for $i\%$ and interpolate; the yield is 11.30%.

---

concept. Suppose that the borrower cannot afford payments of $772.02. Alternatively, we could set up the wrap with monthly payments based on a 30- (rather than a 20-) year amortization period and require a balloon payment of the unpaid balance at the end of 20 years (see Example 9-2). The new monthly payment would be $702.06, with a balloon payment of $53,125 due at the end of the twentieth year. In this case, the wrap lender nets $415.49 per month ($702.06 − $286.57) for 20 years, plus a $53,125 payment at the end of year 20, when the first mortgage fully amortizes. The wrap lender will generally require that the wrap loan be fully paid by the time the first mortgage is retired since the lender's leveraging advantage is eliminated once the lower-interest first mortgage is retired. Note the lower yield in Example 9-2 resulting from extension of the amortization period.

Extended-Term Wrap

A third option for the borrower and the lender is to negotiate a wrap mortgage that has an *extended term and no balloon payment*, as in Example 9-3. Returning to Example 9-2, the $80,000, 10 percent wrap loan would amortize in 30 years at $702.06 per month. With the underlying $40,000 first mortgage fully amortizing in 20 years at $286.57 per month, this option parallels the prior one, except that the

---

EXAMPLE 9-3

EXTENDED-TERM, FULLY AMORTIZED WRAPAROUND MORTGAGE

Existing first mortgage		New wraparound mortgage	
Balance	$40,000	Balance	$80,000
Remaining term	20 years	Term	30 years
Interest rate	6%	Interest rate	10%
Monthly payment	$286.57	Monthly payment	$702.06

1 Funds extended by wrap lender: $40,000
2 Net funds collected by wrap lender
  a Annuity (monthly payment) years 1–20:

$$\$702.06 - \$286.57 = \$415.49$$

  b Annuity (monthly payment) years 21–30:

$$\$702.06$$

3 Yield computation:

$$\$40,000 = \$415.49 \, (PVAF_{i\%/12,240}) + \$702.06 \, (PVAF_{i\%/12,120}) \, (PVF_{i\%/12,240})$$

Solving for the rate, we obtain 12.67%.

---

borrower continues to make regular payments on the wrap loan through years 21 to 30 instead of paying the balloon at the end of year 20. Extending the term of the wrap this way benefits the borrower by lowering the debt service below what it would have been with a simultaneous-term, fully amortized loan and by eliminating the balloon payment at the end of year 20, as with the simultaneous-term, partially amortized loan. Because of the loss of leverage on the underlying 6 percent loan after the twentieth year, the lender's yield on the money advanced is lower than it would have been without the extended-term provision, as Example 9-3 illustrates.

Extended-Term–No-Funds-Advanced Wrap

A fourth option is the wrap with an *extended term but with no funds advanced,* as in Example 9-4. The wraparound mortgage is made in the exact amount of the unpaid balance of the existing first mortgage but is repayable over a longer term than the first. For this type of wrap to be of interest to a borrower, it must result in one benefit: lower monthly payments. For it to be desirable to the lender, it must result in a yield commensurate with the market for the level of risk as-

EXAMPLE 9-4

EXTENDED-TERM, FULLY AMORTIZED WRAPAROUND MORTGAGE
WITH NO FUNDS ADVANCED

Existing first mortgage		New wraparound mortgage	
Balance	$40,000	Balance	$40,000
Remaining term	10 years	Term	30 years
Interest rate	6%	Interest rate	10%
Monthly payment	$444.08	Monthly payment	$351.03

1 Funds extended by wrap lender: net annuity of $93.05 each month for years 1–10.
2 Funds collected by wrap lender: annuity of $351.03 each month for years 11–30.
3 The equation for computing the yield can be set up as follows (PV is zero because no initial funds are advanced):

$$0 = -\$93.05(PVAF_{i\%/12,120}) + \$351.03(PVAF_{i\%/12,240})(PVF_{i\%/12,120})$$

rewriting the equation,

$$\$93.05(PVAF_{i\%/12,120}) = \$351.03(PVAF_{i\%/12,240})(PVF_{i\%/12,120})$$

solving for the rate, we obtain 15.34%.

sumed. The rate on the wrap loan must therefore be higher than that of the first mortgage, which in turn could drive the wrap payments higher than those on the first mortgage if the remaining terms on each are even moderately close. This effect would nullify for the borrower any benefits of payment reduction. As a result, this type of wrap loan is generally used only when there is a large disparity between the remaining term on the first mortgage and the term of the wrap.

As in Example 9-4, suppose a borrower has an existing $40,000, 6 percent loan with 10 years of $444.08 monthly payments remaining. The borrower is experiencing financial difficulties and has found a lender willing to grant a wraparound mortgage at 10 percent for 30 years, simultaneously taking over the payments on the first mortgage. Payments on the wrap loan are $351.03, a $93.05 reduction for the financially distressed borrower. However, during the first 10 years of the wrap, the lender will have a cash *outflow* each month of $93.05 because of making the $444.08 first-mortgage payment. So, even though the wrap lender advances no initial funds, the monthly advances must be made to cover the first mortgage. This type of wraparound mortgage is clearly the riskiest for the lender. See Example 9-4 for the yield computations.

Shorter-Term Wrap

Finally, the wrap loan can be written with a *shorter term* than that remaining on the first mortgage. For such a wrap to be beneficial to both parties, the wrap lender must extend additional funds to the borrower. This wrap entails less risk for the lender because the wrap loan is paid off before the first loan matures, and the yield is enhanced. Conversely, the borrower must shoulder a higher debt service and/or a balloon payment, a higher effective borrowing cost, and a higher risk than with a simultaneous-term wrap loan at the same interest rate.

In Example 9-5, an existing $40,000, 6 percent, 20-year first mortgage with payments of $286.57 is "wrapped" by an $80,000, 10 percent loan that is fully amortized over 15 years at $859.68 per month. At the end of year 15, the borrower will have fully retired the $80,000 debt; however, there is still a $14,823 balance on the first mortgage. Since the first mortgage was assumed by the wrap lender and since the borrower has fully retired personal debt on the wrap loan (which included the first mortgage in its original amount), the buyer should own the property free and clear of the first mortgage debt. Therefore, the wrap lender must extend $14,823 in funds at the end of year 15 to provide the borrower with unencumbered ownership. In this example, the lender extends $40,000 in funds at the beginning of the wrap loan and another $14,823 at the end of year 15 and collects a net payment of $573.11 ($859.68 − $286.57) each month over the intervening term. See Example 9-5 for the yield computations. Alternatively, the wrap

---

EXAMPLE 9-5

SHORTER-TERM, FULLY AMORTIZED WRAPAROUND MORTGAGE

Existing first mortgage		New wraparound mortgage	
Balance	$40,000	Balance	$80,000
Remaining term	20 years	Term	15 years
Interest rate	6%	Interest rate	10%
Monthly payment	$286.57	Monthly payment	$859.68
Balance, EOY 15	$14,823	Balance, EOY 15	0

1 Funds extended by wrap lender
  a $40,000 initially
  b $14,823 at EOY 15 to retire first mortgage
2 Funds collected by wrap lender

$$\$859.68 - \$286.57 = \$573.11 \text{ per month for 15 years}$$

3 Equation is as follows:

$$\$40,000 + \$14,823(\text{PVF}_{i\%/12,180}) = \$573.11(\text{PVAF}_{i\%/12,180})$$

rewriting the equation,

$$\$40,000 = \$573.11(\text{PVAF}_{i\%/12,180}) - \$14,823(\text{PVF}_{i\%/12,180})$$

solving for the rate, we obtain 15.37%.

EXAMPLE 9-6

SHORTER-TERM, FULLY AMORTIZED WRAPAROUND MORTGAGE WITH FIRST
MORTGAGE PAYMENTS INCREASED TO EQUALIZE MATURITY

Existing first mortgage		New wraparound mortgage	
Balance	$40,000	Balance	$80,000
Interest rate	6%	Interest rate	10%
Remaining term (original basis)	20 years	Term	15 years
		Monthly payment	$859.68
Monthly payment (original basis)	$286.57	Balance, EOY 15	0
Revised term	15 years		
Revised monthly payment	$337.54		
Balance, EOY 15	0		

1 Funds extended by wrap lender: $40,000 initially
2 Funds collected by wrap lender:

$$\$859.68 - \$337.54 = \$522.14$$

3 Equation is as follows:

$$\$40,000 = \$522.14(PVAF_{i\%/12,180})$$

solving for the rate, we obtain 13.61%.

lender could increase the payments on the first mortgage from $286.57 to $337.54, which fully amortizes it in 15 years, as Example 9-6 illustrates. This eliminates the necessity of making the balloon payment at the end of year 15 but decreases the lender's yield because of the faster debt retirement of the low-interest first mortgage. (Compare the yield obtained in Example 9-6 with that in Example 9-5).

After-Tax Yield for Wrap Lender: An Example

To illustrate the tax effects of a wrap, consider the following income property example. An investor is considering buying an apartment building for a total price of $650,000, with a $130,000 cash down payment. The existing first mortgage on the property was made 5 years ago for $375,000 at 12 percent interest with monthly payments totaling $47,394 per year, fully amortizing the loan over 25 years. The present amount owed on this mortgage is $358,700.

The investor's proposal is contingent on obtaining a wraparound mortgage for the amount required—$520,000—amortized over 15 years at 14 percent interest with monthly debt service payments totaling $83,100 per year. There is a final balloon payment at the end of year 5.

This investor approaches a private investor in mortgage loans for the necessary funds on the wraparound mortgage. Before making a commitment, the lender must determine the after-tax internal rate of return and the "net" present value on this mortgage, given a required 8 percent after-tax rate of return and a tax rate of 28 percent.

To solve this problem, we first determine the initial cash outlay. The lender must make the $520,000 wrap loan, assume the $358,700 balance on the existing loan, and extend the difference of $161,300 in cash, which the investor will give to the seller along with the down payment ($130,000 + $161,300 + $358,700 = $650,000).

Next, we develop amortization schedules for both loans to determine the net interest the wrap lender earns for each year of the loan. Tables 9-1 and 9-2 are the amortization schedules for the existing and the wraparound loan.

TABLE 9-1 EXISTING MORTGAGE AMORTIZATION SCHEDULE*

Year	Proportion outstanding	Amount outstanding	Debt service	12% Interest (for 25 years)	Principal
0	1.0	$375,000			
1	0.99325	372,469	$47,394	$44,863	$2,531
2	0.98564	369,615	47,394	44,540	2,854
3	0.97707	366,401	47,394	44,180	3,214
4	0.96741	362,779	47,394	43,772	3,622
5	0.95653	358,700	47,394	43,315	4,079
6	0.94427	354,101	47,394	42,796	4,598
7	0.93045	348,919	47,394	42,212	5,182
8	0.91488	343,080	47,394	41,555	5,839
9	0.89733	336,499	47,394	41,555	5,839
10	0.87756	329,085	47,394	40,813	6,581

*See text for assumptions.
Note: Existing loan is initiated at beginning of year 1 (year 0); wrap loan is initiated at beginning of year 6 (end of year 5).

TABLE 9-2 WRAPAROUND MORTGAGE AMORTIZATION SCHEDULE*

Year	Amount outstanding	Debt service	Interest (14% for 15 years)	Principal
0	$520,000			
1	508,140	$83,100	$71,240	$11,860
2	494,620	83,100	69,580	13,520
3	479,207	83,100	67,687	15,413
4	461,636	83,100	65,529	17,571
5	441,605	83,100	63,069	20,031

*See text for assumptions.
Note: Year 1 on this loan coincides with year 6 on the existing loan.

TABLE 9-3   BEFORE-TAX CASH FLOW (BTCF) AND NET INTEREST
EARNED (NIE) ON WRAPAROUND MORTGAGE

Year	Amount loaned	BTCF	NIE
0	$161,300		
1		$ 35,706	$28,444
2		35,706	27,368
3		35,706	26,132
4		35,706	24,716
5		148,226*	23,089

*$112,520 is difference between amount outstanding on wraparound
mortgage and amount outstanding on existing mortgage.

Using the amortization schedules, determine the before-tax cash flows to the
lender and the net interest earned (NIE) each year. The before-tax cash flow is
the debt service received on the wrap loan minus the debt service paid on the
existing loan. The NIE is the interest earned on the wrap loan minus the interest
paid on the existing loan. Table 9-3 illustrates these calculations. Note that BTCF
for year 5 consists of the net balloon payment proceeds, which is the difference
between the balances owing at the end of year 5 plus the net payment proceeds of
$35,706 ($441,605 − $329,085 + $35,706 = $148,226). These are all the figures
necessary for computing the taxes and the ATCFs for each year, as shown in
Table 9-4. Table 9-5 shows the computation of the net present value and the internal rate of return on this loan. Note that the lender will earn more than the
required rate of return given the assumptions.

Yield and Cost-of-Borrowing Considerations

In the examples in previous chapters, yield (to the lender) and effective borrowing costs (to the borrower) were virtually the same. There may be differences,
however, in yield and effective borrowing cost for the parties involved in the
wraparound mortgage. To understand these differences, consider the possible situations in which a wrap may be used and note the perspective of each party involved.

Seller as Wrap Lender   Using the facts from Example 9-1, suppose the situation involves the sale of real estate and the seller will act as the wrap lender. The
before-tax yield to the seller-wrap lender is 13.59 percent on the $40,000 that the
seller has not received on the sale; essentially, the seller has extended $40,000 of
credit to the buyer. The after-tax yield to the seller, however, depends on both
the terms of the wrap loan itself and other rules regarding the installment sale of
property (discussed in the next chapter).

For the borrower in this situation, the effective borrowing cost is simply the
interest rate on the wrap mortgage, which is 10 percent (assuming no points or

TABLE 9-4   TAXES DUE ON WRAPAROUND EARNINGS AND AFTER-TAX CASH FLOWS TO THE WRAP LENDER

Tax computation	Year				
	1	2	3	4	5
Net interest earned	28,444	27,368	26,132	24,716	23,089
× tax rate	0.28	0.28	0.28	0.28	0.28
tax	7,964	7,663	7,317	6,920	6,465

ATCF computation	Year				
	1	2	3	4	5
BTCF	35,706	35,706	35,706	35,706	148,226
− tax	7,964	7,663	7,317	6,920	6,465
ATCF	27,742	28,043	28,389	28,786	141,761

origination fees). The borrower indirectly benefits from the existence of the 6 percent mortgage, but since there is no direct borrower involvement in the underlying loan, it does not affect the effective cost of borrowing.

Third-Party Wrap Lender   Imagine a situation similar to the preceding one, except that a third-party lender enters the picture. This lender extends the $40,000 additional funds to the borrower, the borrower in turn uses these funds to pay off the seller at closing ($40,000 existing mortgage + $40,000 cash from wrap loan + $20,000 down payment = $100,000 purchase price). The seller "cashes out" and is removed from any future financing. The borrower's position is the same as before, with a before-tax borrowing cost of 10 percent. The wrap lender, however, is in the position the seller previously occupied and earns a 13.59 percent before-tax yield (see Example 9-1).

Third-Party Wrap Lender–Owner Refinancing   In the final situation, the owner of real estate requires additional cash and refinances the property with a wraparound mortgage. In our example, the seller is giving up the underlying 6

TABLE 9-5   AFTER-TAX NPV AND IRR ON WRAPAROUND MORTGAGE

Year	Amount loaned	ATCFs	PVF$_{8\%}$	PV
0	$161,300		1.0	($161,300)
1		$ 27,742	0.92593	25,687
2		28,043	0.85734	24,042
3		28,389	0.79383	22,536
4		28,786	0.73503	21,159
5		141,761	0.68058	96,480
			Net present value at 8%	$ 28,604
			IRR	12.90%

percent, $40,000 mortgage and borrowing $40,000 additional cash. The entire cost of obtaining the additional $40,000 cash includes the additional interest now being paid on the $40,000 existing mortgage balance. In this situation then, the owner's before-tax effective borrowing cost is the same as the lender's before-tax yield, approximately 13.59 percent.

Blended-Rate Mortgages

A blended-rate mortgage is one which carries a contract interest rate which is the average between the interest rate on a property's existing mortgage and the current market interest rate on additional funds needed by the borrower.

Blended-rate mortgages were introduced in the late 1970s, when mortgage lenders found themselves paying high rates of interest on deposits while being locked into low-interest bearing mortgages that were issued for up to 30 years. Furthermore, with few funds available in the 1980s, prospective homeowners could not afford the rates offered by mortgage lenders. Thus, the solution to this problem had to not only rearrange the lender's loan portfolio but also be affordable to the lender's customers. The blended-rate mortgages proved to be just that solution. The blended-rate mortgage gained popularity quickly among homeowners and is now offered by lenders such as banks, savings and loan associations, and private mortgage companies.

Once the average, or blend, rate is determined, the blend rate may be as either a fixed-rate loan or an adjustable-rate mortgage with a typical 25- to 30-year maturity.

Blended-rate mortgages may be amortized with monthly payments of principal and interest or they may require interest-only monthly payments with a balloon note due at maturity. These mortgages are usually issued by the same lender who issued the original loan on the property.

To calculate the interest rate on a blended-rate loan, we use the following equation:

Blended rate   = principal outstanding on   ×   interest rate on existing loan
      existing loan
      + new funds to be financed   ×   interest rate on new funds
      = principal outstanding on   +   new funds to be financed
      existing loan

For example, assume that 5 years ago on a $150,000 home a seller had obtained an 8 percent 20-year monthly-payment mortgage for $100,000. A buyer with a $25,000 down payment needs to finance $125,000. Current interest rates are 12 percent. The remaining balance on the old $100,000, 8 percent loan is

$87,526. Thus, the new funds to be financed are $125,000 − $87,526 = $37,474. If the buyer were to get the $125,000 mortgage which blended the old mortgage, the blend's interest rate would be

$$\frac{(\$87,526 \times 0.08) + (\$37,474 \times 0.12)}{\$125,000} = 9.2 \text{ percent}$$

SUMMARY

This chapter examined wraparound mortgages and several ways they can be structured: simultaneous-term with full or partial amortization, extended-term, extended-term with no additional funds, and shorter-term. The legal implications of wraparound mortgages center around usury laws, restrictive clauses in the existing loan, and the mortgage registry tax. These factors, as well as the tax aspects and risks, must all be considered when contemplating the use of a wraparound mortgage. The following chapter discusses another financing tool, the installment sale, which is often used in a wraparound context.

QUESTIONS

1 Define the following terms:
   a wraparound mortgage
   b due-on-sale clause
   c nonassumption clause
   d prepayment penalty
   e usury
   f balloon payment
   g blended-rate mortgage
   h mortgage registry tax
2 Describe the situations in which it would be advantageous to use a wraparound mortgage. How does the wrap mortgage work? Who gets "wrapped"? Who is the "loser" in a wrap mortgage?
3 What unique legal implications does a wraparound mortgage create? From the borrower's perspective, what is the most legal consideration? Lender's perspective?
4 Discuss the income tax implications of a wrap mortgage. Using the example developed in this chapter, explain the after-tax yield to the wrap lender.
5 What are the various categories of wrap mortgages? Describe briefly how each works.
6 Who may act as the lender in a wrap mortgage? Outline how a wrap would work for each party to wrap a loan.
7 When would a buyer want to use a wraparound mortgage? A seller?
8 What additional risks does a wrap lender have that other types of lenders do not?
9 Discuss the wrap mortgage from the borrower's perspective. What are the risks? How would the borrower protect against the risks?
10 How is it possible for the interest rate on a wrap mortgage to be lower than the conventional mortgage rate?
11 Suppose you observed two parcels of real estate that were *exactly* alike, one sold with conventional financing and the other with a wraparound mortgage. Would the selling price be the same for both parcels? Why or why not?
12 Explain how on a wrap the wrap lender's yield and the borrower's cost of borrowing money can be different.

PROBLEMS

1 Suppose a borrower took out a $50,000 loan with an interest rate of 7 percent and a maturity of 20 years. Fifteen years later, the borrower wants to increase indebtedness $20,000. The borrower is willing to pay 11.25 percent on the new wraparound mortgage.
   a Find the monthly payment on the wrap loan.
   b What is the lender's yield?

2 Assume this is a simultaneous-term wraparound mortgage.

Existing first mortgage		New wraparound mortgage	
Balance	$75,000	Balance	$100,000
Remaining term	25 years	Term	25 years
Interest rate	9 percent	Interest rate	11 percent
Monthly payments		Monthly payments	

Calculate:
   a Funds extended by the wrap lender
   b Net funds collected by the wrap lender
   c Yield on the wrap loan

3 Assume this is a simultaneous-term wraparound mortgage with a balloon payment at maturity.

Existing first mortgage		New wraparound mortgage	
Balance	$35,000	Balance	$70,000
Remaining term	15 years	Amortization period	25 years
Interest rate	10 percent	Term	15 years
Monthly payments		Rate	13 percent
		Monthly payments	
		Balloon payment at end	

Calculate:
   a Funds extended by the wrap lender
   b Net funds collected by the wrap lender
   c Yield on the wrap loan

4 Assume this is an extended-term, fully amortized wraparound mortgage.

Existing first mortgage		New wraparound mortgage	
Balance	$50,000	Balance	$100,000
Remaining term	20 years	Term	30 years
Interest rate	8 percent	Interest rate	12 percent
Monthly payment	$418.22	Monthly payment	$1,028.61

Calculate:
   a Funds extended by the wrap lender
   b Net funds collected by the wrap lender
   c Yield on the wrap loan

5 Assume this is an extended-term, fully amortized wraparound mortgage with no funds advanced.

Existing first mortgage		New wraparound mortgage	
Balance	$60,000	Balance	$60,000
Remaining term	10 years	Term	30 years
Interest rate	8 percent	Interest rate	12 percent
Monthly payment	$727.97	Monthly payment	$617.17

Calculate:

a Funds extended by the wrap lender
b Net funds collected by the wrap lender
c Yield on the wrap loan

6 Assume this is a shorter-term, fully amortized wraparound mortgage.

Existing first mortgage		New wraparound mortgage	
Balance	$60,000	Balance	$100,000
Remaining term	20 years	Term	15 years
Interest rate	8 percent	Interest rate	12 percent
Monthly payment	$501.86	Monthly payment	$1,200
Balance, EOY 15	$24,751	Balance, EOY 15	0

Calculate:

a Funds extended by the wrap lender
b Funds collected by the wrap lender
c Yield on the wrap loan

7 Assume this is a shorter-term, fully amortized wraparound mortgage with first mortgage payment increased to equalize maturity.

Existing first mortgage		New wraparound mortgage	
Balance	$60,000	Balance	$100,000
Interest rate	8 percent	Interest rate	12 percent
Remaining term (orig. basis)	20	Term	15
Monthly payments (orig. basis)	$501.86	Monthly payment	$1,200.17
Revised term	15 years	Balance, EOY 15	0
Revised monthly payment	$573.39		
Balance, EOY 15	0		

Calculate:

a Funds extended by the wrap lender
b Funds collected by the wrap lender
c Yield on the mortgage-rate loan

8 A homeowner purchased his home 10 years ago and obtained a 30-year mortgage for $80,000 at 6 percent interest (monthly payments). The home's current selling price is $135,000. A buyer agrees to a blended-rate mortgage at which new funds will be financed at 9.5 percent. What will the buyer's blended rate be?

9 An investor is considering buying an office building for a total price of $1,500,000, with a $200,000 cash down payment. The existing first mortgage on the property was made 5 years ago for $750,000 at 10 percent interest with monthly payments fully amortizing the loan over the 30 years. The investor's proposal is contingent on obtaining a wraparound mortgage for the amount required amortized over 20 years at 12.25 percent interest with monthly payments. There is a final balloon payment at the end of year 5. Determine the after-tax internal rate of return and the net present value of this mortgage, given a required 12 percent after-tax rate of return and a tax rate of 28 percent.

REFERENCES

"The IRS Approach to Wrap-Around Mortgage: A Contradiction of Tax Fundamentals," *The Tax Advisor*, May 1981.

Leteplo, Donald N.: "The Mortgage's Yield in Wraparound Financing," *Real Estate Appraiser and Analyst*, January-February 1979, pp. 23–31.

Mettling, Stephen R.: *Modern Residential Financing Methods: Tools of the Trade*, Chicago Real Estate Co., 1984.

Rosenburg, Menachem: "How to Structure Wrap-Around Mortgages to Allow Installment Method Reporting," *Taxation for Accountants*, vol. 24, January 1980.

"Special Report: How to Use Wrap-Around Financing," *The Mortgage and Real Estate Executives Report*, Spring 1981.

"The Wrap-Around Mortgage: A Critical Inquiry," *UCLA Law Review*, vol. 21, 1974, pp. 15–29.

Wilfred, Jerry: *The Tax Advisor*, February 1986.

INSTALLMENT SALE FINANCING

Generally, the Internal Revenue Code requires that the entire gain from the sale of property be reported when the sale is completed. However, an investor selling and financing property on a deferred-payment basis may use a special method for paying tax on the gain. This special method is the *installment sale,* whereby the buyer pays the seller a series of payments rather than all at once. The installment method relieves the seller of the obligation to pay the tax on income not received and allows the seller to include in gross income only the portion of each principal that is gain.

This chapter explores the mechanics of the installment sale financing method. Specifically, we discuss the basic requirements and provide a detailed example of how the installment method works. Then we compare it to an outright sale and an installment sale offer with a wraparound mortgage.

WHAT IS AN INSTALLMENT SALE?

An installment sale is a financing situation in which the seller is the lender, such as the case of the seller taking a first or a second mortgage or any other junior lien. Often it occurs under an installment contract, with the seller retaining title until all payments have been made. Thus the installment sale is a ''seller'' financing method.

The advantage to the seller is that not all the gain is taxed at the time of sale. The taxes owed are distributed over the life of the installment receipts. For the buyer-borrower, the installment sale is popular since no other third-party lender is involved in the transaction. Installment sale financing is widely used on certain types of real estate and as a tool for increasing the ratio of debt to total property value, thus minimizing the buyer's equity outflows.

This advantage has been dramatically reduced by the Tax Reform Act of 1986, in one respect by the reduction in the tax rates and tax brackets. Prior to 1986 a taxpayer realized a substantial advantage by spreading the gain received from a sale over a period of years rather than recognizing it in one period. In the case of sales greater than $150,000 and dealer, business, or income property, the seller may have to recognize additional gain if he or she has a large amount of other debt. This rule was enacted because some developers had installment receipts pledged as collateral for other loans. Thus, they were receiving the total purchase price without paying the tax on the gain. This amount, termed *allocable installment indebtedness,* forces some of the receipts to be deemed paid before they are actually received.

BASIC REQUIREMENTS

As with any form of financing, the lender in an installment sale must be aware of the basic tax requirements and mechanics involved. The following sections discuss these requirements, including their controversies and rulings. We then work examples to illustrate the mechanics involved.

Reporting the Gain

The effect of the installment method is a spread of the gain and the resulting tax over the years during which the installment payments are received. This result is achieved by applying a *gross profit percentage* to principal payments received each year. The gross profit percentage is the ratio of the gain to the contract price. The gain on an installment sale is determined in the usual manner: The seller's adjusted basis is a long-term capital gain as of the date of sale; it is taxed at the ordinary tax rate. The installment sale method is available only for gains; losses may not be reported by this method.

The *contract price* is the sale price reduced by mortgages or other indebtedness assumed (or taken subject to) by the buyer and payable to a third party. In other words, the contract price is usually the amount the buyer actually pays to the seller: cash, notes, other property, and purchase money mortgages. Also, if any mortgage assumed on (or taken subject to) the purchased property is in excess of the seller's basis, the excess is included in the contract price. Alternatively if the buyer pays off an existing mortgage on the property at the time of sale instead of assuming it, this payment must be included in the contract price.

The gross profit percentage is determined by dividing the gain on the installment sale by the contract price. The percentage is applied to all payments of principal each year to determine the portion of each payment that is reportable as taxable gain. The interest portion of each installment payment is reportable in its entirety as ordinary income, and if no interest is provided for in the agreement, the IRS will "impute" interest; that is, part of the payment will be treated as interest and taxed as ordinary income. If the assumed mortgage on the property is in excess of the seller's adjusted basis in the property, the gain will always be the same as the contract price. Accordingly, the gross profit percentage will be 100 percent, and all installment payments received will be entirely included in income.

Selling Expenses

Commissions and other selling expenses the seller incurs are not deducted when determining the sale price, contract price, or payments in the year of sale. However, a seller who is not a real estate dealer may reduce the gain on the sale by the amount of the selling expenses.

One controversy concerning selling expenses and excess mortgage over basis has been resolved by the temporary regulations issued under the Installment Sale Revision Bill of 1980. The controversy was whether selling expenses should be added to the seller's basis in the property. If the selling expenses are added to the seller's basis, they reduce the amount of any excess mortgage over basis. This reduction is beneficial to the seller because it allows a greater portion of the gain to be deferred when the mortgage assumed exceeds the seller's basis. The temporary regulations take the position that selling expenses should be added to the seller's basis.

Wraparound Mortgages

With a wraparound mortgage (Chapter 9), the buyer gives the seller a mortgage in excess of the existing mortgage on the property and claims not to assume (or take subject to) the existing mortgage. Debate centers around whether the buyer can use a wraparound mortgage to avoid the purchase of the property subject to the existing mortgage. The IRS's view is that when a wraparound mortgage is used, the buyer has taken the property subject to the wrap for tax purposes. The position is the same whether title passes immediately to the buyer or is delayed, as in a wraparound contract for a deed. The use of a wraparound mortgage by the seller in an installment sale creates some unique tax problems that we discuss later in this chapter.

Imputed Interest

Prior to the *imputed interest* laws, installment sales provided for little or no interest and, generally, the purchase price was adjusted upward. This way the seller paid tax on the "interest" income at capital gain rates instead of the ordinary tax rate. The buyer received no interest deduction, but the interest was a part of the basis and was recovered over the property's useful life if it was depreciable property. The advent of imputed interest laws prevented the conversion of unstated interest income to capital gain income.

If a minimum amount of interest is not provided for in an installment payment agreement, the IRS will impute interest. As a result, each installment payment is divided between interest and principal. Accordingly, the interest portion of each payment is ordinary income to the seller and is deductible as interest to the buyer.

The minimum interest rate required to avoid imputed interest is currently 9 percent and subject to change. If the minimum interest is not provided, the IRS imputes a rate 1 percentage point higher than the minimum rate and applies it on a semiannual compound interest basis. Thus if the minimum interest rate is not used, a portion of each installment payment is considered interest (based on semiannual compound interest payment from date of sale), and the remainder is treated as principal.

Other Tax Rules

Traditionally, the installment sale method was available only for sales of real property and casual sales of personal property in excess of $1,000. However, the Installment Sale Revision Bill eliminated the minimum sale price requirement for personal property, and all sales of personal property after October 19, 1980, may use the installment sale method of reporting.

Prior to October 20, 1980, a taxpayer had to elect to use the installment sale method. Now, any sale that requires future payments to the seller is automatically treated as an installment sale. However, if the seller does not want installment sale treatment, the seller may elect to report the entire gain in the year of sale. This may be beneficial if the seller has an unusually low-income year or an expiring net operating loss. For example, a seller may make a sale in July 1984 and receive the entire sale price in 1985. The entire gain would be reported in 1985 according to the installment sale provisions. The seller may receive any percentage (less than 100 percent) of the sale price in the year of sale and still qualify for installment sale treatment.

Related-Person Sales

Persons related to the seller are often used to match a seller wanting an installment sale with a buyer wanting to pay cash. The seller sells the property to a related person on an installment sale basis. In turn, the related buyer sells to the ultimate buyer for cash at neither a gain nor a loss. The related person then pays the seller according to the installment sale agreement. For the purpose of these provisions, Sec. 318(a) of the code defines a related person as the seller's spouse, children, grandchildren, or parents; sales to brothers and sisters do *not* qualify.

As of May 14, 1980, if the seller makes an installment sale to a related person who sells the property within 2 years, the original seller must recognize the balance of personal gain at the time the related person makes the sale. If the property sold is marketable securities, the 2-year rule is inapplicable, and the original seller must recognize the remainder of the gain when the related person makes the sale, regardless of when the sale occurs. So under the new law, a sale to a related person with an immediate resale precludes installment sale reporting.

There are specific exceptions to related-person sales. For instance, if the second sale is an involuntary conversion, it does not trigger income recognition to the original seller. If the IRS establishes to its satisfaction that neither the original nor the second sale "had as one of its principal purposes the avoidance of federal income tax," it does not trigger the accelerated recognition of gain.

INSTALLMENT SALE PROCEDURE AND EXAMPLE

A real estate investor (28 percent tax bracket) is considering the installment sale of an apartment building. The apartment building was purchased 5 years ago at a total cost of $500,000. The investor's depreciable basis was 85 percent of total cost. The straight-line method of depreciation has been used, with a recovery life of 15 years. The investment was financed with a 12 percent mortgage of $375,000 with monthly payments for 25 years. Assume this is the only installment receivable the seller owns. However, the seller's total adjusted basis for all her assets are $600,000, and she has outstanding indebtedness each year of $150,000.

The offer under consideration is a sale price of $650,000, with the buyer assuming the balance of the existing mortgage ($358,700) and making a cash down payment of $130,000, and the seller taking a purchase money mortgage of $161,300 for the remainder at an interest rate of 14 percent and annual payments over 15 years, with a balloon payment for the balance at end of year 5. The annual payment is $26,261. Table 10-1 is the amortization schedule. The portion of the payment attributable to interest is the amount outstanding multiplied by the

TABLE 10-1   AMORTIZATION SCHEDULE—INSTALLMENT SALE EXAMPLE

Year	Amount outstanding	Debt service	Interest	Principal
0	$161,300			
1	157,621	$26,261	$22,582	$3,679
2	153,427	26,261	22,067	4,194
3	148,646	26,261	21,480	4,781
4	143,195	26,261	20,810	5,451
5	136,981	26,261	20,047	6,214

interest rate. In year 1, the interest payment of $22,582 is the amount outstanding at the beginning of the year ($161,300) times the interest rate of 14 percent. The principal portion of the debt-service payment is the debt-service payment reduced by the portion attributable to interest. In year 1, the principal portion of $3,679 is the debt-service payment of $26,261 minus the $22,582 interest portion. The amount outstanding is reduced each year by the principal portion of the debt-service payment.

The present value of after-tax cash flows (PV of ATCFs) from the installment sale is determined in three major steps: (1) the ATCF in year of sale is computed, (2) the ATCF from the installment receipts is calculated, and (3) the ATCFs from the installment sale are discounted.

ATCF in Year of Sale

Table 10-2 shows that the ATCF in the year of sale for the installment sale is $65,104. As illustrated, the ATCF is found by subtracting selling expenses and taxes due in the year of sale from the cash received in that year.

One complication is calculating the tax due in the year of sale. Since the sale is being reported on the installment method, portions of payments received in the year of sale are not necessarily reportable as taxable income. Also, as mentioned, taxable payments in the year of sale do not necessarily have to be in cash (for example, the part of any mortgage the buyer assumes in excess of the seller's basis in the property, increased by the selling expenses). Note that by taking the excess of any mortgage assumed over the seller's basis plus selling expense

TABLE 10-2   AFTER-TAX CASH FLOW IN YEAR OF INSTALLMENT SALE

Down payment (BTCF)	$130,000
− selling expense (SE)	32,500
− taxes*	32,396*
ATCF	65,104

*See Table 10-3.

TABLE 10-3 TAX IN YEAR OF INSTALLMENT SALE

Taxable income:	
Excess of mortgage over adjusted basis and selling expense	$ 0
+ down payment	130,000
payment in year of sale	130,000
× profit percentage*	0.89
taxable portion of principal	115,700
Tax:	
taxable income	115,700
× tax rate	0.28
tax	32,396

*See Table 10-4.

(noncash inflow), the seller's ability to pay the tax due (cash outflow) is adversely affected.

Tax Due in Year of Installment Sale Table 10-3 shows the tax due in the year of the installment sale. The tax is calculated by first multiplying the payment received in the year of sale (excess of mortgage over adjusted basis and selling expense plus down payment) by the *profit percentage* of 89 percent (illustrated in Table 10-4). The profit percentage is equal to the total gain on the sale divided by the contract price. The total gain is the sale price minus selling expenses and the seller's adjusted basis in the property. In our example, the total gain is $259,167. The contract price of $291,301 is the sale price of $650,000 plus any excess mortgage over basis and selling expenses minus the mortgage balance of $358,699 assumed by the buyer. The profit percentage is 89 percent, which is the gain of $259,167 divided by the contract price of $291,301. To determine the portion re-

TABLE 10-4 PROFIT PERCENTAGE ON INSTALLMENT SALE

Total gain:	
Sale price	$650,000
− selling expense	32,500
− adjusted basis	358,333
total gain	259,167
Contract price:	
Sale price	$650,000
+ excess mortgage over basis and selling expenses	0
− mortgage balance assumed	358,699
contract price	291,301
Profit percentage:	
Total gain	$259,167
÷ contract price	291,301
profit percentage	0.89

portable as taxable income, the profit percentage calculated in Table 10-3 will also apply to all future principal payments.

Multiplying the profit percentages by the payment in the year of sale yields the reportable portion of the payment in the year of sale: $115,700. In this example, the long-term capital gain is equal to the taxable portion of the principal of $115,700. Assuming the seller is in a 28 percent tax bracket, the taxes due in the year of sale are $32,396 (0.28 × $115,700).

Allocable Installment Indebtedness

The next step is to compute the seller's allocable installment indebtedness (AII). An installment percentage is derived by dividing the amount of installment receivables by the adjusted basis of all the seller's assets. This percentage is then multiplied by the total amount of debt owed to arrive at the seller's AII. This AII is then deemed to have been ''paid'' to the seller and thus is subject to tax.

In this example, the seller's AII would be $40,325 (Table 10-5). This would be treated as an installment receipt and would be multiplied by the profit percentage to compute the amount of gain to be taxed. The AII is computed each year; however, this is a cumulative amount. For example, if in the first year $75,000 was computed for AII and in the second year $85,000, $10,000 would be the additional amount deemed ''paid'' in the second year. Payments received through the installment agreement are not taxed unless they exceed the cumulative AII total.

ATCF from the Installment Receipts

The third step is the calculation of the ATCFs from the installment receipts in years 1 through 5, as shown in Table 10-6. Determine the ATCF by subtracting the tax due on the installment receipt from the before-tax cash flow (BTCF). The BTCF is the installment payment of $26,261 per year plus a balloon payment of $136,981 in year 5.

Tax Due on the Installment Receipts   The next step is to determine the tax due on the installment payments. Before the tax can be calculated, each installment payment must be separated into interest and principal. Table 10-7 is the amortization schedule for the installment offer.

An explanation of the tax calculations will clarify the necessary steps. AII is

TABLE 10-5   ALLOCABLE INSTALLMENT INDEBTEDNESS

Installments to be paid	$161,300
÷ installments to be paid plus adjusted basis of assets	600,000
installment percentage	26.88
× average quarterly indebtedness	150,000
allocable installment indebtedness	40,325

TABLE 10-6   AFTER-TAX CASH FLOW FROM INSTALLMENT RECEIPTS

	Year				
	1	2	3	4	5
BTCF (debt service	$26,261	$26,261	$26,261	$26,261	$ 26,261
+ balloon payment	0	0	0	0	136,981
− tax*	17,289	6,179	6,014	5,827	35,760
ATCF	8,972	20,082	20,247	20,434	127,482

*See Table 10-7.

TABLE 10-7   TAX DUE ON INSTALLMENT RECEIPTS

	Year				
Taxable income	1	2	3	4	5
Principal portion	$ 3,679	$ 4,194	$ 4,781	$ 5,451	$ 6,214
+ balloon payment	0	0	0	0	13,981
total principal	3,679	4,194	4,781	5,451	143,195
AII	40,325				
total applicable	40,325*	4,194	4,781	5,451	120,975†
× profit percentage	0.89	0.89	0.89	0.89	0.89
amount taxable	39,164	0	0	0	170,668
+ interest	22,582	22,067	21,480	20,810	20,047
taxable income	61,746	22,067	21,480	20,810	127,715
× tax rate	0.28	0.28	0.28	0.28	0.28
tax	17,289	6,179	6,014	5,827	35,760

*Future totals will not be taxed until they exceed $40,325.
†143,195 − (40,325 − 3,679 − 4,194 − 4,781 − 5,451).

always the amount that is taxed first. Therefore, in year 1 the $40,325 computed previously as AII is applied as an installment receipt. However, future principal payments are not taxed until they exceed the cumulative AII. In year 5 when the balloon payment is made, the receipts are greater than AII and are taxed after applying the profit percentage. Interest is added to the taxable capital gain, and both are taxed at the appropriate rate to arrive at the taxes due.

Present Value of ATCF from Installment Sale

To determine how much the installment sale is worth, the investor must calculate the present value of the ATCFs. Table 10-8 shows the total present value of the ATCF for the installment sale offer to be $188,858, assuming a 12 percent rate. The PVs of the individual years are calculated by multiplying the ATCFs by each year's respective PVF. Add these individual PVs to find the total PV of the installment sale. This total PV may be used to compare this installment sale offer with other installment offers or to an outright sale.

TABLE 10-8   PRESENT VALUE OF ATCF FROM INSTALLMENT SALE AT 12% REQUIRED RATE

Year	ATCF	$PVF_{12\%}$	PV
0	65,104	1.0	65,104
1	8,972	0.892857	8,011
2	20,082	0.797194	16,009
3	20,247	0.71178	14,411
4	20,434	0.635518	12,986
5	127,482	0.567427	72,337
		Total present value	$188,858

SELECTING AMONG OFFERS: AN EXAMPLE

To illustrate how to select among different installment sale offers, consider that the real estate investor in our earlier example is still thinking about selling the apartment building. However, in addition to the first installment offer, the investor is now considering an outright sale for $640,000. (*Note:* This sale price is $10,000 less than under the first installment sale.) Obviously, the investor wishes to choose the most beneficial alternative. Accordingly, the offers should be compared on the basis of the present value of their after-tax cash flows, as we show.

First Offer: Installment Sale

Assume the same facts as the example developed earlier in this chapter. The present value to the equity investor was calculated to be $188,858 (Table 10-8).

Second Offer: Outright Sale

For this second offer, again assume the same background information developed earlier. However, this time the offer is for $640,000 payable on completion of the sale. Even though the price has decreased by $10,000, the selling expenses are still estimated at $32,500. As shown in Tables 10-9 and 10-10, calculating present value from outright sale can be broken into three steps, as we did in Chapter 6: (1) calculate the before-tax equity reversion (BTER), (2) calculate the taxes due on the sale, and (3) subtract the taxes due on sale from the BTER to determine the after-tax equity reversion (ATER). Since all cash is received on completion of the sale, ATER is the equivalent of the total present values for this offer.

To calculate the BTER, subtract the $32,500 selling expenses from the $640,000 selling price to derive $607,500 net sales proceeds. Then subtract the $358,699 unpaid mortgage balance from the net sales proceeds to find a BTER of $248,801 (see Table 10-9).

To calculate the taxes due on sale, subtract the selling expenses from the sales price, which is the amount realized ($607,500) in this case. Subtract the adjusted basis of $358,333 from the amount realized to produce a total gain of $249,167.

TABLE 10-9   AFTER-TAX CASH FLOW FROM OUTRIGHT SALE

Selling price	$640,000
− selling expense	32,500
net sales proceeds	607,500
− unpaid mortgage balance	358,699
before-tax equity reversion	248,801
− tax due on sale*	69,767
after-tax equity reversion	179,034

*See Table 10-10.

TABLE 10-10   TAX DUE ON OUTRIGHT SALE

Selling price	$640,000
− selling expense	32,500
amount realized	607,500
− adjusted basis	358,333
total gain	249,167
× tax rate	0.28
tax	69,767

Finally, multiply this amount by the investor's tax rate of 28 percent to find taxes due on sale of $69,767.

The ATCF is then computed as follows: Taxes due on sale of $69,767 are subtracted from the $248,801 BTER to determine the $179,034 ATER (Table 10-9). As pointed out earlier, since all cash is received on completion of the sale, the present value is equal to the ATER, giving a present value of $179,034. If the choice is between the first and second offers, the investor should accept the first (that is, installment sale) because it is worth $9,824 more than the second offer ($188,858 − $179,034 = $9,824).

Third Offer: Installment Sale with a Wraparound Mortgage

Suppose the investor is presented with a third offer, an installment sale that requires the investor to carry a wraparound mortgage. This example is similar to the example in Chapter 9, except that the investor-seller is now acting as the wrap lender; thus, to determine the true impact on the investor, we must consider not only the net interest earned (as we did in Chapter 9) but the portion of principal received along with the tax impacts on it.

Restating our assumptions, the building was purchased 5 years ago at a total cost of $500,000. The investor's depreciable basis was 85 percent of total cost. The straight-line method of depreciation has been used with a recovery life of 15 years. The investment was financed with a 12 percent mortgage of $375,000 with monthly payments totaling $47,394 per year for 25 years. The amount outstanding on the existing first mortgage is $358,700. Again assume this is the only install-ment receivable the seller owns, and the adjusted basis of the seller's total assets is $600,000. Outstanding indebtedness at the end of each year is $150,000.

The installment sale offer is as follows. The sales price is $650,000, with the buyer making a $130,000 cash down payment and signing a wraparound $520,000 loan with the seller. The wraparound loan is made for a term of 15 years at an interest rate of 14 percent, with annual debt-service payments of $84,660 and a balloon payment at the end of year 5. The investor is in the 28 percent marginal tax bracket.

The present value of after-tax cash flow (PV of ATCF) for this offer is best determined by first finding the BTCFs, the net interest earned (NIE), and the net principal. Second, the ATCFs must be determined, and third, the ATCFs must be discounted back to the year of sale.

To determine the BTCFs, the NIE, and the net principal, we must first com-pute the amortization schedules for the existing first mortgage (Table 10-11) and for the wraparound mortgage (Table 10-12). Table 10-13 contains the BTCFs, the NIE, and the net principal. The BTCF is the debt service on the wraparound mortgage less the debt service on the existing first mortgage. In years 1 through 4, this is $84,660 − $47,394 = $37,266. In year 5, one must also take into account the difference between the amounts outstanding on the existing and the wrap-around mortgages. This $112,520 figure is added to $37,266 to derive a BTCF in year 5 of $149,786. Net interest earned and net principal are then derived by sub-tracting the interest and the principal *paid* on the existing mortgage from the in-terest and principal *received* on the wraparound mortgage, respectively. The amount loaned on the wraparound mortgage is found by subtracting the $130,000 cash down payment and the amount outstanding on the first mortgage ($358,700) from the sales price of $650,000 ($650,000 − $130,000 − $358,700 = $161,300).

TABLE 10-11   EXISTING MORTGAGE AMORTIZATION SCHEDULE*

Year	Proportion outstanding	Amount outstanding	Debt service	Interest	Principal
0	1.0	$375,000			
1	0.99325	372,469	$47,394	$44,863	$2,531
2	0.98564	369,615	47,394	44,540	2,854
3	0.97707	366,401	47,394	44,180	3,214
4	0.96741	362,779	47,394	43,772	3,622
5	0.95653	358,700	47,394	43,315	4,079
6	0.94427	354,101	47,394	42,796	4,598
7	0.93045	348,919	47,394	42,212	5,182
8	0.91488	343,080	47,394	41,555	5,839
9	0.89733	336,499	47,394	40,813	6,581
10	0.87756	329,085	47,394	39,980	7,414

*See text for assumptions.

TABLE 10-12   WRAPAROUND MORTGAGE AMORTIZATION SCHEDULE*

Year	Amount outstanding	Debt service	Interest	Principal
0	$520,000			
1	508,140	$84,660	$72,800	$11,860
2	494,620	84,660	71,140	13,520
3	479,207	84,660	69,247	15,413
4	461,636	84,660	67,089	17,571
5	441,605	84,660	64,629	20,031

*See text for assumptions.

TABLE 10-13   BTCF, NET INTEREST EARNED, AND NET PRINCIPAL ON WRAPAROUND MORTGAGE

Year	Amount loaned	BTCF	NIE	Net Principal
0	$161,300			
1		$37,266	$30,004	7,262
2		37,266	28,928	8,338
3		37,266	27,692	9,574
4		37,266	26,276	10,990
5		149,786*	24,649	125,137

*$112,520 is difference between amount outstanding on wraparound mortgage and amount outstanding on existing mortgage.

The second step is to determine the ATCFs. Table 10-14 shows the necessary calculations for determining taxes due on the wraparound mortgage. Total principal is found by adding the net principal and any balloon payments. The net principal is compared with the allocable installment indebtedness (AII), and the greater amount is subject to tax. Since AII is cumulative, subsequent installment receipts are not taxed until they exceed AII. The applicable amount is then multiplied by the gross profit percentage of 0.89 (calculated in Table 10-4). This amount is added to net interest earned to arrive at taxable income. By multiplying this figure by the investor's marginal tax rate, the amount of tax due is determined.

Subtract the taxes from the BTCFs (as shown in Table 10-15) to determine the ATCFs. Finally, discount the ATCFs at 12 percent to get a total present value of $218,395, as shown in Table 10-16.

As shown earlier, if the choice were between the first and second offers, the investor would choose the first offer with a net present value of $188,858. However, the third offer under consideration has a total present value of $218,395. This is worth $39,361 more than the second offer and $29,337 more than the straight installment sale. Therefore, in this example the best results would be obtained from the installment sale with the wraparound mortgage.

TABLE 10-14   TAXES DUE ON WRAPAROUND MORTGAGE

	Year				
	1	2	3	4	5
Net principal portion	$ 7,262	$ 8,338	$ 9,574	$10,990	$ 12,617
+ balloon					112,520
total principal	7,262	8,338	9,574	10,990	125,137
All*	40,325				120,976 ‡
total applicable	40,325	0	0	0	120,976
× profit percentage†	0.89	0.89	0.89	0.89	0.89
Amount taxable	35,889	0	0	0	170,669
+ net interest earned	30,004	28,928	27,692	26,276	24,649
taxable income	65,893	28,928	27,692	26,276	132,318
× 0.28	0.28	0.28	0.28	0.28	0.28
tax	18,450	8,100	7,754	7,357	37,049

*From Table 10-5.
†From Table 10-4.
‡125,137 − (40,325 − 7,262 − 8,338 − 9,574 − 10,990).

TABLE 10-15   ATCF FROM WRAPAROUND MORTGAGE

	Year				
	1	2	3	4	5
BTCF	$37,266*	$37,266*	$37,266*	$37,266*	$ 37,266*
+ balloon					112,520†
− tax‡	18,450	8,100	7,754	7,357	37,049
ATCF	18,816	29,166	29,512	29,909	112,737

*Net difference between debt service on wraparound mortgage and debt service on first mortgage.
†Net difference between principal on wraparound mortgage and principal on first mortgage.
‡See Table 10-14.

TABLE 10-16   PRESENT VALUE OF WRAPAROUND MORTGAGE INSTALLMENT AT 12%

Year	ATCF	$PVF_{12\%}$	PV wraparound
0	$ 74,360	1.0	$74,360
1	18,816	0.892857	16,800
2	29,166	0.797194	23,251
3	29,512	0.711780	21,006
4	29,909	0.635518	19,008
5	112,737	0.567427	63,970
		Net present value	218,395

SUMMARY

This chapter examined the use of the installment sale as a financing method. The basic tax aspects of the installment sale method were reviewed, and several detailed examples of how to select among an installment sale offer, an outright sale, and an installment sale with a wraparound mortgage were provided. Because the real estate investor has more flexibility in the use of the installment method under the new tax law, the wealth-maximizing investor must understand the decision-making implications of each method of disposing of real estate investments.

QUESTIONS

1 Define the following terms:
   a installment sale
   b installment contract
   c gross profit percentage
   d contract price
   e imputed interest
   f net interest earned
   g allocable installment indebtedness

2 Describe how an installment sale works. When would the seller want to use this method? The buyer? What are the basic reasons the seller would find the installment sale advantageous? The buyer?

3 Discuss the basic tax requirements for an installment sale.

4 Outline how the following factors are calculated:
   a after-tax cash flow in the year of installment
   b gross profit percentage
   c after-tax cash flow from the installment receipts
   d allocable installment indebtedness

5 Explain the following statement: The cash flow from the installment receipts is subject to two taxes: ordinary income tax on the interest and taxes on the deferred capital gain.

6 In the example developed in this chapter, the investor had to decide which of two offers to select: an installment sale or an outright sale. Describe how this decision was made. In the example, the installment sale had a higher sale price but the outright sale was considered the better offer. Explain this apparent contradiction.

7 Describe how the installment sale is accomplished with a wraparound mortgage. In the chapter example, this option was the best offer. Explain how this worked in our example. Will this always be the result? Why or why not?

8 Using the analysis in questions 6 and 7, explain the variables on which the decision to select between one offer and another offer depends.

PROBLEMS

1 Rework the installment sale example; however, assume the seller's average indebtedness for years 1 through 5 are $150,000, $175,000, $200,000, $225,000, $250,000, respectively.

2 Discuss the effects of the increasing indebtedness in Problem 1.

3 Recalculate the present value of the cash flows in Table 10-8 at 14 percent and 16 percent. Compare these results with the cash flows from the outright sale (Table 10-9). Has your choice between the installment sale and outright sale changed? Why?

REFERENCES

Kurn, Neal, and Jack O. Nutter, II: "The Installment Sales Revision Act of 1980: In the Name of Simplification Has a Measure of Complexity Been Added?", *Journal of Real Estate Taxation,* Spring 1981, pp. 195–212.

Nelson, Grant S., and Dale A. Whitman: "Installment Land Contracts—A National Viewpoint," *Brigham Young University Law Review,* 1977, pp. 325–362.

Nutter, Jack O., II: "Regulations under the Installment Sales Revision Act," *Journal of Real Estate Taxation,* Fall 1981, pp. 46–56.

Valachi, Donald J.: "Installment Sales of Real Estate and the Wrap-Around Mortgage," *The Appraisal Journal,* vol. 68, January 1980, pp. 9–23.

CONSTRUCTION FINANCING

A construction loan is the method of financing the construction of improvements. Most builder-developers do not have the financial capacity to undertake a project without construction funds. Once the project is completed, the short-term construction loan ends and the builder-developer obtains long-term, permanent financing. Typically, a permanent financing commitment is required before the construction loan is made.

Obviously, the developer must pay for the use of these construction funds. The lender of construction funds bears a substantial portion of the risk of construction, so the interest rate on construction funds is higher than on permanent financing. Because construction financing differs in many ways from permanent financing, this chapter discusses the additional risk and risk analysis, mechanics and loan structure, and tax effects unique to construction financing. We also present a detailed example of the mechanics of a construction financing loan.

WHAT IS A CONSTRUCTION LOAN?

Construction loans differ markedly from permanent loans and thus require a level of expertise and a perspective quite different from those necessary for permanent lending. The permanent loan is secured by real estate that already has value—the building has been constructed and, in the case of income property, is generating a relatively predictable income. In contrast, the construction loan is used to finance the *creation of value*—thus, at the time of loan origination, there is virtually no collateral for the loan, with the exception of the unimproved land. And there is the additional uncertainty that the project may not be completed and therefore not provide sufficient collateral for the loan amount.

STRUCTURING CONSTRUCTION LOANS

As a result of the risk inherent in lending on an uncompleted project, construction loans differ from permanent loans in three ways: the term of the loan, the time frame in which funds are disbursed, and the methods for repayment.

Loan Term

A construction loan is made for the expected length of time that it will take to construct the building and to make other improvements. This is generally a minimum of 6 months for single-family housing to as much as several years for large projects.

Funds Disbursement

As we have seen, permanent loan funds are disbursed in a lump sum at the time of loan origination, typically with repayment in installments over the term of the loan. For construction loans, however, the reverse is generally true: The disbursement is made in installments as work on the project is completed, and repayment is a lump sum at the end of the loan term.

There are three common methods for disbursement of loan funds; the borrower-developer and the lender negotiate the choice. The *stage method* ensures that the economic value being created by construction is "in place" (i.e., completed) and subject to a lender lien as disbursements are made. When predetermined stages of the work have been completed, the lender has the project inspected to verify completion, and a predetermined amount is disbursed to the borrower.

The second method is based on a *draw,* whereby the lender disburses an amount subject to the architect's (or other) verification that the work is in place and completed. The third method is called the *voucher system.* The lender receives invoices from subcontractors for actual work completed to date and makes disbursements (with dual receipts) to the contractor and subcontractors.

Repayment Methods

Most of a construction loan is usually disbursed in installments. However, the construction loan's interest and principal are typically repaid in one lump sum at the end of the loan term. Sometimes, however, accrued interest payments are made during the loan term; these payments are generally considered part of the loan's front-end charges (because of the relative brevity of the construction loan term).

With permanent loans, the lender looks to the property's (or borrower's) income as the source for repayment. With construction loans, *the construction lender is repaid with funds advanced by a permanent lender.* Therefore, the construction lender must have some assurance that permanent loan funds will be forthcoming when the project is completed. There are three basic ways to repay construction loans.

The most common construction loan is made with the knowledge that the borrower (developer) has already signed a note with a permanent lender for the long-term financing of the project, pending the completion of construction. Often, because of geographical, legal, and lending-capacity limitations, certain types of lenders do not make construction loans. Therefore, one lender originates the construction loan, and another lender originates the permanent loan. Generally, a commercial bank or savings and loan association with knowledge of the local market and expertise in construction lending originates the construction loan. Permanent financing is arranged through another, perhaps quite distant, lender (such as a life insurance company). The commitment to fund a long-term, permanent loan, pending completion of construction, is called a *"takeout" commitment* because it takes the construction lender "out" of the picture via payoff of the construction loan.

A second type of repayment involves the lender's making the construction *and* long-term loans. If the borrower under the construction loan is different from the borrower under the permanent loan, as in the case of a developer who will sell the completed project to a known buyer as soon as construction is finished, then both borrowers must be screened prior to loan approval. This combination of construction and long-term loans under one lender is considered less risky because the permanent loan is already guaranteed, but the same lender may actually bear more risk because two loans have been granted on a future event that is susceptible to the default risk inherent in both construction *and* permanent loans.

The third category of construction loan is made without a takeout commitment. The developer and the construction lender take the risk that a permanent lender will not be found prior to the end of the construction loan term. This method is considered extremely risky and is rarely used. The risk is that permanent lenders may not be willing to make a mortgage on the project, thus forcing speculative construction lenders to either foreclose on construction loans or grant long-term financing that they had not anticipated.

The Triparty Buy-Sell Agreement This is an agreement between the construction lender, permanent lender, and borrower to assure the borrower and the construction lender that if all the conditions of the takeout commitment are met, the permanent lender will fund the permanent loan—that is, "purchase" the construction loan. In turn, the construction lender and the borrower make a covenant that they will accept payment on the construction loan only from the permanent lender. This additional agreement in the takeout commitment is often desired by the permanent lender, who must set aside funds for the permanent loan for a long commitment period. In absence of this agreement, the borrower is free to shop around and obtain a takeout commitment from another lender, perhaps at a lower interest rate, and forfeit the commitment fee on the original loan commitment. With the agreement, the permanent lender has greater assurance that the lender will not simply be "used" by the borrower to obtain a construction loan and that there will be no loss of earnings on the funds committed.

Risks in Construction Lending

With permanent loans, the lender bears the risk of inflation and the default risk because of the borrower's inability or unwillingness to repay the loan as agreed. With construction loans, the inflation risk is essentially eliminated in practice, because of the relatively short loan term. The default risk is still a problem, however, but for entirely different reasons. The construction lender is taking the risk that the project might not be completed or that even if it is, the resulting market value will be below the project's cost; both factors can cause the takeout commitment to be retracted and a subsequent default.

One element of a construction lender's risk is *unforeseen construction problems*. Labor strikes, unfavorable weather conditions, structural or design problems, material price increases, and the loss of a contractor or subcontractor contribute to delays and cost overruns. In addition, *poor management*—inefficiency, inexperience, and undercapitalization—contributes to poor planning and results in time and cost overruns.

The following examples illustrate several effects on risk. If the project costs begin to exceed the project value, the construction lender faces the possibility that the borrower-developer will abandon the project before completion rather than invest additional equity capital. The incomplete, unusable structure will not meet the requirements of the takeout commitment, and default on the construction loan will occur.

Alternatively, if the project is completed but its value is lower than projected, the amount of the permanent loan could be reduced (based on the loan-to-value ratio) to an amount insufficient to cover the construction loan payoff. Unless the developer-borrower is able and willing to make up the difference, default on the construction loan will occur.

Finally, time overruns and delays could push the project's completion date beyond the date that the takeout commitment expires, possibly leaving the borrower and the construction lender without their anticipated source of funds for construction loan repayment, again increasing the likelihood of default. Although other scenarios could occur (and undoubtedly have occurred), clearly the risk to the construction lender is quite different institutionally from the permanent lender's risk.

DEALING WITH CONSTRUCTION LOAN RISK

Some construction lenders have become unwilling long-term lenders, because of retraction of takeout commitments. These lenders assumed that since a proposed project had prior approval from the long-term lender, all they had to do was to comply with the takeout commitment terms. Conversely, some long-term lenders, often far removed from the proposed project, believed that if the construction lender (having superior knowledge of the local market) felt comfortable enough about the stipulations in the takeout commitment, then project viability was assured. Hence, either construction lender or permanent lender (or both) failed to properly assess the project's economic feasibility, each believing that the job had been correctly done by the other.

In reality, both parties must shoulder the responsibility. The permanent lender must evaluate the proposed project so that the takeout commitment can be structured to prevent any construction loan risk from being assumed. The construction lender, on the other hand, must do an independent analysis to ensure that the terms of the takeout commitment can indeed be fulfilled. *The construction lender must realize that its position is the same as that of the long-term lender until takeout occurs.*

The greatest risk the construction lender faces is the possibility that the takeout commitment from the permanent lender will not occur. The following problems may prevent the takeout from happening:

1 The plans and specifications as approved for the commitment are not met.

2 The project is not completed on time because of bad weather or inefficient supervision.

3 The project does not meet the zoning or building ordinances, or environmental index and regulations.

4 The appraised value of the project upon completion does not equal the appraised value that was estimated at commitment.

5 There are significant cost overruns during the construction phase. Some variance might be allowed, but significant differences lead to noncommitment.

6 Special conditions, such as construction quality, are not met.

7 The takeout commitment contains lease requirements that are not met.

Several of these risks can be minimized through careful analysis by the construction lender before and during the construction phase. Other risks are beyond the lender's control.

Construction Loan Interest Rate

As we observed earlier, the greater the level of risk, the higher the interest rate charged. To compensate for the increased risk a construction lender bears, construction loan rates generally exceed permanent loan rates. Because of construction loans' increased complexity and high lender involvement in monitoring construction activities, a higher proportion of the construction loan rate is made up of front-end points and origination fees.

The origination fee is often called a *commitment fee* and is usually charged when large projects are being financed. This fee is paid before the construction loan commitment is obtained and is generally nonrefundable if the proposed borrower does not accept the commitment within a predetermined time period.

The interest rate on construction loans is usually a "floating" rate, that is, the rate varies during the construction period based on the lender's cost of funds. Generally, the lender's prime lending rate is used as a basis, with the construction loan interest rate fixed at a predetermined number of "points" above the basis. When the prime rate varies, the construction loan rate varies by the same amount. Since the loan term is short, points and origination fees have a much greater impact on the construction loan's yield (and the borrower's cost) than on a long-term mortgage.

Additions to the Loan-Submission Package

To minimize the additional risk inherent in construction lending, certain additions must be made to the borrower and property analyses of the loan-submission package. Table 11-1 is a checklist for the construction loan application.

Borrower Analysis Recall from Chapter 4 that the lender's two general concerns are that the borrower has both the ability and the willingness to repay the loan. In construction lending, additional concern centers on the *ability* to repay as evidenced by the borrower-developer's past development experience and financial capacity.

Since the financing of construction projects tends to be riskier than the financing of existing projects, the lender requires assurance that the developer has a

TABLE 11-1   CHECKLIST OF PROVISIONS FOR CONSTRUCTION LOANS

1. Definitions
2. Representations and warranties
3. Agreement to borrow and loan
4. Loan documents and borrower's agreement to execute and deliver them
5. Provisions to alter the terms of the note and mortgage for the construction loan
6. Provisions regarding permanent loan commitment
7. Loan expenses
8. Conditions precedent to loan opening (first disbursement)
9. Reserves and deposits
10. Balance provision
11. Periodic disbursements after loan opening
12. Borrower's general agreements
13. Lender's actions and inspections for its own protection
14. Provisions in the event of casualties
15. Conditions precedent to final disbursement
16. Conversion of permanent loan
17. Events of default
18. Remedies
19. Schedule attached to construction loan agreement containing data applicable to particular loan transactions

Source: James A. Douglas and Rosa Koppel: *Real Estate Financing Forms Manual,* Warren, Gorham & Lamont, Boston, 1987, pp. s3–19, s3–23.

successful track record in general and, more importantly, in the development of projects of the type and magnitude for which financing is sought. In addition, construction lenders often require as a condition of the loan commitment that they have approval of both the contractor(s) and the formal building contract, to guard against contractors with poor reputations and vague, ambiguous building contracts.

In case of unforeseen construction problems, resulting slowdowns may require additional funds from the developer. The lender wants assurance that the developer is financially liquid enough to carry the project for a time without reliance on outside funding. Therefore, the development firm must submit a completely audited set of financial statements. If, in the lender's judgment, the firm's financial capacity is insufficient, the lender may require statements about the developer's personal financial status, along with a guarantee that permits the lender to attach a lien to the developer's personal assets in the event of default.

Project Analysis   The lender of a permanent loan on an existing project wants assurance that the project is economically sound, that its value will provide sufficient security for the loan now and in the future, and that the perfection of the lender's first mortgage lien will not be jeopardized. These same general assurances are required in construction lending, but their implementation is much more involved because the improvements do not yet exist.

When a takeout commitment already has been obtained, the construction lender begins the project analysis by analyzing data the permanent lender has compiled. The appraisal report and market analysis are reviewed initially to determine the amount of money to be loaned. The maximum amount of the construction loan is generally determined by the amount of the takeout commitment.

Next, the project's economic feasibility is analyzed. In addition to market and appraisal information provided by the permanent lender, the construction lender requires pro forma (i.e., projected) operating statements from the developer. The lender then analyzes these data by using the tools described in earlier chapters. In addition, the borrower's assumptions used in developing the operating statements are scrutinized. This is the point at which the construction lender's knowledge of local market conditions and trends is a definite advantage. If, in the lender's view, any of the data presented are unrealistic or inadequate, additional operating data or another appraisal may be required. Because rental-income projections frequently are based on leases with certain high-credit tenants, the lender should obtain and examine presigned, verifiable lease documents.

If the project is deemed economically sound, the next step is to ensure that it provides the security necessary for the loan, given its economic value. To accomplish this goal, the improvements must be constructed at or near projected costs. Therefore, the lender requires a detailed cost estimation, which the lender or architect reviews for accuracy. This estimate is compared with the developer's cost estimate. The use of different costs by the developer and the lender may create discrepancies; major differences in costs should be thoroughly investigated. Since a cost estimate is not a guaranteed price, the lender may require *fixed-price contracts* from contractors and subcontractors. This effectively removes from the lender and the developer some of the risk of labor and material price increases and overruns.

At this point, the value and cost of the proposed project are well-documented. However, the building still is not constructed. Although the contractors and subcontractors are hired and the developer's financial capacity, background, and reputation are favorable, there is still risk that the project may not be completed. Contractors and developers may go bankrupt, ceasing operations partway through a project. Consequently, lenders generally require a *performance bond*, which provides for completion of a project in the event that default or breach of contract occurs during construction. Usually, the developer obtains the performance bond from the general contractor, with the lender and the developer designated as co-obligees on the bond.

Up to this point, the lender is fairly well assured that the project will go up as planned and that it will be worth what it costs. However, there is no adequate collateral for the loan if the lender's security interest is impaired. We saw that for loan-submission packages on existing properties, this risk was minimized by the use of title insurance or a lawyer's title opinion. In construction lending as well, the developer is usually required to provide title insurance or a title opinion before construction begins. But there is additional risk because subcontractors, contractors, and material suppliers may file mechanic's liens against the property if they are not paid for their work or materials. These liens may be filed during the construction period and may take precedence over the construction loan.

Therefore, the construction lender may have the title reexamined prior to each disbursement to see that no liens have been filed. With a title insurance policy, the title company often assumes this duty and makes the disbursement if no liens are found. In addition, payment bonds may be required; they guarantee that subcontractors are paid according to the terms of their contracts if the general contractor (or developer) fails to do so, so that mechanic's liens will not be filed. This dual protection (title insurance and payment bond) is the best safeguard against potential impairment of the lender's security.

There is also the possibility that subcontractors may substantially complete their work under the contracts but may leave a small part unfinished. To ensure that this does not occur, the developer may *hold back* a certain percentage of the total amount due the subcontractor until verification that *all* work has been completed. In this event, the lender should also retain the same portion of the money so that the developer has no control over excess funds.

Other Items The permanent lender usually requires in the takeout commitment that prior to takeout a minimum percentage "rent up" of the property has occurred and that the property is operational and producing income. Although this is the developer's job, the construction lender usually requires that all lease rents be assigned to it in the event the developer defaults.

Certain construction projects require an environmental impact statement prior to a building permit's being issued. In addition, zoning status must be verified, and tests of soil load-bearing capacity and surveys may need to be completed.

TAX ASPECTS OF CONSTRUCTION LOANS

Generally, the builder-developer obtains a construction loan in the amount of the takeout commitment. This amount covers most (often all) of the expenses incurred in building the structure and related improvements. Thus, the capital the developer provides is the difference between the estimated project value at completion and the amount of the permanent loan. When the project is completed, permanent financing begins, the construction loan is paid off, and the builder-developer who continues to own and operate the property is for tax purposes treated as any other purchaser of real estate. That is, the cost of the improvements to the land is depreciated over the project's useful life, and interest on the loan and property taxes and other operating expenses are deducted in the year incurred or paid.

Let us assume for a moment that this same reasoning could be applied to construction-period interest and taxes. Under prior law, interest and taxes during construction had to be capitalized and amortized over a 10-year period. Since the construction loan proceeds were used to pay these expenses, the developer had no out-of-pocket cost, yet realized a sizable tax deduction as a result of these expenses for the year(s) of the construction period. The 1976 and 1982 tax revisions reduced this "tax shelter," which was available to individual taxpayers prior to the 1976 act and to corporate taxpayers only from 1976 until 1982. The

Tax Reform Act of 1986 has repealed these provisions and now views interest and taxes occurring during construction as a cost of the property. Therefore, these costs must be depreciated over the appropriate class-life of the property, either 27.5 or 31.5 years. If the property is sold prior to the year in which the expenses are fully amortized, the unamortized portion is added to the seller's adjusted basis in the property in the year of sale.

To illustrate, let us assume that $90,000 of construction-period interest and taxes are deductible at $3,273 per year. Also consider the following additional assumptions:

1 Original cost (basis) of the property is $500,000, of which $400,000 is depreciable.

2 Depreciation is taken at the straight-line rate over a useful life of 27.5 years.

3 The property is sold by the builder-developer at the end of 1989.

4 The builder-developer is a corporate entity.

The adjusted basis of the property at the end of 1989 is computed is follows:

$$\frac{\$490,000 \text{ depreciable basis}}{27.5 \text{ years}} = \$17,818 \text{ annual depreciation deduction}$$

$$\$17,818 \times 3 \text{ years} = \$53,454$$

Original basis	$500,000
− accumulated depreciation deduction	53,454
+ unamortized construction-period expenses	80,188
adjusted basis	526,734

The adjusted basis is then used to determine the gain on the sale.

The largest single expense usually incurred during the construction period is the interest expense on the construction loan. But expenses directly related to the construction loan are deductible. Appraisal fees, brokerage commissions, transfer fees, legal fees, and costs of surveys and title work are generally deductible ratably over the construction loan period. However, if the taxpayer wishes, these other expenses may be added to the property's basis and depreciated along with it, effectively deferring these deductions to future years.

There are several problems with the treatment of *points and origination fees.* The question is, Are they considered expenses related to obtaining and processing the loan, and thus fully deductible in the construction loan period, or are they simply a means by which to raise the yield (i.e., interest)? If the purpose of points and origination fees is to raise the yield, then they are treated as interest and must be amortized. If they represent services the lender provided for processing and monitoring the loan, then they are treated as normal business expenses and are fully deductible when incurred.

Loan commitment fees are *not* considered interest, but simply a charge for keeping a certain amount of funds available for a predetermined amount of time, at a firm price and terms. When a lender makes both the construction and the permanent loans, fees charged as interest must be allocated between the two loans and treated accordingly; fees for lender services must be amortized over the combined terms of both loans.

The tax rules here provide a general knowledge of the treatment of construction-period expenses. *Investors should consult competent tax advisers when analyzing a specific situation.*

CONSTRUCTION LOAN EXAMPLE

Here we illustrate the mechanics of a construction loan for erecting an apartment building.

Background Information

Surety Investment Company has obtained a takeout commitment from Mid-States Life Assurance, Inc. for the permanent loan on a 40-unit garden apartment building it wishes to build on a parcel of land worth, according to a recent appraisal, $312,500. Surety owns the land free and clear. Mid-States has committed to lending $937,500, contingent upon project completion and rent up of 32 units at projected rent levels. With the takeout commitment in hand, John Winston, president of Surety, approaches E. Z. Munny, vice president for construction lending at Fourth National Bank, for a construction loan.

Mr. Winston presents the following information to Mr. Munny:

1 Permanent lender's appraisal report, indicating an estimated market value at completion of $1,250,000

2 Permanent lender's market study, which supports the project's pro forma operating statement data

3 Detailed cost estimates prepared by Surety (summarized in Table 11-2)

The *hard costs* are the costs for "bricks and mortar," the direct costs for the building and land improvements to be constructed. The *soft costs* are the indirect costs related to construction: the design and follow-up inspections of the project and expenses related to interest, origination fees, and carrying costs during the construction period.

The interest amount is based on the assumptions that the total amount borrowed is $937,500 and interest accrues monthly on the unpaid balance, which is increased according to a proposed draw schedule. The interest rate is based on the prime rate plus 2 percent. During the first 6 months, the rate is expected to be 15 percent (prime = 13 percent), and during the last 6 months it is expected to be 13 percent (prime = 11 percent). The loan is due at the end of the 12-month construction period, and the monthly interest payments are added to the loan balance.

Based on this information, Mr. Munny believes the project to be a good in-

TABLE 11-2 SUMMARY OF CONSTRUCTION-COST
ESTIMATES: APARTMENT BUILDING EXAMPLE

Hard costs:	
Building ($20 per sq/ft, 30,000 sq ft)	$600,000
Fixtures	80,000
Landscaping and parking lot	45,000
Water/sewer	65,000
	790,000
Soft costs:	
Closing costs/taxes	$ 15,000
Construction interest	70,362
Loan origination	28,125
Architect/engineer fees	10,000
Inspections	6,000
	129,487
Total construction costs	919,487

vestment for Fourth National and has Surety's cost figures and building plans verified by an architect under contract with Fourth National. The architect confirms that the costs are in line and that the project meets building, zoning, and housing codes. Fourth National Bank now issues a construction loan commitment.

Disbursements and the Draw Schedule

Disbursements under the construction loan proceed as follows. First, the portion of the closing and soft costs the developer incurred up to the date of closing is disbursed by Fourth National at the closing of the construction loan. (These costs are summarized in Table 11-3.) Note that although the origination fee is technically a cost the developer incurred at closing, rather than collecting the fee from the developer and disbursing$52,125, the lender simply reduces the amount of the disbursement by the origination fee.

After the original disbursement, future disbursements are made on a monthly

TABLE 11-3 SUMMARY OF CLOSING AND SOFT COSTS:
APARTMENT BUILDING EXAMPLE

Legal fees	$ 7,500
Engineering	10,000
Title abstract	1,000
Taxes and recording fees	3,000
Origination fee	28,125
Title insurance	2,500
Total	52,125*

*Since $28,125 of this total is the origination fee, $24,000
is the net the developer will receive at closing.

draw basis, depending upon the amount of construction in place at the end of the preceding month. Table 11-4 is the draw schedule prepared over the life of this loan.

Note that at the closing, the initial net cash disbursement made to the developer is $24,000 ($52,125 minus the $28,125 origination fee). The total draw is thus $52,125, and the balance owed is $52,125. There is no interest payment at closing since none has accrued.

For month 1, no construction has been completed; hence no disbursement is made to the developer. However, $652 interest has accrued on the $52,125 balance that has remained outstanding over the month. Since no interest payments are to be made by the developer during the construction period, this amount is added to the previous cumulative loan balance. The interest computation is the monthly interest rate (15 percent/12) times the balance ($52,125), or $652.

For month 2, $145,000 in construction has been completed the previous month. The developer submits architect's verification of this fact and requests a $145,000 disbursement from the bank. The bank makes the indicated disbursement but adds on accrued interest, to derive the total monthly draw and cumulative loan balance of $198,437.

For the remaining 12 months, the computational process remains the same as for month 2. Note, however, that the interest rate changed from 15 to 13 percent at the beginning of month 7, just as anticipated.

Note that there is a cost overrun of $109 on the project. (See the cumulative loan balance in Table 11-4.) Total construction costs were estimated as $919,487

TABLE 11-4 DRAW SCHEDULE FOR CONSTRUCTION LOAN: APARTMENT BUILDING EXAMPLE

Month	Net cash to developer for construction cost	Interest*	Monthly draw‡	Cumulative loan balance
Close	$ 24,000	$ 28,125†	$ 52,125	$ 52,125
1	0	652	652	52,777
2	145,000	660	145,660	198,437
3	125,000	2,480	127,480	325,917
4	100,000	4,074	104,074	429,991
5	100,000	5,375	105,375	535,366
6	75,000	6,692	81,692	617,058
7	75,000	6,683	81,683	698,741
8	50,000	7,567	57,567	756,308
9	50,000	8,191	58,191	814,499
10	50,000	8,821	58,821	873,320
11	25,000	9,458	34,458	907,778
12	20,000	9,831	29,831	937,609
	839,000	98,609	937,609	

*Computed on the previous month's ending balance at 1.25% for months 1 to 6 and 1.083% for months 7 to 12.
†Loan origination fee.
‡Monthly draw includes interest from the disbursements.

(from Table 11-2), and the commitment amount was somewhat higher, $937,500, which was based on a loan-to-value ratio of 75 percent on $1,250,000. The actual $937,609 cost exceeds the commitment amount by $109. In general, if the cumulative loan balance rate increases faster than the percentage of construction completed, a cost overrun may be indicated well in advance of project completion. In this case, the overrun is minor and not of concern to the lender. However, if a substantial cost overrun is indicated, the developer must be prepared to pay the overrun out of personal funds, and if the overrun is large enough, permanent financing may be canceled. Thus, the draw schedule acts as a control device for the lender during the construction period.

Yield (Borrowing Cost)

Since rent up of apartments begins during month 10 and the 80 percent rent-up goal is reached by the end of month 12, takeout occurs as scheduled. At this point, Mr. Munny computes the before-tax yield to Fourth National on the construction loan. At the same time, Mr. Winston compares Surety's actual borrowing cost with his earlier projections. The process is the same in either case: Determine the interest rate that makes the present value of outflow(s) equal to the present value of inflow(s). Table 11-5 illustrates the lender's position; rates of 20 and 19 percent were chosen by trial and error. (The borrower's position is the

TABLE 11-5   PV CALCULATIONS: APARTMENT BUILDING CONSTRUCTION LOAN EXAMPLE

Month	Net outflow	$PVF_{20\%/12}$	$PVF_{19\%/12}$	$PV_{20\%}$	$PV_{19\%}$
			Outflows		
Close	$ 24,000	1.00000	1.0000	$ 24,000	$ 24,000
1	0	0	0	0	0
2	145,000	0.96748	0.96907	140,285	140,515
3	125,000	0.95162	0.95397	118,953	119,246
4	100,000	0.93602	0.93910	93,602	93,910
5	100,000	0.92068	0.92446	92,068	92,446
6	75,000	0.90558	0.91005	67,919	68,254
7	75,000	0.89074	0.89587	66,805	67,190
8	50,000	0.87614	0.88190	43,807	44,095
9	50,000	0.86177	0.86819	43,089	43,408
10	50,000	0.84765	0.85462	42,382	42,731
11	25,000	0.83375	0.81430	20,844	20,358
12	20,000	0.82008	0.82819	16,402	16,564
				770,156	772,717
			Inflows		
12	937,609	0.82008	0.82819	768,914	776,518

TABLE 11-6 INTERPOLATION FOR IRR ON THE CONSTRUCTION LOAN

1	PV of inflows	−	PV of outflows	= flow difference
Discounting at 20%	$768,914	−	$770,156	= −$1,242
Discounting at 19%	$776,518	−	$772,717	= $3,801

2 Sum of absolute values of differences = $1,242 + $3,801 = $5,043

3 Interest rate difference (20 − 19%)	1%
Sum of absolute differences in present values	$5,043
Difference in present value for 19%	$3,801
Ratio of ($3,801 ÷ $5,043) × 1%	0.753718%
19% + 0.753718%	19.753718%

Therefore, the developer's cost of borrowing the construction loan and the yield (to the lender—IRR) is 19.75%.

same, except inflows and outflows are reversed.) In comparing the present value of the inflow with the outflow for each rate, we see that at 20 percent the present value of the outflow exceeds the present value of the inflow; therefore, the 20 percent rate is too high. Conversely, at 19 percent, the present value of the outflow is less than the present value of the inflow, signaling that 19 percent is too low. We know the rate is between 19 and 20 percent.

Interpolation   We can interpolate to estimate the actual rate more accurately, but by a process different from that used previously because we do not have a desired present value to attain. *In this case, we are attempting to make the present value of inflows and outflows equal zero.* First, find the absolute amount that inflows and outflows differ from zero, as shown in Table 11-6. The total difference between 19 and 20 percent is $5,043. Then take the difference at the lower rate ($3,801) and divide it by the total difference of $5,043, to arrive at the percentage distance that separates the rate from 19 percent, which is 0.753718. Multiply this figure by the difference in rates (1 percent) and add it to 19 percent, for a before-tax yield (or borrowing cost) of 19.75 percent.

SUMMARY

This chapter introduced the complex world of construction lending. We concentrated on how construction lending differs from permanent lending in the areas of loan collateral, structure and mechanics, and special risks and how to deal with these factors by fee structuring and additions to the loan-submission package. We also introduced the tax aspects peculiar to construction-period expenses and then illustrated the process via a typical example of a construction loan. In the next chapter, we apply this knowledge of construction loan financing to land-development loans.

QUESTIONS

Define the following terms:

a stage method	e takeout commitment
b draw	f triparty buy-sell agreement
c performance bond	g hard costs
d voucher system	h soft costs

2 Will interest rate on a construction loan typically be lower than the interest rate on a permanent loan? Why? How do these two types of loans work together in the development of real estate?

3 Why are the structure and mechanics of a construction loan different from those of a permanent loan?

4 What are the three accepted construction loan disbursement methods? How does each method work?

5 Identify three ways construction loan repayments may be structured. Which is the least used method, and why?

6 What is the purpose of a triparty buy-sell agreement? What is the most common cause of construction loan default? How can a lender prevent this possibility?

7 What additional borrower and project information does the construction lender usually require? Why is dual protection the *best* protection for the lender?

8 When would the investor-taxpayer elect to have the construction loan expenses added to the property's basis to defer deductions until later years?

9 How does the draw schedule function as a control device for the lender during the construction period?

PROBLEMS

1 Find the yield for this set of draws:

Month	Net outflow	Net inflow
Close	$10,000	—
1	0	—
2	45,000	—
3	32,000	—
4	32,000	—
5	25,000	—
6	20,000	$350,000

2 What are the typical characteristics of a construction loan?

3 Calculate the adjusted basis of the following nonresidential income property at sale:

1 The depreciable basis of the property is $100,000.
2 Construction period interest and taxes are $8,000.
3 The property is to be sold by the builder-developer in 5 years.

REFERENCES

Douglas, James A., and Rosa Koppel: *Real Estate Finance Forms Manual*, Warren, Gorham & Lamont, Boston, 1987.

Feder, Jack M.: "Financing Real Estate Construction: The IRS Challenge to Construction-Period Deductions," *Journal of Real Estate Taxation,* Fall 1980, pp. 3–26.

Harris, Richard: *Construction and Development Financing: 1985 Cumulative Supplement,* Warren, Gorham, & Lamont, Boston, 1985.

Kerngold, Gerald: "Construction Loan Advance and the Subordinated Purchase Money Mortgage," *Fordham Law Review,* December 1981, pp. 313–369.

McMahan, John: *Property Development,* McGraw-Hill, New York, 1976.

Reitz, Curns R.: "Construction Lenders' Liability to Contractors, Subcontractors & Materialmen," *University of Pennsylvania Law Review,* December 1981, pp. 416–459.

LAND-DEVELOPMENT FINANCING

To understand the unique characteristics and risks associated with land-development loans, we must first understand the overall land-investment and land-development process. Then we apply this knowledge to the development lending process by viewing the sources of funds, loan security, structure and mechanics, and methods by which lenders attempt to minimize their risks. Next we consider the unique income tax consequences the land-development process creates for the developer. Finally, a land-development example illustrates the mechanics of land-development financing.

WHAT IS A LAND-DEVELOPMENT LOAN?

A land-development loan is a loan made to a real estate developer for the purposes of acquiring, subdividing, and making improvements to raw, undeveloped land to make it suitable for building housing, industrial facilities, and the like. The finished lots, complete with utilities, access roads or streets, and other on- and off-site improvements, are then sold to builders who, with the aid of construction loans, construct the buildings on the lot. The buildings are then eventually sold to the users, who finance their purchase via permanent loans.

To illustrate the relationship among land-development, construction, and permanent loans, see Figure 12-1, which is a time line for the financing of a typical land development. At year 0, the developer has found a parcel of land believed suitable for development. If the lender agrees, a land-development loan is made to help finance the acquisition and improvements necessary to make the land suitable for building construction and use.

As improvements are completed and in place, disbursements are made. However, although the amount and timing of construction loan repayment are assured by the terms of the takeout commitment, land-development loan repayment oc-

FIGURE 12-1 The lending time line.

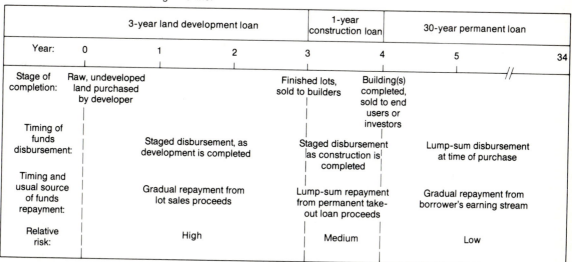

	3-year land development loan			1-year construction loan	30-year permanent loan	
Year: 0	1	2	3	4	5	34
Stage of completion:	Raw, undeveloped land purchased by developer			Finished lots, sold to builders	Building(s) completed, sold to end users or investors	
Timing of funds disbursement:	Staged disbursement, as development is completed			Staged disbursement as construction is completed	Lump-sum disbursement at time of purchase	
Timing and usual source of funds repayment:	Gradual repayment from lot sales proceeds			Lump-sum repayment from permanent take-out loan proceeds	Gradual repayment from borrower's earning stream	
Relative risk:	High			Medium	Low	

curs as lots are sold. As a result, land-development loans tend to be the riskiest of all real estate loans because of the uncertainties associated with the development and sale of the finished lots.

LAND INVESTMENT AND DEVELOPMENT

Before we analyze development financing, let us first examine the general nature of investing in unimproved land. Investing in raw land differs from investing in developed real estate in that raw land generally provides no income from operations over the ownership period. Therefore, investors in raw land must look to the disposition (sale) of the property for the return on their investment. In addition, the absence of operating income means that the investor must bear the carrying costs over the ownership period—real estate taxes, special assessments, debt-service payments—resulting in negative cash flows (except for the cash flow from sale).

Land is vacant because the market has not found it useful due to its location, the demand for land in general, its present condition, or some combination of these factors. The present value of the land reflects its usefulness to the marketplace. Investors purchase vacant land with the expectation that the land value will increase significantly because at some point in the future the land will become more useful (and hence more valuable) than it is today. To make excess returns, the investor must purchase the land before its future becomes known to the market. In doing so, the investor may have to buy and hold the land for 5, 10, or more years to realize substantial profits. During this period, changes in zoning, traffic patterns, population, surrounding land use, and other political, social, and economic factors could render the land much *less valuable* than expected. Although these risks surround all types of real estate investments, they are more acute with unimproved land because the market has not established current use.

Land-Investment Example

Here we illustrate how an investor might analyze a $50,000 parcel of vacant land. Our investor expects to pay cash for the property, hold it for 5 years, and then sell. Through careful analysis of the market, the investor estimates the property will most likely appreciate in value at about 20 percent per year, although similar properties in the area have appreciated from 5 to 40 percent per year. Over the holding period, the only expense will be the real estate taxes, which are based on an assessed value that is 40 percent of market value and a millage (tax) rate of 30. The investor is in the 28 percent tax bracket and expects selling expenses on the property to be 10 percent of the sales price. Given that the investor requires a 10 percent after-tax rate of return, should the land be bought?

Tables 12-1 and 12-2 show the ATCFs and taxes from operations for years 1 through 5. Note that the same format used in earlier chapters is used here, although the analysis in this example is simplified because (1) the land is not ex-

TABLE 12-1   EXPECTED CASH FLOW FROM OPERATION: LAND-INVESTMENT EXAMPLE

	Year				
	1	2	3	4	5
Potential gross income (PGI)	$ 0	$ 0	$ 0	$ 0	$ 0
− vacancy and bad debt allowance (VBD)	0	0	0	0	0
+ miscellaneous income (MI)	0	0	0	0	0
effective gross income (EGI)	0	0	0	0	0
− operating expenses (OE)	(600)	(600)	(600)	(600)	(600)
net operating income (NOI)	(600)	(600)	(600)	(600)	(600)
− debt service (DS)	0	0	0	0	0
before-tax cash flow (BTCF)	(600)	(600)	(600)	(600)	(600)
− taxes (savings) from operation (TO)*	(168)	(168)	(168)	(168)	(168)
after-tax cash flow (ATCF)	(432)	(432)	(432)	(432)	(432)

*See Table 12-2.

TABLE 12-2   EXPECTED TAXES FROM OPERATION: LAND-INVESTMENT EXAMPLE

	Year				
	1	2	3	4	5
Net operating income (NOI)	$(600)	$(600)	$(600)	$(600)	$(600)
− interest on debt (I)	0	0	0	0	0
− depreciation deduction (D)	0	0	0	0	0
− amortized financing costs (AFC)	0	0	0	0	0
+ replacement reserves (RR)	0	0	0	0	0
ordinary taxable income (OTI)	(600)	(600)	(600)	(600)	(600)
× investor's marginal tax rate (τ)	0.28	0.28	0.28	0.28	0.28
taxes (savings) from operation (TO)	(168)	(168)	(168)	(168)	(168)

pected to generate operating income, (2) there are no financing costs or replacement reserves, and (3) land is not depreciable. The operating expenses, net operating incomes, and before-tax cash flows are −$600 for all years. Likewise, the taxable income is −$600, resulting in a tax savings of $168 per year. The after-tax cash flows are −$432 each year for the 5-year holding period.

Tables 12-3 and 12-4 illustrate the expected cash flow from the sale and taxes due on sale. The expected selling price is calculated by using the 20 percent expected annual growth rate [$50,000(1.2)^5 = $124,416]. Since no financing was used, there is no mortgage balance. Also, since the land was not depreciable, the adjusted basis is equal to the original purchase price. The taxes due on sale are $17,353, and the after-tax equity reversion is $94,621.

The net present value for the land investment is computed in Table 12-5 using the investor's required 10 percent after-tax rate of return. The NPV is $7,111, signaling an accept or "invest" decision. The internal rate of return is 12.93 per-

TABLE 12-3 EXPECTED CASH FLOW FROM SALE: LAND-INVESTMENT EXAMPLE

Expected selling price (SP)	$124,416*
− selling expenses (SE)	12,442
net sale proceeds (NSP)	111,974
− unpaid mortgage balance (UM)	0
before-tax equity reversion (BTER)	111,974
− taxes due on sale (TDS)†	17,353
after-tax equity reversion (ATER)	94,621

*At a 20% increase in property value per year.
†See Table 12-4 for computation of taxes due on sale.

TABLE 12-4 EXPECTED TAXES DUE ON SALE: LAND-INVESTMENT EXAMPLE

Taxable income	
Expected selling price (SP)	$ 124,416
− selling expenses (SE)	12,442
amount realized (AR)	111,904
− adjusted basis (AB)	− 50,000
total gain on sale (TG)	61,974

Taxes due on sale	
Taxable income from sale (TIS)	61,974
× investor's marginal tax rate (τ)	0.28
taxes due on sale (TDS)	17,358

TABLE 12-5 NPV AND IRR: LAND-INVESTMENT EXAMPLE

Year	Equity (E)	After-tax cash flow (ATCF)	After-tax equity reversion (ATER)	PVF$_{10\%}$	PV
0	($50,000)			1.0	($50,000)
1		($432)*		0.9091	(393)
2		(432)		0.8264	(357)
3		(432)		0.7513	(325)
4		(432)		0.6830	(295)
5		(432)	$94,621†	+ 0.6209	58,481
				NPV	7,111
				IRR	12.92%

*See Table 12-1.
†See Table 12-3.

TABLE 12-6 AFTER-TAX EQUITY REVERSION (ATER) AT VARIOUS RATES OF INCREASE IN
PROPERTY VALUE: LAND-INVESTMENT EXAMPLE

	Property value appreciation rate (%) per year							
	5	**10**	**15**	**20**	**25**	**30**	**35**	**40**
ATER	$55,352	$66,181	$79,168	$94,621	$112,877	$134,299	$159,283	$188,255

cent, above the required 10 percent rate. Recall that when the NPV is greater
than zero or the IRR is greater than the required rate, the investor should accept
the investment.

Investing in vacant land is obviously "sensitive" to the assumption about the
future value. Table 12-6 contains the ATER at various growth rates, ranging from
the 5 percent minimum to the 40 percent maximum that have been observed in
this market. Table 12-7 shows the various NPVs and IRRs that would occur,
given various appreciation rates from 5 to 40 percent per year. As we see, the
after-tax rate of return and thus the investment decision is quite sensitive to the
uncertainties of appreciation. If financing were included in this example, the sensitivity of NPV and IRR would be much greater, because of leveraging effects.

The Land Developer

Like the investor, the *land developer* may purchase vacant land in the belief that
its value will increase because of market factors. But more importantly, the developer believes that the value can be increased by making improvements to the
land which make the land more useful. If the expected value of the developed
land exceeds the cost of acquiring and developing it (with the values and cost
discounted to the present), then the developer will find it profitable to acquire
and develop the land. To make this determination, let us examine the factors that
the developer must consider.

TABLE 12-7 SENSITIVITY ANALYSIS OF EFFECTS OF
RATE OF APPRECIATION ON NPV AND IRR:
LAND-INVESTMENT EXAMPLE

Rate of appreciation (%)	$NPV_{10\%}$	IRR (%)
5	($17,268)	1.22
10	(10,544)	4.99
15	(2,484)	8.90
20	7,111	12.93
25	18,450	17.05
30	31,751	21.25
35	47,264	25.51
40	65,254	29.82

In evaluating the development potential for a parcel of land, the developer must first analyze the various factors influenced by the land's location. The next step is to evaluate various economic factors to determine expected revenues, costs, and profits, given the locational factors already analyzed.

Location Analysis   The developer's primary consideration when analyzing a development site is the expected market demand for the type of development under study. The developer is trying to answer the question, What is the potential use for the site? Location plays an important role in making this decision.

To determine potential market demand, *land-use patterns* for surrounding property and the community must be considered. The question is, Is the community growing (or likely to grow) in the direction of this site? The answer can be partially determined by examining *natural boundaries,* such as bodies of water or rough terrain, which restrict movement in those directions; *routes of transportation,* along and between which development typically occurs; *population growth* and movement; current *vacancy rates* and the *supply of land;* and *economic base* analysis. All these factors help determine market demand.

Second, the availability of *support services* for the site must be analyzed. The proximity to utilities, access roads, schools, police and fire protection, shopping, and employment should be scrutinized.

Third, the *government regulations* upon the intended use for the site under consideration must be examined. For example, is the site zoned for the developer's intended use? If not, is it reasonable, given the existing political climate, to assume that proper zoning can be obtained? Even if the climate is favorable, the land-use restrictions regarding minimum lot and house sizes, setbacks, signing, and the provisions the developer must make for minimum parking, streets, open space, or recreational areas also must be considered. In addition, building and housing codes and other laws restricting the use or operation of the property, such as rent controls and building moratoriums, must be analyzed.

Finally, the *physical characteristics of the site* itself must be examined. Does the soil have the load-bearing capacity to support the structures intended to be built on it? Do the topography and slope of the land provide proper groundwater drainage? Are the site's aesthetics acceptable for the type of development intended? If any factor is not satisfactory, can changes be made economically to correct the deficiency?

Economic Analysis   To determine the economic feasibility of a proposed development, the analyst uses the market information gathered during the location analysis and specific cost data to estimate the revenues and costs of the proposed project. The *revenues* from the sale of lots are based on the number of lots resulting from the subdividing process and the expected selling prices of those lots. When deciding how to subdivide a development tract, the developer considers the market demand information for the type of development being considered. This information then influences the lot sizes, density requirements, orientation of lots to view, and the amount of land that must be dedicated for streets, parking, and other amenities. Once a proposed plan has been developed, the market values of the lots can be estimated by a comparison to recently sold, equally desirable lots in similar subdivisions in the area.

Generally, more than one initial subdivision plan is prepared. For instance, a developer may have the option of dividing a 150- by 600-foot tract into six 100- by 150-foot lots or eight 75- by 150-foot lots. Assuming the market value is $10,000 for the 100-foot lots and $8,000 for the 75-foot lots, the total revenue for the development, if subdividing 75-foot lots, is $64,000, as opposed to $60,000 for the six-lot development. Ignoring development costs for the moment, it appears that the developer is better off subdividing into eight rather than six lots. However, the relative timing of the sales in the six-lot development could be substantially different from that for the eight-lot development. Suppose that there is a surplus of 75-foot lots in this market but a relative shortage of 100-foot lots. The 100-foot lots would likely sell at a faster rate than the 75-foot lots. Therefore, it is not clear that the developer would be better off with an eight-lot subdivision because when discounted, the present value of future lot sales would be less.

This rate at which lots are purchased is called the *absorption rate*. To illustrate the impact the absorption rate can have on subdivision value, assume that the lots are sold according to the schedule in Table 12-8. As the table illustrates, the present value of the revenues from the subdivision is less with the eight-lot plan because of the slower absorption rate. (We assumed a 20 percent before-tax discount rate.)

Of course, up to this point we have not assessed the *costs of development*. Improvements such as streets, storm sewers, sanitary sewers, water, fire hydrants, natural gas, electricity, and telephone service all must be installed, with connections for each lot. In addition, there are engineering and drafting fees for subdividing and designing these improvements and legal and recording fees for approval of the subdivision and the documents for each individual lot. The costs of real estate taxes, interest on the development loan, and the costs associated with compliance with government regulations must also be considered.

TABLE 12-8   REVENUE COMPARISON: SUBDIVISION EXAMPLE

Month	Six-lot subdivision				Eight-lot subdivision			
	Absorption rate	Total revenue	PVF$_{20\%}$	PV	Absorption rate	Total revenue	PVF$_{20\%}$	PV
1–3	0	0	0	0	0	0	0	0
4–6	1	$10,000	0.9056	$ 9,056	0	0	0	0
7–9	3	30,000	0.8618	25,854	2	$16,000	0.8618	$13,789
10–12	1	10,000	0.8201	8,201	2	16,000	0.8201	13,122
13–15	0	0	0	0	1	8,000	0.7804	6,243
16–18	1	10,000	0.7427	7,427	1	8,000	0.7427	5,942
19–21	0	0	0	0	1	8,000	0.7067	5,654
22–24	0	0	0	0	1	8,000	0.6725	5,380
			Total PV	$50,538			Total PV	$50,130

As with revenues, the magnitude and timing of the costs are important. As we see in the example presented later, the revenues and costs of development are discounted to the present, to determine the present worth of the cash flows. A positive present value indicates the maximum worth of the land to the developer. This is called the *residual land value* and is the maximum price the investor can pay for the land today, given the revenue and costs for the project and the developer's required rate of return. Example 12-1 illustrates the computation of residual land value for an industrial development.

TAX ASPECTS OF LAND DEVELOPMENT

In general, the developer's tax treatment of land-development costs and revenues follows guidelines similar to those used for other types of real estate investments. First, remember that the project does not generate operating income from rents over the holding period; the income received is from the sale of the property. Thus, the tax consequences lie with the gain (or loss) on the sale of the developed lots.

Generally, the process for determining taxes due on sale is the same. The basis is determined and subtracted from the amount realized, yielding the taxable gain.

Due to the characteristics of land development, however, there are areas within the basic tax process that are unique to land development: determining when gain or loss is *recognized* and determining the *amount* of gain or loss.

Recognition of Gain or Loss

Unlike real estate parcels that have been fully developed, lots within a development are usually sold piecemeal over several years. The question thus arises, May the developer postpone the recognition of gain or loss until the last lot is sold? The answer is an unequivocal "no." The developer must "equitably allocate" the development expenses among the lots so that the gain or loss on the sale of each lot is recognized in the year of its sale, although certain expenses may be considered ordinary business expenses and deducted when paid or incurred.

Determining the Amount of Gain or Loss

When determining the amount of gain or loss on the sale, both the deductibility of development costs and their "equitable allocation" must be considered.

Equitable Allocation   This refers to the reasonable apportionment of costs to revenues for each lot within the development. The general guideline used is that since some parcels in a subdivision are worth more than others, they should bear a greater share of the purchase price (basis) and, possibly, of other development costs.

EXAMPLE 12-1

INDUSTRIAL PARK DEVELOPMENT EXAMPLE

A developer wants to acquire a 75-acre tract of land to develop as an industrial park. The developer requires a 16 percent before-tax rate of return on the investment and wants to develop the park and sell sites at an expected selling price of $12,500 per acre. Development costs are expected to be $3,500 per acre for the entire tract. Selling and other holding costs[1] are estimated at $3,000 per acre for the entire tract. Streets and rights-of-way will absorb an estimated 20 percent of the total area. The development is expected to take 3 years, with one-third of the development costs incurred each year. Based on current absorption rates, one-third of the development will be sold each year.

    How much can the developer pay for the tract of land?

    The total site-development cost would be 75 times $3,500, or $262,500. These costs are incurred over a 3-year period, or $87,500 per year. Total sales and other expenses are $225,000 (75 × $3,000), or $75,000 per year over 3 years.

    The total developed acreage is 0.80 × 75 acres, or 60 acres. The total income would be $750,000 (60 × $12,500), or $250,000 per year over 3 years. The net income to the developer would be:

Year	Sale receipts	Development costs	Sale and other expenses	Net income
1	$250,000	$87,500	$75,000	$87,500
2	250,000	87,500	75,000	87,500
3	250,000	87,500	75,000	87,500

    To calculate the value of the land, we discount this net income at the required rate of 16 percent as follows:

Year	Net income	PVF$_{16\%}$	PV
1	$87,500	0.86207	$75,431
2	87,500	0.74316	65,027
3	87,500	0.64066	56,058
		Total PV	$196,516

The developer can thus pay $196,516 for the land, or about $2,600 per acre.

[1]Including the developer's profit.

Allocation and Deductibility of Development Costs Here we examine various categories of development costs, the costs' deductibility, and several commonly accepted allocation methods. *The cost of acquiring the land* is its original basis, and the tax code requires that the allocation of the cost among the various parcels must be made in the year of purchase rather than the year of sale. This rule is intended to prevent the taxpayer from making self-serving allocations in later years to avoid taxes. However, the taxpayer is permitted to change an initial allocation if circumstances occur after acquisition that render the initial allocation unfair.

There are various land-cost allocation methods. The total acquisition cost can be allocated on a *per square foot* or *per acre* basis, if all parcels are approximately equally desirable. When some parcels are more attractive and valuable than others, *relative values* may be established. The developer bears the burden of proof in supporting the relative values.

The cost of *unusable land* must be allocated to the usable lots. Land for streets, parks, playgrounds, schools, and the like, which the developer must dedicate as a condition of subdivision approval, is a cost of doing business for the developer. The original acquisition cost of the entire subdivision must be first divided into usable and unusable portions, with the value of the unusable land allocated equitably over the usable parcels.

Engineering and design costs are generally added to the land cost and allocated on the same basis. However, occasionally these costs may be incurred when investigating possible development sites that are not subsequently purchased. In this instance, these costs are deductible business expenses in the year it is decided *not* to acquire the land.

Off-site improvement costs relate to those improvements that are part of the subdivision but benefit all the lots rather than an individual lot. Such items as streets, main access roads, utility lines, parks, golf courses, clubhouses, swimming pools, and other facilities that are necessary or benefit the entire project are capitalized (i.e., added to land cost) in an equitable fashion, depending on the relative benefit provided by each of these items. These improvements are often allocated on a per parcel, per square foot, or per acre basis.

If the developer retains title to off-site improvements that provide revenue (say a country club), the improvement's costs typically cannot be written off against lot sales. Instead, the cost has to be depreciated over the improvement's useful life.

On-site improvements are costs that benefit a particular lot or lots but not the entire development. To equitably allocate costs, the developer must accurately determine which particular lots benefit from an improvement.

Interest and taxes are generally deductible as business expenses in the year paid or incurred, provided that they are not subject to construction-period interest rules. (Recall that the "construction period" begins on the date construction begins; it does not include the development period, when the land is being readied for construction.) However, the taxpayer may elect to capitalize interest and taxes by adding the appropriate portion to the basis in each lot.

Loan fees and points are treated the same as interest, to the extent that they represent payments for the use or forbearance of funds. The remainder of loan fees and points must be deducted equally over the term of the loan. If the loan is paid off before maturity, the unamortized portion is deductible in the year of sale.

Selling costs incurred in promoting and marketing the finished lots are generally deductible in the year paid or incurred, although a significant amount of advertising and promotion costs incurred before the lots are ready for sale can arguably be capitalized and allocated to the benefited parcels.

In view of the foregoing discussion, it is evident that the developer must perform thoughtful tax planning. The lender too must consider the developer's tax consequences when computing the release price; otherwise, conceivably the developer could be put in a negative cash flow situation each time a lot is sold—the release price paid to the lender combined with the tax due on sale could be greater than the cash inflow from the sale. Typically, developers attempt to reduce their tax liability on early lot sales by writing off as much cost as possible against them, thereby improving cash flows during the project's early stages. In addition, when the developer has the option of capitalizing (i.e., adding to original basis) certain costs or deducting them as expenses in the year incurred, often capitalization is preferred because the property generates no income (and hence, no taxes) until lots are sold. Thus, there is greater benefit from deferring the expense deduction until the year in which income needs to be sheltered. The factor that determines whether to capitalize or expense costs is the extent of the developer's business income generated from other sources during the development period.

RISK ANALYSIS FOR LAND-DEVELOPMENT LOANS

The previous discussion centered on land development in general. We now turn our attention to the unique characteristics of land-development loans.

Sources of Funds

Because of the relatively high risk associated with land-development loans, comparatively fewer commercial lenders are willing and able to make them. Much greater familiarity with the local market, the developer, and land development in general is required. The lenders who do make land-development loans typically finance only 50 to 75 percent of the project cost. As a result, the developer must provide a rather large amount of equity capital or persuade the seller of the land to provide purchase money (record mortgage) financing. The latter arrangement is quite common. The seller owns land that has value but is unusable in its present state. It therefore has a limited market, and financing is difficult (if not impossible) to obtain. For these reasons the seller may be quite willing to provide purchase money financing to the developer. With the lender providing 50 to 75 percent of the funds, and the seller providing, say, an additional 20 to 40 percent, land development can be accomplished with relatively little funding from the developer.

However, lenders want a first-mortgage lien against the property, so the seller must subordinate any purchase money financing to the first mortgage; this puts an additional burden of risk on the seller, so the seller often becomes a de facto partner of the developer and should thus seek competent legal advice before entering into a formal agreement.

Structure and Mechanics

The land-development loan is a unique financing technique because it combines the characteristics of both construction and permanent loans. Like the construction loan, the land-development loan is risky because the security for the loan does not exist. In fact, market demand for the land has not even been established. Even if market studies indicate a strong demand, by the time the property is acquired, government approvals obtained, and improvements completed, the market may have changed for the worse. Other new projects may have been developed, or the economy of the area may be on a downswing. Either factor alone could reduce the demand for the proposed development. In such a situation, the developer and the lender cannot do much but ride out the storm until market conditions improve. There is no takeout commitment with land development—permanent lenders do *not* become involved until the buildings have been constructed and the property is ready for the final user.

Loan Term   The term of a land-development loan should be as long as it takes to develop and sell the building sites. Typically, this time can run from 1 to 3 years up to 6 or 7 years, sometimes longer. The construction timetable and the absorption rate are the key determining factors.

Of course, due to the uncertainties, the land-development loan repayment will likely extend beyond the time originally estimated. It is quite common therefore to provide for this eventuality in the loan document. Generally, the *extension agreement* in development loans requires that the developer pay an extension fee in addition to the accrued interest as consideration for extending the term of the loan.

Funds Disbursement   Disbursement of funds under a land-development loan parallels the method for disbursement of construction loan funds. With both types of loans, funds must be "taken down" or borrowed in stages, usually monthly, as determined by a predesignated percentage of the development work completed and verified. The lender acquires a first lien on the land and all the improvements when they are completed and as the funds are allocated. Both loans also are characterized by the lender requirements of bonding and developer guarantees.

Repayment and the Release Price   Unlike permanent loans, where lenders look to property-borrower income for repayment, and construction loans, where the takeout commitment is the repayment vehicle, land-development loans are expected to be repaid through the sale of the developed sites. When a site is sold, the buyer requires clear, unencumbered title to the lot. The development lender therefore must release lots from the mortgage lien as they are sold and does so upon receipt of a payment, called the *release price*. The release price is the minimum amount of money from each lot sale that the developer must pay to the lender from the sales proceeds. The release price is negotiated between developer and lender and becomes part of the loan agreement.

To compute the release price, the cash outflows disbursed from the loan proceeds are compared with the cash inflows from lot sales. The total proposed principal and interest on the loan over the term are determined and then broken down to an average amount of principal and interest per parcel necessary to retire the debt over the specified term, if lot sales proceed as scheduled. (This process is illustrated by the example later in the chapter.)

Typically, lenders require a release price *greater* than the average principal and interest per parcel. The lender that has extended development funds recognizes that the developer should bear the greatest share of risk. In addition, the lender provides the greater share of front-end money, so there is dual justification for paying back the loan before paying the developer. A release price higher than the average principal and interest per parcel assures the lender that the loan will be repaid before the last lot is sold. Typically, lenders desire the loan to be fully paid by the time 80 percent of the lots are sold; this necessitates a release price that is 0 to 20 percent higher than the average principal and interest per parcel.

As a point of negotiation, the release price is critical to both the developer's and the lender's rate of return. The developer prefers a lower release price to increase cash flows early in the project. The lender, however, prefers a higher release price, for the reasons already mentioned.

A relatively high release price may have a detrimental side effect on the lender's security, however. The success of the project hinges to some extent on the developer's ability to weather the development process's financial ups and downs. A high release price may decrease this ability; therefore, the lender's desire for a high release price must be tempered by the extent to which it will affect the developer's solvency.

Minimizing Development Loan Risks

Much of the Chapter 11 discussion about dealing with construction loan risk applies equally to land-development risk. The financial feasibility of the project is determined by market studies, appraisals, and the developer's financial statement and background. The loan funds are not disbursed until it is ascertained that the improvements are in place. Thus, the lender must monitor the project completion, the cost of which is recouped through front-end points and origination fees. Lenders also generally require a say in contract and contractor approval, personal guarantees from the developer, fixed-price contracts and performance bonds from contractors and subcontractors, title insurance, and payment bonds and holdbacks, just as with construction loans.

As is expected from their inherent risk levels, land-development loans may require a higher yield than other types of real estate loans. In addition, the borrower-analysis portion of the loan-submission package is scrutinized more closely and weighted more heavily, from both a financial and a managerial perspective, because so much of the success of the development hinges on the developer's ability to see the project through to completion. The key elements of the project-analysis portion of the loan-submission package are accurate cost estimates, realistic sales projections derived from market data, and a realistically negotiated release price.

LAND-DEVELOPMENT LOAN EXAMPLE

Landover Development Company (LDC) wishes to develop 55 acres of raw land, improving and subdividing it into 100 single-family residential tracts. LDC has extensively analyzed the market and feels that when the lots are developed, they will sell for $5,000 to $7,000, depending upon each lot's location, size, and view. The average lot price is estimated at $6,000. LDC has studied the absorption rates for similar developments and projects that the absorption (sale) of the lots will take 4 years, according to the annual schedule in Table 12-9. Note that no lots are expected to be sold until the end of year 1 because LDC will not be offering the lots for sale until the development process is completed at the end of year 1.

The price of the land is $225,000. LDC has put down $90,000 to purchase the land, with the remainder to be paid at closing subject to obtaining acceptable financing for the $135,000 balance of the purchase price plus $256,938 of development costs, for a total loan amount of $391,938. Table 12-10 outlines these funding requirements.

At this point, LDC approaches the Clemon Mortgage Company (CMC) for a land-development loan. CMC reviews LDC's background and financial status and the appraisal and market study for the proposed development. Since LDC appears to be a good risk, the projected revenues and costs are in line, and the loan-to-value ratio is within reasonable limits, CMC tentatively agrees to grant a $391,938 loan. CMC requires a 12 percent interest rate and a 2 percent loan origination fee.

Next, CMC requires LDC to estimate the monthly cash draws that will be needed to pay for the work as it is completed (see Table 12-11). The initial draw of $144,938 made at closing is itemized in Table 12-12 and includes payments for the land, initial development expenses, and loan closing fees. Note that the amount disbursed at closing is $144,938 but that the origination fee is added to the loan balance rather than deducted from the proceeds.

TABLE 12-9 ESTIMATED LOT SALES: LDC EXAMPLE

Year	Estimated sales (in lots)	Estimated sales ($)
0 (close)	0	0
1	35	210,000
2	40	240,000
3	15	90,000
4	10	60,000
Totals	100	600,000

TABLE 12-10 TOTAL ESTIMATED FUNDING REQUIREMENTS: LDC EXAMPLE

Land	$225,000
Closing costs	11,250
Taxes	1,688
Engineering, surveys, drafting costs	11,000
Administrative and general expenses	33,000
Other direct costs ($30 per linear foot)	200,000
Total direct project cost	481,938
Less LDC's down payment	90,000
Lender funding required	$391,938

Loan-to-value ratio (assuming project value at completion is $600,000—see Table 12-9):

$$\frac{\$391,938}{\$600,000} = 65.3\%$$

TABLE 12-11 ESTIMATED MONTHLY CASH DRAWS: LDC EXAMPLE

Month	Amount
Closing	$144,938
1	25,000
2	25,000
3	25,000
4	17,500
5	17,500
6	18,000
7	18,000
8	21,000
9	21,000
10	22,000
11	18,500
12	18,500
Total draws	391,938

*See Table 12-12.

The Release Price

With the timing of cash inflows (from lot sales in Table 12-9) and outflows (from loan disbursements in Table 12-11) determined, CMC and LDC can now derive the total principal and interest per parcel so that the *release price* (RP) can be negotiated. Table 12-13 illustrates the process of determining the total principal and interest per parcel. We are trying to determine the amount of the principal and interest per parcel, X, which will make the present value of the draws equal to the present value of the repayments. Column 2 contains the schedule of lot

TABLE 12-12 CLOSING COST: LDC EXAMPLE

Land	$135,000
Appraisals	1,000
Engineering, surveys, drafting costs	1,000
Legal fees	4,416
Title abstract and insurance	2,500
Liability premium	200
Recording fees	100
Real estate taxes	722
Total disbursed at closing	144,938
Origination fee (2%)	7,839
Loan balance at closing	$152,777

sales from Table 12-9, with the number of lots sold multiplied by the principal and interest per lot (X), which is our unknown. This product is the repayment that will occur each year.

Column 3 contains the draw schedule from Table 12-11, except that the draw at closing contains the origination fee of $7,839 as well since it is a borrowing cost

TABLE 12-13 SCHEDULE OF DRAWS AND REPAYMENTS: LDC EXAMPLE

					Present value	
(1) Year	Month	(2) Repayment (lots sold* × X)	(3) Draws	(4) PVF$_{12\%/12}$	(5) 2 × 4 repayment	(6) 3 × 4 draws
0	Closing	0	$152,777†	1.0	0	$152,777
1	1	0	25,000	0.9901	0	24,753
	2	0	25,000	0.9803	0	24,507
	3	0	25,000	0.9706	0	24,265
	4	0	17,500	0.9610	0	16,817
	5	0	17,500	0.9515	0	16,651
	6	0	18,000	0.9420	0	16,957
	7	0	18,000	0.9327	0	16,789
	8	0	21,000	0.9235	0	19,393
	9	0	21,000	0.9143	0	19,201
	10	0	22,000	0.9053	0	19,916
	11	0	18,500	0.8963	0	16,582
	12	35(X)	18,500	0.8874	31.0590(X)	16,418
2	0	40(X)	0	0.7876	31.5040(X)	0
3	0	15(X)	0	0.6989	10.4835(X)	0
4	0	10(X)	0	0.6203	6.2030(X)	0
				Total PVs	79.2495(X)	$385,026

79.2495(X) = $385,026, X = $4,858 = release price

*X = principal and interest per parcel.
†This initial draw includes the $7,839 origination fee.

that must be included in the repayment as part of the interest per parcel. Each repayment or draw is multiplied by the appropriate 12 percent present value factor to determine the present value of inflows (repayment, column 5) and outflows (draws, column 6). Columns 5 and 6 are then totaled and set equal to one another, so that we can solve for X. In doing so, we find that X equals $4,858, the average amount of money required from each lot sale to cover the principal and estimated interest on the loan.

Table 12-14 is the amortization schedule for this loan, based upon the inflows and outflows we have established. Note that two payment columns have been included. The "Payments at P and I" column shows the amortization if repayment is based on the average principal and interest per parcel, $4,858, times the number of lots sold in the period. The "Payments at RP" column is the amortization if repayment is based on a release price of $5,587, which is 1.15 times the average principal and interest per parcel. Note that with repayment at the release price, the loan will be repaid by the end of year 3, about 1 year ahead of the date the final lots are expected to be sold.

Note that the release price is assumed to be 1.15 times the average principal and interest per parcel. But will this release percentage be a problem for the developer because of income taxes resulting from lot sales?

TABLE 12-14 LOAN REPAYMENT SCHEDULE: LDC EXAMPLE

Year	Month	(A) Beginning balance		(B) Draws	(C) Payments† at P and I	(C) Payments† at RP	(D) Interest‡		(E) Ending balance (A + B − C + D)	
1	Close	$ 7,839*		$144,938			$ 0		$152,777	
	1	152,777		25,000			1,528		179,305	
	2	179,305		25,000			1,793		206,098	
	3	206,098		25,000			2,061		233,159	
	4	233,159		17,500			2,332		252,991	
	5	252,991		17,500			2,530		273,021	
	6	273,021		18,000			2,730		293,751	
	7	293,751		18,000			2,928		314,689	
	8	314,689		21,000			3,147		338,836	
	9	338,836		21,000			3,388		363,224	
	10	363,224		22,000			3,632		388,856	
	11	388,856		18,500			3,889		411,245	
	12	411,245		18,500	$170,030	$195,545	4,112		263,827	238,312
2	· · ·	263,827	238,312	0	194,320	223,480	33,460	30,224	102,967	45,056
3	· · ·	102,967	45,056	0	72,870	50,770	13,059	5,714	43,156	0
4	· · ·	43,156	0	0	48,629	0	5,473	0	0	0
Totals				$391,938	485,849	469,795	86,072	70,018		

*Loan origination fee.
†The payments in the At P and I column are derived by multiplying the number of lots sold each year by the average principal and interest per parcel. The payments in the At RP column are computed as the number of lots sold each year times the release price, which is 1.15 times the average principal and interest per parcel. The P and I column is included for comparison only.
‡Interest is computed at a 12% annual rate compounded monthly. Interest is accrued during that period and carried forward in the loan balance. The dual interest, payment, and balance figures result from the two payment schedules.
Note: Draws and payments are assumed to occur at the end of the period.

Developer's After-Tax Cash Flows

To determine these flows, we must calculate the after-tax cash flows to the developer for each year of the development period. We make the following additional assumptions:

1 The developer has no other development projects at this time.
2 Land cost, engineering surveys and drafting charges, administrative and general expenses, and direct costs are included in the basis. They are allocated equally among the lots.
3 Interest expense and taxes are deducted in the year paid.
4 The developer is a cash-basis taxpayer in the 28 percent marginal tax bracket.
5 The $7,839 loan origination fee is considered half interest and half loan-servicing fee.
6 The real estate taxes on the land are $1,688 for year 1; as lots are sold, the taxes the developer owes are expected to be reduced each year by the proportion of lots sold in previous years.

Table 12-15 is the after-tax cash flow computation. At closing, the developer has income of $144,938, the initial loan draw. Expenses incurred at closing include the land purchase of $225,000 plus the other expenses and real estate taxes as shown in Table 12-12, for a total of $234,938. The net amount of −$90,000 represents the developer's equity investment. There are no debt-service outflows or

TABLE 12-15 DEVELOPER'S AFTER-TAX CASH FLOW: LDC EXAMPLE

| | | Year | | | |
	Close	1	2	3	4
Income:					
Sales	$ 0	$210,000	$240,000	$90,000	$60,000
+ loan draws	144,938	247,000	0	0	0
total income	144,938	457,000	240,000	90,000	60,000
Expenses:					
Land purchase	$225,000	$ 0	$ 0	$ 0	$ 0
+ other items at closing	9,216	0	0	0	0
+ direct costs		245,312	0	0	0
+ property taxes	722	1,688	1,013	422	168
total expenses	234,938	247,000	1,013	422	168
Net income (loss)	($90,000)	$210,000	$238,987	$89,578	$59,832
− debt service	0	195,545	223,480	50,770	0
before-tax cash flow	0	14,455	15,507	38,808	59,832
− income taxes*	0	768	2,861	2,781	3,196
after-tax cash flow	(90,000)	13,687	11,646	36,027	56,636

*See Table 12-16.

tax consequences at closing, so the developer's after-tax cash flow is −$90,000, the amount of the equity.

At the end of year 1, the developer has estimated income from lot sales of $210,000 (see Table 12-9). In addition, the total of the loan draws is $247,000, which is the total from Table 12-11 less the draw at closing ($144,938), which we already took into account. Total income for year 1 then is $457,000. Expenses for the year are the direct costs of construction, which are the total loan draws minus the $1,688 property taxes for year 1. The total expenses of $247,000 are deducted from total revenue of $457,000 to derive a net income for the year of $210,000. From this amount is deducted the debt service, which is the release price times the lots sold (see Table 12-14), to obtain the before-tax cash flow.

Tables 12-16 and 12-17 give the computation of taxes. In Table 12-16, we compute the sales price by multiplying the number of lots sold by the $6,000 average

TABLE 12-16 TAXES DUE ON SALE: LDC EXAMPLE

	Year			
	1	2	3	4
Sales price (total)	$210,000	$240,000	$90,000	$60,000
+ selling costs (incl. in basis)	0	0	0	0
net sales proceeds	$210,000	$240,000	$90,000	$60,000
− adjusted basis*	169,460	193,668	72,625	48,417
total gain	40,540	46,332	17,375	11,583
− interest paid	34,080	30,224	5,714	0
− property taxes paid	2,410	1,013	422	168
− amortized financing costs	1,307	1,307	1,307	0
taxable income (loss)	2,743	13,788	9,932	11,415
× tax rate (0.28)	0.28	0.28	0.28	0.28
tax (saving)	768	3,861	2,781	3,196

*See Table 12-17.

TABLE 12-17 ADJUSTED BASIS COMPUTATION: LDC EXAMPLE

Overall basis computation		Annual basis deduction			
Purchase price	$225,000		**Basis per**		**Basis**
+ direct costs	200,000	**Year**	**lot**	**× Lots sold**	**deduction**
+ engineering surveys and drafting	11,000	1	$4841.70	35	$169,460
+ administration and general	33,000	2	4841.70	40	193,668
+ acquisition (closing costs)	11,250	3	4841.70	15	72,625
+ loan service fee	3,920	4	4841.70	10	48,417
Total	$484,170	Totals		100	484,170
÷ # of lots	100				
adjusted basis per lot	4,841.70				

selling price per lot. In this example, selling costs are included in administrative and general expenses. To determine the adjusted basis, we must add the development costs to the original land costs. Note that the acquisition costs are added along with one-half of the original fee: the loan-servicing portion. We then divide the total basis by 100 (the number of lots), to derive the average adjusted basis per lot. We are allocating the basis equally to all lots in this example, but in practice we may need to allocate it differently due to variances in the on-site improvements for each lot. To determine the annual basis deduction, we multiply the average basis per lot by the number of lots sold each year.

Returning to Table 12-16, we subtract the adjusted basis from the net sales proceeds to derive total gain.

However, the investor still may deduct the interest paid on the land-development loan. For year 1, this is the total of the interest accrued up through month 12 (column D, Table 12-14). For years 2 through 4, it is the second single figure listed in column D.

In addition, the investor may deduct the real estate taxes paid each year. For year 1, the deduction is the $1,688 amount plus $722, which was paid at the closing. For years 2 through 4, the taxes are assumed to be reduced each year, because of lot sales in prior years. So for year 2, the expected amounts of taxes is 60/100ths of year 1 taxes ($1,688), or $1,013, since 60 percent of the lots remained in the developer's ownership after year 1 sales. Similarly, year 3 taxes are computed as 25/100ths of year 1 taxes, since 25 percent of the lots remained unsold after year 2 sales. The deduction for year 4 is computed in a similar fashion.

Finally, the interest portion of the loan origination fee may be deducted. Recall that this is one-half of $7,839, which must be amortized equally over the 3-year loan term. The deduction for years 1 through 3 is thus $1,307.

Now the interest, property taxes, and amortized financing costs are deducted from the total gain, to derive the taxable income or loss for each year. This amount is then multiplied by the investor's 28 percent marginal tax rate to derive the tax liability (or savings) for each year.

Returning to Table 12-15, we deduct the income tax from the before-tax cash flow to obtain the after-tax cash flow for each year of the development period.

NPV for the Developer

Table 12-18 shows the calculation for the developer's net present value and IRR. We assume the developer's required IRR is 8 percent; the project's NPV is $2,882, and the IRR is 9.12 percent.

Thus, it appears at this point that the 1.15 release percentage will not be a problem for the developer.

TABLE 12-18 NPV AND IRR COMPUTATIONS: LDC EXAMPLE

Year	Equity	After-tax cash flows	PVF$_{8\%}$	PV
0	($90,000)		1.0000	($90,000)
1		$13,687	0.9259	12,673
2		11,646	0.8573	9,984
3		36,027	0.7938	28,598
4		56,636	0.7350	41,627
			NPV	$ 2,882
			IRR	9.128%

Lender's Before-Tax Yield

To calculate the lender's expected yield on this loan, we must find the rate of interest that equates the outflows with the inflows. Table 12-19 illustrates the process. As a starting point, we know that the contract interest rate is 12 percent and the origination fee is 2 percent. Therefore, we know that the rate must be higher than 12 percent—say, 14 percent. Computing the NPV at 14 percent, we obtain

TABLE 12-19 LENDER'S YIELD: LDC EXAMPLE

Year	Month	Outflow	Inflow	PVF$_{14\%/12}$	PV	PVF$_{15\%/12}$	PV
1	Close	($144,938)		1.0000	($144,938)	1.0000	($144,938)
	1	(25,000)		0.9885	(24,712)	0.9877	(24,691)
	2	(25,000)		0.9771	(24,427)	0.9775	(24,387)
	3	(25,000)		0.9658	(24,145)	0.9634	(24,085)
	4	(17,500)		0.9547	(16,707)	0.9515	(16,652)
	5	(17,500)		0.9437	(16,514)	0.9398	(16,446)
	6	(18,000)		0.9328	(16,790)	0.9282	(16,707)
	7	(18,000)		0.9220	(16,596)	0.9167	(16,501)
	8	(21,000)		0.9114	(19,139)	0.9054	(19,013)
	9	(21,000)		0.9009	(18,918)	0.8942	(18,779)
	10	(22,000)		0.8905	(19,591)	0.8832	(19,430)
	11	(18,500)		0.8802	(13,060)	0.8723	(16,137)
	12	(18,500)	$195,545	0.8701	154,047	0.8615	152,526
2			223,480	0.7570	169,177	0.7422	165,866
3			50,770	0.6586	33,439	0.6394	32,463
				Total NPV	$1,126	Total NPV	($7,311)

Interpolation:
Sum of absolute values of differences: $1,126 + $7,311 = $8,437
Interest rate difference (15 − 14%) = 1%
Difference in present value for 14% = $1,126
Ratio of $1,126 ÷ $8,437 × 1% = 0.00133
14% + 0.133% = 14.13%, lender's yield

$1,126. Since we want an NPV of zero, we know that the 14 percent rate is too low. Trying, say, 15 percent, we obtain an NPV of −$7,311. Thus, we know the rate is between 14 and 15 percent. The interpolation process outlined in Table 12-19 is similar to the interpolation process used on the construction loan example (Chapter 11). The lender's before-tax yield is 14.13 percent.

SUMMARY

This chapter covered land investment, land development, and land-development loans. To help gain an understanding of the special characteristics and risks inherent in land-development loans, we first explained the concepts of land investment and development and the tax considerations peculiar to land development. These concepts were then illustrated by a land-development loan example.

QUESTIONS

1 Define the following terms:
   a absorption rate
   b draw
   c residual land value
   d equitable allocation
   e release price
2 An apartment building complex is to be constructed and ultimately sold to an investor. What is the possible relationship among a construction, a permanent, and a land-development loan? Which loan involves the greatest risk? What is the land-development loan's most unique characteristic?
3 Why is accurate market analysis so important to the land developer? What are common market changes that may substantially reduce the investor's expected rate of return? Why is the estimated future value assumption so "sensitive"?
4 Name the four major components of the location analysis. What is the most crucial local government regulation in the investment decision?
5 Is the statement "The smaller the lot size, the greater the profits" true or false? Why?
6 What is an absorption rate? How does this rate affect the investment decision?
7 What is "unusable land" and how is it "used"? How is the value of unusable land allocated?
8 Why is it necessary to be careful when negotiating a realistic term for the construction loan?
9 What is "released" when the release price is paid? Why should the lender avoid demanding too high a release price?

PROBLEMS

1 An investor might analyze a $65,000 parcel of vacant land. Our investor expects to pay cash for the property, hold it for 10 years, and then sell. The investor estimates the property will most likely appreciate in value at about 25 percent per year, although similar properties in the area have appreciated from 10 to 50 percent per year. Over the holding period, the only expense will be the real estate taxes, which are based on an

assessed value that is 40 percent of market value and a millage (tax) rate of 35. The investor is in the 28 percent marginal tax bracket and expects selling expenses on the property to be 10 percent of the sales price. Given that the investor requires a 14 percent after-tax rate of return, should the land be bought?

2 A developer wants to acquire a 100-acre tract of land to develop as a subdivision with 250 lots. The developer requires a 13 percent before-tax rate of return on the investment and wants to develop the subdivision and sell lots at an expected selling price of $50,000 per lot. Development costs are expected to be $2,000 per lot for the entire tract. Selling and other holding costs (including developer's profit) are estimated to be $1,750 per lot. Streets and rights-of-way will absorb an estimated 15 percent of the total area. The development is expected to take 5 years, with one-fifth of the development costs incurred each year. Based on current absorption rates, one-fifth of the development will be sold each year. How much can the developer pay for the tract of land?

3 A developer wants to acquire a 75-acre tract of land to develop as an industrial park. The developer requires a 14 percent before-tax rate of return on the investment and wants to develop the park and sell sites at an expected selling price of $20,000 per acre. Development costs are expected to be $5,000 per acre for the entire tract. Selling and other holding costs are estimated at $4,000 per acre for the entire tract. The development is expected to take 5 years, with one-fifth of the development costs incurred each year. Based on current absorption rates, one-fifth will be sold each year. How much can the developer pay for the tract of land?

4 An investor expects to pay $150,000 cash for a property, hold it for 3 years, and then sell. The investor estimates the property will appreciate in value at about 10 percent per year. Over the holding period, the only expense will be real estate taxes, which are based on an assessed value that is 25 percent of market value and a millage rate of 20. The investor is in the 15 percent marginal tax bracket and expects selling expenses on the property to be 10 percent of the sales price. Given that the investor requires a 12 percent after-tax rate of return, should the land be bought?

REFERENCES

American Institute of Architects: *Financing Real Estate Development,* Harry A. Goleman (ed.), Aloray, River Vale, N.J., 1974.

Benke, Williams: *All About Land Investment,* McGraw-Hill, New York, 1976.

Broude, Richard F., and Norman Renney: *Cases and Materials on Land Financing,* 2nd ed., Foundation Press, Mineola, N.Y., 1977.

Friedman, Jack P., and Bruce Lindeman: "Sellers-Financed Land Sales," *Journal of the American Society of Farm Managers and Rural Appraisers,* April 1978, pp. 62–67.

Renney, Norman, and Richard F. Broude: *Cases and Materials on Land Financing,* Foundation Press, Mineola, N.Y., 1970.

Seldin, Maury: *Land Investment,* Irwin, Homewood, Ill., 1975.

13

PARTICIPATION MORTGAGES

This chapter discusses two creative financing techniques: the shared-appreciation mortgage and the income-equity participation mortgage. A *shared-appreciation mortgage* loan is used on owner-occupied residential real estate; the borrower agrees to share the property's appreciation with the lender in return for a lower than conventional market interest rate. An *income-equity participation mortgage* applies to income-producing property; the borrower agrees to share with the lender a portion of the investment's income and/or a portion of the property's appreciation in return for a lower than conventional interest rate.

A distinction should be made between participation mortgages and those commonly called simply *loan participations*. The latter term refers to a type of loan whose mortgage amount is so large that one lender cannot or will not fund the debt alone. Thus two or more lenders ''participate'' in the making of one loan. The subject of this chapter is the participation mortgage, which is a variation of the traditional borrower-lender relationship and does not generally involve multiple lenders.

Our discussion begins with the economic conditions that led to the creation of these alternative mortgage techniques, followed by details of the shared-appreciation and the equity participation mortgages. Next, we analyze the risk the unique legal, financial, and tax aspects participation mortgages create. Finally, we provide detailed examples of the shared-appreciation mortgage on a single-family house and an income participation mortgage on an apartment investment, with an added note on convertible mortgages.

WHAT ARE PARTICIPATION MORTGAGES?

Conventional fixed-rate mortgages were the predominant financing technique for real estate from the Depression years of the 1930s through the 1970s. Although these loans met the lender's investment criteria when they were funded, later unexpected inflation dictated that lenders review their mortgage investment criteria to find a hedge against erosion of their capital. As inflation increased during the latter part of the 1970s, homeowners and investors accrued tremendous profit opportunities through the use of leverage. Homeowners' and equity investors' return on equity investments was large as inflation increased the value of real estate. Lenders on real estate, aware that they had made these gains possible, were dissatisfied that they were not sharing in the gains, even though they bore much of the risk if the project failed. In addition, unexpected inflation combined with fixed-rate mortgages caused the lender's ''real'' yield to deteriorate.

The past several years have seen lenders use various alternative financing methods in an attempt to counteract the effects of unexpected inflation on their mortgage loans. As discussed in the previous chapters, among the most common types of alternative financing are the adjustable-rate, graduated payment, renegotiable-rate, and participation mortgages. These alternative financing techniques vary in form and complexity, but they share one objective: to help revive the real estate mortgage market by giving lenders a hedge against unexpected inflation for the debt capital they provide.

Characteristics

With a participation mortgage, the lender in the transaction remains a creditor. The lender does not take partial title to the real estate or become a legal partner with the borrower in the operation or sale of the real estate as the lender would in a joint venture project (discussed in Chapter 14). The additional funds the lender receives, whether they are cash flows or appreciation proceeds, are classified as *contingent interest*.

The lender's participation is tied directly to individual property performance, not to an outside index. In effect, the lender has a preferred equity position, receiving first claim on net earnings in the form of fixed debt service as well as a participation in the equity position. The two major mortgage types in which the lender may participate in profits are the *shared-appreciation* and the *income-equity participation* mortgages.

Shared-Appreciation Mortgages (SAMs)

There are many different forms of shared-appreciation mortgages; the following discussion reviews their typical structure. With a SAM, a borrower receives a mortgage loan at a below conventional interest rate; in return, the lender is allowed to share in the property's appreciation. The interest rate and the lender's share of the appreciation are arrived at by negotiation. The lender's share of appreciation takes the form of the contingent interest and is payable when the property is sold or refinanced or at another agreed-upon time in the property's life.

Typically, the SAM's maximum term is 10 years, although monthly payments may be based on up to a 40-year amortization. If the home is not sold within 10 years, the borrower must refinance the house (after it is appraised) and pay the lender the contingent interest amount. At that time the lender typically guarantees to refinance the loan, including the lender's shared appreciation amount, at the (then) prevailing market rate.

The appreciation amount is calculated by subtracting the original purchase price the borrower paid from the selling price or appraised value. The cost of any home improvements are added to the original purchase price before the appreciation is calculated.

Lenders are attracted to SAMs' property-appreciation feature, which provides a partial hedge against inflation. The main attraction to borrowers is the reduced initial interest rate; the amount of the reduction is a function of the lender's share of the appreciation and the lender's expectation of property appreciation.

Income-Equity Participation Mortgages

An income-equity participation mortgage applies to income-producing property and is similar to a SAM in that the lender can share in the appreciation of the property. Another feature of income-equity participation mortgages is that the lender can also receive a portion of the cash flows resulting from the operation of the investment. In return, the lender gives the borrower a mortgage loan at below conventional rates. The term "equity participation" is a misnomer because the lender does not acquire an ownership interest in the investment. The contract interest rate and the debt-service payment are structured to meet the lender's minimum debt-coverage standards. The participation of the cash flows can be a portion of gross income, net income, or any income in excess of a predetermined break-even point.

The appreciation is computed in a manner similar to that of a SAM, with one important exception. In an income-equity participation mortgage, the participation base is the typical mortgage loan amount, not the original purchase price. In effect, the borrower's down payment becomes part of the appreciation figure from which the lender's share is computed.

Reasons for Participation Mortgages

There are several important reasons for the participation mortgage. With a SAM, the lower initial interest rate enables more borrowers to purchase homes. It also enable lenders to provide the popular fixed-rate mortgage loan yet still retain a hedge against inflation. With income-equity participation mortgages, the lower than market initial interest rate enables borrowers to receive higher loan-to-value ratio mortgages yet still meet the lender's minimum debt-coverage requirements. The lenders' advantage is that they now have a capital investment which is tied directly to the performance of the investment and is not just a fixed return on capital.

RISK ASPECTS OF PARTICIPATION MORTGAGES

To the borrower and the lender, the risks and returns associated with participation mortgages are not nearly so certain as those associated with the conventional fixed-rate loans. This section analyzes the unique legal, financial, and tax risks associated with participation mortgages.

Legal Aspects

Lending institutions which make participation mortgages risk violating usury laws in the particular jurisdiction where the loan is made if the additional interest coupled with the regular interest results in an effective interest rate greater than the maximum legal rate. If the transaction will be subject to the usury limit, the parties should structure the transaction in a manner that will preclude a usury violation. The parties should either appropriate the funds so that they do not take the form of a loan or ensure that the loan is not subject to or is within applicable usury limits.

A second legal consideration is that the loan not be construed to imply a partnership between the borrower and the lender. Applicable statutes may prohibit some lending institutions from engaging in partnerships of this type, and both parties could be subject to unlimited liability in dealings with third parties. Obviously, care must be taken so that the lender is legally construed as a creditor to the transaction.

Finally, lenders may be accused of *redlining*. Redlining is a tactic whereby lenders restrict making loans in less attractive areas and neighborhoods because these places may not offer the appreciation gain of other, more attractive locations. Redlining based on racial considerations is illegal in the United States.

Financial Aspects

Inherent risk-return trade-offs affect both lenders and borrowers in participation mortgages. The lender's desire to enhance loan yield through participation in the property's profits must be balanced against the reduction of the contract interest rate to below the market rate that the lender gives up in return for the participation benefits. Compared with a fixed-rate loan at market rates, all else being equal, the base payments on a participation mortgage are lower; the default risk is lower as a result. But the contingent interest (participation) portion of the lender's return is riskier because of the uncertainties associated with the property's future performance. The basic issues are assessing the risks involved, minimizing them where possible, and then pricing the participation loan accordingly.

Income participations can be structured by designating a portion of effective gross income or net operating income as contingent interest. From the lender's viewpoint, effective gross income may be a more desirable basis because any increases in rents will raise the contingent interest amount. The borrower, however, may find this arrangement detrimental if rent increases occur solely because of increases in operating expenses. This arrangement would cause a decline in cash flows to the borrower at the same time that cash flows to the lender increase. Conversely, the use of net operating income as the basis for contingent interest is better for the borrower; strangely, however, it increases the uncertainty (risk) of the contingent interest to the lender but also lowers the default risk. It is debatable whether these positive and negative changes in the risks directly offset each other.

Equity participation presents similar risk-return trade-offs to the borrower and the lender. In a SAM, the base for determining appreciation is the borrower's purchase price plus permanent improvements. Often, lenders require that only the *value* an improvement adds may be added to the basis. If the cost of the improvement exceeds the value, the borrower loses. Thus, a borrower who wishes to add a home improvement that costs more than it is "worth" to the market, for whatever reason, may find the resulting cost of the improvement even higher.

Common to both income-equity participation and shared-appreciation mortgages is the risk that the property might not appreciate in value over the loan term. This risk could be caused by internal factors relating to the care, upkeep, and/or management of the property or by external market influences. The lender bears the loss of the difference between the expected yield at loan origination and the resulting actual yield. The external influences are not really controllable by the borrower or the lender, but the internal factors are. For this reason, lenders often attempt to minimize their risk by inserting a clause in the mortgage contract allowing property inspections from time to time to ascertain that the borrower is not "committing waste" on (i.e., devaluing) the mortgaged property.

Lenders are exposed to some additional risks with participation loans. For borrowers to agree to a loan that is likely to have balance owing at the end of the loan term, say, 10 years, they will want assurance from the lender that this balance will be able to be refinanced. In agreeing to this condition, however, the lender is exposed to the risk that the borrower or the property may no longer be creditworthy at that time. Thus, the lender could conceivably be forced to refinance a loan that would then be a poor risk.

A possible risk if the borrower obtains junior financing is whether contingent interest on the participation mortgage has priority over junior mortgages and other liens. Since the lender is sharing in "equity," if any, and since equity has not traditionally been part of the debt, conceivably other claims on the equity may gain priority. At present, the issue is unclear. The liquidity of these mortgages is not as certain as it is for more well known, longer-used financing instruments, although there is a secondary market for them that is gaining acceptance.

Finally, lenders who are experiencing poor earnings may find equity participation or shared-appreciation mortgages unsuitable for their portfolios. The lower base interest on the equity participation loan results in lower cash inflows to the lender than the inflows from a standard fixed-rate mortgage. This is expected to be made up on the long run with contingent interest, but it depresses even further in the short run.

Tax Aspects

There are several tax considerations that borrowers and lenders must analyze before engaging in income-equity participation mortgages. Contingent interest paid to the lender under equity participation agreements may not be tax-deductible as interest by the buyer. Interest payments offset income dollar for dollar. Borrowers engaged in income participation mortgages must face the fact that giving a portion of the cash flows and the appreciation to a lender may produce a substantial tax loss. It may be construed that a developer is selling a piece of the action to the lender for a gain.

The deductibility of contingent interest has been the subject of much recent litigation that has been mostly inconclusive. However, in general, if a bona fide, arm's-length debtor-creditor relationship exists, if the contingent interest can be determined with accuracy by the time it is due, and if the termination date when the contingent interest is due is reasonably definite, then it is likely the deduction of contingent interest will be allowed, and the lender's participation amounts will have the same tax effects as the interest payments on any other type of loan.

For example, suppose a mortgage calls for interest payments of $100,000 in a given taxable year. In addition, the lender requires another payment of $20,000, which represents a participation in the net operating income (or gross income or before-tax cash flow). The borrower's total interest deduction would thus be the sum ($120,000) for that taxable year. Also, generally, a lender's participation in the cash flow from sale could be interpreted as an interest payment similar to a prepayment penalty.

PARTICIPATION MORTGAGE EXAMPLES

This section illustrates the mechanics of the shared-appreciation and income participation mortgages. Examples 13-1 and 13-2 detail the general mechanics of these mortgages from the lender's and the borrower's perspectives.

EXAMPLE 13-1

VALUATION OF LENDER'S POSITION IN A PARTICIPATION MORTGAGE

A shopping center is expected to produce the following income:

Year	NOI
1	$100,000
2	105,000
3	103,000
4	108,000
5	110,000

You have approached a lender concerning a mortgage. The lender has agreed to make the loan at an interest rate of 11 percent (annual payments), with debt service of $89,055 each year for 25 years, with a "call" option at the end of year 5, which means that the entire balance is due and payable then. At the end of 5 years, the amount outstanding is $709,174. In addition, the lender wants 5 percent of each year's NOI. If the lender's required rate of return is 12 percent, what is the value of the lender's position?

To solve this type of valuation problem, remember that the value is the present worth of the expected income. The expected income to the lender is as follows:

Year	Debt service	Amount outstanding	Lender's share of NOI	Total lender income	PVF$_{12\%}$	PV
1	$89,055		$5,000	$ 94,055	0.89286	$ 83,978
2	89,055		5,250	94,305	0.79719	75,179
3	89,055		5,150	94,205	0.71178	67,053
4	89,055		5,400	94,455	0.63552	60,028
5	89,055	$709,174	5,500	803,729	0.56743	456,059
					Total PV	$742,297

Multiplying the lender's income each year by the PVF at the required yield of 12 percent results in a total present value of the lender's position of $742,300.

EXAMPLE 13-2

VALUATION OF EQUITY POSITION WITH A PARTICIPATION MORTGAGE

Using the shopping center in Example 13-1, let us determine the value of the equity position with the participation mortgage.

The before-tax cash flows to the equity position are:

Year	NOI	Debt service	Lender's participation	Before-tax cash flow
1	$100,000	$89,055	$5,000	$ 5,945
2	105,000	89,055	5,250	10,695
3	103,000	89,055	5,150	8,795
4	108,000	89,055	5,400	13,545
5	110,000	89,055	5,500	15,445

The shopping center is expected to sell for $1,100,000 at the end of the 5-year holding period. The before-tax equity reversion is thus the net sale price ($1,100,000) minus the unpaid mortgage ($709,174), or $390,826.

Suppose the investor required a before-tax rate of return of 18 percent. The value of the equity position would thus be, the present value of the before-tax cash flows, as follows:

Year	BTCF	BTER	PVF$_{18\%}$	PV
1	$ 5,945		0.84746	$5,038
2	10,695		0.71818	7,681
3	8,795		0.60863	5,353
4	13,545		0.51579	6,986
5	15,445	$390,826	0.43711	177,585
			Total PV	$202,643

Multiplying the equity cash flows by the present factor at the required rate of 18 percent results in a total present value of $202,643 for the equity position.

Adding the value of the lender's position (from Example 13-1) of $742,297 to the value of the equity position of $202,643 yields a total value of the shopping center of $944,940. This is the maximum that could be paid and yield a return to the lender of 12 and 18 percent to the equity investor.

SAM Examples

To understand a SAM's mechanics, see Table 13-1. Table 13-2 is the amortization schedule after 3, 5, 7, and 9 years. The borrower has two options: a fixed-rate mortgage (FRM) or a SAM.

The borrower has the option of a $56,000 SAM at an interest rate of 10 percent and monthly payments of $491.40 for 360 months. To further illustrate the SAM, two percentages of shared appreciation, 33.3 and 50 percent, are assumed. The

TABLE 13-1   SHARED-APPRECIATION MORTGAGE EXAMPLES

	SAM	FRM
Original price	$70,000	$70,000
Mortgage amount	$56,000	$56,000
Interest rate*	10%	13%
Monthly payment	$491.44	$619.47
Percentage share to lender	33.3% and 50%	0
Expected property apprec. rate	0, 5, 7%	0, 5, 7%
Maturity	360 months	360 months
Annual payments	$5,896.80	$7,433.64

*Annual contract rate with monthly compounding.

TABLE 13-2   PROPERTY VALUE AT VARIOUS APPRECIATION RATES: SAM EXAMPLES

Holding period	Expected annual appreciation rate* (%)		
	0	5	7
0	$70,000	$70,000	$70,000
3	70,000	81,054	85,753
5	70,000	89,340	98,179
7	70,000	98,497	112,405
9	70,000	108,593	128,692

*For example, the expected property value at a 5% annual appreciation rate with a 5-year holding period would be

Property value $= (1.05)^5 (70,000)$

Property value $= \$89,340$

assumptions on the expected rate of annual appreciation of the property's value are 0, 5, and 7 percent (shown in Table 13-2).

Table 13-3 contains the total cash flow from the reversion (sale or reappraisal, for example). These cash flows are calculated by subtracting the amount outstanding on the mortgage from the property values in Table 13-2. These cash flows are then split between the borrower and lender, as shown in Table 13-4. We illustrate two different situations: a split of 33.3 percent to the lender and a split of 50 percent to the lender. Obviously, the split would depend upon the SAM agreement.

In our example, suppose the property appreciated at a rate of 5 percent over a 5-year holding period. The cash flows (payments) to the lender would be $491.44 each month for 60 months, the amount outstanding at the end of 5 years $54,079, and, if the lender received 33.3 percent of the total reversion, $14,685 at the end of 5 years.

TABLE 13-3 AMOUNT OUTSTANDING AND TOTAL CASH FLOW FROM REVERSION: SAM EXAMPLES

Holding period	Amount outstanding	Total reversion cash flow at appreciation rate (%)		
		0	5	7
3	$54,964	$15,036	$26,070	$30,789
5	54,079	15,921	35,261	44,100
7	53,004	16,995	45,493	59,401
9	51,688	18,312	56,905	77,004

TABLE 13-4 LENDER'S SHARE OF REVERSION CASH FLOWS: SAM EXAMPLES

	Lender's share					
	33.3%			50%		
Holding period	Expected rate of annual appreciation (%)					
	0	5	7	0	5	7
3	$5,007	$ 8,681	$10,253	$7,519	$13,035	$15,395
5	5,092	11,742	14,685	7,961	17,631	22,050
7	5,659	15,149	19,781	8,598	22,747	29,701
9	6,098	18,949	25,642	9,155	28,453	38,502

Effective Yield on SAMs

Table 13-5 gives the calculated yields on the SAM example. To illustrate how these yields are calculated, suppose the loan called for the lender to receive 33.3 percent of the total equity and the property increased at a rate of 5 percent over a 5-year holding period. In equation form,

$$\$56,000 = PVAF_{i/12.60}(\$491.44) + PVF_{i/12.60}(\$54,079) + PVF_{i/12.60}(\$11,742)$$

The only unknown is the rate. In this example, the yield would be 13.04 percent, as shown in Table 13-5.

An examination of Table 13-5 reveals certain important interrelationships for our examples. As the lender's share of the appreciation increases, the yield also increases. Second, as the holding period increases, the yield decreases. The important factors influencing the lender's yield on a SAM are the property value appreciation rate, the lender's share of the reversion, and the interest rate on the fixed portion of the loan.

TABLE 13-5 YIELDS ON SAM EXAMPLES

Holding period	Lender's share					
	33%			50%		
	Expected rate of annual appreciation (%)					
	0	5	7	0	5	7
3	12.49	14.21	14.91	13.67	16.13	17.13
5	11.38	13.04	13.73	12.11	14.39	15.35
7	10.99	12.49	13.16	11.47	13.58	14.50
9	10.74	12.14	12.80	11.09	13.07	13.92

Comments on SAM Mechanics

In our example, we calculated the lender's share based on the entire equity in the house. Another form of SAM allows the lender to share in the appreciation *above* the original purchase price. Obviously, the yield (holding all else constant) on this type of SAM would be lower than on the example we worked.

Understanding the benefits (and costs) of SAMs requires a knowledge of the important factors influencing the yield. Borrowers and lenders who understand the trade-offs between income and equity participation and the fixed interest rates should be able to determine and negotiate the various components. There are obviously points of indifference among various combinations of these factors.

Income-Equity Participation Example

Now we turn our attention to an example of an income participation mortgage for an income-producing property.

General Mechanics Lender participations are also sometimes called *equity kickers*. Various forms of equity kickers are used in the income property mortgage market such as direct sharing in total revenues collected or in before-tax cash flows (percentage of gross or net income), participation in revenues or operating income after a minimum level, and an escalation participation in rental income or other revenues over time.

An equity participation can also be defined as an arrangement whereby an institutional lender (or lenders, as we later see) acquires an equity interest in the subject property. The lender participates in the future income and receives the contracted debt-service repayment. The lender often accepts a less secure financial position in return. It has been argued that the term *equity participation* is not exactly accurate because generally the lender does not actually receive an "equity" ownership interest. Instead, the lender usually makes a loan, structures the payments to meet the minimum debt-coverage standards, and then requires a participation in gross income, net operating income, or any income over and above a predetermined break-even point. This participation is required to be paid to the lender over a specified number of years called the *lock-in period*. This equity kicker is actually a risk premium the lender earns by modifying under-writer standards (e.g., lowering the initial payments, taking a percentage of the flows, changing the prepayment penalty, and/or taking a percentage of the appre-ciation). Chapter 14 discusses the equity participation whereby the lender ac-quires ownership through a joint venture.

Investment Assumptions   This example assumes that a lender is considering a loan commitment of $9 million at 12 percent interest amortized over 30 years with a balloon payment in 5 years. In addition, the lender will participate in 25 percent of the before-tax equity reversion and 25 percent of the operating before-tax cash flows (to be received from positive cash flows). The developer (borrower) will cover all negative flows.

1 Rent is $20 per square foot and expected to increase 6 percent per year.
2 Building cost is $9,375,000.
3 Land cost is $4 million.
4 Total project cost is $13,375,000.
5 Building size (net rentable area) is 125,000 square feet.
6 Depreciation recovery period using straight-line method is 31.5 years.
7 Operating expenses are $3.50 per square foot, increasing at 4 percent per year.
8 Vacancy and collection loss are 40 percent of potential gross income in year 1; 5 percent thereafter.
9 Selling expenses are 5 percent of gross sales price.
10 Gross sales price is forecast by capping year 5's net operating income at 10.5 percent.
11 Equity investor's marginal tax rate is 28 percent.
12 Holding period is 5 years.
13 Developer's equity is $4,375,000.

Before-Tax Cash Flows   Table 13-6 presents the loan amortization schedule. The beginning loan balance is $9,000,000, the annual debt service is $1,117,293 ($9,000,000 times the mortgage constant), and the interest amounts and the prin-cipal deductions as shown. Note the $8,763,084 balloon due at the end of year 5.

TABLE 13-6   LOAN AMORTIZATION SCHEDULE: PARTICIPATION EXAMPLE

Year	Beginning balance	Debt service	Interest	Principal	End balance
1	$9,000,000	$1,117,293	$1,080,000	$37,293	$8,962,707
2	8,962,707	1,117,293	1,075,526	41,768	8,920,939
3	8,920,939	1,117,293	1,070,512	46,780	8,874,159
4	8,874,159	1,117,293	1,064,899	52,394	8,821,765
5	8,821,765	1,117,293	1,058,612	48,681	8,763,084

TABLE 13-7 EXPECTED CASH FLOW FROM OPERATION: PARTICIPATION EXAMPLE

	Year				
	1	2	3	4	5
Potential gross income (PGI)	$2,500,000	$2,650,000	$2,809,000	$2,977,540	$3,156,192
− vacancy and bad debt allowance (VBD)	1,000,000	132,500	140,450	148,877	157,810
+ miscellaneous income (MI)*	0	0	0	0	0
Effective gross income (EGI)	1,500,000	2,517,500	2,668,550	2,828,663	2,998,382
− operating expenses (OE)	437,500	455,000	473,200	492,128	511,813
net operating income (NOI)	1,062,500	2,062,500	2,195,350	2,336,535	2,486,569
− Debt Service (DS)†	1,117,293	1,117,293	1,117,293	1,117,293	1,117,293
before-tax cash flow (BTCF)	(54,793)	945,207	1,078,057	1,219,242	1,369,276
− lender's share of BTCF (LSBTCF)‡	0	236,302	269,514	304,811	342,319
developer's before-tax cash flow (DBTCF)	(54,793)	708,950	808,543	914,431	1,026,957

*Assumed to be zero for simplicity.
†See Table 13-6.
‡25% of the BTCF and treated as interest to developer. The lender's share is zero in year 1 because of a negative BTCF. The developer bears the total burden.

Table 13-7 computes the expected before-tax cash flows from operations. The effective gross income is found by deducting the vacancy and bad-debt allowance from potential gross income and then adding miscellaneous income. The net operating income is found by subtracting operating expenses from the effective gross income. The before-tax cash flows are found by deducting debt service (from Table 13-6) from the net operating income. The developer's before-tax cash flow is then computed by deducting the lender's share of the before-tax cash flow (25 percent of all positive before-tax flows) from the total before-tax cash flow.

Table 13-8 computes the expected cash flow from sale. The net sale proceeds ($23,680,000) are found by deducting the selling expenses ($1,184,000) from the expected selling price. The before-tax equity reversion ($13,732,916) is calculated by deducting the unpaid mortgage balance ($8,763,084) in the fifth year from the net sales proceeds ($22,496,000). The developer's cash flow from sale

TABLE 13-8 EXPECTED CASH FLOW FROM SALE: PARTICIPATION EXAMPLE

Expected selling price (SP)*	$23,680,000
− selling expenses (SE)	1,184,000
net sale proceeds (NSP)	22,496,000
− unpaid mortgage balance (UM)†	8,763,084
before-tax equity reversion (BTER)	13,732,916
− lender's share of BTER (LSBTER)‡	3,433,229
developer's BTER (DBTER)	10,299,687

*Year 5's NOI capitalized at 10.5%.
†See Table 13-6.
‡25% of the BTER.

TABLE 13-9 LENDER'S CASH FLOWS: PARTICIPATION EXAMPLE

Year	Amount loaned*	Loan receipts†	Participation flows‡	Total cash flows
0	($9,000,000)			($9,000,000)
1		$1,117,293	0	1,117,293
2		1,117,293	236,302	1,353,595
3		1,117,293	269,514	1,386,807
4		1,117,293	304,811	1,422,104
5		9,880,377	3,775,548	13,655,925
				IRR = 19.5%

*At the beginning of year 1, the lender makes a $9 million loan to the developer, which represents outflow for the lender.

†These receipts are the debt-service payments the developer makes in years 1 to 5. In year 5, the outstanding balance is also paid (see Table 13-6).

‡These flows represent the lender's 25% share in the BTCFs (years 1 to 5), and in year 5, the lender also receives 25% of the BTER.

($10,299,687) is then computed by subtracting the lender's share of the before-tax equity reversion ($3,433,229, 25 percent of the BTER) from the before-tax equity reversion ($13,732,916).

Analysis of Lender's Yield The lender's yield can now be computed as shown in Table 13-9. The internal rate of return to the lender (19.5 percent) is found by calculating the rate that equates the lender's outflows (amount loaned −$9,000,000) to the inflows. The lender's inflows are the debt service, the participation amounts, and the unpaid mortgage.

Developer's After-Tax Cash Flows Table 13-10 shows the developer's after-tax cash flows from operations. The taxes from operations (from Table 13-11) are deducted from the developer's before-tax cash flows (Table 13-7). Notice that the interest deductions are the sum of the mortgage interest and lender participation. In year 5 of operations, for tax purposes the lender's share of the cash flow from sale is treated as an interest expense. The tax (or savings) from operations is then

TABLE 13-10 DEVELOPER'S AFTER-TAX CASH FLOWS FROM OPERATIONS: PARTICIPATION EXAMPLE

	Year				
	1	2	3	4	5
Developer's before-tax cash flow (DBTCF)*	($54,793)	$708,905	$808,543	$914,431	$1,026,957
− taxes from operations (TO)†	(88,233)	126,855	156,157	187,378	(740,659)
developer's after-tax cash flow (DATCF)	33,440	582,050	652,386	727,053	1,767,616

*See Table 13-7.
†See Table 13-11.

TABLE 13-11 DEVELOPER'S TAXES FROM OPERATIONS: PARTICIPATION EXAMPLE

	Year				
	1	2	3	4	5
Effective gross income (EGI)	$1,500,000	$2,517,500	$2,668,550	$2,828,663	$2,998,382
− operating expenses (OE)	437,500	455,000	473,200	492,128	511,813
net operating income (NOI)*	1,062,500	2,062,500	2,195,350	2,336,535	2,486,569
− interest on debt (I)†	1,080,000	1,311,827	1,340,026	1,369,710	4,834,160
− depreciation deduction (D)‡	297,619	297,619	297,619	297,619	297,619
− amortized financing costs (AFC)§	0	0	0	0	0
+ replacement reserves (RR)§	0	0	0	0	0
ordinary taxable income (OTI)	(315,119)	453,054	557,705	669,206	(2,645,210)
× developer's marginal tax rate (τ)	0.28	0.28	0.28	0.28	0.28
taxes (savings) from operation (TO)	(88,233)	126,855	156,157	187,378	(740,659)

*From Table 13-7.
†Interest on the debt plus a contingent of "quasi-" interest deduction for the amount of lender's participation (25%) in the BTCFs (see Table 13-7). In year 5, the lender's share of the reversion is deducted as interest.
‡Building cost divided by 31.5.
§Assumed to be zero for simplicity.

found by multiplying the developer's marginal tax rate by the taxable income. (See Table 13-11.)

Table 13-12 calculates the developer's after-tax equity reversion by deducting the taxes due on sale (from Table 13-13) from the developer's before-tax equity reversion. The taxes due on sale are then the product of the total gain on sale and the marginal tax rate.

Analysis of Developer's Yield Table 13-14 first computes the developer's net present value ($441,027) by multiplying the developer's outflows (equity −$4,375,000) and inflows (ATCFs and ATER) by the appropriate present value factors at the required rate of return (20 percent) and summing them. The IRR (22.6 percent) is found by setting the NPV equal to zero and calculating the expected rate of return.

THE CONVERTIBLE MORTGAGE

With income-equity participation mortgages, an ownership interest is not vested in the lender. With joint ventures, however, which are discussed in the next

TABLE 13-12 DEVELOPER'S AFTER-TAX EQUITY REVERSION: PARTICIPATION EXAMPLE

Developer's before-tax equity reversion (DBTER)*	$10,299,687
− taxes due on sale (TDS)†	2,970,547
developer's after-tax equity reversion	7,329,140

*See Table 13-8.
†See Table 13-13.

TABLE 13-13 DEVELOPER'S EXPECTED TAXES DUE ON SALE: PARTICIPATION EXAMPLE

Taxable income	
Expected selling price (SP)	$23,680,000
− selling expenses (SE)	1,184,000
amount realized (AR)	22,496,000
− adjusted basis (AB)*	11,886,905
total gain on sale (TG)	10,609,095

Taxes due on sale	
Total gain on sale	$10,609.095
× investor's marginal tax rate (τ)	0.28
taxes due on sale (TDS)	2,970,547

*AB = total project cost − accumulated depreciation
= $13,375,000 − $1,488,095

TABLE 13-14 DEVELOPER'S NPV AND IRR: PARTICIPATION EXAMPLE

Year	Equity (E)	After-tax cash flow (ATCF)	After-tax equity reversion (ATER)	PVF$_{20\%}$	PV
0	($4,375,000)			1.000000	($4,275,000)
1		33,440		0.83333	27,867
2		582,050		0.69444	404,199
3		652,386		0.57870	377,536
4		727,053		0.48225	350,621
5		1,767,616	7,329,140	0.40188	3,655,804
				NPV	$ 441,027
				IRR	22.6%

chapter, the lender provides debt *and* equity capital and obtains an equity interest in the property. The *convertible mortgage* is a hybrid financing device that fits somewhere between the two types of mortgages: It provides for fixed interest and possibly contingent interest, as does an income-equity participation, but it also provides that the lender has the option, at some specified future date, of converting the mortgage debt into partial or sole equity ownership, typically at a specific option price. The borrower (typically a developer) benefits from the arrangement by obtaining a below-market rate of interest over the loan term, resulting in improved cash flows, and may also realize some appreciation at buy-out. The lender benefits by being able to purchase an attractive equity investment if the project is profitable or to decline the option to do so if it is not. There are numerous and complex legal and tax implications for such an arrangement, so structuring a convertible mortgage must be done very carefully.

SUMMARY

This chapter discussed the financing methods known as participation mortgages. Using these techniques, the lender receives, in addition to the debt service, a percentage of the property's income and/or appreciation in value.

We outlined the general legal, tax, and risk problems for these methods and detailed the mechanics of the shared-appreciation mortgage for single-family houses and the income-equity participation mortgage for income-producing properties. There are numerous ways to structure these methods, depending on the percentage of participation to the lender and the level of income (gross, net, etc.) in which the lender will participate. Finally, we briefly discussed the convertible mortgage, which has the characteristics of an income-equity participation mortgage and a joint venture (discussed in the following chapter).

QUESTIONS

1 Define the following terms:
   a shared-appreciation mortgage
   b income-equity participation mortgage
   c equity kicker
   d call option
   e convertible mortgage
   f contingent interest
2 What factors influence the use of the participation mortgage?
3 Explain the distinction between the shared-appreciation and the income-equity participation mortgages.
4 What are several unique legal, financial, and tax aspects of the participation mortgage?
5 From the borrower's perspective, how is the payment on a shared-appreciation mortgage treated? Income-equity participation mortgage?
6 Suppose you were a mortgage lender. How would you "price" (set the interest rate on) the shared-appreciation or income-equity participation mortgage? Would the interest rate be higher or lower than that of a standard fixed-rate mortgage? Why?
7 Suppose you were a borrower and the lender gave you a choice between a fixed-rate and a shared-appreciation mortgage. How would you decide which one to select? Under what situations would each loan be preferred?
8 Discuss the mechanics of the participation mortgage. How is such a mortgage structured? What problems are created for the lender? The borrower?
9 Using Example 13-1, what is the maximum amount that the lender would loan?

PROBLEMS

1 Compare the monthly and annual payments on the following loans:

	SAM	FRM
Original price	$100,000	$100,000
Mortgage amount	$ 78,000	$ 78,000
Interest rate	12.25%	14.3%
Maturity	25 years	25 years

a Which loan would an investor choose?

b If the loan called for the lender to receive 33.3 percent of the total equity and the property increased at a rate of 3 percent over a 5-year holding period, what would the effective yield be on the SAM?

2 Assume the following about an apartment building with income-equity participation financing:

Purchase price	$425,000
Holding period	5 years
Expected selling price	$505,000
Selling expenses	6%
Net operating income:	
Year 1	$45,000
Year 2	$50,000
Year 3	$52,000
Year 4	$47,000
Year 5	$51,000

Mortgage: $350,000, 20 years, 10 percent base interest plus 5 percent of NOI and 20 percent of sales proceeds less selling expenses. There are no penalties for prepayment. Assume that the share of NOI is paid annually at the year's end. There are no financing costs.

Compute the cash returns to the lender under this participation financing arrangement and calculate the yield.

3 Recompute the lender's yield on the apartment building participation loan with a $10,000 financing cost included.

4 A homeowner purchases a $75,000 home today with a $70,000 SAM at 10 percent amortized over 20 years. The lender's share of the sales proceeds is 40 percent as set forth in the mortgage agreement. Determine the cash flows and yield to the lender under two sets of assumptions:

a The appreciation rate on the property is either 3 percent or 5 percent per year.

b The property is sold and the mortgage is paid off at the end of either 5 years or 10 years.

5 An industrial complex is expected to produce the following income:

Year	NOI
1	$525,000
2	600,000
3	575,000

You have approached a lender concerning a mortgage. The lender has agreed to make a $1,300,000 loan (95 percent LTV) with monthly payments at an interest rate of 13 percent for 30 years, with a "call" option at the end of year 3, which means that the entire balance is due and payable then. In addition, the lender wants 7 percent of each year's NOI. If the lender's required rate of return is 15 percent, what is the value of the lender's position?

6 Using the industrial complex information, determine the value of the equity position with the participation mortgage assuming that the complex is expected to sell for

$1,500,000 net at the end of year 3. The straight-line depreciation method with a 31.5 year recovery period is used. Suppose the investor required a before-tax return of 17 percent.

7 Ms. Y takes out a SAM for the amount of $100,000 at a contract interest rate of 12 percent with monthly payments over 20 years. The lender's share of the proceeds is 25 percent. Determine the cash flows and yield to the lender if (1) the appreciation rate is 4.5 percent per year, and (2) the property is sold and the mortgage paid off at the end of 6 years. Assume that an appraiser determined the value of Ms. Y's residence to be $115,000 at the time of purchase.

8 A condominium complex is expected to produce the following income:

Year	NOI
1	$60,000
2	65,000
3	63,000
4	68,000

You have approached a lender concerning a mortgage. The lender has agreed to make a $50,000 loan at an interest rate of 9.75 percent for 25 years with a call option at the end of year 4. In addition, the lender wants 4 percent of each year's NOI. If the lender's required rate of return is 11 percent, what is the value of the lender's position?

REFERENCES

Chandler, Michael C.: "Equity Participation—Creativity Unlimited," *Real Estate Today,* June 1981, pp. 27–35.

Garrigan, Richard T.: "Real Estate: Equity Participation Mortgages," *Pension World,* September 1982, pp. 96–98.

Mooradian, George T., and Allen L. Rosenblatt: "Characterization of Contingent Payments on Shared Application Mortgages," *The Journal of Taxation,* vol. 57, no. 1, July 1982, pp. 20–22.

Rasmussen, Jim: "Equity Participation: Risks and Returns," *Mortgage Banking,* June 1982, pp. 50–53.

Zorley, Thomas: "Alternative Mortgage Instruments and Lender Risks," *Bankers Magazine,* vol. 169, no. 6, November-December 1981, pp. 61–64.

JOINT VENTURES

/||

Chapter 13 introduced the financing method whereby the lender participates in a real estate project's income by requiring the debt service plus a percentage of the operating and/or reversion cash flows in return for the loan. The lender does not acquire an "equity" interest. This chapter discusses another type of financing method: the *joint venture*. In a joint venture, the lender and the developer-investor form a business partnership to develop or purchase and manage a specific real estate property. We examine the legal, tax, and other problems involved in organizing joint ventures and provide a detailed example of a joint venture.

WHAT IS A JOINT VENTURE?

The joint venture is similar to the participation mortgages described in Chapter 13 in that the lender expects to receive a portion of the cash flows from operation and reversion. Under a joint venture, however, the lender actually acquires an equity ownership interest. Typically, the lender makes the permanent loan as well as advances part of the "equity" required. Thus, the lender usually holds two positions: a debt position as the permanent lender and an equity position. In return for the long-term debt position as the permanent lender and an equity position. In return for the long-term debt, the lender requires the debt service. In return for the equity, the lender requires a portion of the operating and reversion cash flows. The developer provides the expertise in project conception, construction, and management and invests the remaining equity.

Joint ventures are one of the many types of equity participation arrangements. The selection of the entity that will own a real estate project is based on many considerations, including the tax effect of the choice of entity; the riskiness of the project; the desire for control over the development, construction, operation, and disposition of the project; and other legal and practical issues. Therefore, the selection of the joint venture as the vehicle for constructing, owning, and operating a real estate project demands considerable planning.

Many institutional lenders experienced disastrous effects from the unexpected inflation of the 1970s. Conventional methods of financing commercial real estate projects began to diminish and, in some cases, disappear. The typical fixed-rate, long-term mortgage was no longer attractive. Lenders became unwilling to commit large sums of money for long periods of time at prevailing interest rates when it appeared that these funds might yield higher rates of return in alternative investments.

The term *joint venture* originates from the term *joint adventure*. Black's Law Dictionary defines joint adventure as "An association of two or more persons to carry out a single business enterprise for profit, for which purpose they combine their property, money, effects, skill, and knowledge."

Simply stated, a real estate joint venture is typically a business partnership between an institutional lender and a developer that has been organized to share the costs and benefits of a real estate project. Some authorities argue that a joint venture is but a form of partnership, while others state that a joint venture is a distinct form of ownership in and of itself. In addition, the courts have decided that there is an entity known as a joint venture, but they have not been able to distinguish it from a partnership or to offer an adequate definition. Nevertheless, all experts agree that the purpose of the joint venture is for the parties to act together in a particular activity limited by either time or scope.

The typical real estate joint venture is an arrangement between a developer with knowledge and experience but no capital and a lender with the money to invest but no experience. A saying about joint ventures states that the process starts with the lender having the money and the developer having the expertise but ends up with the developer having the money and the lender having the expertise. Therefore, it is extremely important that the *joint venture agreement* between the developer and the lender clearly state the entire understanding of the parties. The following two sections outline the respective roles of these participants in the joint venture.

The Role of the Developer

Generally, the developer conceives the project to be developed. Market studies are done to determine demand, and preliminary cost estimates are prepared to test feasibility. Then the developer, after analysis, examines a parcel of land for zoning requirements and possible title defects, acquires the land (perhaps with an option), and refines the development and operating cost estimates as much as possible. With these preliminary figures, the developer makes certain assumptions concerning the proposed joint venture terms with the lender. After detailed study of cash flows and value, the developer is ready to approach the lender.

Once the lender is willing to participate in the joint venture, the developer's next job is to supervise the construction of the improvements and to coordinate the necessary legal, accounting, architectural, engineering, and other services that are necessary in the project's development. Sometimes the developer is also responsible for leasing and operating the project. However, control of day-to-day operations is an area for negotiation between the developer and the lender. Frequently, the developer assumes the management functions associated with operating the project and receives a fee for this service. But in major matters, the parties will probably want to make a joint decision. Obviously, many conflicts can arise over the operation and disposition of the investment. The operation and disposition factors should be addressed in detail in the joint venture agreement.

The Role of the Lender

The lender's primary function is to provide the financing for the project. If the lender does not make the construction loan, a permanent loan commitment is made so that the developer can arrange elsewhere for construction financing. If the commitment letter is conditioned upon the execution of a joint venture agreement between the permanent lender and the developer, a construction lender may object. The construction lender would prefer that the commitment state that the loan would be callable if the joint venture agreement is not executed within a particular period of time after the permanent loan has been funded.

In addition to financing the project's debt position, the lender also provides some part of the "equity." The transaction should be carefully structured so that usury is not a problem for the lender. (This topic is covered later in more detail).

In exchange for the mortgage and equity contributions, the lender acquires the right to share in the project's income. The benefits may be income participation, equity participation, or tax shelters. For example, the lender may share in effective gross income, net operating income, or before-tax cash flow. Alternatively, the lender could receive a share of the before-tax equity reversion on sale, the proceeds from refinancing, or the tax benefits of the project. Typically, the lender receives a share of cash flows from operation and reversion.

RISK ANALYSIS FOR JOINT VENTURES

As with any other investment arrangement, legal and other risks are associated with the joint venture. Some of the risk-minimization decisions include whether or not the participants should form a separate corporation to enter into the joint venture, the authority of the parties to engage in the transaction, and the entity structure of the joint venture itself. We now examine several of these questions.

Legal Implications

Most lenders entering into a joint venture are institutions, such as banks, savings and loan associations, mutual savings banks, pension funds, life insurance companies, and REITs. For some projects, individual investors may wish to be involved in the role of lender. The role of developer can be performed by a corporation, a partnership, an entrepreneur, or any other type of business entity.

There are many advantages for the developer or lender to form a corporation or subsidiary to enter into the joint venture. First, it may allow the developer to perform market tests without adverse consequences to the parent corporation. If the parent does not want the public to know it is co-owner of a particular project, it can form a subsidiary to protect its identity.

Second, corporations have limited liability. The lender usually wants the developer's personal guarantee concerning the performance of the corporation's or subsidiary's obligations to the lender. The use of the separate corporation protects the developer (or the lender) from third-party claims not related to the joint venture.

Third, if the joint venture is formed as a limited partnership with a separate corporation as coparticipant, the lender may make the mortgage loan without fear of violating the Uniform Limited Partnership Act (ULPA). The ULPA prohibits an individual as limited partner from taking and holding security.

Fourth, where the joint venture is a general partnership, under the Uniform Partnership Act (UPA), the mortgage loan is protected against subordination to the partnership's creditors. Finally, if the developer and the lender corporations can file consolidated income tax returns, neither corporation should encounter any tax problems.

There are two caveats concerning the formation of a subsidiary or separate corporation. First, a court could "pierce the corporate veil" and remove the separate corporation's limited liability advantage. This can occur if the subsidiary is undercapitalized, the parent disregards the corporate entity, or the subsidiary is a "mere instrumentality" of the parent corporation. In any of these situations, the court could hold the parent liable because the subsidiary's debts to the parent are subordinate to the debts of the subsidiary. There is another problem for the lending institution if state law restricts the number and type of subsidiaries the investor may have and the purposes for which they are formed.

Authority to Engage in the Transaction   Typically, the only significant restrictions on the developer's authority to operate are those in the developer's organizational documents. These documents should be reviewed, with additions or amendments made as necessary, to ensure the developer's authority to engage in the transaction.

For the lending institution, however, there are many legislative and regulatory restrictions governing equity participations. An examination of these restrictions is beyond the scope of this book; lenders should seek legal counsel to determine any restrictions that may apply to them.

Usury Considerations   A pervasive problem for lenders that has arisen in these times of high interest is usury. Usury is the practice of collecting on a loan interest that is above the statutory limit. Anything of value a lender receives in connection with making a mortgage loan may be considered interest. Therefore, unless a transaction is exempt under local law, there may be a usury problem. Usury laws do not apply to an institutional investor's simultaneously purchasing a joint venture interest when making the mortgage loan, provided the lender paid a fair market value for the joint venture interest. Usury laws also do not apply if the purchase of the joint venture interest is not a condition for making of the mortgage loan *and* the developer is free to sell the interest to a third party. There are many other ways of avoiding usury when structuring the joint venture, and lenders should thoroughly research this issue before making the loan commitment.

Other Risks   The developer, the lender, or the joint venture itself faces many additional risks. Generally, a joint venturer is jointly and severally liable for all liabilities of the joint venture, just as the partners in a general partnership are liable. However, the reason for selecting the joint venture as a vehicle for the project instead of a "true" partnership is the extent to which one joint venturer can bind the joint venture to third-party liabilities without the consent of the other venturer. The various limitations on authority that each joint venturer may exercise must be explicitly stated in the joint venture agreement. In addition, unlike a partnership, which is usually formed to engage in more than one real estate project, a joint venture is restricted to a single project. Accordingly, the use of a joint venture serves as constructive notice to third parties that the joint venturer, in any case, cannot bind the joint venture for obligations for an unrelated transaction.

Another consideration for the lender is that the role of equity investor is riskier than that of a mortgagee. The equity contribution the lender makes is unsecured. Therefore, the risk of nonrecovery is greater than it would be if the lender merely served as a mortgagee. By making the equity contribution, the lender hopes to receive a greater return on the equity's initial investment in the project because of either anticipated value appreciation at the time of the sale of the property or attractive cash flow benefits.

Both the developer and the lender should perform formal risk analysis, taking into account their respective expected cash flows, the intended holding period, and reversion, to determine the joint venturer's rate of return on the project. Since these two participants in a joint venture usually do not have the same risk-return orientation, the project may prove unpalatable to the developer or to the lender or to both.

Structuring the Joint Venture

To structure the joint venture, different types of ownership schemes may be used. Each method has its own tax consequences, liability exposures, and restrictions. Here we discuss several of these plans.

Typically, joint ventures are corporations, limited partnerships, or general partnerships. Despite a corporation's advantage of limited liability, this entity structure suffers the disadvantages of double taxation and other tax complications. Therefore, most joint ventures are structured as either a limited or a general partnership.

Limited Partnership Limited partnerships in the United States are regulated by case law and the ULPA, which almost all the states have adopted. A limited partnership usually consists of general partners and one or more limited partners. The limited partners have little or no decision-making capability, and their liability is limited to the amount of their investment. However, the ULPA specifically states that a limited partner cannot have control over the business; if the partner does, the liability exposure becomes unlimited. The general partners in the limited partnership have unlimited liability, but they have control over the partnership business and its assets.

From a liability standpoint, the developer is essentially indifferent whether the joint venture is structured as a limited or a general partnership since the developer plays the same role in either case. For the lender, a limited partnership has definite drawbacks. As a limited partner, the lender, by law, must relinquish to the developer (the general partner) the control and management of the joint venture. Accordingly, the lender is caught between limiting its liability and taking part in the control of the business.

General Partnership   The UPA is the authority governing the conduct of general partnerships. The UPA defines a partnership as an association of two or more persons to carry on as co-owners of a business for profit. Unlike a limited partnership, in which the liability of the limited partners is confined to their respective investments, a general partnership exposes all the partners to liability.

Many of the drawbacks of the limited partnership are avoided through the use of the general partnership. The lender, as coventurer, can hold a mortgage on the property of the joint venture and also exercise control over the management of the joint venture. However, there is the disadvantage of unlimited liability. Unless there is understanding to the contrary, such as would be contained in the joint venture agreement, general partners share equally in the project's profits and losses and are liable for the joint venture's debts.

There are other advantages to the limited or general partnership form. For example, real estate may be transferred to the partnership free of tax. In addition, partnerships are not taxable entities, so the various policies and tax determinations are made at the partnership level and passed on to the partners. However, certain tax problems with a partnership must be considered in the joint venture agreement.

Tax Considerations

Since partnerships are not taxed, there are no special tax problems relating to the joint venture itself if it is formed as a partnership.

However, there are several issues that each participant of the joint venture, as a partner, should consider:

1 The joint venture should be structured so that it is taxed as a partnership, not as a corporation.

2 The tax impact on the partner who performs services for the joint venture and receives a disproportionate share of capital or profits must be evaluated.

3 The joint venturer must examine the tax effect of transferring or selling personal interest.

4 The effect the debt has on the basis must be examined.

5 The effects of special allocations of depreciation or other deductions must be examined.

The joint venture agreement allocates the venture's profits and losses. In the absence of such an agreement, a venture's profits and losses are shared equally. However, the Tax Reform Act of 1986 prohibits the deduction of "passive" activity losses and credits against sources of nonpassive activity income. A passive activity can be defined as one of the following:

1 A trade or business activity in which the taxpayer does not materially participate. A taxpayer is deemed a material participant in an activity if it is the taxpayer's principal business. Limited partnerships are automatically treated as passive activities.

2 Any rental activity. A rental activity is one in which the income derived from such comes from payments for the use of tangible property. An exception to the rule involves rental activities in which an individual taxpayer actively participates. The passive rule does not apply as long as the sum of the passive activity loss and the deduction equivalent of the passive activity credit (the amount that would reduce the tax bill for that year by an amount equal to the credit) is not greater than $25,000.

Moreover, when a joint venturer transfers property to the partnership, the basis of the asset remains the same. Accordingly, the depreciation does not change since it is limited to the basis the contributing joint venturer established.

Another consideration is that each partner's initial basis is equal to the amount of cash and property that partner contributes. However, the basis can be changed by the allocation of liabilities to each partner.

Finally, since most joint ventures are formed to develop a new property, such as an office building or a shopping center, all the tax rules concerning the construction period apply. A tax expert's advice is required to fully cover the tax consequences of the joint venture agreement.

THE JOINT VENTURE AGREEMENT

This section outlines several items that should be part of the joint venture agreement.

Equity Contributions

An important consideration for both the developer and the lender is how much equity capital each should contribute. Sometimes the developer has the land to contribute but relatively little, if any, cash. In other cases, the developer may offer the land and split the remaining equity the lender requires. For example, suppose a project will cost $10 million to develop and the lender can provide only a 75 percent loan-to-value ratio. If the land is worth $1 million, the remaining equity that must be divided is $1,500,000. The lender and the developer could each contribute $750,000, or one-half of the remaining equity.

Besides equity contributions, another problem is possible cost overruns. Normally, the developer is responsible for funding cost overruns because ordinarily the lending institution has set a maximum ceiling on its capital contributions, and the lender may insist that any cost overruns the developer bears not be considered equity contributions. This is an area of negotiation. The lender may agree to eliminate these stipulations if the agreement specifies that the lender will be responsible for only a maximum percentage of the original cost estimate.

Construction Financing

The agreement must specify whether the lender is making a construction loan, to be followed by a permanent mortgage on the property, or whether the developer is to obtain alternative construction financing and the lender will provide the takeout commitment.

Title to Property

The UPA allows a partnership to hold title to real property in its name. In states that have not adopted the UPA, title is usually held by partners as tenants in common. If a cotenant dies, the cotenant's undivided interest will pass to the heirs, and the project could continue. However, the heirs may wish to partition the property (ask the court to divide it). If an equitable division of the property is not feasible, the court may require that the property be sold, and either party may be a purchaser at the sale.

Compensation to Developer

When the lender has agreed to contribute equity capital in excess of the amount required to develop the property, this excess can be used to compensate the developer for services in connection with the project's development and construction. The parties must decide how the developer is to receive these funds, either as fees or as capital withdrawals. The same logic applies to the management fees the developer may receive.

Control and Management

If the general partnership vehicle is used in the joint venture, control of the project's day-to-day activities could be the joint responsibility of the lender and the developer. However, the institutional lender may not have a staff with the time or expertise to handle this function. Therefore, the parties may agree to hire an outside management firm to oversee the project, or they may determine that the developer has the staff to perform this task. In any event, a competitive management contract must be executed for these services, whether or not the developer performs the function.

Even though the lender may not wish to be involved in the project's routine management, the lender certainly would want to share in major policy decisions. Accordingly, the agreement should call for unanimous consent of the parties for such decisions as making substantial capital improvements, borrowing additional funds, or selling or refinancing the project.

Participation in Costs and Benefits

As stated, the manner in which the lender shares in the project's costs and benefits is a business decision. The parties may decide to allocate these costs and benefits based on the percentage of equity invested, to share equally, or to provide for the parties' unequal capital contributions through a fair distribution.

The parties may agree to distribute the annual cash flows on the basis of effective gross income, with an equitable distribution of the operating expenses and debt service; or net operating income, with the debt service allocated between the developer and the lender according to the percentage of ownership; or before-tax cash flow. In addition, the lender and the developer would divide the taxable income equitably. The method used should be carefully selected. The agreement should also specify how operating deficits will be handled.

Many lenders insist that the proceeds of sale be distributed to the lender first so that it may recover its capital contributions. However, the lender may agree that its capital contributions may be reduced through the receipt of annual cash flow distributions. After the lender has received its unrecovered capital contributions, the balance of sales proceeds may be distributed first to the developer for its capital contributions, and the remainder in accordance with the percentages of ownership. Another method is to split the before-tax equity reversion and the gain or loss on the sale according to the ownership percentages. In any event, the parties, with the assistance of their respective tax and legal counsel, must specify in the joint venture agreement how the sales proceeds or the proceeds from refinancing will be distributed.

Default Provisions

If either party to the joint venture defaults in making its capital contributions, paying expenses, or the like, the other party should have recourse for bringing action against the defaulting party for damages or specific performance. If the default is the failure to make a capital contribution or other money payment, the nondefaulting party should be able to make the payment on behalf of the defaulting party and thereby purchase a part of the defaulting party's interest. The lender should also define in both the mortgage documents and the joint venture agreement its fiduciary responsibilities to the joint venture so that if the project fails, its rights as mortgagee are protected.

Buy-Sell Provisions and Transfer of Joint Venture Interest

Many joint venture agreements specify that in the event of a major dispute between the parties, either party may purchase the interest of the other. Usually, one party specifies the purchase price, and the other party can either buy the interest or sell its own share at a prorated portion of the purchase price. In addition, the parties should agree to a right of first refusal in the event one of the parties receives an offer to purchase its interest from a third party. The right of first refusal must be on the same terms and conditions as the offer. Typically, however, the venturers will want to stipulate a minimum holding period before any sale or transfer can be made.

The foregoing are just several provisions that should be covered in the joint venture agreement. Other provisions should cover the bankruptcy of one of the parties, the purchase price of a partner's share in the event of death, and other business concerns. For dissolving the joint venture, the UPA or the ULPA rules apply at the time of sale of the project, if the joint venture is structured as a partnership.

JOINT VENTURE EXAMPLE

Following is a detailed analysis of a real estate joint venture that is being formed to develop a project called the Five Points Office Building. The joint venture takes the form of a general partnership between a developer and a permanent lender (Long-Life Insurance Company). The partnership is to be organized immediately, and construction is expected to take 1 year.

Summary of Joint Venture Assumptions

Tables 14-1 to 14-3 summarize the input, equity, and operating and tax assumptions, respectively, for the joint venture.

Development Costs and Financial Data Table 14-1 shows the development costs and financial data. The property is appraised at $2,100,000. Long-Life has

TABLE 14-1 SUMMARY OF INPUT ASSUMPTIONS:
FIVE POINTS OFFICE BUILDING JOINT VENTURE

Development data:	
Construction period	1 year
Appraised value	$2,100,000
Cost breakdown:	
Land	$ 375,000
Hard costs	1,405,000
Construction interest	90,000
Construction loan fee	30,000
Other capital costs (architect, engineering, etc.)	130,000
Property tax during construction	20,000
Total project cost	$2,050,000
Financial data:	
Construction loan:	$1,500,000
Interest rate	12%
Loan fee (2%)	30,000
Term	1 year
Permanent loan:	1,500,000
Interest rate	12%
Loan fee	0
Term/monthly payments	25 years
Annual debt service	$ 189,580

TABLE 14-2   JOINT VENTURE ASSUMPTIONS AND EQUITY REQUIREMENTS:
FIVE POINTS JOINT VENTURE

1   Number of general partners: two, developer and lender.
2   Equity capital contribution: developer—50 percent, lender—50 percent.
3   Cash assessments: developer bears cash assessments due to construction cost overruns; all others are split 50-50.
4   Cash distribution of before-tax cash flow: developer—50 percent, lender—50 percent.
5   Tax profits and losses distribution: developer—50 percent, lender—50 percent.
6   Sale and liquidation of assets: developer—50 percent of before-tax equity reversion, lender—50 percent of before-tax equity reversion.
7   Projected holding period: 1-year construction period; 5 years of operation, then disposition through sale.
8   Developer assumes management of the property.
9   Initial equity requirements:

Total project cost	$2,050,000
+ other applicable fees	0
total cash requirements	2,050,000
− mortgage financing	1,500,000
equity requirements	550,000

Equity requirements breakdown:

Developer (50%)	$275,000	
Lender (50%)	275,000	
		550,000

issued a commitment for the permanent loan of $1,500,000. A construction loan is obtained for $1,500,000 from the ABC Bank (not the participating joint venture lender) for 1 year at at 12 percent interest rate. The total project cost is $2,050,000, which includes a construction loan fee of 2 percent ($30,000). The developer has also obtained prelease commitments for 95 percent occupancy in the new building.

Joint Venture Operation and Equity Requirements   The joint venture comprises two parties: the developer and the (permanent loan) lender (Long-Life). Table 14-2 shows the joint venture agreement. Equity contributions and cash assessments are to be 50 percent each; cash flow distributions and equity-reversion distributions are also 50 percent each. The developer will assume the management responsibilities of the investment. The payment for these services is included as part of the operating expenses. The projected holding period is 6 years: 1 year for the construction period and 5 years of operation. The equity requirement for the developer and the lender is $275,000 each, or $550,000. Of this amount, $375,000 has been used to buy the land, and the remainder is applied to other front-end costs or held in reserve.

At the end of the construction period (1 year), the construction loan is paid off and a permanent loan is secured from Long-Life for $1,500,000 at 12 percent for 25 years (monthly payments). The joint venture lender now receives income from two sources: the debt-service component and the equity cash flows.

TABLE 14-3   OPERATING AND TAX ASSUMPTIONS: FIVE POINTS JOINT VENTURE

Potential gross income (PGI)	$400,000 in year 2 of operation
Income growth rate	5% per year
Vacancy and collection expense (V and CE)	5%
Operating expenses (OE)	40% of effective gross income
Depreciation method	31.5 year straight-line
Depreciation deduction:	
Hard costs	$1,405,000
+ other capital costs	130,000
total amount depreciable	1,535,000
Depreciation deduction per year	$ 48,730

Amortization periods and amounts	Amount	Year	Per year
Construction interest and property taxes	$110,000	10	$11,000
Construction loan fee	30,000	1	30,000

Rent-up period: 95% expected occupancy at start of second year of operation

Projected property value at sale: 10 times NOI

Operating and Tax Assumptions   Table 14-3 contains the operating and tax assumptions. Because the investment is 95 percent preleased, there is no excess vacancy and collection expense during the first year. The depreciable basis (hard costs and other capital costs) are depreciated using the 13.5-year straight-line method. The construction interest and property taxes are amortized over a 10-year period. It is assumed that the project will sell for 10 times its projected net operating income at the end of the holding period.

When evaluating the partners' entire set of financial statements (not shown here), it is important to note the following:

1 In the first year of construction, the developer is a material participant in this project and is allowed to deduct losses or credits against sources of nonpassive activity income. The lender is not deemed a material participant since its principal business activity is the sale of life insurance policies and not the financing of office buildings.

2 Furthermore, during the 5 years of operation, only the developer is allowed a special deduction due to the developer's active participation in the management of the property.

Cash Flows from Operation

Using these assumptions, we can forecast the expected cash flow from operation.

Before-Tax Cash Flow from Operation Table 14-4 contains the expected gross income, operating expenses, and before-tax operating cash flows. The first year is the construction period, so there are no cash flows. The project is expected to generate $380,000 in effective gross income during the second year (the first year after completion). The expected BTCF is $38,420 in year 2 and is expected to increase each year. Table 14-4 also gives the distribution of the cash flows. The developer and the lender each receive 50 percent.

Taxable Income from Operation Table 14-5 summarizes the taxable income from operation. Note that the construction loan fee is tax deductible during the construction year. The construction-period interest and property taxes are amortized at $11,000 each year. The investment is generating a tax loss each year. This shelters all the cash flows from the investment plus the developer's other taxable income since the losses are "passed through" the joint venture. The tax losses decline each year of the holding period. This shelter does not apply to the lender.

After-Tax Cash Flow from Operation Table 14-6 contains the developer's expected after-tax operating flow (ATCF). We assume that the developer is in a 28 percent tax bracket. Thus the tax losses expected (Table 14-5) shelter the developer's other taxable income. In year 1, the ATCF is $5,740, resulting entirely from the tax losses. In year 2, the tax savings is $1,566, resulting in an ATCF of $20,776.

TABLE 14-4 EXPECTED BEFORE-TAX CASH FLOWS: FIVE POINTS JOINT VENTURE

		Year				
	1	2	3	4	5	6
PGI		$400,000	$420,000	$441,000	$463,050	$486,200
− V and CE	(Construction)	20,000	21,000	22,050	23,153	24,310
EGI		380,000	399,000	418,950	439,897	461,890
− OE*	(Year)	152,000	159,600	167,580	175,959	184,756
NOI		228,000	239,400	251,370	263,938	277,134
− DS		189,580	189,580	189,580	189,580	189,580
BTCF		38,420	49,820	61,790	74,358	87,554
Assessments:						
Developer (50%)	$0	$0	$0	$0	$0	$0
Lender (50%)	0	0	0	0	0	0
Distribution of before-tax cash flows:						
Developer (50%)	$0	$19,210	$24,910	$30,895	$37,179	$43,777
Lender (50%)	0	19,210	24,910	30,895	37,179	43,777

*Includes management fee paid to developer.

TABLE 14-5 TAXABLE INCOME FROM OPERATION: FIVE POINTS JOINT VENTURE

	Year					
	1	2	3	4	5	6
NOI	$ 0	$228,000	$239,400	$251,370	$263,938	$277,134
− I	0	179,455	178,165	176,725	175,090	173,260
− D	0	48,730	48,730	48,730	48,730	48,730
− CL fee*	30,000	0	0	0	0	0
− CLIPT†	11,000	11,000	11,000	11,000	11,000	11,000
taxable income	(41,000)	(11,185)	1,505	14,915	29,118	44,144
Distribution of taxable income:						
Developer (50%)	($20,500)	($5,592)	$752	$7,457	$14,559	$22,072
Lender (50%)	(20,500)	(5,592)	752	7,457	14,559	22,072

*Construction loan fee.
†Construction period interest and property taxes.

TABLE 14-6 DEVELOPER'S AFTER-TAX CASH FLOW: FIVE POINTS JOINT VENTURE

	Year					
	1	2	3	4	5	6
BTCF*	$ 0	$19,210	$24,910	$30,895	$37,179	$43,777
− taxes† (savings)	(5,740)	(1,566)	211	2,088	4,077	6,180
ATCF	5,740	20,776	24,699	28,807	33,102	37,597

*See Table 14-4.
†See Table 14-5 for taxable income. Marginal tax rate assumed to be 28%.

Cash Flows from Sale

We now calculate the expected cash flow for the sale of the investment at the end of the holding period.

Before-Tax Equity Reversion Table 14-7 gives the distribution of the cash flow from sale. The expected selling price at the end of year 6 is 10 times the NOI ($277,134). Selling expenses are expected to be 6 percent of the sales price. Long-Life will collect the unpaid loan balance of $1,434,795. The total cash flow from sale is $1,170,265. These proceeds are to be split in half between the developer and Long-Life; each party expects to receive $585,132 from sale of the building.

Taxable Income from Sale Table 14-8 calculates the taxable income from the sale of the investment. The selling expenses are deducted from the sale price to yield the amount realized on the sale. From this amount we deduct the adjusted basis, which yields the total gain of $894,710. The adjusted basis is the original improvements cost ($1,535,000) minus the cumulative depreciation deductions

TABLE 14-7 BEFORE-TAX EQUITY REVERSION FROM SALE:
FIVE POINTS JOINT VENTURE

Expected sales price*	$2,771,340
− selling expenses (6%)	166,280
net sales proceeds	2,605,060
− unpaid mortgage balance	1,434,795
before-tax equity reversion (BTER)	1,170,265

Distribution of before-tax equity reversion:

Developer (50%)	$585,132	
Lender (50%)	585,133	
		1,170,265

*Sale price at end of year 6 is expected to be 10 times that year's NOI.

TABLE 14-8 TAXABLE INCOME FROM SALE:
FIVE POINTS JOINT VENTURE

Sales price	$2,771,340
− selling expenses (6%)	166,280
amount realized	2,605,060
− adjusted basis*	1,710,350
total gain	894,710

Distribution of gain:

Developer (50%)	$447,355	
Lender (50%)	447,355	
		894,710

*The adjusted basis is the original improvements cost ($1,535,000) − the cumulative depreciation deduction ($48,730 per year for 5 years) + the unamortized balance of the construction-period interest and property taxes + land cost ($375,000).

($48,730 per year for 5 years) plus the unamortized balance of the construction-period interest and property taxes ($44,000) plus the land cost ($375,000).

The total gain on the sale is $894,710. This is allocated 50 percent each ($447,355) to the developer and the lender under the joint venture agreement.

After-Tax Cash Flow from Sale Table 14-9 contains the developer's estimate of the after-tax cash flow from the sale of the office building. The developer's share of the before-tax equity reversion is $585,132. Assuming a 28 percent marginal tax rate, the developer's taxes due on sale are $125,259. The resulting after-tax cash flow from sale is $459,873.

TABLE 14-9 DEVELOPER'S AFTER-TAX EQUITY
REVERSION FROM SALE:
FIVE POINTS JOINT VENTURE

Before-tax equity reversion*	$585,132
− taxes due on sale†	125,259
after-tax equity reversion	459,873

See Table 14-7.
†See Table 14-8. Ordinary income tax rate of 28% is
assumed.

Lender's Yield on Joint Venture

Table 14-10 summarizes the lender's expected before-tax flows from the office building joint venture. When the joint venture is organized, the lender must invest $275,000 in equity. At the end of year 1, when construction is completed, the lender advances the permanent loan funds of $1,500,000. The construction loan is paid off from these funds.

Beginning in year 2, the lender receives an annual debt service on the permanent loan of $189,580. This continues for 5 years until the project is sold and the mortgage balance of $1,434,795 is repaid.

The lender is also receiving 50 percent of the before-tax cash flows from the operation of the investment (summarized in Table 14-10). At the end of the holding period (year 6), the office building is sold and the lender receives 50 percent of the expected before-tax equity reversion.

Column 7, Table 14-10 lists the lender's total before-tax cash flows. Suppose the lender has a 14 percent before-tax required rate of return on the composite

TABLE 14-10 LENDER'S BEFORE-TAX CASH FLOWS: FIVE POINTS JOINT VENTURE

(1) Year	(2) Lender's investment	(3) Debt service	(4) Mortgage balance	(5) Lender's share in BTCF*	(6) Lender's share in BTER†	(7) Total cash flow to lender	(8) PVF$_{14\%}$	(9) PV
0	$275,000	$0	$0	$0	$0	($275,000)	1.0	($275,000)
1	1,500,000	0	0	0	0	(1,500,000)	0.877193	(1,315,790)
2	0	189,580	0	19,210	0	208,790	0.769468	160,657
3	0	189,580	0	24,910	0	214,490	0.674972	144,775
4	0	189,580	0	30,895	0	220,475	0.592080	130,439
5	0	189,580	0	37,179	0	226,759	0.519369	117,772
6	0	189,580	1,434,795	43,777	585,133	2,253,285	0.455587	1,026,567
							NPV	($10,580)
							IRR	13.85%

*See Table 14-4.
†See Table 14-7.

TABLE 14-11 DEVELOPER'S NPV AND IRR ON AFTER-TAX CASH FLOWS: FIVE POINTS JOINT VENTURE

Year	Equity	ATCF*	ATER†	PVF$_{15\%}$	PV
0	($275,000)	$ 0		1.0	($275,000)
1	0	5,740		0.8696	4,992
2	0	20,776		0.7561	15,709
3	0	24,699		0.6575	16,240
4	0	28,807		0.5718	16,472
5	0	33,102		0.4972	16,458
6	0	37,597	$459,873	0.4323	215,056
				NPV	$ 9,927
				IRR	15.77%

*See Table 14-6.
†See Table 14-9.

investment. At this rate, the net present value is −$10,580, indicating that the project might not be acceptable. The lender's internal rate of return on the total cash flows is 13.85 percent, which represents the composite rate of return on the mortgage loan at a 12 percent interest rate and the "equity" position. The IRR on the equity position from the BTCF and BTER is about 19.5 percent. The lender would probably, however, make the investment decision based on the expected composite return.

Developer's After-Tax NPV and IRR

Table 14-11 summarizes the developer's after-tax cash flows and shows the computation of the developer's net present value at a required rate of return (after tax) of 15 percent. The developer invests $275,000 in equity. The developer's NPV is $9,927, which indicates that the investment is acceptable at a 15 percent required rate of return. The developer's expected after-tax rate of return (IRR) is about 15.77 percent.

SUMMARY

A joint venture is essentially a partnership between the developer (investor) and the lender. The developer provides the expertise and real estate knowledge; the lender provides the necessary capital. The cash flows from the investment are allocated according to the partnership agreement.

In the next chapter we discuss another popular financing technique, real estate syndication.

QUESTIONS

1 Define the following terms:
  a joint venture
  b joint venture agreement
  c buy-sell provision
  d default provision

2 Describe the similarities and differences between the income-equity participation mortgages (discussed in Chapter 13) and joint ventures.
3 What is the developer's role in a joint venture? The lender's role?
4 What unique legal risks does the joint venture create for the various participants? How are these risks minimized?
5 Discuss the tax aspects of joint ventures.
6 Analyze the types of considerations the joint venture agreement covers. What conflicts between the lender and the developer (investor) does the agreement try to minimize?
7 Discuss how the lender's yield on a joint venture is calculated. What variables influence the yield?
8 What factors would influence how the cash flows (both inflows and outflows) in a joint venture are allocated between the lender and the developer?
9 From the developer's perspective, under what conditions would the joint venture be an attractive financing alternative? From the lender's perspective?
10 What risks does a joint venture create that are not present with the traditional fixed-rate mortgage?

PROBLEMS

1 What is the developer's before-tax NPV and IRR on the Five Points Office Building example if the developer's required rate of return before tax is 13 percent?
2 If selling expenses for the Five Points Office Building were 10 percent of the sales price, how would this affect both the lender's and the developer's yield on the project?
3 Rework the Five Points Office Building example assuming a 60 to 40 percent split rather than the 50 to 50 percent split between the developer and the lender. What are the developer's after-tax NPV and IRR? What is the lender's yield on the joint venture?
4 Assume the following about a real estate joint venture that is being formed to develop a project called Oak Hollow Condominiums. The joint venture takes the form of a general partnership between J. Heartly Developers and American National Bank. The project also involves two limited partners. These are the input assumptions:

Development data:

Construction period	1 year
Appraised value	$1,200,000

Cost breakdown:

Land	$ 250,000
Hard costs	820,000
Construction interest	43,000
Construction loan fee	25,000
Other capital costs	32,000
Property tax during construction	19,000
Total project cost	$1,171,000

Financial data:

Construction loan:	$ 860,000
Interest rate	10%
Loan fee	17,200
Term	1 year
Permanent loan:	860,000
Interest rate	10%
Loan fee	0
Term	20 years/ monthly payments

Joint venture and equity requirements:

1 Number of partners: 4; 2 general partners, 2 limited partners.
2 Equity capital distribution: developer, 40 percent; lender, 40 percent; limited partners, 10 percent each.
3 Cash assessments: developer bears cash assessments due to construction cost overruns; all others are split 50-50.
4 Cash distribution of before-tax cash flows: developer, 40 percent; lender, 40 percent; limited partners, 10 percent each.
5 Tax profits and losses distribution: developer, 40 percent; lender, 40 percent; limited partners, 10 percent each.
6 Sale and liquidation of assets: developer, 40 percent; lender, 40 percent; limited partners, 10 percent each.
7 Projected holding period: 1-year construction period; 3 years of operation, then disposition through sale.
8 Developer assumes management of property.
9 Initial equity requirements:

total project cost	$1,171,000
+ other applicable fees	0
total cash requirements	$1,171,000
− mortgage financing	866,000
equity requirements	$ 311,000

Equity requirements breakdown:

Developer (40%)	$ 124,400	
Lender (40%)	124,400	
Limited partner 1 (10%)	31,000	
Limited partner 2 (10%)	31,000	$ 311,000

Operating and tax assumptions:
Potential gross income (PGI): $250,000 (in year 2)
Income growth rate: 10% per year
Vacancy and collection expenses (V&CE): 5%
Operating expenses (OE): 35% of effective gross income
Construction loan fee: to be amortized over a 1-year period
Depreciation method: 31.5-year straight line
Construction interest and property taxes: to be amortized over a 10-year period
Rent-up period: 95% expected occupancy at start of second year of operation
Projected property value at sale: 10 times NOI
Developer's marginal tax bracket: 28%

Compute the following:
a Expected before-tax cash flows
b Taxable income from operation
c Developer's after-tax cash flow
d Before-tax equity reversion from sale if selling expenses are 5% of the sales price
e Taxable income from sale   f Developer's after-tax equity reversion from sale

5 What is the lender's before-tax yield on the Oak Hollow Condominium project? Compute the developer's before-tax NPV and IRR. The required rate of return for both developer and lender is 11.5 percent.
6 How does the "passive activity" rule apply to the partners in the Oak Hollow Condominium project?

REFERENCES

Barton, Gary J., and Robert E. Morrison: "Equity Participation Arrangements Between Institutional Lenders and Real Estate Developers," *St. Mary's Law Journal,* vol. 12, 1981, pp. 929–1025.

Beck, David M., and Levi R. Darrow: "The Joint Venture: A Technique to Enhance the Return from Corporate Real Estate," *Industrial Development,* vol. 15, November-December 1981, pp. 9–12.

Dilley, Steven C., Vernon Hoven, and James C. Young: *Prentice-Hall Tax Reform Act of 1986 Guide,* Englewood Cliffs, N.J., 1986.

Lottens, Donald M.: "Policing the Financial Marriage," *Business Horizons,* vol. 17, August 1974, pp. 79–86.

Roegge, Frank E., Gerrard J. Talbot, and Robert M. Zinman: "Real Estate Equity Investments and the Institutional Lenders: Nothing Ventured, Nothing Gained," *Fordham Law Review,* vol. 39, 1971, pp. 579–648.

Roulac, Stephen E.: "Structuring the Joint Venture," *Mergers and Acquisitions,* vol. 15, Spring 1980, pp. 4–14.

REAL ESTATE SYNDICATIONS

A syndicate is a group of investors who pool their capital to enhance the quality and quantity of their investments and to reduce their risks through diversification. The syndicate can take various legal forms, but in real estate, the limited partnership is the preferred type of business entity.

This chapter first analyzes the basic structure of real estate syndications and then their legal, financial, and tax features. We examine the securities aspect, the various types of offers a syndicate can supply, and the advantages and disadvantages associated with this form of real estate investing. We conclude with a detailed example of a real estate investment undertaken by a syndicate.

WHAT IS A SYNDICATION?

A real estate syndication is an organization that brings together a group of passive investors who combine their financial resources to acquire, develop, operate, and market real estate investments, such as shopping centers, hotels, apartments or office buildings, or any other type of real estate. Syndications have an equity interest in their investments. Generally, the investors do not have the time, desire, or knowledge necessary to conduct the business of the syndicate. For this they rely on a real estate professional—a sponsor, or *syndicator*—who has the expertise to establish and organize the syndicate, find a suitable property, negotiate for its acquisition, and manage it until disposition.

Organizational Forms

The organizational or business form of the syndication can be a corporation, a joint ownership, or a partnership. A corporate real estate syndication sells shares to raise capital to invest in real estate projects. Investors benefit by the advantages the corporate form offers, such as limited liability and relatively easy marketability of shares, but a major disadvantage is the double taxation of earnings. For this reason, and because tax losses are not passed through to investors, the corporate form is not an attractive medium for real estate syndication.

The joint-ownership form becomes legally cumbersome when a member dies or is disabled. Also, a member's refusing to cooperate for some reason may create a stalemate in the operation or disposition of the investment.

Limited partnerships are the preferred syndicate form. A limited partnership consists of at least one general partner, who is liable for the debts and obligations of the partnership, and at least one limited partner, who is a passive investor and *not* liable for the debts and obligations of the partnership. This form of partnership enables the real estate syndicator to combine his or her skills with the financial resources of passive equity investors to successfully invest in real estate. The limited partnership is not considered a taxable entity, so profits and losses accrue directly to the investors, thus enabling them to take advantage of any tax sheltering effects that an investment may offer. Later we examine the problems possible if the limited partnership takes on too many corporate characteristics and is classified for tax purposes as a corporation. In such a situation, the profits and losses would not directly accrue to the investors. Since the limited partnership is the most popular form, this chapter's discussion revolves around this form of real estate syndication.

Types of Syndicate Offerings

Normally, a sponsor (syndicator) locates a property that appears to be an acceptable investment, secures an option on it, and then solicits the interest of potential investors. The investors, upon receiving the offer, analyze the characteristics of the specific property and decide whether or not to invest. In this type of syndication, a specific property is available for examination, and relevant economic and financial data are available for the investor's consideration.

The syndicator may also offer interests to investors in unspecified properties; this in effect raises capital to purchase real estate before any specific property has been chosen. Such *blind pool* syndications are venture capital funds: The potential investors have no property descriptions or economic or financial data to analyze.

Reasons for Syndication

Syndication provides the passive investor with the benefits of real estate ownership. Syndicate members can participate in larger investments because their funds are pooled. As a result, an investor can purchase "more" real estate through a syndicate than as an individual. Thus, syndication is an attractive method of diversification for the investor.

The individual investor seldom has the knowledge or sophistication to put together the type of property venture that will yield the most benefits. An investor who joins a syndicate becomes associated with a real estate professional who has the experience and knowledge to develop and organize a successful real estate venture.

Under the limited partnership form of syndication, each individual investor is free of personal liability for any obligations the syndicate incurs. The maximum loss an individual investor can sustain is limited to that investor's equity investment. Even if the property is financed with a mortgage, the syndicate typically obtains a *nonrecourse* loan; that is, the limited partners are not personally liable for the debt.

Real estate syndication is a practical alternative to all-or-nothing investments that the individual investor is likely to face. By being able to invest in several different ventures at the same time, the investor decreases the risk of losing the entire investment.

RISK ANALYSIS OF SYNDICATION

The syndication form of equity financing creates unique legal, financial, and tax problems. We now turn our attention to the risks of syndication that the syndicator and the limited partner (investor) must analyze to ensure acceptability.

Keep in mind that the syndication cash flows depend upon the real estate the syndicate acquires. Thus all the basic property analyses discussed in Chapters 5 and 6 must be applied.

Legal Aspects

The syndication form of financing creates legal relationships not found in conventional financing. Specifically, the relationship between the syndicator and the syndication investor must be carefully analyzed.

Form of Business Organization   As mentioned, the syndication is most commonly organized as a limited partnership. This form is popular not only because of the investor's limited liability for the firm's business obligations, but also because the partnership is not a taxable entity: Taxes are paid (or losses claimed) only at the partner level.

Generally, the courts determine the law governing partnerships. Most states have adopted the Uniform Partnership Act (UPA) and the Uniform Limited Partnership Act (ULPA), created by the American Law Institute and the National Conference of Commissioners on Uniform State Laws. The UPA has been adopted by 48 states, the exceptions being Georgia and Louisiana. The ULPA has been adopted in every state except Louisiana. These acts govern, for the most part, the organization, operation, and dissolution of partnerships.

A partnership is an association established by the agreement of two or more persons to carry on as joint owners of a business. An oral agreement is acceptable under law, but it is far better that the agreement be carefully prepared *and in writing*. An oral agreement leads to disputes in proving the exact contents of the contract. A written agreement, stating the articles of partnership, makes clear the obligations of all the parties. Also, tax questions are more easily settled with a written agreement.

The Limited Partnership Agreement   The formation, operation, and dissolution of the syndicate is governed by the agreement between the general and the limited partners. This document is called the *limited partnership agreement*. This agreement must cover many potential conflicts between the syndicator and the syndicate investors, including, for example,

   1 What fees are to be paid to the syndicator
   2 How operating cash flows, taxable income (or deductible losses), and reversion cash flows are to be distributed
   3 How management of the real estate is to be handled
   4 How equity requirements or possible future assessments are to be divided among the limited and general partners

The agreement must cover the entire complex economic and legal relationships between the partners.

Another legal consideration is the death or disability of a partner. Normally, when a limited partner dies, the deceased partner's interest reverts to his or her estate. But the death of a general partner dissolves the partnership, unless the business is continued by a remaining general partner under the right to do so in the partnership certificate, or with the unanimous consent of the remaining partners. The limited partnership agreement must also specify procedures for removing an uncooperative partner and the procedures a partner should follow if she or he decides to sell personal interest in the real estate syndicate.

Securities Aspects

Legal precedent appears to dictate that the limited partner's interest in the typical real estate syndicate is a "security." The Securities Act of 1933 defines a *security* to include an investment contract, later defined by the Supreme Court as a contract, transaction, or scheme whereby a person invests money in a common enterprise and is led to expect profits from the efforts of the promoter or a third party. Therefore, if the promoters or sponsors of a real estate investment offer investors an interest in the profits and losses of the investment, particularly when the investors do not take an active role in the management and operation of the investment, then the promoters are, in effect, offering a security.

Registration with the SEC   The main purpose of the Securities Act of 1933 was to ensure that promoters or sponsors disclosed material facts to investors, to prevent misrepresentation, deceit, or fraud. If the sponsor of a real estate syndication tenders a public offering of shares or interests in a real estate investment through an investment contract (as defined by the Supreme Court) then the sponsor must register those securities with the Securities and Exchange Commission (SEC). Regulation of securities is not limited to the federal level since states have registration requirements of their own (modeled after the federal law) known as *blue-sky laws*. Noncompliance with securities regulations can render an offering illegal and enable investors to rescind the transaction and get their money back.

Exemptions from SEC Registration   Two exemptions primarily claimed in real estate syndications provide that securities need not be registered with regulatory agencies: intrastate and private offering. The *intrastate offering* exemption covers any issue of securities offered and sold only to residents of a single state by a person or corporation who is a resident or does business in this same state. The issuer of the securities must conduct at least 80 percent of its business in the state, and no security may be offered to a resident of another state. If either of these elements is violated, the intrastate exemption is lost for the entire issue.

The *private offering exemption* gives sponsors an opportunity to offer interests in a real estate syndication to a few investors who are considered sophisticated enough to not require the protection of the Securities Act of 1933. There can be no more than 35 purchasers of the securities, and general solicitation of offerees is not allowed.

There are several other methods that sponsors of real estate syndications can use to avoid registration, among them Regulation A, a type of "short-form" registration, or Rule 240, which exempts registration if the aggregate capital amount raised is under $500,000.

This brief discussion has, of course, only touched the surface of the securities aspects of real estate syndication.

Tax Considerations

A major risk the limited partnership is subject to is of being classified as a corporation for tax purposes. Treasury regulations define four characteristics that distinguish a partnership from a corporation. A partnership is classified as a corporation if it meets more than two of the following four corporate characteristics: (1) continuity of life, (2) centralization of management, (3) limited liability, and (4) easy transferability of interest. A limited partnership has the characteristics of centralized management and limited liability, so the limited partnership must not give the appearance of possessing continuity of life or easy transferability of interest. The special tax rules concerning passive activity income discussed in Chapter 14 apply here as well.

Limited Partner's Depreciable Basis   Another item that affects a syndication's tax status is the type of mortgage loan on the investment. This factor is important because the partner's maximum tax loss is limited by the amount of the partner's tax basis, but this tax basis includes both the equity invested and the pro rata portion of the syndication's nonrecourse loans. If the loan is considered nonrecourse, then in effect the limited partners can write off more than 100 percent of their invested capital.

Syndication Fees   Other tax items that must be considered are certain fees the limited partnership incurs. These fees are not deductible in the year they are incurred. Organization fees associated with the syndication must be amortized on a period no shorter than 60 months.

Special Allocations   The economic arrangements of real estate partnerships have become increasingly complex. The tax shelter area in particular has witnessed creative attempts to allocate tax consequences among partners. For example, many real estate partnerships provide separate allocations for each of the following items:

1 Taxable profits and losses
2 Cash flows from operation
3 Obligations to contribute funds
4 Distributions from refinancing of the property
5 Liquidating distributions following disposition of the property

Besides these five allocations, some items may be shared differently in different periods or at different levels of income. Allocation decisions must be made at the time the partnership is organized. *Special allocation* occurs when some of the items listed are allocated in a different manner, for example, giving one partner more of the tax losses and another more of the cash flows.

The Internal Revenue Code provides that a special allocation of income, gain, loss, deduction, or credit, or items thereof, will be respected if the allocation has *substantial economic effect*. If it does not, it will be ignored and the partners' distributive shares will be determined in accordance with the partners' interests in the partnership, which are determined by considering all ''facts and circumstances.'' Relevant facts and circumstances include a partner's relative rights to distribution of capital upon liquidation and the partner's relative interest in cash flow.

Treasury regulations provide that an allocation has *substantial economic effect* if it may actually affect the dollar amount of the partners' shares of the total partnership income or loss independently of tax consequences. A partner's economic interest in a partnership consists of her interest in capital and her interest in income. Generally, a partner's interest in capital (or the value of that interest) at any moment is the amount she would receive if the partnership assets were converted to cash at their fair market value, all debts paid, and the balance distributed to the partners according to the terms of the partnership agreement.

Substantial economic effect means that if you allocate $1 of income to partner A, the allocation is valid only if A's capital account, i.e., his right to receive a distribution of money or other property from the partnership, has been enhanced by $1. From this, the following fairly simple mechanical test has been developed to determine whether an allocation has an economic effect:

1 The partnership agreement provides for the maintenance of capital accounts for each partner.

2 Each partner's capital account is credited with his contributions and his share of income and debited for his distributions and his share of losses and deductions.

3 Upon liquidation of the partnership or a partner's withdrawal, distributions of cash or other property (at fair market value) will be made in strict accordance with the balances in the capital accounts at the time.

Partner's Adjusted Basis Upon sale, for tax purposes we must compute the partner's adjusted basis. In a partnership with special allocations, the adjusted basis is the original equity contributed plus assessments, plus the partner's interest in taxable income earned each year, less any share in taxable losses, less any share in cash distributions made during each year of ownership.

SYNDICATION EXAMPLE

Following is a detailed analysis of a private real estate syndication project that is being formed to develop the Five Points Office Building. The syndication takes the form of a limited partnership, with eight limited partners and the Cambron Investment Group (a general partnership) as the general partner. The partnership is to be organized immediately, and construction is expected to take 1 year.

Development Costs and Financial Data

Table 15-1 summarizes development costs and financial data. The property has been appraised at $2,100,000. A construction loan for $1,500,000 has been obtained from the Second State Bank at a fee of 2 percent, payable at closing. A permanent loan for the same amount has been secured from the State Pension Fund, at a loan fee of 4 percent, also payable immediately. Cambron has obtained prelease commitments for over 50 percent of the office space in the new building and is expected to complete 75 percent of the leasing at the end of the construction period.

Partnership Facts and Equity Requirements

Table 15-2 shows the financial aspects of the partnership agreement and the equity requirements of the general and limited partners. The total equity requirement is $620,000, with the general partner contributing 10 percent ($62,000) and the eight limited partners contributing 90 percent ($558,000), or $69,750 each.

Taxable income and tax losses are distributed in the same proportion as equity contributions: 10 percent to the general partner and 90 percent to the limited partners. Future cash assessments are also funded in the same proportion as equity contributions. Concerning cash disbursements, the limited partners are to receive a 7 percent (noncumulative) preferential return on all equity and assessments.

TABLE 15-1 COST AND FINANCING DATA: FIVE POINTS OFFICE BUILDING

Development data:	
Construction period	1 year
Appraised value	$2,100,000
Cost breakdown:	
Land	$ 375,000
Hard costs	1,405,000
Construction interest	90,000
Construction loan fee	30,000
Permanent loan fee	60,000
Other capital costs (architect, engineering, etc.)	130,000
Property tax during construction	20,000
Total costs	$2,110,000
Financing data:	
Construction loan:	$1,500,000
Interest rate	12%
Loan fee (2%)	30,000
Term	1 year
Permanent loan:	$1,500,000
Interest rate	12%
Loan fee (4%)	$60,000
Term/monthly payments	25 years
Annual debt service	$189,580

TABLE 15-2   PARTNERSHIP ASSUMPTIONS AND EQUITY REQUIREMENTS: FIVE POINTS SYNDICATE

1 Number of partners: two, one general and eight limited.
2 Equity capital contribution: general partner—10 percent, limited partners—90 percent (11.25 percent each).
3 Cash assessments: to be funded in the same proportion as equity contributions.
4 Cash distribution from operations: limited partners to receive a noncumulative, preferential, 7 percent return on all equity and assessments to date; any excess cash flows are to be distributed 50 percent to limited partners and 50 percent to general partner.
5 Tax profits and losses are to be distributed 90 percent to limited partners and 10 percent to general partner without regard to cash flow.
6 Sale and liquidation of assets: after the payment of selling expenses and the remaining mortgage balance, each partner (general and limited) to receive all equity invested plus any assessments; any excess is to be split 75 percent to limited partners and 25 percent to general partner.
7 Projected holding period: 1-year construction period; 5 years of operation, then disposition through sale.
8 Initial equity requirement:

Total project cost	$2,110,000
+ syndicate organizational fee	10,000
total cash requirements	2,120,000
− mortgage financing	1,500,000
equity requirement	620,000
General partner (10%)	62,000
Limited partner	558,000
Investment per limited partner	$69,750

9 Marginal tax rates:

General partner	28%
Limited partners	28%

Any excess operating cash flows are to be distributed 50-50 between the general partner and the limited partners.

After the real estate has been sold and liquidated and the selling expenses deducted and the mortgage balance paid, all partners (general and limited) are to first recover their equity and assessments. Any excess funds from disposition are to be distributed 75 percent to the limited partners and 25 percent to the general partner. The projected holding period for the investment is 6 years. This includes a 1-year construction period and 5 years of operation.

Operating and Tax Assumptions

Table 15-3 shows Cambron's projections regarding operations and tax deductions. Assumptions are made concerning potential gross income and projected income growth, vacancy and collection losses, operating expenses, and the depreciation method. Cambron is to be paid a management fee of 5 percent of effective gross income for managing the investment. Note that in the first year of operations after construction, it is assumed that the project will be only 75 percent oc-

TABLE 15-3 OPERATING AND TAX ASSUMPTIONS: FIVE POINTS SYNDICATE

Potential gross income (PGI)	$400,000 in year 1 of operation
Rental growth rate	5% per year
Vacancy and collection expenses (V and CE)	5%
Operating expenses (OE)	40% of effective gross income
Depreciation method	31.5-year straight-line
Depreciation deduction:	
Hard costs	$1,405,000
+ other capital costs	130,000
total amount depreciable	$1,535,000
Depreciation deduction per year	$48,730
Management fee	5% of effective gross income

Amortization periods and amount	Amount	Years	Per year
Construction interest and property taxes	$110,000	10	$11,000
Syndicate organizational fee	10,000	5	2,000
Construction loan fee	30,000	1	30,000
Permanent loan fee	60,000	25	2,400

Rent-up period: 1 year; 75 percent occupancy in year 1 of operations

Projected property value at sale: 10 times NOI

cupied and that the project will sell for 10 times its projected net operating income at the end of the holding period.

Table 15-3 also summarizes the period over which loan fees, organization fees, and construction-period interest and property taxes are amortized for federal income tax purposes. These are deductions that cannot be expensed during the year they are paid but must be amortized over periods ranging from 1 to 10 years.

Cash Flows from Operation

We now turn our attention to calculating the expected cash flows from operation.

Before-Tax Cash Flows from Operation Table 15-4 gives the expected cash flows over the 6-year holding period. There is no income during the construction year, the first year of the holding period. The vacancy and collection expense during the second year is 25 percent because the lease arrangements are incomplete. There is a negative before-tax cash flow (−$24,580) in year 2 because of the excessive vacancy and collection loss deduction. To make up the deficit, a cash assessment of $2,458 is levied against the general partner and $22,122 against the limited partners ($2,765 each).

TABLE 15-4 EXPECTED BEFORE-TAX CASH FLOWS: FIVE POINTS SYNDICATE

	Year					
	1	2	3	4	5	6
PGI	$0	$400,000	$420,000	$441,000	$463,050	$486,200
− V and CE	0	100,000	21,000	22,050	23,153	24,310
EGI	0	300,000	399,000	418,950	439,897	461,890
− OE	0	120,000	159,600	167,580	175,959	184,756
− management fee	0	15,000	19,950	20,948	21,995	23,095
NOI	0	165,000	219,450	230,422	241,943	254,039
− DS	0	189,580	189,580	189,580	189,580	189,580
BTCF	0	(24,580)	29,870	40,842	52,363	64,459

Assessments:
General partner	$ 2,458
Limited partners	22,122
Per limited partner	2,765

Distribution of before-tax cash flows:
	3	4	5	6
Preferential return to limited partners	$ 29,870	$40,609	$40,609	$40,609
Excess	0	233	11,754	23,850
50% to general partner	0	116	5,877	11,925
50% to limited partners	0	117	5,877	11,925

Total distribution:
	3	4	5	6
General partner	$ 0	$ 116	$ 5,877	$11,925
Limited partners	29,870	40,726	46,486	52,534
Per limited partner	3,734	5,091	5,811	6,567

The $29,870 cash flow in year 3 is disbursed entirely to the limited partners. Recall that the limited partners are to receive a return of 7 percent on their equity and assessments before any disbursements are made to the general partner. In this case the limited partners' equity is $580,000 ($558,000 + $22,122), and 7 percent of $580,122 is $40,609. Any cash flows under $40,609 are paid entirely to the limited partners. Any cash flows in excess of $40,609 are split 50-50 between the limited partner and the general partner. Excess cash flows are realized in years 4 to 6 and are disbursed in this manner.

Taxes from Operation Table 15-5 shows the taxable income and tax computations. There are tax losses in year 1 because of deductions for interest and loan fees. Note that taxable income is negative for each year, except year 5, indicating tax losses. These losses are distributed 90 percent to the limited partners and 10 percent to the general partner. We assume that each partner is in a 28 percent tax bracket.

After-Tax Cash Flow from Operation Table 15-6 presents the after-tax cash flow (ATCF) from the operation of the investment for each limited partner; Table 15-7 presents the ATCF data for the general partner. The tax savings realized on

TABLE 15-5 TAXES FROM OPERATION: FIVE POINTS SYNDICATE

	Year					
	1	2	3	4	5	6
NOI	$ 0	$165,000	$219,450	$230,422	$241,943	$254,039
− I	0	179,455	178,165	176,725	175,090	173,260
− D	0	48,730	48,730	48,730	48,730	173,260
− CL fee	30,000	0	0	0	0	48,730
− CLIPT	11,000	11,000	11,000	11,000	11,000	0
− permanent loan fee	0	2,400	2,400	2,400	2,400	11,000
− syndicate organizational fee	2,000	2,000	2,000	2,000	2,000	50,400*
						2,000
taxable income	(43,000)	(78,585)	(22,845)	(10,433)	2,723	(31,351)
Distribution of taxable income:						
General partner gain (loss)	($ 4,300)	($ 7,859)	($ 2,285)	($ 1,043)	$ 272	($ 3,135)
× tax rate	0.28	0.28	0.28	0.28	0.28	0.28
taxes (savings)	(1,204)	(2,201)	(640)	(292)	76	(878)
Per limited partner gain (loss)	($ 4,838)	($ 8,841)	($ 2,570)	($ 1,174)	$ 306	($ 3,527)
× tax rate	0.28	0.28	0.28	0.28	0.28	0.28
taxes (savings)	(1,355)	(2,475)	(720)	(329)	86	(988)

*The total remaining balance of the permanent loan fee, $50,400 ($60,000 − $9,600), is deducted in year 6, the final year in the holding period.

TABLE 15-6 AFTER-TAX CASH FLOW FROM OPERATION PER LIMITED PARTNER: FIVE POINTS SYNDICATE

	Year					
	1	2	3	4	5	6
BTCF*	$ 0	($2,765)	$3,734	$5,091	$5,811	$6,567
− taxes†	(1,355)	(2,475)	(720)	(329)	86	(988)
ATCF	1,355	(290)	4,454	5,420	5,725	7,555

*See Table 15-4.
†See Table 15-5.

TABLE 15-7 GENERAL PARTNER'S AFTER-TAX CASH FLOW FROM OPERATION: FIVE POINTS SYNDICATE

	Year					
	1	2	3	4	5	6
BCTF*	$ 0	($2,458)	$ 0	$116	$5,877	$11,925
− taxes†	(1,204)	(2,201)	(640)	(292)	76	(878)
ATCF	1,204	(257)	640	408	5,801	12,803

*See Table 15-4.
†See Table 15-5.

the tax losses experienced each year are added to the before-tax cash flows. The tax savings are a result of the sheltering effect of tax losses applied to the partner's passive income from other sources. Note that ATCF is expected to increase each year. Again note that this investment is a passive activity. Therefore, these losses can only result as a tax shelter if the investor also has passive income. Losses over and above passive income must be carried forward to succeeding years.

Cash Flow from Sale

The syndicate is expected to sell the office building at the end of 5 years of operation (year 6 of the syndicate's life). We now calculate the cash flow from the expected sale.

Before-Tax Cash Flow from Sale Table 15-8 shows the distribution of expected cash flows from sale. The expected sale price ($2,540,400) is 10 times the net operating income ($254,040 in Table 15-5) in year 6. The sales price less the selling expense (6 percent) and unpaid mortgage balance results in an expected before-tax equity reversion (BTER) of $953,181. Recovery of equity and assessments has priority on the BTER, and any excess proceeds are distributed 25 percent to the general partner and 75 percent to the limited partners. The total cash distribution is $141,858 to the general partner and $101,415 to each limited partner (see Table 15-8).

TABLE 15-8 BEFORE-TAX CASH FLOWS FROM SALE: FIVE POINTS SYNDICATE

Sales price	$2,540,400	
− selling expense (6%)	152,424	
net sale proceeds	2,387,976	
− unpaid mortgage balance	1,434,795	
before-tax equity reversion	953,181	
Recovery of equity and assessments: BTER		$953,181
Limited partners: original equity	558,000	
Assessment	22,122	
General partner: Original equity	62,000	
Assessment	2,458	643,580
Excess proceeds from sale		309,601
Disbursement of excess proceeds from sale:		
25% to general partner	$77,400	
75% to limited partners	232,201	
Total	309,601	
Total cash distribution:		
General partner	$141,858	
Limited partners	811,323	
Total	953,181	

Total cash distribution per limited partner: $811,323 ÷ 8 = $101,415

TABLE 15-9 COMPUTATION OF LIMITED PARTNER'S ADJUSTED BASIS: FIVE POINTS SYNDICATE

	Year							
	0	**1**	**2**	**3**	**4**	**5**	**6**	**Total**
Share in equity	$69,750							$69,750
Assessments	0	$ 0	$2,765	$ 0	$ 0	$ 0	$ 0	2,765
Net income	0	0	0	0	0	306	0	306
Net losses	0	4,838	8,841	2,570	1,174	0	3,527	(20,950)
Cash distribution	0	0	0	3,734	5,091	5,811	6,565	(21,201)
							Limited partner's adjusted basis	$30,670

TABLE 15-10 COMPUTATION OF GENERAL PARTNER'S ADJUSTED BASES: FIVE POINTS SYNDICATE

	Year							
	0	**1**	**2**	**3**	**4**	**5**	**6**	**Total**
Share in equity	$62,000							$62,000
Assessments	0		$2,458					2,458
Net income	0	$ 0	0	$ 0	$ 0	272	$ 0	272
Net losses	0	4,300	7,859	2,285	1,043	0	3,135	(18,622)
Cash distribution	0	0	0	0	116	5,877	11,925	(17,918)
							General partner's adjusted basis	$28,190

Adjusted Basis and Taxes Due on Sale Table 15-9 presents the computation of the limited partner's adjusted basis. Table 15-10 is the computation of the general partner's adjusted basis. The adjusted basis is the original equity contributed, plus assessments, plus the partner's share in taxable income earned each year, less any share in tax losses, less any share in cash distributions made during each year of ownership. The adjusted basis for each individual partner is $30,670, and the adjusted basis for the general partner is $28,190. The adjusted basis is used to determine the taxes due on sale for each partner.

Tables 15-11 and 15-12 illustrate the determination of the taxes due on sale for the limited partner and the general partner, respectively. The cash distribution from sale less the adjusted basis results in the taxable gain. The resulting taxes due on sale are $19,809 per limited partner and $31,827 for the general partner.

TABLE 15-11 TAXES DUE ON SALE PER LIMITED PARTNER: FIVE POINTS SYNDICATE

Cash distribution from sale (BTER)	$101,415
− adjusted basis	30,670
total gain	70,745
× marginal tax rate	0.28
taxes due on sale	19,809

TABLE 15-12 TAXES DUE ON SALE FOR GENERAL PARTNER:
FIVE POINTS SYNDICATE

Cash distribution from sale (BTER)	$141,858
− adjusted basis	28,190
taxable gain	113,668
× marginal tax rate	0.28
taxes due on sale	31,827

After-Tax Cash Flows from Sale Tables 15-13 and 15-14 give the after-tax cash flow from the sale for the limited partner and the general partner, respectively. Each limited partner is expected to receive $81,606 from the sale of the project. The general partner is expected to receive $110,031.

Limited Partner's NPV and IRR

Table 15-15 shows the calculation of the net present value and internal rate of return per limited partner. The assumed required rate of return is 12 percent. At this required rate, the net present value is −$13,741, which indicates that the investment is not acceptable to the limited partner. The internal rate of return is 7.67 percent.

General Partner's NPV and IRR

Table 15-16 gives the net present value computations for the general partner at a required rate of 13 percent. The investment is acceptable to the general partner

TABLE 15-13 AFTER-TAX CASH FLOW FROM SALE PER
LIMITED PARTNER: FIVE POINTS SYNDICATE

Before-tax equity reversion*	$101,415
− taxes due on sale†	19,809
after-tax equity reversion	81,606

*See Table 15-8.
†See Table 15-11.

TABLE 15-14 GENERAL PARTNER'S AFTER-TAX CASH FLOW
FROM SALE: FIVE POINTS SYNDICATE

Before-tax equity reversion*	$141,858
− taxes due on sale†	31,827
after-tax equity reversion	110,031

*See Table 15-8.
†See Table 15-12.

TABLE 15-15   NPV PER LIMITED PARTNER: FIVE POINTS SYNDICATE

Year	Equity	ATCF	ATER	PVIF$_{12\%}$		PV
0	($69,750)			1.0		($69,750)
1		1,355		0.8929		1,210
2		(290)		0.7972		(231)
3		4,454		0.7118		3,170
4		5,420		0.6355		3,444
5		5,725		0.5674		3,248
6		7,555	$81,606	0.5066		45,168
					NPV	($13,741)
					IRR	7.67%

TABLE 15-16   NPV FOR GENERAL PARTNER: FIVE POINTS SYNDICATE

Year	Equity	ATCF	ATER	PVIF$_{13\%}$		PV
0	($62,000)			1.0		($62,000)
1		$ 1,204		0.8850		1,066
2		(257)		0.7830		(201)
3		640		0.6930		444
4		408		0.6130		250
5		5,801		0.5430		3,150
6		12,803	$110,031	0.4800		58,960
					NPV	$ 1,669
					IRR	13.53%

since the net present value is $1,669. The expected rate of return is about 13.53 percent for the general partner.

In this example, the investment is acceptable for the general partner but not acceptable for the limited partner. We now address the issue of how this conflict can be resolved.

Cash Flow Distribution in a Syndication

Obviously, the rate of return on the investment depends on the expected cash inflows and outflows. The magnitude of these cash flows depends on the distribution decision. In our example, the general partner (syndication) could make the investment more attractive to the limited partners by giving them more of, say, the reversion cash flows.

Table 15-17 illustrates this principle. The value of the limited partner's equity position is simply the sum of the present value of the individual cash flows, which are the operating before-tax cash flows and the before-tax cash flow from sale, minus the taxes from operation and sale. In this example, the taxes from operation are negative, indicating a tax saving each year.

Discounting the component cash flows at the 12 percent required rate yields total present value of $56,009. Of this total present value, the cash flows from

TABLE 15-17   HOW DISTRIBUTION OF CASH FLOWS AFFECTS LIMITED PARTNER'S EQUITY VALUE

	Operation		Sale		$PV_{12\%}$	
Year	BTCF	Taxes	BTER	Taxes	BTCF	Taxes
			Cash flow			
0						
1	$ 0	($1,355)				($1,210)
2	(2,765)	(2,475)			(2,204)	(1,973)
3	3,734	(720)			2,658	(512)
4	5,091	(329)			3,235	(209)
5	5,811	86			3,297	49
6	6,567	(988)	$101,415	$19,809	3,327	(501)
				Total PV	10,313	(4,356)

Limited partner's equity value	PV	Proportion of PV
PV of BTCF	$ 10,313	0.18
− PV of taxes (operation)	− (4,356)	(0.08)
+ PV of BTER	51,377	0.92
− PV of taxes (sale)	− 10,035	0.18
total PV of LP position	$ 56,011	1.00

operation represent about 18 percent, the tax savings about 8 percent, the before-tax reversion about 92 percent, and the taxes due on sale about −18 percent. Since the large proportion of the total present value to the limited partner is from the reversion (about 74 percent), the investment could obviously be made more attractive by giving the limited partner more of the reversion cash flows.

The syndicate's and limited partners' requirements must be met for the investment to be attractive to each party. Reallocation of the cash flow distribution is often necessary to reach each participant's objective.

SUMMARY

This chapter discussed and illustrated the mechanics and use of real estate syndications as a form of real estate financing. Syndications create many unique tax, legal, and other risk elements for the investor.

QUESTIONS

1 Define the following terms:
   a syndicate
   b syndicator
   c blind pool
   d limited partner
   e nonrecourse loan
   f limited partnership agreement
   g security
   h blue-sky laws
   i intrastate offering

2 Describe how a real estate syndication works. What is the syndicator's role?

3 What are several key differences among the various syndication offerings?

4 What unique legal problems does a real estate syndication create? What are the advantages and disadvantages of various forms of business organization?

5 What is the purpose of the limited partnership agreement? What items does the agreement cover?

6 Discuss the securities aspects of real estate syndication. What are the purposes of security laws? What types of syndications are exempt from these laws?

7 What unique tax problems do syndications create?

8 Using Table 15-9, explain how the limited partner's adjusted basis is determined.

9 Using Table 15-17, explain how the distribution of cash flows from a real estate syndication affect the cash flows to the limited partner. Analyze the relationship between Table 15-17 and Table 15-15. How would the total present value of the limited partner's position (Table 15-17) be calculated using Table 15-15?

10 Suppose you were a real estate syndicator. How would you decide how to allocate the cash flow in a syndication?

11 Obtain a copy of a real estate syndication prospectus (either public or private offering). Analyze this prospectus by using the principles discussed in this chapter.

PROBLEMS

1 What are the general partner's and limited partner's before-tax NPV and IRR on the Five Points Office Building project if their before-tax rates of return are 15 and 12 percent, respectively?

2 Congress decided to raise personal taxes to the point where the highest marginal tax bracket would be 50 percent. Rework the Five Points Office Building example assuming that both the general partner and limited partner fall into the 50 percent bracket.

3 If operating expenses for the Five Points Office Building increase by 2 percent per year from $120,000 in year 2, what are the limited and the general partner's after-tax NPV and IRR?

4 Assume that both the limited and the general partner's required rate of return is 15 percent. Compute NPV. Also, show how the distribution of cash flows affects the limited partner's equity value.

5 Refer to the Oak Hollow Condominium project in the problem section of Chapter 14. Assume the same facts as before except there is only one general partner—the Finance Investment Group—instead of two. The split between the investors takes the form of 60 percent general partner, 20 percent each limited partner. There is a syndicate organizational fee of $15,000. The management of the complex is performed by an outside company for a fee of 5 percent of EGI. Furthermore, limited partners require a 7 percent preferential return on cash distributions from operations. Compute the following:

a After-tax cash flow if all investors are in the 28 percent tax bracket

b Cash flow from sale

6 Using the facts in problem 5, determine the limited and the general partner's NPV and IRR on the Oak Hollow Condominium Project.

7 How does the "passive activity" rule apply to the partners in the Oak Hollow Condominium project?

REFERENCES

Arnold, Alvin L.: *Real Estate Syndication Manual,* Warren, Gorham and Lamont, New York, 1984.

Bernstein, Jay B.: *The Professional Syndicator: A Guide for Creating Limiting Partnerships,* Kendall/Hunt, Dubuque, Iowa, 1981.

Miller, Daniel A.: *How to Invest in Real Estate Syndicates,* Irwin, Homewood, Ill., 1978.

Smith, Larry J.: "Syndications Bring Benefits to Small Investors," *Mortgage Banking,* November 1981, pp. 52–55.

LEASES AND SALE-LEASEBACK FINANCING

This chapter examines the use of leases as a financing method. Lease financing creates many unusual legal, tax, and other risk considerations not found in the other methods. There are many decision situations in which lease financing might be used. For example, a developer could lease the land for a shopping center or office building rather than purchasing it fee simple. Another type of lease financing is the so-called *sale-leaseback*. As the name implies, real estate is sold by the owner and then "leased back." There are many business reasons why this practice is attractive.

First, we briefly examine lease financing, and then we examine the unique risk aspects of leases and sale-leasebacks. We end with detailed examples of the mechanics of lease financing methods.

WHAT IS LEASE FINANCING?

A *lease* is a legal contract between a tenant (lessee) and an owner (lessor) for the use and possession of real estate (land and/or improvements) for a specified period of time. The lessee promises to make a series of payments (generally called rent) to the lessor. The frequency of rental payments and other conditions are specified within the lease. Obviously, the rental payments can be level or variable, depending upon the contract. When a lease is terminated, the leased real estate reverts to the lessor. Often, the lease gives the tenant the option to buy the real estate or take out a new lease.

In this chapter we are interested in long-term leasing decisions. The lessee agrees to make a series of payments to the lessor and is committed to the lease payments, much like the commitment to make debt-service payments under a mortgage. Failure to make the lease payments is thus the equivalent of default; the lessor "forecloses" on the lease. Long-term leasing arrangements are thus the equivalent of debt financing.

There are three main forms of lease financing: a sale-leaseback arrangement, direct acquisition of an asset under a lease, and leveraged leasing. In a sale-leaseback arrangement, a firm (or individual) sells real estate it owns to another party, and that party leases the real estate back to the seller. The seller receives the sale price and the use of the asset during the term of the lease. In return, the seller contracts to make periodic lease payments and gives title to the real estate to the buyer.

In direct leasing, an investor (developer or individual) acquires the use of real estate it did not previously own. In leveraged leasing, three parties are involved: lessee, lessor (equity participant), and lender. This form of leasing is identical to the others for the lessee, but the lessor acquires the real estate by financing with part equity, with a long-term lender providing the remaining capital. The loan is usually secured by a mortgage on the asset *and* by the assignment of the lease payments.

Why Lease?

There are numerous economic reasons for leasing rather than owning an asset. One is that the investor might require the use of the real estate for only a short period of time. As a result of the transaction's cost, it is cheaper to lease than to own. Another reason is that lease financing provides 100 percent financing. For example, suppose a developer wants to purchase a parcel of land for development. If the developer buys and finances with a conventional mortgage, only a portion of the purchase price may be financed (e.g., 60 to 80 percent). But if the developer leases the land, 100 percent financing is essentially possible. Of course, the developer pays for this increased leverage.

A third reason for leasing is possible tax advantages. When the investor leases the investment, typically the full amount of the lease payment is tax deductible. Alternatively, if the asset were bought, the investor could take a depreciation and a deduction on any interest expense incurred in financing. Thus, which set of deductions is more valuable to the lessee as a tax shield depends on size and timing. Later we examine the consequences in more detail.

Because leasing is an alternative method of financing the investment in a property, the decision maker is thus interested in determining whether lease financing is more (or less) costly than other forms of financing.

Types of Leasing Decision Situations

There are numerous situations in which the valuation and analysis of lease financing methods are used, including the following:

Situation 1. Johnson Industries leased an office building from Maria D. Investor. The current market rental rate on the office building is more than the contract rental rate that Johnson is paying Investor. Johnson has the right to sublease the office building. What is the value of Johnson's leasehold property rights?

Situation 2. Smith Products requires more warehouse space. It has found an acceptable warehouse and is trying to decide whether to acquire the use of the space by leasing it or buying it outright with mortgage financing.

Situation 3. Dan Developer has found a site suitable for development as a shopping center. He has two options: buy the land or lease the land under a long-term lease contract from the seller. Which option should he select?

Situation 4. Jones Manufacturing owns an office building for its headquarters. It wants to continue to occupy the building and is trying to select between two options: continuing to own the building or selling the property to Maria Investor and leasing back the property.

RISK ANALYSIS OF LEASE FINANCING

We illustrated only four of the many decision situations that involve analysis of lease financing versus other financing options. We now turn our attention to the basic legal, tax, and risk conditions of lease financing.

Legal Aspects of Lease Financing

A *lease* is an agreement that transfers the right of possession and use of real estate for a definite period of time. The *lease document* is the written instrument specifying the relationship between the tenant (lessee) and the landlord (lessor). The lessor retains the right to retake possession after the lease term expires. The lessor's interest is the *leased fee;* the lessee's interest is the *leasehold.* In return for the right of use and possession, the lessee pays the lessor rent.

For the most part, the lease is viewed as a contract. Although no special wording is necessary, leases should always be in writing. Indeed, by law, leases with terms of more than 1 year have to be in writing.

Elements of Leases Since leases are governed by contract law, the following elements of a valid contract must be present: The parties must have the capacity to enter into a valid contract; there must be mutual agreement between the parties evidenced by consideration; the lease's objectives must be legal; and the parties must sign the lease. In addition, other items in a lease are a precise description of the premises, the term (length of time) of the lease, and the rental payment required.

Table 16-1 is a summary of typical lease clauses. Many leases also give the lessee the option to purchase the property under specified conditions. The lease may also give the tenant the right to ''sublet'' the property to another. There are numerous methods by which a lease may be terminated, including

1 Expiration of the term
2 Agreement of the parties
3 Destruction or condemnation of the property
4 Default or breach of the leasing terms and conditions

TABLE 16-1   TYPICAL LEASE CLAUSES

1 Parties' names and addresses
2 Exact description of premises
3 Commencement date and termination date
4 Time and amount of rental payment
5 Lessee's acceptance of premises clause
6 Premise-use description clause
7 Covenant to comply with all applicable laws, ordinances, and regulations
8 Covenant listing parties' obligations in payment of taxes, casualty insurance, and other expenses
9 Covenant listing parties' obligations for maintenance, additions, alterations, and improvements
10 Covenant providing for the type and location of signs
11 Covenant providing right of entry by landlord
12 Covenants on assignment and subleasing
13 Covenants on partial or total casualty losses or condemnation
14 Covenants relating to lessee's obligations in the event of holding over after expiration of term
15 Statement of events constituting a default
16 Renewal options and terms
17 Signatures

Tax Aspects of Lease Financing

The tax aspects of lease financing, particularly sale-leaseback, are complicated. In this section we review only some of the major concepts.

Lessee's Perspective   From the lessee's perspective, there are several important tax consequences. Generally, the payments on a lease of property used in a trade or business are tax deductible. For example, if a business rents office space, the rental payments are deductible as operating expenses.

In the situation in which the developer (investor) leases land for a development, the land rent is deductible. This is an attraction over fee ownership since the land is not depreciable. Leasing the land provides the opportunity to "depreciate" the land. Obviously, the rental payments represent a cash outflow to the lessee, and since the lessee does not own the land, the lessee forgoes the benefit of realizing any appreciation in the land value.

On the other hand, since the lessee "owns" the building (improvements), the lessee (developer) will be entitled to the depreciation deductions on the improvements. If a building is upon leased property, its cost must be recovered over the 27½- or 31½-year period. The cost of other improvements to leased property is recovered using the appropriate ACRS class-life.

Lessor's Perspective   From the lessor's perspective, there are also important tax considerations. The rent received is taxable income to the lessor. If the lessee has the right to the depreciation deductions, the lessor cannot take any deductions—only one participant is entitled to depreciate the improvements.

Tax Aspects of Sale-Leaseback   A sale-leaseback involves the sale of real property by the owner to another investor. The other investor then simultaneously leases the property back to the seller on a long-term basis. There are two major types of sale-leaseback financing: sale and leaseback of land but *not* improvements, or sale-leaseback of land *and* improvements.

Under a true sale-leaseback, the seller (lessee) relinquishes economic interest in the property. Thus, the seller gives up the right to the depreciation deductions; this right goes to the buyer (lessor). However, the seller (lessee) can deduct the rental payments.

Under a sale-leaseback, one of the attractions to the buyer is the depreciation deductions. And if the purchaser bought the property using debt financing, the interest payments are also tax deductible.

Other Considerations

There are several potential problems with lease financing, particularly sale-leasebacks. A major risk is that the transaction may be viewed, for tax purposes, as a financing device rather than as a sale and lease. The court cases involving sale-leaseback indicate that from a tax perspective, the transaction could be viewed as a mortgage loan between the purchaser-lessor as the lender and the seller-lessee as the borrower, with the property used as collateral. If the court takes this perspective, the purchaser-lessor would not be allowed depreciation deductions. The purchaser-lessor would also have to treat the interest portion of the lease payments as income. On the other side, the seller-lessee would be unable to deduct all the lease payments or recognize gain (or loss) on the sale. The seller-lessee would take the depreciation deduction. In essence, the sale-leaseback would be treated as a mortgage.

The court cases have identified several factors as important in distinguishing a sale-leaseback from mortgage financing. These factors include determining who holds the equity interest in the property, by examining such points as the reasonableness of the rental payments, the option price if the lessee has the option to repurchase, and the sale price. Also important is the intent of the parties in the transaction. The investor must be sure that the lease contract is written in a form acceptable from a tax perspective.

Types of Leases

There are five basic types of leases as determined by payment method: straight, net, percentage, step-up (or down), and reappraisal rents. With the use of a *straight lease,* rent is usually negotiated at a fixed price (say, per square foot) as determined by location, quantity of space, and use. Escalation clauses are usually included to compensate for increases in insurance, taxes, or other costs. These straight leases are often used by low-volume, small businesses or as an enticement to lure major (anchor) tenants to a new shopping center project, for example.

A *net lease* is similar to a straight lease except for its provisions that the tenant is to pay all operating expenses, taxes, insurance, maintenance, and utilities. Rent in this lease represents the owner's net return. The owner pays only the debt service and perhaps the common-area costs and leaves managerial duties to the tenant.

The *percentage lease* has rents that are determined by a fixed or flat charge (per square foot) plus a negotiated percentage of all sales volume over a specific level. This amount of rent received over the minimum price per square foot is called overage. The *step-up* lease requires periodic increases in the contract rental over the lease term. *Step-down* leases call for periodic decreases in the rents. A *reappraisal* lease calls for periodic reappraisal of rental payments at specified intervals over the term of the lease.

LEASE FINANCING EXAMPLES

This section illustrates several decision-making situations dealing with lease financing. Specifically, we illustrate how to value the lessee's (tenant's) position in a lease (the leasehold estate), how to decide between leasing and acquiring with mortgage financing, the mechanics of the subordinated ground lease, and how to analyze the sale-leaseback decision.

Lease Valuation Examples

The value of the tenant's leasehold estate is the difference between the present value of the market rents and the present value of the contract rents. If the tenant has the right to sublease the property, the tenant would rent to the sublessee at the market rental rate and pay the owner (lessor) the contract rent.

To illustrate, suppose Johnson Industries leased an office building from Maria D. Investor under the following specifics:

Rental space: 100,000 square foot
Contract rent: $10 per square foot per year
Original term: 20 years, with rent payable at the end of the year
Current market rent: $12 per square foot per year
Remaining term: 15 year

Johnson leased the 100,000 square feet at a contract rent of $10 per square foot (net) with a 20-year term. The current market rent is $12 per square foot (net), and the remaining term is 15 years. Johnson's leasehold value is thus the present value of the market rent minus the contract rent, or $2 per square foot per year for 15 years, for a total of $200,000 per year. In equation form, the leasehold value is

$$\text{Leasehold value} = \text{PVAF}_{i,n}(\text{rental difference})$$

At a before-tax discount rate of, say, 15 percent, the leasehold value is

$$\text{Johnson's leasehold value} = 5.84737(\$200,000)$$
$$= \$1,169,474$$

Obviously, the higher (lower) the discount rate, the lower (higher) the leasehold value. If the rental payment were not constant, we would find the value of discounting the difference as a series of lump sums.

To further illustrate the concepts of lease valuation, consider that an investor owns a 10,000-square-foot warehouse. The contract rent is $8 per square foot (net) per year, payable in advance. The remaining term on the lease is 10 years, at which time the investor estimates the property will sell for $450,000 (net of selling expenses). What is the value of these lease payments at a discount rate of 12 percent?

The value is the sum of the present value of an *annuity due* of $80,000 per year for 10 years and the present value of the net sale price, in equation form:

$$\text{Lease value} = \text{PVAF}_{12\%,10 \text{ years}}(\text{lease payments}) + \text{PVF}_{12\%,10 \text{ years}}(\text{net sale price})$$
$$= 5.650223(\$80,000)(1.12) + 0.321973(\$450,000)$$
$$= \$506,260 + \$144,888$$
$$= \$651,148$$

This is the value of the *leased fee*.

Continuing our example, suppose the tenant has the right to sublease the warehouse and the market is willing to pay $9.50 per square foot per year for the remaining term of 10 years. What is the value of the tenant's leasehold?

The leasehold value would be the present value of the difference between the market rent ($9.50) and the contract rent ($8), or $1.50 per square foot per year for 10 years, payable at the beginning of the year. In equation form:

$$\text{Value of leasehold} = \text{PVAF}_{12\%,10}(\$15{,}000)(1 + 0.12)$$
$$= 5.650223(\$15{,}000)(1.12)$$
$$= \$94{,}925$$

Thus the value of the tenant's leasehold is $94,925. Obviously, the sublessee could rent out the warehouse to someone else and possibly create a leasehold estate. Often the leasehold is viewed as riskier than the leased fee and thus is discounted at a higher rate.

Leasing versus Mortgage Financing Example

Another decision for the real estate investor is whether to acquire the rights to a real estate investment by leasing the property or by buying the property using debt financing. This is often referred to as the *own-versus-lease decision*. To make the decision, we must compute the present value of the cost of each alternative and then select the option with the lowest costs.

Recall from our earlier discussion that generally the total amount of the lease payment is tax deductible. However, if the investor owns the real estate, the depreciation deduction is allowed. In addition, ownership gives the owner the rights to the cash flow from sale at the end of the holding period. Under the leasing option, the reversion belongs to the lessor.

There are certain limitations to be kept in mind. The IRS may determine that the "lease" is actually a "financing agreement" if the lease payments are not reasonable and an option to purchase is permitted. In the following example, we assume that the tax aspects are allowed.

Input Assumptions   Joan D. Businessperson has decided to invest in a warehouse to store her inventory of auto parts. She is trying to decide whether to finance the investment with a mortgage or by leasing. She has found a 10,000-square foot warehouse that fits the requirements.

If she buys the warehouse, the price will be $150,000. For depreciation purposes, the useful life is 31.5 years on a building value of $120,000 (the estimated land value is $30,000). Businessperson will use the straight-line depreciation method. At the end of the expected holding period of 10 years, the property has an expected net selling price of $125,000. Businessperson will purchase the property with a $100,000 mortgage and $50,000 equity. The mortgage will be an interest-only loan for 10 years with the principal payable at the end of year 10.

TABLE 16-2 COST OF LEASE FINANCING

Year	Lease payment	Tax shield	After-tax cash flow with lease	PV$_{10\%}$
1–10	($21,000)	$5,880	($15,120)	($92,906)

If Businessperson leases the property, the lease payments will be $21,000 on a "triple" net arrangement (meaning that she will pay all operating expenses) for a lease term of 10 years.

The marginal tax rate is 28 percent, and the required after-tax yield is 10 percent. Which option would Joan D. Businessperson select?

Cost of Lease Financing Table 16-2 summarizes the computation of the present value of the cost of lease financing. The lease calls for payments of $21,000 per year. Since these payments are tax deductible and the investor is in a 28 percent tax bracket, the tax saving is $5,880. The after-tax cost of the lease payments is thus $15,120 per year. At a discount rate of 10 percent, the present value of these cash outflows is $92,906 (Table 16-2).

Cost of Mortgage Financing The second option is to finance the investment with part equity ($50,000) and the remainder with a mortgage ($100,000). Table 16-3 summarizes the cash flows associated with this option. Since this is an interest-only mortgage, the annual debt service is simply the interest payment each year ($100,000 × 14 percent). Ownership entitles the investor to a depreciation deduction of $3,810 per year. The resultant amount of income that will be shielded from tax is $17,810. This results in a tax saving of $4,987 per year. Thus the after-tax cost of the loan is $9,013 each year. In year 10, the investor expects to sell the investment for $125,000. Table 16-4 summarizes the computations of the after-tax cash flow from the sale of the warehouse. Note that the ATER is an inflow in year 10. The total cash flows (see Table 16-3) are thus a $50,000 outflow at the time zero, a $9,013 outflow for years 1 through 9, and a $12,319 inflow in year 10. The total present value of this option (financing with debt and equity) is $97,156.

TABLE 16-3 COST OF DEBT FINANCING

Year	Equity	Debt service	Depreciation deduction	Tax savings	After-tax reversion	After-tax cash flows	PV$_{10\%}$
0	($50,000)						($50,000)
1–9		($14,000)	$3,810	$4,987		($ 9,013)	($51,906)
10		(14,000)	3,810	4,987	$21,332	12,319	4,750
							($97,156)

*See Table 16-4.

TABLE 16-4 AFTER-TAX CASH FLOW FROM SALE
AND TAXES DUE ON SALE

Net selling price	$125,000
− unpaid mortgage	100,000
BTER	25,000
− taxes due on sale	3,668
ATER	21,332
Taxes due on sale:	
Net selling price	$125,000
− adjusted basis	111,900
capital gain	13,100
× tax rate	0.28
taxes due on sale	3,668

Lease versus Mortgage To select between the lease financing and mortgage-equity financing, we simply select the option with the least present value cost. In this example, the present value of the lease is $92,906. The present value of the financing option is $97,156. Thus the lease financing option is preferred.

Subordinated Ground Lease Example

As the term implies, in a *ground lease,* the lessor (owner), in return for a contract rent and the right to regain exclusive use of the property when the lease ends, gives the lessee (tenant) the exclusive use of a parcel of land for the term of the lease. In the typical situation, the owner of the land may have neither the desire nor the capability to develop the property. Thus, the owner leases the land to a developer (tenant) and when the lease expires retains the right to the residual value of any improvements placed on the land. From the developer's perspective, there is the attraction of acquiring the right of use without high initial outlays.

In most cases, the developer will request that, as part of the ground lease, the lessor agree to subordinate the land to any mortgage on the proposed improvements. This is often referred to as a *leasehold* mortgage, which in effect means that the mortgage lender has first priority and, in the event of default, the lender would obtain title to both the improvements and the land. As a result, the landowner (lessor) requires a higher rental payment to compensate for the additional risk.

The following example illustrates a subordinated ground lease. A real estate investor is considering developing a "strip" shopping center. Table 16-5 summarizes the assumptions. The expected net operating income is $82,500 per year and is forecast to remain constant over the 5-year holding period. The total value of the project is $750,000. The investor can lease the land for $14,250 per year with a 40-year term. The landowner is willing to subordinate to the first mortgage. The investor can borrow $500,000 on a mortgage at an interest rate of 12 percent, with annual payments for 24 years.

The cost of the building is $600,000 and is depreciable over a 31.5-year life using the straight-line method. Thus, the depreciation deduction is $19,048 per year.

TABLE 16-5 SUMMARY OF ASSUMPTIONS: SUBORDINATED GROUND LEASE EXAMPLE

1 Type of investment	Neighborhood shopping center
2 Estimate total property value	$750,000
3 Expected net operating income	$82,500 per year
4 Income growth rate	0% per year
5 Debt financing:	
Loan amount	$500,000
Interest rate	12%
Maturity (annual payments)	24 years
Debt service (annual)	$64,231
6 Ground lease:	
Rental (lease payments)	$14,250 per year
Lease term	30 years
7 Building costs	$600,000
8 Depreciation:	
Method	Straight-line
Life	31.5 years
9 Holding period	5 years
10 Total value at end of holding period	$750,000
11 Value of land at end of holding period	$150,000
12 Investor's selling expenses	$30,000
13 Investor's marginal tax rate	28%

At the end of the 5-year holding period, the investor estimates the total property value (same as original value) at $750,000, with the land valued at $150,000. The value of the investor's position (building) is estimated to be $600,000, with selling expenses of $30,000. In essence, the investor is going to sell the leasehold estate. The investor's marginal tax rate is 28 percent.

After-Tax Cash Flow from Operation Table 16-6 contains the investor's expected after-tax cash flow from operation. The expected net operating income of $82,500 per year minus the debt service of $64,230 and the ground lease payment of $14,250 yields a BTCF of $4,020 per year. Table 16-7 contains the expected taxable income and taxes from operation for each year of the holding period.

TABLE 16-6 INVESTOR'S AFTER-TAX CASH FLOW: SUBORDINATED GROUND LEASE EXAMPLE

	Year				
	1	2	3	4	5
Net operating income	$82,500	$82,500	$82,500	$82,500	$82,500
− debt service	64,230	64,230	64,230	64,230	64,230
− ground lease	14,250	14,250	14,250	14,250	14,250
BTCF	4,020	4,020	4,020	4,020	4,020
− taxes (savings)*	(3,023)	(2,881)	(2,722)	(2,544)	(2,344)
ATCF	7,043	6,901	6,742	6,564	6,364

*See Table 16-7.

TABLE 16-7 TAXABLE INCOME AND TAXES FROM OPERATION: SUBORDINATED GROUND LEASE EXAMPLE

	Year				
	1	2	3	4	5
Net operating income	$82,500	$82,500	$82,500	$82,500	$82,500
− interest	60,000	59,492	58,924	58,287	57,574
− ground lease	14,250	14,250	14,250	14,250	14,250
− depreciation	19,048	19,048	19,048	19,048	19,048
taxable income	(10,798)	(10,290)	(9,722)	(9,085)	(8,372)
× tax rate	0.28	0.28	0.28	0.28	0.28
taxes (savings)	(3,023)	(2,881)	(2,722)	(2,544)	(2,344)

Note that the investment is generating a tax loss (savings) for the investor each year. Since the investor "owns" the building, she is entitled to the depreciation deductions.

After-Tax Cash Flow from Sale Table 16-8 contains the expected cash flow from the sale of the investor's position (the leasehold) at the end of the 5-year holding period. The expected value of the building (leasehold position) is $600,000, with selling expenses of $30,000. The unpaid mortgage debt is $473,127. The taxes due on sale are calculated in Table 16-9. The adjusted basis is the total original building cost ($600,000) minus the cumulative depreciation deductions. The expected ATER is $78,606.

NPV of Investor's Position The investor's net present value and rate of return are calculated in Table 16-10. At a required rate of return of 8 percent (after-tax), the NPV is −$24,875, indicating that the investment is not acceptable to the investor. The expected rate of return is 2.68 percent. If the investor's required rate of return were 2.68 percent or less, the investment would be acceptable.

There are several inputs that would make the investment more attractive if the investor could alter them. If the ground rent were lower, the NPV would in-

TABLE 16-8 AFTER-TAX CASH FLOW FROM SALE: SUBORDINATED GROUND LEASE EXAMPLE

Selling price	$600,000
− selling expenses	30,000
net sale price	570,000
− unpaid mortgage	473,127
before-tax equity reversion	96,873
− taxes due on sale*	18,267
after-tax equity reversion	78,606

*See Table 16-9.

TABLE 16-9 TAXES DUE ON SALE:
SUBORDINATED GROUND LEASE EXAMPLE

Selling price	$600,000
− selling expenses	30,000
amount realized	570,000
− adjusted basis	504,760
total gain	65,240
Taxes due on sale:	
Total gain	65,240
× tax rate	0.28
taxes due on sale	18,267

TABLE 16-10 INVESTOR'S NPV POSITION: SUBORDINATED GROUND LEASE EXAMPLE

Year	Equity	ATCF	ATER	PVF$_{18\%}$		PV
0	($100,000)			1.0		($100,000)
1		7,043		0.9259		6,521
2		6,901		0.8573		5,916
3		6,742		0.7938		5,352
4		6,564		0.7350		4,825
5		6,364	$78,606	0.6806		57,831
					NPV	(24,875)
					IRR	2.68%

crease. Likewise, the financing terms on the mortgage affect the NPV. Also, if the investor revised the forecast of future selling price, the NPV and IRR would change.

Sale-Leaseback Example

In a sale-leaseback financing arrangement, an investor acquires (or owns) a property, sells it to another party, and then leases it back from that party for an agreed series of lease payments. Often a repurchase (option) agreement is also included, which allows the investor (seller-lessee) to buy back the property at some negotiated price and time from the other party (buyer-lessor). Other names for a sale-leaseback include *purchase-and-leaseback* and *liquidating lease*.

Sale-leaseback financing can be used on both existing and undeveloped properties. On occasion, a developer may agree to buy a site to be chosen by the lessee, construct a building according to plans, turn the finished product over to the lessee, and then arrange a sale-leaseback with a lender. The sale-leaseback contract results in sale of the property and delivery of equitable and legal title to the buyer. The lease agreement is then drafted and signed by all parties. The participants must clearly set forth the terms of possible repurchase options, repurchase prices, and cancellation privileges.

Reasons for Sale-Leaseback There are various reasons or advantages why a lessee or lessor may desire a sale-leaseback. For example, if the lessee is a corporation, the following reasons apply:

1 Extra funds are provided for expansion and/or for working capital at a lower cost and for a longer time than is possible from other sources.
2 The released funds can be invested elsewhere at a higher return.
3 The financial plan is simplified and makes possible the use of less debt.
4 Corporations (or individuals) not skilled in real estate management can pass on these duties to the purchaser.
5 There are tax advantages (as previously discussed).

To illustrate the general mechanics of a sale-leaseback, consider the following example.

Input Assumptions The Packard Company occupies and owns free and clear of any debt the Hewlett office building and plans to occupy it for another 20 years. The current book value of the land is $110,000, and the current book value of the building is $310,000 (for tax purposes). The Packard Corporation is considering two options:

1 Continuing to own and occupy the Hewlett building for 20 years and then selling it
2 Negotiating a sale-leaseback arrangement with an investor

Packard is depreciating the building at $31,000 per year using the straight-line method. In 10 years the building will be completely depreciated for tax purposes. Under the sale-leaseback arrangement, the leasing company will pay Packard $1,250,000 cash for the land and the building and lease it back to Packard at $120,000 per annum for 20 years (*payments on lease due at the beginning of each year*), with no option to repurchase. The (net) lease stipulates that Packard (lessee) will pay all property taxes and maintenance costs on the building and land. Packard projects the property's market value of $2 million (up from $1,250,000 at this time) at the end of the 20-year lease. Packard's ordinary tax rate is 34 percent.

Under the option of retaining ownership, the tax benefits from depreciation begin 1 year from now and continue for 10 years. Under the sale-leaseback (option 2), the lease payments begin now and continue for 19 years (20 lease payments). The appropriate discount rate is 10 percent. Should Packard retain ownership of the building (option 1) or negotiate for a sale-leaseback with the investor (option 2)?

Continue to Own With option 1, Packard will retain the depreciation tax shield for the next 10 years. This is

$$\text{Depreciation tax shield} = \text{tax rate} \times \text{depreciation per year}$$

$$= 0.34 \times \$31,000$$

$$= \$10,540$$

The present value of the tax shield at 10 percent for 10 years is $64,764.

Under option 1, Packard owns the building and land. Thus when the property is sold at the end of 20 years for $2 million, the book value will be $110,000 (due to full depreciation of the building). The present value of the after-tax proceeds is

$$\text{Taxable gain on future sale} = \text{sale price} - \text{adjusted basis}$$
$$= \$1,890,000$$

$$\text{Tax due on sale} = \text{taxable gain on sale} \times \text{tax rate}$$
$$= \$1,890,000 \times 0.34$$
$$= \$642,600$$

$$\text{After-tax cash flow from future sale} = \text{sale price} - \text{tax due on sale}$$
$$= \$2,000,000 - \$642,600$$
$$= \$1,357,400$$
$$\text{Present value of after-tax cash flow} = \text{PVF}_{10\%,20}(\$1,357,400)$$
$$= 0.14864(\$1,357,400)$$
$$= \$201,764$$

Sale-Leaseback   Under option 2, Packard receives a sale price of $1,250,000. The after-tax proceeds are

$$\text{Taxable gain} = \text{selling price} - \text{book value of land and building}$$
$$= \$1,250,000 - (\$110,000 + \$310,000)$$
$$= \$830,000$$

$$\text{Tax due on sale} = \text{taxable gain} \times \text{tax rate}$$
$$= \$830,000 \times 0.34$$
$$= \$282,200$$

$$\text{After-tax proceeds from sale now} = \text{before-tax proceeds} - \text{tax due on sale}$$
$$= \$1,250,000 - \$282,200$$
$$= \$967,800$$

Under option 2, Packard must pay lease rental payments of $120,000 per year for 20 years, payable at the beginning of the year. The after-tax cost of these rents per year is

$$\text{After-tax cost of lease payments} = (1 - \text{tax rate}) \times \text{lease payment}$$
$$= (1 - 0.34) \times \$120,000$$
$$= \$79,200$$

The present value of these lease payments (annuity due) at 10 percent is $741,701.

Comparing Options   To select between the two options, we simply compare the present value of the costs and benefits. If Packard continues to occupy the building (option 1), there will be two benefits: the present value of the depreciation tax savings of $64,764 and the present value of the future sale of $201,764. Under the sale-leaseback option, Packard will receive the after-tax proceeds from sale today of $967,800. The costs will be the present value of the after-tax lease payments, $741,701.

The net effect of sale leaseback over continue to own is:

Present value of after-tax proceeds from sale today	$967,800
− present value of lease payment	741,701
− present value of forgone depreciation tax shield	64,764
− present value of forgone future sale proceeds	201,764
net advantage of sale-leaseback	(40,429)

Since the costs exceed the benefits from sale today, we should accept the continue-to-own option.

Obviously the decision depends on the assumptions. The higher the selling price today, the more attractive the sale-leaseback. The higher the lease rental payments on the lease, the less attractive the sale-leaseback. The higher the future expected value of the property, the less attractive the sale-leaseback.

SUMMARY

This chapter introduced the use of leases as a financing method. There are numerous situations in which leasing might be attractive. Essentially, the borrower must compare lease financing with other financing methods to determine the least costly option.

Lease financing creates many unique legal and tax problems. The techniques presented in this chapter should give the borrower-lender a *basic* understanding of how to analyze lease financing. Competent advice should be sought before deciding whether to use this method.

QUESTIONS

1 Define the following terms:

a lease
b lessee
c lessor
d sale-leaseback
e leasehold
f leased fee

g net lease
h percentage lease
i ground lease
j leasehold mortgage
k subordinated ground lease

2 Describe how leasing a parcel of real estate can be used as a financing method. Why would an investor decide to lease rather than own a parcel of real estate?

3 Under what types of situations would leasing be a viable financing option?

4 Discuss several unique legal problems lease financing creates. Using Table 16-1, analyze several of the typical clauses in a typical long-term lease document.

5 What unique tax problems are involved in lease financing?

6 Discuss several alternative ways to determine lease payments. Under what situations might the net lease be used? The percentage lease?

7 Outline how you would value the tenant's claim on a real estate investment. When might a tenant want to sell its leasehold position?

8 What is a leased fee? How is it valued?

9 Outline how a real estate developer would use a ground lease.

10 Describe how a sale-leaseback transaction works. Under what situations might it be used? What are some of its unique tax problems?

PROBLEMS

1 Suppose ABC Medical Corporation leased office space from XYZ Investors under the following specifics:

Rental space: 25,000
Contract rent: $7.50 per square foot per year
Original term: 10 years, with rent payable at end of year
Current market rent: $8 per square foot per year
Remaining term: 8 years

Find ABC Medical Corporation's leasehold value at a before-tax discount rate of 10 percent.

2 Consider an investor who owns a 12,500-square-foot building. The contract rent is $6 per square foot (net) per year, payable in advance. The remaining term on the lease is 13 years, at which time the investor estimates the property will sell for $250,000. Selling expenses are expected to be 4 percent of the sales price. What is the value of these lease payments at a discount rate of 11 percent? What would be the value of the lease payments if the contract rent were payable at the end of each year?

3 Suppose the tenant in the preceding problem has the right to sublease the building. The market is willing to pay $7.33 per square foot per year for the remaining term. What is the value of the tenant's leasehold?

4 Consider the following assumptions for a subordinated ground lease:

Type of investment: warehouse
Estimated total property value: $100,000

Expected net operating income: $52,000 per year
Income growth rate: 3.5 percent per year
Debt financing
Loan amount: $90,000
Interest rate: 13.5 percent
Maturity (monthly payments): 20 years
Ground lease
Rental: $6,000 per year
Lease term: 25 years
Building costs: $92,000
Depreciation
Method: straight-line
Life: 31.5 years
Holding period: 4 years
Total value at end of holding period: $135,000
Value of land at end of holding period: $15,000
Investor's selling expenses: $11,000
Investor's marginal tax rate: 28 percent

Calculate the NPV of the investor's position if his after-tax required rate of return is 12 percent.

5 Sean B. Kelly has decided to invest in an office building. He is trying to decide whether to finance the 5,000-square-foot building with a mortgage or by leasing.

If he buys the building, the price will be $80,000. Kelly will use the straight-line depreciation method with a useful life of 15 years. At the end of the expected holding period of 7 years, the building has an expected selling price of $105,000. Selling expenses are expected to be 10 percent of the sales price. Kelly will purchase the property with a $65,000, 20-year, 10 percent FRM. The remaining $15,000 will be financed with equity.

If Kelly leases the property, the lease payments will be $10,000 on a "triple" net arrangement for a lease term of 5 years.

The marginal tax rate is 28 percent, and the required after-tax yield is 9 percent. Which option should Sean B. Kelly select?

6 Shopping Investors occupies and owns free and clear of any debt the Happy Shopper Shopping Center and plans to occupy it for another 10 years. The current book value of the land is $250,000, and the current book value of the building is $750,000 (for tax purposes). Shopping Investors is considering two options:

a Continuing to own and occupy the Happy Shopper Shopping Center for 10 years and then selling it

b Negotiating a sale-leaseback arrangement with an investor

Shopping Investors is depreciating the building at $150,000 per year using the straight-line method. Under the sale-leaseback arrangement, the leasing company will pay Shopping Investors $2,500,000 cash for the land and the building and lease it back to Shopping Investors at $250,000 per annum for 10 years (payments on lease due at the beginning of each year) with no option to repurchase. The (net) lease stipulates that Shopping Investors (lessee) will pay all property taxes and maintenance costs on the building and land. Shopping Investors projects the property's market value of $3,000,000 at the end of the 10-year lease. Shopping Investors' ordinary tax rate is 34 percent. The appropriate discount rate is 12 percent. Should Shopping Investors retain ownership of the building or negotiate for a sale-leaseback with the investor?

7 Consider the following assumptions:

Type of investment: office building
Estimated total property value: $50,000
Expected net operating income: $12,000 per year
Income growth rate: 0 percent per year
Debt financing
Loan amount: $42,000
Interest rate: ZIM
Maturity: 60 months
Ground lease
Rental: $7,500
Lease term: 25 years
Building costs: $37,000
Depreciation
Method: straight-line
Life: 31.5 years
Holding period: 10 years
Total value at end of holding period: $65,000
Value of land at end of holding period: $23,000
Investor's selling expenses: 4 percent of total value at end of holding period
Investor's marginal tax rate: 28 percent

Calculate the NPV of the investor's position if her after-tax required rate of return is 9 percent.

8 A real estate investor has leased a parcel of land from its owner under the following specifics:

Parcel size: 250 feet × 100 feet
Contract rent: $10 per front foot per year
Original term: 25 years, with rent payable at beginning of year
Current market rent: $9.50 per front foot per year
Remaining term: 15 years

Find the investor's leasehold value at a before tax-discount rate of 12 percent.

9 Ms. X owns a 25,000-square-foot warehouse. The contract rent is $12 per square foot (net) per year, payable in advance. The original term of the lease issued in 1980 was 30 years. Eight years later, Ms. X estimates the property will sell for $1,400,000 net of selling expenses.

a What is the value of these lease payments at a discount rate of 13 percent?

b Suppose the tenant has the right to sublease the warehouse and the market is willing to pay $15 per square foot per year for the remaining term. What is the value of the tenant's leasehold?

10 J. D. Rockefollow has decided to invest in a parcel of land. He is trying to decide whether to finance the property with a mortgage or by leasing.

If he buys the land, the price will be $250,000. At the end of the expected holding period of 5 years, the parcel has an expected net selling price of $375,000. Rockefollow will purchase the property with a $230,000, 30-year, 14 percent FRM. The remaining $20,000 will be financed with equity.

If Rockefollow leases the property, the lease payments will be $50,000 on a "triple" net arrangement for a lease term of 5 years.

The marginal tax rate is 28 percent, and the required after-tax yield is 12 percent. Which option should Rockefollow choose?

REFERENCES

DeCotto, Louis A.: "Sale and Leaseback: A Hollow Sound When Tapped?", *Tax Law Review,* vol. 37, no. 1, Fall 1981, pp. 1–50.

Harmchik, P. J., and N. E. Shertz: "Sale Leaseback Transactions Involving Real Estate: A Proposal for Defined Tax Rules," *Southern California Law Review,* vol. 55, May 1987, pp. 833–894.

Hawk, James J.: "Land Purchase-Leaseback/Leasehold Loan: An Old Idea Whose Time has Come," *Real Estate Issues,* vol. 6, no. 2, Fall-Winter 1981, pp. 21–24.

"Sale and Leasebacks as a Tax Shelter," *Utah Law Review,* 1981, pp. 843–867.

Shenkel, William M.: "Net Leases: A Critical Review," *Journal of Property Management,* May-June 1981, pp. 146–152.

CHAPTER **17**

OTHER FINANCING METHODS

Throughout the earlier chapters we outlined many financing methods. Here we describe various other forms of financing. Although several of these financing methods are relatively new, others have been used for some time. They are placed together in this chapter because they are all relatively simple to explain and understand; each method does not require an entire chapter. Thus this chapter of "other" financing methods is really a series of self-contained minichapters, each one describing the financing method, outlining its unique financial, legal, and tax aspects, and offering a computational example.

Although an entire chapter has not been devoted to each of these other methods, this in no way implies that the methods are little-used, ineffective, or unimportant financing tools. Indeed, several of them may be the primary financing methods of the future.

ASSUMPTION FINANCING

Mortgage loan *assumption* refers to a borrower-buyer's assuming or "taking over payments on" an existing mortgage. The buyer pays the difference between the selling price and the mortgage balance outstanding at the time of takeover and assumes the existing mortgage, including all the covenants, terms, and conditions that were originally agreed to.

Unique Aspects of Loan Assumptions

A loan assumption may be an attractive financing device in some instances. The interest rate on new loans may have risen substantially over the rate on an existing assumable mortgage. In addition, title, transfer, and loan origination fees are often lower when a loan is being assumed than when a new loan is originated.

Legal and Financial Aspects The first step when contemplating the assumption of an existing loan is to determine whether or not the loan may be assumed. Generally, the parties to a mortgage, as with any other legal contract, may assign their respective interests to another party, *in the absence of any agreement to the contrary*. Thus lenders are free to sell (assign) their interests, as they do in the second mortgage assumptions, provided that it is not forbidden to do so in the mortgage contract by so-called *nonassignment, nonassumption,* or *due-on-sale* clauses (see Chapter 3). These clauses generally stipulate that if the property is sold, the balance of the mortgage is immediately due and payable (that is, the acceleration clause is invoked).

Due-on-sale clauses were rarely used until rising interest rates became a serious threat to lenders' portfolio yields. It became undesirable to have long-term, low-interest mortgages on the books, so lenders used the due-on-sale clauses to increase the turnover of these older low-interest mortgages and to allow the money to be loaned out at the current higher rate. Property owners with below-market-rate loans realized that this benefit was accruing to them. In addition, if the market rate ever dropped below the mortgage's contract rate, the borrower was free to refinance at the lower rate (assuming there were no prepayment restrictions). Thus, lenders became strong proponents of due-on-sale clauses, and borrowers (aided by consumer groups) strongly opposed the clauses. Currently, the issue is being litigated, with opponents (borrowers) claiming, among other things, that due-on-sale clauses unfairly restrict consumers from selling their equity interest. Fearing foreclosure and/or litigation, borrowers either avoid assuming mortgages with due-on-sale clauses altogether or attempt to circumvent the clauses. For example, by covert arrangement between buyer and seller, some mortgages are being assumed without the lender being notified. Similarly, long-term lease-with-option-to-buy contracts with lease terms similar to those in the mortgage have been negotiated; officially, there has been no "sale," so the lender presumably cannot call the loan due. At this writing, the issue has not been completely resolved; these attempts to circumvent due-on-sale clauses are viewed as risky undertakings for both buyer and seller. Before committing to assumption financing, parties should seek competent legal counsel.

Other considerations are the rights and responsibilities of the buyer and the seller after the loan is assumed. The new borrower (buyer) is bound by all the terms and conditions of the original mortgage; that is, payment due dates, balloon payments, tax and insurance escrow requirements, late fees, rate and/or payment adjustments, restrictive clauses, and the like are all binding on the new borrower. For this reason, before agreeing to assume an existing loan, an individual should examine copies of the loan documents.

The seller in assumption financing, while assigning the rights and responsibilities under the mortgage to the buyer, generally is not relieved of liability for these responsibilities, unless the lender specifically agrees to this condition. Lenders make mortgage loans largely based on borrowers' ability and inclination to repay them. Since the original borrower submitted to a qualification procedure, the lender may be unwilling to relieve liability unless the new borrower submits to the qualification procedure and is deemed an adequate credit risk.

Once the legal implications of assumptions have been resolved, the financial aspects must be examined. We mentioned the effect of below-market-rate loans on the value of the lender's mortgage loan portfolio. The market value of any given mortgage is simply the present value of the remaining payment stream, discounted at the current market rate. For example, suppose a lender has an 8 percent mortgage with an outstanding balance of $50,000 and 216 payments (18 years $\times$ 12) at $437.48 per month. The current market rate is 12 percent. What is the value of this mortgage to the lender?

$$\text{Market value of mortgage} = \text{payment}(\text{PVAF}_{12\%/12,216})$$
$$= \$437.48(88.34309)$$
$$= \$38,648$$

The $50,000 mortgage is thus worth only $38,648, a "discount" of $11,352. If the lender wanted to sell the loan in the secondary market, it would bring only its discounted value.

The benefit of the $11,352 discount essentially accrues to the borrower for the period of time he holds the loan, and to his assigners if the loan is subsequently assumed. For example, if the borrower decides to sell the property and the loan is assumable, the borrower may ''sell'' both the property and its below-market financing. Since the financing terms cannot be changed from what were originally agreed upon, the benefit of the below-market interest rate may be capitalized into the property's purchase price, under the reasoning that the buyer may be willing to pay a premium for a property that has below-market financing available compared with one that does not. Returning to our previous example, suppose the buyer is attempting to determine the worth of the lower-interest, 8 percent loan to him. If a new $50,000, 12 percent loan has payments of $565.98 for 18 years, the borrower is saving the difference between $565.98 and $437.48, or $128.50, each month for 18 years. Discounting this payment differential to the present at the current 12 percent rate yields $11,352, the same as the lender's discounted value. This implies that if the seller raises the price of the property by $11,352 over its market value to capture the benefits of the low-interest loan, the borrower will be just as well off under an assumption as if a new loan were obtained and the market value were paid for the property. Thus, if the price were increased by less than $11,352, the buyer would be better off with the assumption financing, and vice versa. This assumes, of course, that the loan is held (thus the payment differential ''benefit'' continues) for the entire maturity.

In practice, it is debatable whether sellers can build all this benefit into the purchase price. Buyers in a particular market may not perceive that they will obtain the entire benefit should the property be sold before maturity, which may result in the loans being paid off. In our example, if the seller raises the price of the property by $11,352 with a loan assumption, the entire amount of the benefit accrues to the seller. If the price is not raised at all with a loan assumption, the entire benefit accrues to the buyer. In either case, the lender suffers the entire amount of the loss. Typically, sellers may gain only as much benefit as the market is willing to pay, based on the benefits it expects to receive.

Tax Aspects   The tax issues relating to mortgage assumption are not unique since they depend upon the nature of the original mortgage, which may or may not have unique tax issues associated with it. However, mortgage assumptions are often combined with installment sales (Chapter 10), wraparound mortgages (Chapter 11), and tax-deferred exchanges, where special tax consequence arise.

Assumption Financing Example

The following income property example illustrates the impact of assumption financing. You are considering purchasing a real estate investment that you forecast will have an NOI of $47,600 for each of the next 5 years. You plan to hold the property for 5 years, during which time you expect the property value (net of selling expense) to appreciate 20 percent. You are considering two financing options: obtaining a new loan for 75 percent of value at 14 percent interest for 25 years, or paying the seller his equity and assuming the mortgage that he executed 5 years ago. The mortgage amount at time of execution was $300,000, and the terms were 12 percent interest rate with 300 monthly payments.

If your required rate of return is 16 percent (before-tax), what is the value of the property to you under each financing option? To solve this problem we use the basic valuation formula:

$$V = V_M + V_E$$

where V = value of property
$\quad V_M$ = value of mortgage
$\quad V_E$ = value of equity

First, let us consider the new loan option. The value of the mortgage V_M is V times the loan-to-value ratio, or $0.75(V)$. The value of the equity V_E is the value of the before-tax cash flows plus the value of the before-tax equity reversion, both discounted to the present at the investor's required rate of return. Thus,

$$V = 0.75(V) + \text{PVAF}_{16\%,5}[\$47,600 - \text{MC}_{14\%/12,300}(V)0.75]$$
$$+ \text{PVF}_{16\%,5}[1.2(V) - \text{proportion outstanding}_{14\%/12,300,\text{EOY5}}(V)0.75]$$
$$= 0.75(V) + 3.274294[\$47,600 - 0.108338(V)] + 0.4761130[0.473981(V)]$$

Solving for V,

$$V - 0.75(V) + 0.35473(V) - 0.225669(V) = \$155,856$$
$$0.379061(V) = \$155,856$$
$$V = \$411,163$$

Note that we do not have to know or assume the property's current value—this is our single unknown, and the equation can be solved for V as shown.

Now consider the option with mortgage assumption. Here the value of the mortgage is determined by finding the current balance, which is the present value of the remaining payment stream discounted at the mortgage interest rate:

$$V_M = \$3,159.67(\text{PVAF}_{12\%/12,240})$$
$$= \$3,159.67(90.81942)$$
$$= \$286,959$$

Returning to our original equation, $V = V_M + V_E$, we have

$$V = \$286,959 + \text{PVAF}_{16\%,5}(\text{NOI} - \text{DS})$$
$$+ \text{PVF}_{16\%,5}(1.2V - \text{UM})$$
$$= \$286,959 + 3.274294(\$47,600 - \$37,916)$$
$$+ 0.476113[1.2(V) - 263,268]$$

$$V - 0.571335(V) = \$193,322$$
$$0.428665V = \$193,322$$
$$V = \$450,986$$

Thus, the investor may pay up to \$411,163 for the investment if it is financed with a new loan, or \$450,986 if it is financed under the existing mortgage, and earn the required 16 percent before-tax rate of return. If the seller asks these respective prices, the investor would be indifferent to either option. However, if the asking price is \$411,163 under either option, the investor is better off opting for the loan assumption. This is an unlikely possibility, however, since the seller realizes the benefit of the lower-interest existing loan to a buyer and will raise the asking price accordingly. The investor will likely pay a premium for the property, up to the perceived value of obtaining the lower interest rate.

JUNIOR MORTGAGES

Mortgages on real estate may be referred to by their *lien priority;* that is, the order in which they will be paid out of the sale proceeds of the property in the event of default and foreclosure. A first mortgage has first claim to be paid, a second mortgage has second claim, and so on. All mortgages placed subsequent and subordinate to the first mortgage are collectively referred to as *junior mortgages* because their claim against the property is junior to that of the first mortgage.

Junior mortgages are a useful tool in real estate financing. For example, a property owner with a sizable amount of equity and an existing mortgage that has an interest rate below the current market rate may want to refinance the property to obtain cash. Instead of taking out a new first mortgage in an amount sufficient to pay off the existing first mortgage and put the desired amount of cash in hand, the borrower may find a lender willing to grant a second mortgage for just the amount of cash desired, thereby leaving the first mortgage on the property and retaining the benefit of the below-market interest rate.

A junior mortgage is also commonly used in the financing of the purchase of real estate. The buyer may not have sufficient funds to pay the difference between the amount of the first mortgage and the sales price. The shortage may be loaned by a mortgage lender under a second mortgage so that the seller is fully paid. Or, the seller may be willing to grant the second mortgage, thereby allowing the buyer to pay the shortage in installments.

Unique Aspects of Junior Mortgages

Since the status of a mortgage as "junior" refers only to its lien priority, there are few issues that are unique to junior financing. However, the junior lien status does present some risk, default, and foreclosure aspects that affect the determination of the overall effective cost of borrowing.

Legal and Financial Aspects   The junior mortgage lender, whether a lending institution or a seller, is in a riskier position than that of the first mortgagee. If default occurs and the foreclosure sale proceeds are insufficient to cover the balance owed on the first and junior mortgages combined, the mortgages are paid in order of priority until funds are exhausted. Thus, junior mortgagees consider the combined loan-to-value ratio quite important in risk analysis. Similarly, the combined total of the mortgage payments will be considered in the analysis of the borrower's (or property's) ability to carry the additional debt service imposed by the junior mortgage.

In the event the borrower defaults, the junior lender may be placed in a financially and legally awkward position, depending upon the situation and the individual state's laws affecting foreclosure and redemption. Consider, for instance, the situation in which the borrower defaults on the second mortgage but not on the first. The junior lender has the right of foreclosure but cannot compel the first mortgagee to join in the foreclosure action, although the first mortgagee may do so if desired. Generally, the purchaser at the junior foreclosure sale buys the property subject to the first mortgage. However, if the value of the property is less than the amount owing on the first mortgage, there will likely be no bidders.

Where default has occurred on both the first and the second mortgages, it is likely that the lenders will enter into a joint foreclosure action on both mortgages, with the proceeds being used to pay off the lenders according to the priority.

Finally, if default occurs on the first mortgage but not on the second, the first mortgagee may foreclose alone, omitting the junior mortgagee from the action. The foreclosure on the first mortgage does not extinguish the junior lender's rights, but the situation becomes more complicated. The second mortgagee has basically two remedies: foreclosure and redemption. Under foreclosure, the junior lender forecloses subsequent to the first-mortgage foreclosure, but the property is still subject to the amount owed on the first mortgage, even though the original foreclosure sale may have already occurred. (The first mortgage is essentially revived, but only for the purpose of the junior mortgage foreclosure.) If the property's value exceeds that of the first loan balance at the time of foreclosure, then the junior lender is entitled to the excess up to the amount due the junior lender. In the actual foreclosure sale, the purchaser at the original foreclosure sale will likely be among the bidders. If this purchaser had acted knowledgeably in the first place, the purchaser would have known about the junior lien and considered it when bidding at the original sale.

The other remedy for the junior lender who has been omitted from the foreclosure is redemption, whereby the junior lender pays the senior lender at the original foreclosure sale the amount owing on the first mortgage, thereby becoming the holder of two liens, either or both of which may be foreclosed. Since redemption requires the omitted junior lender to come up with a substantial amount of money and since the junior lender cannot use the property as security for a loan to borrow this money, this remedy is not as common, and it seemingly imposes an additional burden on the junior lender that would not have been the case had the junior lender been included in the original foreclosure action.

These foreclosure rules are based on property law in general; their application and use may vary from state to state. In any case, however, the junior lender is in a riskier position than the first lender and will command a commensurately higher interest rate and usually a shorter maturity than the first-mortgage lender. In addition, in some locales, lenders have a policy of not granting second mortgages unless they already have the first loan, because of the cumbersome nature of foreclosure on the junior lien. It is prudent for the seller contemplating carrying a purchaser on a second mortgage to first consult with legal counsel to ascertain the default and foreclosure remedies available in the local area and their practical ramifications. Finally, an alternative way to structure the financing to avoid many of these foreclosure problems is the wraparound mortgage, discussed in Chapter 9.

Tax Aspects   There are no unique tax aspects in junior mortgages. The borrower can deduct interest according to the loan's amortization structure. At present, most junior mortgages are structured as fixed-rate, level-payment loans or as interest-only loans with the principal due at maturity, so there are no unresolved tax issues here as with other forms of loan amortization.

Junior Mortgage Example

We mentioned that the computation of the overall effective cost of borrowing is somewhat unique when two loans are involved. For example, consider a prospective buyer who wishes to buy an $80,000 property and has a down payment of $10,000. A first mortgage in the amount of $60,000 is available at 12 percent interest, with level monthly payments of $631.93 for 300 months. (For the purposes of computing the effective borrowing cost, it does not matter whether this first mortgage is a new loan or an existing mortgage that will be assumed.) The buyer needs a second mortgage of $10,000 to complete the transaction. Suppose the seller (or third-party lender) is willing to grant a 15 percent, $10,000 second mortgage with a level monthly payment of $161.33 that will amortize the loan in 10 years. What is the buyer's overall effective borrowing cost?

To solve this problem we set the total present value of the financing, $70,000, equal to the present value of the payment stream and solve for the rate that will make the discounted value of the payment stream equal to $70,000. The payment stream is $161.93 + $631.93 = $793.26 per month for the remainder of the first mortgage, assuming it is not prepaid. Thus,

$$\$70{,}000 = \$793.26(\text{PVAF}_{i\%/12,120}) + \$631.93(\text{PVAF}_{i\%/12,180})(\text{PVF}_{i\%/12,120})$$

We must solve for i by trial and error. We know that the actual rate will be higher than 12 percent but lower than 15 percent. Also, since the total of the loans is dominated by the 12 percent first mortgage, the overall rate will be closer to 12 than to 15 percent. So we will try, say, 12 and 13 percent present value facts, as Table 17-1 illustrates. Note that the net present value of 12 percent is a negative number, showing us that the present worth of the outflows (payments) exceeds

TABLE 17-1   OVERALL COST OF BORROWING: JUNIOR MORTGAGE EXAMPLE

Month	Total payment	×	PVAF	×	PVF	=	PV	PVAF	×	PVF	=	PV
					12%					**13%**		
1–120	$793.26		69.70052				$55,291	66.97442				$53,128
120–300	631.93		83.32166		0.30299		15,953	79.03626		0.27444		13,707
						Total PV	$71,244				Total PV	$66,835

Interpolation:

$PV_{12\%}$	$71,244	$PV_{12\%}$	$71,244
$- PV_{13\%}$	66,835	− Desired PV	70,000
Difference	4,409	Difference	1,244

$$\frac{\$1,244}{\$4,409} = 0.28 \quad 0.28 \times 1\% \text{ difference in rate} = 0.28\%$$

$$12\% + 0.28\% = 12.28\%$$

the present worth of the inflow ($70,000). At 13 percent, the converse is true. Thus, we know the rate is between 12 and 13 percent. By interpolation, we have an overall cost of borrowing of 12.28 percent on the combined loans. If the borrower had the option of obtaining a first mortgage of $70,000 so that a second mortgage was not needed, the borrower would be better off with this option if the interest rate on the $70,000 first mortgage was less than 12.28 percent. The borrower would be better off with the $60,000 first mortgage and $10,000 second-mortgage option if the rate was higher than 12.28 percent.

BUYDOWN MORTGAGES

A buydown mortgage is simply a fixed rate, level-payment loan with an additional twist: A third party, typically the developer or seller, at loan origination pays the lender a fee to essentially "buy down" the interest rate for the borrower for the first few years of the loan. The effect for the borrower is similar to that for a graduated-payment mortgage (see Chapter 8). The payments are lower initially, with one or more stepped increases over typically the first 3 to 5 years, finally leveling off for the remaining loan term. The difference is that the borrower's reduced payments are based on a below-market interest rate for the period of time that the rate is "bought down."

Buydowns are used to attract buyers of new or existing homes during periods of high interest rates. The attractiveness to the purchaser is twofold: The lower interest rate initially appears to be a desirable feature, and the lower initial payments allow a borrower to qualify for a higher loan (hence, a more expensive home) than the borrower could afford under a standard fixed-rate mortgage. The cost of the buydown to the seller or developer, however, may likely be built into the selling price of the home, thus partially or completely negating for the purchaser any positive effects of a buydown.

Unique Aspects of Buydown Mortgages

In most cases, buydowns present few additional problems from the standard fixed-rate conventional loan they are derived from. However, the unusual payment structure raises certain financial, legal, and tax issues that must be examined.

Legal and Financial Aspects To fully understand the unique aspects of a buydown loan, we first must understand its mechanics. Suppose a borrower wants to purchase a new $80,000 home, putting down $20,000 cash and financing the remaining $60,000 with a 30-year loan. The current market interest rate is 15 percent. Suppose, however, that the developer offers to buy down the interest rate to 13 percent for the first 3 years of the loan. Under this plan, the borrower's payments would be based on a 13 percent, 30-year, $60,000 mortgage for the first 3 years and on a 15 percent, 30-year, $60,000 mortgage for the remaining term. Thus, the monthly payment for the first 3 years is

$$\$60,000 \times MC_{13\%/12,360} = \text{payment}$$
$$= \$663.72$$

and for years 4 to 30 is

$$\$60,000 \times MC_{15\%/12,360} = \$758.67$$

The difference in the payments, $94.95, is essentially "made up" by the developer. The effect is similar to that of discount points, which were explained in Chapter 2. With discount points, the party paying the points is essentially "buying down" the interest rate for the entire term of the loan, rather than for just the first few years.

The developer's (or seller's) cost is computed by discounting the payment "shortages" back to the present at the required interest rate. Thus, for our example,

$$\text{Payment shortage} \times PVAF_{15\%/12,36} = \text{developer's (seller's) cost}$$
$$\$94.95 \times 28.84727 = \$2,739$$

Since the discount is an added cost to the seller or developer, there is a strong incentive to raise the price of the property and thereby recoup part or all of this cost. However, note that the seller and developer are not the only ones who can pay this fee; often the buyer's parents or other relatives pay the buydown fee.

Occasionally, the *buyer* pays the fee to qualify for a more expensive home. For example, suppose in our previous illustration that the buyer has $20,000 cash to put down on an $80,000 house. The payments on a fixed-rate, level-payment loan of $60,000 at 15 percent interest are $758.67. But suppose the buyer has another option, putting only 10 percent ($8,000) down and using the $12,000 balance of the cash to buy down the interest rate to, say, 9.9 percent for years 1 through 5 of the loan. Level payments on a 15 percent, 30-year loan of $72,000 are $910.40. With the rate bought down to 9.9 percent, payments on the same loan are $626.54, a difference of $283.86. The present value of this difference, discounted at 15 percent for 5 years, is $11,932, or nearly the $12,000 of cash remaining after the $8,000 down payment. Thus, a buyer who has a large down payment but an income level insufficient to afford payments of $758.67 on a standard level-payment mortgage may use part of her or his cash to buy down the interest rate to 9.9 percent and payments to $626.54, which may be enough to make the property affordable at this time. This assumes, of course, that the buyer's income will increase over the 5 years of the buydown such that the $910.40 payment will be affordable at that time.

From the lender's perspective, there is no difference in effective yield between a buydown and a conventional level-payment loan, provided that payoff does not occur prior to the end of the buydown period. If payoff does occur before then, the effect of the discount or buydown fee is similar to that of any front-end discount: It raises the lender's effective yield above what was expected. For this reason, buyers, developers, and others who pay buydown fees often request that the loan agreement declare that the payer or buyer is the "owner" of the buydown fee, which is held in escrow for the express purpose of making up the payment differential during the buydown period. If the loan is paid off before the end of the buydown period, the unused balance in the escrow account reverts to the payer or buyer, as determined by the loan agreement.

The question may arise whether the payer of the buydown fee must pay it all at loan origination. Could the developer, for instance, make up the payment differential each month during the buydown period, rather than pay the discounted value up front? This arrangement could create legal problems if the developer defaults. A borrower current with his or her portion of the payment could find foreclosure occurring because of the developer's default. As a result, buydown fees are *always* collected at loan origination either as a direct fee paid to the lender or as an amount deposited into an escrow account and paid out to the lender as required.

Liquidity Problems   The FNMA imposes several restrictions on the structuring of buydowns to make them acceptable to the secondary mortgage market. A lender who desires a mortgage portfolio with maximum liquidity will structure the buydowns within these current limitations:

1 The seller's contribution is limited to (a) 10 percent of the lesser of the sales price or appraised value, for loans with a loan-to-value ratio of 90 percent or less, or (b) 6 percent of the lesser of the sales price or appraised value, for loans with a loan-to-value ratio greater than 90 percent.

If the seller's contribution exceeds these limits, the excess is treated as sales concession and the value of the property is adjusted accordingly:

2 The borrower's effective interest rate cannot increase by more than 1 percent per year during the buydown period.

3 Buydown loans on one- to four-family properties are permissible. The buydown may be on certain adjustable-rate and graduated-payment, adjustable-rate loans, as well as on conventional fixed-rate mortgages. Buydowns on fixed-rate second mortgages are also permissible.

Tax Aspects Because of their unique structuring, buydowns creates certain tax issues related to the amounts and timing of interest income and expense for lender, borrower, and payer of the buydown fee.

When the developer pays the buydown fee, it is likely that the deposit may be treated as an ordinary business expense deduction. If the seller pays the buydown fee, the fee will likely be treated in the same fashion as discount points. The buyer would be able to deduct only the interest he or she actually paid.

From the lender's perspective, the fee might be considered as income when received. However, if the borrower is designated as the "owner" of the funds pledged into an escrow account, the interest payments paid out of the account in addition to those paid out of the borrower's pocket might be deductible. Also, since the lender in this case does not receive interest payments in advance, but monthly, as with an ordinary level-payment loan, the interest income would not have to be accounted for until received. The refundability of the fee in the event of early debt retirement also may have a bearing on the treatment of buydown fees as interest.

Clearly, buydown mortgages raise several tax issues, many of which have yet to be resolved at this writing. Borrowers, lenders, developers, and other prospective parties to a buydown agreement should seek advice from competent tax counsel before entering into a buydown agreement.

BUYDOWN EXAMPLE

A developer is offering a buydown loan whereby the interest rate will be bought down for the first 3 years of the mortgage. The rate for year 1 will be 12 percent; year 2, 13 percent; year 3, 14 percent; and years 4 through 30, the market rate of 15 percent. A buyer is considering purchasing one of the developer's new homes, which is priced at $100,000. The borrower expects to put down $20,000 and finance $80,000. We wish to determine the borrower's monthly payment, the developer's buydown fee, and the buyer's effective borrowing cost (before-tax). (Note that we assume the lender earns the market rate of 15 percent on this loan—thus borrowing cost and yield are *not* the same here.)

To calculate the borrower's payments, we proceed as follows:

Year 1: $\$80{,}000 \times \text{MC}_{12\%/12,360} = \text{payment}$

                                  $\$80{,}000 \times 0.0102861 = \$822.89$

Year 2: $\$80{,}000 \times \text{MC}_{13\%/12,360} = \text{payment}$

                                  $\$80{,}000 \times 0.011062 = \$884.96$

Year 3: $$\$80,000 \times MC_{14\%/12,360} = \text{payment}$$

$$\$80,000 \times 0.011849 = \$947.90$$

Years 4–30: $$\$80,000 \times MC_{15\%/12,360} = \text{payment}$$

$$\$80,000 \times 0.01264 = \$1,011.56$$

Figure 17-1 illustrates this loan's payment schedule. The area beneath the $1,011.56 line is the total amount the lender receives. The unshaded portion is the amount the borrower pays, and the shaded portion is the amount the developer must make up. Since the developer pays this fee at loan origination, we must calculate the present value of these payment shortages to determine the buydown fee:

$$\text{Buydown fee} = \text{PV year 1 shortage} + \text{PV year 2 shortage} + \text{PV year 3 shortage}$$

$$
\begin{aligned}
PV &= \$1,011.56 - \$822.89(PVAF_{15\%/12,12}) \\
&\quad + \$1,011.56 - \$884.96(PVAF_{15\%/12,24} - PVAF_{15\%/12,12}) \\
&\quad + \$1,011.56 - \$947.90(PVAF_{15\%/12,36} - PVAF_{15\%/12,24}) \\
&= \$188.67(11.07931) + \$126.60(20.62423 - 11.07931) \\
&\quad + \$63.66(28.84727 - 20.62423) \\
&= \$2,090.33 + \$1,800.84 + \$523.48 \\
&= \$4,415
\end{aligned}
$$

Table 17-2 illustrates the calculation of the borrower's effective cost. Since we know that the cost is less than 15 percent but greater than 12 percent, we initially try, say, 14 percent. Our desired PV is $80,000, and the PV at 14 percent is $81,508. Thus, the 14 percent rate is too low. Trying 15 percent, we find the PV is $76,178. Interpolating, we find the borrower's effective cost is 14.29 percent if the loan is held to maturity. If the loan is paid off early, however, the borrower's cost is reduced because of the greater effect of the reduced interest in the early years of the loan.

Note that this loan meets FNMA's requirements for secondary market trading: The seller (developer's) loan fee is $4,415, well within the 10 percent maximum contribution allowed on a mortgage with a loan-to-value ratio of 90 percent or less; and the borrower's interest cost increases 1 percent per year, which is FNMA's limit.

ZERO INTEREST MORTGAGES (ZIMs)

The zero interest mortgage (ZIM) is structured with no interest charges whatsoever, i.e., the entire amount of each payment the borrower makes is directly credited to principal reduction. The recently introduced ZIM is used by developers to attract buyers to new housing or condominium development. The borrower typically pays one-third or more of the purchase price as a down payment, with

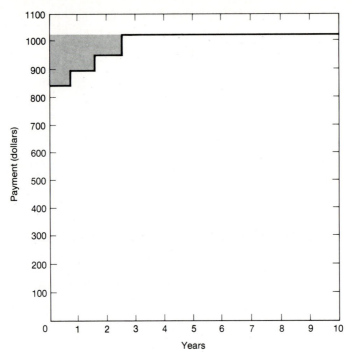

FIGURE 17-1   Payment schedule illustration: buydown example.

the balance "borrowed" on a ZIM with level monthly payments over a 5- to 7-year amortization period.

Unique Aspects of ZIMs

At first glance, the ZIM appears to offer substantial benefits to the buyer-borrower: Although a minimum one-third down payment is generally required, the borrower has the property paid for in, say, 5 years. However, economic analysis suggests that in many cases, the ZIM may offer no real financial benefits to the borrower and may create other problems as well.

Legal and Financial Aspects   As deceptively simple as the ZIM appears, to understand its full impact we must examine why it was created. Developers, faced with many unsold homes in a tight money market and with foreclosure on their construction loans imminent, needed a financing vehicle whose attractiveness would create additional sales and thereby improve cash flows. The developer who carries ZIM financing receives the large down payment that, when applied to the balance of the construction loan, may be enough to appease the lender, and allow the construction loan to be extended for an additional 5 years, the ZIM's

TABLE 17-2   BUYER'S EFFECTIVE COST OF BORROWING AT $PV_{14\%}$ AND $PV_{15\%}$: BUYDOWN EXAMPLE

Year	×	Monthly payment	×	$PVAF_{14\%/12}$	×	$PVF_{14\%/12}$	=	$PV_{14\%}$
1		$822.89		11.13746		1.00000		$9,165
2		884.96		11.13746		0.87006		8,575
3		947.90		11.13746		0.75701		7,992
4–30		1,011.56		83.71478		0.65865		55,776
						Total $PV_{14\%}$		$81,508

Year	×	Monthly payment	×	$PVAF_{15\%/12}$	×	$PVF_{15\%/12}$	=	$PV_{15\%}$
1		$822.89		11.07931		1.00000		$9,117
2		884.96		11.07931		0.86151		8,446
3		947.90		11.07931		0.74220		7,795
4–30		1,011.56		78.57078		0.63941		50,820
						Total $PV_{15\%}$		$76,178

Interpolation:

$PV_{14\%}$	$81,508	$PV_{14\%}$	$81,508
$- PV_{15\%}$	76,178	Desired PV	80,000
Difference	5,330	Difference	1,508

$$\frac{\$1,508}{\$5,330} = 0.29 \times 1\% \text{ difference in rate} = 0.29\%$$

$$14\% + 0.29 = 14.29\%$$

typical period. Of course, this arrangement is costly to the developer because interest is accruing on the money the developer borrowed (the construction loan) and not on the ZIM. However, the cost of the ZIM to the developer can be reduced by significantly increasing the selling price of the property.

For the developer who makes arrangements with an outside lender to provide ZIM funds, the effect is similar. The developer receives the down payment from the buyer, who obtains a ZIM for the remainder of the purchase price from the designated lender. The lender, of course, does not loan money interest-free. The face amount of the ZIM must be discounted according to the lender's current required yield. For instance, suppose a borrower buys a home priced at $75,000, putting down $25,000 and financing the remaining balance of $50,000 with a 5-year ZIM. The lender currently requires a before-tax yield of 15 percent. The ZIM payments of $833.33 over 60 months must be discounted to give the lender the required 15 percent yield. Thus, the present value of this $833.33 monthly annuity to the lender can be calculated as follows:

$$PV \text{ of loan to lender} = \$833.33 \times PVAF_{15\%/12,60 \text{months}}$$
$$= \$833.33 \times 42.03459$$
$$= \$35,029$$

At closing the developer receives the $25,000 down payment and the discounted value of the loan—$35,029—for a total of $60,029, or $14,971 less than the $75,000 asking price.

As the example illustrates, ZIM financing is an expensive proposition for the developer unless the selling price is increased to absorb all or part of the discount. However, even if we raise the selling price in our example by $15,000 (the approximate cost of the discount), to $90,000, the developer still will not recoup the entire financing cost. With a $90,000 price, the down payment is $30,000, with $60,000 financed with a ZIM for 5 years, with monthly payments of $1,000. The value of the loan to the lender is

$$\text{PV of loan to lender} = \$1,000 \times \text{PVAF}_{15\%/12,60 \text{ months}}$$
$$= \$1,000 \times 42.03459$$
$$= \$42,035$$

Adding $42,035 to the $30,000 down payment, we see that the developer's total price is $72,035, nearly $3,000 short of the property's value. In fact, the price would have to be raised to about $93,700 for the developer to recoup all charges and receive $75,000 in cash for the home:

$$\text{Price} \times \text{loan-to-value ratio} = \text{loan amount}$$
$$\$93,700 \times 0.67 = \$62,466$$

$$\text{Loan amount} \div \text{number of payments} = \text{monthly ZIM payment}$$
$$\$62,466 \div 60 = \$1,041.10$$

$$\text{PV of loan to lender} = \$1,041.10 \times \text{PVAF}_{15\%/12,60 \text{ months}}$$
$$= \$1,041.10 \times 42.03459$$
$$= \$43,762$$

$$\text{Loan proceeds} + \text{down payment} = \text{cash to developer}$$
$$\$43,762 + \$31,234 = \$74,996 \approx \$75,000$$

Since the developer is shouldering a portion of the finance costs rather than passing them on to the buyer, this method of financing is typically offered only when sales are lagging.

From the lender's perspective, the ZIM is an attractive investment vehicle. The loan is relatively short-term, compared with the standard 25- to 30-year home mortgage; thus amortization occurs rapidly. Interest is earned at the time of loan origination through the discounting process; if the loan is paid off before it matures, the lender is not required to rebate any of the discount to the developer or borrower, and thus yield is enhanced significantly above expectations. The loan-to-value ratio, at a maximum of 66⅔ percent, is quite low. Although it is likely based on an inflated value, the loan-to-value ratio will not exceed the standard 80 percent even if the purchase price is increased up to 20 percent above market-value. To illustrate, suppose our home, valued at $75,000, is increased by 20 percent, to a price of $90,000. The borrower pays one-third down ($30,000), leaving a balance of $60,000 to be financed with a ZIM. When compared with the actual value of the home, the ratio of the $60,000 loan to the $75,000 value is exactly 80 percent. Recall from our earlier example, however, that this 20 percent increase is not enough to cover the entire financing cost; the price must be raised to $93,700, an increase of $18,700, or about 24.9 percent. However, since the price can be raised $15,000 without exceeding generally accepted loan-to-value ratio requirements, it is possible for the developer to build most of the financing cost into the home's purchase price and still obtain lender financing.

Will a buyer, however, pay $93,700 for a $75,000 home to get the benefit of a ZIM? It is doubtful. There is such a strong incentive for the developer to raise the price of the home enough to cover the financing cost that the buyer ends up paying a very high price for a ZIM. Furthermore, a purchase price well above market value will be a disadvantage for a borrower who is forced to sell soon after purchase, say, because of a job transfer.

For example, to obtain a ZIM, suppose the borrower in our example pays $93,700 for a property valued at $75,000. If this borrower has to sell at, say, the end of the first year of the loan, there will be a potential loss of equity. Table 17-3 illustrates this loan's amortization schedule. At the end of year 1, there is a $49,973 balance remaining on the ZIM. The borrower has paid in a $31,234 down payment. To merely recoup this equity investment (ignoring transaction costs), the property must sell for $81,207, $5,207 more than its value 1 year earlier. A standard fixed-rate, level-payment mortgage on the real $75,000 value would at least provide a return of original equity plus whatever amortization has occurred over the year, assuming no change in the property value.

The effective borrowing cost is significantly increased with an early payoff as well. The borrowing cost of the $62,466 ZIM paid off at the end of year 1 is calculated by setting the real value of the borrowed funds, $43,762, equal to the income stream. Thus,

$$\$43,762 = \$1,041.10(\text{PVAF}_{i\%/12,12}) + \$49,973(\text{PVAF}_{i\%/12,12})$$
$$i = 40.31\%$$

nearly triple the yield if held to maturity.

TABLE 17-3   AMORTIZATION SCHEDULE: $93,700 PURCHASE PRICE WITH $62,466, 5-YEAR ZIM

Year	Price paid	One-third down payment	Debt service	End-of-year loan balance
0	$93,700	$31,234		$62,466
1			$12,493	49,973
2			12,493	37,480
3			12,493	24,987
4			12,493	12,494
5			12,493	0

Of course, if the borrower were able to pass on the benefit of the ZIM to the new buyer through an assumption of the ZIM, the buyer would be willing to pay an above-market purchase price for this benefit, thus allowing the original borrower to recoup much of the inflated purchase price paid at loan origination. Unfortunately for the borrower, nonassumption or due-on-sale clauses are typically inserted into ZIMs, precluding this benefit for the borrower.

Although ZIMs are an effective sales tool for the developer and an attractive, relatively low-risk investment for the lender, it is doubtful that they provide any advantage to the borrower if the price is increased to cover all (or nearly all) the financing costs the developer incurs. This principle is developed further in the example at the end of this section.

Tax Aspects The current tax laws and rulings present another consequence for the borrower on a ZIM. Since the single most important tax effect of any mortgage is the interest deduction, at first glance it may appear that there is no interest deduction on a ZIM because no interest is presumed to be paid. This assumption is incorrect, however, because Sec. 483 of the Internal Revenue Code permits interest to be *imputed* into the payments at a rate (as of 1982) of 10 percent. This means that the difference between the total face amount of the payments, $62,466, is compared with the present value of the payments discounted at the allowable 10 percent rate, which is $49,000. The difference of $13,466 is the total amount of imputed interest allowable, which must be prorated evenly over the 60 loan payments to arrive at the annual interest deduction. Therefore, $13,466 ÷ 60 = $224.44 of interest per payment.

Each $1,041.10 payment, then, consists of (for tax purposes) $224.44 of interest and $816.66 of principal. The annual interest deduction is computed as $224.44 per month × 12 months = $2,693.

Although the interest deduction and resulting tax benefits are not lost completely under a ZIM, they are reduced significantly when compared with other, more straightforward types of financing because of two factors. First, the ZIM-imputed interest is prorated equally, whereas the interest on other types of financing is front-ended such that interest is high during the early years of the loan and lower during the ending years. Since most mortgages historically remain outstanding for only 5 to 7 years, a considerable amount of the interest deduction is lost in the early years of a ZIM when compared with other types of loans. Second, the 10 percent rate at which interest is imputed may be considerably lower than the current market interest rate, upon which the premium selling price and loan discount are presumably based.

Another tax issue that has not been fully resolved is the effect that imputed interest has on the adjusted basis at the time of sale. Although there will be no immediate tax consequence for the owner-occupant who sells the present residence and buys another home of essentially equal or greater value within 24 months, the basis adjustment, if any, may ultimately affect the homeowners' tax liability. As of this writing, the IRS's position is not clear.

When the tax effects of ZIMs are added to the legal and financial aspects, it may be that the borrower is worse off with a ZIM than, for example, a fixed-rate conventional loan. The following example helps put this statement into perspective.

ZIM Example

This example uses the facts from the earlier examples in this section. Our goal is to determine the expected after-tax return to a prospective homebuyer attempting to decide between a standard fixed-rate mortgage and a ZIM. We assume a worst-case situation for the buyer here; that is, we assume that the developer is passing on the *entire* financing cost to the buyer in the form of a higher sales price.

The facts are:

1 Present value of the home is $75,000.
2 Conventional loan terms are 15 percent interest, 20-year term. The developer will sell for a $75,000 price if conventional financing is obtained.
3 ZIM terms are one-third down ($31,234) on a purchase price of $93,700; $62,466 to be financed with a ZIM for 5 years.
4 We assume the home will be held for the entire 20-year term of the conventional loan.
5 We assume the buyer will put down $31,234 under either financing alternative and that the buyer is in the 28 percent marginal tax bracket.

Table 17-4 illustrates the buyer's after-tax cash flows under the ZIM. At year 0, the buyer puts in $31,234 equity, and during the first 5 years makes payments totaling $12,493 annually ($1,041.10 × 12). When multiplied by the homebuyer's 28 percent tax bracket, the $2,693 interest deduction (computed in the "Tax Aspects" section) provides $754 of income tax savings each year. When the pos-

TABLE 17-4   BUYER'S AFTER-TAX CASH FLOWS: ZIM FINANCING

	Equity investment	Debt service	Interest payment	Tax savings	ATCF
0	$31,234				$31,234
1		12,493	$2,693	754	11,739
2		12,493	$2,693	754	11,739
3		12,493	$2,693	754	11,739
4		12,493	$2,693	754	11,739
5		12,493	$2,693	754	11,739

IRR calculation:

$$\$75,000 = \$31,234 + \$11,739(\text{PVAF}_{i\%,5})$$
$$\$43,766 = \$11,739(\text{PVAF}_{i\%,5})$$
$$\text{PVAF}_{i\%,5} = 3.728$$
$$i = 10.65\%$$

itive tax savings are added to the negative before-tax cash flows, the result is an after-tax cash flow of −$11,739 per year for years 1 through 5.

The next step is to solve for the IRR, assuming the present value is the $75,000 value of the home and setting this equal to the payments made to obtain it, as shown in the lower part of the table. As indicated, the after-tax cost of borrowing is 10.65 percent. Next, we must calculate the after-tax cash flows for the conventional loan, as shown in Table 17-5. This table is more involved than Table 17-4 because the loan runs for 20 years and the interest deduction (hence the tax savings) changes each year. Note that we are assuming the buyer makes the same equity investment as required under the ZIM but obtains the property at the $75,000 cash price. Thus, the amount needed to be financed is only $43,766, resulting in monthly payments of $576.31 ($6,916 annually).

To help the borrower decide between the ZIM and a conventional loan, we can do one of two things: First, we can determine the IRR for the conventional loan, as we did in Table 17-4 for the ZIM. If the IRR for the conventional loan is *less than* the 10.65 percent rate on the ZIM, then the conventional loan is the better buy, and vice versa. However, because of the large number of years used in the analysis, finding the IRR for the conventional mortgage would be very tedious, even with a calculator. Fortunately, there is another method that will yield the results needed to make the decision.

TABLE 17-5 BUYER'S AFTER-TAX CASH FLOWS: CONVENTIONAL FINANCING*

Year	Equity investment	Debt service	Interest payment	Tax savings†	ATCF
0	$31,234				$31,234
1		$6,916	$6,540	$1,831	5,085
2		6,916	6,479	1,814	5,102
3		6,916	6,409	1,795	5,121
4		6,916	6,328	1,772	5,144
5		6,916	6,233	1,745	5,171
6		6,916	6,124	1,715	5,201
7		6,916	5,996	1,679	5,237
8		6,916	5,848	1,637	5,279
9		6,916	5,677	1,590	5,326
10		6,916	5,478	1,534	5,382
11		6,916	5,246	1,469	5,447
12		6,916	4,978	1,394	5,522
13		6,916	4,667	1,307	5,609
14		6,916	4,305	1,205	5,711
15		6,916	3,886	1,080	5,828
16		6,916	3,398	951	6,388
17		6,916	2,833	793	6,123
18		6,916	2,177	610	6,506
19		6,916	1,415	396	6,520
20		6,916	531	149	6,767

*$75,000 purchase price, 15% interest rate, $31,234 down payment, $43,766 mortgage for 20 years.
†At 28% marginal tax rate.

Recall that at the internal rate of return, the present value of the outflows exactly equals the present value of the inflows; that is, NPV = 0. So, if we discount the outflows on the conventional loan at the 10.65 percent rate, the total present value of the discounted outflow will

1 Equal $75,000 if the rate on the conventional loan is equal to 10.65 percent, and either option may be chosen
2 Be less than $75,000 if the rate on the conventional loan is less than 10.65 percent, in which case the conventional loan is the better choice
3 Be greater than $75,000 if the rate on the conventional loan is greater than 10.65 percent, in which case the ZIM is better

Table 17-6 illustrates the discounting process. Since the present value of the outflows, $75,007, is equal to the present value of the inflow (the $75,000 house), the borrower is indifferent. The borrower is paying $75,007 for a property worth $75,000 when the payments are discounted at the ZIM rate. Thus, the effective after-tax cost of the conventional loan is the same as that of the ZIM.

This example may be somewhat unrealistic for many borrowers, however, since homes are generally held for only 5 to 7 years. Assume the borrower in our example holds the property only 5 years and then sells it for $92,000, with selling costs equal to 5 percent of the price. Also, we assume there are no tax conse-

TABLE 17-6   NPV COMPUTATIONS

Year	Equity	ATCF	PVF$_{10.65\%}$	PV
0	($31,234)		1.0000	($31,234)
1		(5,085)	0.9038	(4,596)
2		(5,102)	0.8168	(4,167)
3		(5,121)	0.7382	(3,780)
4		(5,144)	0.6671	(3,432)
5		(5,171)	0.6029	(3,118)
6		(5,201)	0.5449	(2,834)
7		(5,237)	0.4924	(2,579)
8		(5,279)	0.4450	(2,349)
9		(5,326)	0.4022	(2,142)
10		(5,382)	0.3635	(1,956)
11		(5,447)	0.3285	(1,789)
12		(5,522)	0.2969	(1,639)
13		(5,609)	0.2683	(1,505)
14		(5,711)	0.2425	(1,385)
15		(5,828)	0.2191	(1,277)
16		(6,388)	0.1981	(1,265)
17		(6,123)	0.1790	(1,096)
18		(6,306)	0.1618	(1,020)
19		(6,520)	0.1462	(953)
20		(6,787)	0.1321	(894)
			Total PV	(75,007)

PV of house − PV of payments = NPV of conventional loan
$75,000 − $43,776   = $31,224

TABLE 17-7   EQUITY REVERSION UNDER ZIM AND CONVENTIONAL FINANCING:
END YEAR 5

	ZIM	Conventional
Sales price	$92,000	$92,000
− selling expenses (5%)	4,600	4,600
− taxes due on sale*	0	0
− outstanding mortgage balance	0	41,177
ATER	87,400	46,223

*We assume the homeowner purchases another residence within the 24-month time
period and thus owes no tax on the sale.

quences on the sale because another residence is purchased. Let us see whether
the ZIM is of any benefit in this case.

The after-tax cash flows for the ZIM and conventional loans for years 0
through 5 are obtained from Tables 17-4 and 17-5, respectively, as before. Table
17-7 develops the equity reversions for both situations. Table 17-8 summarizes
the cash flows for the ZIM and conventional loans, respectively, and shows the
borrower's IRR in each case. Although both loans show negative rates of return
(because the property generates no income and hence there is a negative cash
flow during ownership), the ZIM is the better alternative under these assumptions because it has the *least* negative (i.e., largest) IRR.

Thus, the benefits of a ZIM to the borrower are particularly sensitive to the
holding period as well as the tax considerations. The buyer is well-advised to
thoroughly analyze and compare a proposed ZIM with other available financing
before making the borrowing decision.

GROWING EQUITY MORTGAGES (GEMs)

The growing equity mortgage (GEM) is generally based upon a fixed-rate, conventional mortgage with a 25- to 30-year term. The monthly payments for the first
year are based upon the original term at the contract interest rate. Subsequent
yearly payments are increased by a predetermined percentage (typically 2 to 5
percent each year) for either the remainder of the loan term or a specified number
of years. The increase in the payment is applied to the reduction of the principal
balance each month, the end result being a substantial reduction in the loan term.

Unique Aspects of GEMs

In some ways, the GEM resembles a graduated-payment mortgage (GPM), with a
fixed interest rate and payments increasing annually by a predetermined amount.
The difference is that although the GEM begins with a payment sufficient to amortize the loan, the GPM does not; thus, the GEM does not suffer from the "negative amortization" risk associated with GPMs.

TABLE 17-8 BORROWER'S CASH FLOWS AND IRR: SALE AT END YEAR 5

	ZIM				Conventional			
Year	ATCF	+	ATER	=	Total	ATCF	+	ATER	=	Total
0	($31,234)				($31,234)	($31,234)				($31,234)
1	(11,739)				(11,739)	(5,085)				(5,085)
2	(11,739)				(11,739)	(5,102)				(5,102)
3	(11,739)				(11,739)	(5,121)				(5,121)
4	(11,739)				(11,739)	(5,144)				(5,144)
5	(11,739)		$87,400		(75,661)	(5,171)		$46,223		41,052
IRR 0.94%					IRR 5.66%					

The GEM appears attractive to lenders in that risk is reduced by these loans' rapid amortization and shorter terms. For the borrower, the attraction is a shorter-term loan resulting in a mortgage-free home much sooner than with other financing options. The GEM does present some financial, legal, and tax issues that, while not particularly unique, must be considered when making the financing decision.

Legal and Financial Aspects Unlike many alternative forms of mortgage instruments, the GEM presents few new legal issues, except that financial disclosure (truth-in-lending) regulations require that the mortgage note clearly specify the basis (term, interest rate) for the initial payments, the annual percentage increase in the payment, and the effect of the increased payments on the principal balance.

As stated earlier, the GEM is generally based upon a fixed-rate conventional loan. However, GEMs can be combined with any other type of interest structure or repayment pattern: varying-rate, graduated-payment, and FHA-VA fixed-rate, and GPMs, among others. All that is required for the loan to be classified as a GEM is an annual increase in the monthly payment in excess of that required on the underlying mortgage. Of course, when based upon these other forms of loans, the GEM is affected by *their* unique characteristics.

From the lender's perspective, however, GEM loans must be structured within FNMA guidelines to ensure that these loans can be traded on the secondary market. At this writing, these guidelines are the following:

1 The loans must be secured by a first mortgage on a one- to four-family dwelling.

2 FHA-insured, VA-guaranteed, or conventional loans are eligible.

3 The underlying mortgage must have a fixed interest rate, but either level or graduated payments based on a predetermined percentage increase are acceptable; however, in no event can the *total* annual payment increase (resulting from the increase on an underlying GPM plus the increase under the GEM) exceed 7.5 percent.

4 Payment increases under the GEM portion must be applied directly to the unpaid principal balance.

5 Annual GEM payment increases of from 2 to 5 percent are acceptable.

6 GEM increases may be specified for either the first 10 years of the loan (with level payments beginning in year 11), or for the entire loan term.

7 Buydown plans that comply with FNMA's buydown requirements and are approved by the FHA or VA are acceptable.

The biggest restriction under these guidelines is that FNMA does not accept GEMS based on a varying-interest-rate loan. However, if liquidity is of relatively little concern to the lender, a GEM loan may be structured with a varying-rate loan as its basis (within applicable state regulations, of course). This offshoot of the GEM, typically called an *accelerated-equity mortgage* (AEM), gives the lender the added advantage of an interest rate that is somewhat tied to the lender's cost of funds.

The GEM's payment increase each year raises the same default-risk issue plaguing the GPM: Will the buyer have the increased income to afford the increased payment? This risk is likely quite low in many cases, since the maximum increase FNMA allows is 5 percent. And since borrowers typically spend one-third of their take-home income on housing, it requires an income increase of only 1.67 percent to cover a 5 percent increase in one's mortgage payment:

$$\begin{array}{ccccc} \text{Increase in} & \times & \text{mortgage payment} & = & \text{income increase needed} \\ \text{mortgage payment} & & \text{as \% of income} & & \text{to cover 5\% increase} \\ & & & & \text{in house payment} \\ 5\% & \times & 0.33 & = & 1.67\% \end{array}$$

Finally, because GEMs are typically based upon fixed-rate instruments, many lenders hold them in disfavor, preferring mortgage instruments with rates that can be varied according to the lender's cost of funds. As noted, however, lenders who structure GEMs around varying-rate mortgages may not presently sell them in the secondary market.

Despite its disadvantages, the GEM is seen by some as a major financial method. It is gaining in popularity for three reasons. First, the high inflation rate of the 1970s seems to have abated, changing borrowers' expectations. Where, previously, gains in equity caused by mortgage amortization were small compared with inflationary gains, the current expectation of lower inflation in housing combined with increased wariness of expensive debt are making the GEM a fast-growing financing instrument. Although borrowers seem to view the situation this way, lenders' interest rates still seemingly contain a large inflation component, resulting in mortgage interest rates substantially above the 7 to 9 percent rates common in the 1960s and 1970s.

These relatively high rates of interest highlight an interesting phenomenon that occurs when the payment increase resulting from a shortened term on a lower-interest loan is compared with that for a higher-interest loan. For example, let us compare the payment increase resulting from a 7 percent, level-payment loan of $50,000 being shortened from a 25- to a 15-year term to the payment increase re-

TABLE 17-9   EFFECT OF INTEREST RATES AND SHORTENED MATURITIES ON MONTHLY PAYMENTS

	7% loan	14% loan
Loan amount	$50,000	$50,000
Monthly payments (25-year term)	$353.39	$601.88
Monthly payments (15-year term)	$449.41	$665.87
Payment increase	$96.02	$63.99
Payment increase as percentage of 25-year payment	$\dfrac{\$96.02}{\$353.39} = 27\%$	$\dfrac{\$63.99}{\$601.88} = 10.6\%$

sulting from shortening the same loan at 14 percent. Table 17-9 illustrates the computations. As the table shows, both the absolute (dollar amount) increase in payments and the percentage increase is *lower* with the higher-interest loan. Although the results with a GEM differ because of the graduated-payments stream, the basic principle still holds true: *It costs relatively less to shorten the term on a high-interest mortgage compared with a lower-interest mortgage.* This is the second reason for the GEM's popularity.

The third reason results from the shorter terms of these loans, usually no more than 15 years. There is a lower expectation of default risk and interest rate risk because of the shorter term, making the GEM more attractive to the lender, who may offer the GEM at an interest rate 1 or 2 percentage points lower than that for a comparable 30-year mortgage.

Tax Aspects   The GEM loan creates no unique income tax issues. Interest accrues, is paid, and is deductible in the same manner as under a fixed-rate mortgage; thus, the same tax considerations apply. However, because of a GEM's reduced term and higher amortization, the amount and duration of the interest deductions are reduced accordingly.

When the decision is being made whether to finance under a GEM loan or, say, a fixed-rate, level-payment mortgage, taxes will not likely affect the decision as long as the amount borrowed and the before-tax cost of borrowing are the same under either loan and the borrower's marginal tax rate and the market's inflation expectations do not change over the life of the loans.

GEM Example

To understand the mechanics of a GEM, let us make a side-by-side comparison between a fixed-rate, 15 percent, 30-year loan and a GEM based on a 15 percent, 30-year level-payment mortgage, with payments graduated upward at 4 percent per year. Both loans are for the principal sum of $100,000.

Table 17-10 is the annual amortization schedules for both loans. The fixed-rate, level-payment mortgage is amortized in the usual manner (as described in Chapter 2). The GEM loan amortizes in a similar fashion, but the debt service increases by 4 percent each year from the previous year. Note that the first year's

TABLE 17-10 LEVEL PAYMENT VERSUS GEM AMORTIZATION SCHEDULES: GEM EXAMPLE

| | $100,000, 15%, Fixed-Rate, Level-Payment Mortgage | | | | $100,000, 15% GEM | | |
Year	Debt service	Principal	Interest	Ending balance	Debt service	Principal	Interest	Ending balance
0				$100,000				$100,000
1	$15,173	$ 185	$14,988	99,815	$15,173	$ 185	$14,988	99,815
2	15,173	215	14,958	99,600	15,780	866	14,914	98,949
3	15,173	250	14,923	99,350	16,411	1,681	14,730	97,268
4	15,173	290	14,883	99,060	17,068	2,655	14,413	94,613
5	15,173	337	14,836	98,723	17,751	3,814	13,937	90,798
6	15,173	391	14,782	98,332	18,461	5,137	13,324	85,661
7	15,173	454	14,719	97,878	19,199	6,805	12,394	78,856
8	15,173	527	14,646	97,351	19,967	8,722	11,245	70,134
9	15,173	612	14,561	96,739	20,766	10,981	9,785	59,153
10	15,173	710	14,463	96,029	21,596	13,635	7,961	45,518
11	15,173	824	14,349	95,205	22,460	16,753	5,707	28,765
12	15,173	957	14,216	94,248	23,359	20,410	2,949	8,355
13	15,173	1,111	14,062	93,137	8,632	8,355	277	0
14	15,173	1,290	13,883	91,847				
15	15,173	1,497	13,676	90,350				

debt service and amortization are identical for both loans, but the subsequent payment increases provide much faster amortization under the GEM. The actual maturity of the GEM is 12 years and 5 months, as compared with 30 years for the level-payment mortgage. Note also the compounding effect of increasing the principal each year, resulting in the substantially reduced maturity.

REVERSE ANNUITY MORTGAGES (RAMs)

The *reverse annuity mortgage* (RAM) has disbursement and repayment patterns exactly opposite those of typical real estate mortgages; that is, funds are advanced to the borrower in the form of annuity payments over the loan term. At the end of the term, the accumulated principal and interest balance is due and payable to the lender. This type of loan is usually held by retirees who wish to use the sizable equity in their often mortgage-free homes to supplement their retirement income. The annuity the borrower receives each month provides supplemental income, and the loan is paid at or before maturity from the proceeds of the sale of the home or from the borrower's estate at death.

Unique Aspects of RAMs

Despite the obvious advantages for retired, fixed-income borrowers, the unique structuring of RAMs creates the potential for additional risk and possible undesirable consequences for the borrower and the lender.

Legal and Financial Aspects By its nature, the RAM loan balance increases over time, possibly causing the loan-to-value ratio to increase as well, depending upon changes in the property's value over time. As a result, lenders must be particularly cautious in structuring RAMs so that the balance owing at maturity is well within acceptable loan-to-value ratio guidelines. The problem is that the loan balance at maturity can be predicted with absolute certainty, but the expected value of the property at maturity cannot. Consequently, lenders tend to be more cautious in structuring RAMs by making the loan term relatively short, say, 10 to 15 years, with relatively low loan-to-value ratios, say, 50 to 60 percent, based on the property's current market value.

Because RAMs are usually made to older persons, prudent lenders take steps to ensure reasonably swift, certain repayment of the loan in the event of the borrower's death. Since a borrower's estate may take many months to be settled, lenders often require the borrower to provide a life insurance policy in the amount of the mortgage balance, naming the lender as beneficiary, so that the loan can be paid off promptly when the borrower dies. This, coupled with the unique tax aspects now discussed, may make the RAM more costly compared with other borrowing alternatives.

Tax Aspects RAM's tax aspects primarily center around the timing of interest deductions for the borrower and interest income for the lender. The RAM's structure is such that accrued interest is added to the loan balance periodically but is not deductible by the borrower until paid at loan maturity; thus, the borrower has a sizable lump-sum deduction in the year the loan is paid off. In the example at the end of this section, the borrower has a total of $21,526 of interest due and deductible in the year the loan is due. However, the ability of the borrower (who is typically on a low, fixed income) to benefit from such a sizable tax deduction in 1 year is limited, compared with the tax benefits derived under a standard level-payment mortgage, where accrued interest is paid each month and deductible each year as the loan amortizes.

From the lender's perspective, other tax consequences arise. If the lender uses the accrual method of accounting, each tax year's accrued interest (which is added to the loan balance when monthly disbursements are made) is treated as interest income, even though the lender receives no monies until loan payoff. Thus, the lender has a taxable event in years when only disbursements are made and no income is received.

The consequences for a lender using the cash basis of accounting are similar to that for the borrower. Interest is included in taxable income when paid—thus the lender must account for all the interest when received, possibly creating adverse effects due to shift to a higher marginal tax bracket, especially if several RAMs are retired during the same taxable year.

As of this writing, the IRS's position is as stated above. But before the RAM can become a popular financing alternative, some changes in the accounting for interest earned or paid will have to be made to reduce the negative tax consequences to the borrower and the lender.

RAM Example

Suppose a retired couple wants to increase their monthly retirement income by mortgaging their home on a reverse annuity mortgage. Their home is valued at $90,000 and is mortgage-free. They approach their local lender, which advises them that the loan can be granted for a 10-year period at a 50 percent loan-to-value ratio with interest at 12 percent annually. The *maximum loan amount* is thus 50 percent × $90,000, or $45,000. This is the total amount of principal and interest that will be owed at the end of the 10-year maturity.

The amount of the *monthly annuity* that would be paid to the borrowers is computed as follows:

$$\$45,000 \times SFF_{12\%/12, 120months} = annuity$$
$$\$45,000 \times 0.004347 = \$195.62$$

The retirees would thus receive $195.62 each month, tax-free, to supplement their income over the next 10 years. As noted before, however, if the loan is paid off at the end of year 10 as scheduled, the borrowers will have a sizable interest deduction for that year. To calculate the *interest deduction,* recall that the total amount owing at the end of year 10 is $45,000. The total principal amount the borrowers receive is $195.62 per month × 120 months = $23,474. Subtracting

TABLE 17-11 ANNUAL DISBURSEMENT AND AMORTIZATION SCHEDULE: RAM EXAMPLE

Year	Borrowed principal	Accrued interest	End-of-year balance
1	$ 2,347	$ 134	$ 2,481
2	2,347	448	5,276
3	2,347	803	8,426
4	2,347	1,202	11,975
5	2,347	1,653	15,975
6	2,347	2,160	20,482
7	2,347	2,731	25,569
8	2,347	3,375	31,282
9	2,347	4,101	37,730
10	2,347	4,919	44,996
Totals	23,470	21,526	

the $23,474 of principal from the total $45,000 debt yields an interest amount of $21,526, which is an itemized deduction for year 10. Unless the borrowers have at least $21,526 of other taxable income that year, a portion of this deduction will be of no benefit to them.

Table 17-11 shows the annual disbursement and amortization schedule. Note that to derive the end-of-year balance, the principal borrowed each year is added to the accrued interest.

To illustrate the tax effects on the lender, consider first the situation with an accrual-basis lender in the 34 percent tax bracket. The lender would disburse not only the annuity but 34 percent of the accrued interest in the form of taxes for each year. This concept is illustrated in Table 17-12. The $2,347.44 annuity is added to the tax, which is the deferred interest for the year times the 0.34 tax rate. The total disbursement is the sum of these numbers.

TABLE 17-12 LENDER'S AFTER-TAX CASH FLOWS: RAM EXAMPLE, ACCRUAL-BASIS LENDER

Year	Annuity	+	Taxes	=	Total	Income
1	($2,347)		(46)		($2,393)	
2	(2,347)		(152)		(2,499)	
3	(2,347)		(273)		(2,620)	
4	(2,347)		(409)		(2,756)	
5	(2,347)		(562)		(2,909)	
6	(2,347)		(734)		(3,081)	
7	(2,347)		(929)		(3,276)	
8	(2,347)		(1,148)		(3,495)	
9	(2,347)		(1,394)		(3,741)	
10	(2,347)		(1,672)		(4,019)	$45,000
IRR 9.05%						

TABLE 17-13   LENDER'S AFTER-TAX CASH FLOWS: RAM EXAMPLE, CASH-BASIS LENDER

Year	Disbursements annuity	Gross income	Tax	Net income
1	($2,347)			
2	(2,347)			
3	(2,347)			
4	(2,347)			
5	(2,347)			
6	(2,347)			
7	(2,347)			
8	(2,347)			
9	(2,347)			
10	(2,347)	$45,000	$7,319	$37,681
After-tax IRR 10.15%				

Contrast the results in Table 17-12 with those for a cash-basis lender (Table 17-13). Note that the entire tax is paid when the interest is received at the end of year 10. The tax is the total interest amount, $21,526, times the 0.34 percent tax rate, yielding $7,319. Thus, the lender nets $37,681 after taxes at the end of year 10, less the $2,347 annuity paid in year 10. Although the after-tax yield of 10.15 percent for this lender is higher than that for the accrual-basis lender because of the tax deferment until year 10, remember that we are assuming the lender's tax rate for year 10 does not increase because of the sudden inflow of $21,526 in interest income. Although one RAM such as this would probably not change the lender's cash-basis tax bracket, the retiring of several RAMs in any given year could create a more severe tax consequence.

SUMMARY

As noted, the other financing methods discussed in this chapter can be valuable financing tools. Loan assumptions and junior mortgages have been around a long time, but with the advent of due-on-sale clauses, the number of assumable loans will likely decline in the future. Buydowns and zero interest mortgages (ZIMs) are relatively new concepts and are similar to each other in that with a zero interest mortgage, the interest rate is bought down to zero. The growing equity mortgage (GEM) is another recent phenomenon, similar to a GPM but without the negative amortization. The reverse annuity mortgage (RAM) is essentially an instrument created for a special borrower—the lower, fixed-income retiree—and allows the borrower to live on the equity in his or her home.

All these methods have created unique financial, legal, and tax issues, some of which have yet to be resolved at this writing. However, they provide some additional, possibly beneficial, financing alternatives for the real estate investor and lender.

QUESTIONS

1 Define the following terms:
   a assumption
   b due-on-sale clause
   c junior mortgage
   d buydown mortgage
   e zero interest rate mortgage
   f growing equity mortgage

2 Suppose the selling price of two houses are identical in every aspect except that one home is financed with a conventional mortgage and the other with an assumption. Would you expect the selling price to be the same? Why or why not?

3 Discuss several unique aspects of junior mortgages. Under what situations would second (or third or fourth) mortgages be used?

4 What is a buydown mortgage? What is being "bought" down? How does this mortgage work? Under what situation is it likely to be used?

5 Outline how a zero interest rate mortgage works. Why do you think that the term *zero* is a misnomer?

6 What is a growing equity mortgage? What are the similarities between a GEM and the graduated-payment mortgage discussed in Chapter 8? What are the differences?

7 Analyze the reverse annuity mortgage. When is it likely to be used?

8 Suppose you are considering buying a house and have the choice of an assumption, a standard fixed-rate mortgage, a GEM, a ZIM, or any of the other financing methods discussed. How would you select from among all the options? If possible, collect some data on the financing methods offered in your market and analyze the various terms of each type.

PROBLEMS

1 Consider this assumption financing problem. You are planning to purchase a piece of real estate that you forecast will have an NOI of $65,000 for each of the next 5 years. During that time in which you are "holding" the property, you expect it to appreciate in value 15 percent. Two financing alternatives are available to you: (1) a new loan for 75 percent of value at 12 percent interest for 25 years, or (2) paying the sellers their equity and assuming the mortgage they executed 5 years ago. Their mortgage amount at the time they initiated it was $300,000, and the terms were 13 percent interest rate with 300 monthly payments. Your required rate of return is 15 percent. What is the value of the property to you under each financing option?

2 A buyer would like to buy a new $80,000 home just completed by a local builder. To facilitate sales, the builder is offering a buydown program which buys down the best available mortgage money by 2 interest points for a period of 4 years. The best available financing is 15 percent for 30 years (monthly payments). Assume the buyer puts $15,000 down. Compute both the buyer's and the builder's monthly payment.

3 The seller of a $45,000 condominium offers a no-interest-rate loan to you, an interested buyer. The seller requires one-third down (equity) and the remainder to be paid off in 60 equal monthly installments. The lender's required rate of interest is 12 percent. Compute the monthly payment and the present value of this loan.

4 Make a side-by-side comparison of a $50,000, 14 percent, 30-year, fixed-rate loan and a GEM with the same principal amount and interest rate but with payments that increase at 5 percent per year for 5 years and level off in the sixth year. What is the actual maturity of the GEM?

5 A couple wishes to obtain a reverse annuity mortgage of $57,000 against their home, which is presently free and clear. The lender offers them a 10-year mortgage at 10.5 percent interest.

   a What will the amount of the annuity be?

   b Set up the amortization schedule for this loan.

6 Contrast the tax effects of the preceding problem on an accrual-basis lender and a cash-basis lender. Both lenders are in the 34 percent tax bracket.

7 Consider a prospective buyer who wishes to purchase a $1,250,000 office building with a 10 percent down payment. A first mortgage in the amount of $950,000 is available at 16 percent interest for 30 years. A third-party lender is willing to grant a second mortgage for the remaining amount at 19 percent for 10 years. What is the buyer's overall effective borrowing cost?

8 Consider the following three loans of $100,000:

   1 A 30-year fixed-rate mortgage at the rate of 12 percent

   2 A 15-year fixed-rate mortgage at the rate of 9.5 percent

   3 A 25-year growing equity mortgage at the rate of 11 percent

Calculate the total interest and principal paid on each loan over the first 5 years. Pick which loan you think is the best.

9 Tom and Jane want to buy a house for $60,000. They have equity of $10,000. The current mortgage rate is 10.5 percent for a 30-year mortgage. Property taxes and insurance add another $50 per month to their housing expenses. Their total monthly income is $1,700.

   a Can they qualify for the loan if the lender requires a total housing-expense-to-income ratio of 0.275?

   b Suppose the builder is willing to buy the interest rate down to 9 percent for the first 3 years of the loan. What is Tom and Jane's new payment? Can they qualify?

   c What is the builder's payment each month?

   d Suppose the builder decides to give the lender a lump sum. How much would the lender require?

10 Suppose a developer wished to offer "zero interest financing" on her $105,000 duplexes, with the loan being fully paid over 5 years. The lender's required rate of interest is 12.75 percent.

   a What are the borrower's monthly payments?

   b What is the present value of this loan?

   c What is the discount fee charged to the developer?

   d Assume the following:

   1 Conventional loan terms are 10 percent, 20-year term. The developer will sell for the $105,000 price if conventional financing is obtained.

   2 The home will be held for the entire 20-year term of the conventional loan.

   3 Under either alternative, the buyer makes no down payment. He is in the 28 percent marginal tax bracket.

Which financing alternative should the buyer choose?

11 Suppose a prospective buyer wishes to purchase a piece of property for $150,000 and has $25,000 for a down payment. There is an existing $60,000, 8 percent loan on the property with payments of $401.86 for 20 more years. The buyer would like to assume this loan but needs $65,000 to make the $150,000 purchase. The seller is willing to grant a second mortgage of $65,000 at 13 percent for 10 years with monthly payments. Under these conditions, what is the buyer's effective borrowing cost?

12 Suppose a borrower may assume the present $50,000, 8.5 percent mortgage with 25 years of monthly payments, or he may take out a new loan of $50,000 at the current 10.5 percent rate for 25 years. How much more is the property worth with the assumable loan?

REFERENCES

Britton, James A., Jr., and Lewis O. Kerwood: *Financing Income-Producing Real Estate—A Theory and Casebook,* McGraw-Hill, New York, 1977.
"Junior Lien Financing—Five Varieties and the Advantages They Offer," *Mortgage Banker,* vol. 38, no. 8, May 1978, pp. 41ff.
Strum, Brian J. (ed.): *Financing Real Estate During the Inflationary 80's* American Bar Association, New York, 1981.
"Swaps and Wraps," *Taxes—The Tax Magazine,* vol. 58, April 1980, pp. 43–51.
Vidger, Leonard P: *Borrowing and Lending on Residential Property,* Lexington Books, Lexington, Mass., 1981.

PART # THREE

REAL ESTATE
FINANCING DECISIONS

In the previous chapters, we have discussed the basics of real estate financing. Part One dealt with the fundamentals of mortgage mechanics, the legal aspects of mortgage lending, and the basics of mortgage underwriting. Part Two analyzed a variety of real estate financing methods and techniques.

Part Three discusses real estate finance decision making. The real estate financing process involves a variety of decision situations such as the optimal combination of debt and equity, the refinancing decision, pricing mortgage loans, and managing a mortgage portfolio. Chapter 18 discusses the borrower's perspective, and Chapter 19 analyzes some of the decisions that lenders must make in the real estate financing process.

LEVERAGE, RISK, AND DECISION MAKING

The previous chapters discussed the analysis of the borrowing-lending decision and the variety of financing methods. We examined the various techniques both the borrower and the lender use to make the decision.

In this chapter we first examine the concept of financial leverage. One major attraction of real estate as an investment is the use of debt to increase the expected equity rate of return. However, the risk to the equity position also increases. Thus, a major decision for the borrower involves the amount of debt and equity to use. These concepts are examined in detail. Next, the analysis of risk from the lender's perspective is discussed. The last section outlines how the borrower can make several of the many financial decisions, such as refinancing.

FINANCIAL LEVERAGE AND RISK

A large portion of a real estate purchase can be financed with the use of debt. Typically, 70 to 80 percent, but often as much as 90 percent, of the total cost is debt, with the remainder being equity funds. An investor's use of debt in a real estate investment is referred to as *financial leverage*.

This section demonstrates the impact of the use of debt for the equity investor when making the investment decision. The basic concept to remember is that the use of debt changes the expected rate of return and the risk to the equity position. This risk is called *financial risk*. Real estate investors are familiar with the use of debt financing to "leverage" the rate of return to equity on a real estate investment. Before we discuss why debt financing is so widespread, however, let us review several basic concepts of financial leverage.

The "economics" of a real estate investment revolve around the investment's financial structure. An investment should be considered for its financial components—debt and equity—rather than its physical components—buildings and land. The physical real estate is certainly important in the determination of value, but the feasibility of an investment most often hinges on the financial aspects of debt and equity.

The investor must also remember that each financial component has a cost. The cost of debt is usually called *interest* (which represents the required return to the lender). The equity cost is called the required return on the equity. To be feasible, an investment must produce enough "return" (cash inflow) to pay the cost of each component.

Financial leverage involves the use of funds for which investors pay a fixed cost in the hope of increasing their equity return. Leverage has two outcomes: positive or negative. Positive leverage results when the cost of borrowing is less than the overall rate of return on the investment. Negative leverage is when the opposite is true.

To illustrate how an investor can interplay the cost of each component, consider the following simple example. An investor in a 28 percent tax bracket has the opportunity to buy an apartment building at a total cost of $500,000. The investment has an expected constant net operating income of $60,000 per year. The investor anticipates holding the investment for 5 years and then selling it for the same amount as the original purchase price ($500,000). The investment will be depreciated for tax purposes, using the straight-line method over a 27.5 year life. The depreciable basis is $412,500, and the depreciation deduction is $15,000 per year.

The investor has two financing options:

Financing option 1. 100 percent equity
Financing option 2. $375,000 mortgage at a 12 percent interest rate with interest-only payment with balloon in 5 years; debt service is $45,000 per year (interest only)

Impact of Borrowing on Equity Rate of Return

To illustrate the impact of borrowing on the equity rate of return, let us calculate the internal rate of return to the equity position under each financing option. First we must calculate the cash flows under each option.

Cash Flows: Financing Option 1: The after-tax cash flow (ATCF) from operation under financing option 1 is $47,400 each year. This is the net operating income ($60,000) minus the debt service ($0) minus the taxes from operation ($17,600). The taxable income is calculated by using the net operating income ($60,000) minus the interest ($0) minus the depreciation deduction ($15,000). Multiplying the taxable income ($45,000) by the tax rate (28 percent) results in taxes of $12,600. Since net operating income and depreciation are expected to stay constant, ATCF will be a constant $47,400 per year.

On the sale at the end of year 5, the investor expects an after-tax equity reversion (ATER) of $479,000. This is calculated by using the expected net sale price ($500,000) minus the unpaid mortgage ($0) minus the taxes due on sale ($21,000). The taxes due on sale will be the amount realized ($500,000) minus the adjusted basis ($425,000), yielding a total gain of $75,000. Multiplying the total gain by the tax rate results in the taxes due on sale. The adjusted basis is the original total cost ($500,000) minus the cumulative depreciation deduction ($15,000 per year for 5 years).

Rate of Return to Equity: Financing Option 1 Now we can calculate the investor's expected rate of return. The cash flow is summarized as

Year	Equity	ATCF	ATER
0	($500,000)		
1		$47,400	
2		$47,400	
3		$47,400	
4		$47,400	
5		$47,400	$479,000

The investor invests $500,000 and expects to receive the ATCF each year and the ATER on sale. The internal rate of return on these cash flows is 8.78 percent. This is the rate that will make the present value of the inflow exactly equal to the $500,000 outflow.

Cash Flows: Financing Option 2 What happens under the second financing option? The ATCF flow is expected to be $15,000 each year. This is the NOI ($60,000) minus the debt service ($45,000) minus the taxes ($0).

On the sale of the investment, the ATER is expected to be $104,000. This is the selling price ($500,000) minus the unpaid mortgage ($375,000) minus taxes due on sale ($21,000). The taxes due on sale are not affected by the financing option.

Rate of Return to Equity: Financing Option 2 The investor's internal rate of return under financing option 2 is calculated on the following cash inflows:

Year	Equity	ATCF	ATER
0	($125,000)		
1		$15,000	
2		$15,000	
3		$15,000	
4		$15,000	
5		$15,000	$104,000

The investor invests $125,000. The rate of return on these cash flows is now 9.20 percent. Notice that the rate of return on equity has increased (from 8.78 to 9.20 percent).

Basic Rule for Financial Leverage Our simple example illustrates the basic rule of financial leverage:

> The use of debt will increase the rate of return on equity as long as the after-tax cost of debt is less than the after-tax rate of return on the total investment without debt.

In our example, the after-tax cost of debt is 8.64 percent. The after-tax cost of the debt is the interest rate (12 percent) times 1 minus the investor's marginal tax rate (28 percent). In equation form,

$$\text{After-tax cost of debt} = i(1 - \tau)$$

where i = before-tax interest rate
τ = marginal tax rate

Substituting,

$$\text{After-tax cost of debt} = 0.12(1 - 0.28) \qquad \text{or 8.64 percent}$$

Impact of Borrowing on Risk

The use of debt is not without its "price." This price is the increased financial risk to which the equity position is exposed. This risk is the probability that the debt obligations will not be met. The debt position has priority over the equity position. The equity position is the "residual" and bears the impact of the risk of borrowing. In the example, a small decline in the expected cash flows had a larger impact on the return to equity with rather than without the use of debt.

How Much Debt?

The difficult questions facing the borrower is the optimal amount of debt to use in financing the investment. In our previous example, we saw that the use of debt increased the return on equity from 8.78 to 9.20 percent. And we noted that the equity position is also subject to more risk with the use of debt. Is there any "net" benefit to the use of debt?

Let us return to our example. If, with the use of debt, the borrower's *required* rate of return increases from 8.78 to 9.20 percent, there is no benefit. At a required rate of return of 8.78 percent without debt, the net present value is zero. At a required rate of return of 9.20 percent with the use of debt, the net present value is still zero. Thus, there would be no "net" benefit.

Suppose, however, that with the use of debt the investor decides that the required rate of return with debt is 9 percent. In this case, there is a net benefit since at this rate the net present value will be positive. If all investors, however, used this required rate of return, they would bid up the value of the real estate, thus forcing the net present value back to zero.

The moral is that if you want the benefits, you have to pay the price. The increased equity return is possible only because of the greater risk to which the equity position is exposed.

RISK FROM LENDER'S PERSPECTIVE

The preceding section illustrated the impact of the use of debt on the rate of return and risk to the equity position. We now examine how the lender views the risk in making the lending decision.

It is important to remember that from the lender's perspective the mortgage loan is an investment. For example, if the lender makes a $100,000 loan, the $100,000 represents the amount of equity that the lender has to invest. As in any investment decision, the lender is willing to make the loan only if the *expected* yield to the lender is equal to the lender's *required* rate of return. For example, suppose the lender required a yield of 12 percent but the borrower is willing to pay only 10 percent. Obviously, the lender will not make the investment, that is, loan $100,000 to the borrower. What risks does the lender face (and try to minimize) when making a mortgage loan?

Default Risk

A major risk from the lender's viewpoint is the possibility that the borrower will not meet the requirements of the mortgage contract. This is called *default risk*. The most common form of default occurs when the borrower does not make the payments required under the mortgage. There are many reasons for default. Sometimes the borrower is unable to make payments because of job loss, illness, and so forth. Sometimes the value of the collateral (real estate) declines to an amount below the amount of the mortgage debt, which increases the probability of default. And sometimes default arises from other reasons, such as the borrower's not making the insurance payments or paying property taxes.

Inflation (Interest Rate) Risk

The lender also faces *inflation risk,* which is the risk that the lender may be repaid in dollars that have less purchasing power. Consider the following simple example.

A lender is considering making a loan of $1,000 for 1 year. There is no expected inflation, and the lender requires a 5 percent "real" rate of return. Thus, at the end of 1 year, the lender expects to receive $1,050 ($1,000 principal plus $50 interest). Suppose, however, that inflation has actually been 5 percent over the 1-year period. How much does the lender receive? Obviously, the lender gets $1,050, but since there has actually been 5 percent inflation, the "real" rate of return is 0 percent. To stay even, the lender would have to receive $1,100.

Now suppose that the lender had expected 5 percent inflation. What would have occurred? The interest rate would have been 10 percent (5 percent real rate plus 5 percent expected inflation premium). The important point is that if inflation is expected, the interest rate required should reflect these expectations. As with all investments, however, the actual outcome may be different from the expected. If *actual* inflation is greater than *expected,* the borrower will pay back the lender in deflated dollars. If actual inflation is less than expected, the lender wins at the expense of the borrower.

Many alternative financing methods have been devised to help protect borrowers and lenders from changes in the level of expected inflation. The inflation premium also creates problems from the borrower's perspective.

FINANCIAL DECISION MAKING

The real estate investor (borrower or lender) must make many decisions. This section discusses several of these decisions, such as mortgage discounts and refinancing.[1]

Mortgage Discounts for Early Repayment

To illustrate the decision-making situations the effects of inflation create, consider the following example. Suppose a lender made a mortgage loan of $50,000 at a 9 percent interest rate with 25-year maturity and monthly payments of $419.60. After 5 years, the market rate is 12 percent and the lender would like the bor-

---

[1] For a more detailed discussion and more examples, see C. F. Sirmans and Austin J. Jaffe, *The Complete Real Estate Investment Handbook,* 4th ed., Prentice-Hall, Englewood Cliffs, N.J., 1988.

rower to repay the loan. However, the borrower has little incentive to do so. Thus, the lender is willing to offer the borrower a "discount," that is, let the borrower repay less than the mortgage balance. The lender can then reinvest this amount at the higher market rate. What is the maximum amount of discount the lender would be willing to offer?

To find this discount, we must calculate the amount outstanding on the mortgage, which is the present value of the remaining payments:

$$\text{Amount outstanding} = \$419.60 \ \frac{1 - [1/(1.0075)^{240}]}{0.0075}$$
$$= \$46,636$$

At the end of 5 years (60 months), the borrower owes $46,636. At the current market rate of 12 percent, the value of the remaining payments would be

$$\text{Value remaining payments} = \$419.60 \ \frac{1 - [1/(1.01)^{240}]}{0.01}$$
$$= \$38,108$$

The lender would be willing to discount the loan balance from the face value of $46,631 to the market value of $38,108, a difference of $8,523. This is about an 18 percent discount. If the lender could entice the borrower to repay more than $38,108, the lender would gain from the repayment. The $8,523 represents the maximum, or break-even, discount.

Sale or Continue to Operate

One decision the real estate investor faces is continuing to operate versus selling. This section illustrates how to make this decision. A real estate investor (in a 28 percent tax bracket) owns an apartment building investment that was purchased 5 years ago for $500,000. The depreciable basis was $400,000. The investor has been using the straight-line depreciation method with a 27.5-year life. The investment was financed with a $375,000 fixed-rate mortgage at an interest rate of 10 percent, with monthly payments for 25 years. Table 18-1 is the amortization schedule for this mortgage. The investor estimates that the current selling price is $625,000. Selling expenses would be 7 percent of the selling price.

The investor is trying to decide whether to sell or continue to operate for 5 more years. The NOI next year is to be $68,750 and is expected to increase 2 percent per year. The value of the investment is expected to be $675,000 at the end of this additional 5 years, with selling expenses of 7 percent.

Which option should the investor select (sell or continue to operate) if the required after-tax rate of return is 12 percent?

ATER from Sale Today To determine whether to sell or continue to operate, the investor must first compute the after-tax cash flow from sale *now* [after-tax

TABLE 18-1 MORTGAGE AMORTIZATION SCHEDULE: $375,000 LOAN AT 10% WITH 25-YEAR MATURITY, MONTHLY PAYMENTS

Year	Proportion outstanding	Amount outstanding	Debt service	Interest	Principal
0	1.0	$375,000			
1	0.99053	371,449	$40,892	$37,341	$3,551
2	0.98007	367,526	40,892	36,969	3,923
3	0.96851	363,191	40,892	36,557	4,335
4	0.95574	358,403	40,892	36,104	4,788
5	0.94164	353,115	40,892	35,604	5,288
6	0.92606	347,273	40,892	35,050	5,842
7	0.90884	340,815	40,892	34,434	6,458
8	0.88983	333,686	40,892	33,763	7,129
9	0.86882	325,808	40,892	33,014	7,878
10	0.84561	317,104	40,892	32,188	8,704

TABLE 18-2 EXPECTED CASH FLOW FROM SALE TODAY

Expected selling price (SP)	$625,000
− selling expenses (SE)	43,750
net sale proceeds (NSP)	581,250
− unpaid mortgage balance (UM)	353,115
before-tax equity reversion (BTER)	228,135
− taxes due on sale (TDS)*	43,113
after-tax equity reversion (ATER)	185,022

*See Table 18-3.

TABLE 18-3 EXPECTED TAXES DUE ON SALE TODAY

Taxable income	
Expected selling price (SP)	$625,000
− selling expenses (SE)	43,750
amount realized (AR)	581,250
− adjusted basis (AB)	427,275
total gain on sale (TG)	153,975

Taxes due on sale	
Total gain on sale (TG)	153,975
× investor's marginal tax rate (τ)	0.28
taxes due on sale (TDS)	43,113

equity reversion (ATER)]. Table 18-2 shows this by subtracting the selling expenses, unpaid mortgage balance (from Table 18-1), and taxes (from Table 18-3) from the selling price. Table 18-3 computes the taxes using the standard procedure. Table 18-2 is the amortization schedule for the loan that was originated *5 years ago*. In other words, the amount outstanding today is the unpaid mortgage in year 5 of the loan ($353,115).

Cash Flows from Continuing to Operate Tables 18-4 and 18-5 compute the after-tax cash flows and taxes from continuing to operate. Table 18-4 computes the after-tax flows (for years 1 to 5) by subtracting the debt service and taxes (Table 18-5) from net operating income.

ATER from Continuing to Operate Table 18-6 computes the ATER from sale if the investor continues to operate and sells 5 years from now. The ATER is equal to the selling price minus the selling expenses, unpaid mortgage ($317,104) balance and taxes (from Table 18-7).

TABLE 18-4 EXPECTED CASH FLOW FROM CONTINUING TO OPERATE

	Year				
	1	2	3	4	5
Net operating income (NOI)	$68,750	$70,125	$71,528	$72,958	$74,417
− debt service (DS)	40,892	40,892	40,892	40,892	40,892
before-tax cash flow (BTCF)	27,858	29,233	30,636	32,066	33,525
− taxes (savings) from operation (TO)*	5,363	5,921	6,502	7,112	7,751
after-tax cash flow (ATCF)	22,495	23,312	24,134	24,954	25,774

*See Table 18-5.

TABLE 18-5 EXPECTED TAXES FROM CONTINUING TO OPERATE

	Year				
	1	2	3	4	5
Net operating income (NOI)	$68,750	$70,125	$71,528	$72,958	$74,417
− interest on debt (I)	35,050	34,434	33,763	33,014	32,188
− depreciation deduction (D)	14,545	14,545	14,545	14,545	14,545
− amortized financing costs (AFC)	0	0	0	0	0
+ replacement reserves (RR)	0	0	0	0	0
ordinary taxable income (OTI)	19,155	21,146	23,220	25,399	27,684
× investor's marginal tax rate (τ)	0.28	0.28	0.28	0.28	0.28
taxes (savings) from operation (TO)	5,363	5,921	6,502	7,112	7,751

TABLE 18-6   EXPECTED CASH FLOW FROM SALE IN 5 YEARS

Expected selling price (SP)	$675,000
− selling expenses (SE)	47,250
net sale proceeds (NSP)	627,750
− unpaid mortgage balance (UM)	317,104
before-tax equity reversion (BTER)	310,646
− taxes due on sale (TDS)*	76,496
after-tax equity reversion (ATER)	234,150

*See Table 18-7.

TABLE 18-7   EXPECTED TAXES DUE ON SALE IN 5 YEARS

Taxable income	
Expected selling price (SP)	$675,000
− selling expenses (SE)	47,250
amount realized (AR)	627,750
− adjusted basis (AB)	354,550
total gain on sale (TG)	273,200
Taxes due on sale	
Total gain on sale (TG)	273,200
× investor's marginal tax rate (τ)	0.28
taxes due on sale (TDS)	76,496

Differential Cash Flows   Table 18-8 illustrates the differential after-tax cash of continuing to operate versus selling today. To reach the differential flows, the cash flows from selling today are subtracted from the flows from continuing to operate. Notice that the differential at time zero is negative, which indicates the forgone cash flow from sale if the investor decides to continue to operate.

NPV and IRR of Continuing to Operate   Table 18-9 is the calculation of the NPV (at 15 percent) of continuing to operate. The differential after-tax cash flow is multiplied by the present value factors. The NPV is a positive $11,537, which indicates "continue to operate." The IRR is calculated as 16.71 percent, and with this information we can formulate the following decision criteria.

1 If the opportunity rate is less than 16.71 percent, continue to operate.

2 If the opportunity rate is greater than 16.71 percent, sell (do not continue to operate).

The opportunity rate is that rate of return an investor can receive on an alternative investment of equal risk. Since the NPV in this case is positive, the investor can conclude that continuing to operate is the best option since the present value of the inflows from operating exceed the present value of the flow from selling.

TABLE 18-8 DIFFERENTIAL AFTER-TAX CASH FLOWS OF CONTINUING TO OPERATE VERSUS SALE TODAY

Year	ATCF from continuing to operate	ATCF from sale today	Differential cash flows
0	$ 0	$185,022	($185,022)
1	22,495	0	22,495
2	23,312	0	23,312
3	24,134	0	24,134
4	24,954	0	24,954
5	259,924	0	259,924

TABLE 18-9 NPV AND IRR OF CONTINUING TO OPERATE VERSUS SALE TODAY

Year	Differential ATCF	$PVF_{15\%}$	PV
0	($185,022)	1.0	($185,022)
1	22,495	0.8696	19,562
2	23,312	0.7561	17,626
3	24,134	0.6575	15,868
4	24,954	0.5718	14,260
5	259,924	0.4972	129,234
		Net present value	$ 11,537
		IRR	16.71%

The Refinancing Decision

Often, the real estate investor-owner faces the question of whether or not to refinance a property. There may be several reasons the investor-owner is thinking of refinancing. For example, the owner-borrower may have the opportunity to take out a new loan at an interest rate lower than that of the existing mortgage. Alternatively, the investor may have the opportunity to buy another investment and is considering refinancing an existing property to take advantage of the opportunity.

This section analyzes the refinancing decision. We first examine the decision for owner-occupied properties and then look at the refinancing of income properties. Basically, the decision-making process is the same for both property types.

Refinancing Owner-Occupied Property Example

To make the refinancing decision, we must know the variables associated with (1) the terms of the existing mortgage and (2) the terms of the new loan. These terms include the interest rate, payment, maturity, prepayment penalty or other costs of paying off the old loan; financing costs (such as points and legal fees), interest rate, maturity, and payment for the new loan.

To illustrate, suppose a borrower makes a mortgage loan for $50,000 at a 12 percent interest rate for 30 years, with monthly payment of $514.30. After 5 years, interest rates fall and a new loan is available at 10.5 percent for 25 years with monthly payment of $461.01. The amount outstanding on the existing mortgage is $48,831, and a 5 percent prepayment penalty ($2,442) must be paid. In addition, the lender making the new loan requires financing costs of 3 percent, including origination fees and points, for a total of $1,464. Should the borrower refinance?

To analyze this question, we must determine the costs and the benefits associated with refinancing; they are in Table 18-10. The total costs of refinancing are $3,907, which includes the prepayment penalty on the old loan and the financing costs on the new loan. The benefits are the difference between the payment on the old mortgage and the payment on the new loan at the lower interest rate. This savings is $53.29 per month for 300 (25 × 12) months.

The issue facing the borrower is simply, Does the present value of the savings (benefit) exceed the costs of refinancing? Another way to think about the issue is, Do the benefits (savings) justify investing $3,907 in refinancing? Suppose the borrower has an opportunity investment rate of 14 percent. Now we can calculate the present value of the benefits (see Table 18-10) as $4,427. The net present value is $520, which indicates that refinancing is acceptable given our assumptions.

Alternatively, we could calculate the internal rate of return on the $3,907 outflow versus the $53.29 per month inflow. This rate would be 16.06 percent of the investment. If our opportunity rate is 14 percent, then the "investment" in refinancing is attractive since the rate of return is 16.06 percent.

TABLE 18-10   COSTS AND BENEFITS OF REFINANCING*

Costs of refinancing:	
Prepayment penalty on existing loan	$2,442
+ financing costs on new loan	1,465
total costs to refinance	3,907
Benefits of refinancing:	
Monthly payments on existing loan	$514.30
− monthly payments on new loan	461.01
monthly savings due to refinancing	53.29

$$\text{Present value of benefits} = \text{monthly savings } (\text{PVAF}_{14\%/12,300})$$
$$= \$53.29 \,(83.072960)$$
$$= \$4,427$$

$$\text{Net present value of refinancing} = \text{present value of benefits} - \text{costs}$$
$$\text{to refinance}$$
$$= \$4,427 - \$3,907$$
$$= \$520$$

*See text for assumptions.

Impact of Holding Period   Suppose, however, that the owner does not plan to hold the mortgage for the entire 25-year maturity. For example, the owner forecasts the property will be owned for only 10 more years. In that event, the monthly savings from refinancing will occur for only 120 months instead of the entire 300 months, as in the previous example. This shorter holding period will tend to make refinancing less attractive.

To illustrate, with a 10-year holding period, the savings in payment will be $53.29 per month for 120 months. The costs of financing do not change—it still costs the borrower $3,907 to refinance. There is another difference that must be taken into account: the difference between the existing and the new loan balances. Since there is a difference in the interest rates, the two loans will have different amortization rates.

At the end of a 10-year holding period, the existing mortgage will have a remaining life of 15 years (180 months). The amount outstanding will be $42,852. The balance on the new loan after a 10-year holding period will be $41,705. Thus, the difference between the balances is a savings of $1,147.

The total benefits from refinancing are $53.29 each month for 10 years plus $1,147 at the end of 10 years. Do these savings justify an outflow (investment) of $3,907? To answer this question, we can compute the net present value at the opportunity rate of 14 percent:

$$
\begin{aligned}
\text{NPV} &= \text{present value savings} - \text{costs} \\
&= \text{PVAF}_{14\%/12,120}(\$53.29) + \text{PVF}_{14\%/12,120}(\$1,147) - \$3,907 \\
&= 64.40542(\$53.29) + 0.24860(\$1,147) - \$3,907 \\
&= -\$189.69
\end{aligned}
$$

Obviously, the net present value is lower than previously since the benefits are not as large. It is negative, indicating that refinancing is not attractive. Note that the time period the borrower (owner) expects to hold the mortgage is an important factor in the refinancing decision. The other important factors are the difference between the old and the new loan's interest rates, the financing costs on the old and new loans, and the owner's opportunity rate of investment.

Refinancing Income Property Example

Consider the following fairly complex example, which illustrates all the important points to consider when making the refinancing decision for an income property. A real estate investor is considering refinancing a property that was purchased 3 years ago for $100,000. The investment was financed with a $75,000 mortgage at a 10 percent interest rate, 20-year maturity, with monthly payments. Table 18-11 is the mortgage amortization schedule for the existing loan. At the time of the origination, financing costs were 2 percent of the amount borrowed (0.02 × $75,000, or $1,500 origination fees). The loan calls for prepayment penalties of 3 percent of the outstanding balance. At the time of purchase, $85,500

TABLE 18-11 MORTGAGE AMORTIZATION SCHEDULE FOR EXISTING LOAN

Year	Proportion outstanding	Amount outstanding	Debt service	Interest	Principal
0	0.94498	$70,874			
1	0.92267	69,200	$8,685	$7,011	$1,674
2	0.89802	67,352	8,685	6,837	1,848
3	0.87080	65,310	8,685	6,643	2,042
4	0.84072	63,054	8,685	6,429	2,256
5	0.80750	60,563	8,685	6,194	2,491

was allocated to a depreciable amount using the straight-line depreciation method with a 27.5 year recovery life. The depreciation deduction is $3,109 per year. The remaining $14,500 was the nondepreciable land value.

The investment is expected to generate a net operating income of $12,500 this coming year, and this income is expected to increase 2 percent per year. The investment's current market value is $120,000.

The investor can refinance with a $90,000 new loan at an interest rate of 12 percent with 20-year-maturity, monthly payments. Financing costs (legal fees, appraisal costs, etc.) are 2 percent ($1,800) of the amount borrowed ($90,000 × 0.02). Prepayment penalties are 7 percent. Table 18-12 is the mortgage amortization schedule for this new loan for the next 5 years. The annual debt service is $11,891.

The investor anticipates holding the investment for 5 more years, at which time the expected selling price will be $140,000 with 5 percent selling expenses. The investor is in a 28 percent tax bracket. The investor's opportunity rate of return is 14 percent after tax. Should the investor refinance?

Basic Tax Rules of Refinancing Several general tax rules related to financing should be kept in mind. First, costs of placing a mortgage against an income property are *not* deductible in the year paid. They must be amortized on a straight-line basis over the life of the mortgage as a deduction against ordinary taxable income from operation. If an income property is sold (or refinanced) prior to the matu-

TABLE 18-12 MORTGAGE AMORTIZATION SCHEDULE FOR NEW LOAN

Year	Proportion outstanding	Amount outstanding	Debt service	Interest	Principal
0	1.00000	$90,000			
1	0.98718	88,846	$11,891	$10,737	$1,154
2	0.97273	87,546	11,891	10,591	1,300
3	0.95646	86,081	11,891	10,426	1,465
4	0.93811	84,429	11,891	10,240	1,651
5	0.91744	82,570	11,891	10,032	1,859

TABLE 18-13 EXPECTED AFTER-TAX CASH FLOW WITHOUT REFINANCING

	Year				
	1	2	3	4	5
Net operating income (NOI)	$12,500	$12,750	$13,005	$13,265	$13,530
− debt service (DS)	8,685	8,685	8,685	8,685	10,502†
before-tax cash flow (BTCF)	3,815	4,065	4,320	4,580	3,028
− taxes (savings) from operations (TO)*	648	764	890	1,023	402
after-tax cash flow (ATCF)	3,167	3,301	3,430	3,557	2,626

*See Table 18-14.
†This is the debt service of $8,685 plus the 3 percent prepayment penalty ($1,817).

rity, the unamortized amount is deductible in the year of sale (or refinancing) against ordinary taxable income. Second, borrowed money is not taxable income. Thus, the net amount of equity liquidated as a result of refinancing is not taxable income. Third, prepayment penalties are deductible as interest in the year of sale (or refinance) against ordinary taxable income from operations. Fourth, the interest paid on indebtedness is tax-deductible.

Also, it is important to understand that financing costs represent a *cash outflow* when they are incurred. Likewise, prepayment penalties are cash outflows.

Step 1: After-Tax Cash Flows The first task is to calculate the after-tax cash flows with and without refinancing. Table 18-13 contains the expected after-tax cash flows from operation without refinancing. The NOI is $12,500 and is expected to grow at a 2 percent rate. The debt service on the existing loan (from Table 18-11) is $8,685. Notice that in year 5 there is a 3 percent prepayment penalty ($1,817), which is deducted as a cash outflow. Table 18-14 contains the taxes

TABLE 18-14 EXPECTED TAXES FROM OPERATION WITHOUT REFINANCING

	Year				
	1	2	3	4	5
Net operating income (NOI)	$12,500	$12,750	$13,005	$13,265	$13,530
− interest (I)*	7,001	6,837	6,643	6,429	8,011†
− depreciation (D)‡	3,109	3,109	3,109	3,109	3,109
− amortized financing costs (AFC)§	75	75	75	75	975
taxable income (TI)	2,315	2,729	3,178	3,652	1,435
× tax rate (τ)	0.28	0.28	0.28	0.28	0.28
taxes (savings) from operations (TO)	648	764	890	1,023	402

*From Table 18-11.
†This is the interest in year 5 ($6,194) plus the penalty of $1,817 (0.03 × $60,563).
‡Depreciable amount of $85,500 divided by 27.5-year life.
§Original fees of $1,500 deductible over 20-year maturity. In year 5, the unamortized balance is deductible.

TABLE 18-15 EXPECTED AFTER-TAX CASH FLOW FROM SALE
IN YEAR 5 WITHOUT REFINANCING

Expected selling price (SP)	$140,000
− selling expenses (SE)	7,000
net sale proceeds (NSP)	133,000
− unpaid mortgage balance (UM)	60,563
before-tax equity reversion (BTER)	72,437
− taxes due on sale (TDS)*	16,204
after-tax equity reversion (ATER)	56,233

*See Table 18-16.

from operation without refinancing. Tables 18-15 and 18-16 give the after-tax cash flow from sale in year 5 (the anticipated holding period) and the taxes due on sale at the end of the holding period.

Tables 18-17 to 18-19 contain the after-tax cash flow from operation and future sale if the project is refinanced. Notice that the new debt service is $11,891. Also note that in year 5 there is a prepayment penalty of $2,477 (see Table 18-17) on the new loan. The new loan involves $1,800 in financing costs that are amortized, for tax purposes, over the new loan maturity of 20 years at $90 per year. In year 5 (see Table 18-18), the unamortized balance is deductible against taxable income. Notice that as a result of refinancing, the investment is generating a tax shelter because of the higher interest payments on the new loan. This tax shelter does not necessarily mean, however, that refinancing is attractive. Note that in Table 18-19, the taxes due on sale in year 5 are the same with and without refinancing. Refinancing does not influence the taxes due on sale.

Table 18-20 contains the net after-tax proceeds to the investor from refinancing. The new loan amount is $90,000, from which the investor pays off the exist-

TABLE 18-16 EXPECTED TAXES DUE ON SALE IN YEAR 5
WITHOUT REFINANCING

Taxable income	
Expected selling price (SP)	$140,000
− selling expenses (SE)	7,000
amount realized (AR)	133,000
− adjusted basis (AB)*	75,128
total gain on sale (TG)	57,872
Taxes due on sale	
Total gain on sale (TG)	57,872
× investor's marginal tax rate (τ)	0.28
taxes due on sale (TDS)	16,204

*Original cost ($100,000) minus cumulative depreciation deduction ($24,872).

TABLE 18-17   EXPECTED AFTER-TAX CASH FLOW WITH REFINANCING

	Year				
	1	2	3	4	5
Net operating income (NOI)	$12,500	$12,750	$13,005	$13,265	$13,530
− debt service (DS)	11,891	11,891	11,891	11,891	14,368*
before-tax cash flow (BTCF)	609	859	1,114	1,374	(838)
− taxes (savings) from operations (TO)†	(402)	(291)	(174)	(49)	(988)
after-tax cash flow (ATCF)	1,011	1,150	1,288	1,423	1,826

*Includes prepayment penalty of $2,477 on the new loan (3% of $82,570).
†See Table 18-17.

TABLE 18-18   EXPECTED TAXES FOR OPERATIONS WITH REFINANCING

	Year				
	1	2	3	4	5
Net operating income (NOI)	$12,500	$12,750	$13,005	$13,265	$13,530
− interest (I)*	10,737	10,591	10,426	10,240	12,509†
− depreciation (D)	3,109	3,109	3,109	3,109	3,109
− amortized financing costs (AFC)‡	90	90	90	90	1,440
taxable income (TI)	(1,436)	(1,040)	(620)	(174)	(3,528)
× tax rate (τ)	0.28	0.28	0.28	0.28	0.28
taxes (savings) from operations (TO)	(402)	(291)	(174)	(49)	(988)

*From Table 18-12.
†Includes the $2,477 prepayment penalty.
‡This is the financing costs of $1,800 divided by the 20-year maturity, resulting in a deduction of $90 per year. In year 5, the unamortized balance of the financing costs is deductible.

TABLE 18-19   EXPECTED AFTER-TAX CASH FLOW FROM SALE IN YEAR 5 WITH REFINANCING

Expected selling price (SP)	$140,000
− selling expenses (SE)	7,000
net sale proceeds (NSP)	133,000
− unpaid mortgage balance (UM)	82,570
before-tax equity reversion (BTER)	50,430
− taxes due on sale (TDS)*	16,204
after-tax equity reversion (ATER)	34,226

*See Table 18-16.

ing loan balance of $70,874. The investor also incurs prepayment penalties of $2,126 (3 percent of $70,874) from paying off the old loan. However, since the penalty is deductible as interest, the after-tax cost of these penalties is $1,531 ($2,126 minus the tax deduction of 28 percent of $2,126). The new loan involves financing costs of $1,800 (legal fees, appraisal fees, etc.) that the investor must pay. The net proceeds from refinancing is thus $16,152.

TABLE 18-20 AFTER-TAX PROCEEDS FROM REFINANCING

New loan amount	$90,000
− old loan amount	70,874
− prepayment penalty (after-tax) on old loan*	1,531
− financing costs new loan	1,800
+ tax savings from financing costs of old loan†	357
net proceeds from refinancing	16,152

*If the old loan is paid off, there is a 3% penalty of the amount outstanding ($70,874), or $2,126. This is deductible as interest; thus the after-tax cost (with a 28% tax bracket) is $1,531 (72% of $2,126).

†With the original loan, financing costs were $1,500. We have taken $75 each year for 3 years as a tax deduction. As a result of refinancing, the tax-payer is allowed to deduct the unamortized balance of $1,350. If the investor is in a 28% tax bracket, this deduction results in a tax savings of $357.

Step 2: The Differential Cash Flows The second step in the refinancing decision process is to calculate the differential cash flows, as in Table 18-21. At time zero (the present), if the investment is refinanced, the investor receives a net after-tax cash inflow of $16,152 (from Table 18-20). If the investment is not refinanced, the investor receives no proceeds. Thus, the difference (cash inflow with refinancing minus cash inflow without refinancing) is a cash inflow of $16,153. In year 1, if the investment is refinanced, the investor will receive an expected cash inflow of $1,011. If the investment is not refinanced, the expected cash inflow is $3,167. The difference is thus $2,156 ($1,011 − $3,167). The investor therefore has to "pay" $2,156 for the refinancing decision in year 1. Continuing with Table 18-21, the differential ACTF is negative each year except the year of refinancing. Thus, the investor receives $16,152 but has to "pay" each year for the refinancing as a result of a lower after-tax cash inflow.

It is important to understand that the differential after-tax cash flows consider all the relevant factors that influence the refinancing decision except the "opportunity" rate at which the refinancing proceeds can be invested. Thus, differential cash flows are the "numbers" on which the refinancing decision should be based.

TABLE 18-21 DIFFERENTIAL AFTER-TAX CASH FLOWS: REFINANCE VERSUS NOT REFINANCE

Year	ATCFs with refinancing	ATCFs without refinancing	Differential ATCFs
0	$16,152	$ 0	$ 16,152
1	1,011	3,167	(2,156)
2	1,150	3,301	(2,151)
3	1,288	3,430	(2,142)
4	1,423	3,557	(2,134)
5	36,052†	58,859†	(22,807)

*From Table 18-20.
†Includes operating and reversion cash flows in year 5.

TABLE 18-22 NET PRESENT VALUE AND INTERNAL RATE OF RETURN
ON DIFFERENTIAL CASH FLOWS: REFINANCE VERSUS
NOT REFINANCE

Year	Differential cash flows*	PVF$_{14\%}$	PV
0	$ 16,152	1.00000	$ 16,152
1	(2,156)	0.8772	(1,891)
2	(2,151)	0.7694	(1,655)
3	(2,142)	0.6750	(1,446)
4	(2,134)	0.5921	(1,263)
5	(22,807)	0.5194	(11,846)
		Net present value	(1,949)
		IRR	17.25%

*From Table 18-21.

Step 3: The Decision Criteria   Now that we have calculated the expected after-tax cash inflows and outflows, with and without refinancing, we next apply the decision criteria. As we said earlier, there are two methods for making the decision: (1) calculating the net present value of the differential cash flows or (2) calculating the rate of return on the differential. Table 18-22 shows the net present value (NPV) and internal rate of return (IRR) on the differential cash flows. The investor receives $16,152 from the decision to refinance but must pay out $2,156 in year 1, $2,151 in year 2, $2,142 in year 3, $2,134 in year 4, and $22,807 in year 5 in differential cash flows.

Suppose the investor's opportunity rate is 14 percent. Table 18-22 shows the NPV to be −$1,949 at this rate. So the investor would *not* accept the refinancing decision. This obviously implies that not refinancing is more attractive for our problem. The internal rate of return is 17.25 percent on the differential cash flows, which means that the opportunity rate must be at least 17.25 percent before refinancing would be acceptable given our assumptions. Since our initial assumption was an opportunity rate of 14 percent, we would not refinance since the "cost" of refinancing is 17.25 percent and our opportunity rate is 14 percent.

Sensitivity Analysis   Table 18-23 shows the sensitivity of the refinancing decision in our example at various opportunity rates. Notice that at a rate less than 17.25 percent, the investor does not refinance, given the assumptions in the example. At opportunity rates greater than 17.25 percent, refinancing becomes acceptable. The present value of the after-tax cash flows with and without refinancing declines as the opportunity rate increases. At a rate of 17.25 percent (the IRR on the differential), the net present value is zero. At a higher rate than 17.25 percent, the present value of cash inflows with refinancing exceeds that without refinancing. Of course, this 17.25 percent rate is for the example we have calculated. But in general, the greater the opportunity rate, the more attractive

TABLE 18-23 NET PRESENT VALUE OF CASH FLOWS AT VARIOUS OPPORTUNITY RATES: REFINANCE VERSUS NOT REFINANCE

Opportunity rate (%)	Present value of cash flows with refinancing	Present value of cash flows without refinancing	NPV
0	$57,097	$72,293	($15,196)
4	50,202	60,548	(10,346)
8	44,670	50,997	(6,327)
12	40,270	43,547	(3,277)
16	36,675	37,359	(684)
20	33,734	32,278	1,456
24	31,311	28,074	3,237

refinancing becomes. The rate, however, depends on the loan proceeds and the differential after-tax cash flows from the two options.

SUMMARY

This chapter discussed several situations borrowers and lenders face when making the real estate financing decision. Both the borrower and the lender use the same basic criteria to analyze decisions, such as whether or not to refinance, whether to sell or continue to own an investment, and whether to offer a discount for early repayment.

The next several chapters discuss the various financing methods and techniques. These alternatives (to the traditional fixed-rate mortgage) are designed to solve the numerous problems facing both borrowers and lenders in the real estate market.

QUESTIONS

1 Define the following terms:
   a financial leverage
   b financial risk
   c inflation risk
   d default risk
   e refinance
2 Explain how the use of debt can increase the expected rate of return on the equity position.
3 What happens to the risk to the equity position as debt is used in the financing of an investment?
4 Suppose you can buy an investment for $500,000 all cash, with an expected yield of 12 percent. Alternatively, you can borrow $375,000 and put in $125,000 of equity. Under this option, the rate of return on the equity is 14 percent. Which option would you choose? Why?
5 What risks does the lender take when a mortgage loan is made? If you were a lender, how would you try to deal with the risks?

6 Suppose you are willing to loan me $10,000 for 1 year, at the end of which I have to repay you $11,200. You expect 8 percent inflation during this period. Suddenly, inflation expectations increase to 10 percent during this year. How much would you require me to repay? Suppose we had already made the loan for the $11,200 repayment and inflation expectations changed and you suddenly had to sell the loan to another lender. How much could you sell it for?

7 Suppose you loan me $10,000 for 1 year and I repay you $11,200. However, actual inflation was 10 percent. What was your "real" rate of return?

8 Discuss how you would make the decision to sell an investment or continue to operate and sell in the future. Using the example in Table 18-9, explain the concept of the differential cash flow between sale and continue to operate. What does the net present value of this differential mean? Calculate net present value at rates of 18 and 20 percent. Explain these net present values.

9 Explain the basic principles of the refinancing decision. Describe the steps you would take for making this decision. Under what conditions would it always pay the borrower to refinance? Not refinance?

10 Using the example developed in this chapter, write the equation for making the refinancing decision. (*Hint:* use the cash flows in Table 18-22 as the beginning and substitute in the equations.)

PROBLEMS

1 An investor has two financing options:

Option 1: 100 percent equity
Option 2: $650,000 mortgage at a 10 percent interest rate with interest-only payment with balloon in 3 years; debt service is $65,000 per year (interest only)

The investor is in the 28 percent tax bracket and has the opportunity to buy an office complex at a total cost of $1,000,000. The investment has an expected constant net operating income of $100,000 per year. The investor anticipates holding the investment for 3 years and then selling it for 5 percent above the original purchase price. The investment will be depreciated for tax purposes, using the straight-line method over a 31.5-year life. The depreciable basis is 75 percent of the purchase price. Which option should the investor choose?

2 Calculate the after-tax cost of debt for problem 1.

3 Suppose a lender made a mortgage loan of $75,000 at an 11 percent interest rate with 30-year maturity. After 7 years, the market rate is 13.5 percent and the lender would like the borrower to repay the loan. What is maximum amount of discount the lender would be willing to offer?

4 A real estate investor (in the 28 percent tax bracket) owns a shopping mall that was purchased 2 years ago for $2,500,000. The depreciable basis was $2,000,000. The investor has been using the straight-line depreciation method with a 31.5-year life. The investment was financed with a fixed-rate mortgage at 9 percent for 20 years. The LTV ratio was 95 percent. The current selling price is $2,750,000. Selling expenses would be 5 percent of the selling price.

   The investor is trying to decide whether to sell or continue to operate for another year. The NOI next year is to be $300,000. The value of the investment is expected to be $2,850,000 at the end of next year, with selling expenses of 5 percent. Should the investor sell or continue to operate if the required after-tax rate of return is 10 percent?

5 Suppose a borrower makes a mortgage loan for $1,000,000 at an 11 percent interest rate for 25 years. After 5 years, interest rates fall and a new loan is available at 9.25 percent for 20 years. A 5 percent prepayment penalty must be paid on the old loan. In addition, the lender making the new loan requires financing costs of 3 percent, including origination fees and points. Should the borrower refinance if the borrower's opportunity rate is 13 percent?

6 Suppose that in problem 5, the owner of the property forecasts that it will be owned for only 6 more years. With this new information, should the borrower refinance?

7 A real estate investor is considering refinancing a property that was purchased 2 years ago for $250,000. The investment was financed with a $225,000 mortgage at a 13 percent interest rate, 25-year maturity, with monthly payments.

At the time of origination, financing costs were 2 percent of the amount borrowed. The loan calls for prepayment penalties of 3 percent of the outstanding balance. At the time of purchase, $200,000 was allocated to depreciable amount using the straight-line depreciation method with a 31.5-year recovery life.

The investment is expected to generate a net operating income of $31,000 this coming year, and this income is expected to increase 5 percent per year. The investment's current market value is $300,000. The investor can refinance with a $235,000 new loan at an interest rate of 14 percent with a 25-year maturity, monthly payments. Financing costs are 2 percent of the amount borrowed. Prepayment penalties are 7 percent.

The investor anticipates holding the investment for 3 more years, at which time the expected selling price will be $315,000 with 5 percent selling expenses. The investor is in the 28 percent tax bracket. The investor's opportunity rate of return is 15 percent after tax. Should the investor refinance?

REFERENCES

Edwards, Charles E., Philip L. Cooley, and Robert H. Zerbst: "Evaluating Financial Leverage: Theory vs. Practice," *Real Estate Appraiser and Analyst,* March-April 1979, pp. 8–10.

Sevy, Haim, and Marshall Sarnat: *Capital Investment and Financial Decisions,* 2d ed., Prentice-Hall International, Inc., London, 1982.

Montgomery, J. Thomas: "Leverage," *Appraisal Journal,* October 1977, pp. 589–600.

Van Horne, James C.: *Financial Management and Policy,* 5th ed., Prentice-Hall, Englewood Cliffs, N.J., 1980.

Zerbst, Robert H., Charles E. Edwards, and Philip L. Cooley: "Evaluation of Financial Leverage for Real Estate Investments," *Real Estate Appraisers,* July-August 1977, pp. 7–11.

MANAGING
A MORTGAGE PORTFOLIO

Although the funds for mortgages are ultimately obtained from the savings in the economy, financial institutions, such as banks, savings and loan associations, life insurance companies, and others, play a key role in the flow of these savings in the financial markets. Recent years have been a dynamic period for the suppliers of real estate credit. The mortgage interest rates have been volatile, new government programs have been introduced, and numerous mortgage instruments have been designed. All these factors have created new problems for the financial institutions and their managers.

The purpose of this chapter is to introduce the supply side of the mortgage market: to describe the institutions participating in the mortgage market and to discuss the problems facing the financial managers of the mortgage market financial institutions.

The chapter is divided into three major sections. The first section describes the various financial institutions operating in the primary mortgage market. The second section discusses the characteristics of the secondary mortgage market and its institutions. The third section discusses the decisions facing the financial managers of the financial institutions in the mortgage market.

It should be noted at this point that we use the same basic decision-making tools for mortgage portfolio decisions as we used for other investments. After all, the mortgage lender is simply an investor in mortgages. Thus, the expected cash inflows and outflows, appropriate risk-return level, and resultant NPV must be determined in order to arrive at an accept or reject decision for the mortgage as an investment.

THE PRIMARY MORTGAGE MARKET

The primary mortgage market is made up of borrowers and lenders involved in originating mortgage loans. In Chapter 18, we examined the demand side of the market—the borrowers. Now we turn to an analysis of the supply side of the primary mortgage market—the lending institutions.[1]

Table 19-1 shows total mortgage debt outstanding by type of property and type of holder for year-end 1987. Savings and loan associations and commercial banks are clearly the largest mortgage lenders. These two institutions hold about half of the $2.75 trillion in outstanding mortgage debt. The data show that in 1987 savings and loan associations held a dominant 29.9 percent share of the outstanding mortgage debt. Their closest competitors, commercial banks, held only 19.8 percent share of the outstanding debt.

Table 19-1 also indicates the major role of federal credit agencies in the primary mortgage market. Typically, federal agencies are thought of as part of the secondary market, while in fact several are primary market lenders. In 1987 over $808 million of outstanding mortgage debt was supported by government agencies or government-backed mortgage pools and trusts.

Table 19-2 shows total originations of one- to four-family, multifamily, commercial, and farm mortgages by the nine most important primary mortgage market originators in 1987. The data listed there give further evidence that savings

---

[1] For a good discussion of the lender's viewpoint of the mortgage market, see Kenneth J. Thygerson and Dennis J. Jacobe, *Mortgage Portfolio Management,* U.S. League of Savings Associations, Chicago, 1978.

TABLE 19-1   MORTGAGE DEBT OUTSTANDING BY TYPE OF PROPERTY AND TYPE OF HOLDER
(End of Second Quarter 1987, Millions of Dollars)

Type of holder	One- to four-family	Multi-family	Commer-cial	Farm	Total
All holders	1,770,953	266,913	615,264	91,800	2,744,930
Savings and loan associations	567,262	105,649	149,804	502	823,217
Commercial banks	251,701	33,585	243,399	13,890	542,575
Life insurance companies	12,832	20,820	154,192	10,245	198,089
Federal agencies	123,999	19,654	8,553	44,292	196,498
Mortgage pools and trusts	597,819	14,396	126	67	612,408
Individuals and others	108,442	72,809	59,190	22,804	335,245

Source: Federal Reserve Board of Governors: *Federal Reserve Bulletin,* December 1987, p. A39.

TABLE 19-2   TOTAL ORIGINATION OF MORTGAGES FOR EACH MAJOR LENDER BY TYPE OF PROPERTY
(Millions of Dollars)

Lender	One- to four-family	Multi-family	Commercial	Farm	Total	Percent of total
Savings and loan associations	180,882	19,362	20,136	5	220,385	32.05
Commercial banks	123,500	8,413	107,906	5,038	244,857	35.61
Mortgage companies	116,659	3,231	3,304	0	123,194	17.92
Life insurance companies	3,388	3,756	29,593	857	37,594	5.47
Mutual savings banks	34,523	4,348	6,254	1	45,126	6.56
Private pension funds	2	0	222	0	224	0.03
State and local retirement funds	16	37	276	0	329	0.05
Federal credit agencies	2,837	1,215	516	2,259	6,827	1.00
State and local credit agencies	678	7,800	489	35	9,002	1.31
	462,485	48,162	168,696	8,195	687,538	100.0

Source: U.S. Department of Housing and Urban Development: "News Release," HUD No. 88-24 for the 12 months ending November 1987, November 1987.

and loan associations and commercial banks are the largest mortgage market lenders. Of originations totaling over $687 billion in 1987, savings and loan associations originated 32.1 percent, while commercial banks originated 35.6 percent. All other primary market lenders originated only 32.2 percent of the market.

Table 19-3 gives a breakdown of financial assets of the four major types of financial institutions at the end of December 1987. Those included are savings and loan associations, commercial banks, mortgage banking companies, mutual savings banks, and life insurance companies.

Savings and Loan Associations

The substantial role played by savings and loan associations in the mortgage market is not surprising, since their charters (federal and state) have, in the past, re-

TABLE 19-3 FINANCIAL ASSETS OF PRIVATE INSTITUTIONS

Financial Assets	Savings and loan associations		Mutual savings banks		Commercial banks		Life insurance companies	
	Millions of dollars	Percent	Millions of dollars	Percent	Millions of dollars	Percent	Millions of dollars	Percent
Mortgages	140,590	24.9	128,217	63.9	150,427	89.3	200,382	53.8
Cash and reserves	137,769	24.4	4,939	2.4	—		—	
Governmental securities	—	—	13,549	6.8	—		87,279	23.5
Corporate bonds	—	—	18,803	9.4	—			
Other	285,578	50.7	35,200	17.5	17,940	10.7	84,390	22.7
Total assets	563,937	100.0	200,708	100.0	168,367	100.0	372,051	100.0

Source: Federal Reserve Board of Governors: *Federal Reserve Bulletin,* December 1987, pp. A26, A27.

quired that they be functionally specialized in residential mortgages. Associations chartered by the federal government have not been authorized to invest in commercial and industrial loans, corporate bonds and paper, or equities and are subject to limits on the percentage of assets they can invest in multifamily and nonresidential mortgages as well as on the types of consumer loans and municipal bonds they can purchase. The constraints have virtually guaranteed a high degree of participation of savings and loan associations in the residential mortgage market.

Commercial Banks

Commercial banks are the most diversified of all the primary mortgage lenders, being able to invest in virtually all U.S. debt-credit instruments. The role played by a particular commercial bank in the mortgage market varies, since each bank's managers have the freedom to determine the role of mortgages in their institution's asset portfolio. Suburban and small-town banks invest a higher percentage of their assets in residential mortgages than large money-center banks do. Commercial banks tend to hold a higher percentage of their total mortgages in multifamily and nonresidential mortgages than savings and loan associations as a result of this greater asset freedom.

Life Insurance Companies

Life insurance companies as a group are also large investors in residential mortgages. However, as the data in Table 19-2 indicate, they also invest heavily in multifamily and commercial loans. Unlike depository-type institutions, life insurance companies cannot take deposits in their loan origination offices to offset their direct lending costs. Today, the life insurance companies are the second largest holder of commercial mortgages. Of their total $198 billion invested in mortgages at the end of 1987, $13 billion is in one- to four-family mortgages, while

$154 billion and $21 billion, respectively, are invested in nonresidential and mul-tifamily mortgages.

Mutual Savings Banks

Mutual savings banks are state-chartered institutions and are more restricted than commercial banks. However, they are substantially less restricted than a feder-ally chartered savings and loan association. Their charter permits them to pur-chase corporate bonds, paper, and equities and to participate in nearly all types of consumer credit. Savings banks are, as a result, substantially more diversified than savings and loan associations but less diversified than commercial banks, holding 64 percent of their assets in mortgages. Because most savings bank assets are concentrated in the northeast, where population and the demand for mort-gages have been declining, they tend to be active purchasers of out-of-state mort-gages. They are also relatively active multifamily and nonresidential mortgage holders.

Mortgage Banking Companies

Mortgage banking companies, sometimes known as mortgage companies or mort-gage dealers, are primarily originators of, not investors in, mortgages. In contrast to the activity of financial institutions, the mortgage banker's principal activity is originating and servicing residential and income-property mortgage loans for in-stitutional investors. Since mortgage bankers are essentially mortgage merchan-disers, they usually hold mortgages in their portfolios for a fairly short time. Nor-mally, they only hold mortgages until an investor is found or a delivery date occurs. A mortgage banker occasionally originates mortgages without having a purchase commitment from an investor. This occurs when the mortgage company believes interest rates will decline or remain level when short-term financing costs provide the firm with a profit from carrying these assets.

Mortgage Brokers

Mortgage brokers, in contrast to mortgage bankers and other financial institu-tions, are not originators of or investors in mortgages. Mortgage brokers never invest their own capital in a mortgage: They are strictly agents. Mortgage bro-kers' primary activity is to originate real estate loans for banks, life insurance companies, and other institutions. They provide the services of processing loan information for borrowers and analyzing mortgage investments for lenders. They do not administer or service the loan once it has been made.

THE SECONDARY MORTGAGE MARKET

Since the latter half of the 1960s, the secondary mortgage market has become an important part of the overall mortgage market, particularly the residential mortgage market. The *secondary mortgage market* is a term used to refer to those federal agencies and private corporations involved in the buying and selling of existing mortgage loans and providing credit to primary lenders (loan originators). Since many of the entities involved in the secondary market are also active primary mortgage participants, it is often difficult to precisely delineate secondary market operations. The clearest distinction can be made at the point of loan origination, which is where the primary lender operates. Lenders who buy or accept a mortgage loan that they did not originate are considered to be operating in the secondary market.

Role of the Secondary Mortgage Market

The key role played by the secondary mortgage market is to provide liquidity to the holders of long-term mortgages and potential investors in residential mortgages. By purchasing mortgages from primary market loan originators, the secondary market attempts to provide a means by which long-term investors (such as savings and loans, commercial banks, etc.) can convert mortgage loans to cash. Without the secondary market operations, long maturities and limited liquidity associated with mortgage lending would severely limit a primary lender's ability to issue new mortgages with any flexibility. This increased liquidity is designed to increase the efficiency of mortgage market operations, leading to better funds flows in the mortgage market.

Table 19-4 shows the purchases and sales of one- to four-family and multifamily mortgage loans for 9 major lending institutions in 1987. Almost all are both buyers and sellers of mortgage loans. Table 19-5 shows the amount and percentage of mortgage purchases and sales of all types of property: one- to four-family, multifamily, commercial, and farm. The data in both tables illustrate that the bulk

TABLE 19-4   PURCHASES OF ONE- TO FOUR-FAMILY AND MULTIFAMILY MORTGAGE LOANS
(Millions of Dollars)

	One- to four-family		Multifamily	
Lender	Purchases	Sales	Purchases	Sales
Commercial banks	20,873	48,305	3,886	79
Mutual savings banks	2,939	13,679	73	165
Savings and loan associations	58,163	124,287	2,770	3231
Life insurance companies	1,258	1,169	136	7
Mortgage companies	53,105	169,887	664	4705
State and local retirement funds	1,116	245	168	25
Federal credit agencies	22,291	5,333	1,440	1100
Mortgage pools	26,980	282	5,362	0
State and local credit agencies	4,130	1	71	0
Total	190,855	363,188	14,570	9,312

Source: HUD No. 88-24 for 12 months ending November 1987, U. S. Department of Housing and Urban Development: "News Release," November 1987.

TABLE 19-5   PURCHASES AND SALES OF MORTGAGE LOANS BY PROPERTY TYPE

Property type	Purchases		Sales	
	Amount (millions of dollars)	Percent	Amount (millions of dollars)	Percent
One- to four-family	190,855	77.98	363,188	94.94
Multifamily	14,570	5.95	9,312	2.43
Commercial	39,076	15.97	9,994	2.61
Farm	258	0.10	63	0.02
Total	244,759	100.0	382,557	100.0

Source: HUD No. 88-24 for the 12 months ending November 1987, U.S. Department of Housing and Urban Development: "News Release," November 1987.

of secondary mortgage market trading occurs in home mortgages. Almost 79 percent of the purchases and 95 percent of the sales involve home mortgages.

The secondary mortgage market provides a mechanism to facilitate the transfer of funds from capital-surplus to capital-deficient areas of the country. It helps to stabilize the various supply and demand conditions across different regions of the country. Without the secondary mortgage market, investors with surplus funds might experience difficulty in placing those funds in mortgages. Likewise, in areas with a lack of supply of funds available for mortgages, the secondary market provides a mechanism whereby the financial institution can easily convert its mortgages into cash. Since many secondary lenders also participate in other financial markets, the secondary market also provides to all mortgage market participants information about how the total financial market evaluates the relative risk and return on mortgages compared with those of other financial instruments.

One of the main criticisms of the secondary mortgage market is that its institutions (especially the government-backed agencies) are tapping the credit markets for funds and as a result are reducing the resources available to primary lenders. Thus these agencies may be posing a threat to the continuing growth of the private intermediaries in the mortgage market.

Participants in the Secondary Mortgage Market

Until the early 1970s, only government-backed institutions were involved in the secondary mortgage market. These agencies typically operate through the primary mortgage lenders and include the Federal National Mortgage Association (FNMA, now a quasi-public corporation often referred to as *Fannie Mae*), the Government National Mortgage Association (GNMA, often referred to as *Ginnie Mae*), Federal Home Loan Mortgage Corporation (FHLMC, *Freddie Mac*), and the Federal Home Loan Bank System (FHLB). Table 19-6 shows the amount of mortgage debt supported by these agencies for the years 1980 through 1987. To-

TABLE 19-6 RESIDENTIAL DEBT SUPPORTED BY FEDERAL CREDIT AGENCIES
(Millions of Dollars)

Agency	1980	1981	1982	1983	1984	1985	1986	1987
Federal National Mortgage Association	55,185	58,749	70,052	7,594	83,720	9,896	93,563	91,637
Government National Mortgage Association	2,817	2,715	2,165	2,165	2,165	2,165	2,165	1,965
Federal Home Loan Mortgage Corporation	2,536	5,480	4,524	6,793	10,270	11,926	13,589	12,309
Federal Home Loan banks	41,258	54,131	55,967	48,930	65,085	74,447	88,752	100,976
Total	101,796	72,357	132,708	132,482	161,240	182,434	198,069	206,887

Source: Federal Reserve Board of Governors: *Federal Reserve Bulletin,* December 1987.

gether these agencies supported almost $207 billion in residential mortgage debt in 1987.

These agencies and their privately supported counterparts raise capital by selling various types of *mortgage-backed securities*. In other words, the capital raised is used to purchase (invest in) existing mortgages. Table 19-7 lists the ma-

TABLE 19-7 PRIMARY INSTITUTIONS AND TRADING VEHICLES USED IN THE SECONDARY MORTGAGE MARKET

Primary institutions	Primary trading vehicles

Private depository institutions
  Savings and loan associations
  Commercial banks
  Mutual savings banks
  Credit unions
	Whole mortgage loans
	Private-issue mortgage participations
	GNMA pass-through securities
	FHLMC participation certificates
	FHLMC-guaranteed mortgage bonds

Federal credit agencies
  Federal National Mortgage Association (FNMA)
  Federal Home Loan Mortgage Corporation (FHLMC)
  Government National Mortgage Association (GNMA)
  Farmers Home Administration
	Private-issue mortgage pass-through securities
	Private-issue mortgage-back bonds
	Industrial development bonds
	CMOs
	REMICs

State agencies
  State housing finance agencies
  State mortgage finance agencies	

Other private institutions
  Mortgage banking companies
  Life insurance companies
  Private and government pension funds
  Mortgage investment trusts
  Trust funds
  Bond brokerage firms	

Source: K. J. Thygerson and F. J. Jacobe: *Mortgage Portfolio Management,* United States League of Savings Associations, Chicago, 1978, p. 116.

TABLE 19-8   TERMS AND YIELDS IN PRIMARY AND SECONDARY MORTGAGE MARKETS, 1982–1987

	1982	1983	1984	1985	1986	1987
Primary market terms*						
Purchase price (thousands of dollars)	94.6	92.8	96.8	104.8	118.1	135.11
Amount of loan (thousands of dollars)	69.8	69.5	73.7	77.4	862	99.07
Loan/value ratio (%)	76.6	77.1	78.7	77.1	752	75.3
Fees and charges† (percentage of loan amount)	2.95	2.40	2.64	2.53	2.66	2.25
Contract rate (%)	14.47	12.20	11.87	11.12	9.57	8.97
Primary market yields						
FHLBB series‡	15.12	12.66	12.37	11.58	10.02	9.26
HUD series§	15.79	13.43	12.28	9.89	9.84	
Secondary market yields						
FHA mortgages (HUD series)	15.12	12.66	12.37	12.24	9.80	9.78
GNMA securities	14.68	12.25	13.13	11.61	9.06	9.00

*Weighted averages based on sample surveys of conventional mortgages of new homes originated by major institutional lender groups; compiled by the FHLBB in cooperation with the FDIC.

†Includes all fees, commissions, discounts, and points paid by the borrower or the seller in order to obtain a loan.

‡Average effective interest rates on loans closed, assuming prepayment at the end of 10 years.

§Average contract rates on new commitments for conventional first mortgages, rounded to the nearest 5 basis points; from Department of Housing and Urban Development.

Source: Federal Reserve Board of Governors: *Federal Reserve Bulletin,* December 1987, p. A38.

jor institutions, both public and private, involved in the secondary mortgage market and the various types of trading instruments used to transfer mortgage assets. Note that many of the institutions listed participate actively in the primary mortgage market. The terms and yields on selected securities in the secondary market and on conventional mortgages for 1982 through 1987 are shown in Table 19-8. Mortgage-backed securities will be discussed at the end of this chapter.

DECISION SITUATIONS FACING MORTGAGE INVESTORS

The financial managers working for the various financial institutions in the mortgage market are faced with a wide variety of problems in the management of their institutions' mortgage portfolios. Financial managers must make decisions concerning the origination of mortgages in the primary market and the buying and selling of existing mortgages in the secondary market. These are investment decisions. An investment can be defined generally as a certain cash outflow (in this case, the mortgage loan) in return for an uncertain future cash inflow (the mortgage payments). In either market, the financial managers' investment decisions should be designed to maximize the lender's mortgage portfolio yield over the long run. There are a variety of decisions that financial managers must make to maximize the portfolio yields from investing in either or both the primary and secondary mortgage markets.

Primary Mortgage Market Decisions

In the case of a primary mortgage market investment, a lender receives a borrower's promise to repay the principal investment plus some agreed-upon interest charge or, in the case of default, the rights and title to the mortgaged property. Therefore, in the primary mortgage market a financial manager's investment decision must include not only an analysis of the mortgage market and the lender's current mortgage portfolio but also the value of the real estate to be mortgaged and the credibility and ability of the borrower to repay the loan commitment. We will examine six types of primary mortgage market decisions: existing-loan decisions, timing decisions, pricing decisions, new-loan decisions, servicing decisions, and default and foreclosure decisions.[2]

Existing-Loan Decisions   Existing-loan decisions involve the maximization of the portfolio yield on existing mortgages. Until the mid-1960s mortgage rates moved in a very narrow band—rarely fluctuating more than 0.5 percent in any 1 year. Once a mortgage was originated and the concern over default eliminated, it was essentially forgotten. Today, however, low-interest mortgages have a very damaging effect on earnings, substantially lowering portfolio yields for long-term lenders.

Instead of holding a mortgage for 10, 20, and 30 years, it has become far more important for mortgage portfolio managers to devise methods of encouraging the prepayment or refinancing of these mortgages. One method is to offer the borrowers a discount for full or even partial prepayment of their old mortgage loans. Another method is to allow borrowers to repay their old mortgages and have additional cash by taking out a second mortgage at an interest rate somewhere between the old rate and current market rates.

If a mortgage market financial manager can encourage the prepayment or refinancing of a 1972, 6.5 percent mortgage loan, he or she is in a position to convert an asset yielding 6.5 percent into an asset earning 1987 mortgage rates of 11 to 13 percent. Mortgage portfolio managers must continually work to design methods of converting older low-earning assets into higher-earning assets.

For example, suppose a mortgage lender holds several old 6 percent loans in its portfolio and wishes to offer an incentive to the borrowers to pay them off because the current market rate is 12 percent. The question is, How much of a discount can be offered to the borrower? The answer depends not only on the loan interest rate and current market rate but also on the number of months remaining on the loan. What we need to find is the maximum discount the lender can offer the borrower and still break even.

Suppose one of these loans has 180 months (15 years) of payments remaining. The loan amount originally was $40,000, amortized over 30 years at $239.82 per month. We first calculate the balance outstanding today.

---

[2] Thygerson and Jacobe discuss similar decision areas in Kenneth J. Thygerson and Dennis J. Jacobe, op. cit.

$$\text{Balance outstanding} = \$239.82(\text{PVAF}_{6\%/12,180})$$
$$= \$19,982$$

Thus, this loan is really only "worth" $19,982 to the lender. That is, if the lender was offered $19,982 by the borrower today instead of monthly payments of $239.82 for the next 15 years, it would be just as well off. The lender could afford to offer the borrower a discount equal to the difference between the amount owed on the contract, $28,420, and the $19,982 value, and still break even. This discount of $8,438, which amounts to 29.7 percent of the outstanding balance, is the most the lender can pay. Of course, paying this discount offers no advantage to the lender. If the borrower can be enticed to pay the loan off with, say, a $5,000 discount, then the lender benefits by $3,438.

Timing Decisions   Timing decisions are involved with determining when to make or commit to making a mortgage loan. Because of the increased volatility of mortgage interest rates in the late 1960s and throughout the 1970s, mortgage lenders can no longer assume that rates 6, 12, or 18 months from the present will be the same. Should the lender invest in a long-term mortgage or in some other type of instrument, such as a shorter-term U.S. Treasury note? Although many lenders are restricted to a few regulated investments, the decision when to make and/or commit to making mortgage investments has become an extremely important one for the financial managers of mortgage-lending institutions.

Let us illustrate the importance of timing decisions with a brief example. Suppose a mortgage lender is faced with the following decision: It can invest a large sum of available capital "long," that is, in long-term mortgages at 10 percent interest, or "short," in 90-day Treasury bills at 8 percent. If the lender chooses the second option, we assume the money will be invested in mortgages at the end of 90 days. The decision, of course, rests on the expectation of the lender with regard to future mortgage interest rates. If mortgage rates are expected to decline in the future, the lender will likely choose the first option, because the manager believes that investing in mortgages now will provide a greater yield over the long run. On the other hand, if the manager expects mortgage interest rates to rise appreciably, she will likely choose the second option, lending (to the government) at a lower rate in the short run to get the expected benefit of a higher overall yield in the long run. Although a detailed example is beyond the scope of this text, the decision is made just as with any other investment: The expected cash inflows and outflows are estimated, and the IRR (yield) and/or NPV are calculated.

Pricing Decisions   Pricing decisions, as the name implies, involve the analysis and pricing of mortgage commitments. The mortgage market financial manager must determine the interest rate to be charged and the mortgage instrument to be used. A host of peripheral pricing decisions are also involved. The financial manager must determine the initial charges to be levied on the borrower, prepayment penalties, loan maturities, and, for some instruments, the variability of interest rates and maturities (VRM, RRM) and possible increases in the mortgage payments (GPM).

Pricing strategies must also include the borrower's desire to minimize mortgage costs and the lender's desire to maximize portfolio yields. The financial manager must establish prices such that the lender's risks and required returns are accounted for without pricing the lender out of the market. A careful analysis of the supply and demand for mortgage funds is required to establish a viable pricing strategy.

Servicing Decisions   Servicing is the management or administration of a loan. It includes the collection of the payments on a loan. In addition to the monthly mortgage payment of principal and interest, the borrower will often remit to the lender an amount needed to cover real estate taxes and insurance. The servicer (lender) will keep these payments in an escrow account and later pay them to the appropriate creditors. Servicing responsibilities also include such procedures as record keeping and defaulted loan follow-up. Servicing provides a large percentage of the lender's income. This return is generated by a servicer's retaining a certain fraction of the principal balance collected monthly.

New-Loan Decisions   New-loan decisions involve an analysis of the lender's risk of making a new mortgage commitment. Mortgage lenders attempt to maximize the return on their investments—subject to acceptable risk levels. In addition to pricing and timing risks, the lender's risk in making the loan is obviously related to the borrower's characteristics and credibility. The risk of a loss in the case of default depends on the value of the mortgaged property. The financial manager must therefore be able to determine both the probability of a borrower's defaulting on his or her mortgage commitment and the value of the property in case of default.

Default and Foreclosure Decisions   A borrower defaults when he or she fails to pay the underlying debt or perform some other obligation required by the mortgage. The most common types of occurrences causing a default include

1 Failure to pay monthly installments of principal and interest
2 Failure to pay taxes on the property
3 Failure to maintain adequate insurance on the property
4 Failure to maintain the physical condition of the property
5 Selling of the mortgaged property
6 Death of the borrower

When a borrower defaults, the lender usually works with the borrower to resolve the problem. Some lenders allow the borrower to cure any default by satisfying the back payments, interest, and penalties without instigating legal action.

The lender may even agree to extend the loan's payment period or alter the terms of payment.

If the problem (and default) cannot be solved, the lender has the right to foreclose, that is, the borrower's title to the property is taken and the property is sold to pay off the debt. In most states, the lender's right to foreclosure takes two basic forms: foreclosure by judicial sale and foreclosure by power of sale. Chapter 3 contains a complete description of the types of foreclosure available to lenders.

Regardless of the type of foreclosure, it can be an expensive process, involving administrative and institutional costs. On the administrative side, the mortgage lender must incur the time, paperwork, and other costs involved in closely monitoring the borrower and the mortgaged property in order to protect its interests properly. Besides these direct administrative costs, foreclosures also include costs associated with the way lending institutions' policies are affected by the foreclosure process. Before a potential borrower ever walks through the lender's front door, the lender is well aware of the administrative costs associated with foreclosure. The lender knows from its records what percentage of borrowers default on their loans, how often foreclosure procedures have to be used, how much these procedures cost, and the amount that foreclosure costs reduce the lender's average return on mortgage loans. Because lenders are aware of all these factors, they tailor their lending policies accordingly. If foreclosures did not reduce a lender's return, it would lend more money and do so at reduced interest rates. Thus, while foreclosure protects the mortgage borrower by forcing the lender to go through judicial processes to take over the mortgaged property, these same processes hinder borrowers because they result in lenders' providing less borrowable money at higher interest rates.

The probability of a borrower's defaulting on a mortgage loan is generally considered to be a function of five factors: the borrower's character, the borrower's capacity to repay the loan, the borrower's financial position, the collateral offered for the loan, and any economic conditions affecting the borrower's ability to fulfill his or her obligations. These factors are often referred to as the five C's of credit: character, capacity, capital, collateral, and conditions. Chapter 4 contains a complete description of borrower analysis.

The lender's risk of loss on a mortgage investment also depends on the value of the mortgaged property. Generally, the lending institution employs an appraiser to estimate property values and then makes the investment decision in light of the determined value. We discussed valuation and appraisal in greater detail in Chapter 5.

Secondary Mortgage Market Decisions

The second category of decisions facing the financial manager of a financial institution are those associated with the purchase, sale, and packaging of mortgage loans in the secondary mortgage market. Because they involve existing mortgage loans, secondary mortgage market investment decisions are usually entirely market-related. Little or no borrower analysis takes place. We will examine three generalized decision areas for investment in the secondary mortgage market: market analysis, pricing, and mortgage securitization.[3]

Market Analysis Decisions   Financial market analysis decisions involve the financial manager's analysis of an institution's lending markets in order to evaluate the opportunities and/or demand for secondary mortgage market transactions. The lender should not ignore the lending markets outside a given geographical location—especially if greater returns or lower risks can be found elsewhere. The secondary mortgage market allows credit-surplus areas to supplement the mortgage funds in credit-deficient areas, providing an additional investment outlet for some of the funds available in credit-surplus areas. Many financial institutions in credit-deficient areas have made the decision to respond to large credit demands by taking advantage of the opportunity to originate loans in the primary market for subsequent resale in the secondary market. In this way, the lenders in deficient areas, acting as intermediaries, benefit from the origination and servicing fees associated with mortgage banking operation without actually having to loan nonexistent funds.

Federal and state agencies operating in the secondary market have also influenced the behavior of mortgage lenders and mortgage bankers. Mortgage lenders realize that federal and state credit agencies have a preferred position in attracting funds for mortgage purchases. Federal agencies have government backing, and state agencies generally pay a tax-exempt return on their funds. As a result, many mortgage lenders who would normally only lend up to their available resources may now decide to lend above that level in contemplation of selling the excess mortgages to a federal or state mortgage credit agency. Lenders are given many incentives for selling mortgages to these agencies.[4]

1 The lending requirements of a large-scale builder who might otherwise be served by many lenders can be accommodated by one lender.

2 Lenders can maintain a more even work flow in their origination department by selling mortgages at times when their own resources are committed and the lending department is not busy.

3 Good builders or developers can be appeased by assurances that they will always have funds available despite local conditions.

4 Lenders in a capital-short area can continue to satisfy local demands despite inadequate local resources.

5 Lenders can increase profits through additional closing-cost income and servicing fees associated with additional mortgages and/or by the sale of mortgage loans to the secondary market at a favorable yield.

---

[3] The discussion of secondary mortgage market decisions draws heavily on Thygerson and Jacobe, op. cit., pp. 4–8.
[4] This list was drawn from Thygerson and Jacobe, op. cit., pp. 4–8.

In the primary mortgage market, lenders are willing to undertake the risks associated with a mortgage commitment because of their personal knowledge of the security. The primary lender has the property inspected and appraised and is also better able to keep in touch with the debt-paying habits of the borrower by performing the loan-servicing operations. The operations of the secondary mortgage market inherently prohibit this personal touch. As a result, the rapid growth in secondary mortgage market transactions has both facilitated and necessitated the standardization of mortgage contracts, but it also has other implications for financial institutions. Standardized instruments lower the skill levels required to service mortgage contracts and encourage advances in the origination and servicing of mortgage portfolios.

Pricing Decisions   One the financial manager has determined that secondary mortgage market transactions are feasible, an evaluation of pricing and potential profitability must be made. Pricing and yield calculations for the secondary mortgage market are complicated by a variety of factors. Secondary mortgage market transactions often involve loan discounts or premiums, varying assumptions about loan life, servicing agreements, and other special arrangements in cases of delayed or slow payments, default, and foreclosures. The financial manager must be fully aware of the impact the various provisions can have on the price and yields of secondary mortgage market transactions.

In the past decade, there has been a significant amount of activity in the development of new securities for use in the secondary mortgage market. The various different types of mortgage-backed instruments available were listed in Table 19-7. The successful financial manager must have a comprehensive understanding of the factors affecting prices and yields on these investments. For any security under consideration, the financial manager should be concerned with the following characteristics of the investment: (1) the liquidity of the issue, (2) the tax implications, (3) the expected yield, (4) the denomination of the security issued, (5) the issue's default risk, (6) the means of payment of principal and interest, (7) the arrangements for handling slow payments and defaults, and (8) the expected life or maturity of the issue.

The financial manager must also face decisions regarding the servicing of loans bought and sold on the secondary market. Loan servicing in the secondary market involves billing, record keeping, and payment collection, duties that are usually retained by the institution which originated the loan. Oftentimes, borrowers never become aware that the local lender has sold their respective loans because the billing and payment-collection responsibilities are retained by their lender.

There are obvious advantages to buyers and sellers of mortgages in letting the seller retain the loan-servicing function. If the purchasing lender is quite distant from the mortgage property, payment-collection and foreclosure procedures are likely to be more effective if kept locally. The local (selling) lender benefits by charging a fee for servicing the sold loans, which provides a stable income for covering the lender's fixed and semifixed costs during nonpeak business periods.

Economic studies have demonstrated that properly priced mortgage loan servicing can result in significant income to the servicing institution. Mortgage-servicing contracts include provisions for origination fees and initial charges, mortgage maturities, default procedures, and calculating the loan amount on which the fees are based. The servicing fees are usually determined as a percentage of the unpaid loan balance and are payable each month of the servicing period (loan maturity).

It is important for the lender active in the secondary mortgage market to understand the economics of the mortgage loan–servicing decision and thus negotiate the best possible price for this service (or least price if a purchaser).

To illustrate the mechanics of pricing secondary market transactions, consider the following simplified example. A mortgage lender with a surplus of loanable funds due to a slow housing market wishes to purchase existing mortgages in the secondary mortgage market. The lender is considering purchasing a package of three mortgages from a lender in another state. The terms of these mortgages are as follows:

Loan 1. $40,000 remaining balance, 9 percent interest, 24 years of payments remaining at $339.47 per month, 30-year original term
Loan 2. $30,000 remaining balance, 9 percent interest, 20 years of payments remaining at $269.92 per month, 25-year original term
Loan 3. $25,000 remaining balance, 9 percent interest, 18 years of payments remaining at $234.11 per month, 25-year original term

As is customary with transactions of this type, the out-of-state lender (who originated the loans) will retain the responsibility for loan servicing. To simplify calculations, we assume the loan-servicing fee requested by the seller is 0.25 percent of the outstanding loan balance at the beginning of each year and is payable each year at that time.

Although the maturity of the three loans varies from 18 to 24 years, experience and intuition tell us that the loans will likely be paid off several years prior to maturity. (As we already are aware, shortening the loan maturity may significantly alter the yield on a mortgage.) The question is, Can we justify an assumption about remaining loan life from currently available data? Research has shown that mortgage loan lives are not at all predictable. However, convention in the secondary market typically assumes a 10- to 12-year life for new or relatively unseasoned mortgages. Since the mortgages in our example have been seasoned from 5 to 7 years, we arbitrarily assume an expected remaining loan life of 6 years for the package.

If the purchaser's required yield on this type of package is 12 percent, what is the most than can be paid for the package?

The general formula for determining this value is as follows:

$$\text{Value of loan package} = \text{PV of loan payments} + \text{PV of loan payoffs}$$
$$(\text{EOY6}) - \text{PV of servicing fees}$$

To determine the present value of the loan payments, we add the payments on the loans together and discount them to the present at the 12 percent required rate for the 6-year assumed loan life:

$$\text{PV of loan payments} = (\$339.47 + \$269.92 + \$234.11)(\text{PVAF}_{12\%/12,72})$$
$$= \$843.50(51.150039)$$
$$= \$43,145$$

To determine the present value of the loan payoffs, we must individually compute the balances 6 years hence, add them together, and discount them to the present at the 12 percent required rate:

Loan 1: $\text{Loan payoff (EOY6)} = \$339.47(\text{PVAF}_{9\%/12,216})$
$$= \$339.47(106.78686)$$
$$= \$36,251$$

Loan 2: $\text{Loan payoff (EOY6)} = \$269.62(\text{PVAF}_{9\%/12,168})$
$$= (\$269.92)(95.33456)$$
$$= \$25,733$$

Loan 3: $\text{Loan payoff (EOY6)} = \$234.11(\text{PVAF}_{9\%/12,144})$
$$= \$234.11(87.87109)$$
$$= \$20,572$$

Total of loan payoffs (EOY6) $= \$36,251 + \$25,733 + \$20,572$
$$= \$82,556$$

Present value of loan payoffs $= \$82,556(\text{PVF}_{12\%/12,72})$
$$= \$82,556(0.48850)$$
$$= \$40,329$$

Finally, we must compute the present value of loan-servicing fees. We need to calculate each year's fees for the package and then discount these back to the present at the 12 percent required rate. The general formula for each year's fee is

Servicing fee (year t) $= 0.25\%(\text{balance of loan, EOY } t - 1)$
$$= 0.0025\{(\text{monthly payment})\text{PVAF}_{9\%/12,12[n-(t-1)]}\}$$

where $n =$ the years remaining on the loan at purchase
$t =$ the year for which the fee is being calculated

(Also, because the fee is computed on the beginning-of-year balance, the -1 factor must be inserted.)

For the first year, the initial servicing fee is simply 0.25 percent of the loan balances at purchase ($95,000), or $237.50. For the second year, we must compute the fee for each loan separately, using the formula above:

$$\begin{aligned}
\text{Loan 1 fee (year 2)} &= 0.0025(\$339.47)(\text{PVAF}_{9\%/12,(24\text{-}1)12}) \\
&= 0.0025(\$339.47)(116.37811) \\
&= \$98.77
\end{aligned}$$

$$\begin{aligned}
\text{Loan 1 fee (year 3)} &= 0.0025(\$339.47)(\text{PVAF}_{9\%/12,(24\text{-}2)12}) \\
&= 0.0025(\$339.47)(114.78759) \\
&= \$97.42
\end{aligned}$$

The remaining loan-servicing fees for all three loans are computed in a similar fashion. Table 19-9 lists these fees according to the time they are paid, which is $(t-1)$ years since they are paid at the beginning of each year. The present value of servicing fees is $1,034.

We may now insert our computations for the present values of the payments, payoffs, and servicing fees into our general equation.

$$\begin{aligned}
\text{Value of loan package} &= \$43,145 + \$40,329 - \$1,034 \\
&= \$82,440
\end{aligned}$$

Thus, the purchaser would be willing to pay as much as $82,440 for this loan and still earn the required 12 percent yield.

Although this problem assumed a 12 percent before-tax required rate, decisions on loan purchases and sales in the secondary market are often based on income tax considerations for buyer and seller, which are beyond the scope of this text. Suffice it to say that the tax impacts may be significant enough to warrant after-tax (rather than before-tax) analysis.

Mortgage Securitization   Mortgage securitization involves the "pooling" of a group of mortgages as collateral for the issuance of securities—bonds, certificates, or notes. Each mortgage-backed security (MBS) represents an undivided interest in the pool. Investors receive a pro rata share of the interest, principal, and prepayment amounts collected from the mortgages.

The market for mortgage-backed securities developed out of the guarantees issued in the 1970s by federal agencies such as the GNMA, the FNMA, and the

TABLE 19-9   LOAN-SERVICING FEES, SECONDARY MORTGAGE MARKET EXAMPLE

Year paid	Loan 1	+	Loan 2	+	Loan 3	=	Total fee	×	PVF$_{12/12}$	=	PV
0	$100.00		$75.00		$62.50		$237.50		1.00000		$ 237.50
1	98.77		73.60		61.04		233.41		0.88745		207.14
2	97.42		72.06		59.45		228.93		0.78757		180.30
3	95.94		70.38		57.70		224.02		0.69892		156.57
4	94.32		68.54		55.80		218.66		0.62026		135.63
5	92.56		66.53		53.71		212.80		0.55045		117.14
Total present value											$ 1,034.28

FHLMC. Since then, the market for mortgage securities has undergone dramatic changes. In 1984, more than $1.8 trillion of real estate mortgage debt has the potential to be securitized, up from $21 billion for the years 1970 through 1975, inclusive.

Mortgage-backed securities offer distinct advantages to potential investors. For example, a buyer of mortgage-backed securities may make a mortgage investment of whatever magnitude he chooses without examining each mortgage individually. Furthermore, mortgage-backed securities usually carry investment rating (as bonds do); therefore, these pools can be actively traded, thus increasing liquidity.

There are several different types of mortgage-backed securities. However, possibilities other than the ones discussed here may exist.

Pass-through certificates are issued and sold by mortgage companies with a guarantee that a federal agency or some private insurer will meet the scheduled monthly payments to investors. Since most mortgages have prepayment clauses, the amount of these payments and the maturities of the securities are uncertain. Thus, an investor's prorated share and the maturity of the certificate depend on when prepayment occurs.

The most common form of pass-through certificate is the Ginnie Mae pass-through. Since GNMA is a subdivision of the Department of Housing and Urban Development, this type of certificate carries the full faith and credit of the U.S. government as guarantee of payment. Similar certificates have been issued by FNMA and FHLMC. These offer the guarantee of the affiliated federal agency. Certificates issued by private mortgage companies or conduits carry a bank letter of credit of the services of a private insurer to guarantee timely payment. In recent history, however, some of these insurers have failed and caused substantial losses to investors.[5]

Mortgage-backed bonds are bonds whose payments are backed by a mortgage or a pool of mortgages as collateral. Mortgage-backed bonds are quite similar to ordinary corporate bonds. The investor receives principal repayment at maturity and interest payments at semiannual intervals. Such securities were originally designed to attract funds at a lower cost than that of issuing pass-through certificates. However, the issuer must be prepared to assume the risk of losses or gains if there is a timing difference between the flow patterns of the bonds and mortgages dues to a change in interest rates or if prepayment occurs.

The *collateralized mortgage obligation* (CMO) is a special type of mortgage-backed security which envelops some of the characteristics of the mortgage-backed bond. A pool of mortgages is assembled as collateral, and several classes of bonds are issued instead of one. Terms specify that each bond has a fixed semiannual interest payment and that all principal payments (including prepayments) go to the highest class of bonds until these bonds are paid off. After the

[5] This discussion draws heavily on Sherman J. Marsel: *Real Estate Finance*, Harcourt Brace Jovanovich, San Diego, 1987.

first class is retired, principal payments are then applied to the next highest class of bonds until they have been paid off also, and so on, until all classes of the original issues are retired.

Collateralized mortgage obligations were designed for investors who prefer semiannual payments and shorter maturities than those offered by pass-through certificates and mortgage-backed bonds. On the supply side of the market, CMOs provide their issuers advantages that no other mortgage-backed security can offer: (1) There is no timing difference between bond and mortgage flows; thus interest rate risk is diminished; and (2) the maturities of CMOs can be structured to meet market demands (they are usually very short, 1 to 4 years).

The *real estate mortgage investment conduit* (REMIC) is a mortgage-backed security created by the Tax Reform Act of 1986. REMIC provisions are intended to reduce the tax considerations involved in mortgage securities. Previously, entities which issued multiple classes of investor interests backed by a mortgage pool were subject to double taxation. The creation of a REMIC avoids this situation.

REMIC interests can take the form of bonds, certificates, corporate stock, or partnership interests. Investor participation consists of one or more classes of regular interest and one class of residual interest. Regular interests operate like CMOs. A pool of mortgages is assembled as collateral, and several classes of securities (in terms of payoff priority) can then be issued. The residual interest is made up of only one class of interest and is defined as any interest which is not a regular interest. Payments are made on a pro rata basis to all holders.

Mortgage Pass-Through Example[6]   Assume that Jan B. Investor purchases a GNMA pass-through certificate. The original amount of the GNMA 9 percent pool at the time of the origination was $500,000. A servicing fee of 0.50 percent serves to reduce the GNMA coupon rate one-half of 1 percent lower than on the pool's collateral of mortgages. Thus, the pool actually consists of 9.50 percent mortgage loans. The original term of the pool was 30 years and has aged 10 years (120 months) since the time of origination.

To calculate the interest due to the investors in the 121st month, we must first find the remaining balance at the end of month 120:

$$\text{Remaining balance}_{120} = \text{original pool amount} \times \text{proportion outstanding}$$

$$= \text{original pool amount}\left[1 - \frac{(1 + i\%/12)^{120} - 1}{(1 + i\%/12)^{360} - 1}\right]$$

$$= \$500,000\left[1 - \frac{(1 + 0.09/12)^{120} - 1}{(1 + 0.09/12)^{360} - 1}\right]$$

$$= \$500,000 \times 0.8942974$$

$$= \$447,149$$

---

[6] This example is similar to that found in Frank J. Fabozzi, *The Handbook of Mortgage Backed Securities,* Probus Publishing, Chicago, 1985.

Thus,

$$\text{Interest }_{i\%/12, 121} = \text{remaining balance}_{120} \left(\frac{i}{12} - \frac{0.005}{12} \right)$$

$$= \$447,149 \left(\frac{0.09 - 0.005}{12} \right)$$

$$= \$3,167.31$$

Monthly principal payment calculation, assuming no prepayments, is also quite easy:

$$\text{Principal} = \text{balance}_{120} - \text{balance}_{121}$$

$$= \$447,149 - \$500,000 \left[1 - \frac{(1 + 0.09/12)^{121} - 1}{(1 + 0.09/12)^{360} - 1} \right]$$

$$= \$447,149 - \$446,479$$

$$= \$670$$

The total monthly payment in month 121 is

$$\text{Interest} + \text{principal} = \$3,167.31 + 670$$

$$= \$3,837.31$$

This amount is then split on a pro rata basis between Jan B. Investor and all other certificate holders in the GNMA pool.

We now complicate matters by assuming that prepayment occurs at a rate of 0.3 percent per month beginning in month 120 (time t). First, calculate the adjustment to the balance caused by the prepayment:

$$\text{Adjustment to balance} = 1 - \left[\frac{\text{prepayment rate}}{100} \right]$$

$$= 1 - \left[\frac{0.3}{100} \right]$$

$$= 0.997$$

The mortgage balance at time t assuming prepayment is

$$\text{Balance assuming prepayment} = \text{proportion outstanding}_{120}$$
$$\times \text{(adjustment to balance)}^t$$

Using our same assumptions as before,

$$\text{Balance assuming prepayment} = 0.8942974(0.997)^{120}$$
$$= 0.8942974 \times 0.6972989$$
$$= 0.6235926$$

We then must adjust our original pool amount of $500,000. The formula is

$$\text{Adjusted pool amount} = \frac{\text{original pool amount}}{\text{balance assuming prepayment}}$$
$$= \frac{\$500,000}{0.6235926}$$
$$= \$801,802$$

With the original pool amount adjusted for prepayment, the calculations for principal and interest can now be conducted using the previously introduced methods.

SUMMARY

In this chapter, we discussed the supply side of the primary and secondary mortgage markets. First we examined the characteristics of financial institutions operating in the primary mortgage market and the role of and participants in the secondary mortgage market. We also discussed the interrelationship between the primary and secondary markets and the fact that many institutions participate actively in both markets.

Then we examined the decisions that financial managers must make with regard to investment decisions in the primary and secondary mortgage markets. For the primary market, we examined decisions concerning existing loans; the pricing, servicing, and timing of new loans; default and foreclosure decisions; and the basics of borrower analysis. The secondary market decisions we looked at involved market analysis, pricing, and mortgage securitization.

QUESTIONS

1 Define the following terms:
  a servicing   e CMO
  b pass-through certificates   f REMIC
  c secondary mortgage market   g 5 C's of credit
  d foreclosure by power of sale
2 Discuss the purpose of the financial market in general and the mortgage market.
3 What is the role of financial intermediaries in the financial market and the mortgage market?
4 What is the distinction between the primary and secondary mortgage markets? What is the role of the secondary market? Does the secondary market increase, in total, the supply of mortgage funds, i.e., does it cause a shift in the supply curve? Why?
5 What are some of the basic characteristics of the lender in the primary mortgage market?
6 What government agencies are involved in the secondary market? What is their role?

7 What are the problems facing financial intermediaries in the primary and secondary mortgage markets?

8 Which primary mortgage market lenders concentrate on residential markets? Why?

9 Which institutions are the major lenders of mortgage funds?

10 Why are savings and loan associations the largest holder of residential mortgages?

11 What is a mortgage broker? How does a mortgage broker differ from a mortgage banker?

12 What are some of the primary mortgage market decisions that must be made by the lender?

13 Why are existing loans now causing problems for long-term lenders?

14 What factors are considered in determining the probability of a borrower's defaulting on a mortgage loan?

15 What are some of the rules of thumb used by institutions to evaluate borrowers?

16 What are some of the incentives institutions have for selling mortgages in the secondary mortgage market?

PROBLEMS

1 With the information provided in Table 19-10 answer the following:

a For 1982, what was the average difference in the effective interest rate (yield) when going from a 75 percent to 80 percent loan-to-price (i.e., loan-to-value) ratio? What is the average difference between 90 and 95 percent L/V? What do these differences represent?

b For the months of January, April, July, and October 1982, plot the effective interest rates as a function of the loan-to-value ratio (i.e., put interest rates on the vertical axis, L/V on the horizontal axis). What is the nature of the relationship of L/V to yield? Be thorough.

TABLE 19-10 COMMITMENT RATES AND LENDING POLICY ON CONVENTIONAL HOME MORTGAGE
LOANS WITH 25-YEAR MATURITY
(Effective Interest Rate, 10-Year Life)

| Month | Loan-to-price ratio | | | | |
	50%	75%	80%	90%	95%
January	17.31	17.23	17.35	17.56	17.72
February	17.47	17.50	17.52	17.75	17.90
March	17.49	17.51	17.54	17.72	17.83
April	17.37	17.39	17.41	17.59	17.64
May	17.26	17.28	17.29	17.46	17.50
June	17.14	17.16	17.16	17.35	17.39
July	17.21	17.23	17.23	17.44	17.50
August	16.99	17.01	17.02	17.20	17.25
September	16.17	16.18	16.18	16.31	16.26
October	15.60	15.62	15.59	15.74	15.78
November	14.62	14.63	14.59	14.77	14.70
December	14.20	14.22	14.21	14.38	14.35

Source: Federal Home Loan Bank Board: *Federal Home Loan Bank Board Journal,* vol. 16, March 1983, p. 36.

2 Recall the example of a proposed secondary market transaction given in the chapter. Assume that the loans are newly originated by the selling lender, and as a result the prospective purchaser revises the remaining loan life assumption. Determine the new value of the loan to the lender.

3 Suppose you are in the business of buying second mortgages and contracts for deeds. Currently you require a before-tax yield of 18 percent based on the riskiness of these types of investments. Not included in this rate are your initial costs of transferring the loan, assumption fees, title opinions, document drafting, transfer taxes, and other such costs. These costs generally amount to $100 plus 0.50 percent of the outstanding loan balance. You are approached by an individual who holds a second mortgage originated 2 years ago. The loan was in the original amount of $20,000 at 10 percent interest, with monthly payments based on a 20-year amortization but with a balloon payment at the end of year 6. How much will you offer for this mortgage?

4 In Table 19-11 the contract interest rates and discount points offered by lenders in one locale on a particular date are listed.

    a Without doing any financial calculations, determine which lenders are the most (and the least) competitive.

    b Determine the yield on each mortgage offered by each lender assuming a 10-year loan life and a 6-year loan life. Assume the interest rate on the ARM increases at 0.50 percent per year for the first 5 years and that the payments increase accordingly.

    c Rank the lenders on the basis of their yields for each type of loan under both loan-life assumptions. Are the rankings the same for the various loan types and loan lives? Give possible reasons for your answer.

5 Suppose in the chapter example that you are the selling lender and wish to put a price on the loan-servicing fee. Your estimated annual costs of servicing one loan are as follows:

Direct labor	$29.56
Computer costs	6.50
Other equipment cost	0.70
Telephone	2.10
Postage	1.50
Supplies	1.75
General and administrative overhead	30.00
Total	$72.11

TABLE 19-11 CONTRACT INTEREST RATES AND DISCOUNT POINTS

	30-year fixed rate		Adjustable rate	
Lender	Interest rate (%)	Discount points	Initial interest rate (%)	Discount points
Acme Savings Bank	13.25	3	12.50	3
Lenders Mortgage Corporation	12.50	1	12.25	2
Citizens Bank	12.50	1½	11.25	1
Deal Savings and Loan	12.62	1	11.50	1
First National Mortgage	12.37	2	12.25	2
Mutual State Federal	12.50	2½	12.25	1½

These costs are expected to increase at 6 percent per year due to inflation and are paid at the end of each year. Assuming your required rate of return is 12 percent, is a servicing fee of 0.25 percent acceptable to you? (*Hint:* Determine the present value of the differential cash flows.)

6 You are a mortgage lender who made several 30-year, 8 percent loans 5 years ago. Mortgage interest rates are currently 14 percent. You feel that several borrowers can be enticed to pay off their mortgages if offered a discount of 10 percent on their outstanding balance. Assuming these loans, on average, have an expected life of 5 years, should you offer a 10 percent discount for early repayment?

7 Rework the mortgage pass-through example assuming that the collateral for the pool consists of $250,000 of 12 percent mortgage loans.

REFERENCES

Boykin, James H.: *Financing Real Estate,* Lexington Books, Lexington, Mass., 1979.

Dennis, Marshall W.: *Fundamentals of Mortgage Lending,* Reston Publishing Co., Reston, Va., 1978.

Fabozzi, Frank J.: *Mortgage Backed Securities,* Probus Publishing, Chicago, 1987.

Fabozzi, Frank J.: *The Handbook of Mortgage Backed Securities,* Probus Publishing, Chicago, 1985.

Lederman, Jess: *The Secondary Mortgage Market,* Probus Publishing, Chicago, 1987.

Maisel, Sherman J.: *Real Estate Finance,* Harcourt Brace Jovanovich, San Diego, 1987.

Thygerson, K. J., and D. J. Jacobe: *Mortgage Portfolio Management,* U.S. League of Savings Associations, Chicago, 1978.

Van Horne, James C.: *Financial Market Rates and Flows,* Prentice-Hall, Englewood Cliffs, N.J., 1978.

Appendix

REAL ESTATE FINANCE TABLES

The tables presented in this appendix are used in making real estate finance decisions. There are three sets of tables:

Table 1. Present Value of $1 Factors (Annual Compounding)
Table 2. Mortgage Constant (Monthly Compounding)
Table 3. Proportion Outstanding of $1 (Monthly Compounding)

TABLE 1 PRESENT VALUE OF $1 (ANNUAL COMPOUNDING)

	Interest rate (%)			
Year	6.00	6.25	6.50	6.75
1	0.94339623	0.94117647	0.93896714	0.93676815
2	0.88999644	0.88581315	0.88165928	0.87753457
3	0.83961928	0.83370649	0.82784909	0.82204643
4	0.79209366	0.78466493	0.77732309	0.77006692
5	0.74725817	0.73850817	0.72988084	0.72137416
6	0.70496054	0.69506652	0.68533412	0.67576034
7	0.66505711	0.65418025	0.64350621	0.63303076
8	0.62741237	0.61569906	0.60423119	0.59300305
9	0.59189846	0.57948147	0.56735323	0.55550637
10	0.55839478	0.54539432	0.53272604	0.52038068
11	0.52678753	0.51331230	0.50021224	0.48747605
12	0.49696936	0.48311746	0.46968285	0.45665203
13	0.46883902	0.45469879	0.44101676	0.42777708
14	0.44230096	0.42795180	0.41410025	0.40072794
15	0.41726506	0.40277817	0.38882652	0.37538917
16	0.39364628	0.37908533	0.36509533	0.35165262
17	0.37136442	0.35678619	0.34281251	0.32941698
18	0.35034379	0.33579877	0.32188969	0.30858733
19	0.33051301	0.31604590	0.30224384	0.28907478
20	0.31180473	0.29745497	0.28379703	0.27079605
21	0.29415540	0.27995762	0.26647608	0.25367312
22	0.27750510	0.26348952	0.25021228	0.23763289
23	0.26179726	0.24799014	0.23494111	0.22260693
24	0.24697855	0.23340248	0.22060198	0.20853108
25	0.23299863	0.21967292	0.20713801	0.19534527
26	0.21981003	0.20675099	0.19449579	0.18299323
27	0.20736795	0.19458917	0.18262515	0.17142223
28	0.19563014	0.18314274	0.17147902	0.16058289
29	0.18455674	0.17236964	0.16101316	0.15042893
30	0.17411013	0.16223025	0.15118607	0.14091703
31	0.16425484	0.15268729	0.14195875	0.13200659
32	0.15495740	0.14370569	0.13329460	0.12365957
33	0.14618622	0.13525241	0.12515925	0.11584034
34	0.13791153	0.12729639	0.11752042	0.10851554
35	0.13010522	0.11980837	0.11034781	0.10165391
36	0.12274077	0.11276081	0.10361297	0.09522614
37	0.11579318	0.10612783	0.09728917	0.08920482
38	0.10923885	0.09988501	0.09135134	0.08356423
39	0.10305552	0.09400942	0.08577590	0.07828031
40	0.09722219	0.08847946	0.08054075	0.07333050
41	0.09171905	0.08327478	0.07562512	0.06869368
42	0.08652740	0.07837627	0.07100950	0.06435005
43	0.08162962	0.07376590	0.06667559	0.06028108
44	0.07700908	0.06942673	0.06260619	0.05646939
45	0.07265007	0.06534280	0.05878515	0.05289873
46	0.06853781	0.06149911	0.05519733	0.04955384
47	0.06465831	0.05788151	0.05182848	0.04642046
48	0.06099840	0.05447672	0.04866524	0.04348521
49	0.05754566	0.05127221	0.04569506	0.04073556
50	0.05428836	0.04825619	0.04290616	0.03815978

TABLE 1 PRESENT VALUE OF $1 (ANNUAL COMPOUNDING) (*Continued*)

	Interest rate (%)			
Year	7.00	7.25	7.50	7.75
1	0.93457944	0.93240093	0.93023256	0.92807425
2	0.87343873	0.86937150	0.86533261	0.86132181
3	0.81629788	0.81060280	0.80496057	0.79937059
4	0.76289521	0.75580680	0.74880053	0.74187525
5	0.71298618	0.70471497	0.69655863	0.68851532
6	0.66634222	0.65707689	0.64796152	0.63899333
7	0.62274974	0.61265911	0.60275490	0.59303326
8	0.58200910	0.57124392	0.56070223	0.55037889
9	0.54393374	0.53262837	0.52158347	0.51079247
10	0.50834929	0.49662319	0.48519393	0.47405334
11	0.47509280	0.46305192	0.45134319	0.43995670
12	0.44401196	0.43175004	0.41985413	0.40831248
13	0.41496445	0.40256414	0.39056198	0.37894430
14	0.38781724	0.37535118	0.36331347	0.35168844
15	0.36244602	0.34997779	0.33796602	0.32639299
16	0.33873460	0.32631962	0.31438699	0.30291692
17	0.31657439	0.30426072	0.29245302	0.28112940
18	0.29586392	0.28369298	0.27204932	0.26090895
19	0.27650833	0.26451560	0.25306913	0.24214288
20	0.25841900	0.24663459	0.23541315	0.22472657
21	0.24151309	0.22996232	0.21898897	0.20856294
22	0.22571317	0.21441708	0.20371067	0.19356190
23	0.21094688	0.19992269	0.18949830	0.17963981
24	0.19714662	0.18640810	0.17627749	0.16671908
25	0.18424918	0.17380709	0.16397906	0.15472769
26	0.17219549	0.16205789	0.15253866	0.14359878
27	0.16093037	0.15110293	0.14189643	0.13327033
28	0.15040221	0.14088851	0.13199668	0.12368476
29	0.14056282	0.13136458	0.12278761	0.11478864
30	0.13136712	0.12248446	0.11422103	0.10653238
31	0.12277301	0.11420462	0.10625212	0.09886996
32	0.11474113	0.10648449	0.09883918	0.09175866
33	0.10723470	0.09928624	0.09194343	0.08515885
34	0.10021934	0.09257458	0.08552877	0.07903374
35	0.09366294	0.08631663	0.07956164	0.07334918
36	0.08753546	0.08048171	0.07401083	0.06807348
37	0.08180884	0.07504122	0.06884729	0.06317724
38	0.07645686	0.06996850	0.06404399	0.05863317
39	0.07145501	0.06523870	0.05957580	0.05441594
40	0.06678038	0.06082862	0.05541935	0.05050203
41	0.06241157	0.05671666	0.05155288	0.04686963
42	0.05832857	0.05288267	0.04795617	0.04349850
43	0.05451268	0.04930785	0.04461039	0.04036984
44	0.05094643	0.04597468	0.04149804	0.03746621
45	0.04761349	0.04286684	0.03860283	0.03477142
46	0.04449859	0.03996908	0.03590961	0.03227046
47	0.04158747	0.03726721	0.03340428	0.02994938
48	0.03886679	0.03474798	0.03107375	0.02779525
49	0.03632410	0.03239905	0.02890582	0.02579606
50	0.03394776	0.03020890	0.02688913	0.02394066

TABLE 1 PRESENT VALUE OF $1 (ANNUAL COMPOUNDING) (*Continued*)

	Interest rate (%)			
Year	8.00	8.25	8.50	8.75
1	0.92592593	0.92378753	0.92165899	0.91954023
2	0.85733882	0.85338340	0.84945529	0.84555423
3	0.79383224	0.78834494	0.78290810	0.77752114
4	0.73502985	0.72826322	0.72157428	0.71496196
5	0.68058320	0.67276048	0.66504542	0.65743629
6	0.63016963	0.62148775	0.61294509	0.60453912
7	0.58349040	0.57412263	0.56492635	0.55589804
8	0.54026888	0.53036732	0.52066945	0.51117061
9	0.50024897	0.48994672	0.47987968	0.47004194
10	0.46319349	0.45260667	0.44228542	0.43222247
11	0.42888286	0.41811240	0.40763633	0.39744595
12	0.39711376	0.38624702	0.37570168	0.36546754
13	0.36769792	0.35681018	0.34626883	0.33606211
14	0.34046104	0.32961679	0.31914178	0.30902263
15	0.31524170	0.30449588	0.29413989	0.28415874
16	0.29189047	0.28128950	0.27109667	0.26129539
17	0.27026895	0.25985173	0.24985869	0.24027162
18	0.25024903	0.24004779	0.23028450	0.22093942
19	0.23171206	0.22175315	0.21224378	0.20316269
20	0.21454821	0.20485280	0.19561639	0.18681627
21	0.19865575	0.18924046	0.18029160	0.17178507
22	0.18394051	0.17481798	0.16616738	0.15796328
23	0.17031528	0.16149467	0.15314965	0.14525360
24	0.15769934	0.14918676	0.14115176	0.13356652
25	0.14601790	0.13781687	0.13009378	0.12281979
26	0.13520176	0.12731350	0.11990210	0.11293774
27	0.12518682	0.11761063	0.11050885	0.10385080
28	0.11591372	0.10864723	0.10185148	0.09549498
29	0.10732752	0.10036696	0.09387233	0.08781148
30	0.09937733	0.09271774	0.08651828	0.08074619
31	0.09201605	0.08565149	0.07974035	0.07424937
32	0.08520005	0.07912378	0.07349341	0.06827528
33	0.07888893	0.07309356	0.06773586	0.06278187
34	0.07304531	0.06752292	0.06242936	0.05773045
35	0.06763454	0.06237683	0.05753858	0.05308547
36	0.06262458	0.05762294	0.05303095	0.04881423
37	0.05798572	0.05323135	0.04887645	0.04488665
38	0.05369048	0.04917446	0.04504742	0.04127508
39	0.04971341	0.04542675	0.04151836	0.03795410
40	0.04603093	0.04196467	0.03826577	0.03490032
41	0.04262123	0.03876644	0.03526799	0.03209225
42	0.03946411	0.03581195	0.03250506	0.02951011
43	0.03654084	0.03308263	0.02995858	0.02713573
44	0.03383411	0.03056132	0.02761160	0.02495240
45	0.03132788	0.02823217	0.02544848	0.02294474
46	0.02900730	0.02608053	0.02345482	0.02109861
47	0.02685861	0.02409287	0.02161734	0.01940102
48	0.02486908	0.02225669	0.01992382	0.01784002
49	0.02302693	0.02056045	0.01836297	0.01640461
50	0.02132123	0.01899349	0.01692439	0.01508470

TABLE 1   PRESENT VALUE OF $1 (ANNUAL COMPOUNDING) (*Continued*)

Year	Interest rate (%) 9.00	9.25	9.50	9.75
1	0.91743119	0.91533181	0.91324201	0.91116173
2	0.84167999	0.83783232	0.83401097	0.83021570
3	0.77218348	0.76689457	0.76165385	0.75646077
4	0.70842521	0.70196299	0.69557429	0.68925811
5	0.64993139	0.64252906	0.63522767	0.62802561
6	0.59626733	0.58812728	0.58011659	0.57223290
7	0.54703424	0.53833161	0.52978684	0.52139672
8	0.50186628	0.49275204	0.48382360	0.47507674
9	0.46042778	0.45103162	0.44184803	0.43287175
10	0.42241081	0.41284359	0.40351419	0.39441617
11	0.38753285	0.37788887	0.36850611	0.35937692
12	0.35553473	0.34589370	0.33653526	0.32745050
13	0.32617865	0.31660751	0.30733813	0.29836036
14	0.29924647	0.28980092	0.28067410	0.27185454
15	0.27453804	0.26526400	0.25632337	0.24770346
16	0.25186976	0.24280458	0.23408527	0.22569791
17	0.23107318	0.22224675	0.21377651	0.20564730
18	0.21199374	0.20342952	0.19522969	0.18737795
19	0.19448967	0.18620551	0.17829195	0.17073162
20	0.17843089	0.17043983	0.16282370	0.15556411
21	0.16369806	0.15600900	0.14869744	0.14174407
22	0.15018171	0.14280000	0.13579675	0.12915177
23	0.13778139	0.13070938	0.12401530	0.11767815
24	0.12640494	0.11964245	0.11325598	0.10722383
25	0.11596784	0.10951254	0.10343012	0.09769825
26	0.10639251	0.10024031	0.09445673	0.08901891
27	0.09760781	0.09175315	0.08626185	0.08111062
28	0.08954845	0.08398457	0.07877795	0.07390489
29	0.08215454	0.07687375	0.07194333	0.06733931
30	0.07537114	0.07036499	0.06570167	0.06135700
31	0.06914783	0.06440731	0.06000153	0.05590615
32	0.06343838	0.05895406	0.05479592	0.05093955
33	0.05820035	0.05396253	0.05004193	0.04641417
34	0.05339481	0.04939362	0.04570039	0.04229081
35	0.04898607	0.04521155	0.04173552	0.03853377
36	0.04494135	0.04138357	0.03811463	0.03511050
37	0.04123059	0.03787970	0.03480788	0.03199134
38	0.03782623	0.03467249	0.03178802	0.02914928
39	0.03470296	0.03173684	0.02903015	0.02655971
40	0.03183758	0.02904973	0.02651156	0.02420019
41	0.02920879	0.02659015	0.02421147	0.02205029
42	0.02679706	0.02433881	0.02211093	0.02009138
43	0.02458446	0.02227808	0.02019263	0.01830650
44	0.02255455	0.02039184	0.01844076	0.01668018
45	0.02069224	0.01866530	0.01684087	0.01519834
46	0.01898371	0.01708494	0.01537979	0.01384815
47	0.01741625	0.01563839	0.01404547	0.01261790
48	0.01597821	0.01431432	0.01282692	0.01149695
49	0.01465891	0.01310235	0.01171048	0.01047558
50	0.01344854	0.01199300	0.01069779	0.00954495

TABLE 1 PRESENT VALUE OF $1 (ANNUAL COMPOUNDING) (*Continued*)

	Interest rate (%)			
Year	10.00	10.25	10.50	10.75
1	0.90909091	0.90702948	0.90497738	0.90293454
2	0.82644628	0.82270247	0.81898405	0.81529078
3	0.75131480	0.74621540	0.74116204	0.73615420
4	0.68301346	0.67683936	0.67073487	0.66469905
5	0.62092132	0.61391325	0.60699989	0.60017973
6	0.56447393	0.55683742	0.54932116	0.54192301
7	0.51315812	0.50506795	0.49712323	0.48932100
8	0.46650738	0.45811152	0.44988527	0.44182483
9	0.42409762	0.41552065	0.40713599	0.39893890
10	0.38554329	0.37688948	0.36844886	0.36021571
11	0.35049390	0.34184987	0.33343788	0.32525121
12	0.31863082	0.31006791	0.30175374	0.29368055
13	0.28966438	0.28124073	0.27308031	0.26517431
14	0.26333125	0.25509364	0.24713150	0.23943504
15	0.23939205	0.23137745	0.22364842	0.21619417
16	0.21762914	0.20986617	0.20239676	0.19520918
17	0.19784467	0.19035480	0.18316449	0.17626111
18	0.17985879	0.17265741	0.16575972	0.15915225
19	0.16350799	0.15660536	0.15000879	0.14370406
20	0.14864363	0.14204568	0.13575456	0.12975536
21	0.13513057	0.12883962	0.12285481	0.11716059
22	0.12284597	0.11686133	0.11118082	0.10578835
23	0.11167816	0.10599668	0.10061613	0.09551995
24	0.10152560	0.09614211	0.09105532	0.08624826
25	0.09229600	0.08720373	0.08240301	0.07787654
26	0.08390545	0.07909635	0.07457286	0.07031741
27	0.07627768	0.07174272	0.06748675	0.06349202
28	0.06934335	0.06507276	0.06107398	0.05732914
29	0.06303941	0.05902291	0.05527057	0.05176446
30	0.05730855	0.05353552	0.05001861	0.04673992
31	0.05209868	0.04855830	0.04526571	0.04220309
32	0.04736244	0.04404381	0.04096445	0.03810662
33	0.04305676	0.03994903	0.03707190	0.03440779
34	0.03914251	0.03623495	0.03354923	0.03106798
35	0.03558410	0.03286617	0.03036129	0.02805235
36	0.03234918	0.02981058	0.02747628	0.02532944
37	0.02940835	0.02703908	0.02486542	0.02287082
38	0.02673486	0.02452524	0.02250264	0.02065086
39	0.02430442	0.02224512	0.02036438	0.01864637
40	0.02209493	0.02017698	0.01842930	0.01683645
41	0.02008630	0.01830111	0.01667810	0.01520221
42	0.01826027	0.01659965	0.01509330	0.01372660
43	0.01660025	0.01505637	0.01365910	0.01239423
44	0.01509113	0.01365657	0.01236118	0.01119117
45	0.01371921	0.01238691	0.01118658	0.01010490
46	0.01247201	0.01123530	0.01012361	0.00912406
47	0.01133819	0.01019074	0.09016163	0.00823843
48	0.01030745	0.00924331	0.00829107	0.00743876
49	0.00937041	0.00838395	0.00750323	0.00671672
50	0.00851855	0.00760449	0.00679026	0.00606475

TABLE 1   PRESENT VALUE OF $1 (ANNUAL COMPOUNDING) (*Continued*)

	Interest rate (%)			
Year	11.00	11.25	11.50	11.75
1	0.90090090	0.89887640	0.89686099	0.89485459
2	0.81162243	0.80797879	0.80435963	0.80076473
3	0.73119138	0.72627307	0.72139877	0.71656799
4	0.65873097	0.65282973	0.64699441	0.64122415
5	0.59345133	0.58681324	0.58026405	0.57380237
6	0.53464084	0.52747257	0.52041619	0.51346969
7	0.48165841	0.47413265	0.46674097	0.45948070
8	0.43392650	0.42618665	0.41860177	0.41116841
9	0.39092477	0.38308912	0.37542760	0.36793594
10	0.35218448	0.34434977	0.33670636	0.32924916
11	0.31728331	0.30952789	0.30197880	0.29463013
12	0.28584082	0.27822731	0.27083301	0.26365112
13	0.25751426	0.25009197	0.24289956	0.23592941
14	0.23199482	0.22480177	0.21784714	0.21112252
15	0.20900435	0.20206901	0.19537860	0.18892395
16	0.18829220	0.18163506	0.17522744	0.16905947
17	0.16963262	0.16326747	0.15715466	0.15128364
18	0.15282218	0.14675728	0.14094588	0.13537686
19	0.13767764	0.13191665	0.12640886	0.12114260
20	0.12403391	0.11857677	0.11337118	0.10840501
21	0.11174226	0.10658586	0.10167818	0.09700672
22	0.10066870	0.09580751	0.09119120	0.08680691
23	0.09069252	0.08611911	0.08178583	0.07767956
24	0.08170498	0.07741044	0.07335052	0.06951191
25	0.07360809	0.06958242	0.06578522	0.06220305
26	0.06631359	0.06254599	0.05900020	0.05566269
27	0.05974157	0.05622112	0.05291497	0.04981001
28	0.05382160	0.05053584	0.04745738	0.04457272
29	0.04848793	0.04542547	0.04256267	0.03988610
30	0.04368282	0.04083188	0.03817280	0.03569226
31	0.03935389	0.03670282	0.03423569	0.03193938
32	0.03545395	0.03299130	0.03070466	0.02858110
33	0.03194050	0.02965510	0.02753781	0.02557593
34	0.02877522	0.02665627	0.02469759	0.02288674
35	0.02592363	0.02396069	0.02215030	0.02048030
36	0.02335462	0.02153770	0.01986574	0.01832689
37	0.02104020	0.01935973	0.01781681	0.01639990
38	0.01895513	0.01740200	0.01597920	0.01467553
39	0.01707670	0.01564225	0.01433112	0.01313247
40	0.01538441	0.01406045	0.01285302	0.01175165
41	0.01385983	0.01263861	0.01152738	0.01051601
42	0.01248633	0.01136055	0.01033845	0.00941030
43	0.01124895	0.01021173	0.00927216	0.00842085
44	0.01013419	0.00917908	0.00831583	0.00753544
45	0.00912990	0.00825086	0.00745815	0.00674312
46	0.00822513	0.00741650	0.00668892	0.00603411
47	0.00741003	0.00666652	0.00599903	0.00539965
48	0.00667570	0.00599238	0.00538030	0.00483191
49	0.00601415	0.00538641	0.00482538	0.00432385
50	0.00541815	0.00484171	0.00432769	0.00386922

TABLE 1   PRESENT VALUE OF $1 (ANNUAL COMPOUNDING) (*Continued*)

	Interest rate (%)			
Year	12.00	12.25	12.50	12.75
1	0.89285714	0.89086860	0.88888889	0.88691796
2	0.79719388	0.79364686	0.79012346	0.78662347
3	0.71178025	0.70703506	0.70233196	0.69767048
4	0.63551808	0.62987533	0.62429508	0.61877648
5	0.56742686	0.56113615	0.55492896	0.54880397
6	0.50663112	0.49989858	0.49327018	0.48674410
7	0.45234922	0.44534395	0.43846239	0.43170208
8	0.40388323	0.39674294	0.38974434	0.38288433
9	0.36061002	0.35344582	0.34643942	0.33958699
10	0.32197324	0.31487378	0.30794615	0.30118580
11	0.28747610	0.28051117	0.27372991	0.26712710
12	0.25667509	0.24989859	0.24331547	0.23691982
13	0.22917419	0.22262681	0.21628042	0.21012844
14	0.20461981	0.19833123	0.19224926	0.18636669
15	0.18269626	0.17668706	0.17088823	0.16529196
16	0.16312166	0.15740496	0.15190065	0.14660041
17	0.14564434	0.14022713	0.13502280	0.13002254
18	0.13003959	0.12492395	0.12002027	0.11531932
19	0.11610678	0.11129083	0.10668468	0.10227878
20	0.10366677	0.09914550	0.09483083	0.09071289
21	0.09255961	0.08832561	0.08429407	0.08045489
22	0.08264251	0.07868651	0.07492806	0.07135689
23	0.07378796	0.07009934	0.06660272	0.06328770
24	0.06588210	0.06244930	0.05920242	0.05613100
25	0.05882331	0.05563412	0.05262437	0.04978359
26	0.05252081	0.04956269	0.04677722	0.04415396
27	0.04689358	0.04415385	0.04157975	0.03916094
28	0.04186927	0.03933528	0.03695978	0.03473254
29	0.03738327	0.03504256	0.03285314	0.03080492
30	0.03337792	0.03121832	0.02920279	0.02732143
31	0.02980172	0.02781142	0.02595803	0.02423187
32	0.02660868	0.02477632	0.02307381	0.02149168
33	0.02375775	0.02207245	0.02051005	0.01906136
34	0.02121227	0.01966365	0.01823116	0.01690586
35	0.01893953	0.01751773	0.01620547	0.01499411
36	0.01691029	0.01560599	0.01440486	0.01329855
37	0.01509848	0.01390289	0.01280432	0.01179472
38	0.01348078	0.01238565	0.01138162	0.01046095
39	0.01203641	0.01103398	0.01011700	0.09027800
40	0.01074680	0.00982983	0.00899289	0.08022883
41	0.00959536	0.00875709	0.00799368	0.00729830
42	0.00856728	0.00780141	0.00710549	0.00647299
43	0.00764936	0.00695003	0.00631599	0.00574101
44	0.00682978	0.00619157	0.00561421	0.00509181
45	0.00609802	0.00551587	0.00499041	0.00451601
46	0.00544466	0.00491392	0.00443592	0.00400533
47	0.00486131	0.00437766	0.00394304	0.00355240
48	0.00434045	0.00389992	0.00350493	0.00315069
49	0.00387540	0.00347431	0.00311549	0.00279440
50	0.00346018	0.00309516	0.00276932	0.00247841

TABLE 1   PRESENT VALUE OF $1 (ANNUAL COMPOUNDING) (*Continued*)

Year	Interest rate (%)			
	13.00	**13.25**	**13.50**	**13.75**
1	0.88495575	0.88300221	0.88105727	0.87912088
2	0.78314668	0.77969290	0.77626191	0.77285352
3	0.69305106	0.68847055	0.68393120	0.67943167
4	0.61331873	0.60792102	0.60258255	0.59730256
5	0.54275994	0.53679560	0.53090974	0.52510115
6	0.48031853	0.47399170	0.46776188	0.46162739
7	0.42506064	0.41853572	0.41212501	0.40582628
8	0.37615986	0.36956796	0.36310573	0.35677035
9	0.33288483	0.32632933	0.31991695	0.31364427
10	0.29458835	0.28814952	0.28186515	0.27573122
11	0.26069765	0.25443666	0.24833934	0.24240107
12	0.23070589	0.22466813	0.21880118	0.21309985
13	0.20416450	0.19838246	0.19277637	0.18734052
14	0.18067655	0.17517215	0.16984702	0.16469497
15	0.15989075	0.15467739	0.14964495	0.14478678
16	0.14149624	0.13658048	0.13184577	0.12728508
17	0.12521791	0.12060086	0.11616368	0.11189898
18	0.11081231	0.10649083	0.10234685	0.09837273
19	0.09806399	0.09403164	0.09017344	0.08648152
20	0.08678229	0.08303014	0.07944796	0.07602771
21	0.07679849	0.07331580	0.06999821	0.06683754
22	0.06796327	0.06473801	0.06167243	0.05875828
23	0.06014448	0.05716381	0.05433694	0.05165563
24	0.05322521	0.05047577	0.04787396	0.04541154
25	0.04710195	0.04457022	0.04217970	0.03992224
26	0.04168314	0.03935560	0.03716273	0.03509647
27	0.03688774	0.03475108	0.03274249	0.03085404
28	0.03264402	0.03068528	0.02884801	0.02712443
29	0.02888851	0.02709517	0.02541675	0.02384565
30	0.02556505	0.02392510	0.02239361	0.02096321
31	0.02262394	0.02112591	0.01973005	0.01842920
32	0.02002119	0.01865423	0.01738331	0.01620149
33	0.01771786	0.01647172	0.01531569	0.01424307
34	0.01567953	0.01454457	0.01349400	0.01252138
35	0.01387579	0.01284289	0.01188899	0.01100781
36	0.01227937	0.01134030	0.01047488	0.00967719
37	0.01086670	0.01001351	0.00922897	0.00850742
38	0.00961655	0.00884195	0.00813125	0.00747905
39	0.00851022	0.00780746	0.00716410	0.00657499
40	0.00753117	0.00689400	0.00631198	0.00578021
41	0.00666475	0.00608742	0.00556121	0.00508151
42	0.00589801	0.00537521	0.00489975	0.00446726
43	0.00521948	0.00474632	0.00431696	0.00392726
44	0.00461901	0.00419101	0.00380349	0.00345254
45	0.00408762	0.00370067	0.00335109	0.00303520
46	0.00361736	0.00326770	0.00295250	0.00266830
47	0.00321020	0.00288539	0.00260132	0.00234576
48	0.00283292	0.00254780	0.00229192	0.00206221
49	0.00250701	0.00224972	0.00201931	0.00181293
50	0.00221859	0.00198650	0.00177913	0.00159378

TABLE 1 PRESENT VALUE OF $1 (ANNUAL COMPOUNDING) (*Continued*)

	Interest rate (%)			
Year	14.00	14.25	14.50	14.75
1	0.87719298	0.87527352	0.87336245	0.87145969
2	0.76946753	0.76610374	0.76276196	0.75944200
3	0.67497152	0.67055032	0.66616765	0.66182309
4	0.59208028	0.58691494	0.58180581	0.57675215
5	0.51936866	0.51371111	0.50812734	0.50261625
6	0.45558655	0.44963773	0.44377934	0.43800981
7	0.39963732	0.39355600	0.38758021	0.38170789
8	0.35055905	0.34446915	0.33849800	0.33264304
9	0.30750794	0.30150472	0.29563144	0.28988501
10	0.26974381	0.26389910	0.25819340	0.25262310
11	0.23661738	0.23098390	0.22549642	0.22015085
12	0.20755910	0.20217409	0.19694010	0.19185259
13	0.18206939	0.17695763	0.17200009	0.16719180
14	0.15970999	0.15488633	0.15021842	0.14570092
15	0.14009648	0.13556790	0.13119513	0.12697248
16	0.12289165	0.11865899	0.11458090	0.11065139
17	0.10779969	0.10385908	0.10007065	0.09642823
18	0.09456113	0.09090510	0.08739795	0.08403332
19	0.08294836	0.07956683	0.07633009	0.07323165
20	0.07276172	0.06964274	0.06666383	0.06381843
21	0.06382607	0.06095644	0.05822169	0.05561519
22	0.05598778	0.05335356	0.05084863	0.04846640
23	0.04911209	0.04669896	0.04440929	0.04223651
24	0.04308078	0.04087436	0.03876540	0.03680742
25	0.03779016	0.03577625	0.03387372	0.03207618
26	0.03314926	0.03131400	0.02958403	0.02795310
27	0.02907830	0.02740832	0.02583758	0.02436000
28	0.02550728	0.02398977	0.02256557	0.02122876
29	0.02237481	0.02099761	0.01970792	0.01850001
30	0.01962702	0.01837866	0.01721216	0.01612201
31	0.01721669	0.01608635	0.01503246	0.01404968
32	0.01510236	0.01407996	0.01312878	0.01224373
33	0.01324768	0.01232381	0.01146618	0.01066992
34	0.01162077	0.01078671	0.01001414	0.00929840
35	0.01019366	0.00944132	0.00874597	0.00810318
36	0.00894181	0.00826374	0.00763840	0.00706160
37	0.00734369	0.00723303	0.00667109	0.00615390
38	0.00688043	0.00633088	0.00582628	0.00536287
39	0.00603547	0.00554125	0.00508846	0.00467353
40	0.00529427	0.00485011	0.00444407	0.00407279
41	0.00464410	0.00424517	0.00388128	0.00354927
42	0.00407377	0.00371569	0.00338976	0.00309305
43	0.00357348	0.00325224	0.00296049	0.00269547
44	0.00313463	0.00284660	0.00258558	0.00234899
45	0.00274968	0.00249156	0.00225810	0.00204705
46	0.00241200	0.00218079	0.00197218	0.00178392
47	0.00211579	0.00190879	0.00172243	0.00155462
48	0.00185595	0.00167071	0.00150431	0.00135479
49	0.00162803	0.00146233	0.00131381	0.00118064
50	0.00142810	0.00127994	0.00114743	0.00102888

TABLE 1   PRESENT VALUE OF $1 (ANNUAL COMPOUNDING) (*Continued*)

Year	Interest rate (%)			
	15.00	15.25	15.50	15.75
1	0.86956522	0.86767896	0.86580087	0.86393089
2	0.75614367	0.75286678	0.74961114	0.74637657
3	0.65751623	0.65324666	0.64901397	0.64481778
4	0.57175325	0.56680838	0.56191686	0.55707799
5	0.49717674	0.49180771	0.48650810	0.48127688
6	0.43232760	0.42673120	0.42121914	0.41578996
7	0.37593704	0.37026568	0.36469189	0.35921379
8	0.32690177	0.32127174	0.31575056	0.31033589
9	0.28426241	0.27876073	0.27337711	0.26810876
10	0.24718471	0.24187482	0.23669014	0.23162744
11	0.21494322	0.20986969	0.20492652	0.20011010
12	0.18690715	0.18209952	0.17742556	0.17288129
13	0.16252796	0.15800392	0.15361521	0.14935749
14	0.14132866	0.13709668	0.13300018	0.12903455
15	0.12289449	0.11895590	0.11515167	0.11147693
16	0.10686477	0.10321553	0.09969841	0.09630836
17	0.09292589	0.08955795	0.08631897	0.08320377
18	0.08080512	0.07770754	0.07473504	0.07188231
19	0.07026532	0.06742520	0.06470566	0.06210134
20	0.06110028	0.05850343	0.05602222	0.05365127
21	0.05313068	0.05076219	0.04850409	0.04635099
22	0.04620059	0.04404529	0.04199488	0.04004405
23	0.04017443	0.03821717	0.03635920	0.03459529
24	0.03493428	0.03316023	0.03147983	0.02988794
25	0.03037764	0.02877244	0.02725526	0.02582112
26	0.02641534	0.02496524	0.02359763	0.02230766
27	0.02296986	0.02166181	0.02043085	0.01927228
28	0.01997379	0.01879550	0.01768905	0.01664991
29	0.01736851	0.01630846	0.01531519	0.01438438
30	0.01510305	0.01415051	0.01325991	0.01242711
31	0.01313309	0.01227810	0.01148044	0.01073616
32	0.01142008	0.01065345	0.00993977	0.00927530
33	0.00993050	0.00924377	0.00860586	0.00801322
34	0.00863522	0.00802063	0.00745097	0.00692287
35	0.00750889	0.00695933	0.00645105	0.00598088
36	0.00652947	0.00603846	0.00558533	0.00516707
37	0.00567780	0.00523945	0.00483578	0.00446399
38	0.00493722	0.00454616	0.00418682	0.00385658
39	0.00429323	0.00394461	0.00362495	0.00333182
40	0.00373324	0.00342265	0.00313849	0.00287846
41	0.00324630	0.00296976	0.00271731	0.00248679
42	0.00282287	0.00257680	0.00235265	0.00214841
43	0.00245467	0.00223584	0.00203692	0.00185608
44	0.00213449	0.00193999	0.00176357	0.00160353
45	0.00185608	0.00168329	0.00152690	0.00138534
46	0.00161398	0.00146055	0.00132199	0.00119683
47	0.00140346	0.00126729	0.00114458	0.00103398
48	0.00122040	0.00109960	0.00099068	0.00089329
49	0.00106122	0.00095410	0.00085799	0.00077174
50	0.00092280	0.00082785	0.00074285	0.00066673

TABLE 1 PRESENT VALUE OF $1 (ANNUAL COMPOUNDING) (*Continued*)

	Interest rate (%)			
Year	16.00	16.25	16.50	16.75
1	0.86206897	0.86021505	0.85836910	0.85653105
2	0.74316290	0.73996994	0.73679751	0.73364544
3	0.64065767	0.63653328	0.63244421	0.62839010
4	0.55229110	0.54755551	0.54287057	0.53823563
5	0.47611302	0.47101549	0.46598332	0.46101553
6	0.41044225	0.40517462	0.39998568	0.39487411
7	0.35382953	0.34853731	0.34333535	0.33822194
8	0.30502546	0.29981704	0.29470846	0.28969759
9	0.26295298	0.25790713	0.25296863	0.24813498
10	0.22668360	0.22185559	0.21714046	0.21253532
11	0.19541690	0.19084352	0.18638666	0.18204310
12	0.16846284	0.16416647	0.15998855	0.15592557
13	0.14522659	0.14121847	0.13732923	0.13355509
14	0.12519534	0.12147825	0.11787916	0.11439408
15	0.10792701	0.10449742	0.10118383	0.09798108
16	0.09304053	0.08989026	0.08685307	0.08392470
17	0.08020735	0.07732495	0.07455199	0.07188411
18	0.06914427	0.06651609	0.06399313	0.06157097
19	0.05960713	0.05721814	0.05492972	0.05273745
20	0.05138546	0.04921990	0.04714998	0.04517126
21	0.04429781	0.04233970	0.04047208	0.03869059
22	0.03818776	0.03642125	0.03473999	0.03313969
23	0.03292049	0.03133011	0.02981973	0.02838517
24	0.02837973	0.02695063	0.02559634	0.02431278
25	0.02446528	0.02318334	0.02197110	0.02082465
26	0.02109076	0.01994266	0.01885932	0.01783696
27	0.01818169	0.01715497	0.01618825	0.01527791
28	0.01567387	0.01475697	0.01389550	0.01308601
29	0.01351196	0.01269416	0.01192747	0.01120857
30	0.01164824	0.01091971	0.01023817	0.00960049
31	0.01004159	0.00939330	0.00878813	0.00822312
32	0.00865654	0.00808026	0.00754346	0.00704335
33	0.00746253	0.00695076	0.00647507	0.00603285
34	0.00643322	0.00597915	0.00555800	0.00516732
35	0.00554588	0.00514335	0.00477082	0.00442597
36	0.00478093	0.00442439	0.00409512	0.00379098
37	0.00412149	0.00380593	0.00351512	0.00324710
38	0.00355301	0.00327392	0.00301727	0.00278124
39	0.00306294	0.00281627	0.00258994	0.00238222
40	0.00264047	0.00242260	0.00222312	0.00204044
41	0.00227626	0.00208396	0.00190826	0.00174770
42	0.00196230	0.00179265	0.00163799	0.00149696
43	0.00169163	0.00154206	0.00140600	0.00128219
44	0.00145831	0.00132651	0.00120687	0.00109824
45	0.00125716	0.00114108	0.00103594	0.00094068
46	0.00108376	0.00098158	0.00088922	0.00080572
47	0.00093427	0.00084437	0.00076328	0.00069012
48	0.00080541	0.00072634	0.00065517	0.00059111
49	0.00069432	0.00062481	0.00056238	0.00050631
50	0.00059855	0.00053747	0.00048273	0.00043367

TABLE 1 PRESENT VALUE OF $1 (ANNUAL COMPOUNDING) (*Continued*)

Year	Interest rate (%)			
	17.00	17.25	17.50	17.75
1	0.85470085	0.85287846	0.85106383	0.84925690
2	0.73051355	0.72740168	0.72430964	0.72123728
3	0.62437056	0.62038522	0.61643374	0.61251574
4	0.53365005	0.52911320	0.52462446	0.52018322
5	0.45611115	0.45126925	0.44648890	0.44176919
6	0.38983859	0.38487783	0.37999055	0.37517553
7	0.33319538	0.32825401	0.32339622	0.31862041
8	0.28478237	0.27996078	0.27523082	0.27059058
9	0.24340374	0.23877252	0.23423900	0.22980092
10	0.20803738	0.20364394	0.19935234	0.19516001
11	0.17780973	0.17368353	0.16966156	0.16574099
12	0.15197413	0.14813094	0.14439282	0.14075668
13	0.12989242	0.12633769	0.12288751	0.11953858
14	0.11101916	0.10775070	0.10458511	0.10151896
15	0.09488817	0.09189825	0.08900861	0.08621568
16	0.08110100	0.07837804	0.07575201	0.07321926
17	0.06931709	0.06684694	0.06446979	0.06218196
18	0.05924538	0.05701231	0.04586791	0.05280846
19	0.05063708	0.04862458	0.04669609	0.04484795
20	0.04327955	0.04147085	0.03974135	0.03808743
21	0.03699107	0.03536960	0.03382243	0.03234601
22	0.03161630	0.03016597	0.02878505	0.02747008
23	0.02702248	0.02572790	0.02449791	0.02332915
24	0.02309614	0.02194278	0.02084929	0.01981244
25	0.01974029	0.01871452	0.01774407	0.01682585
26	0.01687204	0.01596121	0.01510134	0.01428947
27	0.01442055	0.01361297	0.01285220	0.01213543
28	0.01232525	0.01161021	0.01093805	0.01030610
29	0.01053440	0.00990210	0.00930898	0.00875253
30	0.00900376	0.00844529	0.00792253	0.00743314
31	0.00769553	0.00720280	0.00674258	0.00631265
32	0.00657737	0.00614312	0.00573837	0.00536106
33	0.00562169	0.00523933	0.00488372	0.00455292
34	0.00480486	0.00446851	0.00415635	0.00386660
35	0.00410672	0.00381110	0.00353732	0.00328373
36	0.00351002	0.00325040	0.00301049	0.00278873
37	0.00300001	0.00277220	0.00256212	0.00236835
38	0.00256411	0.00236435	0.00218052	0.00201134
39	0.00219155	0.00201650	0.00185577	0.00170814
40	0.00187312	0.00171983	0.00157938	0.00145065
41	0.00160096	0.00146681	0.00134415	0.00123198
42	0.00136834	0.00125101	0.00114396	0.00104626
43	0.00116952	0.00106696	0.00097358	0.00088855
44	0.00099959	0.00090999	0.00082858	0.00075461
45	0.00085435	0.00077611	0.00070517	0.00064085
46	0.00073021	0.00066193	0.00060015	0.00054425
47	0.00062411	0.00056454	0.00051076	0.00046221
48	0.00053343	0.00048149	0.00043469	0.00039253
49	0.00045592	0.00041065	0.00036995	0.00033336
50	0.00038968	0.00035023	0.00031485	0.00028311

TABLE 1 PRESENT VALUE OF $1 (ANNUAL COMPOUNDING) (*Continued*)

	Interest rate (%)			
Year	18.00	18.25	18.50	18.75
1	0.84745763	0.84566596	0.84388186	0.84210526
2	0.71818443	0.71515092	0.71213659	0.70914127
3	0.60863087	0.60477879	0.60095915	0.59717160
4	0.51578888	0.51144084	0.50713852	0.50288135
5	0.43710922	0.43250811	0.42796500	0.42347903
6	0.37043154	0.36575738	0.36115189	0.35661392
7	0.31392503	0.30930857	0.30476953	0.30030646
8	0.26603816	0.26157173	0.25718948	0.25288965
9	0.22545607	0.22120231	0.21703753	0.21295970
10	0.19106447	0.18706326	0.18315404	0.17933449
11	0.16191904	0.15819303	0.15456037	0.15101852
12	0.13721953	0.13377846	0.13043069	0.12717349
13	0.11628773	0.11313189	0.11006809	0.10709346
14	0.09854893	0.09567179	0.09288447	0.09018397
15	0.08351604	0.08090638	0.07838352	0.07594439
16	0.07077630	0.06841977	0.06614643	0.06395317
17	0.05997992	0.05786027	0.05581977	0.05385530
18	0.05083044	0.04893046	0.04710529	0.04535184
19	0.04307664	0.04137883	0.03975130	0.03819102
20	0.03650563	0.03499266	0.03354540	0.03216086
21	0.03093698	0.02959211	0.02830836	0.02708283
22	0.02621778	0.02502504	0.02388891	0.02280659
23	0.02221845	0.02116282	0.02015942	0.01920555
24	0.01882920	0.01789668	0.01701217	0.01617310
25	0.01595695	0.01513461	0.01435626	0.01361945
26	0.01352284	0.01279883	0.01211499	0.01146901
27	0.01146003	0.01082353	0.01022362	0.00965811
28	0.00971189	0.00915309	0.00862752	0.00813315
29	0.00823042	0.00774046	0.00728061	0.00684897
30	0.00697493	0.00654584	0.00614398	0.00576755
31	0.00591096	0.00553560	0.00518479	0.00485689
32	0.00500929	0.00468126	0.00437535	0.00409001
33	0.00424516	0.00395879	0.00369228	0.00344422
34	0.00359759	0.00334781	0.00311585	0.00290039
35	0.00304881	0.00283113	0.00262941	0.00244244
36	0.00258373	0.00239419	0.00221891	0.00205679
37	0.00218960	0.00202469	0.00187250	0.00173203
38	0.00185560	0.00171221	0.00158017	0.00145855
39	0.00157254	0.00144796	0.00133347	0.00122826
40	0.00133266	0.00122449	0.00112529	0.00103432
41	0.00112937	0.00103551	0.00094962	0.00087101
42	0.00095710	0.00087569	0.00080136	0.00073348
43	0.00081110	0.00074054	0.00067626	0.00061767
44	0.00068737	0.00062625	0.00057068	0.00052014
45	0.00058252	0.00052960	0.00048159	0.00043801
46	0.00049366	0.00044787	0.00040640	0.00036885
47	0.00041836	0.00037874	0.00034296	0.00031061
48	0.00035454	0.00032029	0.00028941	0.00026157
49	0.00030046	0.00027086	0.00024423	0.00022027
50	0.00025462	0.00022906	0.00020610	0.00018549

TABLE 1   PRESENT VALUE OF $1 (ANNUAL COMPOUNDING) (*Continued*)

Year	Interest rate (%)			
	19.00	19.25	19.50	19.75
1	0.84033613	0.83857442	0.83682008	0.83507307
2	0.70616482	0.70320706	0.70026785	0.69734703
3	0.59341581	0.58969146	0.58599820	0.58233572
4	0.49866875	0.49450017	0.49037507	0.48629288
5	0.41904937	0.41467520	0.41035570	0.40609009
6	0.35214233	0.34773602	0.34339389	0.33911490
7	0.29591792	0.29160253	0.28735891	0.28318572
8	0.24867052	0.24453042	0.24046770	0.23648077
9	0.20896683	0.20505696	0.20122820	0.19747872
10	0.17560238	0.17195552	0.16839180	0.16490916
11	0.14756502	0.14419750	0.14091364	0.13771120
12	0.12400422	0.12092034	0.11791937	0.11499891
13	0.10420523	0.10140070	0.09867729	0.09603250
14	0.08756742	0.08503203	0.08257514	0.08019415
15	0.07358606	0.07130569	0.06910054	0.06696798
16	0.06183703	0.05979513	0.05782472	0.05592315
17	0.05196389	0.05014266	0.04838888	0.04669992
18	0.04366713	0.04204836	0.04049279	0.03899784
19	0.03669507	0.03526068	0.03388518	0.03256605
20	0.03083619	0.02956870	0.02835580	0.02719503
21	0.02591277	0.02479556	0.02372870	0.02270984
22	0.02177544	0.02079292	0.01985665	0.01896437
23	0.01829869	0.01743641	0.01661645	0.01583664
24	0.01537705	0.01462173	0.01390498	0.01322475
25	0.01292189	0.01226141	0.01163596	0.01104363
26	0.01085873	0.01028210	0.00973721	0.00922224
27	0.00912498	0.00862231	0.00814829	0.00770124
28	0.00766805	0.00723045	0.00681865	0.00643110
29	0.00644374	0.00606327	0.00570599	0.00537044
30	0.00541491	0.00508450	0.00477488	0.00448471
31	0.00455034	0.00426373	0.00399572	0.00374506
32	0.00382382	0.00357546	0.00334370	0.00312740
33	0.00321329	0.00299829	0.00279807	0.00261161
34	0.00270025	0.00251429	0.00234148	0.00218088
35	0.00226911	0.00210842	0.00195940	0.00182120
36	0.00190682	0.00176806	0.00163967	0.00152083
37	0.00160237	0.00148265	0.00137211	0.00127001
38	0.00134653	0.00124332	0.00114821	0.00106055
39	0.00113154	0.00104261	0.00096084	0.00088563
40	0.00095087	0.00087431	0.00080405	0.00073957
41	0.00079905	0.00073317	0.00067285	0.00061759
42	0.00067147	0.00061482	0.00056305	0.00051574
43	0.00056426	0.00051557	0.00047117	0.00043068
44	0.00047417	0.00043235	0.00039429	0.00035965
45	0.00039846	0.00036255	0.00032995	0.00030033
46	0.00033484	0.00030403	0.00027611	0.00025080
47	0.00028138	0.00025495	0.00023105	0.00020944
48	0.00023645	0.00021379	0.00019335	0.00017489
49	0.00019870	0.00017928	0.00016180	0.00014605
50	0.00016698	0.00015034	0.00013540	0.00012196

TABLE 1 PRESENT VALUE OF $1 (ANNUAL COMPOUNDING) (*Continued*)

	Interest rate (%)			
Year	20.00	20.25	20.50	20.75
1	0.83333333	0.83160083	0.82987552	0.82815735
2	0.69444444	0.69155994	0.68869338	0.68584460
3	0.57870370	0.57510182	0.57152977	0.56798724
4	0.48225309	0.47825515	0.47429357	0.47038281
5	0.40187757	0.39771738	0.39360877	0.38955098
6	0.33489798	0.33074211	0.32664628	0.32260951
7	0.27908165	0.27504541	0.27107535	0.26717144
8	0.23256804	0.22872799	0.22495913	0.22125999
9	0.19380670	0.19021039	0.18668808	0.18323809
10	0.16150558	0.15817912	0.15492786	0.15174997
11	0.13458799	0.13154189	0.12857084	0.12567285
12	0.11215665	0.10939034	0.10669779	0.10407689
13	0.09346388	0.09096910	0.08854589	0.08619205
14	0.07788657	0.07564998	0.07348206	0.07138058
15	0.06490547	0.06291059	0.06098097	0.05911435
16	0.05408789	0.05231649	0.05060661	0.04895598
17	0.04507324	0.04350644	0.04199719	0.04054326
18	0.03756104	0.03617999	0.03485244	0.03357620
19	0.03130086	0.03008731	0.02892318	0.02780637
20	0.02608405	0.02502063	0.02400264	0.02302805
21	0.02173671	0.02080718	0.01991921	0.01907085
22	0.01811393	0.01730327	0.01653046	0.01579367
23	0.01509494	0.01438941	0.01371822	0.01307964
24	0.01257912	0.01196625	0.01138442	0.01083200
25	0.01048260	0.00995114	0.00944765	0.00897060
26	0.00873550	0.00827538	0.00734037	0.00742907
27	0.00727958	0.00688181	0.00650653	0.00615244
28	0.00606632	0.00572292	0.00539961	0.00509519
29	0.00505526	0.00475918	0.00448101	0.00421962
30	0.00421272	0.00395774	0.00371868	0.00349451
31	0.00351060	0.00329126	0.00308604	0.00289400
32	0.00292550	0.00273702	0.00256103	0.00239669
33	0.00243792	0.00227610	0.00212534	0.00198483
34	0.00203160	0.00189281	0.00176376	0.00164376
35	0.00169300	0.00157406	0.00146370	0.00136129
36	0.00141083	0.00130899	0.00121469	0.00112736
37	0.00117569	0.00108856	0.00100804	0.00093363
38	0.00097974	0.00090525	0.00083655	0.00077319
39	0.00081645	0.00075280	0.00069423	0.00064033
40	0.00068038	0.00062603	0.00057613	0.00053029
41	0.00056698	0.00052061	0.00047811	0.00043916
42	0.00047248	0.00043294	0.00039677	0.00036370
43	0.00039374	0.00036003	0.00032927	0.00030120
44	0.00032811	0.00029940	0.00027326	0.00024944
45	0.00027343	0.00024898	0.00022677	0.00020658
46	0.00022786	0.00020706	0.00018819	0.00017108
47	0.00018988	0.00017219	0.00015617	0.00014168
48	0.00015823	0.00014319	0.00012960	0.00011733
49	0.00013186	0.00011908	0.00010756	0.00009717
50	0.00010988	0.00009903	0.00008926	0.00008047

TABLE 1

PRESENT VALUE OF $1 (ANNUAL COMPOUNDING) (*Continued*)

	Interest rate (%)			
Year	21.00	21.25	21.50	21.75
1	0.82644628	0.82474227	0.82304527	0.82135524
2	0.68301346	0.68019981	0.67740351	0.67462442
3	0.56447393	0.56098953	0.55753376	0.55410630
4	0.46650738	0.46267178	0.45887552	0.45511811
5	0.38554329	0.38158497	0.37767532	0.37381365
6	0.31863082	0.31470926	0.31084389	0.30703380
7	0.26333125	0.25955403	0.25583859	0.25218382
8	0.21762914	0.21406518	0.21956674	0.20713250
9	0.17985879	0.17654860	0.17330596	0.17012936
10	0.14864363	0.14560709	0.14263865	0.13973664
11	0.12284597	0.12008832	0.11739807	0.11477342
12	0.10152560	0.09904192	0.09662392	0.09426975
13	0.08390545	0.08168405	0.07952586	0.07742895
14	0.06934335	0.06736829	0.06545338	0.06359668
15	0.05730855	0.05556148	0.05387110	0.05223546
16	0.04736244	0.04582390	0.04433835	0.04290387
17	0.03914251	0.03779291	0.03649247	0.03523932
18	0.03234918	0.03116941	0.03003496	0.02394400
19	0.02673486	0.02570673	0.02472013	0.02377331
20	0.02209493	0.02120143	0.02034578	0.01952633
21	0.01826027	0.01748571	0.01674550	0.01603805
22	0.01509113	0.01442121	0.01378231	0.01317294
23	0.01247201	0.01189378	0.01134346	0.01081966
24	0.01030745	0.00980930	0.00933618	0.00888679
25	0.00851855	0.00809015	0.00768410	0.00729921
26	0.00704013	0.00667228	0.00632436	0.00599524
27	0.00581829	0.00550292	0.00520524	0.00492422
28	0.00480850	0.00453849	0.00428415	0.00404454
29	0.00397397	0.00374308	0.00352605	0.00332200
30	0.00328427	0.00308708	0.00290210	0.00272854
31	0.00271427	0.00254604	0.00238856	0.00224110
32	0.00224320	0.00209983	0.00196589	0.00184074
33	0.00185388	0.00173182	0.00161802	0.00151190
34	0.00153214	0.00142830	0.00133170	0.00124181
35	0.00126623	0.00117798	0.00109605	0.00101997
36	0.00104647	0.00097153	0.00090210	0.00083776
37	0.00086485	0.00080126	0.00074247	0.00068809
38	0.00071475	0.00066084	0.00061108	0.00056517
39	0.00059070	0.00054502	0.00050295	0.00046421
40	0.00048819	0.00044950	0.00041395	0.00038128
41	0.00040346	0.00037072	0.00034070	0.00031316
42	0.00033344	0.00030575	0.00028041	0.00025722
43	0.00027557	0.00025217	0.00023079	0.00021127
44	0.00022774	0.00020797	0.00018995	0.00017353
45	0.00018822	0.00017152	0.00015634	0.00014253
46	0.00015555	0.00014146	0.00012867	0.00011707
47	0.00012855	0.00011667	0.00010590	0.00009615
48	0.00010624	0.00009622	0.00008716	0.00007897
49	0.00008780	0.00007936	0.00007174	0.00006487
50	0.00007257	0.00006545	0.00005905	0.00005328

TABLE 1 PRESENT VALUE OF $1 (ANNUAL COMPOUNDING) (*Continued*)

	Interest rate (%)			
Year	22.00	22.25	22.50	22.75
1	0.81967213	0.81799591	0.81632653	0.81466395
2	0.67186240	0.66911731	0.66638900	0.66367735
3	0.55070689	0.54733522	0.54399102	0.54067401
4	0.45139909	0.44771797	0.44407431	0.44046763
5	0.36999925	0.36623147	0.36250964	0.35883310
6	0.30327808	0.29957585	0.29592623	0.29232839
7	0.24858859	0.24505182	0.24157244	0.23814940
8	0.20376114	0.20045138	0.19720199	0.19401173
9	0.16701733	0.16396841	0.16098122	0.15805436
10	0.13689945	0.13412549	0.13141324	0.12876119
11	0.11221266	0.10971410	0.10727611	0.10489710
12	0.09197759	0.08974569	0.08757234	0.08545589
13	0.07539147	0.07341160	0.07148762	0.06961783
14	0.06179629	0.06005039	0.05835724	0.05671514
15	0.05065269	0.04912098	0.04763856	0.04620378
16	0.04151860	0.00148076	0.03888862	0.03764055
17	0.03403164	0.03286769	0.03174582	0.03066440
18	0.02789479	0.02688564	0.02591495	0.02498118
19	0.02286458	0.02199234	0.02115506	0.02035127
20	0.01874146	0.01798965	0.01726944	0.01657944
21	0.01536185	0.01471546	0.01409750	0.01350668
22	0.01259168	0.01203718	0.01150816	0.01100340
23	0.01032105	0.00984637	0.00939442	0.00896408
24	0.00845988	0.00805429	0.00766891	0.00730271
25	0.00693433	0.00658837	0.00626034	0.00594925
26	0.00568387	0.00538926	0.00511048	0.00484664
27	0.00465891	0.00440840	0.00417182	0.00394838
28	0.00381878	0.00360605	0.00340557	0.00321661
29	0.00313015	0.00294973	0.00278006	0.00262045
30	0.00256570	0.00241287	0.00226943	0.00213479
31	0.00210303	0.00197372	0.00185260	0.00173914
32	0.00172379	0.00161449	0.00151233	0.00141681
33	0.00141295	0.00132065	0.00123455	0.00115422
34	0.00115815	0.00108029	0.00100780	0.00094031
35	0.00094931	0.00088367	0.00082269	0.00076603
36	0.00077812	0.00072284	0.00067158	0.00062406
37	0.00063780	0.00059128	0.00054823	0.00050840
38	0.00052279	0.00048366	0.00044754	0.00041417
39	0.00042852	0.00039563	0.00036534	0.00033741
40	0.00035124	0.00032363	0.00029823	0.00027488
41	0.00028790	0.00026473	0.00024346	0.00022393
42	0.00023599	0.00021654	0.00019874	0.00018243
43	0.00019343	0.00017713	0.00016224	0.00014862
44	0.00015855	0.00014489	0.00013244	0.00012107
45	0.00012996	0.00011852	0.00010811	0.00009864
46	0.00010652	0.00009695	0.00008826	0.00008035
47	0.00008731	0.00007931	0.00007204	0.00006546
48	0.00007157	0.00006487	0.00005881	0.00005333
49	0.00005866	0.00005306	0.00004801	0.00004345
50	0.00004808	0.00004341	0.00003919	0.00003539

TABLE 1 PRESENT VALUE OF $1 (ANNUAL COMPOUNDING) (*Continued*)

Year	Interest rate (%)			
	23.00	**23.25**	**23.50**	**23.75**
1	0.81300813	0.81135903	0.80971660	0.80808081
2	0.66098222	0.65830347	0.65564097	0.65299459
3	0.53738392	0.53412046	0.53088338	0.52767240
4	0.43689749	0.43336346	0.42986508	0.42640194
5	0.35520122	0.35161335	0.34806889	0.34456722
6	0.28878148	0.28528467	0.28183716	0.27843816
7	0.23478169	0.23146829	0.22820823	0.22500053
8	0.19087942	0.18780389	0.18478399	0.18181861
9	0.15518652	0.15237638	0.14962266	0.14692413
10	0.12616790	0.12363195	0.12115195	0.11872657
11	0.10257553	0.10030990	0.09809875	0.09594066
12	0.08339474	0.08138734	0.07943218	0.07752781
13	0.06780060	0.06603435	0.06431756	0.06264873
14	0.05512244	0.05357757	0.05207899	0.05062524
15	0.04481499	0.04347064	0.04216923	0.04090928
16	0.03643495	0.03527030	0.03414512	0.03305801
17	0.02962191	0.02861688	0.02764787	0.02671354
18	0.02408286	0.02321856	0.02238694	0.02158670
19	0.01957956	0.01883859	0.01812708	0.01744380
20	0.01591834	0.01528486	0.01467780	0.01409600
21	0.01294174	0.01240151	0.01188486	0.01139071
22	0.01052174	0.01006208	0.00962336	0.00920461
23	0.00855426	0.00816396	0.00779220	0.00743807
24	0.00695468	0.00662390	0.00630947	0.00601056
25	0.00565421	0.00537436	0.00510888	0.00485702
26	0.00459692	0.00436054	0.00413675	0.00392486
27	0.00373733	0.00353796	0.00334959	0.00317161
28	0.00303848	0.00287056	0.00271222	0.00256291
29	0.00247031	0.00232905	0.00219613	0.00207104
30	0.00200838	0.00188970	0.00177824	0.00167357
31	0.00163283	0.00153322	0.00143987	0.00135238
32	0.00132751	0.00124399	0.00116589	0.00109283
33	0.00107927	0.00100933	0.00094404	0.00088310
34	0.00087746	0.00081893	0.00076440	0.00071361
35	0.00071338	0.00066444	0.00061895	0.00057666
36	0.00057998	0.00053910	0.00050118	0.00046599
37	0.00047153	0.00043740	0.00040581	0.00037655
38	0.00038336	0.00035489	0.00032859	0.00030429
39	0.00031167	0.00028795	0.00026607	0.00024589
40	0.00025339	0.00023363	0.00021544	0.00019870
41	0.00020601	0.00018956	0.00017444	0.00016056
42	0.00016749	0.00015380	0.00014125	0.00012975
43	0.00013617	0.00012478	0.00011437	0.00010485
44	0.00011071	0.00010125	0.00009261	0.00008472
45	0.00009001	0.00008215	0.00007499	0.00006846
46	0.00007318	0.00006665	0.00006072	0.00005532
47	0.00005949	0.00005408	0.00004916	0.00004471
48	0.00004837	0.00004388	0.00003981	0.00003613
49	0.00003932	0.00003560	0.00003223	0.00002919
50	0.00003197	0.00002888	0.00002610	0.00002359

TABLE 1 PRESENT VALUE OF $1 (ANNUAL COMPOUNDING) (*Continued*)

	Interest rate (%)			
Year	24.00	24.25	24.50	24.75
1	0.80645161	0.80482897	0.80321285	0.80160321
2	0.65036420	0.64774968	0.64515088	0.64256770
3	0.52448726	0.52132771	0.51819348	0.51508433
4	0.42297360	0.41957964	0.41621966	0.41289325
5	0.34110774	0.33768985	0.33431298	0.33097655
6	0.27508689	0.27178258	0.26852448	0.26531187
7	0.22184426	0.21873849	0.21568232	0.21267484
8	0.17890666	0.17604708	0.17323881	0.17048084
9	0.14427957	0.14168779	0.13914764	0.13665798
10	0.11635449	0.11403444	0.11176517	0.10954548
11	0.09383427	0.09177822	0.08977122	0.08781201
12	0.07567280	0.07386577	0.07210540	0.07039039
13	0.06102645	0.05944931	0.05791598	0.05642516
14	0.04921488	0.04784653	0.04651886	0.04523059
15	0.03968942	0.03850827	0.03736455	0.03625698
16	0.03200759	0.03099257	0.03001168	0.02906372
17	0.02581258	0.02494372	0.02410577	0.02329757
18	0.02081659	0.02007543	0.01936207	0.01867540
19	0.01678758	0.01615729	0.01555186	0.01497026
20	0.01353837	0.01300385	0.01249145	0.01200021
21	0.01091804	0.01046588	0.01003330	0.00961941
22	0.00880487	0.00842324	0.00805887	0.00771095
23	0.00710070	0.00677927	0.00647299	0.00618112
24	0.00572637	0.00545615	0.00519919	0.00495481
25	0.00461804	0.00439127	0.00417606	0.00397179
26	0.00372423	0.00353422	0.00335426	0.00318380
27	0.00300341	0.00284444	0.00269419	0.00255214
28	0.00242210	0.00228929	0.00216400	0.00204581
29	0.00195331	0.00184249	0.00173816	0.00163992
30	0.00157525	0.00148289	0.00139611	0.00131457
31	0.00127036	0.00119347	0.00112137	0.00105376
32	0.00102449	0.00096054	0.00090070	0.00084470
33	0.00082620	0.00077307	0.00072345	0.00067711
34	0.00066629	0.00062219	0.00058109	0.00054278
35	0.00053733	0.00050076	0.00046674	0.00043509
36	0.00043333	0.00040302	0.00037489	0.00034877
37	0.00034936	0.00032436	0.00030112	0.00027958
38	0.00028182	0.00026106	0.00024186	0.00022411
39	0.00022728	0.00021011	0.00019427	0.00017965
40	0.00018329	0.00016910	0.00015604	0.00014401
41	0.00014781	0.00013610	0.00012533	0.00011543
42	0.00011920	0.00010953	0.00010067	0.00009253
43	0.00009613	0.00008816	0.00008086	0.00007417
44	0.00007753	0.00007095	0.00006495	0.00005946
45	0.00006252	0.00005710	0.00005216	0.00004766
46	0.00005042	0.00004596	0.00004190	0.00003821
47	0.00004066	0.00003699	0.00003365	0.00003063
48	0.00003279	0.00002977	0.00002703	0.00002455
49	0.00002644	0.00002396	0.00002171	0.00001968
50	0.00002133	0.00001928	0.00001744	0.00001578

TABLE 1   PRESENT VALUE OF $1 (ANNUAL COMPOUNDING) (*Continued*)

Year	Interest rate (%)			
	25.00	25.25	25.50	25.75
1	0.80000000	0.79840319	0.79681275	0.79522863
2	0.64000000	0.63744766	0.63491056	0.63238857
3	0.51200000	0.50894025	0.50590483	0.50289350
4	0.40960000	0.40633952	0.40311142	0.39991530
5	0.32768000	0.32442277	0.32120432	0.31802410
6	0.26214400	0.25902018	0.25593969	0.25290187
7	0.20971520	0.20680254	0.20393601	0.20111481
8	0.16777216	0.16511180	0.16249881	0.15993225
9	0.13421773	0.13182579	0.12948113	0.12718270
10	0.10737418	0.10525013	0.10317221	0.10113933
11	0.08589935	0.08403204	0.08220893	0.08042889
12	0.06871948	0.06709145	0.06550513	0.06395935
13	0.05497558	0.05356603	0.05219532	0.05086231
14	0.04398047	0.04276729	0.04158990	0.04044717
15	0.03518437	0.03414554	0.03313936	0.03216474
16	0.02814750	0.02726191	0.02640586	0.02557832
17	0.02251800	0.02176599	0.02104053	0.02034062
18	0.01801440	0.01737804	0.01676536	0.01617544
19	0.01441152	0.01387468	0.01335885	0.01286317
20	0.01152922	0.01107759	0.01064451	0.01022916
21	0.00922337	0.00884438	0.00848168	0.00813452
22	0.00737870	0.00706138	0.00675831	0.00646881
23	0.00590296	0.00563783	0.00538511	0.00514418
24	0.00472237	0.00450126	0.00429092	0.00409080
25	0.00377789	0.00359382	0.00341906	0.00325312
26	0.00302231	0.00286932	0.00272435	0.00258697
27	0.00241785	0.00229087	0.00217080	0.00205724
28	0.00193428	0.00182904	0.00172972	0.00163597
29	0.00154743	0.00146031	0.00137826	0.00130097
30	0.00123794	0.00116592	0.00109822	0.00103457
31	0.00099035	0.00093087	0.00087507	0.00082272
32	0.00079228	0.00074321	0.00069727	0.00065425
33	0.00063383	0.00059338	0.00055559	0.00052028
34	0.00050706	0.00047376	0.00044270	0.00041374
35	0.00040565	0.00037825	0.00035275	0.00032902
36	0.00032452	0.00030200	0.00028108	0.00026164
37	0.00025961	0.00024111	0.00022397	0.00020807
38	0.00020769	0.00019251	0.00017846	0.00016546
39	0.00016615	0.00015370	0.00014220	0.00013158
40	0.00013292	0.00012271	0.00011331	0.00010464
41	0.00010634	0.00009707	0.00009028	0.00008321
42	0.00008507	0.00007822	0.00007194	0.00006617
43	0.00006806	0.00006245	0.00005732	0.00005262
44	0.00005445	0.00004986	0.00004567	0.00004185
45	0.00004356	0.00003981	0.00003639	0.00003328
46	0.00003484	0.00003179	0.00002900	0.00002646
47	0.00002788	0.00002538	0.00002311	0.00002104
48	0.00002230	0.00002026	0.00001841	0.00001673
49	0.00001784	0.00001618	0.00001467	0.00001331
50	0.00001427	0.00001292	0.00001169	0.00001058

TABLE 2   MORTGAGE CONSTANT (MONTHLY COMPOUNDING)

	Interest rate (%)			
Year	6.00	6.25	6.50	6.75
1	0.08606643	0.08618138	0.08629642	0.08641154
2	0.04432061	0.04443334	0.04454625	0.04465933
3	0.03042194	0.03053534	0.03064900	0.03076292
4	0.02348503	0.02359982	0.02371495	0.02383043
5	0.01933280	0.01944926	0.01956615	0.01968346
6	0.01657289	0.01669115	0.01680993	0.01692921
7	0.01460855	0.01472870	0.01484944	0.01497076
8	0.01314143	0.01326350	0.01338623	0.01350964
9	0.01200575	0.01212976	0.01225452	0.01238002
10	0.01110205	0.01122801	0.01135480	0.01148241
11	0.01036703	0.01049495	0.01062377	0.01075349
12	0.00975850	0.00988837	0.01001921	0.01015103
13	0.00924723	0.00937904	0.00951190	0.00964580
14	0.00881236	0.00894610	0.00908096	0.00921693
15	0.00843857	0.00857423	0.00871107	0.00884909
16	0.00811438	0.00825194	0.00839075	0.00853080
17	0.00783101	0.00797045	0.00811121	0.00825327
18	0.00758162	0.00772293	0.00786561	0.00800965
19	0.00736083	0.00750398	0.00764856	0.00779455
20	0.00716431	0.00730928	0.00745573	0.00760364
21	0.00698857	0.00713534	0.00728363	0.00743343
22	0.00683074	0.00697928	0.00712939	0.00728105
23	0.00668847	0.00683875	0.00699065	0.00714414
24	0.00655978	0.00671177	0.00686543	0.00702071
25	0.00644301	0.00659669	0.00675207	0.00690912
26	0.00633677	0.00649211	0.00664918	0.00680795
27	0.00623985	0.00639682	0.00655555	0.00671601
28	0.00615124	0.00630980	0.00647016	0.00663227
29	0.00607005	0.00623018	0.00639213	0.00655585
30	0.00599551	0.00615717	0.00632068	0.00648598
31	0.00592695	0.00609012	0.00625515	0.00642199
32	0.00586380	0.00602844	0.00619496	0.00636330
33	0.00580553	0.00597161	0.00613959	0.00630940
34	0.00575170	0.00591919	0.00608858	0.00625982
35	0.00570190	0.00587076	0.00604154	0.00621417
36	0.00565577	0.00582598	0.00599811	0.00617208
37	0.00561300	0.00578453	0.00595797	0.00613325
38	0.00557331	0.00574611	0.00592083	0.00609739
39	0.00553643	0.00571048	0.00588644	0.00606424
40	0.00550214	0.00567740	0.00585457	0.00603357
41	0.00547022	0.00564666	0.00582501	0.00600517
42	0.00544050	0.00561809	0.00579758	0.00597887
43	0.00541279	0.00559150	0.00577210	0.00595449
44	0.00538696	0.00556675	0.00574842	0.00593187
45	0.00536285	0.00554370	0.00572641	0.00591088
46	0.00534033	0.00552221	0.00570593	0.00589139
47	0.00531930	0.00550217	0.00568687	0.00587328
48	0.00529964	0.00548347	0.00566912	0.00585645
49	0.00528125	0.00546602	0.00565258	0.00584081
50	0.00526405	0.00544973	0.00563717	0.00582626

TABLE 2   MORTGAGE CONSTANT (MONTHLY COMPOUNDING) (*Continued*)

Year	Interest rate (%)			
	7.00	**7.25**	**7.50**	**7.75**
1	0.08652675	0.08664204	0.08675742	0.08687288
2	0.04477258	0.04488600	0.04499959	0.04511336
3	0.03087710	0.03099153	0.03110622	0.03122116
4	0.02394624	0.02406240	0.02417890	0.02429574
5	0.01980120	0.01991936	0.02003795	0.02015696
6	0.01704901	0.01716931	0.01729011	0.01741142
7	0.01509268	0.01521518	0.01533828	0.01546195
8	0.01363372	0.01375846	0.01388387	0.01400994
9	0.01250628	0.01263328	0.01276102	0.01288950
10	0.01161085	0.01174010	0.01187018	0.01200106
11	0.01088410	0.01101561	0.01114801	0.01128129
12	0.01028381	0.01041756	0.01055226	0.01068792
13	0.00978074	0.00991671	0.01005370	0.01019172
14	0.00935401	0.00949218	0.00963143	0.00977177
15	0.00898828	0.00912863	0.00927012	0.00941276
16	0.00867208	0.00881458	0.00895828	0.00910317
17	0.00839661	0.00854122	0.00868709	0.00883421
18	0.00815502	0.00830172	0.00844973	0.00859904
19	0.00794192	0.00809068	0.00824079	0.00839224
20	0.00775299	0.00790376	0.00805593	0.00320949
21	0.00758472	0.00773747	0.00789166	0.00804727
22	0.00743424	0.00758893	0.00774510	0.00790273
23	0.00729919	0.00745579	0.00761389	0.00777348
24	0.00717760	0.00733605	0.00749605	0.00765756
25	0.00706779	0.00722807	0.00738991	0.00755329
26	0.00696838	0.00713043	0.00729407	0.00745927
27	0.00687815	0.00704194	0.00720734	0.00737430
28	0.00679609	0.00696157	0.00712868	0.00729736
29	0.00672130	0.00688843	0.00705720	0.00722756
30	0.00665302	0.00682176	0.00699215	0.00716412
31	0.00659059	0.00676089	0.00693284	0.00710639
32	0.00653341	0.00670523	0.00687870	0.00705377
33	0.00648098	0.00665427	0.00682921	0.00700575
34	0.00643283	0.00660755	0.00678392	0.00696188
35	0.00638856	0.00656467	0.00674243	0.00692176
36	0.00634783	0.00652528	0.00670437	0.00688503
37	0.00631031	0.00648906	0.00666944	0.00685138
38	0.00627571	0.00645573	0.00663735	0.00682052
39	0.00624379	0.00642502	0.00660785	0.00679220
40	0.00621431	0.00639672	0.00658071	0.00676620
41	0.00618707	0.00637061	0.00655572	0.00674230
42	0.00616188	0.00634652	0.00653270	0.00672034
43	0.00613857	0.00632427	0.00651148	0.00670013
44	0.00611699	0.00630370	0.00649191	0.00668153
45	0.00609701	0.00628470	0.00647386	0.00666441
46	0.00607848	0.00626712	0.00645720	0.00664864
47	0.00606131	0.00625085	0.00644182	0.00663411
48	0.00604538	0.00623580	0.00642760	0.00662071
49	0.00603060	0.00622186	0.00641447	0.00660836
50	0.00601688	0.00620894	0.00640234	0.00659697

TABLE 2 MORTGAGE CONSTANT (MONTHLY COMPOUNDING) (*Continued*)

Year	Interest rate (%)			
	8.00	**8.25**	**8.50**	**8.75**
1	0.08698843	0.08710406	0.08721978	0.08733559
2	0.04522729	0.04534140	0.04545567	0.04557012
3	0.03133637	0.03145182	0.03156754	0.03168351
4	0.02441292	0.02453044	0.02464830	0.02476650
5	0.02027639	0.02039625	0.02051653	0.02063723
6	0.01753324	0.01765556	0.01777838	0.01790171
7	0.01558621	0.01571106	0.01583649	0.01596249
8	0.01413668	0.01426407	0.01439213	0.01452084
9	0.01301871	0.01314867	0.01327935	0.01341077
10	0.01213276	0.01226526	0.01239857	0.01253268
11	0.01141545	0.01155048	0.01168639	0.01182317
12	0.01082453	0.01096207	0.01110056	0.01123997
13	0.01033074	0.01047077	0.01061179	0.01075381
14	0.00991318	0.01005566	0.01019919	0.01034376
15	0.00955652	0.00970140	0.00984740	0.00999449
16	0.00924925	0.00939650	0.00954491	0.00969447
17	0.00898257	0.00913214	0.00928292	0.00943489
18	0.00874963	0.00890148	0.00905457	0.00920890
19	0.00854501	0.00869909	0.00885446	0.00901109
20	0.00836440	0.00852066	0.00867823	0.00883711
21	0.00820428	0.00836266	0.00852239	0.00868345
22	0.00806178	0.00822223	0.00838406	0.00854724
23	0.00793453	0.00809700	0.00826087	0.00842610
24	0.00782054	0.00798497	0.00815082	0.00831806
25	0.00771816	0.00788450	0.00805227	0.00822144
26	0.00762598	0.00779417	0.00796380	0.00813483
27	0.00754280	0.00771278	0.00788421	0.00805705
28	0.00746759	0.00763930	0.00781247	0.00798705
29	0.00739946	0.00757286	0.00774770	0.00792396
30	0.00733765	0.00751267	0.00768913	0.00786700
31	0.00728148	0.00745807	0.00763610	0.00781552
32	0.00723038	0.00740848	0.00758801	0.00776892
33	0.00718382	0.00736338	0.00754435	0.00772670
34	0.00714137	0.00732232	0.00750469	0.00768840
35	0.00710261	0.00728491	0.00746861	0.00765363
36	0.00706719	0.00725079	0.00743576	0.00762204
37	0.00703480	0.00721964	0.00740584	0.00759332
38	0.00700516	0.00719119	0.00737855	0.00756718
39	0.00697800	0.00716518	0.00735366	0.00754338
40	0.00695312	0.00714139	0.00733094	0.00752171
41	0.00693030	0.00711961	0.00731019	0.00750195
42	0.00690936	0.00709968	0.00729122	0.00748393
43	0.00689013	0.00708141	0.00727389	0.00746749
44	0.00687248	0.00706467	0.00725803	0.00745248
45	0.00685626	0.00704932	0.00724352	0.00743879
46	0.00684135	0.00703524	0.00723024	0.00742628
47	0.00682764	0.00702232	0.00721808	0.00741485
48	0.00681502	0.00701046	0.00720695	0.00740440
49	0.00680342	0.00699958	0.00719675	0.00739486
50	0.00679274	0.00698958	0.00718740	0.00738613

TABLE 2   MORTGAGE CONSTANT (MONTHLY COMPOUNDING) (*Continued*)

	Interest rate (%)			
Year	9.00	9.25	9.50	9.75
1	0.08745148	0.08756745	0.08768351	0.08779966
2	0.04568474	0.04579953	0.04591449	0.04602962
3	0.3179973	0.03191621	0.03203295	0.03214994
4	0.02488504	0.02500392	0.02512314	0.02524269
5	0.02075836	0.02087990	0.02100186	0.02112424
6	0.01802554	0.01814986	0.01827469	0.01840002
7	0.01608908	0.01621624	0.01634398	0.01647230
8	0.01465020	0.01478022	0.01491089	0.01504220
9	0.01354291	0.01367577	0.01380936	0.01394367
10	0.01266758	0.01280327	0.01293976	0.01307702
11	0.01196080	0.01209930	0.01223865	0.01237884
12	0.01138031	0.01152156	0.01166373	0.01180681
13	0.01089681	0.01104078	0.01118572	0.01133163
14	0.01048938	0.01063602	0.01078368	0.01093235
15	0.01014267	0.01029192	0.01044225	0.01059363
16	0.00984516	0.00999697	0.01014990	0.01030392
17	0.00958804	0.00974235	0.00989781	0.01005440
18	0.00936445	0.00952119	0.00967911	0.00983820
19	0.00916897	0.00932808	0.00948840	0.00964991
20	0.00899726	0.00915867	0.00932131	0.00948517
21	0.00884581	0.00900945	0.00917434	0.00934047
22	0.00871174	0.00887754	0.00904461	0.00921293
23	0.00859268	0.00876057	0.00892974	0.00910017
24	0.00848664	0.00865655	0.00882775	0.00900020
25	0.00839196	0.00856382	0.00873697	0.00891137
26	0.00830723	0.00848096	0.00865599	0.00883227
27	0.00823125	0.00840679	0.00858361	0.00876169
28	0.00816300	0.00834027	0.00851882	0.00869861
29	0.00810158	0.00828051	0.00846071	0.00864215
30	0.00804623	0.00822675	0.00840854	0.00859154
31	0.00799628	0.00817834	0.00836164	0.00854613
32	0.00795116	0.00813468	0.00831942	0.00850534
33	0.00791035	0.00809526	0.00828138	0.00846865
34	0.00787341	0.00805965	0.00824708	0.00843563
35	0.00783993	0.00802744	0.00821612	0.00840589
36	0.00780957	0.00799830	0.00818815	0.00837909
37	0.00778203	0.00797190	0.00816288	0.00835491
38	0.00775701	0.00794798	0.00814002	0.00833309
39	0.00773428	0.00792628	0.00811934	0.00831338
40	0.00771361	0.00790661	0.00810062	0.00829559
41	0.00769482	0.00788874	0.00808366	0.00827950
42	0.00767772	0.00787252	0.00806829	0.00826496
43	0.00766214	0.00785779	0.00805436	0.00825180
44	0.00764796	0.00784440	0.00804173	0.00823990
45	0.00763505	0.00783223	0.00803028	0.00822913
46	0.00762327	0.00782117	0.00801989	0.00821938
47	0.00761254	0.00781110	0.00801046	0.00821056
48	0.00760276	0.00780194	0.00800190	0.00820256
49	0.00759384	0.00779361	0.00799413	0.00819532
50	0.00758570	0.00778603	0.00798707	0.00818877

TABLE 2 MORTGAGE CONSTANT (MONTHLY COMPOUNDING) (*Continued*)

Year	Interest rate (%)			
	10.00	10.25	10.50	10.75
1	0.08791589	0.08803220	0.08814860	0.08826509
2	0.04614493	0.04626040	0.04637604	0.04649185
3	0.03226719	0.03238469	0.03250244	0.03262045
4	0.02536258	0.02548281	0.02560338	0.02572428
5	0.02124704	0.02137026	0.02149390	0.02161795
6	0.01852584	0.01865216	0.01877897	0.01890628
7	0.01660118	0.01673064	0.01686067	0.01699127
8	0.01517416	0.01530677	0.01544002	0.01557390
9	0.01407869	0.01421442	0.01435086	0.01448801
10	0.01321507	0.01335390	0.01349350	0.01363387
11	0.01251988	0.01266175	0.01280446	0.01294799
12	0.01195078	0.01209565	0.01224141	0.01238804
13	0.01147848	0.01162628	0.01177502	0.01192469
14	0.01108203	0.01123269	0.01138434	0.01153696
15	0.01074605	0.01089951	0.01105399	0.01120948
16	0.01045902	0.01061519	0.01077242	0.01093070
17	0.01021210	0.01037091	0.01053081	0.01069178
18	0.00999844	0.01015980	0.01032228	0.01048585
19	0.00981259	0.00997642	0.01014139	0.01030747
20	0.00965022	0.00981643	0.00998380	0.01015229
21	0.00950780	0.00967631	0.00984599	0.01001679
22	0.00938246	0.00955318	0.00972507	0.00989810
23	0.00927182	0.00944466	0.00961867	0.00979382
24	0.00917389	0.00934877	0.00952481	0.00970199
25	0.00908701	0.00926383	0.00944182	0.00962093
26	0.00900977	0.00918846	0.00936829	0.00954924
27	0.00894098	0.00912144	0.00930304	0.00948574
28	0.00887960	0.00906176	0.00924504	0.00942940
29	0.00882477	0.00900854	0.00919341	0.00937934
30	0.00877572	0.00896101	0.00914739	0.00933481
31	0.00873178	0.00891853	0.00910634	0.00929517
32	0.00869238	0.00888051	0.00906968	0.00925983
33	0.00865703	0.00884646	0.00903690	0.00922831
34	0.00862527	0.00881594	0.00900759	0.00920017
35	0.00859672	0.00878856	0.00898134	0.00917503
36	0.00857105	0.00876398	0.00895783	0.00915256
37	0.00854793	0.00874190	0.00893676	0.00913246
38	0.00852712	0.00872206	0.00891787	0.00911448
39	0.00850836	0.00870423	0.00890092	0.00909839
40	0.00849146	0.00868818	0.00888570	0.00908397
41	0.00847621	0.00867375	0.00887204	0.00907106
42	0.00846246	0.00866075	0.00885978	0.00905949
43	0.00845005	0.00864905	0.00884876	0.00904912
44	0.00843885	0.00863851	0.00883886	0.00903982
45	0.00842873	0.00862902	0.00882995	0.00903148
46	0.00841959	0.00862047	0.00882195	0.00902400
47	0.00841134	0.00861276	0.00881476	0.00901730
48	0.00840388	0.00860581	0.00880829	0.00901128
49	0.00839715	0.00859954	0.00880247	0.00900587
50	0.00839106	0.00859389	0.00879723	0.00900103

TABLE 2 MORTGAGE CONSTANT (MONTHLY COMPOUNDING) (*Continued*)

	Interest rate (%)			
Year	11.00	11.25	11.50	11.75
1	0.08838166	0.08849831	0.08861505	0.08873188
2	0.04660784	0.04672399	0.04684032	0.04695681
3	0.03273872	0.03285723	0.03297601	0.03309503
4	0.02584552	0.02596710	0.02608901	0.02621125
5	0.02174242	0.02186731	0.02199261	0.02211832
6	0.01903408	0.01916237	0.01929116	0.01942043
7	0.01712244	0.01725417	0.01738646	0.01751932
8	0.01570843	0.01584358	0.01597937	0.01611579
9	0.01462586	0.01476441	0.01490366	0.01504360
10	0.01377500	0.01391689	0.01405954	0.01420295
11	0.01309235	0.01323752	0.01338350	0.01353029
12	0.01253555	0.01268393	0.01283317	0.01298326
13	0.01207527	0.01222677	0.01237918	0.01253248
14	0.01169054	0.01184508	0.01200055	0.01215696
15	0.01136597	0.01152345	0.01168190	0.01184131
16	0.01109000	0.01125033	0.01141165	0.01157396
17	0.01085381	0.01101687	0.01118096	0.01134606
18	0.01065050	0.01081620	0.01098295	0.01115073
19	0.01047464	0.01064288	0.01081218	0.01098251
20	0.01032188	0.01049256	0.01066430	0.01083707
21	0.01018871	0.01036171	0.01053578	0.01071088
22	0.01007223	0.01024746	0.01042374	0.01060106
23	0.00997008	0.01014742	0.01032581	0.01050523
24	0.00988027	0.01005962	0.01024002	0.01042142
25	0.00980113	0.00998240	0.01016469	0.01034798
26	0.00973127	0.00991435	0.01009844	0.01028351
27	0.00966950	0.00985429	0.01004008	0.01022682
28	0.00961480	0.00980121	0.00998859	0.01017691
29	0.00956629	0.00975423	0.00994312	0.01013292
30	0.00952323	0.00971261	0.00990291	0.01009410
31	0.00948497	0.00967570	0.00986733	0.01005981
32	0.00945093	0.00964294	0.00983581	0.01002950
33	0.00942063	0.00961383	0.00980786	0.01000269
34	0.00939364	0.00958796	0.00978308	0.00997896
35	0.00936958	0.00956494	0.00976107	0.00995794
36	0.00934811	0.00954445	0.00974153	0.00993931
37	0.00932896	0.00952621	0.00972417	0.00992280
38	0.00931186	0.00950996	0.00970874	0.00990816
39	0.00929659	0.00949548	0.00969502	0.00989517
40	0.00928294	0.00948257	0.00968282	0.00988364
41	0.00927075	0.00947106	0.00967196	0.00987341
42	0.00925984	0.00946079	0.00966230	0.00986432
43	0.00925009	0.00945163	0.00965369	0.00985625
44	0.00924137	0.00944345	0.00964604	0.00984908
45	0.00923356	0.00943615	0.00963921	0.00984271
46	0.00922658	0.00942964	0.00963314	0.00983705
47	0.00922033	0.00942382	0.00962773	0.00983202
48	0.00921473	0.00941862	0.00962291	0.00982755
49	0.00920973	0.00941398	0.00961861	0.00982358
50	0.00920524	0.00940984	0.00961478	0.00982005

TABLE 2   MORTGAGE CONSTANT (MONTHLY COMPOUNDING) (*Continued*)

	Interest rate (%)			
Year	12.00	12.25	12.50	12.75
1	0.08884879	0.08896578	0.08908286	0.08920003
2	0.04707347	0.04719031	0.04730731	0.04742448
3	0.03321431	0.03333384	0.03345363	0.03357366
4	0.02633384	0.02645675	0.02658000	0.02670358
5	0.02224445	0.02237099	0.02249794	0.02262530
6	0.01955019	0.01968044	0.01981118	0.01994240
7	0.01765273	0.01778671	0.01792124	0.01805632
8	0.01625284	0.01639051	0.01652881	0.01666772
9	0.01518423	0.01532555	0.01546755	0.01561023
10	0.01434709	0.01449199	0.01463762	0.01478398
11	0.01367788	0.01382626	0.01397543	0.01412538
12	0.01313419	0.01328597	0.01343857	0.01359200
13	0.01268666	0.01284173	0.01299766	0.01315446
14	0.01231430	0.01247254	0.01263168	0.01279172
15	0.01200168	0.01216299	0.01232522	0.01248837
16	0.01173725	0.01190150	0.01206670	0.01223283
17	0.01151216	0.01167923	0.01184726	0.01201624
18	0.01131950	0.01148927	0.01166001	0.01183170
19	0.01115386	0.01132620	0.01149951	0.01167378
20	0.01101086	0.01118565	0.01136141	0.01153812
21	0.01088700	0.01106410	0.01124218	0.01142120
22	0.01077938	0.01095869	0.01113896	0.01132016
23	0.01068565	0.01086704	0.01104937	0.01123262
24	0.01060382	0.01078717	0.01097144	0.01115662
25	0.01053224	0.01071744	0.01090354	0.01109052
26	0.01046952	0.01065646	0.01084427	0.01103294
27	0.01041449	0.01060305	0.01079247	0.01098272
28	0.01036613	0.01055621	0.01074713	0.01093885
29	0.01032359	0.01051510	0.01070741	0.01090049
30	0.01028613	0.01047896	0.01067258	0.01086693
31	0.01025311	0.01044718	0.01064201	0.01083754
32	0.01022398	0.01041921	0.01061515	0.01081178
33	0.01019827	0.01039457	0.01059156	0.01078919
34	0.01017557	0.01037286	0.01057080	0.01076936
35	0.01015550	0.01035371	0.01055254	0.01075196
36	0.01013776	0.01033682	0.01053647	0.01073668
37	0.01012206	0.01032191	0.01052232	0.01072325
38	0.01010817	0.01030875	0.01050986	0.01071146
39	0.01009588	0.01029713	0.01049887	0.01070108
40	0.01008500	0.01028686	0.01048919	0.01069196
41	0.01007536	0.01027779	0.01048066	0.01068394
42	0.01006682	0.01026977	0.01047314	0.01067689
43	0.01005926	0.01026268	0.01046650	0.01067068
44	0.01005255	0.01025642	0.01046065	0.01066522
45	0.01004661	0.01025088	0.01045549	0.01066041
46	0.01004134	0.01024598	0.01045093	0.01065618
47	0.01003667	0.01024164	0.01044692	0.01065246
48	0.01003253	0.01023781	0.01044337	0.01064918
49	0.01002886	0.01023442	0.01044024	0.01064629
50	0.01002560	0.01023142	0.01043748	0.01064375

TABLE 2   MORTGAGE CONSTANT (MONTHLY COMPOUNDING) (*Continued*)

	Interest rate (%)			
Year	13.00	13.25	13.50	13.75
1	0.08931728	0.08943461	0.08955203	0.08966953
2	0.04754182	0.04765933	0.04777701	0.04789486
3	0.03369395	0.03381449	0.03393529	0.03405633
4	0.02682750	0.02695174	0.02707632	0.02720123
5	0.02275307	0.02288126	0.02300985	0.02313884
6	0.02007411	0.02020629	0.02033896	0.02047211
7	0.01819196	0.01832815	0.01846489	0.01860218
8	0.01680726	0.01694740	0.01708816	0.01722953
9	0.01575359	0.01589762	0.01604231	0.01618768
10	0.01493107	0.01507889	0.01522743	0.01537668
11	0.01427611	0.01442761	0.01457987	0.01473289
12	0.01374625	0.01390131	0.01405717	0.01421383
13	0.01331210	0.01347059	0.01362992	0.01379007
14	0.01295264	0.01311442	0.01327707	0.01344056
15	0.01265242	0.01281736	0.01298319	0.01314987
16	0.01239988	0.01256783	0.01273668	0.01290640
17	0.01218614	0.01235697	0.01252869	0.01270129
18	0.01200433	0.01217787	0.01235231	0.01252764
19	0.01184898	0.01202510	0.01220211	0.01238001
20	0.01171576	0.01189431	0.01207375	0.01225405
21	0.01160114	0.01178198	0.01196370	0.01214627
22	0.01150226	0.01168525	0.01186911	0.01205379
23	0.01141676	0.01160177	0.01178761	0.01197428
24	0.01134267	0.01152956	0.01171727	0.01190577
25	0.01127835	0.01146700	0.01165645	0.01184666
26	0.01122244	0.01141273	0.01160378	0.01179558
27	0.01117376	0.01136557	0.01155812	0.01175138
28	0.01113133	0.01132456	0.01151849	0.01171310
29	0.01109432	0.01128885	0.01148406	0.01167992
30	0.01106200	0.01125774	0.01145412	0.01165113
31	0.01103375	0.01123060	0.01142807	0.01162613
32	0.01100904	0.01120693	0.01140539	0.01160441
33	0.01098743	0.01118626	0.01138564	0.01158554
34	0.01096851	0.01116820	0.01136842	0.01156913
35	0.01095193	0.01115242	0.01135341	0.01155485
36	0.01093741	0.01113863	0.01134031	0.01154243
37	0.01092468	0.01112657	0.01132889	0.01153161
38	0.01091352	0.01111601	0.01131891	0.01152220
39	0.01090373	0.01110678	0.01131021	0.01151400
40	0.01089514	0.01109870	0.01130261	0.01150685
41	0.01088761	0.01109163	0.01129598	0.01150063
42	0.01088100	0.01108543	0.01129018	0.01149521
43	0.01087519	0.01108001	0.01128512	0.01149048
44	0.01087010	0.01107526	0.01128069	0.01148636
45	0.01086563	0.01107110	0.01127683	0.01148277
46	0.01086170	0.01106746	0.01127345	0.01147965
47	0.01085825	0.01106427	0.01127050	0.01147692
48	0.01085522	0.01106147	0.01126792	0.01147454
49	0.01085256	0.01105903	0.01126567	0.01147247
50	0.01085023	0.01105688	0.01126369	0.01147066

TABLE 2   MORTGAGE CONSTANT (MONTHLY COMPOUNDING) (*Continued*)

	Interest rate (%)			
Year	14.00	14.25	14.50	14.75
1	0.08978712	0.08990479	0.09002255	0.09014039
2	0.04801288	0.04813107	0.04824943	0.04836795
3	0.03417763	0.03429918	0.03442098	0.03454303
4	0.02732648	0.02745205	0.02757795	0.02770419
5	0.02326825	0.02339806	0.02352828	0.02365890
6	0.02060574	0.02073985	0.02087443	0.02100948
7	0.01874001	0.01887839	0.01901730	0.01915676
8	0.01737150	0.01751408	0.01765726	0.01780103
9	0.01633370	0.01648038	0.01662772	0.01677571
10	0.01552664	0.01567731	0.01582868	0.01598074
11	0.01488666	0.01504118	0.01519644	0.01535243
12	0.01437127	0.01452949	0.01468849	0.01484825
13	0.01395103	0.01411280	0.01427538	0.01443874
14	0.01360490	0.01377006	0.01393603	0.01410282
15	0.01331741	0.01348580	0.01365501	0.01382504
16	0.01307699	0.01324843	0.01342070	0.01359379
17	0.01287476	0.01304908	0.01322424	0.01340022
18	0.01270383	0.01288087	0.01305874	0.01323743
19	0.01255876	0.01273835	0.01291876	0.01309998
20	0.01243521	0.01261719	0.01279998	0.01298355
21	0.01232967	0.01251388	0.01269889	0.01288465
22	0.01223929	0.01242558	0.01261264	0.01280045
23	0.01216173	0.01234995	0.01253892	0.01272860
24	0.01209504	0.01228505	0.01247578	0.01266720
25	0.01203761	0.01222928	0.01242163	0.01261465
26	0.01198808	0.01218127	0.01237512	0.01256961
27	0.01194532	0.01213992	0.01233514	0.01253097
28	0.01190836	0.01210425	0.01230074	0.01249779
29	0.01187639	0.01207346	0.01227110	0.01246928
30	0.01184872	0.01204687	0.01224556	0.01244476
31	0.01182474	0.01202388	0.01222353	0.01242366
32	0.01180396	0.01200401	0.01220452	0.01240549
33	0.01178594	0.01198681	0.01218812	0.01238985
34	0.01177030	0.01197192	0.01217395	0.01237637
35	0.01175673	0.01195903	0.01216171	0.01236475
36	0.01174495	0.01194786	0.01215113	0.01235473
37	0.01173472	0.01193818	0.01214198	0.01234609
38	0.01172583	0.01192980	0.01213408	0.01233864
39	0.01171811	0.01192253	0.01212724	0.01233222
40	0.01171140	0.01191623	0.01212133	0.01232667
41	0.01170557	0.01191077	0.01211622	0.01232189
42	0.01170050	0.01190603	0.01211179	0.01231776
43	0.01169609	0.01190192	0.01210796	0.01231419
44	0.01169226	0.01189836	0.01210465	0.01231112
45	0.01168893	0.01189527	0.01210179	0.01230846
46	0.01168603	0.01189259	0.01209931	0.01230617
47	0.01168351	0.01189026	0.01209716	0.01230419
48	0.01168132	0.01188824	0.01209530	0.01230248
49	0.01167941	0.01188649	0.01209369	0.01230100
50	0.01167776	0.01188497	0.01209230	0.01229973

TABLE 2   MORTGAGE CONSTANT (MONTHLY COMPOUNDING) (*Continued*)

Year	Interest rate (%)			
	15.00	**15.25**	**15.50**	**15.75**
1	0.09025831	0.09037632	0.09049442	0.09061259
2	0.04848665	0.04860551	0.04872454	0.04884374
3	0.03466533	0.03478788	0.03491068	0.03503373
4	0.02783075	0.02795764	0.02808486	0.02821241
5	0.02378993	0.02392136	0.02405319	0.02418542
6	0.02114501	0.02128102	0.02141749	0.02155443
7	0.01929675	0.01943728	0.01957835	0.01971994
8	0.01794541	0.01809037	0.01823592	0.01838206
9	0.01692434	0.01707361	0.01722353	0.01737407
10	0.01613350	0.01628693	0.01644105	0.01659585
11	0.01550915	0.01566659	0.01582474	0.01598361
12	0.01500877	0.01517003	0.01533204	0.01549478
13	0.01460287	0.01476778	0.01493346	0.01509988
14	0.01427040	0.01443876	0.01460790	0.01477780
15	0.01399587	0.01416750	0.01433990	0.01451308
16	0.01376770	0.01394239	0.01411787	0.01429411
17	0.01357700	0.01375458	0.01393292	0.01411203
18	0.01341691	0.01359717	0.01377819	0.01395997
19	0.01328198	0.01346475	0.01364826	0.01383250
20	0.01316790	0.01335299	0.01353881	0.01372534
21	0.01307117	0.01325841	0.01344636	0.01363500
22	0.01298897	0.01317820	0.01336812	0.01355869
23	0.01291899	0.01311004	0.01330176	0.01349410
24	0.01285929	0.01305203	0.01324539	0.01343936
25	0.01280831	0.01300258	0.01319745	0.01339290
26	0.01276470	0.01296039	0.01315663	0.01335342
27	0.01272738	0.01292434	0.01312183	0.01331984
28	0.01269540	0.01289352	0.01309215	0.01329126
29	0.01266797	0.01286716	0.01306681	0.01326692
30	0.01264444	0.01284459	0.01304517	0.01324617
31	0.01262424	0.01282525	0.01302667	0.01322848
32	0.01260688	0.01280868	0.01301086	0.01321339
33	0.01259197	0.01279447	0.01299733	0.01320051
34	0.01257916	0.01278229	0.01298575	0.01318952
35	0.01256813	0.01277184	0.01297585	0.01318014
36	0.01255865	0.01276287	0.01296737	0.01317212
37	0.01255050	0.01275517	0.01296011	0.01316528
38	0.01254348	0.01274857	0.01295389	0.01315943
39	0.01253744	0.01274289	0.01294856	0.01315443
40	0.01253224	0.01273802	0.01294400	0.01315016
41	0.01252777	0.01273384	0.01294009	0.01314651
42	0.01252391	0.01273025	0.01293674	0.01314339
43	0.01252060	0.01272716	0.01293387	0.01314072
44	0.01251774	0.01272451	0.01293141	0.01313844
45	0.01251528	0.01272223	0.01292931	0.01313649
46	0.01251316	0.01272028	0.01292750	0.01313483
47	0.01251134	0.01271860	0.01292595	0.01313340
48	0.01250977	0.01271715	0.01292463	0.01313219
49	0.01250841	0.01271591	0.01292349	0.01313114
50	0.01250725	0.01271484	0.01292252	0.01313025

TABLE 3 PROPORTION OUTSTANDING OF $1 (MONTHLY COMPOUNDING, TERM = 15 YRS)

Holding Period	Interest rate (%)			
	6.00	6.25	6.50	6.75
1	0.95758333	0.95843190	0.95926784	0.96009119
2	0.91255049	0.91419007	0.91580777	0.91740361
3	0.86474012	0.86710253	0.86943710	0.17174379
4	0.81398091	0.81698623	0.81996090	0.82290476
5	0.76009099	0.76364635	0.76717119	0.77066517
6	0.70287725	0.70687556	0.71084605	0.71478825
7	0.64213470	0.64645317	0.65074871	0.65502074
8	0.57764567	0.58214430	0.58662655	0.59109173
9	0.50917911	0.51369897	0.51821000	0.52271149
10	0.43648968	0.44085111	0.44521147	0.44957006
11	0.35931692	0.36331755	0.36732410	0.37133595
12	0.27738431	0.28079688	0.28422046	0.28765456
13	0.19039829	0.19296834	0.19555122	0.19814661
14	0.09804715	0.09949050	0.10094363	0.10240640
15	0.00000000	0.00000000	0.00000000	0.00000000
	7.00	7.25	7.50	7.75
1	0.96090202	0.96170040	0.96248639	0.96326008
2	0.91897765	0.92052992	0.92206051	0.92356946
3	0.87402255	0.87627338	0.87849625	0.88069117
4	0.82581765	0.82869944	0.83155000	0.83436920
5	0.77412802	0.77755944	0.78095918	0.73432698
6	0.71870174	0.72258608	0.72644086	0.73026571
7	0.65926868	0.66349200	0.66769015	0.67186261
8	0.59553921	0.59996833	0.60437846	0.60876899
9	0.52720273	0.53168304	0.53615173	0.54060814
10	0.45392619	0.45827919	0.46262838	0.46697308
11	0.37535250	0.37937312	0.38339721	0.38742417
12	0.29109870	0.29455238	0.29801513	0.30148644
13	0.20075419	0.20337363	0.20600461	0.20864680
14	0.10387866	0.10536027	0.10685108	0.10835093
15	0.00000000	0.00000000	0.00000000	0.00000000
	8.00	8.25	8.50	8.75
1	0.96402153	0.96477083	0.96550805	0.96623329
2	0.92505686	0.92652279	0.92796733	0.92939057
3	0.88285815	0.88499720	0.88710835	0.88919164
4	0.83715696	0.83991319	0.84263780	0.84533075
5	0.78766260	0.79096583	0.79423647	0.79747432
6	0.73406023	0.73782407	0.74155690	0.74525837
7	0.67600889	0.68012849	0.68422093	0.68828576
8	0.61313932	0.61748884	0.62181698	0.62612318
9	0.54505160	0.54948147	0.55389709	0.55829786
10	0.47131264	0.47564640	0.47997371	0.48429393
11	0.39145337	0.39548424	0.39951616	0.40354855
12	0.30496583	0.30845282	0.31194690	0.31544761
13	0.21129987	0.21396349	0.21663732	0.21932103
14	0.10985968	0.11137716	0.11290323	0.11443773
15	0.00000000	0.00000000	0.00000000	0.00000000

TABLE 3 PROPORTION OUTSTANDING OF $1 (MONTHLY COMPOUNDING, TERM = 15 YRS) (*Continued*)

Holding Period	Interest rate (%)			
	9.00	9.25	9.50	9.75
1	0.96694663	0.96764816	0.96833797	0.96901616
2	0.93079262	0.93217358	0.93353356	0.93487268
3	0.89124712	0.89327485	0.89527490	0.89724734
4	0.84799198	0.85062146	0.85321916	0.85578507
5	0.80067921	0.80385098	0.80698948	0.81009459
6	0.74892817	0.75256602	0.75617163	0.75974473
7	0.69232253	0.69633082	0.70031022	0.70426033
8	0.63040689	0.63466757	0.63890471	0.64311778
9	0.56268314	0.56705233	0.57140484	0.57574009
10	0.48860643	0.49291059	0.49720578	0.50149141
11	0.40758081	0.41161237	0.41564264	0.41967105
12	0.31895444	0.32246691	0.32598455	0.32950688
13	0.22201429	0.22471677	0.22742812	0.23014801
14	0.11598050	0.11753137	0.11909020	0.12065681
15	0.00000000	0.00000000	0.00000000	0.00000000
	10.00	**10.25**	**10.50**	**10.75**
1	0.96968283	0.97033807	0.97098199	0.97161469
2	0.93619106	0.93748882	0.93876610	0.94002304
3	0.89919225	0.90110974	0.90299991	0.90486286
4	0.85831920	0.86082155	0.86329215	0.86573105
5	0.81316619	0.81620418	0.81920847	0.82217899
6	0.76328508	0.76679245	0.77026661	0.77370737
7	0.70818077	0.71207117	0.71593119	0.71976050
8	0.64730631	0.65146981	0.65560782	0.65971990
9	0.58005750	0.58435652	0.58863661	0.59289723
10	0.50576686	0.51003157	0.51428494	0.51852641
11	0.42369703	0.42772001	0.43173946	0.43575480
12	0.33303340	0.33656366	0.34009718	0.34363348
13	0.23287612	0.23561209	0.23835560	0.24110632
14	0.12223105	0.12381275	0.12540175	0.12699789
15	0.00000000	0.00000000	0.00000000	0.00000000
	11.00	**11.25**	**11.50**	**11.75**
1	0.97223628	0.97284686	0.97344655	0.97403545
2	0.94125978	0.94247646	0.94367325	0.94485029
3	0.90669871	0.90850760	0.91028966	0.91204502
4	0.86813828	0.87051390	0.87285799	0.87517062
5	0.82511567	0.82801848	0.83088739	0.83372236
6	0.77711455	0.78048796	0.78382746	0.78713290
7	0.72355878	0.72732573	0.73106107	0.73476452
8	0.66380561	0.66786453	0.67189627	0.67590043
9	0.59713787	0.60135801	0.60555718	0.60973488
10	0.52275541	0.52697141	0.53117386	0.53536223
11	0.43976551	0.44377104	0.44777087	0.45176447
12	0.34717211	0.35071259	0.35425448	0.35779732
13	0.24386390	0.24662803	0.24939837	0.25217458
14	0.12860100	0.13021091	0.13182747	0.13345050
15	0.00000000	0.00000000	0.00000000	0.00000000

TABLE 3 PROPORTION OUTSTANDING OF $1 (MONTHLY COMPOUNDING, TERM = 15 YRS) (*Continued*)

Holding Period	Interest rate (%)			
	12.00	12.25	12.50	12.75
1	0.97461368	0.97518135	0.97573857	0.97628547
2	0.94600774	0.94714577	0.94826454	0.94936424
3	0.91377385	0.91547629	0.91715251	0.91880269
4	0.87745189	0.87970190	0.88192075	0.88410857
5	0.83652340	0.83929052	0.84202373	0.84472307
6	0.79040416	0.79364113	0.79684372	0.80001183
7	0.73843584	0.74207479	0.74568114	0.74925469
8	0.67987664	0.68382455	0.68774381	0.69163411
9	0.61389066	0.61802407	0.62213465	0.62622201
10	0.53953601	0.54369470	0.54783779	0.55196481
11	0.45575133	0.45973095	0.46370283	0.46766648
12	0.36134066	0.36488405	0.36842706	0.37196924
13	0.25495635	0.25774334	0.26053524	0.26333171
14	0.13507985	0.13671534	0.13835681	0.14000410
15	0.00000000	0.00000000	0.00000000	0.00000000
	13.00	13.25	13.50	13.75
1	0.97682216	0.97734876	0.97786538	0.97837216
2	0.95044502	0.95150708	0.95255059	0.95357573
3	0.92042699	0.92202559	0.92359870	0.92514650
4	0.88626548	0.88839164	0.89048717	0.89255224
5	0.84738859	0.85002032	0.85261836	0.85518277
6	0.80314541	0.80624440	0.80930876	0.81233847
7	0.75279524	0.75630263	0.75977669	0.76321727
8	0.69549512	0.69932655	0.70312812	0.70689957
9	0.63028571	0.63432537	0.63834061	0.64233104
10	0.55607529	0.56016876	0.56424478	0.56830290
11	0.47162142	0.47556717	0.47950327	0.48342927
12	0.37551017	0.37904942	0.38258658	0.38612122
13	0.26613245	0.26893713	0.27174543	0.27455705
14	0.14165705	0.14331548	0.14497925	0.14664817
15	0.00000000	0.00000000	0.00000000	0.00000000
	14.00	14.25	14.50	14.75
1	0.97886921	0.97935665	0.97983460	0.98030320
2	0.95458269	0.95557167	0.95654285	0.95749643
3	0.92666919	0.92816697	0.92964006	0.93108867
4	0.89458702	0.89659167	0.89856638	0.90051134
5	0.85771364	0.86021108	0.86267519	0.86510610
6	0.81533351	0.81829388	0.82121959	0.82411067
7	0.76662425	0.76999749	0.77333691	0.77664241
8	0.71064064	0.71435110	0.71803072	0.72167929
9	0.64629633	0.65023613	0.65415011	0.65803796
10	0.57234272	0.57636380	0.58036575	0.58434819
11	0.48734471	0.49124917	0.49514221	0.49902342
12	0.38965294	0.39318133	0.39670601	0.40022657
13	0.27737168	0.28018900	0.28300871	0.28583052
14	0.14832210	0.15000087	0.15168432	0.15337229
15	0.00000000	0.00000000	0.00000000	0.00000000

TABLE 3 PROPORTION OUTSTANDING OF $1 (MONTHLY COMPOUNDING, TERM = 20 YRS) *(Continued)*

Holding Period	Interest rate (%)			
	6.00	6.25	6.50	6.75
1	0.97330201	0.97405373	0.97478893	0.97550780
2	0.94495735	0.94643855	0.94788944	0.94931026
3	0.91486445	0.91704710	0.91918843	0.92128864
4	0.88291549	0.88576515	0.88856526	0.89131592
5	0.84899598	0.85247109	0.85589121	0.85925628
6	0.81298440	0.81703549	0.82102891	0.82496438
7	0.77475170	0.77932061	0.78383182	0.78828481
8	0.73416089	0.73917983	0.74414357	0.74905132
9	0.69106652	0.69645714	0.70179733	0.70708608
10	0.64531420	0.65098644	0.65661507	0.66219889
11	0.59673996	0.60259098	0.60840688	0.61418629
12	0.54516978	0.55108264	0.55697010	0.56283068
13	0.49041886	0.49626119	0.50208850	0.50789928
14	0.43229102	0.43791352	0.44353138	0.44914313
15	0.37057798	0.37581283	0.38015258	0.38629590
	7.00	**7.25**	**7.50**	**7.75**
1	0.97621050	0.97689721	0.97756813	0.97822344
2	0.95070125	0.95206268	0.95339481	0.95469794
3	0.92334794	0.92536660	0.92734486	0.92928303
4	0.89401726	0.89666942	0.89927259	0.90182698
5	0.86256626	0.86582115	0.86902098	0.87216585
6	0.82884166	0.83266054	0.83642087	0.84012254
7	0.79267911	0.79701427	0.80128993	0.80550574
8	0.75390236	0.75869602	0.76343168	0.76810876
9	0.71232244	0.71750550	0.72263440	0.72770832
10	0.66773671	0.67322741	0.67866991	0.68406320
11	0.61992787	0.62563030	0.63129235	0.63691281
12	0.56866292	0.57446540	0.58023675	0.58597563
13	0.51369203	0.51946527	0.52521757	0.53094753
14	0.45474728	0.46034241	0.46592710	0.47149995
15	0.39154142	0.39678781	0.40203377	0.40727797
	8.00	**8.25**	**8.50**	**8.75**
1	0.97886334	0.97948803	0.98009771	0.98069259
2	0.95597234	0.95721834	0.95843623	0.95962637
3	0.93118140	0.93304031	0.93486008	0.93664109
4	0.90433283	0.90679041	0.90920002	0.91156195
5	0.87525584	0.87829111	0.88127183	0.88419821
6	0.84376547	0.84734964	0.85087505	0.85434175
7	0.80966142	0.81375673	0.81779147	0.82176548
8	0.77272675	0.77728517	0.78178360	0.78622166
9	0.73273652	0.73768829	0.74259296	0.74743994
10	0.68940629	0.69469826	0.69993823	0.70512537
11	0.64249050	0.64802433	0.06351320	0.65895611
12	0.59168073	0.59735080	0.60298463	0.60858104
13	0.53665377	0.54233496	0.54798979	0.55361700
14	0.47705960	0.48260469	0.48813391	0.49364597
15	0.41251914	0.41775600	0.42298731	0.42821183

TABLE 3 PROPORTION OUTSTANDING OF $1 (MONTHLY COMPOUNDING, TERM = 20 YRS) (*Continued*)

Holding Period	Interest rate (%)			
	9.00	9.25	9.50	9.75
1	0.98127290	0.98183883	0.93239061	0.98292847
2	0.96078906	0.96192467	0.96303354	0.96411603
3	0.93838370	0.94008831	0.94175532	0.94338515
4	0.91387657	0.91614422	0.91836529	0.92054019
5	0.88707049	0.88988894	0.89265385	0.89536557
6	0.85774982	0.86109939	0.86439062	0.86762370
7	0.82567867	0.82953096	0.83332233	0.83705281
8	0.79059902	0.79491541	0.79917059	0.80336437
9	0.75222866	0.75695863	0.76162937	0.76624048
10	0.71025890	0.71533809	0.72036227	0.72533081
11	0.66435208	0.66970018	0.67499952	0.68024927
12	0.61413889	0.61965710	0.62513462	0.63057045
13	0.55921535	0.56478365	0.57032075	0.57582552
14	0.49913961	0.50461360	0.51006674	0.51549785
15	0.43342835	0.43863568	0.44383266	0.44901814
	10.00	10.25	10.50	10.75
1	0.98345262	0.98396328	0.98446070	0.98494509
2	0.96517250	0.96620334	0.96720891	0.96818960
3	0.94497823	0.94653500	0.94805592	0.94954145
4	0.92266934	0.92475319	0.92679220	0.92878684
5	0.89802443	0.90063082	0.90318514	0.90568784
6	0.87079887	0.87391637	0.87697651	0.87997961
7	0.84072244	0.84433132	0.84787960	0.85136743
8	0.80749661	0.81156721	0.81557610	0.81952328
9	0.77079160	0.77528242	0.77971265	0.78408208
10	0.73024311	0.73509864	0.73989692	0.74463751
11	0.68544865	0.69059691	0.69569336	0.70073736
12	0.63596363	0.64131324	0.64661842	0.65187833
13	0.58129688	0.58673379	0.59213525	0.59750029
14	0.52090581	0.52628949	0.53164784	0.53697981
15	0.45419100	0.45935015	0.45449452	0.46962306
	11.00	11.25	11.50	11.75
1	0.98541668	0.98587572	0.98632242	0.98675702
2	0.96914580	0.97007790	0.97098630	0.97187139
3	0.95099208	0.95240827	0.95379053	0.95513936
4	0.93073762	0.93264504	0.93450962	0.93633190
5	0.90813934	0.91054014	0.91289072	0.91519159
6	0.88292602	0.88581612	0.88865032	0.89142905
7	0.85479504	0.85816265	0.86147055	0.86471903
8	0.82340877	0.82723263	0.83099497	0.83469593
9	0.78839052	0.79263785	0.79682396	0.80094879
10	0.74932001	0.75394406	0.75850938	0.76301569
11	0.70572829	0.71066561	0.71554881	0.72037741
12	0.65709220	0.66225927	0.66737886	0.67245031
13	0.60282799	0.60811746	0.61336786	0.61857838
14	0.54228439	0.54756061	0.55280753	0.55802424
15	0.47473476	0.47982862	0.48490368	0.48995901

TABLE 3 PROPORTION OUTSTANDING OF $1 (MONTHLY COMPOUNDING, TERM = 20 YRS) *(Continued)*

Holding Period	Interest rate (%)			
	12.00	12.25	12.50	12.75
1	0.98717975	0.98759084	0.98799054	0.98897906
2	0.97273357	0.97357325	0.97439083	0.97518671
3	0.95645525	0.95773872	0.95899030	0.96021049
4	0.93811243	0.93985177	0.94155049	0.94320917
5	0.91744329	0.91964636	0.92180137	0.92390890
6	0.89415278	0.89682198	0.89943716	0.90199884
7	0.86790845	0.87103916	0.87411156	0.87712607
8	0.83833568	0.84191444	0.84543245	0.84888998
9	0.80501235	0.80901465	0.81295576	0.81683578
10	0.76746278	0.77185048	0.77617864	0.78044717
11	0.72515099	0.72986918	0.73453163	0.73913805
12	0.67747301	0.68244638	0.68736990	0.69224308
13	0.62374826	0.62887676	0.63396319	0.63900691
14	0.56320987	0.56836358	0.57348458	0.57857209
15	0.49499369	0.50000685	0.50499763	0.50996521
	13.00	13.25	13.50	13.75
1	0.98875663	0.98912350	0.98947988	0.98982600
2	0.97596132	0.97671504	0.97744828	0.97816146
3	0.96139983	0.96255884	0.96368806	0.96478801
4	0.94482838	0.94640874	0.94795084	0.94945528
5	0.92596954	0.92798390	0.92995258	0.93187623
6	0.90450757	0.90696391	0.90936844	0.91172176
7	0.88008314	0.88298325	0.88582688	0.88861456
8	0.85228736	0.85562490	0.85890300	0.86212203
9	0.82065484	0.82441313	0.82811084	0.83174822
10	0.78465602	0.78880517	0.79289464	0.79692449
11	0.74368819	0.74818182	0.75261878	0.75699891
12	0.69706547	0.70183666	0.70655630	0.71122403
13	0.64400730	0.64896378	0.65387582	0.65874291
14	0.58362537	0.58864373	0.59362650	0.59857303
15	0.51490878	0.51982759	0.52472089	0.52958797
	14.00	14.25	14.50	14.75
1	0.99016210	0.99048838	0.99080509	0.99111243
2	0.97885498	0.97952924	0.98018464	0.98082158
3	0.96585924	0.96690227	0.96791764	0.96890589
4	0.95092268	0.95235366	0.95374883	0.95510881
5	0.93375547	0.93559096	0.93738335	0.93913329
6	0.91402448	0.91627723	0.91848064	0.92063537
7	0.89134682	0.89402422	0.89664734	0.89921677
8	0.86528243	0.86838463	0.87142911	0.87441636
9	0.83532553	0.83884307	0.84230116	0.84570018
10	0.80089480	0.80480571	0.80865736	0.81244994
11	0.76132213	0.76558836	0.76979757	0.77394977
12	0.71583959	0.72040269	0.72491314	0.72937074
13	0.66356459	0.66834043	0.67307004	0.67775305
14	0.60348274	0.60835505	0.61318942	0.61798535
15	0.53442184	0.53924076	0.54402519	0.54878084

TABLE 3   PROPORTION OUTSTANDING OF $1 (MONTHLY COMPOUNDING, TERM = 25 YRS) (*Continued*)

Holding Period	Interest rate (%)			
	6.00	6.25	6.50	6.75
1	0.98219961	0.98285404	0.98348901	0.98410484
2	0.96330133	0.96460523	0.96587224	0.96710293
3	0.94323745	0.94518261	0.94707565	0.94891721
4	0.92193607	0.92451070	0.92702022	0.92946525
5	0.89932087	0.90250913	0.90562163	0.90865890
6	0.87531081	0.87909239	0.88278995	0.88640384
7	0.84981986	0.85416943	0.85842918	0.86259922
8	0.82275669	0.82764339	0.83243693	0.83713712
9	0.79402432	0.79941114	0.80470393	0.80990215
10	0.76351981	0.76936294	0.77511359	0.78077086
11	0.73113384	0.73738199	0.74354154	0.74961123
12	0.69675037	0.70334396	0.70985505	0.71628201
13	0.66024621	0.66711655	0.67391252	0.68063215
14	0.62149055	0.62855893	0.63556284	0.64250006
15	0.58034452	0.58752121	0.59464482	0.60171291
	7.00	7.25	7.50	7.75
1	0.98470187	0.98528044	0.98584091	0.98638363
2	0.96829783	0.96945753	0.97058261	0.97167369
3	0.95070794	0.95244856	0.95413977	0.95578234
4	0.93184648	0.93416462	0.93642044	0.93861472
5	0.91162152	0.91451015	0.91732550	0.92006832
6	0.88993450	0.89338242	0.89674817	0.90003239
7	0.86667973	0.87067099	0.87457337	0.87838732
8	0.84174386	0.84625715	0.35067709	0.85500387
9	0.81500537	0.82001329	0.82492567	0.82974243
10	0.78633396	0.79180223	0.79717511	0.80245216
11	0.75558990	0.76147652	0.76727019	0.77297013
12	0.72262333	0.72887765	0.73504368	0.74112031
13	0.68727362	0.69383522	0.70031535	0.60671254
14	0.64936847	0.65616607	0.66289096	0.66954137
15	0.60872315	0.61567330	0.62256122	0.62938488
	8.00	8.25	8.50	8.75
1	0.98690896	0.98741726	0.98790890	0.98838426
2	0.97273137	0.97375628	0.97474907	0.97571037
3	0.95737704	0.95892466	0.96042602	0.96188194
4	0.94074832	0.94282209	0.94483694	0.94679380
5	0.92273941	0.92533965	0.92786993	0.93033119
6	0.90323578	0.90635911	0.90940319	0.91236891
7	0.88211336	0.88575208	0.88930416	0.89277034
8	0.85923778	0.86337919	0.86742856	0.87138642
9	0.83446355	0.83908913	0.84361936	0.84805452
10	0.80763306	0.81271759	0.81770563	0.82259717
11	0.77857566	0.78408622	0.78950137	0.79482077
12	0.74710651	0.75300137	0.75880411	0.76451406
13	0.71302543	0.71925279	0.72539349	0.73144653
14	0.67611564	0.68261222	0.68902968	0.69536669
15	0.63614236	0.64283185	0.64945163	0.65600012

TABLE 3   PROPORTION OUTSTANDING OF $1 (MONTHLY COMPOUNDING, TERM = 25 YRS) *(Continued)*

Holding Period	Interest rate (%)			
	9.00	9.25	9.50	9.75
1	0.98884369	0.98928757	0.98971628	0.99013018
2	0.97664084	0.97754114	0.97841192	0.97925387
3	0.96329327	0.96466088	0.96598564	0.96726842
4	0.94869362	0.95053738	0.95232608	0.95406073
5	0.93272441	0.93505061	0.93731083	0.93950616
6	0.91525719	0.91806900	0.92080536	0.92346735
7	0.89615141	0.89944825	0.90266177	0.90579294
8	0.87525339	0.87903015	0.88271746	0.88631615
9	0.85239498	0.85664121	0.86079373	0.86485318
10	0.82739230	0.83209120	0.83669413	0.84120146
11	0.80004420	0.80517151	0.81020269	0.81513781
12	0.77013065	0.77565343	0.78108205	0.78641626
13	0.73741101	0.74328614	0.74907125	0.75476577
14	0.70162204	0.70779463	0.71388346	0.71988765
15	0.66247581	0.66887732	0.67520336	0.68145276
	10.00	**10.25**	**10.50**	**10.75**
1	0.99052966	0.99091507	0.99128679	0.99164518
2	0.98006764	0.98085391	0.98161334	0.98234661
3	0.96851012	0.96971163	0.97087386	0.97199770
4	0.95574238	0.95737206	0.95895084	0.96047979
5	0.94163768	0.94370654	0.94571387	0.94766084
6	0.92605604	0.92857258	0.93101814	0.93339389
7	0.90884280	0.91181241	0.91470288	0.91751537
8	0.88982711	0.89325127	0.89658963	0.89984325
9	0.86882022	0.87269563	0.87648024	0.88017492
10	0.84561364	0.84993119	0.85415472	0.85828490
11	0.81997703	0.82472059	0.82936885	0.83392222
12	0.79165593	0.79680099	0.80185149	0.80680758
13	0.76036924	0.76588128	0.77130163	0.77663012
14	0.72580642	0.73163908	0.73738507	0.74304388
15	0.68762443	0.69371739	0.69973078	0.70566381
	11.00	**11.25**	**11.50**	**11.75**
1	0.99199061	0.99232343	0.99264401	0.99295270
2	0.98305437	0.98373730	0.98439604	0.98503126
3	0.97308405	0.97413383	0.97514793	0.97612726
4	0.96195997	0.96339248	0.96477840	0.96611881
5	0.94954863	0.95137844	0.95315146	0.95486892
6	0.93570107	0.93794090	0.94011466	0.94222360
7	0.92025107	0.92291120	0.92549701	0.92800978
8	0.90301323	0.90610070	0.90910684	0.91203288
9	0.88378063	0.88729838	0.89072921	0.89407423
10	0.86232247	0.86626826	0.87012312	0.87388800
11	0.83838119	0.84274636	0.84701835	0.85119790
12	0.81166946	0.81643744	0.82111191	0.82569333
13	0.78186667	0.78701129	0.79206408	0.79702520
14	0.74861514	0.75409856	0.75949392	0.76480111
15	0.71151579	0.71728613	0.72297433	0.72857997

TABLE 3 PROPORTION OUTSTANDING OF $1 (MONTHLY COMPOUNDING, TERM = 25 YRS) (*Continued*)

Holding Period	Interest rate (%)			
	12.00	12.25	12.50	12.75
1	0.99324985	0.99353579	0.99381088	0.99407544
2	0.98564360	0.98623371	0.98680222	0.98734975
3	0.97707270	0.97798515	0.97886550	0.97971461
4	0.96741479	0.96866744	0.96987783	0.97104703
5	0.95653202	0.95814199	0.95970004	0.96120742
6	0.94426904	0.94625225	0.94817456	0.95003728
7	0.93045080	0.93282140	0.93512292	0.93735670
8	0.91488007	0.91764968	0.92034303	0.92296144
9	0.89733458	0.90051145	0.90360605	0.90661964
10	0.87756388	0.88115179	0.88465282	0.88806809
11	0.85528576	0.85928279	0.86318988	0.86700797
12	0.83018222	0.83457919	0.83888490	0.84310008
13	0.80189492	0.80667357	0.81136156	0.81595935
14	0.77002009	0.77515090	0.78019368	0.78514861
15	0.73410273	0.73954235	0.74489867	0.75017161
	13.00	13.25	13.50	13.75
1	0.99432980	0.99457429	0.99480922	0.99503490
2	0.98787693	0.98838436	0.98887265	0.98934239
3	0.98053335	0.98132258	0.98208315	0.98281590
4	0.97217612	0.97326615	0.97431818	0.97533324
5	0.96266532	0.96407497	0.96543757	0.96675434
6	0.95184172	0.95358920	0.95528105	0.95691858
7	0.93952411	0.94162652	0.94366530	0.94564184
8	0.92550627	0.92797888	0.93038066	0.93271300
9	0.90955352	0.91240898	0.91518736	0.91789001
10	0.89139876	0.89464604	0.89781116	0.90089539
11	0.87073806	0.87438120	0.87793846	0.88141096
12	0.84722552	0.85126204	0.85521055	0.85907198
13	0.82046748	0.82488655	0.82921723	0.83346021
14	0.79001596	0.79479606	0.79948932	0.80409620
15	0.75536114	0.76046732	0.76549028	0.77043021
	14.00	14.25	14.50	14.75
1	0.99525164	0.99545974	0.99565949	0.99585117
2	0.98979416	0.99022852	0.99064605	0.99104728
3	0.98352164	0.98420119	0.98485535	0.98548490
4	0.97631237	0.97725658	0.97816688	0.97904426
5	0.96802646	0.96925511	0.97044147	0.97158670
6	0.95850310	0.96003593	0.96151835	0.96295165
7	0.94755752	0.94941372	0.95121182	0.95295320
8	0.93497729	0.93717496	0.93930742	0.94137607
9	0.92051831	0.92307365	0.92555741	0.92797102
10	0.90390000	0.90682632	0.90967567	0.91244941
11	0.88479988	0.88810638	0.89133170	0.89447708
12	0.86284730	0.86653754	0.87014376	0.87366706
13	0.83761628	0.84168624	0.84567095	0.84957131
14	0.80861721	0.81305293	0.81740398	0.82167104
15	0.77528736	0.78006204	0.78475463	0.78936555

TABLE 3 PROPORTION OUTSTANDING OF $1 (MONTHLY COMPOUNDING, TERM = 30 YRS) (*Continued*)

Holding Period	Interest rate (%)			
	6.00	6.25	6.50	6.75
1	0.98771988	0.98828204	0.98882275	0.98934254
2	0.97468236	0.97581037	0.97689693	0.97794298
3	0.96084070	0.96253649	0.96417242	0.96574972
4	0.94614532	0.94840881	0.95059572	0.95270746
5	0.93054357	0.93337241	0.93610977	0.93875710
6	0.91397953	0.91736885	0.92065367	0.92383540
7	0.89639386	0.90033591	0.90416245	0.90787473
8	0.87772354	0.88220738	0.88656677	0.89080276
9	0.85790168	0.86291278	0.86779269	0.87254210
10	0.83685725	0.84237713	0.84776126	0.85300999
11	0.81451484	0.82052058	0.82638830	0.83211790
12	0.79079441	0.79725818	0.80358395	0.80977113
13	0.76561095	0.77249951	0.77925235	0.78586841
14	0.73887423	0.74614830	0.75329121	0.76030139
15	0.71048844	0.71810215	0.72559141	0.73295419
	7.00	7.25	7.50	7.75
1	0.98984190	0.99032143	0.99078166	0.99122312
2	0.97894947	0.97991738	0.98084767	0.98174133
3	0.96726963	0.96873345	0.97014248	0.97149804
4	0.95474545	0.95671119	0.95860622	0.96043208
5	0.94131590	0.94378777	0.94617437	0.94847738
6	0.92691552	0.92989563	0.93277740	0.93556256
7	0.91147414	0.91496216	0.91834039	0.92161051
8	0.89491650	0.89890930	0.90278260	0.90653793
9	0.87716191	0.88165315	0.88601701	0.89025483
10	0.85812383	0.86310350	0.86794987	0.87266399
11	0.83770950	0.84316341	0.84848013	0.85366036
12	0.81581940	0.82172863	0.82749891	0.83313051
13	0.79234688	0.79868715	0.80488885	0.81095183
14	0.76717752	0.77391851	0.78052352	0.78699192
15	0.74018866	0.74729326	0.75426665	0.76110772
	8.00	8.25	8.50	8.75
1	0.99164636	0.99205193	0.99244038	0.99281223
2	0.98259937	0.98342278	0.98421255	0.98496968
3	0.97280149	0.97405417	0.97525746	0.97641271
4	0.96219039	0.96388275	0.96551081	0.96707624
5	0.95069857	0.95283972	0.95490266	0.95688925
6	0.93825293	0.94085038	0.94335684	0.94577427
7	0.92477432	0.92783366	0.93079047	0.93364676
8	0.91017698	0.91370150	0.91711336	0.92041448
9	0.89436808	0.89835833	0.90222731	0.90597680
10	0.87724704	0.88170037	0.88602546	0.89022391
11	0.85870496	0.86361496	0.86839153	0.87303600
12	0.83862391	0.84397976	0.84919891	0.85428234
13	0.81687613	0.82266199	0.82830984	0.83382030
14	0.79332330	0.79951745	0.80557437	0.81149425
15	0.76781560	0.77438960	0.78082928	0.78713439

TABLE 3 PROPORTION OUTSTANDING OF $1 (MONTHLY COMPOUNDING, TERM = 30 YRS) (*Continued*)

Holding Period	Interest rate (%)			
	9.00	9.25	9.50	9.75
1	0.99316803	0.99350831	0.99383359	0.99414438
2	0.98569517	0.98639001	0.98705517	0.98769163
3	0.97752131	0.97858462	0.97960401	0.98058084
4	0.96858068	0.97002583	0.97141335	0.97274492
5	0.95880136	0.96064090	0.96240978	0.96410990
6	0.94810468	0.95035010	0.95251262	0.95459432
7	0.93640456	0.93906600	0.94163320	0.94410835
8	0.92360690	0.92669270	0.92967402	0.93255307
9	0.90960873	0.91312508	0.91652793	0.91981940
10	0.89429744	0.89824786	0.90207711	0.90578719
11	0.87754984	0.88193463	0.88619208	0.89032401
12	0.85923120	0.86404678	0.86873051	0.87328395
13	0.83919414	0.84443232	0.84953592	0.85450618
14	0.81727747	0.82292458	0.82843630	0.83381351
15	0.79330487	0.79934084	0.80524261	0.81101066
	10.00	10.25	10.50	10.75
1	0.99444121	0.99472458	0.99499496	0.99525286
2	0.98830035	0.98888228	0.98943835	0.98996949
3	0.98151646	0.98241220	0.98326939	0.98408933
4	0.97402221	0.97524688	0.97642058	0.97754495
5	0.96574320	0.96731160	0.96881701	0.97026133
6	0.95659728	0.95852364	0.96037550	0.96215497
7	0.94649367	0.94879137	0.95100370	0.95313293
8	0.93533207	0.93801331	0.94059911	0.94309177
9	0.92300171	0.92607710	0.92904789	0.93191639
10	0.90938019	0.91285828	0.91622368	0.91947867
11	0.89433233	0.89821903	0.90198620	0.90563600
12	0.87770876	0.88200672	0.88617971	0.89022968
13	0.85934448	0.86405231	0.86863128	0.87308311
14	0.83905722	0.84416861	0.84914896	0.85399969
15	0.81664563	0.82214830	0.82751962	0.83276064
	11.00	11.25	11.50	11.75
1	0.99549874	0.99573307	0.99595629	0.99616886
2	0.99047660	0.99096056	0.99142225	0.99186252
3	0.98487330	0.98562258	0.98633841	0.98702202
4	0.97862160	0.97965213	0.98063811	0.98158110
5	0.97164645	0.97297426	0.97424660	0.97546531
6	0.96386415	0.96550516	0.96708005	0.96859091
7	0.95518130	0.95715107	0.95904450	0.96086382
8	0.94549367	0.94780714	0.95003456	0.95217827
9	0.93468500	0.93735609	0.93993208	0.94241538
10	0.92262556	0.92566673	0.92860457	0.93144150
11	0.90917062	0.91259235	0.91590351	0.91910644
12	0.89415869	0.89796884	0.90166232	0.90524134
13	0.87740960	0.88161265	0.88569425	0.88965644
14	0.85872232	0.86331848	0.86778991	0.87213839
15	0.83787257	0.84285671	0.84771449	0.85244743

TABLE 3 PROPORTION OUTSTANDING OF $1 (MONTHLY COMPOUNDING, TERM = 30 YRS) (*Continued*)

Holding Period	Interest rate (%)			
	12.00	12.25	12.50	12.75
1	0.99637121	0.99656374	0.99674688	0.99692100
2	0.99228219	0.99268208	0.99306298	0.99342566
3	0.98767459	0.98829730	0.98889129	0.98945768
4	0.98248262	0.98334416	0.98416719	0.98495314
5	0.97663219	0.97774902	0.97881755	0.97983949
6	0.97002977	0.97142864	0.97275953	0.97403437
7	0.96261127	0.96428904	0.96589933	0.96744428
8	0.95424065	0.95622402	0.95813072	0.95996306
9	0.94480842	0.94711364	0.94933344	0.95147023
10	0.93417996	0.93682239	0.93937124	0.94182899
11	0.92220353	0.92519721	0.92808990	0.93088405
12	0.90870820	0.91206521	0.91531472	0.91845912
13	0.89350132	0.89723108	0.90084791	0.90435407
14	0.87636583	0.88047418	0.88446546	0.88834173
15	0.85705713	0.86154530	0.86591370	0.87016419
	13.00	13.25	13.50	13.75
1	0.99708651	0.99724378	0.99739315	0.99753498
2	0.99377087	0.99409934	0.99441176	0.99470883
3	0.98999756	0.99051200	0.99100202	0.99146863
4	0.98570342	0.98641939	0.98710239	0.98775372
5	0.98081654	0.98175033	0.98264248	0.98349456
6	0.97525511	0.97642363	0.97754180	0.97861141
7	0.96892603	0.97034667	0.97170827	0.97301286
8	0.96172333	0.96341377	0.96503662	0.96659409
9	0.95352641	0.95550436	0.95740643	0.95923494
10	0.94419806	0.94648092	0.94867997	0.95079763
11	0.93358210	0.93618651	0.93869974	0.94112422
12	0.92150079	0.92444214	0.92728561	0.93003360
13	0.90775186	0.91104357	0.91423156	0.91731816
14	0.89210513	0.89575781	0.89930197	0.90273983
15	0.87429865	0.87831905	0.88222739	0.88602571
	14.00	14.25	14.50	14.75
1	0.99766961	0.99779737	0.99791856	0.99803349
2	0.99499120	0.99525953	0.99551442	0.99575648
3	0.99191279	0.99233546	0.99273755	0.99311995
4	0.98837465	0.98896640	0.98953018	0.99006713
5	0.98430810	0.98508461	0.98582554	0.98653230
6	0.97963426	0.98061208	0.98154656	0.98243935
7	0.97426241	0.97545888	0.97660418	0.97770016
8	0.96808832	0.96952145	0.97089556	0.97221269
9	0.96099218	0.96268042	0.96430190	0.96585879
10	0.95283629	0.95479829	0.95668599	0.95850166
11	0.94346237	0.94571662	0.94788934	0.94998291
12	0.93268854	0.93525285	0.93772891	0.94011911
13	0.92030573	0.92319664	0.92599324	0.92869791
14	0.90607364	0.90930565	0.91243814	0.91547338
15	0.88971610	0.89330065	0.89678151	0.90016082

INDEX